D1809206

Cuba
Handbook

Sarah Cameron

Footprint Handbooks

*I am sitting by the bay in Cienfuegos and the
temperature is over ninety, though the sun has been
down for an hour... The light here is wonderful just
before the sun goes down: a long trickle of gold and
seabirds are dark patches on the pewter swell. The big
white statue in the Paseo which looks in daylight like
Queen Victoria is a lump of ectoplasm now.*

Graham Greene *Our Man in Havana*

Footprint Handbooks

®

6 Riverside Court, Lower Bristol Road
Bath BA2 3DZ England
T 01225 469141 F 01225 469461
E mail handbooks@footprint.cix.co.uk

ISBN 1 900949 12 1 ISSN 1369-1422
CIP DATA: A catalogue record for this book is
available from the British Library

In North America, published by

PASSPORT BOOKS
NTC/Contemporary Publishing Company

4255 West Touhy Avenue, Lincolnwood
(Chicago), Illinois 60646-1975, USA
T 847 679 5500 F 847 679 2494
E mail NTCPUB2@AOL.COM

ISBN 0-8442-4948-3
Library of Congress Catalog Card
Number: 97-76425
Passport Books and colophon are registered
trademarks of NTC/Contemporary Publishing
Company

Every effort has been made to ensure that
the facts in this Handbook are accurate.
However travellers should still obtain
advice from consulates, airlines etc about
current travel and visa requirements and
conditions before travelling. The editors
and publishers cannot accept responsibilty
for any loss, injury or inconvenience,
however caused.

Maps - the black and white text maps are
not intended to have any political
significance.

Cover design by Newell and Sorrell;
photography by Tony Stone; and La Belle
Aurore

Production: Design by Mytton Williams;
Secretarial assistance Rhoda Williams;
Typesetting by Jo Morgan, Ann Griffiths
and Alex Nott; Maps by Sebastian Ballard,
Kevin Feeney and Aldous George; Proofread
by Rod Gray.

Printed and bound in Great Britain by
Clays Ltd., Bungay, Suffolk

Cubana
Your best route to Cuba

Montreal
Toronto
Mexico City
San Jose
Panama
Bogota
Caracas
Quito
Guayaquil
Lima
Rio De Janiero
Santiago De Chile
Montevideo
Buenos Aires
Cancun
Sao Paulo
Montego Bay
Kingston
St. Martin
Santo Domingo
Point-a-Pitre
Berlin
Manchester
London
Brussels
Moscow
Frankfurt
Paris
Rome
Las Palmas
Santiago De Compostela
Barcelona
Madrid
Lisbon

HAVANA
VARADERO
CIEGO DE AVILA
CAMAGUEY
LAS TUNAS
HOLGUIN
BAYAMO
BARACOA
MANZANILLO
SANTIAGO DE CUBA
GUATANAMO

Cubana offers more connections to Cuba from more parts of the world than any other airline.

Whether you're planning a holiday or a business trip, we'll ensure it gets off to a perfect start. Cuba is one of the most diverse islands in the Caribbean, offering everything from the historic architecture and vibrant nightlife of Havana, to spectacular sandy beaches and dramatic mountain scenery. Wherever you go, you'll receive a warm welcome from the friendly, laid-back Cubans.

Visit Cuba soon. Just ask your travel agent about Cubana's unbeatable service.

CUBANA
Bringing the world to Cuba

Contents

4

Cuba

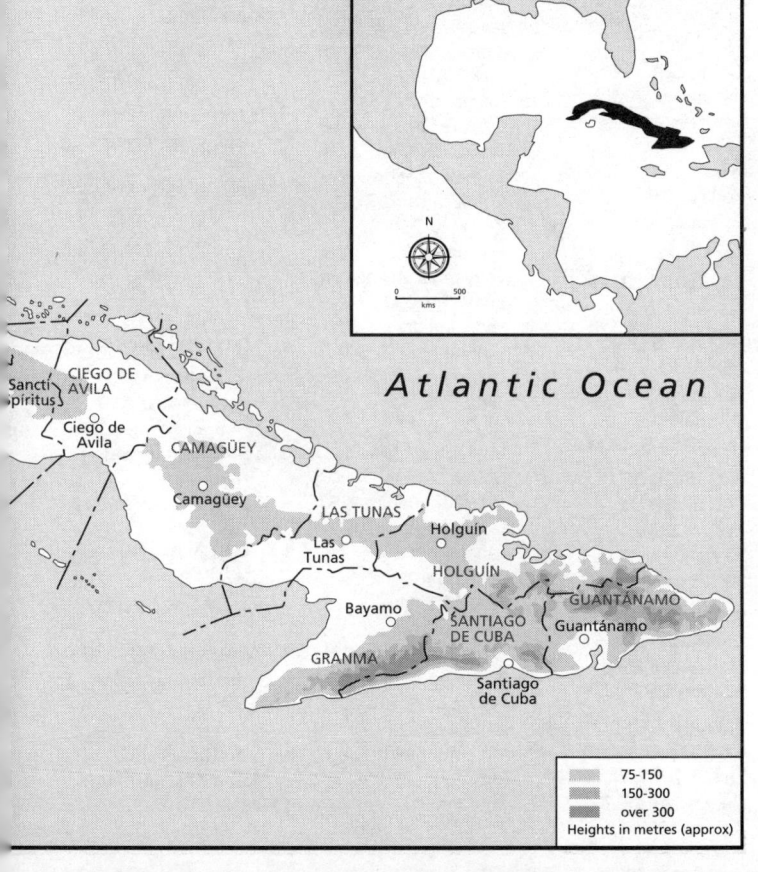

The author

Sarah Cameron

Following a degree in Latin American studies and a year living in Colombia and travelling the continent, Sarah Cameron did the one thing she had vowed not to do – she went to work for a bank. For the next 13 years she combined economics with her interest in Latin America, learning the intricacies of debt rescheduling and the fallibilities (or foolishness) of economic forecasting. But travelling was still in the blood and Sarah spent her spare time moonlighting for the *South American Handbook* as a sub-editor, traveller and researcher. In 1990 she decided to part company with the world of finance and devote more time to the Handbooks. Together with Ben Box she wrote the *Caribbean Islands Handbook*, which she edits annually, she is joint editor of the *Mexico & Central American Handbook* and occasional sub-editor of the *South American Handbook*, while keeping an eye on the economic data in all three and in the new single country *Handbooks* for South America. After persistent badgering the publishers allowed her to write a *Cuba Handbook*, the first single country *Handbook* for the Caribbean, a region which she knows and loves well. When she is not travelling around the Caribbean Basin gathering information and experiences for the *Handbooks*, Sarah retreats to her 17th century farmhouse in rural Suffolk, to write it all down and work as mother, groom and kennel maid to two daughters, horses and many other animals.

The team

For substantial contributions to the text the editor would like to thank:

Angie Todd, a translator for the English language edition of *Granma International*, who has been living in Havana since June 1994 and is the Cuba correspondent for the *Caribbean Islands Handbook*. Angie has carried out extensive research, mostly on her bicycle, on Havana and its development, and has checked and re-checked all the details on transport, accommodation and other areas of crucial importance to travellers.

Gavin Clark, a freelance writer and traveller, who covered the eastern end of the island as well as writing the sections on art, literature and architecture.

Mark Wilson, a geographer and journalist resident in Trinidad and Tobago, who travelled in the west of Cuba, wrote the sections on geology and climate, and supplied information on fauna and flora.

Specialist contributors

Dave Willets for music; Catherine Davies for cinema; Martha Watkins Gilkes and Eleonora de Sabata for diving; Patrick Symmes for Che Guevara information; Nicole Bichard for the Isla de la Juventud; Lila Haines for the Isla de la Juventud and extraneous economic information; Meic Haines for Afro Cuban religion; Hilary Emberton and Arnaldo Iglesias for research on several colonial cities; Eileen Morris for first hand experience of the Cuban health service and links between Canada and Cuba; David Snashall for health.

Cuba

Everybody's image of Cuba is different. For some the allure is of a tropical paradise: bounty bar scenes of palm trees swaying over endless dazzling white beaches and a stunning torquoise-blue sea.

Others remember its past decadence: thousands visiting the island attracted by sun, sea and sex, helped by the tittle-tattle stories of Hemingway and Greene – cheap rum, gambling, wild dances and cigars being rolled on the thighs of dusky maidens. All this set against the background of the beautiful architecture of the colonial cities.

Then again there are the revolutionaries: Hatuey (an Indian chief), José Martí, Castro and Che Guevara whose poster has been plastered across countless walls by students the world over. This is perhaps the most powerful image of them all: Cuba freeing itself from its colonial past and then daring to stand up to the most powerful country in the world. Despite (or because of) the US embargo and the dire state of the Cuban economy over the last few years, Cuba remains determined to survive and will not be bullied. However, Castro is no longer shutting the door against his former opponents. In January 1998 for instance few around the world will have missed the Pope berating Cuba's human rights record on the one hand and the USA trade embargo on the other whilst a bemused (and elegantly suited) Castro clapped his approval at the Pope's jokes across a Plaza de Revolución crowded with worshippers.

For financial reasons, Cuba now has no choice but to greet tourists with open arms. It is doing this with great charm and there can be little doubt that apart from the obvious delights of the sun and beaches, the Cubans will ensure that any visit will be truly memorable. 1998 is the centenary of the expulsion of Spain as colonial ruler. The year will see many celebrations, conference and fiestas commemorating the history of the two countries and their renewed friendship. January 1999 will be the 40th anniversary of the Revolution when Fidel Castro led his freedom fighters to power and expelled the dictator Batista. Will you be there to celebrate? Whatever your political opinions about communism and human rights the relative merits of capitalism and private ownership, it has to be acknowledged that Cubans today have a better health service, education system and employment record than any other country in Latin America.

Cuba is a fun place to visit and tourists are being attracted for many different reasons. It might be simply that cheap packages are on offer and it is a good place to get some Caribbean sun and sand, or a more political reason: go before Castro dies, you never know what might happen afterwards. Some are attracted by the music, the colonial architecture, the landscape, the birdwatching, or the scuba diving (yes, 'scuba Cuba'). Even those famous fifties cars have many admirers. Whatever the reason, no one will leave the island without being affected by the pulsating rhythms of the music and dance, the racial mixture which has produced such creativity and exuberance in the arts and entertainment without being diverted into advertising, billboards and neon lights. And, of course, you haven't lived until you've learned to dance the rumba.

Sarah Cameron

Acknowledgements

Much additional help has been received in the preparation of this edition. All contributions have been tremendously helpful and are duly acknowledged at the end in **Rounding up**.

We try as hard as we can to make each Footprint Handbook as up-to-date and accurate as possible but, of course, things always change. Many people write to us with new information, amendments or simply comments. Please do get in touch. In return we will send you details of our special guidebook offer.
See page 338 for more information.

Where to go

Everybody who goes to Cuba does so for his or her own particular reason, looking for some personal benefit which will differ from anyone else's. We make no attempt here to be prescriptive; tastes vary in travel as in everything else, and we try to set out the facts and descriptions as objectively as possible to allow you to make your own judgement on what you would like to do. There are, however, a number of places which are perennial favourites and you might like to consider.

The **colonial cities** are among the best examples in the world of Spanish architecture of the 18th and 19th centuries. **Havana**, the capital, is crumbling, eroded by the sea air and past lack of money for repairs but, on the other hand, the old city is still intact, unadulterated by modern skyscrapers or advertising or neon lights. Current restoration work is progressing steadily and the magnificence of the old palaces is being revealed in all its glory. **Trinidad** is even more a piece of the past, stuck in a time warp with its cobbled streets, fine churches, plantation owners' palaces and low colonial houses with picturesque patios. Most of the original seven *villas*, or towns, founded by Diego de Velázquez: **Bayamo, Baracoa, Santiago de Cuba, Puerto Príncipe (Camagüey), Sancti Spíritus, Trinidad and Havana**, have their colonial centres intact. Typically there is a central square with a church and a town hall, and streets radiate out from it on the grid system.

Impressive mansions were built by the planter and merchant classes, many of which are museums today.

The **Cuban countryside** is famous for its sugar plantations and the rolling green hills of cattle ranches and no trip to the island is complete without a drive in the country. The **mountains of the Sierra Maestra** offer some dramatic landscape and many historical associations with the wars of independence and the Revolution of the 1950s. The pine-clad mountains roll down to pretty, **unspoilt beaches** all along the eastern Caribbean coast stretching from **Cabo Cruz** to **Cabo Maisí**. This far eastern tip of Cuba, where Columbus first made landfall, is fascinating, both for the attractions of **Baracoa** and the fauna and flora of the area, with an amazing number of endemic species. The central **Escambray mountains**, which rise above Trinidad, are so invigorating that a health farm, or hospital hotel, has been built there, although most people go for the scenery, the rivers, caves and waterfalls. **Pinar del Río** in the west is on most tour itineraries, a small provincial city set amid some of the most extraordinary landscape of limestone hills and caves with tobacco fields everywhere you look. For birdwatching, the **Zapata peninsula** should not be missed and nature lovers will want to visit the national parks, biosphere reserves and other protected areas around the island.

For **beaches**, **Varadero** is world class, with its broad stretch of sand running all along the peninsula, but for those who

Tourism in Cuba

Cuba first became a holiday destination for wealthy Americans over a century ago. The textile magnate, Dupont, developed the resort area of Varadero from 1880, and it became fashionable for east coast Americans to spend the winter in the Bahamas or Cuba. Some came in large yachts, others stayed in the first hotels, By 1915, there were 72 hotels, more than a third of them in Havana, and leisure activities such as polo or fishing were available. Between the wars Cuba was visited by film stars and other famous names, many of whom can be seen in photos on the walls of one of the bars of the *Hotel Nacional*, built in the 1930s. Havana gained a reputation for gambling, drinking and prostitution; the mafia moved in and several hotels were built with their money, protected by the dictatorship. At this time Ernest Hemingway was one of the most well-known frequent visitors, enjoying the rum and deep sea fishing and becoming an expatriate resident. By the 1950s tourism was the second largest earner of foreign exchange after sugar and the island received over 300,000 tourists a year, most of them American. In the 1960s, when jet travel promoted mass tourism, Cuba was left in the cold because of the 1959 Revolution and the US boycott, American tourists went to Puerto Rico and the Bahamas instead, while Europeans went to Spain. Hotels fell into disrepair, standards declined, service was minimal and the tourism sector gave way to the all-important task of achieving a 10-million tonne sugar harvest. The only new hotels were built in the Soviet style, huge concrete blocks, with a heavy style of architecture.

The collapse of the Soviet bloc forced the Cuban government urgently to seek new sources of foreign exchange and a concerted effort has been made to develop tourism again. Foreign investment in joint ventures has been promoted in the 1990s to secure capital, management skills and training. The new resorts, many of which have Spanish or Canadian participation, are among the best in the Caribbean, mostly competing for the package charter holiday business, rather than the luxury, intimate, hideaway hotels found on islands such as St Barts or the Grenadines. However, tourism has been developed in isolation from the rest of the economy; there is very little local sourcing even for building materials, furniture or linen because of poor quality and inefficiency in state industries. The contradictory desire to maintain the centralized economy while getting into bed with foreign investors has produced distortions. There is a huge gap between those who have access to dollars and those who live in the peso economy, which has encouraged highly skilled professionals such as doctors to give up their training and become waiters or tourist guides. At the same time there is resentment at being physically excluded from tourist enclaves and beaches such as Varadero; Cubans who do not work there are stopped at check points and turned away if they do not have the right papers. Tourists also find the situation confusing; package holiday visitors spend only dollars while independent travellers cope with pesos .

Despite the economic problems and distortions, however, Cuba is one of the friendliest and safest tourist destinations in the Caribbean. Once off the beaten tourist trail you will find that everyone is interested in you, keen to help and generous with their own limited resources. Take a bottle of rum to a street party and you will be friends for life with the musicians and dancers. Offer fruit or lunch to your neighbour on a long distance train or bus and you can strike up a conversation which will teach you more about Cuba than you can ever read in a guide book. Now that it is legal to stay with Cuban families, albeit only those who are registered with the state and pay taxes, it is much easier to make contact and have direct dealings with Cubans, even if their initial interest in you is as a walking provider of dollars.

prefer a quieter resort, **Guardalavaca** is a good alternative. Then there are the **cays**, low-lying, sandy islets hugging the northern coast, only a handful of which have been developed and are perfect for escapism. Divers prefer the cays off the southern coast and the former prison island, Isla de la Juventud.

SUGGESTED ITINERARIES

An important thing to remember is that Cuba is a big island, the largest in the Caribbean and nearly as big as England. Just as you could not hope to cover England in a 2-week trip, do not plan to do too much in Cuba if that is all the time you have got. You will also be limited by transport, or rather the lack of it, unless you hire a car, which is an expensive option. You should expect to have to take advantage of opportunities as they come up and your transport will probably be a combination of bus (public bus and tour bus), train and hired private car where appropriate. If your time is restricted you should decide which end of the island you would prefer to see in detail and fly to either Havana or

Santiago de Cuba and start from there. If you have got all the time in the world then start at one end of Cuba and work your way to the other. An excellent road runs all the way from Havana to Santiago down the centre of the island, passing through many of the important cities, with side roads off to other places of interest. You could return to your starting point by plane or train, again depending on the time available.

The following suggested routes will give you a rough idea of how much time to allow in any particular region, although obviously you could spend far longer depending on your interests.

1. **Havana**: you need at least a day just to see the old city and 2-3 days to get round all the major sites in the suburbs. If you are using the capital as a base for day trips out to the countryside or the beaches along the coast, then a week is needed.

2. **Pinar del Río**: frequently done as a day trip from Havana on a whistle stop bus tour which does not do justice to this western province, home of some of the best tobacco and cigars in the world. A more leisurely pace would allow a night at Las Terrazas with walks in the rainforest and a visit to the orchid gardens at Soroa, and 2 further nights at Pinar del Río or Viñales, with excursions to the *mogotes*, the caves, beaches and the Guanahacabibes National Park in the extreme west. With your own transport, you can drive a circular route and see much of the province.

3. **Matanzas**: much of Matanzas province is accessible only by hired car or tour bus, notably the Zapata peninsula, which again is usually visited as a day trip from Havana or Varadero. To get a good overview of the province you should spend 2 or 3 nights in Varadero, giving yourself time to sit on the beach as well as indulging in an excursion to the cays and a trip inland to Cárdenas and caves in the area, followed by 2 nights in either Playa Larga

or Playa Girón, with visits to Guamá, the Bay of Pigs and some birdwatching in the Ciénaga de Zapata.

4. **Trinidad**: day trips to Trinidad are rushed and unsatisfactory, particularly as the best time to see the town is after the tour buses have gone home. With the best part of a week to spare, get a bus or train to Santa Clara, last resting place of Che Guevara; next day get yourself to Sancti Spíritus, another colonial city of great charm, and visit the Zaza dam; then travel to Trinidad, preferably by hiring a private car and driver so that you can visit the Valley of the Sugar Mills and stop for sightseeing on the way; stay at least 2 nights in Trinidad, giving yourself time to explore the town and get up into the Escambray mountains; you might also like to spend some time on the beach at Ancón before travelling to Cienfuegos to take in more colonial architecture, a fortress and another beach. The return trip to Havana could take in the Bay of Pigs and the Zapata peninsula if you have your own car.

5. **Camagüey**: the central towns of Camagüey, Ciego de Avila and Las Tunas are often missed because travellers concentrate on one end of the island or the other and skip the bits in between. Nevertheless, Camagüey is a priceless colonial gem of a town and well worth a day's exploration. From here you can take in a couple of nights on the beach at Playa Santa Lucía. Similarly, Ciego de Avila, only 110 km from Camagüey, warrants a day of sightseeing and is the jumping off point for the beach resort of Cayo Coco.

6. **Santiago de Cuba**: 2 weeks are needed to do justice to the eastern end of the island, allowing time to see the city, do day trips to places like La Gran Piedra, Parque Baconao and El Cobre, a round trip west along the coast to where the revolutionaries disembarked and on to Manzanillo and Bayamo, followed by an easterly round trip to Guantánamo, Baracoa, Holguín and the beaches of Guardalavaca, before returning to Santiago through the mountains.

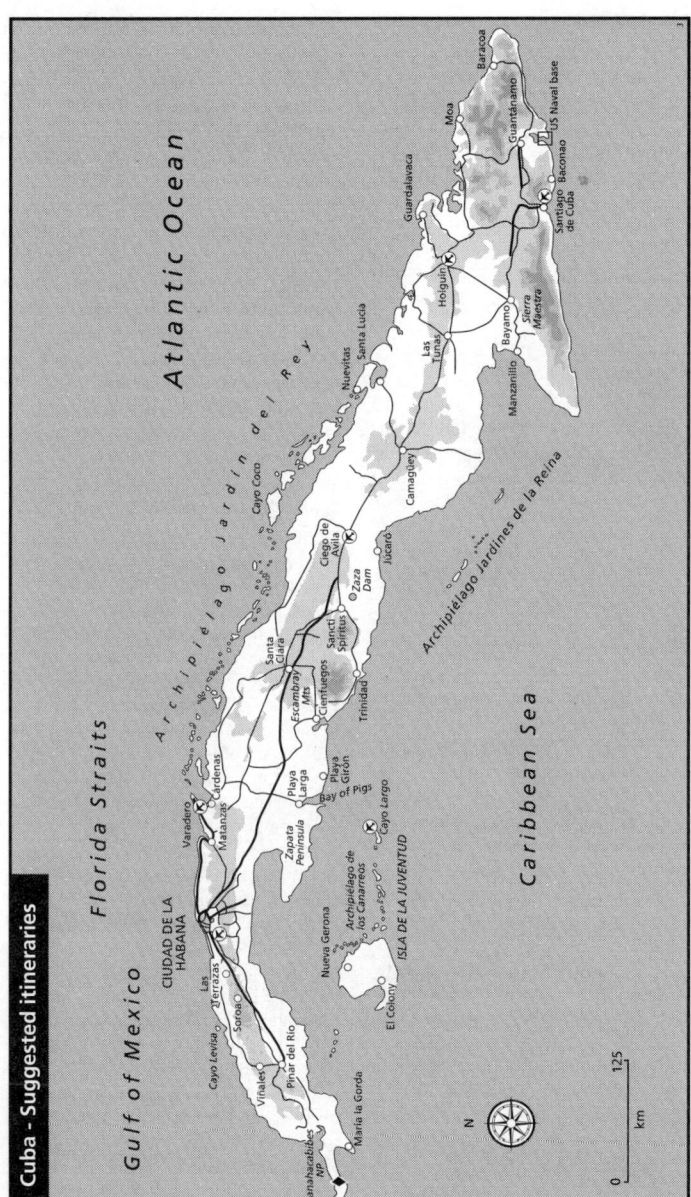

Cuba - Suggested itineraries

How to go

GETTING AROUND

The shortage of fuel and spare parts in Cuba have led to difficulties in the supply of long distance transport and this has been a major headache for independent travellers in the past. The problems are easing now, however, and you can generally get to anywhere you want if you know how to arrange it.

New buses, paid for in dollars, are being introduced on long distance routes between cities commonly visited by foreigners to supplement the existing bus network used by Cubans. Tour buses are flexible, allowing you to stay a night or two in, say, Pinar del Río, before rejoining the tour for the return to Havana.

The express train between Havana and Santiago de Cuba is generally fast and reliable, but other rail journeys are fraught with difficulties and generally are subject to breakdowns and long delays. Internal flights are frequent and efficient but generally only link Havana with other towns, so you can not crisscross the island by air.

Roads are good and there is little traffic except in Havana, which is a bit of a nightmare if you have just arrived. Out of the city, however, roads are empty and you can travel for miles without seeing another vehicle. Car hire is available, although you may not get the car you want unless you arrange it in advance from abroad. The disadvantage of car hire is that it is expensive and filling stations are not always conveniently located, but you will have the freedom of going where you want, when you want and you will have the roads almost to yourself. A good way of getting around and meeting the people is to hire a private car with driver to take you out for a day. He will want to be paid in dollars, but if there are two or three of you it can work out cheaper and more enjoyable than taking an organized excursion on a tour bus.

PRACTICALITIES

There is no centralized tourist office in Cuba. For information you have to go to one of the state travel companies, such as Rumbos or Fantástico, who have desks in most hotels. They are generally good, informative, multi-lingual and will not hard sell you one of their own tours.

The unit of currency is the peso. There is an official exchange rate of 1 peso = US$1, but tourists use the floating rate in the Cadecas (exchange houses) of around 21-23 pesos = US$1. Other currencies can be changed in Havana and banks in large cities, but the US dollar is king and accepted as legal tender. Most people need only change a minimum of US$5-10 for incidental expenses such as stamps, food bought from street stalls and books. All accommodation, restaurants and transport are charged in dollars except for some places to eat and some bus journeys off the beaten track. Note that although the US currency is accepted, travellers' cheques drawn on a US bank are not, see **Information for travellers** (page 290) for details.

The best hotels are those with foreign investment or foreign management contracts, which are found in the resort areas. However, there are hotels to suit most budgets, even if at the lower end they are basic. Cubans stay in peso hotels, which are rarely available to foreigners. A growing segment of the market is the private sector. It is now legal to stay with a Cuban family and rent a room or apartment as long as the family is registered and pays taxes. The price of a room is usually around US$15-25 but you will have to pay more if you are introduced to the family by a tout, so that he gets his commission.

Food is not Cuba's strong point, although the supply of fresh food has improved. Hotels tend to serve buffet meals which can get tedious after a while, but breakfast is usually good and plentiful and you can stock up for the day. The best meals at reasonable prices are to be had in the private restaurants, known as *paladares*, where you can get items paid for in dollars which are not available to Cubans on their ration cards. Vegetarians find Cuba particularly difficult; even the beans are often cooked with meat fat.

Rum is the national drink and all cocktails are rum-based. There are several brand names and each has a variety of ages, so you have plenty of choice. Beer is good and there are regional varieties which come in bottles or cans. Tobacco is of course excellent but remember that all the best leaves go into cigar making, rather than cigarettes. Make sure you buy the best to take home and don't get tricked into buying fakes, you may not get them through Customs. The locally grown coffee is good, although hotels often manage to make it undrinkable in the mornings.

Spanish is the official language, spoken fast with some consonants dropped. In the main tourist areas you will find staff often speak several languages, but off the beaten track you will need Spanish or very efficient sign language.

Most hotels have facilities for international calls and faxes which you can use even if you are not staying there. Phone cards are now used elsewhere and can work out quite economical. Cuba does not have a reputation for good communications; it can take time to get a line and e-mail is rare, but things are gradually improving with help from foreign telecommunications companies. The downside is that numbers and codes are frequently changing.

WHEN TO GO

The high season is mid-December to mid-April, when there are more dry days, more sunshine and less humidity. The season for hurricanes and tropical storms begins in August and can go on until the end of November, but a serious hurricane does not come every year by any means.

HEALTH

For anyone travelling overseas, health is a key consideration. With sensible precautions the visitor to Cuba should remain as healthy as at home. There are general rules to follow which should keep you in good health when travelling in Cuba. These are dealt with in the full health section on page 318.

Before you travel make sure you take out adequate insurance. Have a check up with your doctor, if necessary, and arrange your immunizations well in advance. There are no vaccinations demanded by immigration officials in Cuba, but you would do well to be protected by vaccination against typhoid, polio, tetanus and hepatitis A if you are going to be travelling rough in rural areas. There is no malaria in Cuba but lots of mosquitoes in the wetlands so take insect repellent.

The most common affliction of travellers to any country is probably diarrhoea. Shellfish are always a risk, although not common in Cuba. Fruit should be washed or peel it yourself. Avoid raw food, undercooked food (including eggs) and reheated food. Food that is cooked in front of you and offered hot all through is generally safe.

Tap water is safe in most areas of Cuba, but bottled water is widely available if you prefer. Cuba has a high quality national health service and is one of the healthiest countries in Latin America and the Caribbean. Travel in Cuba poses no health risk to the average visitor provided sensible precautions are taken.

The climate is hot; Cuba is a tropical country and protection against the sun will be needed. Take a high factor sun screen, apply it regularly and stay out of the midday sun. Children need to be particularly well protected and wear a hat. The breeze at the beach is deceptive, you may not feel hot, but the sun will burn very quickly.

On returning home, report any symptoms to your doctor and say exactly where you have been.

SINGLE TRAVELLERS

Whether you are a man or a woman travelling on your own, you will be approached by *jineteros/as* looking to make a quick buck out of you. Be careful who you allow to become attached to you, for obvious reasons, and if you choose to have a companion make sure that the terms and conditions are fully understood by both parties. Single men and women are targeted by Cubans of the opposite sex, not only for their dollars, but also as a way out of the country if they can find a marriage partner. Within Cuba, it is often difficult to enter hotels if you are accompanied by a Cuban, or even a foreigner who looks like a Cuban. Single women will encounter the usual macho attitudes found in all Latin American countries and can expect to receive stares and comments on their attributes. Rape is not common, but the usual precautions should be taken to avoid getting into a compromising situation.

DISABLED TRAVELLERS

Servimed runs special hotel hospitals for people with special needs such as physiotherapy, kidney dialysis or other treatment, but outside these centres there are few facilities for people with disabilities. In the resort areas such as Varadero, some of the new hotels have been built with a couple of rooms adapted for people in wheelchairs, but the older, state-run, three-star hotels usually have no facilities. It is advisable to book in advance with a good tour company who can arrange everything to suit your needs and ensure that the right transport is available for transfers and excursions.

GAY AND LESBIAN TRAVELLERS

Cuba has in the past been notoriously homophobic and after the Revolution many homosexuals were sent to hard labour camp to be 'rehabilitated'. The Mariel exodus was characterized as being the flight of criminals and homosexuals, who could no longer stand their human rights being flouted. However, in the latter part of the 1980s and in the 1990s, attitudes have gradually changed and although Cuba is still a macho society, there is more tolerance of gays just as there is more religious freedom. The film, *Fresa y Chocolate* (see **Cuban cinema** page 80), has done much to stimulate debate and acceptance. For an excellent account of Cuban attitudes to homosexuals, before and after the Revolution and up to the present, read Ian Lumsden's *Machos, Maricones and Gays, Cuba and Homosexuality*, published by the Temple University Press, Philadelphia and Latin American Bureau, London. Gay travellers will not generally encounter any problems in Cuba, there are no laws against homosexuality and physical assaults are rare.

Adventure tourism

TREKKING, hiking, rafting and bird watching are elements of adventure or nature travel which are still in their infancy in Cuba but are likely to be heavily promoted in the near future. The island's plentiful fauna and flora, its mountains, cays and wetlands and its expanding system of national parks and other protected areas are perfect for getting close to nature. Hunting lodges still attract those who enjoy blasting ducks out of the sky and sport fishing is available in many marinas, but in the last few years the emphasis has been on looking and not touching, as in bird watching and scuba diving. The state travel agencies are opening specialist operations for organized tours with expert staff on hand to advise on biology, botany or forestry. So far there is Ecotur, which offers tours and is involved in conservation; Ecocuba, which is a joint venture between Cubatur and the Costa Rican tour company Tikal and operates mostly in the Sierra del Rosario; and Cubamar, which runs 'camp sites', or lodges, around the country for Cubans and foreigners.

Facilities are limited and many sports are simply unavailable. Traditionally, tourists have been expected to spend their time on the beach, with sightseeing excursions to colonial cities and night time forays into bars and clubs. More activities are now being developed, however, and those seeking water sports are unlikely to be disappointed.

WALKING

The three main mountain ranges are excellent for hill walking in a wide range of tropical vegetation where many national parks are being established and trails demarcated. The highest peaks are in the Sierra Maestra in the east, where there are also many historical landmarks associated with the wars of independence and the revolution. A 3-day walk will take you from Alto del Naranjo up the island's highest peak, Pico Turquino, and down to the Caribbean coast at Las Cuevas, giving you fantastic views of the mountains and the coastline. The Sierra del Escambray, in the centre of the island, is conveniently located just north of the best preserved colonial city: Trinidad, and there are some lovely walks in the hills, along trails beside rivers, waterfalls and caves. The mountains of the west of the island, the Sierra del Rosario and the Sierra de los Organos, have some of the most unusual geological features, notably the large number of caves and the limestone *mogotes*, straight sided, flat topped hills rising from the midst of tobacco fields and looking almost Chinese, particularly in the early morning mist. Good large scale maps are non-existent and you are advised to take a guide when embarking on long walks. Not only will this prevent you getting lost, but you will learn a lot more about your surroundings, as many of the guides are professional botanists or ornithologists. It is not advisable to take off for a long walk on your own in Cuba.

The first months of the year are the best for walking, as they are drier, less humid and not so hot. However, temperature varies with the altitude and the higher you get in the Sierra Maestra, the cooler it will become, so take appropriate clothing. Also remember that in the rain forest there are few days when it does not rain, so expect to get wet. The months from August to November are the wettest, when the risk of hurricanes or tropical storms increases, but you can still encounter days when there is plenty of sunshine and you can get out for a good walk. It is best to start early, before it gets too hot. Always carry plenty of drinking water, some food and suntan lotion.

MOUNTAIN BIKING

Cycling in Cuba is a very rewarding way of seeing the countryside. Much of the island is flat or undulating and relatively easy for cyclists. There are organized tours if you want to go with a party, but this is not necessary if you are prepared to put in a bit of planning beforehand. Most people prefer to cycle in the west and the centre of the island, avoiding the mountains of the Sierra Maestra in the east. Roads are generally good and there is very little traffic; it is not uncommon to have a whole motorway to yourself but watch out for sleeping dogs or coffee beans spread out to dry. You will encounter many Cubans on bicycles, often with side cars attached, or towing little carts, all adapted to carry the entire family because of the shortage of fuel for cars. It is perfectly acceptable to hitch a ride on a truck with your bicycle if you get tired, wait for a ride at one of the out of town road junctions where the *Amarillos* organize lifts for everybody.

Finding accommodation in the right places may be a problem if you have not planned a route carefully beforehand. Finding food is also a frequent complaint from cyclists, so stock up on fruit and other foodstuffs sold at the roadside when you find it. Carry plenty of water, but do not be afraid to stop and ask to refill your bottle at a house or roadside café. Cool, loose fitting clothing and plenty of high factor suntan lotion is essential, cycling is an extremely hot activity in Cuba and you must start off early in the morning if you are to cover any great distance before the day gets too hot.

SAILING

The management of marinas in Cuba is split between several companies: Cubanacán owns Marlin Marinas y Náuticas and the Hemingway Marina, and there are also the Puertosol chain and Gaviota. Marlin Marinas has 13 diving centres around the country and watersports activities in 31 hotels. They are currently developing recreational sailing and live-aboard yachts, with a fleet of about 20 boats based in places like Guardalavaca, Santiago de Cuba and Cienfuegos. Puertosol has six marinas, three diving centres and a nautical equipment store, and they operate in Cayo Largo del Sur, Tarará, Isla de la Juventud (*Hotel El Colony*) and María La Gorda, amongst other places. They have 22 live-aboard yachts and operate the *Tortuga* floating hotel in the Jardines de la Reina. Gaviota's main marina is at the tip of the Hicacos peninsula, Varadero, and they currently concentrate on day trips into the Cayo Piedra National Park. Their other marina is in Estero Ciego, Bahía de Naranjo, near Guardalavaca, where there is a dolphinarium and docking facilities.

Not many 'yachties' (people who live and travel on their own boats) visit the island because of the political difficulties between Cuba and the USA. The US administration forbids any vessel, such as a cruise ship, cargo ship or humble yacht from calling at a US port if it has stopped in Cuba. This effectively prohibits anyone sailing from the US eastern seaboard calling in at a Cuban port on their way south through the Caribbean islands, or vice versa. It is better to rent a bareboat yacht from a Cuban marina and sail around the island, rather than include it in a Caribbean itinerary. It would be worthwhile to invest in *The Cruising Guide to Cuba*, by Simon Charles (Cruising Guide Publications, Box 1017, Dunedin, FL 34697-1017, USA, T 813-733 5322, F 813-734 8179) before embarking.

FISHING

Cuba has been a fisherman's dream for many decades, not only for its deep sea fishing, popularized by Ernest Hemingway, but also for its freshwater fishing in the many lakes and reservoirs spread around the island. **Freshwater fishing** is mostly for the largemouth bass (*trucha*), which grow to a great size in the Cuban lakes. Horizontes is the travel company to contact for accommodation and fishing packages, which can be arranged all year round. The main places are Maspotón, in Pinar del Río, where you can fish in La Juventud reservoir or in the mouth of the Río Los Palacios or Río Carraguao; Laguna del Tesoro in the Ciénaga de Zapata, where there is a wide variety of fish; Presa Alacranes in Villa Clara province, which is the second largest reservoir in the country; Presa Zaza, in Sancti Spíritus, the largest artificial lake in Cuba, where the record catch of *trucha* is 16.5 lbs; Lago La Redonda, near Morón in Ciego de Avila province, where the clear waters hold such a concentration of fish that a group of US fishermen were able to catch 5,078 *trucha* in 5 days; and in the province of Camagüey on the Porvenir, Muñoz and Mañana de Santa Ana dams. Equipment can be hired, but serious fishermen will prefer to bring their own and a large quantity of insect repellent. **Deep sea fishing** can be organized at most marinas around the island although most of the tournaments and the best facilities are at the Marina Hemingway, just west of Havana. The waters are home to a variety of beaked fish: marlin, swordfish, tarpon, sawfish, yellowfin tuna, dorado, wahoo, shark and a host of others are all caught here. Varadero is a good point from which to go fishing and take advantage of the Gulf Stream which flows between Key West in Florida and Cuba, but records have been broken all along the northern coast in the cays of the Archipiélago de Sabana and the Archipiélago de Camagüey. There is also good fishing off the south coast around the Isla de la Juventud and Cayo Largo. **Bonefishing** is best done off the south coast in the Archipiélago de los Jardines de la Reina, or off Cayo Largo.

SHOOTING

If you think fishing is bad and an unnecessary waste of life, then you will not be pleased to hear that hunting and shooting birds is a popular sport in Cuba and enjoyed by a certain sort of foreigner. It takes place at most of the lodges for freshwater fishing, such as Maspotón or Morón and can also be arranged by Horizontes. All equipment and dogs are for hire and a hunting licence must be purchased. If you want to use your own equipment you must get a permit to bring it into the country. The hunting season for most birds is 15 September to 30 March, except for white crowned ring dove, which is from 15 August to 30 September. The unfortunate victims of this sport include the mourning dove, the white winged dove, migrant ducks, snipe, guinea fowl, pheasant and quail.

Diving and marine life

Cuba's marine environment is pristine compared with most Caribbean islands, where there has often been overharvesting and overdevelopment of the dive industry. The majority of coral reefs are alive and healthy and teeming with assorted marine life. The Government has established a marine park around the Isla de la Juventud and much marine life is protected around the entire island, such as turtles, the manatee and coral. There are three main marine platforms, the Archipiélago del Rey (Sabana-Camagüey), the Archipiélago de la Reina and the Archipiélago de los Canarreos. The first one has the greatest diversity of marine species and is being explored and classified with the aim of making it a protected zone. There are believed to be some 900 species of fish, 1,400 species of molluscs, 60 species of coral, 1,100 species of crustaceans, 67 species of sharks and rays and four types of marine turtles around the island, as well as the manatee (see box, page 27).

The main dive areas are Isla de la Juventud, Varadero, Faro de Luna, María La Gorda, Santa Lucía and Santiago de Cuba. New areas are being developed as hotels are built around the island. Most areas offer a variety of diving, including reefs and walls and an assortment of wrecks, from remains of ancient Spanish ships to many modern wrecks sunk as dive sites. Cuban diving is a new frontier in the Caribbean and has much to offer the adventurous or trainee diver.

SCUBA CUBA

Heading west from Havana, all along the northwest coast of Cuba there is a long chain of small islets, or cays. One which has recently been discovered by scuba divers is **Cayo Levisa**, where there is now a hotel. You get there by a 15-minute boat ride from Palma Rubia, which is in turn 2 hours by car, 125 km from Havana. The reef runs parallel to the cay and it drops off to over 50m. There are about 15 dive sites frequently dived, of between 15-35m deep and boat dives are no more than half an hour away. The underwater scenery is characterized by big sponges and enormous black coral trees. Angel fish are very numerous, as are barracuda and schools of jacks. The current is generally quite gentle so it is an ideal place for beginners and experts alike. There are several bits and pieces of old galleons, most of which have been covered by corals. The dive shop is Diving World, staffed by Cubans, who use 10-12m wooden boats to take out 8-14 divers at a time. They offer CMAS courses in English and Spanish.

In the far west of the island, **María la Gorda** offers some of the best diving in a warm, sheltered bay where visibility is good all year round. The coral formations, sponges and gorgonians are quite spectacular and the fish are plentiful, including barracuda, moray eels, lobsters, grunts, groupers and even whale sharks at certain times of the year. Most dive sites, which include bits of old Spanish galleons, caves, tunnels and drop-offs, stretch along the coast from La Bajada to Cabo Corrientes. As in most of Cuba, you do a morning dive, return to shore for lunch and then go out again on the boat in the afternoon. There is little else to do in this area other than dive, which, if you are not on a package, will cost you US$30 per tank and US$7.50 a day to hire equipment. Fresh water cave diving in blue holes is also possible though not on offer as an organized activity.

Due east of María la Gorda, now moving along the south coast of Cuba, is Cuba's most famous and long-established dive spot, the **Isla de la Juventud**. From the marina on the west coast you can reach 56 buoyed dive sites, count over 40 varieties of coral and swim through tunnels, deep canals and valleys. It takes about 45 minutes by boat to reach Cabo Francés, which is where many of the best diving places are. The west side of the island is protected from the prevailing winds so that the water is normally calm with temperatures ranging from 24° in winter to 28° in summer.

There are many exciting dive sites stretching east of the Isla de la Juventud along the **Archipiélago de los Canarreos**, but these are really only possible on a liveaboard (some of which come from the Cayman Islands). The string of low lying cays, with sandy beaches, mangroves, clear water and colourful reefs has trapped many ships in the past. Divers have found the remains of over 70 ships and there is an area near Cayo Avalos, called Bajo de Zambo, which is full of them. Several would have been looking for turtle meat and today you can still find Green, Hawksbill and Ridley turtles, which are protected now in Cuba.

At the eastern end of the archipelago is the resort island of **Cayo Largo**, a flat, sandy island surrounded by some lovely beaches and turquoise water. You have to be keen on the water to come here, as there is nothing much else to do, and some 30 dive sites have been identified. There are two main diving areas: south of the island along the reefs Los Ballenatos and on the nearby Cayo Rosario there are some pretty coral patches rising from a sandy bottom in shallow water, rich in fish with easy diving, ideal for novice divers; north of the island, in the Golfo de Cazones, there is a deep drop-off with steep walls, ridges and caves where you can find large pelagic and black coral but there is often a strong current so this is only really suitable for expert divers.

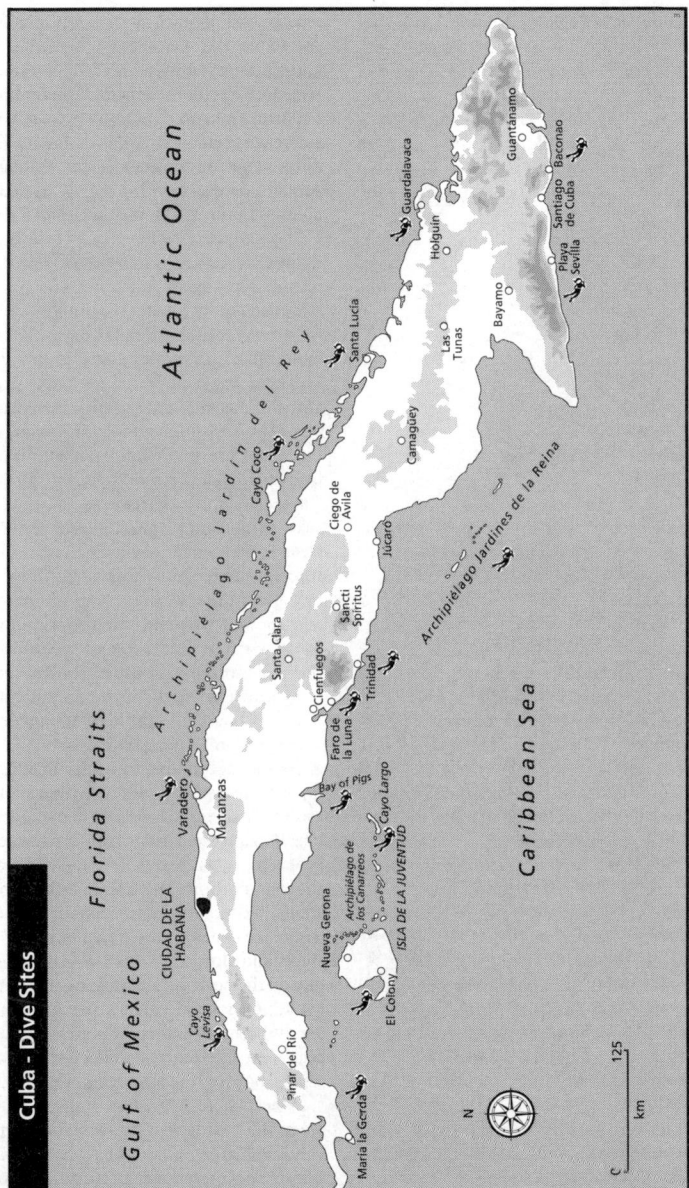

Cuba - Dive Sites

Action Sport Diving Center is based at Playa Sirena, T/F 5-48300, offering a full range of PADI courses (US$350 for open water), US$60 for two dives in a day, snorkelling, full day trips and night dives.

Diving from **Punta Perdix (Bay of Pigs)** is an easy beach entry if you are in the area, although there is no dive shop or anything else in this remote part. Nearby there is a 15-18m long Fisheries Division shipwreck, sitting in 20m of water on a sand slope. The wreck was intentionally sunk by the government in 1995. The boat, known as a Cayo Largo boat, was built in the early 1980s from concrete and wire. Cuba is well known for building ships like this, which are expected to have a life of around 10 years and then gutted, with everything of use being removed for a newer model. These 'throw away' boats used to be sunk in deep water, but as diving developed as a sport on the islands, the wrecks were placed in shallow waters to allow divers to explore them.

Faro de Luna, near Cienfuegos, has over 18 reef sites and a variety of modern wrecks, including seven sunk as diving sites just outside the harbour. One of the best is *Camaronero II*, a shrimp boat only 5 minutes from the dive shop at *Hotel Faro de Luna* (Carretera de Pasacaballo Km 18, Playa Rancho Luna, Cienfuegos). Most of the wrecks have been stripped of everything, but the *Camaronero II* still has her propellers which makes an interesting photo site. 22m long, she was built of steel around 1974 and was sunk deliberately between 1983-84 in 18m of water, totally intact. The wreck is adorned with small coral growth, small gorgonias and sponges and seasonally large schools of red snapper, grouper, hog fish and jacks are found there. However, during the rainy season the visibility is not good as she lies near the mouth of the river. Other wrecks are the *Camaronero I*, an 8m wreck lying in shallow water close to shore but very broken up; the cargo ships, *Panta I* and *II*, sunk in 1988; the *Barco R Club*, a

20m cement and steel passenger ship sunk in 1992 in 8m; the 20m passenger boat *Barco Arimao* also sunk in 1992 in 18m and the steel fishing boat *Itabo* sunk in 1994 in 12m. There are also numerous reef sites in this area and the dive shop has identified over a dozen, of which the best include El Bajo in 4m, El Laberinto, La Guasa and Rancho Luna II all in 12m, and La Corona in 15m (well known as divers often see whale sharks around this site).

Jardines de la Reina is an archipelago of 3,000 sq km of islets and mangroves 80 km south of the province of Camagüey. Unapproachable for years as they were Castro's favourite fishing spot, these islands have now been declared a natural park. There are birds, iguanas, turtles and loads of fish (and mosquitoes, bring insect repellent). You get there by boat from Júcaro, 1 hour drive from Ciego de Avila, and then 5 hours by boat to the Jardines. A floating hotel, the *Tortuga*, 50m by 15m, has eight cabins with a/c and en suite facilities and two new compressors on board. It is moved from place to place every 6 months or so to reduce the impact on the reef. There is also basic accommodation on board the old and slow 20m liveaboards, *Fantasía* and *Explorador*, which can accommodate eight people. However, the crew is very efficient and helpful, food is good with fresh fish and bread baked every day. The boats stay anchored for 2-3 days in one place or are used for a 6-night trip away from the *Tortuga*. Another boat, the 25m *MV Boca del Toro*, operates out of Trinidad but offers diving all along the archipelago. The boat is refurbished but accommodation is basic with room for 12, simple but plentiful food. There are about 40 dive sites along the southwest side of the archipelago. The reef runs parallel to the shore and usually drops down in three 'steps': the first at 10-15m, very exposed to the surf; a second at 20m on a sandy bottom, and a third that starts at 40-45m and drops downward. You will find all the

The Manatee

There are manatee, or sea cow (*trichechus manatus latirostrisis*), in the waters around Cuba, but they are rare and protected. Once thought by sailors to be mermaids, they are actually a distant relative of the elephant and in appearance are a far cry from the beautiful sirens who in Greek mythology lured mariners to their deaths. The manatee is the largest vegetarian living in the sea, it can weigh over 1,360kg and measure up to 4 metres. Its body is a huge oval shape, rather like an outsize sea lion, with a bulbous nose, small eyes, two forelimbs and a paddle tail. It is warm blooded, suckles its young and surfaces to breathe air every 4-5 minutes. The two fore limbs each have five bones and may once have been used for some other purpose many thousands of years ago but evolution has reduced them to flippers. Both sexes reach maturity at around seven years old and mate with several partners. The female is in sole charge of the young once the calf is born at the end of a 13-month gestation and it will keep close to its mother for two years. Calves are usually about 1 metre long at birth and weigh about 37kg. Sometimes there are twins. They can see, hear and swim immediately, rising three times a minute to

breathe and keeping close to the surface. Manatees are very shy but docile and completely harmless. Once they get used to people they can be inquisitive and approach you, but it is extremely unlikely that in Cuba you will ever be able to swim with the manatees like you can with the captive dolphins.

reef fishes here, tarpons and at one site there is shark feeding. The sea is often rough. Avalon Dive Centre instructors can teach CMAS and NAUI courses.

Santiago de Cuba offers a great deal of diving with four dive shops along the coast. To the east of the city: Bucanero (*Club Amigo Bucanero*, Carretera a Baconao Km 4, Arroyo La Costa), Daiquirí Dive Centre (*Hotel Daiquirí*, Carretera a Baconao), Sigua Dive Centre (Carretera a Baconao Km 28), and to the west: Sierra Mar (*Hotel Sierra Mar*, Playa Sevilla, Guamá). The Sierra Maestra mountains all along this south-facing Caribbean coast offer a foretaste of what is to be found underwater, where the island platform gently shelves to a depth of 35m and then the ocean wall drops straight down to a depth of over 1,000m in the channel between Cuba and Haiti. Popular wreck sites near the Sigua Dive Centre include the 30m passenger ship, *Guarico*, lying in

15m. She lies on her port side with the mast covered in soft sponges. A ferry/tug wreck lies upside down in 35m of water and the two vessels together span around 150m. The metal structure is covered with large yellow and purple tube sponges. The 35m *Spring Coral* lies in 24m. Most of the structure is still intact with a great deal of marine growth offering many photo opportunities. An unusual site dived by Bucanero and the Daiquirí Dive Centre is the Bridge. In 1895 a large bridge broke and fell into the sea in 12m, along with a train. Later a ship sank and was blown into the bridge underwater, adding to the mass of structures. The Sierra Mar Dive Shop offers a special wreck dive on the *Cristóbal Colón*, a Spanish ship lying on a slope in 9-27m. She was badly damaged by gunfire in 1898 by the US Navy during the Battle of Santiago in the Spanish American War after a long chase. Although initially beached, attempts to refloat her were abandoned. This is an excellent shore dive with hardly any current, although in the wet season visibility is affected by runoff from the Sierra Maestra. There are four other wrecks in shallow water and are ideal for a snorkel.

Heading northwest now along the Atlantic coast back towards Havana, at **Guardalavaca**, there are a couple of dive shops at the resort hotels. They dive the reef and wall just offshore with mostly boat dives. There is lots of life here underwater, you can see lobsters, moray eels, huge crabs and angelfish as well as a variety of small, colourful, tropical fish, grouper, snapper, triggerfish, eagle rays, tarpon and sometimes sharks. This area is not particularly recommended during the wet season as the sea is rough, visibility deteriorates, you have to wade and swim out to the boat with all your gear and entry and exit is tricky with high waves (the author felt rather seasick!).

Santa Lucía sank in 1905 on a slope of 7-27m and is home for a host of marine life, including eight massive bull sharks, who have been hand fed by the dive masters from Sharks Friends Dive Shop (*Hotel Cuatro Vientos*) since the early 1980s (very exciting to watch). Other wrecks include the *Sanbinal*, in 17m and the British steel ship, *Nuestra Señora de Alta Gracia*, sunk around 1973 and completely intact, allowing divers to penetrate the entire ship, entering the engine room where all the machinery is still in place. An exciting historical site is Las Anforas, under an old fort dating from 1456. The fort was attacked several times by pirates and artefacts from Spanish ships are scattered across the sea bed. Four anchors were seen on one dive, with the largest being at least 2m. Further west along the archipelago, there is also good diving at **Cayo Coco**, where the water is beautifully clear and there is a wide variety fish found in large quantities, including snappers, jacks, tarpon and grouper.

Varadero is one of the most developed areas for diving. There are several sites around the offshore cays suitable for novice or advance divers and it is an attractive ride on the boat past the beautiful islets, which are good for snorkelling and picnics. Interesting sites include the wreck of the *Neptune*, a 60m steel cargo ship thought to be German, lying in only 10m. This is home to a number of fish including four massive green moray eels and four very large, friendly French angelfish. The wreck is very broken up, but the boilers are still intact and there are places where the superstructure (shaft and propeller) is in good condition and interesting to explore with good photo sites. Among the many reef dive sites in the area are Clara Boyas (Sun Roof), a massive 60 sq m coral head in 20m of water with tunnels large enough for three to four divers to swim through. These connect with upward passages where the sunlight can be seen streaming through. Another site, Las Brujas (the Witches) is only 6m deep. Large coral heads protrude from the sandy bottom, with coral holes and crevices, adorned with sea fans, home for large schools of snappers. Playa Coral is a site on a 2 km barrier reef west of Varadero, beginning at Matanzas Bay, with a large variety of fish and coral. This is usually a shore dive, although if you go over the wall, where you can find black coral and gorgonians in deep water, it can be a boat dive. If you are based in Varadero on a dive package, you may be offered a trip to Playa Girón for good shore diving, and to the Saturno Caves for an inland cave dive as part of your package.

Dive shops and equipment

All dive shops are government owned in Cuba, but run as joint ventures with foreign investors. There are three main companies, the largest (14 dive shops) is Cubanacán (Marlin). The others are Puerto Sol and Gaviota. Most staff speak Spanish, English and often other languages. There is nearly always a German, Italian or French speaking member of staff, depending on where most of their diving customers come from. Diving is usually done as part of all-inclusive packages, although dives can be booked direct with dive shops for around US$35, including all equipment. Most companies use European dive gear. In Europe for details on dive packages contact Cubanacán UK Ltd, Skylines, Unit 49, Limeharbour, Docklands, London E14 9TS, T 0171 537 7909, F 537 7747.

Diving supplies are very limited. Basic rental gear is available, but if you use your own you should be prepared with all spares needed for diving and photography (batteries, film, replacement parts such as a regulator mouthpiece etc) as these are either not available or excessively expensive. In the summer months, on the south of the island, tiny jelly fish may abound and can cause nasty stings on areas not covered by a wet suit. A tropical hood is a good idea to protect the neck and face in jelly fish season, often referred to as *agua mala*, or 'bad water'. A well-stocked first aid kit is recommended, for although the medical profession is well-trained, supplies are limited. Things you might like to take for precautionary purposes include antibiotics for possible ear or sinus infections, nasal sprays, ear drops,

antihistamine cream, diarrhoea remedies and seasickness pills. Remember, however, that decongestants and antihistamine will make you sleepy and you should not dive after taking this sort of medicine. Other common problems such as sunburn, cuts and abrasions from scraping against coral, and fire coral stings can be treated with preparatory remedies brought from home, but be particularly careful to avoid infection from any lesions and make sure you are up to date with your anti-tetanus injections. Best to avoid touching any coral (which will die if you do anyway) and not go poking about in holes and overhangs where you might get stung or bitten by something you can't see. Havana has a *Hyperbaric Medicine Centre* and Varadero uses a chamber at the main hospital at Cárdenas, both staffed by doctors trained in hyperbaric medicine. There is also a recompression chamber at the *José Castillo Duany Military Hospital* in Santiago de Cuba and at the *Hotel Colony* on the Isla de la Juventud.

Dives can sometimes be delayed for a variety of reasons, including limited available fuel, Coast Guard clearance to depart port, etc, so patience is needed.

Horizons

THE LAND

GEOLOGY AND LANDSCAPE

Geologically at least, Cuba is part of North America; the boundary between the North American and Caribbean plates runs east-west under the Caribbean Sea to the south of the island. Along the plate margin is a deep underwater rift valley, which runs between Cuba and Jamaica. This feature is quite close to the Cuban coast to the south of the Sierra Maestra, with water plunging to 6,000m deep only a few miles offshore. Earth movements along the plate boundary make the eastern region of Cuba the most earthquake-prone part of the country, with well-known earthquakes including Bayamo in 1551 and Santiago de Cuba in 1932.

Current plate movements are pushing Cuba to the west and the Caribbean plate to the east. What is now the Sierra Maestra in southern Cuba was probably joined 40 million years ago to geologically similar areas on the north coast of Haiti and the Dominican Republic. Plate movements since then have caused a displacement of around 400 km. Cuba is also being tilted gradually to the north. The northern coastline is gradually emerging from the sea. Old coral reefs have been brought to the surface, and now form much of the coastline, so that much of the northern coast consists of coral limestone cliffs and sandy beaches. A short way inland, old cliff lines marking stages of coastal emergence form a series of coral terraces, one of which runs just north-east of the *Hotel Nacional* in Havana. There are well-developed series of old cliff lines and coral terraces on the southeast tip of the island near Baracoa and to the west of Santiago near Cabo Cruz. By contrast the southern coastline is being gradually submerged, producing a series of wetlands and mangroves running from the Ensenada de Cortés in the west to the Gulf of Guacanayabo in the east, with fewer sandy beaches than the north of the island.

During the geologically recent glacial periods of the last million years, sea level worldwide fell by about 120m, as much of the world's water was locked up in the northern ice sheets. The shallow seas which now form Cuba's continental shelf were dry land, and the coastline generally followed the line of Cuba's 4000-plus offshore islands: the Sabana island chain to the north and the Canarreos and Jardines de la Reina to the south. At this time, central Cuba was separated from the Bahamas by a narrow channel, about 32 km wide.

Cave systems which formed during glacial periods in what were then coastal limestone plains have since been flooded by the sea. In coastal areas such as the western Guanahacabibes peninsula and Playa Girón, there are small, deep lakes known to English-speaking geologists as Blue Holes where these submerged cave systems meet the surface.

There is no clear agreement about Cuba's more distant geological origins. The curve of the island follows the line of a collision in the Cretaceous period around 100 million years ago between an arc of volcanic islands and the stable Bahamas platform which then formed the southern edge of the North American plate. There is disagreement about whether this arc faced north or south, and about how the collision took place. But the powerful forces associated with the process produced a complex pattern of folding and faulting, while many rocks were greatly altered by heat and pressure. Many of Cuba's rocks predate this collision. These include the Caribbean's only Pre-Cambrian rocks, metamorphics more than 900 million years old in the province of Santa Clara; and the Jurassic limestones, around 160 million years old, which form the Sierra de los Organos.

After the collision, what is now Cuba was submerged for long periods, and there were new deposits of limestone and other rocks. For most of the tertiary period, from 35 million years ago, Cuba was a series of large islands and shallow seas, emerging as a single land mass by the start of the Pliocene period 5 million years ago. Limestones of various types cover about two-thirds of the island. In most areas, there is a flat or gently rolling landscape. The most common soils, both formed on limestone, are terra rossa, stained bright red by iron oxides, and vertisols, black, fertile, and developing deep cracks during the dry season.

There are three main mountain areas in the island. In the west, the Cordillera de Guaniguanico is divided into the Sierra del los Organos in the west, with thick deposits of limestone which have developed a distinctive landscape of steep-sided flat-topped mountains; and the Sierra del Rosario in the east, made up partly of limestones and partly of lavas and other igneous rocks. Another mountainous area in central Cuba includes the Escambray mountains north of Trinidad, a double dome structure made up of igneous and metamorphic rocks, including marble.

The Sierra Maestra in east Cuba has Cuba's highest mountains, rising to Pico Turquino (1,974m) and a rather different geological history, with some rocks formed in an arc of volcanic activity around 50 million years ago. Older rocks include marble, and other metamorphics. The country's most important mineral deposits are in this area; nickel mined near Moa is the third most important foreign currency earner, after sugar and tourism.

For those interested in further information on the physical and human geography of Cuba, the Nuevo Atlas Nacional de Cuba (Geocuba, Calle F y 13, Havana, T 323494) provides a beautifully produced series of detailed thematic maps on every possible topic down to the distribution of ants and spiders, with informative commentaries.

CLIMATE

Like most Caribbean islands, Cuba has a tropical marine climate, with temperatures averaging 22°-26°C over most of the country, and rainfall generally around 1,000-1,400 mm. The rainfall total sounds high by European standards but is achieved by high intensity showers, not a slow steady drip. Havana and most coastal areas have rain on fewer than 80 days a year. Rainfall is more than 2,000 mm in the three mountainous areas of western, central and eastern Cuba; the highest total of 3,400 mm is recorded in the highest parts of the Sierra Maestra, where the mountain climate also produces lower temperatures of around 16°C. By contrast, the coastline south of the Sierra Maestra, around Guantánamo Bay, is a rain shadow area with rainfall around 600 mm and the highest average temperatures in the country.

Completely cloudless days are most common in the dry season, which runs from December to April. Because Cuba is relatively close to the North American

Hurricane Lili

After several days of hesitation, during which Cubans frantically speculated and evacuated, Hurricane Lili finally moved towards the Cuban coast on 17 October 1996. It was at first thought that she would pass over the island to the W of Havana through Pinar del Río; the next forecast was that the route would be to the E and hit Matanzas. Once she got started and headed due N over Isla de la Juventud, it was assumed she would strike Havana, wreaking untold damage to the fragile colonial city. However, she changed course at the last minute, and, having reached the coast veered SE again towards Trinidad and sharply NE across Villa Clara province to the Atlantic Ocean and on to the Bahamas. There was extensive damage to crops and housing, but no one was killed because of highly efficient civil defence procedures involving evacuation of the most vulnerable areas. Heaps of rubble for renovation were cleared from the streets of Havana to prevent storm drains being blocked, leaving them cleaner than ever before. Half the buildings in the colonial city were judged to be at risk and 200,000 people were moved from their homes. Tourists were evacuated from Cayo Largo to Varadero and some Havana hotels were emptied, although a few Italian and Spanish visitors professed to be looking forward to the 'adventure' and refused to move. Crop damage was compounded by heavy rain later in October which flooded eastern Cuba and further storms in mid-November affecting the whole country. Several buildings collapsed in Havana while thousands of tonnes of bananas, citrus, rice, sugar and root vegetables were destroyed.

continent, coldfronts in the winter season can also produce heavy rain, strong winds, rough seas and quite low temperatures on the north coast. Lows of 6°-12°C are reached in an average year, and 2°C has been recorded in exceptional conditions. For most of the year, the NE trades keep temperatures comfortable, although summer daytime temperatures of up to 36°C are sometimes recorded. Very hot conditions are most frequent in the eastern interior of the island.

The rainy season runs from May to October, with rainfall slightly lower in the middle of this period (July-August) than in May-June or September-October. Even in the wettest months, most days have dry, relatively clear weather.

Cuba is in the hurricane belt, although the chances of any part of the island being hit in a particular year are quite low, and satellite weather systems give several days' warning of an approaching storm. Hurricane risk is greatest from June to November.

FLORA AND FAUNA

When the Spanish arrived at the end of the 15th century more than 90% of Cuba was covered with forest. When Fray Bartolomé de las Casas visited the island, he said *"La Isla tiene de luengo cerca de 300 leguas y se puede andar toda por debajo de los árboles"* (the island is 300 leagues long and you can walk the length of it beneath the trees). However, clearance for cattle raising and sugar cane reduced this proportion to 54% by 1890 and 14% in 1959, though reafforestation since the Revolution has increased this figure again to 19.5%. 75% of the land is now savannah or plains, 18% mountains and 4% swamps. The mesophytic semi-deciduous tropical woodland which covered most low-lying areas was hardest hit by forest clearance. Besides semi-deciduous woodland, vegetation types include rainforest, coastal and upland scrub, distinctive limestone vegetation found in the Sierra de los Organos and similar areas, savannah vegetation found on nutrient-deficient white silica sands, pine forests, xerophytic coastal limestone woodland, mangroves and other bird-rich coastal wetlands.

Cuba is characterized by extraordinarily high rates of biodiversity and endemism, particularly concentrated in four regions: the Montañas de Moa-Nipe-Sagua-Baracoa, which have the greatest diversity in all the Caribbean and are among the highest in the world, and 30% of the endemic species on the island; Parque Nacional Sierra de los Organos and the Reserva de la Biósfera Sierra del Rosario come a close second, with high rates of endemism, followed closely by the Reserva Ecológica del Macizo de Guamuhaya. There is a high proportion of endemic species, found only in Cuba, one region of Cuba, or in the extreme case of some snail species, only on one small mountain in the Sierra de los Organos. Around half the plant species, 90% of the insects and molluscs, 82% of the reptiles and 74 bird species are endemic.

Why the high proportion of endemics? Cuba has a 5 million year history as an isolated land mass, with species following their own evolutionary path. There are also a number of specialized environments with geological or soil constraints such as chemical toxicity, poor water retention, low nutrient retention, on ultrabasic igneous rocks, silica sands and limestones. By the end of this decade, it is hoped that a catalogue will be completed of all the flora and fauna found in Cuba's protected areas as well as a large percentage of those outside the reserves.

Flora

There are over 7,000 plant species in Cuba, of which around 3,000 are endemic. 950 plant species are endangered, rare, or have become extinct in the last 350 years. Oddities in the plant world include the *pinguicola lignicola*, the world's only carniverous epiphytic plant; the **cork palm** (*microcycas colocoma*), an endemic living fossil which is a threatened species; and the *solandra grandiflora*, one of the world's largest flowers, 10 cm across at the calyx and 30 cm at the corolla.

There are around 100 different palm trees in Cuba, of which 90 are endemic. The **Royal palm** (*roystonea regia*) is one of four species of *roystonia*; it is the national tree and can be seen in the countryside throughout the island. Cubans use the small, purple fruits to feed pigs, as they are oily and nutritious. They develop in bunches below the crown shaft, which can weigh 20-25 kilos. They would naturally drop one by one when ripe, but they are usually harvested before then by *trepadores*, men who skilfully climb the trunk of the palm by means of two slings, one supporting the thigh and another supporting a foot. You can also see many flowering trees, pines, oaks, cedars, etc. Original forest, however, is confined to some of the highest points in the southeast mountains and the mangroves of the Zapata Peninsula.

There are, of course, a multitude of flowers and in the country even the smallest of houses has a flower garden in front. The **orchid** family includes some 300 endemic species, but more are constantly being discovered. You can find orchids all over the island, especially in the mountainous regions, some of which live above 700m. There is one tiny orchid, *pleurothallis shaferi*, which is only 1 cm, with leaves measuring 5 mm and flowers of only 2 mm. The orchidarium at Soroa has over 700 examples of orchids and other flowers. To complement the wide variety of butterflies that can be found in Cuba, the butterfly flower, *mariposa*, a type of jasmin, has been named the national flower.

Fauna

Animal life is also varied, with nearly 14,000 species of fauna, of which 10% could be on the verge of extinction. 250 vertebrate species are endangered, rare or have become extinct in the last 350 years. The total number includes 54 mammals (40% endemic), 330 species of birds (8 genus, 22 species, 32 endemic sub-species), 106 reptiles (81% endemic), 42 amphibians (93% endemic), over 1,700 molluscs (87% endemic), 7,000 insects and 1,200 arachnids, as well as a variety of marine species.

There are no native large mammals but some genera and families have diversified into a large number of distinct island species. These include mammals such as the **hutia** (*capromys*: 10 species, *jutía* in Spanish), **bats** (26 species) and the protected **manatee** with more than 20 breeding groups, mostly in the Ciénaga de Zapata and north of Villa Clara. Reptiles range from three types of crocodiles including the **Cuban crocodile** (*crocodylus rhombifer*) now found only in the Ciénaga de Zapata (there is a farm on the Zapata Peninsula) to iguanas to tiny salamanders. Cuba claims the smallest of a number of animals, for instance the **Cuban pygmy frog** (*eleutherodactylus limbatus*, 12 mm long, one of some 30 small frogs), the **almiquí** (*selenodon cubanus*, a shrew-like insectivore, the world's smallest mammal, found only in the Sierra de Nipe-Sagua-Baracoa, the **butterfly** or **moth bat** (*natalus lepidus*, 186 mm) and the **bee hummingbird** (*mellisuga helenae*, 63 mm long, called locally the *zunzuncito*). The latter is an endangered species, like the **carpintero real woodpecker** (*campephilus principalis*), the **cariara** or **caracara** (*caracara plancus*, a hawk-like bird of the savannah), the **pygmy owl** (*glaucidium siju*), the **Cuban green parrot** (*amazona leucocephala*) and the *fermina*, or **Zapata wren** (*fermina cerverai*). Less attractively, there is also a **dwarf scorpion** (*microtytus fundorai*, *alacrán* in Spanish, 10 mm long).

The best place for birdwatching on the island is the Zapata Peninsula, where 170 species of Cuban birds have been recorded, including the majority of endemic species. In winter the number increases as migratory waterbirds, swallows and others visit the marshes. The area around Santo Tomás contains rare birds such as the **Zapata rail**, the **Zapata wren** and the **Zapata sparrow** (*torreornis inexpectata*, or *cabrerito de la Ciénaga*).

The national bird is the forest-dwelling **Cuban trogon** (*priotelus temnurus*, the *tocororo*), partly because of its blue head, white chest and red underbelly, the colours of the Cuban flag.

Conservation

The first national park, the Parque Nacional Pico Cristal, was established in 1930, but with little regulation and less financing. Conservation only really got started in Cuba with the passing of Law 27 in 1980, which provided funds and legislation to set up more parks. They started in the Sierra Maestra, where there are now 13 parks, reserves and refuges. In 1985 Unesco started working with Cuba in selecting first class sites, collecting data on biodiversity and endemic species, highlighting the need to give priority to conservation and give total protection in some areas. Within a year a coordinating committee had set out financing needs and donations began to some in to develop the first international reserves in Cuba. Four biosphere reserves were established as pilot programmes and education programmes were offered to neighbouring communities on conservation and sustainable development. In 1991 a consultative group was formed which set up a new Sistema Nacional de Areas Protegidas (national system of protected areas) and proposed 73 reserves. Overnight, 12% of Cuba's territory was protected, taking in 96% of vegetation and 321 species of vertebrates. Cuba also ratified the Cartagena Agreement for the protection of the marine environment and certain Unesco conventions on World Heritage sites and Biosphere Reserves. In 1995 a new strategy was adopted, reorganizing the national environmental plan with the formation of 12 institutions. The key agency is the Centro Nacional para las Areas Protegidas (CNAP), which, together with the Centro Nacional para la Administración Ambiental and the Centro Nacional para la Información, now has responsibility for the protection of the natural environment.

Cuba - National Parks

Florida Straits

Gulf of Mexico

CIUDAD DE LA HABANA

Matanzas

19

LA HABANA

PINAR DEL RÍO

8

Pinar del Río

MATANZAS

VILLA CLARA

17

Santa Cla

CIENFUEGOS

Cienfuegos

13

18

10

Nueva Gerona

9

ISLA DE LA JUVENTUD

11

SANC
SPIRIT

N

Caribbean Se

	75-150
	150-300
	over 300

Heights in metres (approx)

0   125
km

A new environmental law passed in 1997 strengthened the legal framework for wildlife conservation. There is now a comprehensive system of protected areas covering 30% of Cuba including its marine platform, and incorporating examples of more than 96% of Cuba's vegetation types, 95% of plant species and almost all terrestrial vertebrates. There are 11 categories of protection: *reserva natural, parque nacional, reserva ecológica, elemento natural destacado, reserva florística manejada, refugio de fauna, parque natural, área natural turística, área protegida recursos manejados, área protegida de uso múltiple* and *área protegida sin categoría*. These protected areas include 14 national parks and four UNESCO biosphere reserves: **Guanahacabibes** in the extreme western tip of the island; the **Sierra del Rosario**, 60 km west of Havana; **Baconao** in the east and **Cuchillas del Toa**. However, not all legally established conservation areas have any infrastructure, personnel or administration in place.

NATIONAL PARKS

Parque Nacional Alejandro de Humboldt (1), 59,771 hectares in the Montañas de Toa, near Moa, ranging in altitude from 20m to 1,168m, now being established with assistance from the German NGO, Green Gold. It is the nucleus of the **Cuchillas del Toa UNESCO Biosphere Reserve**, and is basically the union of a group of reserves: Cupeyal del Norte, Ojito de Agua, Jaguaní, Alto de Iberia, Taco and

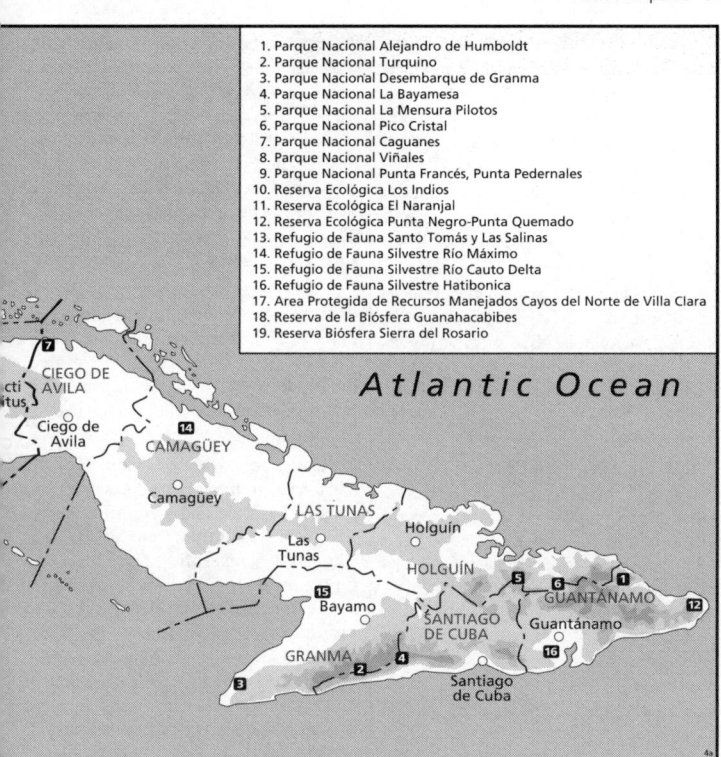

1. Parque Nacional Alejandro de Humboldt
2. Parque Nacional Turquino
3. Parque Nacional Desembarque de Granma
4. Parque Nacional La Bayamesa
5. Parque Nacional La Mensura Pilotos
6. Parque Nacional Pico Cristal
7. Parque Nacional Caguanes
8. Parque Nacional Viñales
9. Parque Nacional Punta Francés, Punta Pedernales
10. Reserva Ecológica Los Indios
11. Reserva Ecológica El Naranjal
12. Reserva Ecológica Punta Negro-Punta Quemado
13. Refugio de Fauna Santo Tomás y Las Salinas
14. Refugio de Fauna Silvestre Río Máximo
15. Refugio de Fauna Silvestre Río Cauto Delta
16. Refugio de Fauna Silvestre Hatibonica
17. Area Protegida de Recursos Manejados Cayos del Norte de Villa Clara
18. Reserva de la Biósfera Guanahacabibes
19. Reserva Biósfera Sierra del Rosario

Yamaniguey. This humid tropical woodland has examples of 16 of Cuba's 28 vegetation types and has the highest rate of endemism, with 150 species found only in this area. Endangered species include the *carpintero real*, the *almiquí*, the Cuban kite (*chondrohierax wilsonii*, known in Spanish as the *gavilán caguarero*), the Cuban parakeet (*aratinga euops*, or *catey* in Spanish), the Cuban parrot (*amazona leucocephala*, or *cotorra* in Spanish) and the manatee.

Parque Nacional Turquino (2), 17,450 hectares in the Sierra Maestra, including Cuba's highest mountain, the 1,974m Pico Turquino, and managed in collaboration with WWF Canada. This park contains humid montane forest and has a high percentage of endemics, *juniperus saxicola* trees, fruit-bearing *rubus turquinensis*, and small frogs, *eleutherodactylus albipes* and *eleutherodactylus turquinensis*.

Parque Nacional Desembarque de Granma (3), the marine terraces of Cabo Cruz, 27,545 hectares managed in collaboration with WWF Canada. This is the world's second biggest series of marine coral terraces, a staircase-like formation of 22 old shorelines and sea cliffs formed on emerging coral coast, with dry tropical forest and mangrove. 58 endemic plant species have been recorded here, and the fauna includes species like the primitive lizard (*cricosaura typica*) and a brightly coloured snail (*ligus vittatus*) which lives in only a small area of the park. There is a network of interpretative paths, archaeological sites with petroglyghs and pictographs, manatees, and diving on the offshore reef.

Parque Nacional La Bayamesa (4) is 21,100 hectares in the Sierra Maestra around Pico Bayamesa, 1,730m, north of Uvero, but there is no administration yet in place.

Parque Nacional La Mensura Pilotos (5) (Pinares de Mayarí), 5,340 hectares in the Altiplanicie de Nipe of pine forests with traditional coffee and livestock farming, while also home to 460 endemic species. There are interpretative paths, some ecotourism and you can see parrots.

Parque Nacional Pico Cristal (6), 15,000 hectares in the Sierra de Cristal of pine forest and broadleaved humid tropical forest, where you can find parrots and nightingales (*myadestes elizebeth*) and possibly the *almiquí*. There is no administration yet in place. This was the first protected area in Cuba, dating from 1930, although it was never managed as such until recently.

Parque Nacional Caguanes (7), 22,690 hectares (5,387 on land and 17,303 under water) in the Cayería Caibarien Caguanes, a group of small islands just offshore. Cayo Caguanes which gives its name to the park has 25 caves on only 1.1 sq km and is joined to the mainland by mangroves. Some caves have endemic invertebrates. They are also sites of prehistoric interest, with cave drawings and dozens of archaeological sites. The Parque is also the home of one of the 10 colonies in Cuba of **sandhill cranes**, known locally as *grulla* (*grus canadensis nesiotes*), a tall, long-legged bird with a long neck which it stretches out in front of it when flying.

Parque Nacional Viñales (8), 13,400 hectares in the Sierra de los Organos, with the distinctive *mogotes*. There is no administration yet in place for these limestone uplands with extensive cave systems (Santo Tomás and Palmarito are believed to be the largest in the Caribbean) and distinctive xerophytic vegetation, where you can find sierra palm (*gausio princeps*), ceibón (*bombracopsis cubensis*) and cork palm (*mycrocicas calocoma*). There are several types of snails which have become so isolated that they live only on one part of a *mogote*.

Parque Nacional Punta Francés, Punta Pedernales (9) is a marine park covering 17,424 hectares of marine platform going down to 200m, with untouched coral formations and abundant flora and fauna. There is no park management as such, but it is looked after by the International Diving Centre at *Hotel Colony*, Isla de la Juventud.

Reserva Ecológica Los Indios (10) is a 3,050-hectare reserve on the white sand plains of Isla de la Juventud, administered in collaboration with WWF Canada. As well as exceptional bird life, there is pine covered savannah with 24 endemics and the carniverous plants of the genera *drosera*, *pinguicola* and *utricularia*. Many plants and trees have adapted to become resistant to fire. As a result of management and protection of the area it is now the site of one of the largest nesting groups of Cuban parrot, and is another of the sites for the sandhill crane.

Reserva Ecológica El Naranjal (11) covers 3,068 hectares in the beautiful Guamuhaya mountains at an altitude of 70-870m, where you can find the Cuban parrot, the Cuban parakeet and the *jutía conga (capromys pilorides)*. Over 600 plant species have been recorded here, of which 22% are endemic and 12 are found nowhere else

Reserva Ecológica Punta Negro-Punta Quemado (12) on the Maisí marine terraces, 3,972 hectares of the world's largest and best developed system of marine coral terraces with 27 levels and the driest natural environment in Cuba, many endemic and some unique plants. A substantial part of the first three levels is included in the reserve. There is no administration yet in place.

Refugio de Fauna Santo Tomás y Las Salinas (13) are two reserves which form the basis of the **Parque Nacional Ciénaga de Zapata**. They are still being defined and established but there is rich bird life here, in what is the largest wetland in the Caribbean. More than 160 species of birds have been recorded. At Las Salinas there are huge populations of waterbirds and at Santo Tomás there are two species found nowhere else in the world, the **Zapata rail**, known as the *gallinuela de Santo Tomás* (*cyanolimnas cerverai*), and the **Zapata wren**, known as ferminia (*ferminia cerverai*). The Zapata rail is dark, with a mixture of olive brown on top, slate grey underneath and on its forehead and cheeks, without any spots or streaks, except for white tips to its flank feathers and conspicuously white under its tail. Its bill is green, with red at its base, it has red feet and very short wings, so it does not fly very well. The Zapata wren measures 16 cm, it has short wings and a long tail, has a spotted head, greyish brown back with black bars and whitish underparts. It lives in the dense bushes and hardly ever flies but it has a loud voice, with a varied, musical warbling.

Refugio de Fauna Silvestre Río Máximo (14), is 12,500 hectares of mangroves on the north Camagüey coast, with saline and fresh water lakes and semi-deciduous coastal woodlands. It is a major site for flamingoes with two colonies of some 4,000 birds and the world's largest nesting population. There is also a large population of the **American crocodile** (*crocodylus acutus*). Largest of all, however, is the number of water fowl which migrate here in season, when tens of thousands of duck (*anas*, 11 species), **glossy ibis** (*plegadis falcinellus*), **white ibis** (*eudocimus albus*) (both known locally as *cocos*), **roseate spoonbill** (*ajaia ajaia*) and other water birds can be seen.

Refugio de Fauna Silvestre Río Cauto Delta (15), just north of Manzanillo, 60,000 hectares of mangroves, hypersaline and freshwater lakes and wetlands, which are very rich in bird life as well as home to flamingoes and the American crocodile.

Refugio de Fauna Silvestre Hatibonica (16), a 5,220-hectare refuge overlooking the US naval base at Guantánamo Bay, with sparsely vegetated hill country and varied fauna including iguanas (*cyclura nubila nubila*) and endemic cacti. Strange wind-blown, variegated rock formations, called *Monitongos*, charactize this arid landscape. There is an interpretative path: Los Monitongos.

Area Protegida de Recursos Manejados Cayos del Norte de Villa Clara (17), 17,500 hectares above and below water down to 20m in the Sabana de Camagüey archipelago. Wildlife includes the second largest colony of manatees in the country around the Cayos del Pajonal, hutia or *jutía rata* (*capromys auritus*) on Cayo Fragoso, flamingoes on Las Picuas, iguanas on Cayo Cobo and various endemic birds and reptiles on Cayo Francés and Cayo Santa María.

Reserva de la Biósfera Guanahacabibes (18), on the extreme western tip of the island covering 101,500 hectares of 'dog-stooth' landscape of bare limestone with scattered pockets of soil and dry coastal evergreen and semi-deciduous woodland. Terraces and beaches are interspersed along the coast. There are two well-established nuclei of the biosphere reserve, Reserva Natural El Veral and Reserva Natural Cabo Corrientes, where an ecological station carries out research.

Reserva Biósfera Sierra del Rosario (19), 25,000 hectares of the Sierra del Rosario mountain range with the best example of evergreen forest in western Cuba. There are three nuclei in the reserve, El Salón, Las Peladas and Las Terrazas, where there is an ecological station and the local community is directly involved with protecting the environment.

Pre-columbian civilizations

The recorded history of the Caribbean islands begins with the arrival of Christopher Columbus' fleet in 1492. Our knowledge of the native peoples who inhabited the islands before and at the time of his arrival is largely derived from the accounts of contemporary Spanish writers and from archaeological examinations as there is no evidence of indigenous written records.

The Amerindians encountered by Columbus in the Greater Antilles had no overall tribal name but organized themselves in a series of villages or local chiefdoms, each of which had its own tribal name. The name now used, Arawak, was not in use then. The term Arawak was used by the Indians of the Guianas, a group of whom had spread into Trinidad, but their territory was not explored until nearly another century later. The use of the generic term, Arawak, to describe the Indians Columbus encountered, arose because of linguistic similarities with the Arawaks of the mainland. It is therefore surmised that migration took place many centuries before Columbus' arrival, but the two groups were not in contact at that time. The time of the latest migration from the mainland, and consequently the existence of the island Arawaks, is in dispute, with some academics tracing it to about the time of Christ (the arrival of the Saladoids) and others to AD 1000 (the Ostionoids).

The inhabitants of the Bahamas were generally referred to as Lucayans, and those of the Greater Antilles as Tainos, but there were many sub-groupings. The inhabitants of the Lesser Antilles were, however, referred to as Carib and were described to Columbus as an aggressive tribe which sacrificed and sometimes ate the prisoners they captured in battle. It was from them that the Caribbean gets its name and from which the word cannibal is derived.

The earliest known inhabitants of the region, the Siboneys, migrated from Florida (some say Mexico) and spread throughout the Bahamas and the major islands. Most archaeological evidence of their settlements has been found near the shore, along bays or streams, where they lived in small groups. The largest discovered settlement has been one of 100 inhabitants in Cuba. They were hunters and gatherers, living on fish and other seafood, small rodents, iguanas, snakes and birds. They gathered roots and wild fruits, such as guava, guanabana and mamey, but did not cultivate plants. They worked with primitive tools made out of stone, shell, bone or wood, for hammering, chipping or scraping, but had no knowledge of pottery. The Siboneys were eventually absorbed by the advance of the Arawaks migrating from the S, who had made more technological advances in agriculture, arts and crafts.

The people now known as Arawaks migrated from the Guianas to Trinidad and on through the island arc to Cuba. Their population expanded because of the natural fertility of the islands and the abundance of fruit and seafood, helped by their agricultural skills in cultivating and improving wild plants and their excellent boatbuilding and fishing techniques. They were healthy, tall, good looking and lived to a ripe old age. It is estimated that up to 8 million may have lived on the island of Hispaniola alone, but there was always plenty of food for all.

Their society was essentially communal and organized around families. The smaller islands were particularly egalitarian, but in the larger ones, where village communities of extended families numbered up to 500 people, there was an incipient class structure. Typically, each village had a headman, called a *cacique*, whose duty it was to represent the village when dealing with other tribes, to settle family disputes and organize defence. However, he had no powers of coercion and was often little more than a nominal head. The position was largely hereditary, with the eldest son of the eldest sister having rights of succession, but women could and did become *caciques*. In the larger communities, there was some delegation of responsibility to the senior men, but economic activities were usually organized along family lines, and their power was limited.

The division of labour was usually based on age and sex. The men would clear and prepare the land for agriculture and be responsible for defence of the village, while women cultivated the crops and were the major food producers, also making items such as mats, baskets, bowls and fishing nets. Women were in charge of raising the children, especially the girls, while the men taught the boys traditional customs, skills and rites.

The Tainos hunted for some of their food, but fishing was more important and most of their settlements were close to the sea. Fish and shellfish were their main sources of protein and they had many different ways of catching them, from hands, baskets or nets to poisoning, shooting or line fishing. Cassava was a staple food, which they had successfully learned to leach of its poisonous juice. They also grew yams, maize, cotton, arrowroot, peanuts, beans, cocoa and spices, rotating their crops to prevent soil erosion. It is documented that in Jamaica they had three harvests of maize annually, using maize and cassava to make breads, cakes and beer.

Cotton was used to make clothing and hammocks (never before seen by Europeans), while the calabash tree was used to make ropes and cords, baskets and roofing. Plants were used for medicinal and spiritual purposes, and cosmetics such as face and body paint. Also important, both to the Arawaks and later to the Europeans, was the cultivation of tobacco, as a drug and as a means of exchange.

They had no writing, no beasts of burden, no wheeled vehicles and no hard metals, although they did have some alluvial gold for personal ornament. The abundance of food allowed them time to develop their arts and crafts and they were skilled in woodwork and pottery. They had polished stone tools, but also carved shell implements for manioc preparation or as fishhooks. Coral manioc graters have also been found. Their boatbuilding techniques were noted by Columbus, who marvelled at their canoes of up to 75 ft in length, carrying up to 50 people, made of a single tree trunk in one piece. It took 2 months to fell a tree by gradually burning and chipping it down, and many more to make the canoe.

The Arawaks had three main deities, evidence of which have been found in stone and conch carvings in many of the Lesser Antilles as well as the well populated Greater Antilles, although their relative importance varied according to the island. The principal male god was Yocahú, *yoca* being the word for cassava and *hú* meaning 'giver of'. It is believed that the Indians associated this deity's power to provide cassava with the mystery of the volcanoes, for all the carvings, the earliest out of shells and the later ones of stone, are conical. The Yocahú cult was wiped out in the Lesser Antilles by the invading Caribs, and in the Greater Antilles by the Spaniards, but it is thought to have existed from about 200 AD.

The main female deity was a fertility goddess, often referred to as Atabeyra, but she is thought to have had several names relating to her other roles as goddess of the moon, mother of the sea, the tides and the springs, and the goddess of childbirth. In carvings she is usually depicted as a squatting figure with her hands up to her chin, sometimes in the act of giving birth.

A third deity is a dog god, named Opi-yel-Guaobiran, meaning 'the dog deity who takes care of the souls of the immediately deceased and is the son of the spirit of darkness'. Again, carvings of a dog's head or whole body have been found of shell or stone, which were often used to induce narcotic trances. Many of the carvings have holes and Y-shaped passages which would have been put to the nose to snuff narcotics and induce a religious trance in the shaman or priest, who could then ascertain the status of a departed soul for a recently bereaved relative.

One custom which aroused interest in the Spaniards was the ball game, not only for the sport and its ceremonial features, but because the ball was made of rubber and bounced, a phenomenon which had not previously been seen in Europe. Catholicism soon eradicated the game, but archaeological remains have been found in several islands, notably in Puerto Rico, but also in Hispaniola. Excavations in the Greater Antilles have revealed earth embankments and rows of elongated upright stones surrounding plazas or courts, pavements and stone balls. These are called *bateyes, juegos de indios, juegos de bola, cercados* or *corrales de indios. Batey* was the aboriginal name for the ball game, the rubber ball itself and also the court where it was played. The word is still used to designate the cleared area in front of houses in the country.

The ball game had religious and ceremonial significance but it was a sport and bets and wagers were important. It was played by two teams of up to 20 or 30 players, who had to keep the ball in the air by means of their hips, shoulders,

heads, elbows and other parts of their body, but never with their hands. The aim was to bounce the ball in this manner to the opposing team until it hit the ground. Men and women played, but not usually in mixed sex games. Great athleticism was required and it is clear that the players practised hard to perfect their skill, several, smaller practice courts having been built in larger settlements. The game was sometimes played before the village made an important decision, and the prize could be a sacrificial victim, usually a prisoner, granted to the victor.

In 1492 Arawaks inhabited all the greater islands of the Caribbean, but in Puerto Rico they were being invaded by the Caribs who had pushed N through the Lesser Antilles, stealing their women and enslaving or killing the men. The Caribs had also originated in South America, from around the Orinoco delta. In their migration N through the Caribbean islands they proved to be fierce warriors and their raids on the Arawak settlements were feared. Many of their women were captured Arawaks, and it was they who cultivated the land and performed the domestic chores. Polygamy was common, encouraged by the surplus of women resulting from the raids, and the Arawak female influence on Carib culture was strong.

Despite rumours of cannibalism reported to Columbus by frightened Arawaks, there appears to be no direct evidence of the practice, although the Spaniards took it seriously enough to use it as an excuse to justify taking slaves. After some unfortunate encounters, colonizers left the Caribs alone for many years. The Arawaks, on the other hand, were soon wiped out by disease, cruelty and murder. The Spanish invaders exacted tribute and forced labour while allowing their herds of cattle and pigs to destroy the Indians' unfenced fields and clearings. Transportation to the mines resulted in shifts in the native population which could not be fed from the surrounding areas and starvation became common. Lack of labour in the Greater Antilles led to slave raids on the Lucayans in the Bahamas, but they also died or committed collective suicide. They felt that their gods had deserted them and there was nowhere for them to retreat or escape. Today there are no full-blooded Arawaks and only some 2,000 Caribs are left on Dominica (there has been no continuity of Carib language or religious belief on Dominica). The 500 years since Columbus' arrival have served to obliterate practically all the evidence of the indigenous civilization.

THE CONTEMPORARY CARIBBEAN

The decisive date in the shaping of the modern Caribbean was 1492, when Christopher Columbus successfully crossed the Atlantic to make landfall in the Antilles. Although Spain did not exert its influence here to the same degree as on the American mainland, the way was open for Europeans to follow Columbus, take possession of, fight over and exploit the islands for profit. Over the following 5 centuries, the population of the region has been imported and almost all traces of the precolumbian past have been removed. Similarly, the majority of food and cash crops grown have been transplanted from elsewhere.

At one stage, the islands were some of the most valuable colonies ever known, but little of the wealth they generated stayed in the region. Being for the most part small, the territories still depend on the outside world for their prosperity (commodity exports, tourism), but with limited regional organization and economic imbalances there is great inequality of reward. Politically the region is disunited. Its own major events, like the Haitian and Cuban Revolutions, the movement towards black consciousness, have had tremendous, lasting impact outside their immediate realm, but at the same time have been engulfed in wider, global concerns.

The culture that the immigrants brought with them is now confronted by influences of global media systems. Ease of travel has also brought cultural pressures, not solely from the incoming tourist, but also from the large number of emigrants who, having sought work abroad, bring home the culture of their adopted countries. Conversely, emigration, the result of the unemployment which followed the decline of labour intensive agriculture, takes Caribbean culture to Europe and North America. At the same time, though, it causes a social structure which is heavily biased towards female heads of families when the men go elsewhere to work.

Yet for all the new cultural clashes, which build up on top of older ones (French spoken on 'English' islands, islands divided between nations), the struggle for a Caribbean identity continues, particularly in the work of writers and artists. Different colours and faiths coexist; the African and European mix to make some of the most vibrant music; the goal of the Jamaican national motto applies to all: "Out of many, one people".

History

SPANISH CONQUEST

Cuba was visited by Cristóbal Colón (Christopher Columbus) during his first voyage to find a westerly route to the Orient on 27 October 1492, and he made another brief stop 2 years later on his way from Hispaniola to Jamaica. Columbus did not realize it was an island when he landed; he had heard from the inhabitants of the Bahamas, where he first made landfall, that there were larger islands to the south where there was gold, and he hoped it was Japan. He arrived on the north coast of 'Colba', but found little gold. He did, however, note the Indians' practice of puffing at a large, burning roll of leaves, which they called 'tobacos'.

The Arawaks told Columbus of the more aggressive Carib tribe and he headed off towards the eastern islands to find them, discovering la Isla Española, or Hispaniola, which occupied the Spanish for the next few years with attempted settlements, feuds, rebellions and other troubles. On future expeditions, more settlers were brought from Spain to Hispaniola, adventurers who wanted to get rich quick and return to Spain. Although most died of tropical diseases, enough survived to impart their own European viruses on the Indians, which decimated the local population. The Spaniards also demanded a constant supply of Indian labour which they were ill-equipped to provide, having previously lived in a subsistence barter economy with no experience of regular work. The Spaniards cruel treatment of the native inhabitants led to

many of them losing the will to live. On the other hand, the need for a steady supply of labour pushed the Spanish into further exploration of the Indies. Slavers went from one island to another in search of manpower. Puerto Rico was conquered in 1508, Jamaica in 1509 and Cuba in 1511. From there they moved on to the mainland to trade in slaves, gold and other commodities.

Cuba was first circumnavigated by Sebastián de Ocampo in 1508, but it was Diego de Velázquez who conquered it in 1511 and founded several towns, called *villas*, including Havana. From Cuba, Velázquez sent out two expeditions in 1517-18 to investigate the Yucatán and the Gulf of Mexico. On the basis of their information he petitioned the Spanish Crown for permission to set up a base there prior to conquest and settlement. However, before the authorization came through from Spain, his commander, Hernán Cortés, set off without permission with 600 men, 16 horses, 14 cannon and 13 muskets to conquer Mexico, leaving Velázquez in the lurch.

The first African slaves were imported to Cuba in 1526. Sugar was introduced soon after but was not important until the last decade of the 16th century. When the British took Jamaica in 1655 a number of Spanish settlers fled to Cuba, already famous for its cigars. Tobacco was made a strict monopoly of Spain in 1717. The coffee plant was introduced in 1748. The British, under Lord Albemarle and Admiral Pocock, captured Havana and held the island in 1762-63, but it was returned

Christopher Colombus, City Museum, Havana

to Spain in exchange for Florida. Up until this point, the colony had been important largely as a refuelling depot for Spanish ships crossing the Atlantic, but the British occupation and the temporary lifting of Spanish restrictions, showed the local landowning class the economic potential of trading their commodities with England and North America.

INDEPENDENCE MOVEMENT

Towards the end of the 18th century Cuba began its transformation into a slave plantation society. After the French Revolution, there were slave revolts in the French colony of Haiti, which became the first independent black republic. French sugar planters fled what had been the most profitable colony in the Caribbean and settled across the water in Cuba, bringing their expertise with them. Cuba soon became a major sugar exporter and after 1793 slaves were imported in huge numbers to work the plantations. The island was under absolute military control with a colonial elite which made its money principally from sugar.

The tobacco monopoly was abolished in 1816 and Cuba was given the right to trade with the world in 1818. Independence elsewhere in the Spanish empire, however, bred ambitions, and a strong movement for independence was quelled by Spain in 1823. By this time the blacks outnumbered the whites in the island; there were several slave rebellions and little by little the Créoles (or Spaniards born in Cuba) made common cause with them. On the other hand, there was also a movement for annexation by the USA, Cuba's major trading partner, supported by many slave owners who had a common interest with the southern states in the American Civil War. The defeat of the South and the abolition of slavery in the USA ended support for annexation.

By the 1860s Cuba was producing about a third of the world's sugar and was heavily dependent on African slaves to do so, supplemented by indentured Chinese labourers in the 1850s and 1860s. Although Spain signed treaties under British pressure to outlaw the Atlantic slave

Museo de Arte Colonial, Habana Vieja

trade in 1817 and 1835, they were completely ignored by the colony and an estimated 600,000 African slaves were imported by 1867. Independence from Spain became a burning issue in Cuba as Spain remained intransigent and refused to consider political reforms which would give the colony more autonomy within the empire.

On 10 October 1868, a créole landowner, Carlos Manuel de Céspedes, issued the *Grito de Yara*, a proclamation of independence and a call to arms, while simultaneously freeing his slaves. The first war of independence was a 10-year rebellion against Spain in the eastern part of the island between 1868 and 1878, but it gained little save a modest move towards the abolition of slavery. In 1870 the Moret Law freed all children of slaves born after 1868 and any slave over 60, but complete abolition was not achieved until 1886. In 1878 the Convention of Zanjón brought the civil war to an end. This enabled Cubans to elect representatives to the Spanish Cortés (parliament) in 1879, but did not suppress the desire for independence. Many national heroes were created during this period who have become revolutionary icons in the struggle against

domination by a foreign power. Men such as de Céspedes, Máximo Gómez and the mulatto General Antonio Maceo, have inspired generations of Cuban patriots and are still revered with statues and street names in nearly every town and city on the island. One consequence of the war was the destruction of much agricultural land and the ruin of many sugar planters. US interests began to take over the sugar plantations and the sugar mills, and as sugar beet became more important in Europe, so Cuba became more dependent on the market for its main crop in the USA.

From 1895 to 1898 rebellion flared up again in the second war of independence under the young poet and revolutionary, José Martí, who had organized the movement from exile in the USA, together with the old guard of Antonio Maceo and Máximo Gómez. José Martí led the invasion but was tragically killed in an ambush in May 1895 when the war had barely begun, and Maceo was killed in 1896. Despite fierce fighting throughout the island, neither the Nationalists nor the Spanish could gain the upper hand. However, the USA was now concerned for its investments in Cuba and was considering its strategic interests within the region. When the US battle-ship *Maine* exploded in Havana harbour on 15 February 1898, killing 260 crew, this was made a pretext for declaring war on Spain. Spain offered the independence fighters a truce but they chose instead to help the USA to defeat the colonial power. American forces (which included Colonel Theodore Roosevelt) were landed, a squadron blockaded Havana and defeated the Spanish fleet at Santiago de Cuba. In December peace was signed and US forces occupied the island. The Nationalists had gained independence from Spain but found themselves under US military occupation for 4 years and then with only limited independence granted to them by the USA.

During the occupation, the USA put the Cuban administration and economy back to rights. It eliminated a famine, introduced improved sanitation and helped to eradicate yellow fever with the scientific discoveries of a Cuban doctor, Carlos J Finlay. State education was introduced, the judiciary was reformed and an electoral system for local and national government was introduced. In 1901 an elected assembly approved a liberal constitution which separated Church and state and guaranteed universal adult male suffrage.

The Republic of Cuba was proclaimed in 1902 and the Government was handed over to its first president, Tomás Estrada Palma, the elected candidate of José Martí's Cuban Revolutionary Party, on 20 May. However, the new Republic was constrained by the Platt Amendment to the constitution, passed by the US Congress, which clearly made it a protectorate of the USA. The USA retained naval bases at Río Hondo and Guantánamo Bay and reserved the right of intervention in Cuban domestic affairs, but granted the island a handsome import preference for its sugar. The USA intervened several times to settle quarrels by rival political factions but, to quell growing unrest and a reassertion of pro-independence and

revolutionary forces, repealed the Platt Amendment in 1934. The USA formally relinquished the right to intervene but retained its naval base at Guantánamo. Resentment against the USA for its political and economic dominance of the island lingered and was a powerful stimulus for the nationalist Revolution of the 1950s.

DICTATORSHIP

Even after the repeal of the Platt Amendment, the USA dominated the Cuban economy. Around two thirds of sugar exports went to the USA under a quota system at prices set by Washington; two thirds of Cuba's imports came from the USA; foreign capital investment was largely from the USA and Cuba was effectively a client state. Yet, despite the money being made out of Cuba, its people suffered from grinding rural poverty, high unemployment, illiteracy and inadequate health care. The good life, as enjoyed by the socialites in the casinos and bars of Havana highlighted the social inequalities in the country. Politics was a mixture of authoritarian rule and corrupt democracy.

From 1924 to 1933 the 'strong man' Gerardo Machado ruled Cuba. He was elected in 1924 on a wave of popularity and set about diversifying the economy and investing in public works projects. However, a drastic fall in sugar prices in the late 1920s led to strikes and protests which he forcefully repressed. In 1928 he 'persuaded' Congress to grant him a second term of office, which was greeted with protests and violence from students, the middle classes and labour unions. Widespread nationalist popular rebellion throughout Machado's dictatorship was harshly repressed by the police force. The USA was reluctant to intervene again, but tried to negotiate a deal with its ambassador. The nationalists called a general strike in protest at US interference, and Machado finally went into exile. The violence did not abate, however, and there were more strikes, mob attacks

Fidel Castro Ruiz

Now in his 70s, Fidel Castro has spent more than half his life as president, jefe and supreme comandante of Cuba. He has passed from being the world's youngest ruler in 1959 to the second longest serving head of state (after King Hussein of Jordan). He has outstayed eight US presidents and survived hundreds of assassination attempts, and is still non-committal about his future, saying he will stay in office as long as his country needs him. It is reported that he still exercises regularly, swims, scuba dives, plays ball games and works long hours, but his speeches are now shorter, quieter and less passionate. His longest speech went on for 7 hours, but Cubans were regularly called upon to listen to his rhetoric for 4-5 hours. Dramatic pauses have replaced the fire and arm waving of his youth, he moves more slowly and on medical advice has given up his trademark cigar. Rumours circulate of heart troubles and arthritis. Nevertheless he still travels to international summit meetings and conventions, and in 1996 was received by the Pope in an historic photo opportunity which made him look almost sprightly in comparison with his host. He has always been instantly recognizable for his beard, now thinning and grey, and his military fatigues, although these are now occasionally replaced when abroad by a sober suit.

Castro's father came from Galicia in Spain. Fidel was born in Cuba in 1926 and became a lawyer, running his own practice until he took up the revolutionary cause. His first armed uprising with 150 insurgents was launched on the Moncada barracks in Santiago de Cuba on 26 July 1953. The attack was repelled, many rebels were killed and the others including Castro faced 15 years' imprisonment on the Isla de Pinos, now the Isla de la Juventud. However, in 1955 the dictator Batista granted an amnesty to political prisoners and Castro chose exile in the USA and later in Mexico, where he met the Argentine, Che Guevara, one of the most influential members of the rebel group. From there he launched his second incursion, sailing from exile on the cabin cruiser, Granma, and landing in Cuba on 2 December 1956 with over 80 revolutionaries, including his younger brother, Raúl, and Che, who fought alongside him. The uprising was crushed by the military but 12 men, including Castro, escaped into the mountains. There they organized the 26 July Movement, named after the 1953 uprising, and began guerrilla warfare while gradually building up popular support. Although Raúl was a Marxist-Leninist, Fidel campaigned on a nationalist platform and only later turned to communism. The campaign slogan was *libertad o muerte*, rather than the subsequently adapted version, *patria o muerte* in 1960 and then *socialismo o muerte*. On 17 March 1958 he called for a general revolt. His popularity and forces had grown steadily and they pushed on towards Havana. On 1 January 1959 Batista fled the country and a provisional government was established. Castro initially renounced office, but was prevailed upon to become prime minister and later president.

and occupations of factories, which the new government was unable to quell. In September 1933 a revolt of non-commissioned officers including Fulgencio Batista, then a sergeant, deposed the government and installed a 5-member committee chosen by the student movement, the Directorio Estudiantil. They chose as president a professor, Dr Ramón Grau San Martín, but he only lasted four months before Batista staged a coup. He then held power through presidential puppets until he was elected president himself in 1940.

Batista's first period in power, from 1933-44, was characterized by nationalist and populist policies, set against corruption and political violence. Batista himself was a mulatto from a poor background who had pulled himself up through the ranks of the military and retained the support of the armed forces. He was also supported by US and Cuban business interests while gaining control of the trade unions by passing social welfare legislation, building low cost housing and creating jobs with public works projects. The students and radical nationalists remained opposed to him, however, and terrorism continued. In 1940 a new Constitution was passed by a constituent assembly dominated by Batista, which included universal suffrage and benefits for workers such as a minimum wage, pensions, social insurance and an 8-hour day.

In 1944 Batista lost the elections to the candidate of the radical nationalists: Dr Ramón Grau San Martín, of the Partido Revolucionario Cubana-Auténtico, who held office in 1944-48. His presidential term benefited from high sugar prices following the Second World War, which allowed corruption and political violence to continue unabated. Grau was followed into the presidency by his protégé, Carlos Prío Socarrás, 1948-52, a term which even more corrupt and depraved, until Batista, by then a self-promoted general, staged a military coup

in 1952. Constitutional and democratic government was at an end. His harshly repressive dictatorship was brought to a close by Fidel Castro in January 1959, after an extraordinary and heroic 3-year campaign, mostly in the Sierra Maestra, with a guerrilla force reduced at one point to 12 men.

REVOLUTION

The dictator, Batista, was opposed by many, but none more effective than the young lawyer, Fidel Castro, the son of immigrants born in Galicia and born in Cuba in 1926. He saw José Martí as his role model and aimed to continue the Revolution he started in 1895, following his ideals. In 1953, the 100th anniversary of José Martí's birth, Castro and a committed band of about 160 revolutionaries attacked the Moncada barracks in Santiago de Cuba on 26 July. The attack failed and although Castro and his brother Raúl escaped, they were later captured and put on trial. Fidel used the occasion to make an impassioned speech denouncing corruption in the ruling class and the need for political freedom and economic independence. The speech has gone down in history for its final phrase, 'History will absolve me', and a revised version, smuggled out of prison on the Isle of Pines, became the basis of a reform programme. In 1955 the Castros were given an amnesty and went to Mexico. There Fidel continued to work on his essentially nationalist revolutionary programme, called the 26 July Movement, which called for radical social and economic reforms and a return to the democracy of Cuba's 1940 constitution. He met another man of ideas, an Argentine doctor called Ernesto Guevara (see box, page 50), who sailed with him and his brother Raúl and a band of 82 like-minded revolutionaries, back to Cuba on 2 December 1956. Their campaign began in the Sierra Maestra in the east of Cuba and after years of fierce fighting Batista fled the country on 1 January 1959.

Ernesto 'Che' Guevara: A traveller's odyssey

Every visitor to Cuba learns to recognize the face of Che Guevara, the Cuban Revolution's unofficial emblem. Che's steely visage gazes down from propaganda posters and wall murals, is featured on stamps and the three-peso note, and is sold to tourists on T-shirts, post cards and refrigerator magnets, completing Guevara's conversion from Socialist icon into name-brand consumer good.

Born in Rosario, Argentina, Ernesto Guevara was a medical student when he began travelling around Latin America by motorcycle, bus, truck and even as a stowaway on ships. In 1956, Guevara was in Guatemala when the CIA toppled that country's elected government. His hopes for peaceful change in the hemisphere were dashed and Guevara found his natural enemy: imperialism. Months later in Mexico he met his natural ally, the exiled Cuban lawyer, Fidel Castro. Guevara joined Castro's invasion force as a doctor, but once in Cuba quickly showed himself a brilliant field commander as well and rose during three years of warfare to lead the guerrilla army's second column.

Argentine stamp

Repeatedly wounded, Che led from the front lines and was lionized by his Cuban soldiers, many of whom would follow him for the rest of their lives. On 27 December 1958, Che's badly outnumbered guerrillas ambushed a troop train at Santa Clara, Cuba, the decisive victory that sealed the fate of the Batista regime. It was the apogee of Guevara's career. Within days he had entered Havana and the realm of revolutionary politics, a field of battle far more dangerous than the mountains of the Sierra Maestra.

Fidel Castro, to universal popular acclaim, entered Havana and assumed control of the island.

COMMUNISM AND THE 1960s

From 1960 onwards, in the face of increasing hostility from the USA, Castro led Cuba into socialism and then communism. Officials of the Batista régime were put on trial in 'people's courts' and executed. The promised new elections were not held. The judiciary lost its independence when Castro assumed the right to appoint judges. The free press was closed or taken over. Trade unions lost their independence and became part of government. The University of Havana, a former focus of dissent, and professional associations all lost their autonomy. The

democratic constitution of 1940 was never reinstated. In 1960 the sugar centrales, the oil refineries and the foreign banks were nationalized, all US property was expropriated and the Central Planning Board (Juceplan) was established. The professional and property-owning middle classes began a steady exodus which drained the country of much of its skilled workers.

CIA-backed mercenaries and Cuban exiles kept up a relentless barrage of attacks, but failed to achieve their objective. In March a French ship carrying arms to Cuba was sabotaged. At the burial of the victims, Castro first used the slogan, 'Patria o Muerte'. Diplomatic relations were re-established with the USSR, North Korea and Vietnam, while China and Cuba signed mutual benefit treaties.

Meanwhile, the USA cancelled Cuba's sugar quota and put an embargo on all imports to Cuba.

At the beginning of 1961, the USA severed diplomatic relations with Cuba and encouraged Latin American countries to do likewise. This was the year of the Bay of Pigs invasion, a fiasco which was to harden Castro's political persuasion. On 14 April 1961, some 1,400 Cuban emigrés, trained by the CIA in Miami and Guatemala set off from Nicaragua to invade Cuba with the US Navy as escort. On 15 April, planes from Nicaragua bombed several Cuban airfields in an attempt to wipe out the air force. Seven Cuban airmen were killed in the raid, and at their funeral the next day, Fidel Castro addressed a mass rally in Havana and declared Cuba to be socialist. On 17 April the invasion flotilla landed at Playa Girón and Playa Larga in the Bahía de Cochinos (Bay of Pigs), but the men were stranded on the beaches when the Cuban air force attacked their supply ships. 200 were killed and the rest surrendered within 3 days. The invaders' aircraft also took a beating when 11 were shot down, including all the B-26 bombers flown from Nicaragua. A total of 1,197 men captured were eventually returned to the USA in exchange for US$53 million in food and medicine. In his May Day speech, Fidel Castro, who had personally taken control of the defence of Cuba, confirmed that the Cuban Revolution was socialist.

The US reaction was to isolate Cuba, with a full trade embargo and heavy pressure on other American countries to severe diplomatic relations. Cuba was expelled from the Organization of American States (OAS) and the OAS imposed economic sanctions. Crucially, however, across the border in both Canada and Mexico, governments refused to toe the line and maintained relations, a policy which has now borne fruit for many Canadian and Mexican companies at the expense of US businesses. Nevertheless, in 1961-62, the trade embargo hit hard,

shortages soon appeared and by March 1962 rationing had to be imposed.

At this stage, Cuba became entangled in the rivalry between the two superpowers, the USA and the USSR. In April 1962, Kruschev decided to send medium-range missiles to Cuba, which would be capable of striking anywhere in the USA, even though all Castro wanted were short-range missiles he could point at Miami to deter invasion. In October, President JF Kennedy ordered Soviet ships heading for Cuba to be stopped and searched for missiles in international waters. This episode, which became known as the 'Cuban Missile Crisis', brought the world to the brink of nuclear war, defused only by secret negotiations between JFK and Kruschev. Kennedy demanded the withdrawal of Soviet troops and arms from Cuba and imposed a naval blockade. Without consulting Castro and without his knowledge, Kruschev eventually agreed to have the missiles dismantled and withdrawn on condition that the West would guarantee a policy of non-aggression towards Cuba. In November, JFK suspended the naval blockade but reiterated US support for political and economic aggression towards Cuba. In the following year he made a speech in Costa Rica, in which he stated "We will build a wall around Cuba", and Central American countries agreed to isolate the island.

Castro's decision to adopt Marxism-Leninism as the official ideology of the Revolution was followed by the fusion of the 26 July Movement with the Communist Party, at that time known as the Popular Socialist Party (PSP). The PSP had opposed the Revolution until the final stages of the overthrow of the Batista dictatorship and it took several years and two purges before the 'old' communists were expunged and the new Communist Party was united behind the new official ideology. In October 1965, a restructured Cuban Communist Party (PCC) was founded and Cuba has been Communist ever since.

Exploding cigars and other 1960s plots

The number of CIA-backed attempts on Castro's life is legendary, the most extraordinary stories so far published being about trying to kill him with an exploding cigar, or putting a special powder in his shoes to make his beard fall out. But, failing to assassinate or maim him, the US administration in the 1960s put an extraordinary amount of effort into trying to discredit him. Many covert plans were put forward to Operation Mongoose, an anti-Castro destabilization project at the Pentagon. One plan, codenamed Operation Dirty Trick, was to blame Castro if anything went wrong with US space flights, specifically John Glenn's flight into orbit in 1962. The Pentagon was to provide 'irrevocable proof' that if anything happened it was the fault of Cuban Communists and their electronic interference. Another idea was to sabotage a US plane and claim that a Cuban aircraft had shot down a civilian airliner. Yet another was to sink a US warship and blame that on Castro. None of these came to anything, but sabotage did take place. Cuban emigré groups received help from a special CIA budget to destroy Castro's Cuba. In 1960, a French ship carrying a cargo of armaments from Belgium was blown up in Havana harbour, killing 81 people and wounding hundreds of others. Pressure was put on British companies by the USA to stop them trading with Cuba. Having 'discouraged' British ships from transporting a cargo of British Leyland buses and spare parts, but having failed to get the deal cancelled, it was therefore more than coincidental that an East German ship carrying the equipment was rammed in the Thames. Cuba has claimed other sabotage, such as supplying asymmetrical ball bearings to damage machinery, and chemical additives in lubricants for engines to make them wear out quickly. As classified documents of the Kennedy administration are released, more bugs keep crawling out of the woodwork.

Economic policy during the 1960s was largely unsuccessful in achieving its aims. After a spell as head of the Central Bank, Che Guevara was appointed Minister of Industry, a key position given that the government wanted to industrialize rapidly to reduce dependence on sugar. However, the crash programme, with help from the USSR, was a failure and had to be abandoned. Sugar was king again but productivity plummeted and there were poor harvests in 1963-64. The whole nation was called upon to achieve a target of 10 million tonnes of sugar by 1970 and everyone spent time in the fields helping towards this goal. It was never reached and never has been, but the effort revealed distortions in the Cuban economy which in effect increased the island's dependence on the Soviet Union. Castro jumped out of the frying pan into the fire, he escaped domination by the USA only to replace it with another superpower.

Rationing is still fierce, and there are still shortages of consumer goods. However, the Revolution's social policies have largely been successful and it is principally these achievements which have ensured the people's support of Castro and kept him in power. Education, housing and health services have been greatly improved and the social inequalities of the 1940s and 1950s have been wiped out. Equality of the sexes and races has also been promoted, a major change in what was a *machista*, racially prejudiced society. Infant mortality fell to 7.3 per 1,000 live births in October 1997, on a par with many industrialized countries. It is claimed that illiteracy has been wiped out. Considerable emphasis is placed on combining productive agricultural work with study: there are over 400 schools and colleges in rural areas where the students divide their time between the fields and the classroom. Education is compulsory up to the age of 17 and free, while access to higher education has been granted to all.

1970s SOVIET DOMINATION

During the second decade of the Revolution, Cuba became firmly entrenched as a member of the Soviet bloc, joining COMECON in 1972. Technicians came from Eastern Europe and Cubans were trained in the USSR. The Communist Party grew in strength and size and permeated all walks of life, influencing every aspect of Cubans' day to day living, while putting more central controls on education and culture. The Revolution was institutionalized along Soviet lines and the Party gained control of the bureaucracy, the judiciary and the local and national assemblies. Communist planners controlled the economy and workers were organized into government-controlled trade unions. A new socialist constitution was adopted in 1976. In 1971-75 the economy grew by about 16% a year, but fell back after then and never recovered such spectacular growth rates again.

Cuba's foreign policy during this period changed from actively fomenting socialist revolutions abroad (such as Guevara's forays into the Congo and Bolivia in the 1960s) to supporting other left wing or third world countries with combat troops and technical advisers. Some 20,000 Cubans helped the Angolan Marxist government to defeat a South African backed guerrilla insurgency and 15,000 went to Ethiopia in the war against Somalia and then the separatist rebellion in Eritrea. Cuban advisers and medical workers went to Nicaragua after the Sandinista overthrow of the Somoza dictatorship in 1979; advisers and workers went to help the left wing Manley government in Jamaica and to the Marxist government in Grenada (until expelled by the US Marines in 1983). In September 1979, Castro hosted a summit conference of the non-aligned nations in Havana, a high point in his foreign policy initiatives.

The decade also marked a period of intellectual debate at home and abroad about the path the Revolution was taking. In 1971 the poet Herberto Padilla was arrested for cultural deviation and forced to confess his crimes against the Revolution. His treatment and cultural censorship brought accusations of Stalinization of cultural life. The Padilla affair split the Hispanic intellectual world, with writers such as Octavio Paz and Carlos Fuentes of Mexico, Mario Vargas Llosa of Peru and Juan Goytisolo of Spain renouncing their support for the Revolution, while Gabriel García Márquez of Colombia and Julio Cortázar of Argentina reaffirmed their support. Free expression was stifled and during this time the best Cuban art and literature was produced by exiles. The debate widened to include civil liberties and political rights, and official secrecy made it difficult to gauge accurately the persecution of political prisoners, religious believers, intellectual opponents and homosexuals.

1980s DISSATISFACTION AND FLIGHT

By the 1980s, the heavy dependence on sugar and the USSR, coupled with the trade embargo, meant that the expected improvements in living standards, 20 years after the Revolution, were not being delivered as fast as hoped and the people were tiring of being asked for ever more sacrifices for the good of the nation. In 1980, the compound of the Peruvian embassy was overrun by 11,000 people seeking political asylum. Castro's answer to the dissidents was to let them go and he opened the port of Mariel for a mass departure by sea. He also opened the prisons to allow prisoners, both political and criminal, to head for the USA in anything they could find which would float. It was estimated that some 125,000 embarked for Miami, amid publicity that it was the criminals, delinquents, homosexuals and mental patients who were fleeing Cuba.

At the same time huge demonstrations were organized in Havana in support of the Revolution. Some relaxation in controls was allowed, however, with 'free markets' opening alongside the official ration system.

This was the decade of the Latin American debt crisis, and Cuba was unable to escape the pressures brought to bear on its neighbours. Development projects in the 1970s had been financed with loans from western banks, in addition to the aid it was already receiving from the USSR. When interest rates went up in 1982, Cuba was forced to renegotiate its US$3.5 billion debt to commercial banks, and in 1986 its debt to the USSR. The need to restrain budget spending and keep a tight control over public finances brought more austerity. The private markets were stopped in 1986 and the people were once more asked for voluntary labour to raise productivity and achieve economic growth. Excess manpower, or unemployment, was eased by sending thousands of Cubans abroad as internationalists to help other developing countries, whether as combat troops or technicians.

The collapse of the Communist system in the Eastern European countries in the late 1980s, followed by the demise of the USSR, very nearly brought the end of Castro's Cuba as well. Exiles in Miami started counting the days until they would re-enter the homeland and Castro's position looked extremely precarious. There were signs that a power struggle was taking place at the top of the Communist Party. In 1989, General Arnaldo Ochoa, a hero of the Angolan campaign, was charged with drug trafficking and corruption. He was publicly tried and executed along with several other military officers allegedly involved. Castro took the opportunity to pledge to fight against corruption and privilege and deepen the process of rectification begun in 1986.

THE SOVIET CONNECTION

Before the collapse of the Soviet system, aid to Cuba from the USSR was traditionally estimated at about 25% of gnp. Cuba's debt with the USSR was a secret; estimates ranged from US$8.5 billion to US$34 billion. Apart from military aid, economic assistance took two forms: balance of payments support (about 85%), under which sugar and nickel exports were priced in excess of world levels and oil imports were indexed against world prices for the previous 5 years, and assistance for development projects. About 13 million tonnes of oil were supplied a year by the USSR, allowing 3 million to be re-exported, providing a valuable source of foreign earnings. By the late 1980s up to 90% of Cuba's foreign trade was with centrally planned economies.

US RELATIONS

Before the Revolution of 1959 the USA had investments in Cuba worth about US$1,000 million, covering nearly every activity from agriculture and mining to oil installations. Today all American businesses, including banks, have been nationalized; the USA has cut off all imports from Cuba, placed an embargo on exports to Cuba, and broken off diplomatic relations. Promising moves to improve relations with the USA were given impetus in 1988 by the termination of Cuban military activities in Angola under agreement with the USA and South Africa. However, developments in Eastern Europe and the former USSR in 1989-90 revealed the vulnerability of the economy (see **The Economy**, page 84) and provoked Castro to defend the Cuban system of government; the lack of political change delayed any further rapprochement with the USA. Prior to the 1992 US presidential elections, President Bush approved the Cuban Democracy Act (Torricelli Bill) which strengthened the trade embargo by forbidding US subsidiaries from trading with Cuba. Many countries, including EC

Castro and the UN

In 1960, Fidel Castro visited the UN for the first time since becoming leader of Cuba. Relations with the USA were becoming sour and the hotels in New York were wary of giving lodging to the new Government in case of reprisals from the Cuban exiles and other potential violence. Hotels refused to accept his booking without a large deposit, which he refused to pay. Undeterred, Castro led his party to buy tents and headed for Central Park, where he intended to pitch camp, declaring he was still a *guerrilla comandante*. They never got there, however, for a young black leader called Malcolm X persuaded them to come with him to Harlem, where he found them rooms in the run down *Hotel Theresa* in the heart of the black district. In addition he promised them security and protection from the emigrés provided by his black Muslims. It was a great occasion and Castro held court at the hotel, receiving eminent visitors such as Nehru and his daughter Indira Ghandi, Nasser, Khruschev and others, while also mingling with 'the masses'. His performance at the General Assembly was memorable, the audience was forced to listen to a speech lasting four and a half hours. 35 years later, he made another visit to the UN and went back to Harlem, although he lodged at the Cuban UN mission. Discarding the sober suit he wore to the UN General Assembly (where he was limited to a 5-minute address but received a longer ovation than the US leader for a speech which expressed the broad resentments of the Third World), he donned his military fatigues and cap and went to talk to an all-ticket audience at the Abyssinian Baptist Church about Cuba's educational and health achievements. Although he was again excluded by polite society, uninvited to President Clinton's reception for 149 heads of state and government and left off the guest list for Mayor Giuliani's dinner party, he was courted by no less than 230 US businessmen and invited to lunch by the Rockefeller family.

members and Canada, said they would not allow the US bill to affect their trade with Cuba and the UN General Assembly voted in November in favour of a resolution calling for an end to the embargo. The defeat of George Bush by Bill Clinton did not, however, signal a change in US attitudes, in large part because of the support given to the Democrat's campaign by Cuban exiles in Miami.

1990'S CRISIS AND CHANGE

In an effort to broaden the people's power system of government introduced in 1976, the central committee of the Cuban Communist Party adopted resolutions in 1990 designed to strengthen the municipal and provincial assemblies and transform the National Assembly into a genuine parliament. In February 1993, the first direct, secret elections for the National Assembly and for provincial assemblies were held. Despite calls from opponents abroad for voters to register a protest by spoiling their ballot or not voting, the official results showed that 99.6% of the electorate voted, with 92.6% of votes cast valid. All 589 official candidates were elected. October 1997 saw the first stage of the third elections for delegates to the municipal assemblies of People's Power (these serve a 2-year term). Delegates are directly nominated in neighbourhood meetings (the PCC does not put forward candidates), and ballot boxes are guarded by primary school children. The electoral process concludes with general elections in 1998, when provincial delegates and national deputies are elected for a 5-year term. The slate consists of up to 50% of the newly elected municipal delegates and the remainder selected by a national commission on the basis of proposals from the mass organizations. In the October 1997 elections, 97.6% of the electorate voted and 92.8% of the votes were valid (7.2% blank or spoiled).

Economic difficulties in the 1990s brought on by the loss of markets in the former USSR and Eastern Europe, together with higher oil prices because of the Gulf crisis, forced the Government to impose emergency measures and declare a special period in peace time. Rationing was increased, petrol became scarce, the bureaucracy was slashed and several hundred arrests were made in a drive against corruption. As economic hardship continued into 1993, Cuba was hit on 13 March by a winter storm which caused an estimated US$1 billion in damage. Agricultural production, for both export and domestic consumption, was severely affected. In mid-1994, economic frustration and discontent boiled up and Cubans began to flee their country. Thousands left for Florida in a mass exodus similar to that of Mariel in 1980 on any craft they could invent. It was estimated that between mid-August and mid-September 30,000 Cubans had left the country, compared with 3,656 in the whole of 1993. In contrast, the number of US visas issued in January-August was 2,059 out of an agreed maximum annual quota of 20,000. Eventually the crisis forced President Clinton into an agreement whereby the USA was committed to accepting at least 20,000 Cubans a year, plus the next of kin of US citizens, while Cuba agreed to prevent further departures.

As the economic crisis persisted, the government adopted measures (some of which are outlined below) which opened up many sectors to private enterprise and recognized the dependence of much of the economy on dollars. The partial reforms did not eradicate the imbalances between the peso and the dollar economies, and shortages remained for those without access to hard currency.

Cuba then intensified its economic liberalization programme, speeding up the opening of farmers' markets throughout the country and allowing farmers to sell at uncontrolled prices once their commitments to the state procurement system were fulfilled. Importantly, the reforms also allowed middlemen to operate. It had been the emergence of this profitable occupation which had provoked the Government to close down the previous farmers' market system in 1986. Markets in manufactured goods and handicrafts also opened and efforts were made to increase the number of self-employed.

US PRESSURE IN THE 1990s

Cuba's foreign policy initiatives in 1994-95 succeeded in bringing international pressure to bear on the USA over its trade embargo. In its third and worst defeat in 1994, the USA lost a resolution in the UN General Assembly which called for an end to the embargo by 101 votes to 2. In 1995 it lost again by 117 votes to 3 and in 1996 by 137 to 3, with many European Union countries shifting from their previous abstentions. In the most recent vote, in November 1997, voting was 143 in favour, 3 against and 17 abstentions. The European Parliament meanwhile adopted a resolution which described the 1992 Torricelli Act as contrary to international law and called for its repeal. The Russian parliament passed a similar motion. However, right wingers in the USA continued to push for further economic pressure on Cuba.

In 1996, another US election year, Cuba faced another crackdown by the US administration. In February, Cuba shot down 2 light aircraft piloted by Miami exiles allegedly over Cuban air space and implicitly confirmed by the findings of the International Civil Aviation Organization (ICAO) report in June. The attack provoked President Clinton into reversing his previous opposition to key elements of the Helms-Burton bill to tighten and internationalize the US embargo on Cuba and on 12 March he signed into law

Sport

🦶 Cuba's attendance at international sporting events has often depended on its relations with the USA and foreign policy considerations. No team was sent to the 1984 Olympic Games, held in the USA, in solidarity with Eastern European countries who did not attend because of security concerns. The 1988 Olympic Games were originally supposed to have been jointly hosted by North and South Korea, but when they were held in Seoul Cuba boycotted the event in protest over the Korean question. The 1992 Games in Barcelona, Spain, were the first in 30 years not to have been affected by any political boycott or ban. Cuba won the baseball competition, the first time baseball had been included as an Olympic sport. All sport in Cuba is amateur, but baseball is the national sport and its baseball team would be a match for any professional side. Cuba did attend the 1996 Olympic Games in Atlanta, USA, despite the US economic embargo and frosty relations between the two governments.

In 1982 Cuba hosted the Central American Games, and in 1991 the Pan American Games. The latter proved rather controversial, given the dire state of the economy set against the need for heavy spending to build 15 stadiums and an Olympic village on the edge of Havana for 6,000 athletes and officials from 39 countries. Castro admitted that if the commitment had not been made in 1986 when times were better, he would not have agreed to host the event, but the commitment had to be honoured. Some 20,000 competitors and spectators flooded Havana, including American baseball scouts seeking new talent.

Amateur athletes in Cuba have frequently been tempted abroad by the lure of fame and fortune. Shortly before the 1991 games, René Arocha, pitcher for the Cuban world championships team which beat the USA by two games to one in an exhibition match, defected in Miami. In 1993, when the Pan American Games were held in Puerto Rico, a record 50 Cubans were reported to have defected, including the gold medallist weightlifters Lino Elías Ocana and Emilio Lara Rodríguez, gymnast Tajedo Cortina, who collected his gold medal and ran to the waiting car of a Cuban exile, baseball pitcher Odalys Hernández, water polo team member Antonio Pérez, and gymnast Roberto Aldazábal, who won one medal but defected before he could win another. In 1996, before the Olympic Games, two boxers and a baseball pitcher defected to the USA. They were Joel Casamayor, the reigning Olympic bantamweight boxing champion, Ramón Garbey, the former light heavyweight world boxing champion, and Rolando Arrojo, the baseball team's star pitcher.

the Cuban Freedom and Democratic Solidarity Act. The new legislation allows legal action against any company or individual benefiting from properties expropriated by the Cuban government after the Revolution. Claims on property nationalized by the Cuban state extended to persons who did not hold US citizenship at the time of the expropriation, thus including Batista supporters who fled at the start of the Revolution. It brought universal condemnation: Canada and Mexico (Nafta partners), the EU, Russia, China, the Caribbean Community and the Río Group of Latin American countries all protested that it was unacceptable to extend sanctions outside the USA to foreign companies and their employees who do business with Cuba. In 1997 the EU brought a formal complaint against the USA at the World Trade Organization (WTO), but suspended it when an EU/US agreement was reached under which Clinton was expected to ask the US

Congress to amend Title IV of the law (concerning the denial of US entry visas to employees and shareholders of 'trafficking companies'). Clinton was also expected to carry on waiving Title III (authorizing court cases against 'trafficking' of expropriated assets).

RECENT EVENTS

A spate of bombings targeted at the tourist industry caused alarm in 1997. The first was in April at the *Meliá Cohiba* in Havana, followed by one in July at the *Capri* and another at the *Nacional*. The *Meliá Cohiba* was hit again in August, while in September three hotels on the seafront were bombed and an Italian was killed by flying glass. In an extraordinarily successful piece of detective work, it only took about a week for the Interior Ministry to announce it was holding a former paratrooper from El Salvador, Raúl Ernesto Cruz León, who confessed publicly on TV to working as a mercenary and planting six bombs. He did not say who he was working for, but it was assumed in Cuba that the Miami-based Cuban American National Foundation (CANF) was behind the bombings.

At the end of July, Cuba successfully resuscitated the (14th) World Festival of Youth and Students, which was held in Havana and attended by over 12,500 delegates, although only 5,000 had been expected. The Festival was financed entirely by private donations and voluntary effort and, despite warnings by their government that their participation contravened the Trading with the Enemy Act,

the US delegation was the largest of all, with 849 Americans attending.

The Cuban Communist Party held its 5th Congress in October 1997, the first since 1991, and timed to coincide with the 30th anniversary of the death of Che Guevara in Bolivia, whose remains were returned to Cuba in July. It stressed the unity of the Cuban people behind the Revolution and Party, the Cuban system of democracy and the changes in the economy, but highlighted issues such as the need for efficiency in relation to maintaining and increasing the slow economic recovery. Immediately afterwards, Cuba began a week of official mourning for Che and his comrades in arms, where vast numbers filed past their remains in Havana and Santa Clara, where they were laid to rest on 17 October. It is likely that nationalism will remain at the forefront of domestic politics in the months leading up to the centenary of the US occupation of Cuba in 1898. Several academic conferences and other events are planned for 1998.

In January 1998 the Pope visited Cuba for the first time. During his 4-day visit he held open air masses around the country, attended by thousands of fascinated Cubans encouraged to attend by Castro. The world's press was represented in large numbers to record the Pope's preaching against Cuba's record on human rights and abortion while also condemning the US trade embargo preventing food and medicines reaching the needy. The visit was a public relations success for both Castro and the Pope.

Culture

RELIGION

The major characteristic of Cuban culture is its combination of the African and European. Because slavery was not abolished until 1886 in Cuba, black African traditions were kept intact much later than elsewhere in the Caribbean. They persist now, inevitably mingled with Hispanic influence, in **religion**: for instance *santería*, a cult which blends popular Catholicism with the Yoruba belief in the spirits which inhabit all plant life. This now has a greater hold than orthodox Catholicism, which has traditionally been seen as the religion of the white, upper class, opposing

independence from Spain in the 19th century and the Revolution in the 1950s.

Church and State were separated at the beginning of the 20th century when Spain was defeated by the USA and a constituent assembly approved a new constitution. The domination of the USA after that time encouraged the spread of Protestantism, although Catholicism remained the religion of the majority. Nevertheless, Catholicism was not as well supported as in some other Latin American countries. Few villages had churches and most Cubans rarely went to mass. Even before the Revolution, the Church was seen as right wing, as most of the

The Cuban Revolution

The Cuban Revolution has had a profound effect on culture both on the island itself and in a wider context. Domestically, its chief achievement has been to integrate popular expression into daily life, compared with the pre-revolutionary climate in which art was either the preserve of an elite or, in its popular forms, had to fight for acceptance. The encouragement of painting in people's studios and through a national art school, and the support given by the state to musicians and film-makers has done much to foster a national cultural identity. This is not to say that the system has neither refrained from controlling what the people should be exposed to (eg much Western pop music was banned in the 1960s), nor that it has been without its domestic critics (either those who lived through the Revolution and took issue with it, or younger artists who now feel stifled by a cultural bureaucracy). Furthermore, while great steps have been made towards the goal of a fully-integrated society, there remain areas in which the unrestricted participation of blacks, women and homosexuals has yet to be achieved. Blacks predominate in sport and music (as in Brazil), but find it harder to gain recognition in the public media; women artists, novelists and composers have had to struggle for acceptance; homosexuals have suffered persecution, particularly in the 1970s, and many gay intellectuals have fled the country. Nevertheless, measures are being taken in the cultural, social and political spheres to rectify this and the 1990s have seen a considerable relaxation in prejudices.

Church of Jesus Miramar, Havana

priests were Spanish and many of them were supporters of General Franco and his fascist régime in Spain. They had an important role in education, particularly the Jesuits, who taught Fidel Castro.

After the Revolution relations between the Catholic Church and Castro were frosty. Most priests left the country and some joined the exiles in Miami, where connections are still strong. By the late 1970s the Vatican's condemnation of the US embargo helped towards a gradual reconciliation. In 1979 the Pope was invited to visit Cuba on his way back from a trip to Mexico, but he also received an invitation from the Cuban exiles in Miami. Caught between a rock and a hard place, the Pope opted to go to the Bahamas instead. In the 1980s, Castro issued visas to foreign priests and missionaries and allowed the import of bibles as well as giving permission for new churches to be built.

In 1994 Cardinal Jaime Ortega was appointed by the Vatican to fill the position left vacant in Cuba since the last cardinal died in 1963. A ban on religious believers joining the Communist Party has been lifted and Protestant, Catholic and other Church leaders have reported rising congregations. In the archdiocese of Havana, there were 7,500 baptisms in 1979 but this figure shot up to 34,800 in 1994.

In 1996 Fidel visited Pope John Paul II at the Vatican and the Pope visited Cuba in January 1998. Castro has stated in the past that there is no conflict between Marxism and Christianity and has been sympathetic towards supporters of liberation theology in their quest for equality and a just distribution of social wealth. During the Pope's visit to Brazil in October 1997, he criticized free market ideology which promotes excessive individualism and undermines the role of society, which he further emphasized in his visit to Cuba. The two septuagenarians clearly share some common ground on the need for social justice, although they are poles apart on the family, marriage, abortion and contraception, let alone totalitarianism and violent revolution. At the Pope's request, Castro decreed 25 December 1997 a public holiday, but for 1 year only. Christmas Day was abolished in the 1960s because it interfered with the sugar harvest; a whole generation has grown up without it and many people were unsure of its religious significance when it was reinstated. Nevertheless, artificial Christmas trees sold out and tinsel was to be found in many homes.

AFRO CUBAN RELIGION

From the mid-16th century to the late 19th, countless hundreds of thousands of African slaves were brought to Cuba. Torn from dozens of peoples between the Gulf of Guinea and southern Angola, speaking hundreds of languages and dialects, they brought from home only a memory of their customs and beliefs as a shred of comfort in their traumatic new existence on the sugar plantations. The most numerous and culturally most influential group were the Yoruba-speaking agriculturalists from the forests of southeast Nigeria, Dahomey and Togo, who became known collectively in Cuba as *lucumí*. It is their pantheon of deities or *orishas*, and the legends (*pwatakis*) and customs surrounding these, which form the basis of the syncretic **Regla de Ocha** cult, better known as **Santería**.

Though slaves were ostensibly obliged to become Christians, their owners, anxious to prevent different ethnic groups from uniting, turned a blind eye to their traditional rituals. The Catholic saints thus spontaneously

The Orishas

Every *toque de santo* begins and ends with the evocation of **Elegguá**, lord of the roads and crossroads and guardian of our destiny, dressed always in red and black. In the calendar of Christian saints he is equated with the Child of Prague. Most powerful *orisha* of all is red-clad **Changó**, lord of fire, thunder, war, drums and virility, who is syncretized with St Barbara. *Santeros* believe he was born of **Yemayá**, alter ego of the Virgin of Regla, Havana Bay's patron saint. Dressed in blue and white, she is mistress of the seas and goddess of motherhood. **Oggún** (St Peter) is another war god and patron of blacksmiths. Brother to **Changó**, he is also his rival for the affection of **Yemayá**'s sensual dancing sister **Ochún**, the yellow-clad goddess of rivers and springs, beauty and sexual love. Christianized as the Virgin of Charity of El Cobre, she is Cuba's patron saint. Her shrine at the Basilica of El Cobre outside Santiago de Cuba is always filled with fragrant *mariposas*, the national flower, and the walls are hung with countless offerings from those whose prayers have been answered, including crutches, sachets of Angolan earth brought by returning veterans, a medallion left by Fidel Castro's mother after his safe return from the guerrilla struggle, and Hemingway's Nobel Prize. **Olofi** or **Olorun**, syncretized as both the Eternal Father and the Holy Spirit, is the supreme creator of all things, but, say *santeros*, takes little interest in our world, and long ago handed over the care of it to **Obatalá** who, dressed all in white like his devotees or *hijos* (children), is god of peace, truth, wisdom and justice. In Christian guise he is Our Lady of Mercy. His son is **Orula** (colours: yellow and green), syncretized as St Francis of Assisi and others. Known also as **Ifá**, he is the ancient, implacable lord of divination. Unlike other *orishas*, who 'descend on' and possess their *hijos*, he communicates only with the *babalawo* or priest who interprets his predictions. Divination of what the future holds is a central feature of Regla de Ocha, and may be achieved through casting the *ékuele*, a set of eight pieces of turtle or coconut shell. Other popular *orishas* include **Oyá** (St Teresa of Avila), mistress of the winds and lightning, queen of the cemetery; and **Babalú Ayé**. Dressed in bishop's purple, covered in sores, limping along on crutches and followed by stray dogs, he is the deity of leprosy and venereal and skin diseases. Every 17 December thousands of his followers, including the halt and lame and those fulfilling a promise in thanks for a favour received, make the pilgrimage to the chapel of St Lazarus, his Christian manifestation, at El Rincón on the southern outskirts of Havana.

merged or syncretised in the *lucumí* mind with the *orishas* whose imagined attributes they shared.

While the Yoruba recognise 400 or more regional or tribal *orishas*, their Cuban descendants have forgotten, discarded or fused together most of these, so that today barely two dozen regularly receive tribute at the rites known as *toques de santo*.

Santería, which claims to have at least as many believers as the Catholic Church in Cuba, in all walks of life including Communist Party members, enshrines a rich cultural heritage. For every *orisha* there is a complex code of conduct, dress (including colour-coded necklaces) and diet to which his or her *hijos* must conform, and a series of chants and rhythms played on the sacred *batá* drums.

Santería is non-sectarian and non-proselytizing, co-existing peacefully with both Christianity and the **Regla Conga** or **Palo Monte** cult brought to Cuba by *congos*, slaves from various Bantu-speaking regions of the Congo basin. Indeed many people are practising believers in both or all three. Found mainly in Havana and Matanzas provinces, **Palo Monte** is a much more fragmented and impoverished belief system than **Regla de Ocha**, and has borrowed aspects from it and other sources. Divided into several sects, the most important being the *mayomberos*, *kisimberos* and *briyumberos*, it is basically animist, using the forces of nature to perform good or evil magic and predict the future in ceremonies involving rum, tobacco and at times gunpowder. The focus of its liturgy is the *nganga*, both a supernatural spirit and the earthenware or iron container in which it dwells along with the *mpungus* or saints. **Regla Conga** boasts a wealth of complex magic symbols or *firmas*, and has retained some exciting drum rhythms.

The **Abakuá Secret Society** is, as its name suggests, not a religion but a closed sect. Open to men only, and upholding traditional *macho* virtues, it has been described as an Afro-Cuban freemasonry, though it claims many non-black devotees. Found almost exclusively in Havana (particularly in the Guanabacoa, Regla and Marianao districts), and in the cities of Matanzas, Cárdenas and Cienfuegos, it has a strong following among dockworkers; indeed, outsiders often claim its members have *de facto* control over those ports. Also known as *ñañiguismo*, the sect originated among slaves brought from the Calabar region of southern Nigeria and Cameroon, whose Cuban descendants are called *carabalí*. Some **ñáñigos** claim the society was formally founded in 1836 in Regla, across the bay from Havana, but there is evidence that it already existed at the time of the 1812 anti-slavery conspiracy. **Abakuá** shares with freemasonry the fraternal aims of mutual assistance, as well as a series of seven secret commandments, secret signs and arcane ceremonies involving special vestments.

● **Reading list**
There is a vast array of reading matter on the subject of Afro Cuban religions, most of which is in Spanish. Those listed here which are published in Cuba are mostly available in dollars at large hotel bookstores (eg at the *Habana Libre*), or at Librería Fernando Ortiz (opposite the *Habana Libre*, esquina 23 y L), or possibly at La Moderna Poesía in Old Havana, esquina Obispo y Bernaza. Ediciones Unión has its own bookshop at UNEAC (Unión de Escritores y Artistas de Cuba) headquarters on Calle 17 351, esquina H, Vedado. Casa de las Américas is on Avenida 3 y G, Vedado. Letras Cubanas has its own bookshop in the Palacio del Segundo Cabo, O'Reilly 4 (in the Plaza de Armas, Old Havana).

Fernando Ortiz, *Los negros esclavos*, Editorial de Ciencias Sociales, La Habana (1987); *Los bailes y el teatro de los negros en el folklore de Cuba*, Letras Cubanas, La Habana (1985).

Lydia Cabrera, *El Monte: Igbo, Finda, Ewe Orisha, Vititi Nfinda*, Colección del Chichirekú, Ediciones Universal, 3090 SW 8th Street, Miami, Florida, e-mail ediciones@kampung.net (1992, first published Havana 1954); *Reglas de Congo: Palo monte mayombe*, Ediciones CR, Miami, Florida (1979).

Natalia Bolívar, *Los orishas en Cuba*, Editorial Unión, La Habana.

Natalia Bolívar Aróstegui & Carmen González Díaz de Villegas, *Mitos y leyendas de la comida afrocubana*, Colección Echú Bi, Editorial de Ciencias Sociales, La Habana (1993).

Miguel Barnet, *Cultos afrocubanos: la regla de Ocha, la regla de Palo Monte*, Ediciones Unión, La Habana (1995).

Samuel Feijóo, *Mitología cubana*, Editorial Letras Cubanas, La Habana (1985).

Enrique Sosa Rodríguez, *Los ñáñigos*, Casa de las Américas, La Habana (1982).

Agenor Martí, *Mis porfiados oráculos*, Fuentetaja Ediciones, Madrid (1992).

Migene González-Wippler, *Santería – the religion: a legacy of faith, rites and magic*, Llewelyn Publications, St Paul, Minnesota (1994); *Legends of santería*, Llewelyn Publications, St Paul, Minnesota (1994).

Rafael A Núñez Cedeño, *The Abakuá secret society in Cuba: language and culture*, Hispania, vol 71, no 1 (1988).

Art

Until the 19th century Cuban artists were mainly concerned with emulating the styles fashionable in Spain at the time, to gain favour with their colonial rulers. In the 19th century painters began to develop styles that were endemic to the island, among them Valentín Sans Carta and Juan Borrero. The latter was remarkable for his prolific output, though an early death at only 19 cut short his career. He was most famous for his portraits, two of which now hang in the Museo Nacional Palacio de Bellas Artes (closed for major refurbishments until the end of 20th century). Estéban Chartrand (1840-1883) painted landscapes influenced by the French style of the previous century.

Victor Manuel's
Gypsy Girl from the Tropics, 1929

Wilfredo Lam 1902-82

Wilfredo was the last of eight children born to Lam Yam, a shopkeeper in Sagua La Grande who had emigrated to Cuba from Canton via San Francisco and Mexico, and his second wife, a mulatto with some Amerindian blood. The family was sufficiently prosperous for Wilfredo to be educated in Havana, where he received some art training, and then to be sent to Spain for further education in 1923. His early work was relatively conservative, with some Cubism influence. He was still in Spain during the Spanish Civil War and fought on the Republican side, taking part in the defence of Madrid. After a spell in hospital with an intestinal infection he moved to France, where he was introduced to Picasso, with whom he became friends, even sharing an exhibition with him in New York in 1939. He was also introduced to André Breton and Benjamin Péret, leaders of the Surrealist movement, and encouraged by them to explore primitive art, imposing on him a vision of what they thought he should be like, based on his background and appearance. In 1940, Lam fled Paris, travelling mostly by foot to Bordeaux, then on to Marseilles and in 1941 to Martinique, where he was interned. During his spell in the French Antilles, he met Aimé Cesaire, the poet, who had just published fragments of *Cahier d'un retour au pays natal*, a hugely influential work which started the *négritude* movement. Lam took seven months to get back to Cuba, where he was distressed to see how all men of colour aped white men and wanted lighter skins. He resolved to 'thoroughly express the negro spirit' and adopted a new style of painting which was African influenced and caused quite a stir in Cuba. His painting, *The Jungle*, was widely acclaimed, and much of his work sprung from a visit to Haiti to research Afro-Caribbean customs and voodoo ceremonies, which sharpened his imagery. Most of Lam's work was designed for a non-Latin American audience and he lived in New York, Cuba, Paris and Genoa with his Swedish wife. He opposed Batista and welcomed Castro's Revolution, recruiting intellectual support for Castro in Europe.

One of the artists known for his major contribution to the emerging Cuban style of painting was Leopoldo Romañach, though even at the end of the 19th century, when Impressionism was revolutionizing painting in France, the Cuban style still retained its roots in the academic tradition of landscape and portrait painting.

It was the 1920s which saw Cuban artists finally developing their own avant-garde movement; the art magazine '*avance*' made its appearance in 1927. Víctor Manuel's (1897-1969) 1924 painting '*Gitana Tropical*', with its echoes of Cézanne and Gaugin, caused a sensation when the public first saw it. Now it has become the painting which symbolizes the beginning of modernism in Cuban art. US encroachment on the failing Cuban sugar industry in the 1920s led to a new nationalism among artists and intellectuals, with painters looking to Afro-Cuban images for inspiration. Eduardo Abela (1889-1965) and Jorge Arche were two of the better-known painters working from the late 1920s to early 1930s.

The decade of the 1940s belonged to Wilfredo Lam (1902-1982), still Cuba's most famous painter. He spent many years in France and Spain, becoming friends with Picasso and André Bréton, who introduced him to primitive art. Lam blended synthetic cubism, African masks and surrealism to create an essentially Cuban vision. Although he did most of his major work in Cuba, he always intended to show those outside

Latin America the reality there. One of his contemporaries, Amelia Peláez (1896-1968), looked west for her inspiration, to the mural painting of Mexico. Her brightly coloured murals can be seen in the Tribunal de Cuentas building and the Office of the Comptroller in Havana. It was this divergence of influences that characterized Cuban art during the 1940s: the expressionist paintings of Carlos Enríquez; René Portocarrero (1912-1985), with his big colourful paintings incorporating Afro-Cuban imagery, one of the few painters not to be influenced by the movements in Europe; and the unique vision of Wilfredo Lam.

The 1950s and 1960s saw a big influence on painting of imagery from the cinema; a major group of artists around this time were known as the 'Grupo de los Once', and included Luis Martínez Pedro, Raúl Milián and Sandú Darie.

The revolution had a strong influence on developments in the art world. The first national art school was founded in the early 1960s, and in 1976 the Escuela Superior de Arte was founded. These institutions gave more people access to the serious study of applied art. Raúl Martínez (1927-95), was the most well-known of the Cuban Pop Artists. Unlike their North American contemporaries, the imagery of Cuban Pop Art came from the ubiquitous faces of revolutionaries, seen on murals all over Cuba.

The 1970s was the most difficult era for artists in Cuba, with many political restrictions on their work; of the few that made it past the censors, Flavio Garciandia was the most notable, producing paintings mixing abstract and figurative styles.

The 1980s, as in most countries, saw the emergence of conceptual art, with the formation of many alternative groups, such as 'Artecalle' – street art. there was also the 'Puré' group, the most important member being Toirac. Though most of the better-known artists were now abroad, the art scene still flourished. Some, like the sculptor Alejandro Aguilera, distorted patriotic symbols in a confrontational way. As in other parts of the world, the 1980s were a decade in which everything was questioned and deconstructed.

The 1990s have seen the rise of performance art as a means of expression. Carlos Garaicoa is one of the bigger names in this field, already having taken part in the 1997 Havana Biennial along with Tania Brugrera, who had also exhibited in the 1996 Sao Paulo Biennal. Many alternative galleries have sprung up recently, the best being 'Aglutinador', run by two well-known artists from the 1980s, Sandra Ceballos and Esequiel Suárez. The gallery is in their house in the Vedado area of Havana.

The 1990s have also seen a return to painting, after the vogue for installation of the 1980s. This reflects the economic need, during the special period, for artists to make saleable objects again, though it also has its conceptual roots in post-modernism.

Until the Museo Nacional Palacio de Bellas Artes reopens in the early 21st century, the only state-run galleries now open in Havana are the Centro de Desarrollo de las Artes Visuales, and the Wilfredo Lam centre, which has shows by contemporary artists. You can also see some small exhibitions of avant-garde work at the Casa de Las Américas. Look out for the many small private galleries around Habana Vieja and Centro Habana as well.

Architecture

The oldest house in Cuba still standing today is Diego de Velázquez's residence in Santiago, built in 1522. However, the most important architectural works of the 16th century were the forts of Havana and Santiago, built in response to the many pirate attacks Cuba suffered. The original fort on the site of the **Castillo de la Real Fuerza** in Havana was burnt to the ground in 1555 by the French pirate Jacques de Sores. Felipe II commissioned a new fortress but the work was delayed when the architect was replaced in 1562 by Francisco de Calona, who completed the reconstruction in 1582. The building is a technological marvel, considering the primitive resources available when it was built: the walls are 6m thick and 10m high, with huge triangular bulwarks at each corner; a drawbridge leads over the wide moat to the vaulted interior. The early 17th century saw the construction of two castles in Havana and Santiago, by the Italian Juan Bautista Antonelli. They are both known as **Castillo del Morro**, and both still stand. Also built in the 17th century were the Havana city walls: 1.5m thick and 10m high, they ran for nearly 5,000m around the edge of the bay. A few fragments remain at Calle Egido y Avenida del Puerto.

Baroque

The most notable baroque building in Havana is the **cathedral**; completed in 1777, it features an eccentric, undulating façade,

Cathedral of Havana

Casa de la Obrapía

asymmetrical towers, and wooden-ribbed vaulting over its three naves. The increased power enjoyed by the church in the 17th and 18th centuries led to bishops such as Diego Evelino de Compostela having a big say in city planning, with the result that many churches were built during this period. The gardens of Evelino's house in Calle Compostela, Havana were the site of the first baroque church in Havana, **Iglesia de Nuestra Señora de Belén**, completed in 1718 and currently under restoration. The classic baroque façade features a nativity scene framed within a shell. Diego de Compostela also built the **Colegio de San Francisco de Sales** in Havana. A typical central patio, surrounded by thick columns and slatted doors, receives rainbows of light from the 'mediopuntos' – semicircular windows with fan-shaped stained glass.

San Francisco de Asís church in Habana Vieja was rebuilt in the baroque style in 1730. A 40m tower was also added, making it one of the highest religious buildings in Latin America. The building is no longer a church; only the exterior of the building, in particular the Escorial style of the façade, retains the baroque splendour of its day.

Colonial Mansions

A series of large, airy rooms on the first floor surrounded the central patio, based on the Sevillian style; the ground floor was reserved for warehouses and shops, and the *entresol*, between the ground and first floors, was where the slaves lived. Ornate carved *rejas* adorned the windows, and half-doors set with coloured glass divided the rooms. A good example in Havana is **Casa de La Obra Pía**, on Obrapía and Mercaderes.

Neo-Classical

The first neo-classical building in Havana was the **Templete**, a small doric temple on the Plaza de Armas. In the early 19th century the cathedral in Havana had its baroque altars removed, and replaced with neo-classical ones by Bishop Juan José de Espada. There are three fine neo-classical buildings in Matanzas: the cathedral, the **Iglesia de San Pedro Apóstol**, and the theatre. Many elaborate country houses were built around this time, for example **Quinta de Santovenia** near Havana, now

Malecón

an old people's home. Its inlaid marble floor, fountains and wrought-iron *rejas* are typical of the neo-classical period. The **Palacio de Aldama** (Amistad y Reina in Centro Habana) has a stunning neo-classical interior with fine decorated ceilings. It is now the Instituto de Historia de Cuba.

20th Century

One of the most notable art nouveau buildings is the **Palacio Velasco**, on Capdevila esquina Agramonte in Centro Habana. Built in 1912, it is now the Spanish Embassy. There are also many good examples of art deco in Havana; the best is the **Edificio Bacardí**, built in 1929 by the founder of Bacardi rum, and the neo-renaissance **Casino Español**, now the Palacio de Los Matrimonios, on Paseo Martí in Centro Habana. The **Capitolio** was the brainwave of former dictator Machado, who sought to demonstrate his allegiance to the US by erecting a copy of the Capitol building in Washington DC. Built in 1932, it has a 62m dome and a 120m entrance hall.

More examples of 1930s architecture can be seen in Santiago, where there are some attractive art-deco buildings on the Malecón, as well as the **Palacio Nacionalista**. The **Vista Alegre** neighbourhood, begun in 1906, contains some outstanding examples of art nouveau, notably the **Palacio de Pioneros**. This pink building on Manduley entre 9 y 11 was one of the Bacardí family residences.

Aquiles Capablanca was the most popular architect of the 1950s. His **Tribunal de Cuentas** in Havana is one of the most admired 20th century buildings in Latin America. He also built the Office of the Comptroller, in Plaza de la República. Both buildings feature murals by well-known artist Amelia Peláez. Capablanca employed many elements inspired by le Corbusier, whose influence can also be seen in residential work of the 1950s; conical designs called paraboloids were incorporated in the roof, whose purpose was to allow fresh air to circulate in the building. These avant-garde designs were combined with a revival of the colonial construction around a central patio, which hadn't been used for 70 years. The *Tropicana* nightclub, built by Max Borges Jr in 1952, was another work of stunning originality: exotic, sinuous curves on the shell-like structure are combined with tropical vegetation and the architect's own sculptures.

Post-Revolution

The revolution saw less construction of new buildings than the conversion of former emblems of the Batista dictatorship into more functional buildings for public benefit. This happened with the **Moncada Garrison** in Santiago, now a school and museum, and the **Capitolio** in Havana, now a library and museum. Some new structures did appear, such as the **School of Plastic Arts**: started in 1961 by Ricardo Porro, and completed after his defection by Vittorio Garatti in 1965, it has been described as resembling a stretched-out woman's body, with breast-like domes and curved walkways. Another good example of post-revolution creativity is the *Coppelia* ice-cream parlour, by Mario Girona, completed in 1966.

Soviet influence and materials after the Revolution saw the appearance of the grey monolithic buildings associated with the former USSR. However, the negative aura of such buildings in Eastern Europe has often much to do with the climate. Many of such buildings in Cuba, for example state-run hotels built during the 1960s and 1970s, have such wide open-plan interiors and vast windows, often coloured with modernist stained glass, that the effect is entirely positive, allowing light and air to move freely through the building. The *Hotel Sierra Maestra* in Bayamo and the *Hotel Guacanayabo* in Manzanillo are good examples of this.

An excellent way to get an overall picture of the architecture of Havana is to visit the Maqueta de La Habana, on Calle 28 113 entre 1 y 3, Miramar. This is a detailed model of the city with a scale of 1m = 1 km, covering all its buildings dated by colour from the colonial period to the present.

Bibliography

A History of Latin American Art and Architecture, Leopoldo Castedo.
Havana, Portrait of a City, Juliet Barclay.

Literature

The earliest known work of Cuban literature was a poem called '*Espejos de paciencia*', published in 1605 by Silvestre de Balboa. An epic canto about the struggles between a Spanish bishop and a French pirate, it is an esteemed work for its time, though it now retains only historical value. Early schools of writers in Cuba were too influenced by Spanish literature to produce anything essentially Cuban; not until the first half of the 19th century did poets begin to formulate a voice of their own: the first collection of verse by a native Cuban was Ignacio Valdés Machuca's '*Ocios poéticos*', published in 1819.

José María Heredia y Heredia (1803-39) is considered the turning point for Cuban letters. His '*Meditación en el teocalli de Chobula*' (1820) marked the beginning of Romanticism, not only in Cuba, but in the Spanish language. He was also the first of many Cuban writers to be involved in the struggle for independence. He was expelled from the country for his part in anti-colonial conspiracies, and wrote most of his work while in exile in Mexico and the USA.

Cuba's most prolific woman writer was Gertrudis Gómez de Avellaneda (1814-73). Her anti-slavery novel '*Sab*' (1841) was the first of its kind to be published anywhere in Latin America, its theme predating '*Uncle Tom's Cabin*' by a decade. A glut of abolitionist novels followed, the most notable being '*Cecilia Valdés*' (1882) by Cirilio Villaverde. The poet Domingo Delmonte led a protest against Cuba's continued acceptance of slavery after its official abolition in 1815, and many writers had to publish their anti-slavery novels in New York.

The most influential figure in Cuba's struggle for independence was José Martí (1853-95). He was deported to Spain in 1880 for his part in the independence movement (see box, **José Martí**, page 71). He later died in battle during the second War of Independence in 1895. He wrote 'Versos Sencillos' (1891), based on the drama of his own life, while in exile in the USA. Martí also wrote highly acclaimed prose, which appeared in political journals published in Argentina and Venezuela. Many of his prophesies about Cuba's political future have been fulfilled.

Two poets associated with the transition from romanticism to modernism are Enrique Hernández Miyanés and Julián del Casal (1863-93). The latter, influenced by Baudelaire, praised the value of art over nature in *Hojas al Viento* (Leaves in the Wind, 1890) His posthumous '*Bustos y Rimas*' (Busts and Rhymes 1893), has been compared to the great Nicaraguan poet Rubén Darío. Another important modernist poet was Regina Eladio Boti y Barreiro. Although she only published three collections of verse, she was responsible for taking Cuban poetry from modernism to post-modernism.

In the 1920s the '*negrismo*' movement began, which created non-intellectual poetry based on African dance rhythms. The poet Lydia Cabrera has dedicated her life to research of Afro-Cuban culture. As well as numerous stories, in which she created a prose based on the magical-mythical beliefs passed orally through black folklore, she published many books on the ethnography and linguistics of Afro-Cubans. The negrismo group consisted of poets both black and white, although its most famous member, Nicolás Guillén Batista (1902-89), was mulatto. '*Motivos de son*' (1930), in which he incorporated African rhythms in his *son* poetry, is considered his best work. He joined the Communist party, and after the Revolution was made president of the Union of

Cuban Writers, and declared the National Poet by Castro.

Two of Guillén's former colleagues on the Communist newspaper '*Hoy*' were the writers Lino Novas Calvo and Carlos Montenegro. Novas Calvo is recognised as one of the finest short story writers in Latin America. He used the narrative techniques of Hemingway and Faulkner to capture the feel of Havana slang. He was the first of many writers to go into voluntary exile with the instalment of Castro's regime. *La Luna Nona y Otros Cuentos* (The Ninth Moon, 1942) is his best collection. Carlos Montenegro's '*Hombres Sin Mujer*' (Life Without Women) has been compared to Céline and Genet. He was jailed for life aged 18 for killing a sailor who sexually assaulted him. The novel is based on the sexual exploits of his 15 years in prison.

The major writers at the time of the 1959 revolution were the novelists Virgilio Piñera (1914-79) and Alejo Carpentier (1904-80) (see box, **Alejo Carpentier**, page 72), and the poet José Lezama Lima. All publishers were merged into the National Printing Press, with Alejo Carpentier as manager. The founder of 'Magic Realism', Carpentier's early novels are among the most highly rated in Latin American literature. Many are available in English, including '*Los Pasos Perdidos*' (The Lost Steps), the most accessible of his richly Baroque tales, which weave aesthetic fantasy with powerful twists and turns in the plots.

José Lezama Lima (1910-76) scandalised post-revolution Cuba with his novel *Paradiso* (Paradise, 1966), a thinly-disguised account of his homosexual experiences. Primarily a poet, Lezama was one of the driving forces behind the *criollismo* movement of the 1940s and 1950s. His rebellious, apolitical stance is an inspiration to the young Cuban poets of today, who seek to create a non-politicized poetry with a more spiritual dimension.

One of the most famous dissident novelists was Reinaldo Arenas (1943-90).

José Martí (1853-1895)

Born into a poor family in Havana, José Martí dedicated his life from a young age to rebellion against the colonial Spanish rule. A strong influence on him was the head of his school, the poet and freedom fighter Rafael Mendive. It was his connection with Mendive that was used as evidence for Martí's sentence of forced labour for his part in the 1868 Independence Conspiracy while still a boy. The experience of gross injustice, slaving in the sun with old men and young boys chained at the ankles, implanted in the young Martí a lifelong commitment to the struggle for independence from Spanish rule.

Martí's sentence was commuted to exile. He was sent to Spain in 1871-74, where aged 18 he wrote the first of many political essays, *'El presidio político de Cuba'*, in which he denounced the sufferings of his fellow Cubans at the hands of an authoritarian colonial rule. He completed his studies in Spain, and then went to Mexico to become editor of *'Revista Universal'*. From there his continued period of exile found him teaching at the University of Guatemala in 1877. He then lived in Venezuela until 1881 and the last years of his exile were spent in the USA. He left in 1895 to join the liberation movement in Cuba, where he was welcomed as a political leader. Tragically, he was killed on 19 May that year while fighting in the War of Independence at Boca de Dos Ríos near Santiago.

José Martí's work was primarily concerned with the liberation of Cuba, but many of his poems focused on nature, with Man at the centre engaged in a continual process of betterment. He combined a love of poetry with a desire for his prose work to have some effect on the world; all his energies were directed towards securing a future in which justice and happiness could flourish. Though one of the greatest modernist poets, he did not share other modernists' views that the role of poetry was outside conventional society.

Martí also differed from his contemporaries in his rejection of contemporary European literature. He saw pre-Columbian culture as having far more importance to a Latin American poet. His views were expanded upon in his essay *'Nuestra América'*, in which he welcomed the contributing force of Indians and blacks in contemporary culture.

Martí set the tone for all his poetry with his 1882, *'Ismaelillo'*, demonstrating the simplicity and sincerity he felt was lacking in current Spanish poetry. He developed this style in 1878 with *'Versos libres'*, and later in his most admired collection *'Versos sencillos'* (1891), in which the upheavals of his own life were his biggest inspiration. Martí is perhaps best known in Europe by the song *'Guantanamera'* – an adaptation by Pete Seeger of Martí's verse, put to the melody of Joseíto Fernández. In Cuba, however, he is the figure head of Cuban liberation and has become an icon, deliberately exploited by Castro, of anti-coloni-
alism, independence and freedom.

Alejo Carpentier (1904-1980)

👣 Alejo Carpentier was born in Lausanne, Switzerland, of Franco-Russian parents, but grew up and was educated in Cuba, studying music and architecture at the University of Havana. When only 20, he was made editor of an avant-garde Cuban literary review, 'Carteles', became involved in poetry in the Afro-Cuban movement and joined the 'Grupo Minorista', a literary group. Carpentier's search for a new form of specifically Latin American literature led him to the 'Indigenista' writers such as Romulo Gallegos (Venezuela) and Miguel Angel Asturias (Guatemala). He believed that writers should look around them more at the essentially non-European aspects of their culture, in particular at the tradition of oral story-telling prevalent in all Latin America. Carpentier believed that this inward-looking would reveal 'lo Real Maravilloso', or Magic Realism.

Carpentier wrote his first novel 'Ecué-Yamba-O!' (Lucumí for 'Praise be to God') during a period of imprisonment in 1927 for petitioning against the dictator Machado. It portrays the surviving ethnic traditions of black Cubans, in particular their religious cults. Having escaped from Cuba on a false passport, he lived in Paris from 1928-39, where he wrote musical scenarios and a ballet, while following the Surrealist movement. After reading Spengler's 'Decline of the West', and on his return to Cuba, Carpentier visited Haiti, where his ideas crystallized: here was an example, in the slaves' 1791 movement for independence, of social change brought about without the help of European ideas of enlightenment. Carpentier made this the subject of his second novel 'El Reino de este mundo' (1949).

In 1945-59, Carpentier left Cuba again to live in Caracas, where he worked as a journalist. During this time he wrote 'La Música en Cuba', which is now rather dated but still worth reading, and travelled up the Orinoco, which gave him the inspiration for his third novel.

'Los pasos perdidos' (1953) is about a New York-based composer who flees his dull existence on a trip to the most primitive regions of the American subcontinent. He settles in a tiny colony deep in the Amazon jungle, and begins to discover how simple life becomes without the trappings of modern civilization. Only when the narrator begins to compose music again does he come up against a major obstacle: there is a dire shortage of paper in the village. He is forced to choose between living the primitive life (in utopia) without Art, or returning to a city to get some paper, risking his re-acceptance on his return to the jungle community. This novel is now considered his seminal work on lo real maravilloso, with Latin America as a surreal place where all ages of history co-exist.

After the Revolution, Carpentier returned to Cuba and wrote 'El Siglo de las Luces' (1962), a passionate testimony to the new Socialist state but set in 1790-1809 and dealing with the impact of the French Revolution on the Caribbean. He was one of the few writers of the pre-Revolution years to gain favour with the new government, and was made manager of the state publishing house. In 1966 he went to Paris as the Cuban Ambassador, where he lived until his death in 1980. He continued to write, but his best work was already behind him.

Today Carpentier holds an important position among Latin American authors as the founder of Magic Realism; his early works show a remarkable richness of language and are studded with cultural references from pre-Columbian times to the Parisian avant-garde. The above-mentioned novels are all available in English.

Dogged by state security for most of his youth, he was imprisoned several times as a dissident and a homosexual, and only managed to publish his novel, '*El mundo alucinado*' (Hallucinations, 1971) by smuggling the manuscript out of the country through foreign friends. He finally escaped to Miami in the Mariel exodus, but, suffering from AIDS, he committed suicide in New York. His memoirs, '*Antes que anochezca*' (Before night falls) were published posthumously. This and his other works are available in translation. Also available in English are the works of Guillermo Cabrera Infante, who now lives and works in England. In 1959 he founded '*Lunes*', the literary supplement to the newspaper '*Revolucion*', but within 2 years it had been phased out by the government. Cabrera Infante's novel '*Tres tristes tigres*' (Three Trapped Tigers, 1965) won a prestigious Spanish literary award in 1965, the year he left Cuba. It was Herberto Padilla's favourable review of this book which sparked off the famous 'Padilla Affair'. He was imprisoned as a counter-revolutionary and forced to make a public confession of crimes he had not committed, a humiliating act which caused an outcry among the intellectuals of Europe.

As a reaction to the political restrictions placed on writers after the Revolution, a movement sprang up in the sixties of experimental literature, influenced by the French avant-garde and North American pop culture. Severo Sarduy, who left Cuba for Paris immediately after the Revolution, was the leading member; his '*De dónde son los cantantes?*' (From Cuba with a Song, 1967), with its complex layering of cultural history and linguistic puzzles, is still regarded as a classic by Cuban intellectuals. Sarduy became a citizen of France in 1967 and lived there until his death in 1993.

Nowadays Cuban writers find it easier to express their ideas in public. Havana has its first legally-recognized literary group, and there is talk of a private publishing house being established in the near future. At the centre of the group is Reina María Rodríguez, a poet who is already gaining admiration outside Cuba. Some of these young poets and writers see themselves as carrying on where literature left off after the 1960s, when the repressive measures of the Revolution induced a state of creative inertia and self-censorship.

Music and dance

There are few countries in the world with so rich a musical heritage as Cuba. No visitor can fail to be moved by the variety of sounds which surround them, whether it be a street corner rumba or a septeto in the Casa de la Trova. Music is everywhere – it seems that nothing can happen without it.

The story of Cuban music begins long before the founding of modern Cuba, in Africa and Spain. But it was in Cuba itself, in the villages, the dockyards, in the mountains and on the streets that a new Cuban identity was forged through music. Musical forms which have their roots in Angola have been transformed with Spanish styles; songs from Andalucía have been influenced and enriched by African rhythms and instruments. The result is a feast for any music lover.

The centrepiece of Cuban music is surely the *son*. Son is played by Cuba's oldest musicians and by its youngest, proving that the longest lasting tradition in Cuban music is, in fact, innovation. Son began its life in rural Oriente where old songs from Spain combined with African call-and-response choruses. The syncopated notes of the guitar and *tres* (a small guitar like instrument) contributed to early styles such as *Guaracha*, full of satire and humour, the *Guajira*, including the famous 'Guajira Guantanamera', and *Nengón*, which soon developed, with the addition of bongo, maracas and marimbula, into the style known as *Son Changüí*. From Guantánamo (where Changüí is still strong), the son reached Havana, where by the late 1920s Ignacio Piñero had formed his Septeto Nacional. Their sones not only featured his exceptional vocal improvisations (honed in the large choral societies called *Coros de Clave*), but added a hot trumpet to the central rhythm of the *clave*. Nicolás Guillén busied himself composing sones and son was now recognised as the sound of Cuba (in Europe and the USA it was mistakenly called 'the Rumba'). The *septeto* style is still heard today in the popular music bars and *Casas de la Trova*. Piñero continued to innovate by mixing styles, creating Guajira Son, Bolero Son (also popularized by Santiago's Miguel Matamoros) and even Pregón Son which used Havana street cries, including the famous 'Echalé Salsita.

A new development in the 1930s was Arsenio Rodriguez' *Conjunto* style which marked the beginning of modern Salsa. To the traditional Septeto came conga drums, timbales (or 'Paila'), piano and more trumpets. This 'big band' son made much of the final, wild call-and-response or '*montuno*' section of the song. The later *Descargas* were improvised jam sessions over strong paila, conga and bongo rhythms which had major influences on US jazz.

During the 1950s, Beny Moré emerged as *Sonero Mayor*, updating the son once more with contemporary styles, from jazz to mambo and cha cha cha. Along with the arrival of such artists as Celia Cruz, Miguel Cuní and Félix Chapottín, son was ensured a place in the early years of the Revolution.

Elio Reve spent the 60s and 70s creating a modern Changüí, revived with the aid of bassist Juan Formell, who later went on to found the exceptional and ever popular Los Van Van.

The new generation of *soneros* have continued this 'tradition of innovation' with such groups as NG La Banda displaying bewildering talent on their tours across the globe, while Adalberto Alvarez carries the torch for a more rootsy son. The 'child' of son – Latin salsa – has

Buying music

Obviously on your return from Cuba you will want to transform your little room into the local Casa de la Trova and invite all the neighbours round for a *traguito* of Havana Club rum. Luckily there is a large choice of music on sale, on video, cassette and CD. The state record company EGREM has shops alongside recording studios in the main towns. Every hotel should stock tapes at least of the major artists. Thanks to a distribution deal with a French company, much of the EGREM back catalogue is seeing the light of day again under the name of ARTEX, in a series of well balanced compilations and major reissues. Artex is involved in all cultural marketing so they too have shops in every town centre which stock posters, crafts and books alongside the sound and vision. The dollar shops such as Cubalse will also have a good range. The series *'El Son Es Lo Más Sublime'* features an extensive history of the genre and there are excellent series on rumba, danzón, bolero, Cuban jazz, conga and folkloric styles as well as the latest by Van Van, El Médico and the others. These should also be for sale, along with recordings by house bands, in the Casas de la Trova. Occasionally the booksellers on street corners and in the plaza will have old vinyl discs (probably unplayable) and you might even chance upon one of the newly emerging second hand record stores for those rare *'descarga'* sessions. These are sometimes worth it for the sleeves alone. You'll need to know the dollar/peso exchange rate to buy, though. If you fancy a go yourself, EGREM shops stock a range of mass produced Afro-Cuban instruments: conga drums, bongos, claves and suchlike, which are reasonably priced, especially compared with prices in Europe. You'll need to watch your baggage allowance though (and your back muscles as you stagger home). If you don't have time for record shopping, or you want to brush up on your *son* before you go, the Latin American craft shop Tumi (Tumi Music Ltd, 8/9 New Bond Street Place, Bath, BA1 1BH, T 01225 462367, F 01225 444870) are now distributing the best of EGREM's compilations in Britain. There are also three wonderful and all-embracing compilations: *'Cuban Counterpoint – A History of Son Montuno'*, *'A Carnival of Cuban Music'* and *'Afro-Cuba, An Anthology'* all out on the Rounder label. Just out on the Blue Jacket label, packaged in a cigar box, is *'Cuba I am Time'*, a compilation of four CDs with an 112-page book. It's difficult to find a book purely about Cuban music in English. The best at the moment is the study of salsa *'Havana Heat, Bronx Beat'* by Hernando Calvo Ospina. If your Spanish is up to it, you could try the short essays (and lovely pen sketches) *'Música por El Caribe'* by Helio Orovio. María Teresa Linares' *'La Música y El Pueblo'* is a classic and the African roots are brilliantly explored in *'Los Cabildos y la Fiesta Afrocubanos del Día de Reyes'* by Cuba's pioneering ethnologist Fernando Ortíz. All these should be adequate for the new lending library attached to your recently opened 'Casa de la Trova experience'. The neighbours will be ecstatic...

returned to Cuba in style with Isaac Delgado, 'El Chévere de la Salsa'.

While son was appearing in Cuba's countryside, an African rhythm known as the Yuka, which had survived on the sugar plantations, was joining forces with the Spanish *Décima* and livening up the ports of Havana and Matanzas. This style soon came to be known as **rumba**. African rhythms were played on whatever came to hand: boxes used to pack fish or candles gave a good tone. Characters such as 'Mama'buela' were created in mime and singers commented on current events or battled with each other for honours. This Rumba de Cajón also involved the stately *Yambú* dance, where following the vocal section, a couple would mime courtship.

Soon the rhythms passed onto drums, the large Tumba providing a solid bass, the Conga a repeated cross rhythm which was accompanied by brilliant improvisations on the small Quinto. To this was added a pair of claves and a struck length of bamboo known as the Guagua or Cata. The more sexual dance form known as *Guaguancó* (still the main rumba style) demanded more rapid playing. Great *rumberos* emerged, such as Florencio Calle, Chano Pozo, Estéban Latrí and Celeste Mendoza as well as groups who specialised in rumba, such as Los Papines, Conjunto de Clave y Guaguancó and the well-travelled Muñequitos de Matanzas who used the rhythms of the Abakuá religion in their rumbas. The Muñequitos also play the Matanzas style known as Columbia. This rumba echoes African solo dancing, involving an element of danger such as the use of knives. Even faster playing underpins a singing style which makes use of Bantu phrases and ends in a call-and-response.

Rumba is a playfully competitive art form. The rhythms have got faster, break dancing and karate moves have been incorporated into the dance, *rumberos* sing about the special period; in this way rumba survives as a true reflection of Cuban street life.

Matanzas is also the birthplace of the *danzón*. The popular 'Típica' orchestras, influenced by the great cornettist Miguel Faílde, added subtle African rhythms to the European Contradanza, along with a call-and-response 'montuno' section, creating a balance between formal dance and syncopated rhythm, almost a Cuban 'ragtime'. The *Orquesta Típica* slowly changed, adding piano and further percussion, while the 1920s saw a new arrival, the *Charanga Francesa*, which was another

Alicia Alonso and the Ballet Nacional de Cuba

Although there was dancing in Cuba during the Spanish colonial period, with occasional visiting theatre companies from Spain, ballet as such was not seen until 1842, when the great Romantic ballerina Fanny Elssler appeared with her sister and partner at the Teatro Tacón. After that there were occasional performances by touring companies including a visit by Anna Pavlova in 1917. Home-bred ballet started with the ballet evenings of the Sociedad Pro-Arte Música in 1931. The Sociedad also housed the conservatory with a ballet class which produced Alicia Alonso and the two Alonso brothers, Alberto and Fernando, amongst other outstanding dancers and choreographers of their generation.

Alicia Alonso has been the most influential Cuban dancer and ballet director ever, having made her name on the world stage before returning to Cuba to take charge of the development of ballet there. Born Alicia Ernestina de la Caridad del Cobre Martínez Hoyo in Havana on 21 December 1921, she studied in Havana and at the School of American Ballet in New York. Her first jobs were in Broadway musicals but in 1940 she became a member of the Ballet Theatre and temporarily joined the Sociedad Pro-Arte Música in Havana. She suffered periods off work because of a detached retina but returned to the Ballet Theatre in 1943 as ballerina. In 1948 she set up her own company in Havana, the Ballet Alicia Alonso, which was followed by a school in 1950. However, she continued to dance abroad, both with the American Ballet Theatre and as a guest of many other companies.

Alonso is known for her classical style and flawless technique, but she has also successfully interpreted modern roles. In New York she worked a lot with the choreographer, Anthony Tudor, who once said of her during a rehearsal, "Oh, this excitable, temperamental Cuban, very savage, very primitive, you should try to be development of the típica, featuring wooden flute and strings as well as paila.

This was the beginning of a style developed by many contemporary Cuban groups such as Orquesta Aragón, Original de Manzanillo, Cándido Fabre and his group, Los Van Van and the Charanga Habanera.

During the 1940s and 1950s, Orestes López ('Cachao') and the violinist Enrique Jorrín created the new Mambo and Cha cha cha styles directly from Danzón. These driving rhythms are still popular all over Cuba, and were fundamental to the explosion of Latin music and dance worldwide.

The *Canción Habanera* is regarded as the first truly Cuban vocal style. Emerging in the 1830s as a mixture of the so called 'Tongo Congo' rhythm and Spanish melodies, it had its greatest exponent in Eduardo Sánchez. *Habaneras* were also composed by Eduardo Lecuona, a pianist who was internationally feted during the 1930s and 40s.

Another *Canción* style, involving simply a singer and a guitar, was developed during the 19th century in Oriente by Pepe Sánchez. His simple, beautiful songs such as 'Rosa No 1' and 'Rosa No 2' inspired others such as María Teresa Vera and the remarkable Sindo Garay who claimed to be the only man who had shaken the hand of both Jose Martí and Fidel Castro! The romantic style known as *Bolero* soon developed from canción.

Realising the potential for expression offered by canción, young musicians like Silvio Rodríguez, Sara González and Pablo Milanés created the *Nueva Trova*. Their songs reflect the path of the Revolution, Silvio's 'Playa Girón' telling its own story. 'Pablito' is an exceptional composer and interpreter, especially of Guillén's poetry.

more educated!" Knowing that his remarks were hurtful, he asked when she would start crying. "Never!" came the reply, and she kept her promise. In fact, Tudor loved her superb technique, her spirit and her combination of vulnerability and defiance, but believed that her natural expressiveness and her tendency to show all her emotion in her face was vulgar and needed to be restrained. He held that the movement itself should show the expression. A compromise was reached. One of Alonso's most famous roles was, like Fanny Elssler, that of *Giselle,* but she has created roles in Tudor's *Undertow* (1945), Alberto Alonso's *Romeo and Juliet* (1946), Balanchine's *Theme and Variations* (1947), de Mille's *Fall River Legend* (1948), and the title role in Alberto Alonso's *Carmen* (1967).

Alicia married Fernando Alonso, a dancer and ballet director, and brother of the dancer and choreographer, Alberto Alonso. The three of them worked to establish the company, Ballet Alicia Alonso, which in 1955 became the Ballet de Cuba and then in 1961 the Ballet Nacional de Cuba. The company became a showpiece for the Revolutionary Government and frequently toured abroad, even to the USA in 1978. The young dancers brought on by the dance school have a high reputation for their technique and artistic interpretation and many have won medals at international competitions. In Havana they perform at the Teatro García Lorca, with a repertory of classical ballets, folklore-based works and modern dance. Several important ballets have been especially created for the company, including Alberto Alonso's *El Güije* and *Un retablo para Romeo y Julieta*, J García's *Majismo,* José Parés' *Un Concierto en Blanco y Negro*, Jorge Lefèbre's *Edipo Rey* and A Méndez' *Nos Veremos Ayer Noche, Margarita*. Alberto Alonso's *Carmen* was originally created for the Bolshoi Ballet, but has become part of the repertory of the Ballet Nacional de Cuba.

The Afro Trail

It is not so long since traditionalist believers were scandalized when the renowned jazz and salsa band *Irakere* started to use the sacred *cueros batá* (the three drums used in **Santería** rites) on stage. In these times, when all's fair in the scramble for tourist dollars, you may well find a more-or-less disneyfied all-singing all-dancing version of lucumí or congo ceremonies on offer as part of your hotel's entertainment. Enjoy the spectacle but season liberally with salt. Alternatively you can witness expertly choreographed but largely genuine performances of Yoruba and Congo devotional and profane song and dance, as well as the intricacies of the *real* rumba in all its variants, at the *Sábado de la Rumba* sessions put on by the **Conjunto Folklórico Nacional** on Saturday afternoons at their Calle 4 headquarters in Vedado (see box, **Music in Havana**, box page 124). Despite the colourful trappings, this is only incidentally a spectacle for tourists, who are regularly outnumbered by the Cubans fervidly chorusing the *santero* chants in Yoruba and swaying to the infectious *guaguancó*. The **Casa de Africa** (Obrapía 157, entre San Ignacio y Mercaderes, Old Havana, Tuesday-Sunday 1300-2000) is a pleasant and untaxing way to get a glimpse of the wealth of African cultures, in Cuba and in Africa itself. As well as small collections from various African countries, it houses the Afro-Cuban devotional artifacts collected by the late Don Fernando Ortiz, the founding father of Afro-Cuban ethnographic studies. Also worth a visit: the **Museo Municipal de Regla** (Martí 158, entre Facciolo y Piedra, Regla, Monday-Saturday 0930-1830, Sunday 0900-1300). The most atmospheric way to reach Regla is by *lanchita* (ferry) across the bay from the terminal near the Plaza de Armas. The collection of history of African religions in Cuba, formerly in the **Museo Histórico de Guanabacoa** (Martí 108, entre Versalles y San Antonio) in the district popularly regarded as the Mecca of Afro-Cuban cults, is now in the Casa de Africa. Any *habanero* afflicted by aches and pains or generally down in the mouth will sooner or later be advised: "what you need is a trip to Guanabacoa."

Cuban jazz is exceptionally healthy. *Orquesta Irakere* continue to renew themselves, inspired by the pianistic genius of Jesús 'Chucho' Valdéz, while *Grupo Afro-Cuba* fuse jazz with traditional Cuban rhythms, including the *bata* drums of Santería. Among the generation of the 1980s and 1990s the incredible pianist Gonzalo Rubalcaba is supreme, composing pieces using danzón rhythms amongst others. The annual Jazz Festival in Havana was for years attended by Dizzy Gillespie, whose influence is evident in the playing of Cubans such as Arturo Sandóval, and has recently heard British jazzers giving their all.

The rhythms and songs of *santería* remain strong across the island. The three African *bata* drums are regarded as the most complex of all to master and the rhythms, each assigned to a particular deity, accompany the singing in old Yoruba. Merceditas Valdés is loved throughout Cuba for her interpretation of these songs. Meanwhile, 'bembe' parties on Saints' days are accompanied by singing and drumming. The singer Lázaro Ros has developed a band, Síntesis, who combine traditional *santería* music effectively with jazz rock.

The music of the Cuban **carnival**, recently revived following the debilitating effects of the Special Period, is truly exhilarating. Both Havana and Santiago have their own styles of *conga*, the thunderous music which drives on the parade. During February in Havana, the conga drums, bells and bass drums of groups

Music on Cuban TV

A most encouraging aspect of Cuban culture is that live music is paramount. Rather than tinny speakers placed high up on walls, most cafés, hotels, bars and even airports will have a live band serenading the punters. However, those who find themselves in front of a (working) television will not be disappointed. Music is everywhere. In Cuba there is a host of specials on Cubavision to look out for. 'Must see' for salsa fans is *'Mi Salsa'* on Sunday nights which regularly showcases a top Cuban band as well as showing the latest salsa artists on video. This follows on from *'Palmas y Cañas'*, the *campesino* programme which features rural son and the *'controversio'* style of musical debate, as well as advice on herbal teas... Tuesday night has both *'Encuentro'*, a collection of music from across Latin America, and *'A Capella'* which shows old film of Cuban greats such as Matamoros or Tata Güinés. On Wednesday you can hear Cuban stars talk about their influences in *'Tiempos'* whilst *'En FM'* on Friday nights is the 'Top of the Pops' of Cuban music – the 'chart' is compiled by phone-in requests. Anyone who has struggled with a Cuban phone will realise what a triumph of patience this is. Saturday night kicks off with the excellent *'Contacto'*, a two-hour arts magazine which has a regular live band and discussion with top musicians. A wonderful *'Contacto'* moment occurred when Ken Loach (in Havana for the film festival) enjoyed the music and then proceeded to struggle with inane 'are you liking Cuba' questions, having previously sat in silence during an in-depth discussion (in Spanish) with Gutiérrez Alea on the influence of Italian New Realism on revolutionary Cuban Cinema! *'Contacto'* is followed by the hugely popular comedy show *'Sabadazo'*; Los Van Van, La Charanga or other star bands finish off the show with a blast of brilliant son. Along with whole nights dedicated to musical rallies, Christmas specials and New Year concerts, TV is a great chance to see the bands you might have missed live. If you can't get near a TV, Saturday radio (Rebelde) rocks to some great salsa. Go on, have a night in.

such as Los Dandy or La Jardinera support brass players as they belt out popular melodies, the lanterns spinning in the dancers' hands. In Santiago, each barrio is represented by massed ranks of *bocué* drums, bass drums and brake drums. The cloaked and masked revellers of Los Hoyos and San Agustín sing in response to the wailing *corneta china*, a remnant of Cuba's Chinese communities. Other bands' *paseos*, combine brass players with the usual barrage of percussion during the late July festivities.

The carnival procession usually features the old *Cabildos* whose drums keep alive the original rhythms of Africa. In Oriente, the *Tumbas Francesas* parade the rhythms and dances developed by Africans in Haiti before the 18th Century revolution forced yet another move across the ocean.

All of this music can be heard in Cuba now: at the Casas de La Trova, at the Focos Culturales, in the theatres and the cafés, in the parks, the backyards and on the streets. From changüí to cha cha cha, from rumba to bolero, from son to santería, the music of Cuba is gloriously, vibrantly alive.

Cinema

One of the great success stories of the Cuban Revolution is the Cuban film industry. The Film Institute, known familiarly as ICAIC (Cuban Institute of Cinematographic Art and Industry) was set up by the new Government in March 1959, only three months after the victory of the Revolution. Headed by Alfredo Guevara, it aimed to produce, distribute, and show Cuban films to as wide a domestic audience as possible, to train filmmakers and technicians, and to promote film culture generally. Open to anyone with an interest in film, excepting pro-Batista collaborationists, the Institute built up an industry with an international reputation within 10 years, virtually from scratch.

Before the Revolution films had been made in Cuba by foreign companies or amateurs. The staple diet of the Cuban filmgoer, even in 1959, was Hollywood movies. In the early 1960s, after the Bay of Pigs episode (1961) and the missile crisis (1962), several film directors (including Nestor Almendros), cinematographers and technicians, left the island taking their precious equipment with them. Adequate government funding, which depended on the fluctuating Cuban economy, and state of the art training and technology, became critical problems following the US trade embargo. The majority of the crew working on Tomás Gutiérrez Alea's comedy 'The Twelve Chairs', for example (the assistant director, director of cinematography, camera operator, focus puller, camera assistant, and continuity girls), were first-timers. Yet in learning to make the most of their

scant resources the Cuban filmmakers introduced striking new techniques which, in addition to their youthful enthusiasm, improvisation and revolutionary focus, created a forceful impact on the world of film. Five Cuban films won international awards in 1960 alone. As Francis Ford Coppola remarked, "We don't have the advantage of their inconveniences". Measures such as the launch of the film journal *Cine cubano*, the inauguration of the Havana Cinemateca (1960), a national network of film clubs, and a travelling cinema (*cinemóvil*) showing films to peasants in remote rural districts, the nationalization of the film distribution companies, and the 1961 literacy campaign enabling 700,000 viewers to read the subtitles of undubbed foreign films for the first time, placed cinema at the forefront of revolutionary cultural innovation. Even the posters, designed under the auspices of ICAIC by individual artists, became world famous.

The types of films made during the 1960s were national, nonconformist and cheap. ICAIC aimed to keep as independent criteria as possible over what constituted 'art' and encouraged imaginative, popular films, directly relevant to the revolutionary process and challenging the mass culture of acquiescent consumption. The preferred format was the documentary shot on 8 mm or 16 mm film (40 were made in 1965), honed to perfection by Santiago Alvarez, but there were a good number of excellent features too: *Cuba Baila* (Cuba Dances), *Historias de la Revolución* (Stories of the Revolution), *El Joven Rebelde* (The Young Rebel, based on a script by Zavattini), *La Muerte de un Burócrata* (Death of a Bureaucrat) and *Aventuras de Juan Quinquin* (The Adventures of Juan Quinquin), the most popular feature in Cuba of all time, until the release of *Fresa y Chocolate* (Strawberry and Chocolate).

In 1967 the film director Julio García Espinosa published his seminal essay 'For an Imperfect Cinema' which, with

Tomás Gutiérrez Alea (1928-1996)

👣 The two most famous Cuban films, *Memorias del Subdesarrollo* (Memories of Underdevelopment,1968), on the role of the intellectual in society, and *Fresa y Chocolate* (Strawberry and Chocolate, 1993), on gay issues in Cuba, were made by the director who has contributed more than any other to Cuban cinema. Tomás Gutiérrez Alea made over twelve features and thirteen shorts/documentaries. His films vary from the hilarious *La Muerte de un Burócrata* (Death of a Bureaucrat, 1966) to the sentimental romance *Hasta Cierto Punto* (Up to a Point, 1984). Except for *Cartas del Parque* (Letters from the Park, 1988), based on a screenplay by Gabriel García Márquez, they all have a sharp critical edge. Gutiérrez Alea started filming in 1947, then studied at the Centro Sperimentale in Rome in 1953. His first serious work was a 1955 documentary on the charcoal workers, confiscated by the Batista police. During the Revolution he played a leading part organizing the cinema section of the Revolutionary army and made (with García Espinosa) the first post-victory documentary, *Esta Tierra Nuestra* (This Our Land). His first feature film, *Historias de la Revolución* (Stories of the Revolution) dates from 1960. Since then, he has won many international awards. Retrospectives of his work have been shown across the world (including San Francisco, New York, Toronto, and New Delhi). Repeatedly, particularly in the late 1980s, he was refused entry into the USA. Yet in 1994, *Fresa y Chocolate* was nominated for an Oscar in the best foreign film category. Made primarily for a domestic market, it stages the dramatic encounter between a young Communist student and a gay intellectual. Both are patriotic Cubans, but while the student embraces the culture of Che and Fidel, the intellectual identifies with the refined art world of pre-revolutionary Cuba. Each learns from the other, but the intellectual, hounded by the authorities, finally seeks political asylum in Europe. Gutiérrez Alea's last film, the road movie *Guantanamera* (1995), which returns to the macabre comedy format of *La Muerte de un Burócrata*, was completed shortly before his death. The leading actress in both films was his wife, Mirta Ibarra.

the work of Octavio Getino and Fernando Solanas in Argentina and Glauber Rocha in Brazil, laid the basis of the New Latin American cinema movement, also known as Third Cinema, a key concept in film culture today. Cuban cinema reached its highpoint in 1968 with groundbreaking films such as *Lucía* (Lucia) and *Memorias del Subdesarrollo* (Memories of Underdevelopment) and, in 1969, *La Primera Carga al Machete* (The First Charge of the Machete). Cuban filmmakers, a number of whom had been trained in the Centro Sperimentale in Rome in the 1950s were influenced predominantly by Italian Neorealism, French New Wave Cinema and *cinéma verité* – British Free Cinema (Tony Richardson and Lindsay Anderson), and the Soviet classics. Films shot on location with hand held cameras featuring ordinary people engaged in a revolutionary process have remained the trademarks of classic Cuban cinema ever since.

By the 1970s, however, uncomfortable questions were being asked about the appropriateness of avant-garde art for the needs of the Cuban mass public. Tensions between creative artists and government bureaucrats exploded in the Padilla affair (1970), resulting in a 5-year government clamp down. ICAIC's production programme was reduced to three features a year, while young, often amateur filmmakers (average age 36) were favoured over the more experienced. Nevertheless, important films were produced, tending to focus on women's issues, historical

Films

🖎 If you know Spanish (and even if you don't) the following comedies are a must: *La Muerte de un Burócrata* (Death of a Bureaucrat, Gutiérrez Alea, 1966), in which a worker is mistakenly buried with his identity card. His widow needs it to claim her pension but when the family try to exhume the body officially they are caught up in a Kafkian tangle of bureaucracy forcing them to dig up the body themselves. When the body starts to smell , they try to bury it again, with hilarious results. This is a side-splitting, but no less serious, criticism of state officialism. The social satire *¡Plaff!* (Splat!, Juan Carlos Tabio, 1988) picks up on the same theme. A woman dies of a heart attack when an egg is thrown at her. Who threw the egg and why? This parody of a detective film delves deep into social issues such as the Cuban housing crisis and the scarcity of resources, while lampooning 'imperfect cinema'. The preference for foreign imports is ridiculed when a home-made polymer made from pig shit at the Institute of Excrement is proved to be far superior to a Canadian brand. The highlight of the film, however, is when the director of the Institute asks for a new filing cabinet, to store the letters he has written asking for a new filing cabinet. *Adorables Mentiras* (Adorable Lies, Gerardo Chijona, 1991) is a much more poignant comedy. An unsuccessful script-writer tries to impress a young street-walker by pretending to be a film director, while she in turn deceives him by pretending to be a professional actress. The complex web of sex, lies and audiotape unravels when the writer's wife, who thinks he's gay, is delighted to find out he is having an affair with a woman. But the objective of this apparently farcical charade is deadly serious. Cuban society of the 1980s is shown to be rife with petty corruption, resulting from self-delusion and material constraints. Young people are urged to face reality and get on with life, even if it means painful compromise.

and/or multiracial themes (particularly slavery and African-Cuban culture), with a view to consolidating a strong, cohesive sense of national identity. The black film director Sergio Giral's *El Otro Francisco* (The Other Francisco) and Gutierrez Alea's *La Ultima Cena* (The Last Supper), both depicting the courage and resistance of Cuban slaves, black director Sara Gómez's *De Cierta Manera* (One Way or Another), highlighting the problem of machismo among black men, and Solás' *Retrato de Teresa* (Portrait of Teresa), denouncing sexist attitudes in post-revolutionary society, all date from this period.

In 1976 the Ministry of Culture was set up, ushering in yet another episode in Cuban film history. In 1982 Julio García Espinosa took over from Alfredo Guevara as the Head of ICAIC, and ICAIC was incorporated into the Ministry. Until 1980 it had been self-financing. Nevertheless, de-

spite the increasing influence of the Hollywood format (favouring sentimental melodrama and romance), perhaps indicative of a deeper crisis of belief, films still tended to be critical of Cuban social reality. Production figures increased to some six features a year during the 1980s, many of these co-productions with countries such as Mexico and Spain. By the end of the 1980s there were 60 million filmgoers, each Cuban visiting a cinema on average six times a year. The Cuban audiences, mostly young white collar workers, technicians and specialists, tend to be educated and demanding. A network of video clubs and libraries were set up in the 1980s to meet their needs.

In the late 1980s, ICAIC recovered its independence and was restructured on the basis of three 'creation groups' each under an experienced film director in charge of encouraging and training young filmmakers. But, as Cuba moved into the 'Special Period' (1990-1994) in response to the fall of the Eastern block and the intensified US trade embargo, ICAIC faced another crisis. After the release of a controversially critical film, *Alicia en el Pueblo de Maravillas* (Alice in Wonderworld), in a climate of political tension, moves were made to incorporate the Institute into Radio and Television, directly controlled by the Central Committee of the Communist Party. This strategy was actively resisted by leading filmmakers, such as Gutiérrez Alea, the plans were scrapped, and Alfredo Guevara was appointed director once more. Paradoxically, at a time when resources were scarcer than ever before, ICAIC produced its most successful film ever, *Fresa y Chocolate* (Strawberry and Chocolate 1993), suggesting, perhaps, that the best Cuban films are made when circumstances are at their worst.

The Economy

Following the 1959 revolution, Cuba adopted a Marxist-Leninist system. Almost all sectors of the economy were state controlled and centrally planned, the only significant exception being agriculture, where some 12% of arable land was still privately owned. The country became heavily dependent on trade and aid from other Communist countries, principally the USSR (through its participation in the Council of Mutual Economic Aid), encouraged by the US trade embargo. It relied on sugar, and to a lesser extent nickel, for nearly all its exports. While times were good, Cuba used the Soviet protection to build up an impressive, but costly, social welfare system, with better housing, education and health care than anywhere else in Latin America and the Caribbean. The collapse of the Eastern European bloc, however, revealed the vulnerability of the island's economy and the desperate need for reform. A sharp fall in gdp of 35% in 1990-93, accompanied by a decline in exports from US$8.1 billion (1989) to US$1.7 billion (1993), forced the Government to take remedial action and the decision was made to start the complex process of transition to a mixed economy.

Transformation of the unwieldy and heavily centralized state apparatus has progressed in fits and starts. The Government is keen to encourage self-employment to enable it to reduce the public sector workforce, but Cuban workers are cautious about relinquishing their job security. Some small businesses have sprung up, particularly in the tourism sector (see box page 88). Free farm produce markets were permitted in 1994 and these were followed by similar markets at deregulated prices for manufacturers, including goods produced by state enterprises and handicrafts. Cubans are now allowed to hold US dollars and in 1995 a convertible peso at par with the US dollar was introduced, which is fully exchangeable for hard currencies.

Although commercial relations with market economies were poor in the late 1980s, because of lack of progress in debt rescheduling negotiations, Cuba has made great efforts in the 1990s to improve its foreign relations. The US trade embargo and the associated inability to secure finance from multilateral sources has led the Government to encourage foreign investment, principally in joint ventures. All sectors of the economy, including sugar and real estate, are now open to foreign investment and in some areas majority foreign shareholdings are allowed. About US$1,500 million was registered between 1990-94, in areas such as tourism, oil and mining. Some 400 foreign companies are now established in Cuba, with capital from 38 countries in 26 economic sectors. In 1996 Cuba attracted US$2 billion in foreign investment and the number of joint ventures rose to 260. The leading investors are from Spain, Canada, France, Italy and Mexico, in that order. Bilateral investment promotion and protection agreements have been signed with 12 nations including Italy, Spain, Germany and the UK. Under new legislation passed in 1996, free-trade zones are being established, the first one

Cuba fact file

Geography The Cuban archipelago (110,992 sq km) is made up of the island of Cuba (105,007 sq km), the Isla de la Juventud (2,200 sq km) and around 4,195 cays and islets (3,715 sq km). It lies in the entrance to the Gulf of Mexico with the Atlantic to the north and the Caribbean to the south. Haiti is 77 km across the Windward Passage, Jamaica 140 km across the Columbus Straits, the USA 180 km across the Florida Straits, and Mexico 210 km across the Straits of Yucatán. It is the largest of the Caribbean Islands and larger than Portugal or Guatemala. It is a long country, measuring 1,250 km from Punta de Quemado in the far east to Cabo de San Antonio in the far west. At its narrowest point it is only 31 km from Mariel bay to Majana, while at its widest it is 191 km from Tararacos beach in the north of Camagüey to La Punta de Camarón Grande on the southern coast of Granma Province. The northern coast measures 3,209 km and the southern coast 2,537 km, with more than 80 bays and 288 beaches. Principal mountain ranges: Sierra Maestra, Guamuhaya, Guaniguanico. Highest mountain: Pico Turquino (Santiago de Cuba) 1,974m. Longest river: Cauto, 343.4 km.

Population 11,038,000 (1996), 65th largest in the world. Density 99.4 per sq km. Annual growth rate 0.8% (1991-96). Birth rate per 1,000 population 14.0 (1993). Urban 72.8% (1990). Male 50.2% (1996). Ethnic composition: mixed 51%, white 37%, black 11%, other 1% (1994).

Health Infant mortality 7.3 per 1,000 live births (October 1997), the lowest in Latin America. 56,925 doctors, 1 per 193 inhabitants. 80,684 hospital beds, 1 per 134 persons (1994). Life expectancy (1990-95), male 73.9 years, female 77.6 years. Caloric intake as % of FAO requirement, 123%.

Language Spanish.

National holidays 1 January, Liberation Day, anniversary of the Revolution; 1 May, International Labour Day; 26 July, National Rebellion Day; 10 October, start of the Wars of Independence.

National flower *Mariposa*, butterfly flower, a jasmine, symbol of purity and rebellion in the Wars of Independence.

National bird *Tocororo*, Cuban trogon, with the red, white and blue colours of the Cuban flag.

National tree *Palma real*, Royal palm, typical of the Cuban landscape.

Economy Gross national product US$17,972 million (1996), per capita US$1,628.

Tourism 1,001,739 visitors (1996). Tourism receipts US$850 million (1994).

at Havana with others to follow at Cienfuegos, Mariel and Wajay, outside Havana. 75% of production must be exported but the rest can be sold in Cuba on the dollar market. Employees will be paid in pesos. By mid-1997, 35 foreign companies had applied for licences to operate.

Structure of production

Sugar is the major crop, providing about 70% of export earnings. However, the industry has consistently failed to reach the targets set. Cuba's dream of a 10 million tonne raw sugar harvest has never been reached. Poor weather and shortages of fertilizers, oil and spare parts cut output to 3.3 million tonnes in 1994-95, but it recovered to 4.4 million in 1995-96. Sugar mills have been converted to use bagasse as fuel, but the canefields use large quantities of oil for machinery to cut and transport the cane. Earnings from sugar exports are devoted to purchasing oil. Trade agreements with the ex-USSR, involving oil and sugar, survived US pressure on Russia to end oil shipments in order to receive US aid. A new sugar minister was appointed in 1997: General Ulises Rosales del Toro, who picked up his machete and went to work alongside his new army of 400,000 sugar workers, in a bid to shake up the sector. Several mills were shut 'temporarily' and workers laid off, to improve efficiency at a time of low harvests. It was too late to improve the 1997-98 crop, forecast to be between 3.8 million and 4.2 million tonnes, much the same level as the 1996-97 harvest, but it is hoped that the conditions can be created for a recovery of production from the 1998-99 season onwards.

Citrus is now the second most important agricultural export contributing about 4% of revenues. Cuba became a member of the International Coffee

Health

Free health care is provided to all Cubans by the state as their right. In the 1960s the state took on the task of curing the population of many infectious diseases, despite having lost half of its 6,000 doctors who left the country after the revolution. Mortality rates were high and attention was focused on eradicating specific diseases, improving ante-natal and post-natal care and training large numbers of doctors and other health care workers. Health facilities in operation before the revolution were consolidated into a single state health system. In the 1970s there was more emphasis on community health care, and polyclinics were set up with specialist services around the country. Positive results were soon evident as mortality rates fell and life expectancy rose. By the 1980s, policy had shifted again, this time towards preventive medicine rather than curative care. Mass immunisation programmes were carried out and screening became regular practice. In 1985 the Family Doctor programme was started to take pressure off the hospitals and clinics and provide continuity of care. Each doctor cares for 120 families, providing them with primary care and if necessary referring them to the intermediate level of polyclinics or specialist hospitals. The family doctors also collect health and social information on all their patients, providing the state with a database on the health of each community and ultimately the nation.

The results of this attention to health care are staggering. Cubans may be poor and live in inadequate housing but their health is equal to that of industrialized countries. 95% of the population has been vaccinated against 11 diseases and several, such as polio, diphtheria, measles and mumps, have been eliminated. Between 1986 and 1993, the entire population was tested for the AIDS virus. In October 1997 the infant mortality rate was reduced to record low of 7.3 per 1,000

Agreement in 1985 and produces about 22,000 tonnes of **coffee** a year but exports are minimal. **Tobacco** is a traditional crop with Cuban cigars world famous, but this too has suffered from lack of fuel, fertilizers and other inputs. Production fell to about 13,800 tonnes, a third of previous levels, but is recovering with the help of Spanish credits and importers from France and Britain. The 1996 crop was some 34,500 tonnes, from which about 65 million cigars were produced for export, earning over US$100 million.

Diversification away from sugar is a major goal, with the emphasis on production of **food** for domestic use because of the shortage of foreign exchange for imports. The beef herd declined from an average 5.2 million head in 1979-81 to 4 million in the first half of the 1990s because of the inability to pay for imports of grains, fertilizers and chemicals.

Production is now less intensive, with smaller herds on pastures, and numbers are beginning to rise again. Similarly, milk production is also increasing.

In October 1993, in a new agricultural reform process, the Cuban state handed over more than 28,250 sq km of land in usufruct to workers in state enterprises. Thus the newly created basic units of cooperative production (UBPCs) now possess approximately 25% of the country's land surface, or 42% of Cuba's arable land. Taking into account the longer-running cooperative systems and land given to *campesino* families to cultivate coffee and tobacco, the total non-state utilization of land has risen to 67.3%. The opening of farmers markets in 1994 has helped to stimulate diversification of crops and greater availability of foodstuffs, although shortages still remain.

live births (Australia 5.7, 1996; Argentina 28.8, 1995; Brazil 57.2, 1995; Germany 5.6, 1995; Spain 6.0, 1994; USA 8.0, 1995). As a result of the intensive training of doctors to meet health programmes, there is now a better doctor: patient ratio than anywhere except Israel.

Health care is now also an export item. Cuba's expertise is sought by developing countries world wide. Cuban doctors work abroad in teams to provide specific services and foreign medical students come to Cuba to receive training. The Carlos J Finlay Medical Detachment was set up in the 1980s to prepare community doctors and in the first graduation year it included 147 graduates (out of a total of 3,440 that year) from 45 different countries. The Detachment was named after the 19th century Cuban physician who discovered the mosquito vector of yellow fever. In 1996 South Africa requested the services of 600 English-speaking Cuban doctors under a three-year contract to make up a shortfall caused by the emigration of South African doctors. Cuban emergency medical teams have helped overseas with hurricane relief and other natural disasters, and foreign patients come to Cuba to receive specialist treatment not available in their own countries. Some 16,000 people, mostly children, victims of the Chernobyl nuclear disaster, have been treated by Cuban medical institutions. Cuba has done more for the Chernobyl victims than all the rest of the world put together. Exports of medicines and vaccines are a substantial item. Brazil has bought the meningitis vaccine from Cuba. In 1996 it was proposed that Cuba's debt to Venezuela, of around US$46 million, should be amortized with revenue earned from medicines exported to that country. An agreement with Vietnam involves the Cuban import of rice in exchange for sales of medical and pharmaceutical products.

Self-employment – Cuban style

When the Cuban government realized it would have to lay off thousands of workers in state enterprises in order to achieve some sort of efficiency, while thousands of others were already idle because of the lack of fuel and spare parts which paralysed industry, it hit upon self-employment as a convenient way to mop up surplus labour. It was hoped that it would boost the income of non-working women and people on pensions, and provide some services the state was unable to offer. Initially cautious, Cubans accepted the scheme as the only way to increase their income from the average state employee's monthly salary of 200 pesos. The positive response led to the categories of work being extended. Craft markets and street vendors appeared on street corners and many families opened their doors to feed tourists and Cubans with small restaurants, known as *paladares*, a term coined from a Brazilian soap opera. The boom was short-lived, however. As soon as the new entrepreneurs started to make money, the authorities saw the need to tax and control them to reduce distinctions in income. Restaurant owners have to buy a licence to operate, they are limited to 12 chairs in their *paladar* and are not permitted to employ anyone other than relatives, who also have to buy a licence. In Feb 1996, tax payments were increased sharply from 500 to 1,000 pesos for restauranteurs, 100 to 400 pesos for taxi drivers and 45 to 500 pesos for car mechanics. No wonder that the number of registered self-employed fell in one month from 208,000 to 205,694. The number of self-employed fell further to 171,860 at the beginning of 1997 and since then taxi drivers came out of the self-employed category in July 1997.

The sudden withdrawal of **oil** supplies when trade agreements with Russia had to be renegotiated and denominated in convertible currencies, was a crucial factor in the collapse of the Cuban economy. Although trade agreements involving oil and sugar remain, Cuba has had to purchase oil from other suppliers, such as Iran and Colombia, with extremely limited foreign exchange. As a result, Cuba has stepped up its own production to 1,287,000 tons in 1994, providing 27% of electricity generation. Foreign companies have been encouraged to explore for oil on and off-shore and investment has borne fruit. Two Canadian companies have found oil in Cárdenas Bay, east of Havana, in a well capable of producing 3,750 barrels a day. Nevertheless, shortages of fuel remain, which, combined with a lack of spare parts for ex-Soviet and Czechoslovakian generating plants, does result in power cuts and unreliable public transport.

Mining is a sector attracting foreign interest and at the end of 1994 a new mining law was passed. A Mining Authority was created and a tax system set up. 40,000 sq km have been allocated for mining ventures and all were expected to have been allocated by the end of 1995. Major foreign investors included Australian (nickel), Canadian (gold, silver and base metals) and South African (gold, copper, nickel) companies. Nickel and cobalt production declined by 11.3% to 26,362 tonnes in 1994, but with greater investment output rose to 43,900 tonnes in 1995 and a record 55,800 tonnes in 1996, nearly half of which came from the Moa Bay plant run as a joint venture between Canadian interests and the Cuban state. Cuba has one small gold mine at Castellanos in Pinar del Río province which produced 200 kg in 1995 and 300 kg in 1996. New, Canadian-backed projects in Pinar del Río at the Hierro Mantua site will produce gold and copper, and on Isla de la Juventud, gold and silver.

Tourism is now a major foreign exchange earner and has received massive investment from abroad with many joint ventures. New hotel projects are coming on stream and many more are planned. An estimated 5,000 new or renovated rooms came into use in 1996, bringing the total available to foreign visitors to 33,600. Most of the development has been along the Varadero coast, where large resort hotels attract beach package tourism. By the year 2000, Cuba aims to have 50,000 hotel rooms, of which 33,000 will be in beach resorts and 10,000 in cities. Despite political crises, numbers of visitors have risen steadily from 546,000 in 1993 to 630,000 in 1994, 741,700 in 1995 and 1,001,739 in 1996. The target is for 2,550,000 tourists a year bringing earnings of about US$3.1 billion.

Recent trends

There has been considerable success in reducing the fiscal deficit, which was bloated by subsidies and inefficiencies. A deficit of 5,000 million pesos in 1993 was cut to 775 million in 1995 and 570 million in 1996, only 2.4% of gdp, reflecting subsidy reductions. More reforms are planned, which may include the removal of subsidies from almost all state enterprises, new legislation on property ownership and commercial practice, development of the tax system and restructuring of the banking system. Financial services will have to be overhauled to cater for the accumulation of capital by owners of small businesses, who currently have to operate in cash. In 1997 legislation was approved to transform the Banco Nacional de Cuba; the Banco Central de Cuba was established on 28 May 1997 to assume the central banking functions of the Banco Nacional, which will continue as a commercial bank.

There are signs that the Cuban economy has turned the corner, although these have yet to be felt by the population in general. In 1994 gdp showed a small growth rate of 0.7%, exports rose by about 3.5% and the black market exchange rate for the US dollar strengthened from 130 to 40 pesos. In 1995 gdp grew stronger by 2.5% and the exchange rate strengthened further to 20 pesos = US$1. 1996 was even better, with growth of 7.8% due to increases in output of nickel, oil, fertilizers, tobacco, sugar, steel and cement as well as greater tourism earnings. The external accounts remain weak, however. Foreign debt hovers around US$14 billion, or 80% of gdp, and Cuba's dependence on high-interest, short-term trade finance is a burden. Cuba is ineligible for long-term development finance from multilateral lending agencies because of the US veto.

CONSTITUTION AND GOVERNMENT

In 1976 a new constitution was approved by 97.7% of the voters, setting up municipal and provincial assemblies and a National Assembly of People's Power. The membership of the Assembly was increased to 589 in 1993, candidates being nominated by the 169 municipal councils, and elected by direct secret ballot. Similarly elected are members of the 14 provincial assemblies. The number of Cuba's provinces was increased from six to 14 as a result of the decisions of the First Congress of the Communist Party of Cuba in December 1975. Dr Fidel Castro was elected President of the Council of State by the National Assembly and his brother, Major Raúl Castro, was elected First Vice-President.

Responsible tourism

Much has been written about the adverse impacts of tourism on the environment and local communities. It is usually assumed that this only applies to the more excessive end of the travel industry such as the Spanish Costas and Bali. However travellers can have an impact at almost any density and this is especially true in areas 'off the beaten track' where local people may not be used to western conventions and lifestyles, and natural environments may be very sensitive.

Of course, tourism can have a beneficial impact and this is something to which every traveller can contribute. Many National Parks are part funded by receipts from people who travel to see exotic plants and animals, El Yunque (Puerto Rico) and the Asa Wright Centre (Trinidad) are good examples of such sites. Similarly, travellers can promote patronage and protection of valuable archaeological sites and heritages through their interest and entrance fees.

However, where visitor pressure is high and/or poorly regulated, damage can occur. This is especially so in parts of the Caribbean where some tour operators are expanding their activities with scant regard for the environment or local communities. It is also unfortunately true that many of the most popular destinations are in ecologically sensitive areas easily disturbed by extra human pressures. Eventually the very features that tourists travel so far to see may become degraded and so we seek out new sites, discarding the old, and leaving someone else to deal with the plight of

local communities and the damaged environment. Fortunately, there are signs of a new awareness of the responsibilities that the travel industry and its clients need to endorse. For example, some tour operators fund local conservation projects and travellers are now more aware of the impact they may have on host cultures and environments. We can all contribute to the success of what is variously described as responsible, green or alternative tourism. All that is required is a little forethought and consideration. It would be impossible to identify all the potential impacts that might need to be addressed by travellers, but it is worthwhile noting the major areas in which we can all take a more responsible attitude in the countries we visit. These include changes to natural ecosystems (air, water, land, ecology and wildlife), cultural values (beliefs and behaviour) and the built environment (sites of antiquity and archaeological significance).

At an individual level, travellers can reduce their impact if greater consideration is given to their activities. For example in most Caribbean countries dress codes are fairly strictly adhered to; shorts and T shirts are OK on the beach but less so when shopping or cashing cheques. Avoid topless or nude bathing except where it is expressly allowed. Do not take photographs of people without permission. Recognition of these cultural cues goes a long way towards reducing the friction that can develop between host and visitor. Collecting or purchasing wildlife curios might have an effect on local ecosystems and may well be illegal under either local or international legislation (see below). Some environmental impacts are caused by factors beyond the direct control of travellers, such as the management and operation of a hotel chain. However, even here it is possible to voice concern about damaging activities and an increasing number of hotels and travel operators are taking 'green concerns' seriously, even if it is only to protect their share of the market.

Environmental Legislation

Legislation may have been enacted to control damage to the environment, and in some cases this can have a bearing on travellers. The establishment of National Parks may involve rules and guidelines for visitors and these should always be followed. In addition there may be local or national laws controlling behaviour and use of natural resources (especially wildlife) that are being increasingly enforced. If in doubt, ask. Finally, international legislation, principally the Convention on International Trade in Endangered Species of Wild Fauna and Flora (CITES), may affect travellers.

CITES aims to control the trade in live specimens of endangered plants and animals and also 'recognizable parts or derivatives' of protected species. Sale of black coral, some hard corals, turtle shells, rare orchids and other protected wildlife is strictly controlled by signatories of the convention. The full list of protected wildlife varies, so if you feel the need to purchase souvenirs and trinkets derived from wildlife, it would be prudent to check whether they are protected. Cuba is a party to CITES and most European countries, the USA and Canada are all signatories. Importation of CITES protected species into these countries can lead to heavy fines, confiscation of goods and even imprisonment. Information on the status of legislation and protective measures can be obtained from Traffic International (T UK 01223 277427; e-mail traffic@wcmc.org.uk).

Green travel companies and information

The increasing awareness of the environmental impact of travel and tourism has led to a range of advice and information services as well as spawning specialist travel companies who claim to provide 'responsible travel' for clients. This is an expanding field and the veracity of claims needs to be substantiated in some cases. The following organizations and publications can provide useful information for those with an interest in pursuing responsible travel opportunities.

International organizations

Green Flag International aims to work with travel industry and conservation bodies to improve environments at travel destinations and also to promote conservation programmes at resort destinations; provides a travellers' guide for 'green' tourism as well as advice on destinations, T UK 01223 890250.

Tourism Concern aims to promote a greater understanding of the impact of tourism on host communities and environments, T UK 0171-753-3330; e-mail tourconcern@gn.apc.org.

Centre for Responsible Tourism (CRT) co-ordinates a North American network and advises on North American sources of information on responsible tourism: CRT, PO Box 827, San Anselmo, California 94979, USA.

Centre for the Advancement of Responsive Travel (CART) has a range of publications available as well as information on alternative holiday destinations, T UK 01732 352757.

Havana

O F ALL THE capital cities in the Caribbean, Havana has the reputation of being the most splendid and sumptuous. Before the Revolution its casinos and nightlife attracted the mega stars of the day in much the same way as Beirut and Shanghai and remarkably little has changed architecturally since then. There have been no tacky modernizations, partly because of lack of finance and materials. Low level street lighting, relatively few cars (and many of those antiques), no (real) estate agents or Wendyburgers, no neon, no advertising (except for potitical slogans), all give the city plenty of scope for nostalgia. Restoration works in the old part of the city are revealing the glories of the past, although most of the city is fighting a losing battle with the sea air and many of the finest buildings along the sea front are crumbling.

It is not a modern city in the materialist sense and is no good for people for whom shopping and eating well are the central leisure activities. However, it is probably the finest example of a Spanish colonial city in the Americas. Many of its palaces were converted into museums after the Revolution and more work has been done since the old city was declared a UNESCO World Heritage Site in 1982, with millions of dollars of foreign aid and investment. Away from the old city, Habana Vieja, there is also some stunning modern architecture from the first half of the 20th century. There are good views over the city from the top floor restaurant and bar of *Hotel Habana Libre* (the scene of much political activity over the years), the *Hotel Sevilla* and from the lookout at the top of the José Martí monument in the Plaza de la Revolución.

Area 727 sq km; *Population* 2,204,300; *Phone code* 7

Havana, the capital, founded in 1519 on the present site, is situated at the mouth of a deep bay; in the colonial period, this natural harbour was the assembly point for ships of the annual silver convoy to Spain. Its strategic and commercial importance is reflected in the extensive fortifications, particularly on the east side of the entrance to the bay (see below). Notably the shield of Havana depicts three towers and a key, illustrating the importance of the city's defences. Before the Revolution, Havana was the largest, the most beautiful and the most sumptuous city in the Caribbean. Today it is rather run-down, but thanks to the Government's policy of developing the countryside, it is not ringed with shanty-towns like so many other Latin American capitals, although some have reappeared in the 1990s. With its suburbs it has 2.1 million people, half of whom live in housing officially regarded as sub-standard. Many buildings are shored up by wooden planks. Some of it is very old, but the ancient palaces, plazas, colonnades, churches and monasteries merge agreeably with the new.

The old city has been declared a World Heritage Site by the United Nations. The priorities of the city government include the restoration of the historic centre, under the auspices of UNESCO and the City Historian's Office, whose brief is also to rebuild communities in the widest sense of the word, with income from cultural tourism; the restoration of the Malecón,

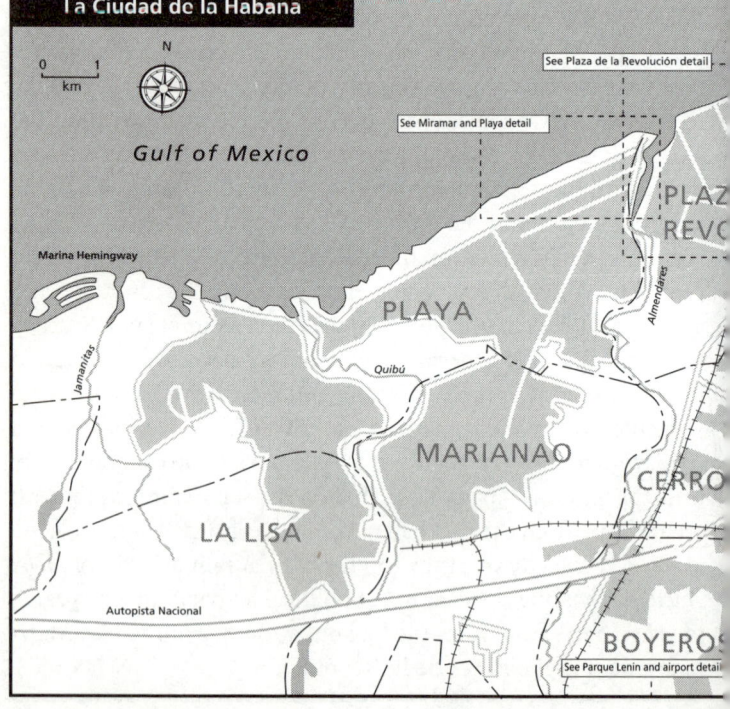

La Ciudad de la Habana

0 1 km

N

See Plaza de la Revolución detail

See Miramar and Playa detail

Gulf of Mexico

Marina Hemingway

Jaimanitas

PLAYA

Quibú

Almendares

PLAZ
REVO

MARIANAO

CERRO

LA LISA

Autopista Nacional

BOYEROS

See Parque Lenin and airport detail

starting from the historic centre, where housing has been badly affected by salination and sea damage; and restoration of the Bosque de la Habana, crossed by the Río Almendares, now suffering from pollution and contamination, but a potentially rich green belt, extending over several kilometres, with the aid of European NGOs. The aim is to create 20 sq m of green space per inhabitant, compared with 1 sq m in 1959 and the current 14 sq m.

ORIENTATION

The centre is divided into five sections, three of which are of most interest to visitors, **Habana Vieja** (Old Havana), **Central Havana** and **Vedado**. The oldest part of the city, around the **Plaza de Armas**, is quite near the docks where you can see cargo ships from all over the world being unloaded. Here are the former **Palace of the Captains-General**, the temple of **El Templete**, and **Castillo de La Real Fuerza**, the oldest of all the forts. From Plaza de Armas run two narrow and picturesque streets, Calles Obispo and O'Reilly (several old-fashioned pharmacies on Obispo, traditional glass and ceramic medicine jars and decorative perfume bottles on display in shops gleaming with polished wood and mirrors). These two streets go west to the heart of the city: **Parque Central**, with its laurels, poincianas, almonds, palms, shrubs and gorgeous flowers. To the southwest rises the golden dome of the **Capitol**. From the northwest corner of Parque Central a wide, tree-shaded avenue, the **Paseo del Prado**, runs to the fortress of **La Punta**; at

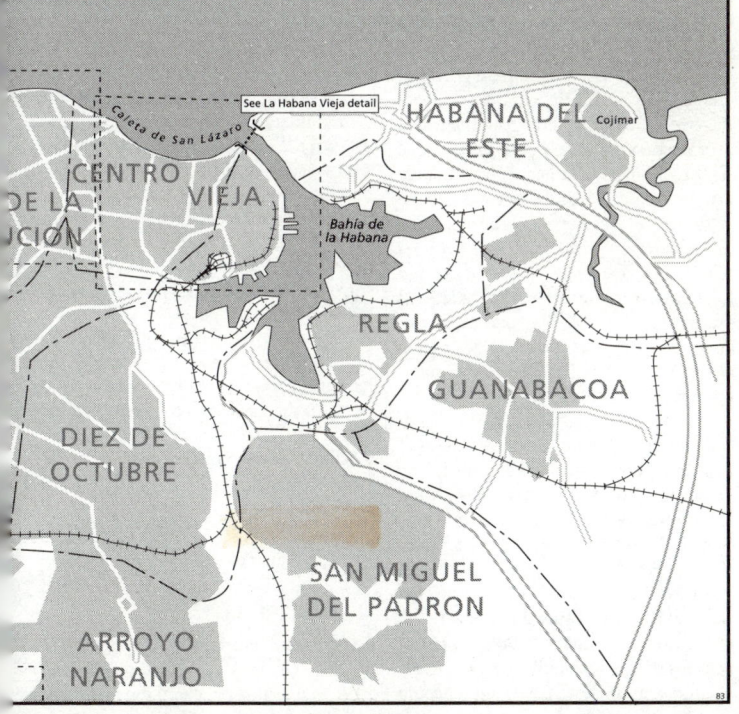

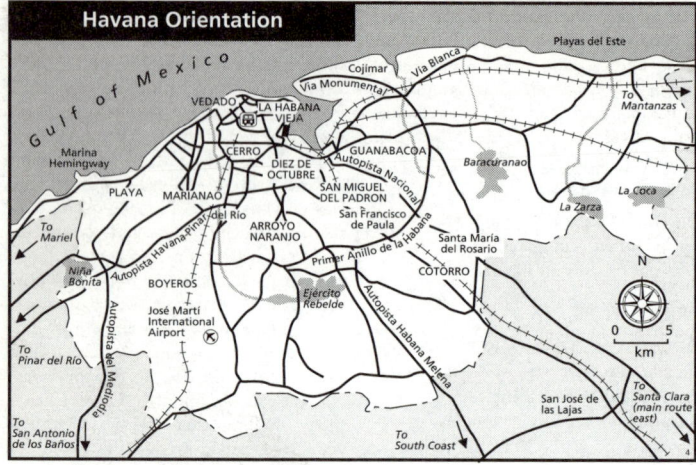

Havana Orientation

its north sea-side end is the **Malecón**, a splendid highway along the coast to the west residential district of Vedado. The sea crashing along the seawall here is a spectacular sight when the wind blows from the north. On calmer days, fishermen lean over the parapet, lovers sit in the shade of the small pillars, and joggers sweat along the pavement. On the other side of the six-lane road, buildings which from a distance look stout and grand, with arcaded pavements, balconies, mouldings and large entrances, are salt-eroded, faded and sadly decrepit inside. Restoration is progressing slowly, but the sea is destroying old and new alike and creating a mammoth renovation task.

Further west, Calle San Lázaro leads directly from the monument to **General Antonio Maceo** on the Malecón to the magnificent central stairway of **Havana University**. A monument to **Julio Antonio Mella**, founder of the Cuban Communist Party, stands across from the stairway. Further out, past **El Príncipe** castle, is **Plaza de la Revolución**, with the impressive monument to **José Martí** at its centre. The large buildings surrounding the square were mostly built in the 1950s and house the principal government ministries. The long grey building behind the monument is the former Justice Ministry (1958), now the headquarters of the Central Committee of the Communist Party, where Fidel Castro has his office. The Plaza is the scene of massive parades and speeches marking important events. It was completely transformed for an open air mass held by the Pope in January 1998 with massive religious paintings suspended over the surrounding buildings. The May Day parade is also held here.

From near the fortress of **La Punta** a tunnel runs east under the mouth of the harbour; it emerges in the rocky ground between the **Castillo del Morro** and the fort of **La Cabaña**, some 550m away, and a 5 km highway connects with the Havana-Matanzas road.

OLD HAVANA (LA HABANA VIEJA)

The street map of Old Havana is marked with numerals showing the places of most interest to visitors.

Castillo del Morro (1)

The Castillo del Morro was built between 1589 and 1630, with a 20m moat, but has been much altered. It stands on a bold headland, with the best view of Havana and is illuminated at night; it was one of the major fortifications built to protect the natural harbour and the assembly of Spain's silver fleets from pirate attack. The flash of its lighthouse, built in 1844, is visible 30 km out to sea. The castle is open to the public Monday-Saturday 0930-1830, Sunday 0900-1300, as a museum with a good exhibition of Cuban history since Columbus. On the harbour side, down by the water, is the **Battery of the 12 Apostles**, each gun named after an Apostle. Entrance fee US$1 for the *parque*, US$3 for the Castillo, US$2 for photographs and US$2 for the lighthouse, open to the public 0830-2030. Every Saturday at around 1000-1100 there is a display of AfroCuban dancing and music. A disco overlooking the harbour and all Havana, taped music and rather touristy, but worth it for the views. There are two restaurants, *La Divina Pastora*, specializing in seafood, and *Los Doce Apóstoles*, with national and European dishes, both open 1145-0045. Access to the Castillo del Morro from any bus going through the tunnel (24 or 40 centavos), board at San Lázaro and Av del Puerto, get off at stop after tunnel, cross the road and climb following the path to the left. Alternatively take a taxi, or a 20-minute walk from the Fortaleza de la Cabaña (see Casablanca below).

Fortaleza de la Cabaña (2)

Built 1763-1774. Fronting the harbour is a high wall; the ditch on the landward side, 12m deep, has a drawbridge to the main entrance. Inside are **Los Fosos de los Laureles** where political prisoners were shot during the Cuban fight for independence. Every night the cannons are fired in an historical ceremony recalling the closing of the city walls in the 17th century to protect it from pirates; this starts at 2045 so that the walls are closed at 2100. Open to visitors 0830-2200, US$3. There are two museums here, one about Che Guevara and another about fortresses

with pictures and models, some old weapons and a replica of a large catapult and battering ram. Access as for Castillo del Morro or via Casablanca.

The **National Observatory** and the railway station for trains to Matanzas are on the same side of the Channel as these two forts, at **Casablanca**, a charming town. It is also the site of a statue to a very human Jesus Christ erected during the Batista dictatorship as a pacifying exercise and reached by a steep, twisting flight of stone steps, starting on the other side of the plaza in front of the landing stage. You can walk from the statue to the Fortaleza (10 minutes) and then on to the Castillo del Morro. Left-hand ferry queue next to the Customs House, opposite Calle Santa Clara (10 centavos).

Castillo de la Punta (3)

Built at the end of the 16th century, a squat building with 2½m thick walls, Castillo de la Punta is open to the public, daily. Entrance (free) through gap in makeshift fencing, custodian with dogs shows you around. Opposite the fortress, across the Malecón, is the monument to Máximo Gómez, the independence leader.

Castillo de la Real Fuerza (4)

This is Cuba's oldest building and the second oldest fort in the New World. It was first built in 1558 after the city had been sacked by buccaneers and rebuilt in 1582. It is a low, long building with a picturesque tower from which there is a grand view. Inside the castle is a museum with armour and ceramics, open daily, 0830-1830, US$1. The downstairs part is used for art exhibitions. Upstairs there is a small shop and cafetería. The Castillo reopened (1994) after renovation. **NB** There are two other old forts in Havana: **Atarés**, finished in 1763, on a hill overlooking the southwest end of the harbour; and **El Príncipe**, on a hill at the far end of Av Independencia (Av Rancho Boyeros), built 1774-1794, now the city gaol. Finest view in Havana from this hill.

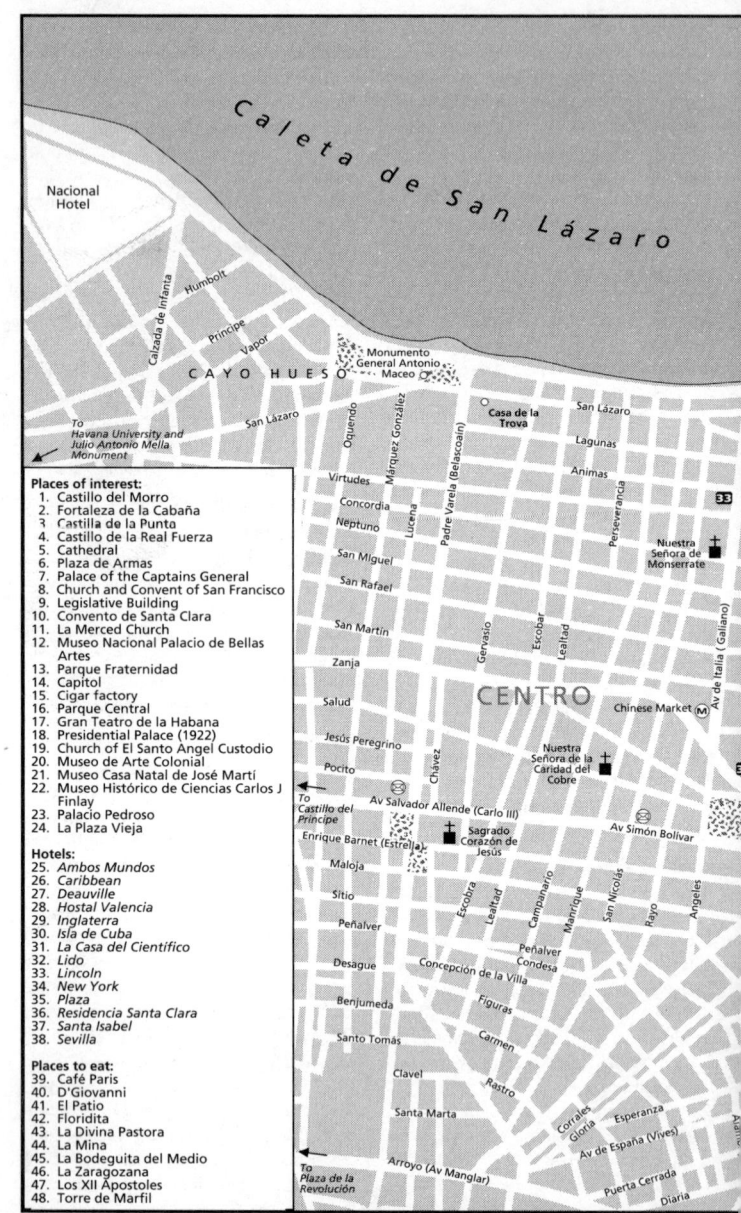

Places of interest:
1. Castillo del Morro
2. Fortaleza de la Cabaña
3. Castilla de la Punta
4. Castillo de la Real Fuerza
5. Cathedral
6. Plaza de Armas
7. Palace of the Captains General
8. Church and Convent of San Francisco
9. Legislative Building
10. Convento de Santa Clara
11. La Merced Church
12. Museo Nacional Palacio de Bellas Artes
13. Parque Fraternidad
14. Capitol
15. Cigar factory
16. Parque Central
17. Gran Teatro de la Habana
18. Presidential Palace (1922)
19. Church of El Santo Angel Custodio
20. Museo de Arte Colonial
21. Museo Casa Natal de José Martí
22. Museo Histórico de Ciencias Carlos J Finlay
23. Palacio Pedroso
24. La Plaza Vieja

Hotels:
25. *Ambos Mundos*
26. *Caribbean*
27. *Deauville*
28. *Hostal Valencia*
29. *Inglaterra*
30. *Isla de Cuba*
31. *La Casa del Científico*
32. *Lido*
33. *Lincoln*
34. *New York*
35. *Plaza*
36. *Residencia Santa Clara*
37. *Santa Isabel*
38. *Sevilla*

Places to eat:
39. Café Paris
40. D'Giovanni
41. El Patio
42. Floridita
43. La Divina Pastora
44. La Mina
45. La Bodeguita del Medio
46. La Zaragozana
47. Los XII Apostoles
48. Torre de Marfil

N

0   250
metres (approx)

CASABLANCA

1

47

43

2

Road Tunnel

C a n a l   d e   E n t r a d a

3

Malecón
San Lázaro   Cárcel

Genio

Refugio

Monumento
Máximo Gómez

Peña Pobre

23

Crespo   Colón   **26**

Trocadero

Aguila

Industria

Bernal

Animas

31

Paseo De Martí (Prado)

Morro

Zulueta

18

Av. de Las Misiones

Cuarteles

Chacón

Tejadillo

19

Av. CM de Céspedes (Del Puerto)

Tacón

5

Virtudes

32

38

12

Empedrado

45 **41**

40

4

San Juan Dios

20

Mercaderes

Neptuno

35

O'Reilly

39

7 **44** **6** **37**

San Miguel

29

16

42

Obispo

25

San Ignacio

Aguiar

48

28

Boulevard

17

46

Obrapía

Cuba

Oficios

n Martín

Industria

Lamparilla

VIEJA

arcelona

14

Amistad

Monserrate

Bernaza

Santo Cristo
del Buen Viaje

Amargura

Teniente Rey (Brasil)

22

Passenger ferry
to Casablanca

15

Dragones

Villegas

Muralla

24

8

San Pedro

13

Aguacate

Compostela

Sol

Porvenir

10
36

Inquisidor

9

Santa Clara

láximo Gómez

30

Corrales

Economía

Cárdenas

Cienfuegos

Apote (Someruelo)

Zulueta

Egido (Av de Bélgica)

Luz

Habana

Centro
Wilfredo Lam

Passenger ferry
to Regla

Factoría

Apodaca

Acosta

Jesús María

Espíritu Santo

Suárez

Gloria

Misión

Merced

11

Revillagigedo

Esperanza

21

Leonor Pérez

Aquila

Estación Central
de Ferrocarriles

San Isidro

Desamparados

E n s e n a d a
d e   A t a r é s

The Cathedral (5)

Construction of a church on this site was begun by Jesuit missionaries at the beginning of the 18th century. After the Jesuits were expelled in 1767 the church was later converted into a cathedral. On either side of the Spanish colonial baroque façade are belltowers, the left one (west) being half as wide as the right (east). There is a grand view from the latter. The church is officially dedicated to the Virgin of the Immaculate Conception, but is better known as the church of Havana's patron saint, San Cristóbal, and as the Columbus cathedral. The bones of Christopher Columbus were sent to this cathedral when Santo Domingo was ceded by Spain to France in 1795; they now lie in Santo Domingo. The bones were in fact those of another Columbus. The Cathedral is open Monday-Tuesday, Thursday-Saturday 0930-1230, Sunday 0830-1230, Mass at 1030. Several days a week there is a handicraft market on the square in front of the Cathedral, and in adjacent streets.

Plaza de Armas (6)

This has been restored to very much what it once was. The statue in the centre is of Carlos Manuel de Céspedes. In the northeast corner of the square is the church of **El Templete** (reopened after renovation late-1997); a column in front of it marks the spot where the first mass was said in 1519 under a ceiba tree. A sapling of the same tree, blown down by hurricane in 1753, was planted on the same spot, and under its branches the supposed bones of Columbus reposed in state before being taken to the cathedral. This tree was cut down in 1828, the present tree planted, and the Doric temple opened. There are paintings by Vermay, a pupil of David, inside. On the north side of the Plaza is the **Palacio del Segundo Cabo**, the former private residence of the Captains General, now housing the Feria Cubana del Libro. Its patio is worth a look. Outside in the Plaza de Armas there is a small book market daily except Monday.

El Templete

Palace of the Captains General

Museo de la Ciudad (7)

On the west side of Plaza de Armas is the former **Palace of the Captains General**, built in 1780, a charming example of colonial architecture. The Spanish Governors and the Presidents lived here until 1917, when it became the City Hall. It is now the **Museo de la Ciudad**, the Historical Museum of the city of Havana (open Monday-Saturday 0930-1830, camera fee US$3) and recommended to visit. The museum houses a large collection of 19th century furnishings which illustrate the wealth of the Spanish colonial community. There are no explanations, even in Spanish. There are portraits of patriots, flags, military memorabilia and a grandly laid out dining room. The building was the site of the signing of the 1899 treaty between Spain and the USA. The arcaded and balconied patio is well worth a visit. The courtyard contains royal palms, the Cuban national tree. Outside is a statue of Ferdinand VII of Spain, with a singularly uncomplimentary plaque. No Spanish king or queen ever came to Cuba. Also in front of the museum is a collection of church bells. An extension to the museum is the **Casa de la Plata**, a silverware collection on Obispo entre Mercaderes y Oficios, fine pieces, jewellery and old frescoes on upper floor, free with ticket to Museo de la Ciudad. The former **Supreme Court** on the north side of the Plaza is another colonial building, with a large patio.

NB It is possible to buy a combined one-day ticket which together with the Museo de la Ciudad allows access to several other museums (see box for further details, page 102).

The Church and Convent of San Francisco (8)

Built in 1608 and in reconstructed 1730, this is a massive, sombre edifice suggesting defence rather than worship. The three-storey tower was both a landmark for returning voyagers and a look-out for pirates. The church is now a concert hall and the convent is a museum containing religious pieces. Restoration work still going on. Open daily 0930-1800, US$2, bell tower with stunning views of the city and port an extra US$1. Most of the treasures were removed by the government and some are in museums.

Legislative Building (9)

The Corinthian white marble building on Calle Oficios south of the Post Office was

The Museum tour: one-day passes

For US$9 you can buy a one-day ticket at the Museo de la Ciudad allowing you entrance to this museum and its Casa de la Plata and the following:

Casa de los Arabes (with restaurant, Al Medina) opposite, on Oficios between Obispo and Obrapía, a lovely building with vines trained over the courtyard for shade, open daily 0930-1830, US$1.

Casa de Africa, on Obrapía 157 between San Ignacio and Mercaderes (Monday-Saturday 1030-1730, Sunday 0930-1230, US$2); small gallery of carved wooden artefacts and handmade costumes.

Vintage Car Museum, Oficios y Jústiz (just off Plaza de Armas, open daily 0900-1900, US$1). There are a great many museum pieces, pre-revolutionary US models, still on the road especially outside Havana, in among the Ladas, VWs and Nissans.

Casa de Guayasimín, Obrapía entre Mercaderes y Oficios, exhibition of works donated to Cuba by Ecuadorean artist Oswaldo Guayasimín (paintings, sculpture and silkscreens) and occasionally other exhibitions. The upstairs part is being converted into studios so that he can work here. Guayasimín painted a famous portrait of Fidel Castro for his 70th birthday with his hands raised.

Casa de México, opposite the above, also called La Casa de Benito Juárez, Obrapía entre Mercaderes y Oficios, a museum of Mexico in a pink building marked with the Mexican flag, open Tuesday-Saturday 1030-1730, Sunday 0930-1230, entrance US$1.

Casa de Simón Bolívar, Mercaderes entre Obrapía y Lamparilla, contains exhibits about the life of the South American liberator, open Tuesday-Saturday 1030-1730, Sunday 0930-1230, US$1.

Casa de Asia, Mercaderes entre Obrapía y Obispo, converted from a solar, a multi-family dwelling with a central courtyard, into what will be an exhibition space of art, furniture and other artefacts donated from the Asian subcontinent. Bonsai plants are being cultivated in the central courtyard, for sale in a shop next door. The funds will be used to set up the museum display.

once the legislative building, where the House of Representatives met before the Capitol was built.

The Convento de Santa Clara (10)

The convent was founded in 1644 by nuns from Cartagena in Colombia. It was in use as a convent until 1919, when the nuns sold the building. In a shady business deal it was later acquired by the government and after radical alterations it became offices for the Ministry of Public Works until the decision was made to restore the building to its former glory. Work began in 1982 with the creation of the Centro Nacional de Conservación, Restauración y Museología

(CNCRM) and is still continuing. The Convent occupies four small blocks in Old Havana, bounded by Calles Habana, Sol, Cuba and Luz, and originally there were three cloisters and an orchard. You can see the cloisters, the nuns' cemetery and their cells. The first cloister has been carefully preserved; the ground floor is a grand porticoed stone gallery surrounding a large patio packed with vegetation, in it are the city's first slaughter house, first public fountain and public baths. The Sailor's House in the second cloister, reputedly built by a sailor for his love-lorn daughter is now a *Residencia Académica* for student groups (and independent travellers if room). The convent is topped by an extensive tiled roof with a stone turret next to the church choir. Open Monday-Friday 0900-1500, US$2 for guided tour in Spanish or French, entrance on Cuba.

La Merced (11)
Construction of this church began 1755, and was still incomplete 1792, when work stopped. Building was completed late in the 19th century. It has an unremarkable exterior and a redecorated lavish interior.

The Museo Nacional Palacio de Bellas Artes (12)
Closed for refurbishment until 2001, it has a large collection of relics of the struggle for independence, and a fine array of modern paintings by Cuban and other artists. Its huge collection of European paintings, from the 16th century to the present, contains works supposedly by Gainsborough, Van Dyck, Velázquez, Tintoretto, Degas, et al. One painting by Canaletto is in fact only half a painting; the other half of the 18th century painting *Chelsea from the Thames* is owned by the National Trust in Britain and hangs in Blickling Hall, Norfolk. It is believed to have been commissioned by the Chelsea Hospital in 1746-48, which is featured in the Cuban half, but the artist was unable to sell it and cut it in two just before he died in 1768. The left hand half was sold to the 11th Marquis of Lothian, whose family owned Blickling Hall, where it has stayed ever since. The right hand half was bought and sold several times until it ended up with a Cuban collector, Oscar Cinetas, who donated it to the museum before the Revolution. The museum also has large chambers of Greek, Roman, Egyptian sculpture and artefacts, many very impressive.

Parque Fraternidad (13)
The park has been landscaped to show off the **Capitol**, north of it, to the best effect. At its centre is a ceiba tree growing in soil provided by each of the American republics. In the park also is a famous statue of the Indian woman who first welcomed the Spaniards: La Noble Habana, sculpted in 1837. From the southwest corner the handsome Avenida Allende runs due west to the high hill on which stands **El Príncipe Castle** (now the city gaol). The **Quinta de los Molinos**, on this avenue, at the foot of the hill, once housed the School of Agronomy of Havana University. The main house now contains the **Máximo Gómez Museum** (Dominican-born fighter for Cuban Independence). Also here is the headquarters of the young writers and artists (Asociación Hermanos Saiz). The gardens are a lovely place to stroll. North, along Calle Universidad, on a hill which gives a good view, is the **University**.

The Capitol (14)
Opened May 1929, the Capitol has a large dome over a rotunda; it is a copy, on a smaller scale, of the US Capitol in Washington. At the centre of its floor is set a 24-carat diamond, zero for all distance measurements in Cuba. The interior has large halls and stately staircases, all most sumptuously decorated. Entrance for visitors is to the left of the stairway, US$1 to go in the halls, US$3 for a tour.

Cigar factory (15)
Partagas on Calle Industria behind the Capitolio, gives tours twice daily, in theory, at 1000 and 1330, US$5. The tour lasts for about an hour and is very interesting. You are taken through the factory and shown the whole production process from storage and sorting of leaves, to packaging and labelling (explanation in Spanish only). Four different brand names are made here; Partagas, Cubana, Ramón Allones and Bolívar (special commission of 170,000 cigars made for the Seville Expo, Spain, 1992). These and other famous cigars can be bought at their shop here, open 0900-1700, and rum, at good prices (credit cards accepted). Cigars are also made at many tourist locations (eg Palacio de la Artesanía, the airport, some hotels).

Museo de la Revolución

Parque Central (16)

Very pleasant with monument to José Martí in the centre.

Gran Teatro de la Habana (17)

A beautiful building but they will not let you look around inside. Go to a performance.

Presidential Palace (1922) (18)

A huge, ornate building topped by a dome, facing Av de las Misiones; now contains the **Museo de la Revolución** (T 62-4091). Open Tuesday-Sunday 1000-1700, entrance US$3, cameras allowed, US$3 extra. (Allow several hours to see it all, explanations are all in Spanish.) The history of Cuban political development is charted, from the slave uprisings to joint space missions with the ex-Soviet Union. The liveliest section displays the final battles against Batista's troops, with excellent photographs and some bizarre personal mementoes, such as a revolutionary's knife, fork and spoon set and a plastic shower curtain worn in the Sierra Maestra campaign. At the top of the main staircase are a stuffed mule and a stuffed horse used by Che Guevara and Camilo Cienfuegos in the same campaign. The yacht *Granma*, from which Dr Castro disembarked with his companions in 1956 to launch the Revolution, has been installed in the park facing the south entrance, surrounded by planes, tanks and other vehicles involved, as well as a Soviet-built tank used against the Bay of Pigs invasion and a fragment from a US spy plane shot down in the 1970s.

The Church of El Santo Angel Custodio (19)

The Jesuits built this church in 1672 on the slight elevation of **Peña Pobre** hill. The original church was largely destroyed by a hurricane in 1844 and rebuilt in its present neo-Gothic style in 1866-71. It has white, laced Gothic towers and 10 tiny chapels, no more than kneeling places, the best of which is behind the high altar. There is some interesting stained glass depicting conquistadors. During the Christmas period some impressive figures around a manger are placed at the entrance.

Museo de Arte Colonial (20)

Plaza de la Catedral (in the former Palacio de los Condes de Casa Bayona), open Monday-Saturday 1000-1800, Sunday 0900-1300, US$2, contains colonial furniture and other items, plus a section on stained glass, exquisite (T 61-1367).

Museo Casa Natal de José Martí (21)

Leonor Pérez 314 entre Picota y Egido, opposite central railway station (Tuesday-Saturday 0900-1700, Sunday 0900-1300, entrance US$1, T 61-3778).

Museo Histórico de Ciencias Carlos J Finlay (22)

Calle Cuba 460 entre Amargura y Brasil (Monday-Friday 0800-1700, Saturday 0900-1500, entrance US$2, T 63-4824).

Palacio Pedroso (23)

This is a beautiful Arab building housing shops and restaurant/bar. It is now the **Palacio de la Artesanía**. Open 0900-0200 Friday-Sunday with traditional dance at 2200; see **Shopping** below, page 125.

La Plaza Vieja (24)

An 18th century plaza, undergoing restoration since February 1996 as part of a joint project by UNESCO and Habaguanex, a state company responsible for the restoration and revival of old Havana. The former house of the Spanish Captain General, **Conde de Ricla**, who retook Havana from the English and restored power to Spain in 1763 can be seen on the corner of San Ignacio and Muralla. As restoration continues, 18th century murals are being uncovered on the external walls of the buildings, many of which boast elegant balconies overlooking the plaza. Art exhibitions in the colonial house on the corner of San Ignacio and Brasil. The newly-restored Cuban Stock Exchange building, **La Lonja**, Oficios and Plaza San Francisco, is worth a look, as is the new cruise ship terminal opposite.

MUSEUMS IN HABANA VIEJA

Numismatic Museum (Calle Oficios 8 entre Obispo y Obrapía, T 63-2521, Tuesday-Saturday 1000-1700, Sunday 1000-1300).

Museo de Finanzas, Obispo y Cuba, in the old Ministry of Finance building, has a beautiful stained-class ceiling in the foyer, Monday-Friday 0830-1700, Saturday till 1230 only.

Museo Nacional de la Música, Cárcel 1, entre Habana y Aguilar, small and beautifully furnished old house; interesting collection of African drums and other instruments from all around the world, showing development of Cuban *son* and *danzón* music (Monday-Saturday 0900-1645, US$2, T 61-9846).

Museo Nacional de Historia Natural is at Obispo 61, Plaza de Armas, open Tuesday-Saturday 1000-1730, Sunday 0900-1230.

La Casa de la Obra-Pía, on the other side of the road, is a furniture museum housed in a yellow building on Obrapía entre Mercaderes y San Ignacio, open Tuesday-Saturday 1030-1730, Sunday 0930-1230, entrance US$1.

Centro Wilfredo Lam, San Ignacio 22, esquina Empedrado, just next to the cathedral, changing exhibition programmes, mostly Cuban artists but also from abroad, eg a Henry Moore exhibition in 1997; when art exhibitions are on it is open Monday-Saturday 1000-1800, US$1.

Centro de Desarrollo de las Artes Visuales, San Ignacio 22 esquina Teniente Rey, also has a variety of art exhibitions.

Nelson Domínguez, the artist, has his own studio/gallery, on Calle Oficios 166, Habana Vieja, open Tuesday-Sunday 1100-1700, and there are several other artists' galleries on Obispo.

Fundación Alejo Carpentier, Empedrado 215 entre Cuba y San Ignacio, just down from the *Bodeguita del Medio*, is a museum of the writer's letters and books, open Monday-Friday 0830-1630, entrance free but donations welcome. Literary courses also available.

MUSEUMS IN CENTRO HABANA

Museo Napoleónico, San Miguel 1159 esquina Ronda (Monday-Saturday 1100-1830, entrance US$2, T 79-1460), houses paintings and other works of art, a specialized library and a collection of weaponry (T 79-1412).

Museo de Artes Decorativas, Calles 17 y Este, Vedado (Wednesday-Sunday 0930-1630, entrance US$2, T 32-0924).

Museo José Martí, Plaza de la Revolución, in base of memorial, beautifully restored and most impressive museum, with lookout accessed by mirrored lift (Monday-Saturday 0900-1600, US$3, lookout US$5 extra).

Postal Museum, Ministry of Communications, Plaza de la Revolución (Monday-Friday 0900-1700, entrance US$1, T 81-5551).

MUSEUMS IN VEDADO

The **Cuban pavilion** (Pabellón Cuba), a large building on Calle 23, Vedado, is a combination of a tropical glade and a museum of social history. It tells the nation's story by a brilliant combination of objects, photography and the architectural manipulation of space.

Casa de la Amistad, Paseo 406, entre 17 y 19, Vedado, a former mansion (see above), a beautiful building with gardens, now operated by ICAP (Cuban Institute for Friendship among the Peoples) and housing the *Amistur* travel agency (see

Cayo Hueso

Cayo Hueso is a barrio lying in a triangle between Infanta, San Lázaro and the Malecón in Centro Habana, dating back to the beginning of the 20th century. It was named by cigar factory workers returning from Key West and has nothing to do with bones (*huesos* in Spanish), although it was once the site of the Espada cemetery and the San Lázaro quarry. La Fragua Martiana houses the remains of the quarry and is a learning centre for children and a place for reflection. There are about 12,000 homes in the barrio, mostly tenements, which have been earmarked for a project to halt their deterioration. The project, initiated in 1995, involves state ministers, organizations and all the neighbours. 18 agencies are involved in renovation of the buildings' exteriors, common areas and technical work, while residents have been sold the materials needed to repair the interiors of their homes. As in Habana Vieja, the project also involves educating the community in its own particular culture and history.

In 1924, the cigar factory workers built a place for their social activities on San Lázaro, which became the site of the José Martí People's University. San Lázaro, with the University of Havana's wide stairway at its top, was the site of fierce and determined student movement demonstrations from the late 1920s onwards. By the mid-1950s, Infanta was the Maginot line where the students faced Batista's troops. On 25 July 1956, Fidel Castro departed from Calle Jovellar 107 for the attack on the Moncada Garrison in Santiago de Cuba. There is a memorial plaque there now.

Cayo Hueso has lots of little alleyways, one of which, Calle Hamel, unites two art forms: music and visual arts. Hamel 1108 is the home of singer-songwriter Angel Díaz and the birthplace of the musical genre known as *filin* (from 'feeling'). It is also home to Salvador González' art studio. Inspired by the history of the neighbourhood, which is no stranger to *santería*, González has painted large African-Cuban murals. Every Friday night, cultural events are held here with poetry, theatre, painting or music. This is a neighbourhood of *filin*, rumba and tango. Calle Hornos was the site of the first cultural circle dedicated to Carlos Gardel (the Argentine maestro of tango), and is another centre for cultural activities. Cayo Hueso has the reputation of being a bit of a rough neighbourhood, maybe because of past neglect, but it is well worth a visit for its rich cultural and historical associations. It is an easy stroll from the *Hotel Nacional*, *Habana Libre* and other nearby hotels.

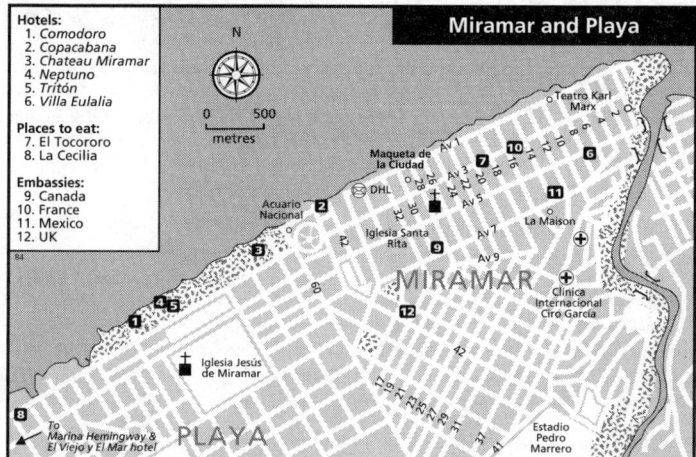

Hotels:
1. *Comodoro*
2. *Copacabana*
3. *Chateau Miramar*
4. *Neptuno*
5. *Tritón*
6. *Villa Eulalia*

Places to eat:
7. *El Tocororo*
8. *La Cecilia*

Embassies:
9. Canada
10. France
11. Mexico
12. UK

Miramar and Playa

MIRAMAR

PLAYA

Tour companies & travel agents page 126). It has a reasonably priced bar, cafetería and tourist shop (0930-1800). The bar and cafetería are open Monday-Friday 1100-2300 (with sextet), Saturday 1100-0200 (with Cuban bands).

The **Cementerio Colón** should be visited to see the wealth of funerary sculpture, including Carrara Marbles; Cubans visit the sculpture of Amelia de Milagrosa and pray for miracles; entry US$1.

The **José Martí** sports ground at the seaward end of Av de los Presidentes on the Malecón is a good example of post-Revolutionary architecture; built in 1961, it shows a highly imaginative use of concrete, painted in primary colours. Refurbishment was to take place in 1997.

SUBURBS
Miramar
is some 16 km west of the capital, and easily reached by bus. To get a good idea of the layout of the city and its suburbs visit the **Maqueta de la Ciudad** (scale model of Havana) on Calle 28 113 entre 1 y 3, open Tuesday-Saturday 1000-1800, US$3. Opened in 1995, this is fast becoming a great attraction. The model covers

Havana and its suburbs as far out as Cojímar and the airport. Colonial buildings are in red, post-colonial pre-Revolution buildings in yellow and post-Revolution buildings in white. Some of the model is difficult to see, especially in the middle, but there is an upper viewing gallery with two telescopes where it is a little easier to see. Good fun, every building is represented, recommended for the end of your stay in Havana so that you can pick out the places you visited.

Marianao
Museo Nacional de la Alfabetización, Av 29E esquina 86, Marianao, vivid history of the 1960 literacy campaign (Monday-Friday 0830-1200, 1300-1600, T 20 8054).

Cubanacán
The **Escuela Superior de Arte**, located in the grounds of the former Havana Country Club in **Cubanacán**, southwest of Miramar, houses schools for different arts and was designed by Ricardo Porro. Architects will be interested in this 'new spatial sensation', which was an ambitious project of the early 1960s. Some parts were not completed and others have been abandoned (they were not

The development of the City

The city of Havana has 200 districts in 15 municipalities, including 14,000 *manzanas* (blocks). These municipalities are: **Playa**, **Marianao** and **La Lisa** in the west; **Boyeros** in the southwest; **Plaza de la Revolución**, **Centro Habana**, **La Habana Vieja**, **Cerro**, **Diez de Octubre** in the centre; south-central **Arroyo Naranjo**; **Regla**, **San Miguel del Padrón** going eastwards; **Cotorro** in the southeast; and in the east, **Playas del Este** and **Guanabacoa**.

From the beginning of the 19th century, the local sugar plantocracy began to move out of the city guarded by defensive walls, and build neo-colonial villas or country estates in what are now the municipalities of Cerro, 10 de Octubre and the high part of Marianao. One example of this architecture is **Quinta del Conde Santo Venia**, built in 1841, now a home for the elderly just behind the Estadio Latino Americano. By the 1850s, the city walls had more or less collapsed and Prado became another extension, making Central Havana the city's burgeoning commercial centre. The Fortaleza de la Cabaña, Atarés and Príncipe forts were constructed at this time, A fine neo-classical example here is the **Palacio de Aldama** opposite the Parque de la Fraternidad. Competition began to come from the west in the 1870s, with the rise of Vedado, which reached its high point in the 1920s, taking over from Cerro, where neo-classical, romantic and art nouveau style small palaces with internal courtyards vied with each other for luxury and originality. The **Casa de la Amistad**, on Paseo, is an example, and the **Colón cemetery** also reflects this bourgeois competitiveness. By 1918, Miramar, on the western outskirts across the Río Almendares, now Playa municipality, began to take over, in another new style: that of beach resorts, exclusive seaside clubs and, of course, casinos. It was the salon of the city, American-style. In the 1950s, the development had reached as far west as the present districts of **Siboney** and **Cubanacán** (now given Indian names in place of their former ones such as the Biltmore and the Country Club) in **Playa**, housing some 300 wealthy families. Many

entirely practical schemes), but you can still visit the Escuela Superior de Artes Plásticas, a series of interlinked pavilions, courtyards and sinuous walkways designed by Porro (which most people describe as laid out in the form of a woman's body, although some see it more as a womb itself, with a cervix-like fountain in the centre). There is also the Escuela Superior de Artes Escénicas, built by an Italian called Gottardi, in the form of a miniature Italian hill-top town, rather claustrophobic and quite unlike Porro's sprawling, 'permeable' designs full of fresh air and tropical vegetation. Porro's Dance School, although part of the same complex, is not accessible via the Country Club (now the Music School, the 1960s Music School by Garatti being now in ruins).

Boyeros
Expocuba completed in January 1989, a sprawling facility southwest of Havana in **Boyeros**, past Lenin Park, near the botanical gardens, features a score of pavilions showing Cuba's achievements in industry, science, agriculture and the arts and entertainment. Open Wednesday-Friday 1400-1600 and Saturday-Sunday 1000-1800 (times subject to change), T 44-7324. Special trains leave from main terminal in Old Havana. Information on times (and special buses) from hotels.

Cerro
South of the centre, in **Cerro** district, is the **Estadio Latinoamericano**, the best place to see baseball (the major league level), entrance 1 peso.

of these completed their journey westwards with the Revolution, by fleeing to Florida. The houses where the wealthy lived in **Miramar** before the Revolution are today occupied by several embassies and government buildings, but there are also many old, abandoned villas. Major building operations took place after the two World Wars in Miramar and after the Korean war (boom periods in terms of sugar and also nickel sales for armaments) in the far western suburbs. This was also the moment for the extension of **Nuevo Vedado**, tower buildings like the Focsa, and the *Hotel Nacional*. The sea was regarded as a threat during most of Havana's history and only became an asset in the 20th century. The **Malecón** seafront drive was built in 1901, the tunnel to Miramar (replacing a bridge) in 1950, and the tunnel leading to **Playas del Este**, on the other side of the bay, in 1958.

The wealthy middle class also built property for rent. 80% of Havana was rented, to other nationals and foreigners. Landlords lived in houses built on the *manzana*, or block architectural style. Those that were built for rent were on a smaller scale, with fewer green areas and small apartments off passage ways dividing up and separating the block style. Working class areas within these suburbs or municipalities were also developed, such as **Pogolotti** (early 1900s in Marianao), and parts of **San Miguel del Padrón**, in 1948. **Buena Vista**, in Nuevo Vedado, was also a poorer area. After the Revolution, construction was concentrated on the rest of the country, which had been largely forgotten. Havana was seen as relatively well-developed in comparison. Exceptions were service buildings, such as the Almeijeras hospital on the Malecón, and educational institutions. A whole section of the bay was also developed for the fishing industry. The municipality of **Havana del Este** is post Revolution; the **Camilo Cienfuegos** housing estate was built in 1959-61 and **Alamar** in 1970. There is also the scientific complex near Siboney in the far west of Miramar, housing a state of the art genetic biology centre and a neurological hospital, among other facilities.

Regla

You can take a ferry from by the Customs House opposite Calle Santa Clara in Old Havana (or the Ruta 6 bus from Zulueta y Virtudes inland) to **Regla**, which has a largely black population and a long, rich and still active cultural history of the Yoruba and *santería* (see **Afro Cuban religion**, page 61). Following the main street which runs north from the landing stage, Martí, the extension room of the **Museo Municipal de Regla** (on the left side of the church), 30m on your left, houses information and objects of Yoruba culture. Open Monday-Saturday 0930-1830, Sunday 0900-1300, US$2. Three blocks further on is the **Casa de la Cultura**, which has very occasional cultural activities (T 9905). At Martí 158 entre Facciolo y Piedra is the Museo Municipal de Regla,

with exhibitions on the history of the municipality (times and entrance as above).

Cojímar

An easy excursion, 15 minutes by taxi, is to **Cojímar**, the seaside village featured in Hemingway's *The Old Man and the Sea*. He celebrated his Nobel prize here in 1954 and his bust is here opposite a small fort. The coastline (no beach) is covered in sharp rocks and is dirty because of effluent from tankers, but it is a quiet, pretty place to relax. *La Terraza* is a restaurant with a pleasant view, reasonably priced seafood meals; photographs of Hemingway cover the walls, open 1200-2300.

● **Accommodation   A3-B** *Panamericano* (Horizontes), Calle A y Av Central, Cojímar, T 33-8810, 68-4101, F 33-8001, 81 room hotel and 421 2/3-room apartments, restaurants, bars, pool.

Guanabacoa

Guanabacoa is 5 km to the east of Havana and is reached by a road turning off the Central Highway. It is a well preserved small colonial town; sights include the old parish church which has a splendid altar; the monastery of San Francisco; the Carral theatre; the Jewish cemetery and some attractive mansions. The **Museo Histórico de Guanabacoa** is a former estate mansion, with slave quarters at the back of the building, Calle Martí 108, between San Antonio and Versalles, T 979117. Closed for repairs in 1997-98, the African religion section has been transferred to Casa de Africa.

● **Transport** Bus Ruta 5 from 19 de Mayo, at the bus terminal opposite the Sala Polivalente Ramón Fonst, or by launch from Muelle Luz (at the end of Calle Santa Clara, Habana Vieja) to the suburb of Regla, then by bus direct to Guanabacoa.

Santa María del Rosario

A delightful colonial town, founded in 1732, 16 km southeast of Havana. It is reached from Cotorro, on the Central Highway, and was carefully restored and preserved before the Revolution. The village church is particularly good. See the paintings, one by Veronese. There are curative springs nearby.

San Francisco de Paula

Hemingway fans may wish to visit his house, 11 km from the centre of Havana, where he lived from 1939 to 1960 (called the **Museo Ernest Hemingway**, T 91-0809, US$3, open 0930-1600, closed Tuesday). The signpost is opposite the Post Office, leading up a short driveway. Visitors are not allowed inside the plain white-washed house which has been lovingly preserved with all Hemingway's furniture and books, just as he left it. But you can walk all around the outside and look in through the windows and open doors, although vigilant staff prohibit any photographs unless you pay US$5 for each one. There is a small annex building with one room used for temporary exhibitions, and

from the upper floors there are fine views over Havana. The garden is beautiful and tropical, with many shady palms. Next to the swimming pool (empty) are the gravestones of Hemingway's pet dogs, shaded by a flowering shrub. Hemingway tours are offered by hotel tour desks for US$35.

PARKS AND ZOOS

Jardín Botánico Nacional de Cuba

Km 3½, Carretera Rocío, south of the city in **Arroyo Naranjo**, beyond Parque Lenín. Open Monday-Friday 0800-1700, US$3, T 44-5525. The garden is well-maintained with excellent collections; it has a Japanese garden with tropical adaptations. Rosa Alvarez, one of the guides, is knowledgeable and speaks some English. There are few signs, so despite the extensive plant collection it is not informative as it might be. There is a good organic vegetarian restaurant (the only one in Cuba) which uses solar energy for cooking, book at the gate and it costs 14 pesos, just turn up at the restaurant and you'll be charged US$12. There is only one sitting for lunch but you can eat as much as you like from a selection of hot and cold vegetarian dishes, with hot and cold drinks. Water and waste food is recycled and the restaurant grows most of its own food. Private taxi from Old Havana US$8, Panataxi US$14. Many hotel tour desks now organize day trips including the lunch.

Zoo

Parque Zoológico Nacional, Km 3, Carretera de Capdevila, Wednesday-Sunday, 0900-1515, T 44-7613. **Parque Zoológico de la Habana**, Av 26, Nuevo Vedado (open daily 0930-1700, US$2).

El Bosque de la Habana

Worth visiting. From the entrance to the City Zoo, cross Calle 26 and walk a few blocks until you reach a bridge across the Almendares. Cross this, turn right at the end and keep going north, directly to the Bosque which is a jungle-like wood.

Hemingway's Havana or Papa Dobles on the Pilar

Marlin fishing, gambling, beautiful prostitutes: these were the things that attracted Ernest Hemingway to Cuba in 1932. At first he stayed at the *Hotel Ambos Mundos* in Havana, but his visits became so frequent that he decided to buy a property. In 1940 he bought Finca Vigía, a 14-acre farm outside Havana. The staff included three gardeners, a Chinese cook and a man who tended to the fighting cocks Hemingway bred.

During WW1, Hemingway set up his own counterintelligence unit at the Finca, calling it 'the Crook Factory'; his plan was to root out Nazi spies in Havana. He also armed his fishing boat, the '*Pilar*', with bazookas and hand grenades. With a crew made up of Cuban friends and Spanish exiles from the Civil War, the *Pilar* cruised the waters around Havana in search of German U-Boats. The project surprisingly had the blessing of the US Embassy, who even assigned a radio operator to the *Pilar*. With no U-Boats in sight for several months, the mission turned into drunken fishing trips for Hemingway, his two sons and his friends.

When Hemingway returned to Cuba after more heroic contributions to the War effort in France, he wrote the book which was to have the biggest impact on the reading public, '*The Old Man and the Sea*', the novel which won him the Pulitzer Prize in 1953. This was a period of particularly heavy drinking for Hemingway: early morning Scotches were followed by numerous Papa Dobles (2½ jiggers of white rum, the juice of half a grapefruit, six drops of maraschino, mixed until foaming) at the *Floridita*, Absinthe in the evening, 2 bottles of wine with dinner, and Scotch and soda till the early hours in the casinos of Havana.

When the political situation under Batista began to grow tense in 1958, a government patrol shot one of Hemingway's dogs at the Finca. By then he was older and wearier than when he had defended the Republicans during the Spanish

Civil War, and he quietly went back to his home in Idaho, from where he heard the news of Fidel Castro's victory. Hemingway made a public show of his support for the Revolution on his return to Cuba. He met Castro during the Marlin fishing tournament, which the new president won.

Hemingway's last days at the Finca were taken up with work on '*The Dangerous Summer*', a long essay about bullfighting, but his thoughts frequently turned to suicide, and he left for Florida in 1960. After the Bay of Pigs US-backed attempted invasion in 1961, the government appropriated the Finca. Hemingway committed suicide in the USA in 1961.

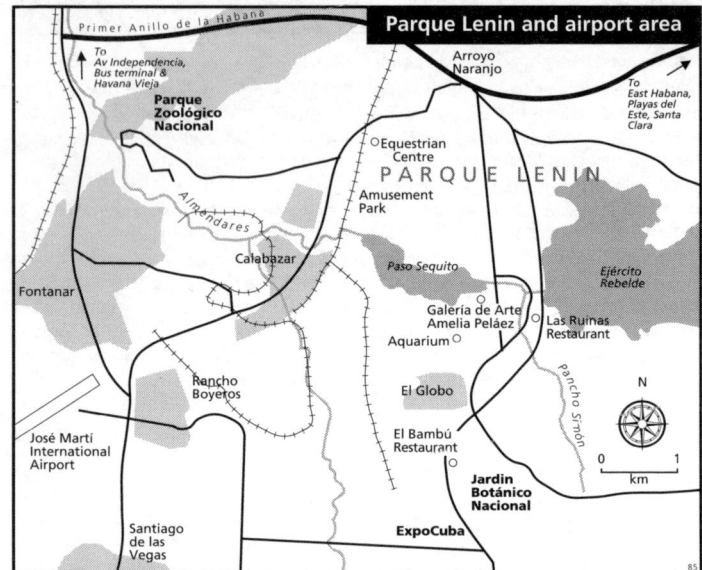

Parque Lenin and airport area

Aquaria

National Aquarium, Calle 60 and Av 1, Miramar, specializes in salt-water fish and dolphins, entrance US$2, while the **Parque Lenín aquarium** has fresh-water fish on show.

BEACHES AND WATERSPORTS

The beaches in Havana, at **Miramar** and **Playa de Marianao** are rocky and generally very crowded in summer (transport may also be difficult and time consuming). The beach clubs belong to trade unions and may not let non-members in. Those to the east, **El Mégano**, **Santa María del Mar** and **Bacuranao**, for example, are much better. To the west of Havana are **Arena Blanca** and **Bahía Honda**, which are good for diving and fishing but difficult to get to unless you have a car.

MARINA HEMINGWAY

Off Avenida 5, 20 minutes by taxi from Havana, is the Marina Hemingway tourist complex, in the fishing village of **Santa Fe**.

Fishing and scuba diving trips can be arranged here as well as other watersports and land-based sports. The Offshore Class 1 World Championship and the Great Island speedboat Grand Prix races have become an annual event in Havana, usually held during the last week in April, attracting power boat enthusiasts from all over the world. In May and June the marina hosts the annual Ernest Hemingway International Marlin Fishing Tournament and in August and September the Blue Marlin Tournament. There are 100 slips with electricity and water and space for docking 400 recreational boats. The resort includes the hotel *El Viejo y El Mar*, a Canadian-Cuban joint venture, restaurants, bungalows and villas for rent, shopping, watersports, facilities for yachts, sports and a tourist bureau. Building continues for more villas and apartments; the new *Jardín del Eden* hotel should be fully operational in 1998 with 316 rooms and suites and other facilities. The Hemingway International Nautical Club is here, a social club for foreign executives based in Cuba. Founded in 1992, it currently has 730 members from 37 countries. The club organizes regattas, sailing schools and excursions as well as the Hemingway Tournament. Excursions include a day trip to the Castillo del Morro in Old Havana with swimming and lunch (US$30); a snorkelling excursion along the reef west of Havana with equipment and lunch (US$35); by yacht to the beaches east of Havana with swimming and lunch (US$45). Shorter trips available as well as scuba diving and fishing trips, T 33-1909. VHF radio channels 16, 72, or 55B 2790.

● **Accommodation** *El Viejo y El Mar*, Calle 248 y Av 5, Santa Fe, T 246336, F 246823, reservations T 246819, pleasant enough hotel on seafront but out of the way and nothing to do unless you are busy at the marina, package tourists come here before going off on excursions, small pool, restaurant with buffet meals, lobby bar, clean, bath tub, tricky shower.

● **Places to eat** Several restaurants and a grocery store at the Marina: *La Tasca*; *Pepe's* at the end of the 'dock'; *Fiesta*, Spanish, OK.

PLAYAS DEL ESTE

Phone code 687

This is the all-encompassing name for a string of beaches within easy reach of Havana. East of the city is the pleasant little beach of **Bacuranao**, 15 km from Havana. At the far end of the beach is a villa complex with restaurant and bar. Then come **Tarará** (famous for its hospital where the Chernobyl victims have been treated), **El Mégano**, and **Santa María del Mar**, with a long, open beach which continues eastwards to **Guanabo** (4 train departures daily in July and August from Estación Cristal, Havana, and buses from Havana), a pleasant, non-touristy beach 27 km from Havana but packed with Habaneros at weekends. Cars roll in from Havana early on Saturday mornings, line up and deposit their cargo of sun worshippers at the sea's edge. The quietest spot is **Brisas del Mar**, at the east end. As a general rule, facilities for

foreigners are at Santa María del Mar and for Cubans at Guanabo. The latter is therefore cheaper. Tourism bureaux offer day excursions (minimum 6 people) for about US$15 per person to the Playas del Este, but for two or more people, its worth hiring a private car for the day for US$20-25. Cheap packages and all-inclusive holidays can be booked here from Canada and Europe, which can be good if you want to combine a beach holiday with excursions to Havana. However, most people report getting fed up after a few days of sitting on the beach here and the food is monotonous, so if you are the sort of person who likes to get out and about, avoid the all-inclusive deals.

● **Accommodation** L1-A2 *Villa Tarará*, T 335510/01, F 335499, 121 a/c units in villas with 2-5 rooms, TV, fridge, porch and parking, at the marina, restaurant, snack bar, grill, disco, watersports; *Los Pinos Villa* (Gran Caribe), Av de las Terrazas 21, Santa María del Mar, T 971361, F 802144, 26 houses, most with pools or near the beach, grill restaurant, popular with Italians, Spanish and French in that order, lots of repeat guests, comfortable, private, good for entertaining friends, very flexible management, multilingual staff; **A2** *Tropicoco Beach Club*, Av Sur y Las Terrazas, Santa María del Mar, T 687-2530, price includes beer, rum, 3 meals, wonderful view of beach but food boring after 2 days, nothing to do but drink and bathe, 188 rooms; **A2-C** *Aparthotel Las Terrazas*, Av de las Terrazas entre C 9 y 10, T 687-4910-16, 154 1-3 bedroomed apartments, each with cooking facilities, fridge, radio

El Jefe

👣 The Spanish poet, Rafael Alberti, once described Castro as 'the most cheerful head of state in the world'. Others have not been so complimentary about El Comandante. Even his daughter, Alina Fernández Revuelta, who left Havana in 1993, referred to him as El Jefe, rather than Papa, and after her departure she called him a 'killer', who had 'failed as a leader, a politician and a human being.'

and TV, in rather unattractive block opposite the beach, 2-tier swimming pool with children's area, restaurant, bar, tourist bureau, disco in separate building, car and moped rental, great location, recommended; **A3** *Itabo*, Laguna Ilabo entre Santa María del Mar y Boca Ciega, T 687-2550/58/80, F 33-5156, all-inclusive, 198 a/c rooms, good accommodation in 4 2-storey buildings around large pool with terrace bar and barbecue, beach reached by footbridge over Itabo lagoon, non-motorized watersports and bicycles included, restaurant, disco, shop; **B** *Hotel Atlántico* (Gran Caribe), Av Las Terrazas, entre 11 y 12, Santa María del Mar, T 687-2506/2561, 92 rooms, also has an *Aparthotel* (opposite the hotel is the self-catering complex's shop selling fresh food, including eggs, bread, cheese and meat). It may be possible to find privately rented apartments in Guanabo for US$15 a night with kitchen, ask around; **C** *Villa Playa Hermosa*, 5 Av y Calle D, T 2774, Guanabo, 33 rooms or chalets, good value, often used by party faithful and honeymooners, pizzería, good quality, US$1-2, rich French pastries US$1, well worth the culinary experience, rents bikes (in poor condition).

● **Places to eat** There are many *paladares* in Guanabo and elsewhere along the coast, reasonable prices. If you are self-catering, there is a farmers' market in Guanabo selling fresh fruit and vegetables 6 days a week.

● **Hospitals & medical services** *Clínica Internacional Habana del Este*, Av de las Terrazas, between *Aparthotel Las Terrazas* and *Hotel Tropicoco* in Santa María del Mar.

● **Watersports** The hotels provide some non-motorized watersports. Marina Tarará, run by Marinas Puertosol, has moorings for 50 boats, VHF communications and provisioning, yacht charters, deep sea fishing and scuba diving, all of which can be arranged through the hotel tour desks.

LOCAL INFORMATION

● **Accommodation**

Prices:
L1 over US$200; **L2** US$151-200; **L3** US$101-150; **A1** US$81-100; **A2** US$61-80; **A3** US$46-60; **B** US$31-45; **C** US$21-30; **D** US$12-20; **E** US$7-11; **F** up to US$6

(Payment for hotels used by tourists is in US$). Foreign tourists should obtain a reservation through an accredited government agent (see **Tour companies & travel agents** page 126). Always tell the hotel each morning if you intend to stay on another day. Do not lose your 'guest card' which shows your name and room number. Tourist hotels are a/c, with 'tourist' TV (US films, tourism promotion), restaurants with reasonable food, but standards are not comparable with Europe and plumbing is often faulty or affected by water shortages.

The Vedado hotels are away from the old centre; the others reasonably close to it. Several important hotel renovation projects have been completed in Old Havana and these are now elegant places to stay. A huge colonial building on the Plaza de Armas has opened as the luxury *Hotel Santa Isabel*, which is the best situated hotel in the old city. *Hotel Ambos Mundos*, Calle Obispo on the corner of San Ignacio, reopened at the

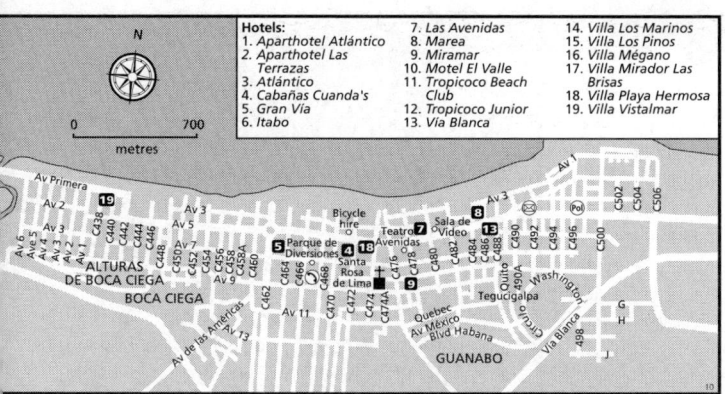

Hotels:
1. Aparthotel Atlántico
2. Aparthotel Las Terrazas
3. Atlántico
4. Cabañas Cuanda's
5. Gran Vía
6. Itabo
7. Las Avenidas
8. Marea
9. Miramar
10. Motel El Valle
11. Tropicoco Beach Club
12. Tropicoco Junior
13. Vía Blanca
14. Villa Los Marinos
15. Villa Los Pinos
16. Villa Mégano
17. Villa Mirador Las Brisas
18. Villa Playa Hermosa
19. Villa Vistalmar

end of 1996 and is well-located: Hemingway lived here for 10 years before moving to La Vigia in 1939. The *Parque Central* on the park of same name was due for inauguration on 14 February 1998.

Vedado and Old Havana

L1-L2 *Nacional de Cuba* (Gran Caribe), Calle O esquina 21, Vedado, T 33-3564-7, F 33-5054/5, 467 rooms, mostly renovated and redecorated 1996-97, good bathrooms with lots of bottles of goodies, some package tours use it at bargain rates, generally friendly and efficient service, faded grandeur, dates from 1930, superb reception hall, note the vintage Otis high speed lifts, steam room, 2 pools, restaurants, bars, shops, exchange bureau, gardens with old cannons on hilltop overlooking the Malecón and harbour entrance, great place to watch people and vehicles, the hotel's tourist bureau is also efficient and friendly; **L1-L2** *Meliá Cohiba* (Sol Meliá), Paseo entre 1 y 3, Vedado, T 33-3636, F 33-4555, international grand luxury, high rise and dominating the neighbourhood, 462 rooms, 120 suites, shops, gym, healthclub, pool, gourmet restaurant, piano bar; **L1-L2** *Santa Isabel*, Baratillo y Obispo, Plaza de Armas, T 33-8201, F 33-8391, 5-star, only 27 rooms, 10 of them suites, height of luxury, restaurant serving Cuban and international cuisine, central patio with fountain and greenery and lobby bar, relax with a cocktail and watch the view from El Mirador, the cafeteria also has a good view of the Palacio de los Capitanes Generales, El Templete and other local sights, great location; **L3** *Victoria* (Gran Caribe), 19 y M, Vedado, T 33-3510, F 33-3109, 31 rooms, small, quiet and pleasant, tasteful if conservative, recommended.

A1 *Habana Libre* (Tryp), L y 23, Vedado, T 33-4011, F 33-3141, 606 rooms in huge block, prices depend on the floor number, remodelled 1997, most facilities are here, eg hotel reservations, excursions, Polynesian restaurant, buffet, 24-hour coffee shop, *Cabaret Turquino* 2200-0400, US$20 per couple, shopping mall under construction, nearly completed end-1997, includes liquor store, cigar shop, jewellery and perfume, handicrafts, shoe shop, Air Jamaica, Photoservice, Banco Financiero Internacional, postal service; **A1** *Habana Riviera* (Gran Caribe), Paseo y Malecón, Vedado, T 33-3733, F 33-3738, 330 rooms, 1950s block, Mafia style, appearance suffers from being so close to the glitzy *Meliá Cohiba*, desolate square outside which together with the hotel entrance is awash with prostitutes after dark, does a good breakfast, no need to eat again all day; **A1-A2** *Inglaterra* (Gran Caribe), Prado 416 esquina San Rafael y San Miguel, T 33-8254, 86 rooms, built in 1875 next to the Teatro Nacional, famous former foreign guests included Sara Bernhardt, Federico García Lorca and Rubén Darío, colonial style, regal atmosphere, beautifully restored, balconies overlook Parque Central, delightful glazed tile pictures by famous and not-so-famous Cuban artists have been set into the pavement in front of the hotel, some single rooms have no windows but at least you won't get woken by the traffic, highly recommended, helpful staff, several of whom speak English, reasonable breakfast, lovely old mosaic tiled dining room, one of four cafés or restaurants with a variety of services and cuisines; **A2** *Presidente* (Gran Caribe), Calzada y G, Vedado, T 33-4075, F 33-3753, 142 rooms, oldest hotel

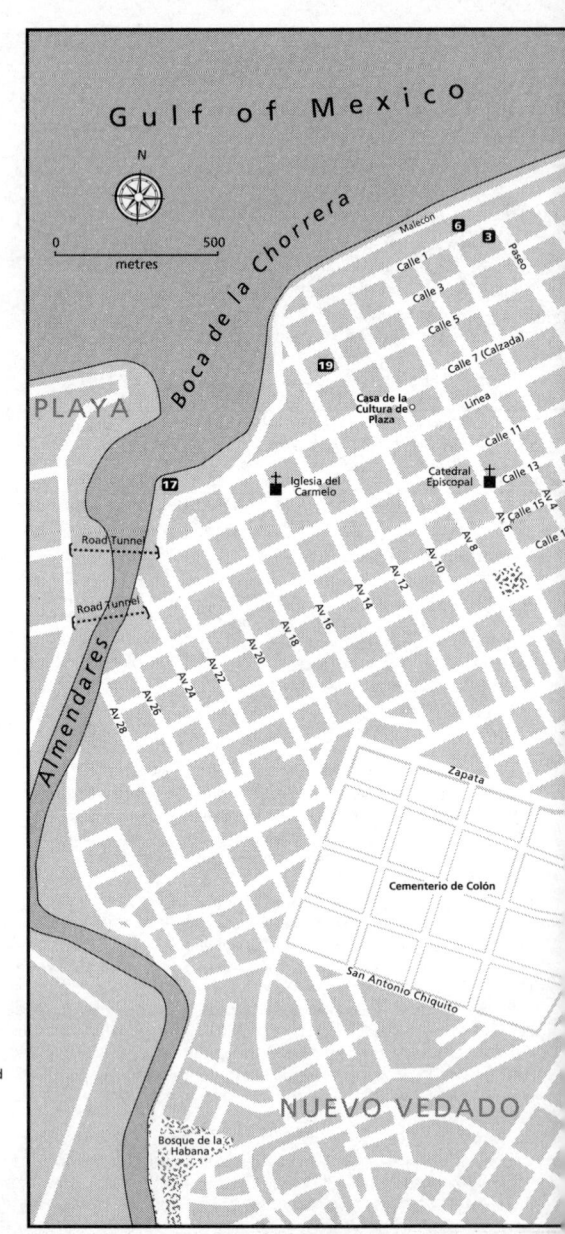

Hotels:
1. *Bruzón*
2. *Capri*
3. *Cohiba*
4. *Colina*
5. *Habana Libre*
6. *Habana Riviera*
7. *Morro*
8. *Nacional*
9. *Presidente*
10. *St. John's*
11. *Vedado*
12. *Victoria*

Places to eat:
13. Casa de la Amistad
14. Coppelia
15. El Conejito
16. La Torre (Focsa)
17. Restaurante 1830

Clubs:
18. Café Cantante
19. Maxim

Plaza de la Revolución

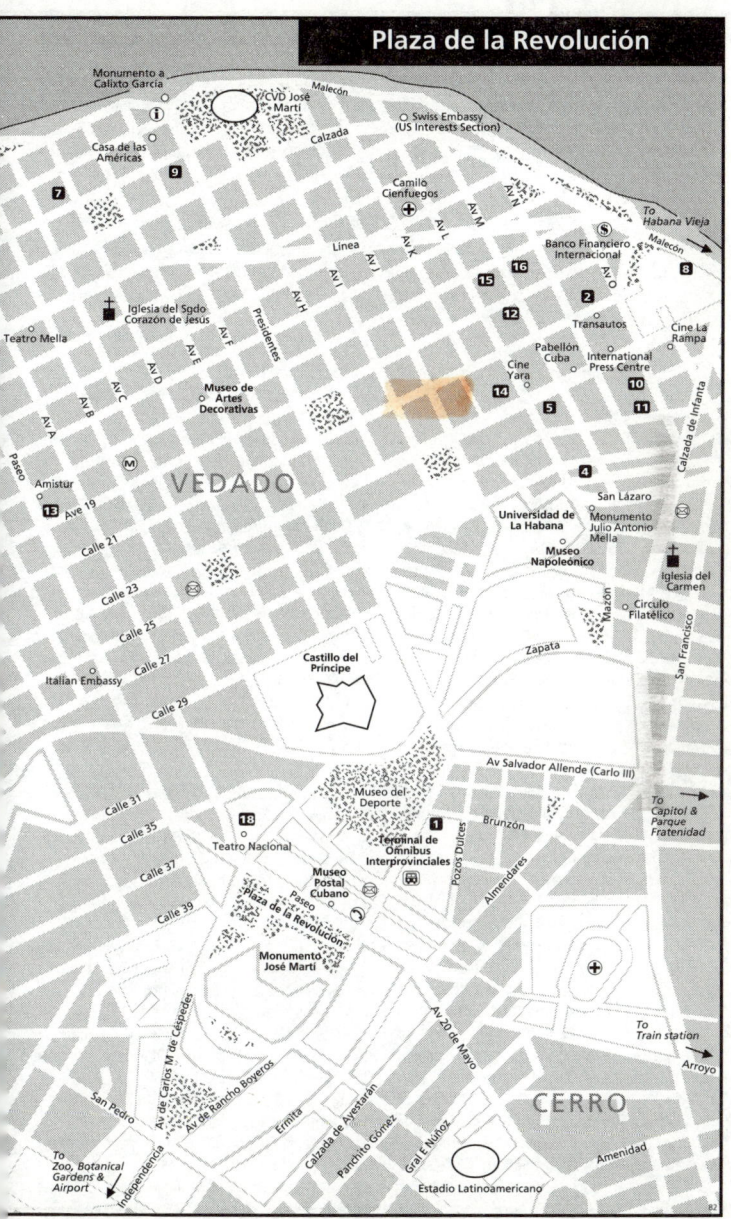

Monumento a
Calixto García

Malecón
CVD José
Marti

Swiss Embassy
(US Interests Section)

Calzada

Casa de las
Américas

9

7

Camilo
Cienfuegos

To
Habana Vieja

Banco Financiero
Internacional

$ **S**

Linea

Av N

Av M

Av L

Av K

Malecón

15 **16**

8

Av J

Iglesia del Sgdo
Corazón de Jesús

Av H

12

Transautos

Cine La
Rampa

Teatro Mella

Av F

Presidentes

Pabellón
Cuba

International
Press Centre

Av D

Av E

Cine
Yara

10

Museo de
Artes
Decorativas

Av C

Av B

Av A

14

5

11

Calzada de Infanta

M

4

Paseo

Amistur

13 Ave 19

VEDADO

San Lázaro

Universidad de
La Habana

Monumento
Julio Antonio
Mella

Calle 21

Museo
Napoleónico

Mazón

Iglesia del
Carmen

Calle 23

Círculo
Filatélico

Calle 25

San Francisco

Italian Embassy

Calle 27

Castillo del
Príncipe

Zapata

Calle 29

Calle 31

Av Salvador Allende (Carlo III)

To
Capitol &
Parque
Fraternidad

Calle 35

18

Museo del
Deporte

Brunzón

Teatro Nacional

1

Calle 37

Museo
Postal
Cubano

Terminal de
Omnibus
Interprovinciales

Pozos Dulces

Almendares

Paseo

Calle 39

Plaza de la
Revolución

Monumento
José Martí

Av Carlos M de Céspedes

Av 20 de Mayo

To
Train station

Arroyo

CERRO

San Pedro

Independencia

Av de Rancho Boyeros

Ermita

Calzada de Ayestarán

Panchito Gómez

Gral F Núñez

Amenidad

To
Zoo, Botanical
Gardens &
Airport

Estadio Latinoamericano

82

Private Accommodation in Havana

Tourists have to pay for accommodation in US dollars in Havana. Cubans use the national Islazul chain. However Cubans may offer you their house, apartment or a room and cook for you. A taxation system for this form of 'self-employment' was introduced in 1997 so that it is now legal. See **Information for travellers**. Private homes vary considerably and can be extremely comfortable or very basic. Because of shortages things often don't work, there may be cold water only, once a day, and the lights often go off. A torch is useful. The families will usually offer you cheap transport too. Remember that rates are likely to be negotiable if you go direct to the owners, or stay for several nights. The owners pay US$5/night/room for each client brought to them by a tout, and taxes and licences are high at US$250/room/month, so profit margins are tight and prices have risen.

in Havana, 1940s furniture, pool, TV, restaurant OK, cafetería, piano bar, nightclub; **A2 Plaza** (Gran Caribe), Ignacio Agramonte No 267, T 62-2006, F 33-8591, 186 rooms, comfortable, street front rooms very noisy, ask for one in the inner courtyard, good breakfast, poor dinner, service generally poor; **A2 Ambos Mundos** (Habaguanex), Obispo, on corner of Mercedes, Old Havana, T 66-9530, F 66-9532, beautifully restored, reopened 1997, Hemingway lived here for 10 years before moving to La Vigia in 1939; **A2 Sevilla** (Gran Caribe), Trocadero 55 y Prado, T 33-8560, 33-8580, F 33-8582, recently restored, 188 marvellous rooms of 1937 vintage on edge of Old Havana, pool, shops, sauna and massage, tourism bureau, buffet restaurant on ground floor, excellent breakfast, elegant restaurant on top floor with great night time views over Vedado and the Malecón; **A2 Capri** (Horizontes), 21 y N, Vedado, T 33-3571/3747, F 33-3750, 215 rooms, showing their age, public areas also with signs of wear and tear, a/c, pool, cabaret, shops, currency exchange, parking, car rental; **A3 Hostal Valencia** (Horizontes), Oficios 53 esquina Obrapía, T 62-3801, Old Havana, joint Spanish/Cuban venture modelled on the Spanish paradores, 12 rooms, each named after a Valencian town, tastefully restored building, nicely furnished, good restaurant (see below); **A3 St John's** (Horizontes), O, entre 23 y 25, Vedado, T 33-3740/4187, F 33-3561, 93 rooms, sparse, a/c, pool, avoid rooms close to noisy nightclub, closed for repairs 1997; **A3 Vedado** (Horizontes), Calle O 244 entre 23 y 25, T 33-4072, F 33-4186, next to St John's, 194 rooms, a/c, pool, restaurants, nightclub; **A3 Deauville**, Galiano y Malecón, T 33-8812, F 33-8148, 148 rooms, noise from Malecón, very tatty, weather damage, poor food.

B Villa Eulalia, Av 5 y Calle 6, Miramar, T 233223/235724/233217, bed & breakfast, dinner can be included for an extra US$5, beautiful villa, very spacious rooms, big shady garden, formerly for visiting Communist Party functionaries, now taking tourists, there is a good paladar about 100m away on Calle 6 y Av 3 if you don't want to eat in, main course starts at US$5; **B** Colina (Horizontes), L y 27, Vedado, T 33-4071, F 33-4104, 79 rooms, hot water, street noise, small rooms, excellent buffet breakfast, open to non-residents US$3, popular with airport Cubatur desk; **B** Lincoln (Islazul), Galiano 164 esquina Virtudes, T 62-8061, 135 rooms, friendly, TV, hot water, a/c, radio, clean, good value, guests are mostly Cuban honeymooners; **B** Morro (Horizontes), Calle 3 entre C y D, Vedado, T 33-3907, F 33-3908, 20 rooms, restaurant and bar.

The **cheaper hotels** are usually hard to get into; often full. **C** Lido (Horizontes), Consulado entre Animas y Trocadero, T/F 33-8814, 65 rooms, a/c, some with TV, not bad for the price, but don't expect hot water in the shower, laundry expensive, done by hand and charged per item, central, slightly dodgy area at night with prostitutes heckling, but 1 block from Prado, very friendly reception, restaurant downstairs food bland and overpriced but breakfast good at US$4, bar and café on roof terrace same menu in somewhat better setting, live music; **C** Caribbean (Horizontes), Paseo Martí 164 esquina Colón (bus 82 from Vedado), T 33-8210 F 66-9479, lobby full of smoke and prostitutes, 36 rooms, only 2 have windows, hot water (sporadic supply), fan and TV, popular with budget travellers but safety standards poor, clean, old city, recommended by some, but avoid noisy rooms at front and lower floors at back over deafening water pump, and beware of theft from rooms, small café serves mostly sandwiches and eggs at a low price; **C** *La Casa del Científico*, Prado 212 esquina Trocadero, Centro Habana, T 624511, beautiful colonial building, as good as the *Inglaterra* but much cheaper, shared bathroom, well renovated, luxurious dining room and lounge in classic style, very pleasant atmosphere, friendly staff, highly recommended; **C-D** *Residencia Santa Clara*, in convent buildings, see page 102, lovely, peaceful, nice café, T 61-2877, 66-9327, F 33-5696; **D** *Isla de Cuba* (Islazul), 169 Máximo Gómez, T 62-1031, refurbished, great character, central, no hot water, noisy disco below but friendly and helpful; nearby is **C-D** *New York* (Islazul) at 156 Dragones, T 62-7001, OK; **D** *Bruzón* (Islazul), on Calle Bruzón No 217, with P Dulces y Independencia, near the Plaza de la Revolución and the bus station, T 70-3531, fan, bath, TV in some rooms, no hot water, drinking water on each floor, back rooms noisy from bus station, staff from sleepy to helpful, club at side, free to guests.

Further west

There is a string of 4-star hotels west along the coast which are used by package tour operators; guests are often here for the first and last nights of their stay in Cuba before being whisked off round the island. They are not particularly convenient for visiting the old city, but you do get a sea view. *Sierra Maestra* is being reconstructed. **L3-A1** *Copacabana*, Av 1 y 44, Marianao, T 240340/2, F 242846, 168 rooms, restaurant, bar and cafeteria, pool and nightly disco 2200-0500; **L3-A1** *Chateau Miramar*, Av 1 y 62, Marianao, T 241952/241926-7, F 240224, 50 rooms, restaurant, 24-hour bar, pool, shops, laundry, fax and translation services, very helpful staff; **L3-A1** *Neptuno-Tritón* complex, Av 1 entre 70 y 80, Marianao, T 241606, F 240244, twin towers, *Neptuno* with 261 rooms, *Tritón* with 130 rooms, restaurant, grill and snack bar in pool area, which transforms into nightclub, marina planned; **L3-A1** *Comodoro*, Av 1 y 84, Marianao, T 245551/240700-1, F 242028, 120 rooms, restaurant, bar, pool. Further west still, is *El Viejo y El Mar*, see above, **Marina Hemingway**, page 112.

To the east

If you have a car, the eastern beaches are good places to stay for visiting Havana (see **Playas del Este**, page 113). The hotels are usually booked up by package tours but you can rent an apartment on the beach away from the main tourist area for US$30. The office is at the end of the main road running along the beach nearest to Havana and furthest from the main hotel area.

Private accommodation

At the top end of the market in **Vedado** are: **Amparo López**, Línea 53, Apartamento 2, entre M y N, T 327003, US$25 for self-contained apartment, large bedroom with fan, double bed, own bathroom, separate entrance, Amparo is a university lecturer and her husband speaks some English; **Don Pepe**, Línea 58, ground floor, beside Japanese Embassy, T 326183, US$25 for a/c bedroom, doctor and dentist couple; **Marta Vitorte**, Calle G 301, Apartamento 14, 14th floor, entre 13 y 15, T 326475, high rise building near corner with Línea, spacious, en-suite bathroom, balcony, great sea view, US$30, Marta is a retired civil servant and speaks some English; **Yovan**, Calle 1 511 entre 23 y 25, T 322173; **Ilka Picard**, Calle 19 606 entre B y C, T 326886; **Guillermina Abreu**, Calle Paseo 126, Piso 13, Apto A, entre 5 y Calzada, T 326401; **Francisco Rodríguez**, Calle 17 558 (bajos) entre C y D, T 325003; **Armando Gutiérrez**, Calle 21 62, Piso 4, Apto 7, esquina M, T 321876; **Patrice Tadeo Capote**, Calle 17 553 entre C y D, T 326761; the Anglican Church is reported helpful in finding private accommodation at around US$12/night, contact the ex-bishop **Emilio Hernández**, who speaks English, at Calle 13 y 6, T 38003. In **Centro Habana**, a recommended family is that of *Julio Massagué Barranco*, an English teacher and very friendly, Escobar 413 entre San Rafael y San José, T 631731, US$10 per person; **Dr Antonio E Clavero Machado**, Calle Lealtad 262, Neptuno y Condordia, US$12 for a nice single room with a/c, private bath with hot shower; **Maritza**, Calle Príncipe 140 entre Espada y Hospital, T 786842, also contact for other rooms and apartments in the area. For a longer stay it is possible to find an apartment for about US$50-100/month.

● **Places to eat**

Restaurants are not cheap. The choice of food is limited to 'dollar' restaurants, recognizable by the credit card stickers on the door, where meals are about US$20-25, paid only in US dollars. Check the bill carefully as overcharging is common in some Havana 'dollar' restaurants, also the bill may not record what you actually ate. As a rule, in Havana, outside the hotels, the 'dollar' places have been the only option, but since 1995 it has been legal for private houses to operate as restaurants, charging for meals in dollars or pesos. Known as *paladares*, they are licensed and taxed and limited to 12 chairs as well as having employment restrictions (see box, page 88). Some very good family-run businesses have been set up, offering a 3-course meal for US$6-8 pp, excellent value. They are not allowed to have lobster or shrimp on the menu as these are reserved for the dollar hotels and the export market. However, if you ask, there are often items available which are not on the menu.

Paladares in Old Havana

Doña Eutimia, Callejón del Chorro, just off Plaza Catedral, highly recommended, open daily 1200-2400; *Bellamar*, Virtudes entre Amistad e Industria, good, US$3 for fish, salad, rice, service slow; *Alhambra*, Virtudes esquina Consulado, open 0800-2400, good meals for US$2-3; *Sevilla's*, Obispo 465, altos, entre Villegas y Aguacate, open from 1130, good seafood but expensive; *La Julia*, O'Reilly 506A, T 62-7438, meals US$6-8, beer US$1, large portions, good creole food, can help with finding accommodation; *Doña Blanquita*, Prado 153 entre Colón y Refugio, near *Hotel Caribbean*, run by English-speaking lawyer; another *paladar* on Malecón 27 entre Prado y Cárcel, 1st floor, you are served on balcony, lovely view of city, bay and prostitutes plying their trade; *Chez Aimée*, upstairs at San Ignacio 68, near Plaza Catedral, T 61-2545, great lobster, shrimp or fish, US$12 for full meal and coffee, friendly, highly recommended; just down the street is *La Moneda* at San Ignacio 77, good for fish with salad, beans and rice with fried banana, around US$8.

Paladares in central Havana

La Guarida, Concordia 418 entre Gervasio y Escobar, T 62-4940, film location for *Fresa y Chocolate*.

Paladares at the Chinese market

At Zanja and Rayo, one block west of Galiano there is a good *paladar* called *El Flamboyán*, where they have a written menu and you can get a good chop suey for US$2; opposite is *Tien Tan* where you can get Chinese meals for US$2-3, open 1200-2100, always full; *El Pacífico*, Zanja y San Nicolás, impressive, looks like a Chinese temple, food can be very good if it is open, if there is water, if there is cooking gas and if there is any food, problems which affect all the restaurants around here, all prices in pesos, therefore very cheap, around US$3-4 for two, eg lobster chop suey for 13 pesos, lemonade 60 centavos, etc.

Paladares in Vedado

Try *Doña Nieves*, Calle 19, entre 2 y 4, T 30-6282, open Tuesday-Sunday, 1200-2400, recommended; *El Helecho*, Calle 6 entre Línea y 11; *El Moro*, Calle 25 1003, entre Paseo y 2; *Los Amigos*, M y 19, opposite *Victoria*, cheap and tasty; *Ex Corde*, Calle 17 entre 2 y 4, really nice place, in pesos or dollar equivalent, also opens Sunday.

Paladares near the university

La Reina, San Lázaro 1214, apto 1, entre M y N, open 1230-0100, T 78-1260, where a plate of food with salad and rice will cost US$5; opposite is *Casa Karlita*, San Lázaro 1207, T 78-3182, both have small signs on street.

Paladares in Nuevo Vedado

Acapulco, Calle 26 659 entre 35 y 37, T 300197; *El Palenque*, Zoológico 110 entre 36 y 38, T 811392, Cuban and Chinese; *Romeo y Julieta*, Av Ulloa 349, esquina Zoológico, T 811170, Italian.

Restaurants in Old Havana

La Bodeguita del Medio, Empedrado 207, near the Cathedral, was made famous by Hemingway and should be visited if only for a drink (*mojito* – rum, crushed ice, mint, lemon juice and carbonated water – is a must, US$4), food poor, expensive at US$35-40 for 2 but very popular, open 1030-0100, T 33-8857; *Floridita*, on the corner of Obispo and Monserrate, next to the Parque Central, T 33-8856, open 1200-0100, was another favourite haunt of Hemingway. It has had a recent face-lift and is now a very elegant bar and restaurant reflected in the prices (US$6 for a daiquiri), but well worth a visit if only to see the sumptuous decor and 'Bogart atmosphere'; *La Zaragozana*, almost next door, Monserrate entre Obispo y Obrapía, oldest restaurant in Havana, international cuisine, good seafood, recommended; *El Patio*, San Ignacio 54 esquina Empedrado, Plaza Catedral, nearby, is recommended for national dishes, open 24 hours, T 61-8504 and *La Mina*, on Obispo esquina Oficios, Plaza de Armas, open 1200-2400, T 62-0216, traditional Cuban food but both have uneven service, waits can be long and cooking gas shortages are common; *Cappuccino* next door is very similar, both have tables and chairs outside with live Cuban music; nearby, *Oasis*, Paseo Martí 256-58, in Arab Cultural Institute, cold a/c, very good hummus and lamb dishes, good music, trio plays old Cuban songs in very relaxed atmosphere, most enjoyable, T 61-4098, open 1000-2400; and *D'Giovanni*, Italian,

Tacón between Empedrado and O'Reilly, lovely old building with patio and terrace, interesting tree growing through the wall, but food very bland. Handicrafts shop in doorway specializes in miniature ornaments; *Al Medina*, Oficios, entre Obrapía y Obispo, Arab food in lovely colonial mansion, dishes priced between US$4-11, nothing extraordinary, some seating on large cushions, show at 2130 Friday, Saturday, also Mosque and Arab cultural centre off beautiful courtyard, open 1200-2300, T 63-0862; *Torre de Marfil*, Mercaderes, entre Obispo y Obrapía, good, inexpensive Cantonese menu, open 1200-2200, T 62-3466; *Hostal Valencia* restaurant *La Paella* features the best paella in Havana, good food, charming, open 1200-2300; *Café París*, Obispo y San Ignacio, serves good and reasonably priced chicken for US$3.50, beer US$1, snacks and pizza around the clock; *Cafetería Torre La Vega*, Obrapía 114, next to the Casa de México, open 0900-1900, does bland chicken and chips US$1.70, better value spaghetti US$0.65, beer US$0.85.

Restaurants in Vedado

El Conejito, Calle M esquina 17, T 32-4671, open 1800-2200, specializes in rabbit, and *La Torre*, 17 y M, at top of Edificio Fosca, T 32-5650, open midday-midnight, poor food but good view, are both quite expensive. In the *Habana Libre Hotel*, try *El Barracón*, traditional Cuban with good fish and seafood at lobby level, open 1200-midnight, T 30-5011, and *Sierra Maestra* restaurant and *Bar Turquino* on the 25th floor (spectacular views of Havana which makes the food acceptable, service bad). Along and near La Rampa there are some cheaper pizzerías and self-service restaurants. *Hanoi*, on Av Brazil, Cuban food, bland combination meal of chicken/fish/pork, mound of rice, black beans, chips is US$4.50, can get busy with groups and then takes an age to get served; *La Azucena China* on Calle Cienfuegos, Chinese food, charges US$1-2 for a main course; *Restaurante 1830*, at far west end of Malecón, overlooks bay, excellent seafood, relatively inexpensive, open air show in gardens at 2200, recommended; *El Ranchón*, Av 19 y 140, Playa, T 23-5838, good barbecued chicken, meats, typical *criolla* cuisine; *Casa de la Amistad*, Paseo entre 17 y 19, 1100-2300, for chicken, snacks and pizza.

Restaurants in Miramar

El Tocororo (national bird of Cuba), excellent food at US$40-50 a head, Calle 18 y Av 3, Miramar, T 24-2209, open Monday-Saturday 1230-2400, old colonial mansion with nice terrace, recommended as probably the best restaurant in town; *La Cecilia*, Calle 5 entre 110 y 112, Miramar, good international food, mostly in open air setting, recommended, open 1200-2400, T 24-1562.

Restaurants in Casablanca

La Divina Pastora, fish restaurant, Fortaleza de la Cabaña, open 1230-2300, T 33-8341, expensive, food praised; *Los XII Apostoles*, nearby on Vía Monumental, fish and good criollo food, good views of the Malecón.

Restaurants in Parque Lenín

Las Ruinas, Calle 100 esquina Cortina Presa in Parque Lenín, Cuba's most exclusive restaurant, and aptly named for its prices, is most easily reached by taxi; try to persuade the driver to come back and fetch you, as otherwise it is difficult to get back, open 1200-2400, T 44-3336.

Restaurants in Playa

La Ferminia, Av 5, entre 182 y 184, T 33-6555, international, elegant, lovely gardens, expensive. At Marianao beach there are also some cheaper bars and restaurants.

Vegetarians

There is little choice and we have received many reports that a vegetarian travelling in Cuba is bound to lose weight. Your best bet is the restaurant in the Jardín Botánico, *El Bambú*, see above, where lunch is served around 1400.

A visit to the *Coppelia* open-air ice-cream parlour, 23 y L, Vedado, is recommended, open 1000-midnight, payment in pesos, you might have to queue for an hour or so, not unpleasant in the shade, or pay in dollars to avoid the queue, US$2 for small portion. The parlour found movie fame in *Strawberry and Chocolate*. The building is a good example of the architectural creativity of the post-Revolutionary years, by Mario Girona, 1966. Alternatively, sample the Coppelia ice-cream in the tourist hotels and restaurants and some dollar food stores.

There are many **street stalls** and places where you can pick up snacks, pizza etc. Note that their prices are listed in pesos even though there is a $ sign posted. These can work out very cheap and are good for filling a hole at lunchtime, although don't expect a culinary masterpiece.

● Bars

Visitors find that ordinary bars *not* on the tourist circuit will charge them in dollars, if they let foreigners in at all. If it is a local bar and the Cubans are all paying in pesos, you will have to pay in US dollars. Even so, the prices in most places are not high by Caribbean standards.

The bar not to miss in Old Havana is *La Bodeguita* (see above, also for *La Floridita*). *Lluvia de Oro*, Calle Obispo esquina Habana, good place to drink rum and listen to loud rock music or salsa, also food, open 24 hours. Try a *mojito* in any bar. Tour groups are often taken to *O'Reilly*, on the street of the same name, for a *mojito*, pleasant upstairs, with balcony and musicians. *Bar Montserrate*, Av de Bélgica y Obrapía, beer US$1, *mojito* US$2, plenty of flavour but not very generous shot of rum, hot dogs US$2.50, filling meal featuring unidentifiable meat in breadcrumbs US$4, interesting to sit and watch comings and goings, high level of prostitutes/girls, though bar staff seem to have unwritten agreement whereby girls are allowed in with a foreigner, of if they buy a drink, but if girl to punters ratio gets too high, some of the girls have to leave, hustling is not excessive though. The trendy new place to go is the *Habana Café* in the *Meliá Cohiba*, which has replaced the bombed out disco, now a 1950s theme place with old cars, small Cubana plane hanging from the ceiling, memorabilia on the walls, Bene Moré music and large screen showing brilliant film of old Cuban musicians and artistes, expensive and meals not recommended, turkey burger or veggie burger US$6, *limonada* US$2, beer US$1.75, but *the* place to go, entrance to the left of the main hotel entrance, open 1200-0100, live music at weekends 2230-0100. *Casa de la Amistad*, Paseo 406 (see above), bar with a beautiful garden extension, tasty cheap light meals optional, very peaceful surroundings. For Graham Greene *aficionados*, go to the *Hotel Sevilla*, have a drink and tapas in the courtyard by the fountain and fantasize about Wormold from *Our Man in Havana* being recruited into MI6 in the gents.

● **Airlines**
All are situated in Havana, at the seaward end of Calle 23 (La Rampa), Vedado: eg Cubana, for international sales, Calle 23 64, esquina Infanta, T 33-4949/50, F 3-6190, for national sales, Calle Infanta esquina Humboldt, Centro Habana, T 706714 and phone numbers above; Aeroflot, Calle 23 64, esquina Infanta, T 33-3200/3759, F 33-3288. Iberia, Calle 23 72, T 33-5041/2, F 33-5041/2; Mexicana, T 33-3531/2, F 33-3729. Lacsa has an office in the *Habana Libre* which sells tickets for cash only, T 33-3114/3187, F 33-3728. Air Jamaica also has an office in the *Habana Libre* complex. If staying at Old Havana, allow sufficient time if you need to visit an airline office before going to the airport.

● **Banks & money changers**
Banco Nacional and its branches. For dollar services, credit card withdrawals, TCs and exchange, **Banco Financiero Internacional**, Línea esquina O, T 33-3423/4, F 33-3006, open Monday-Friday 0800-1500, last day of the month until 1200, branch in *Habana Libre* complex, T 33-3429, F 33-3795, same times, and another branch in Miramar, Calle 18 111 entre 1 y 3, T 33-2058, F 33-2458. Exchange bureau in *Hotel Nacional*, open 0800-1200, 1230-1930. **Banco Internacional de Comercio**, Ayestarán esquina Paseo, Plaza de la Revolución, open 0830-1400. (See also under **Currency**, page 290.)

● **Embassies and consulates**
All in Miramar, unless stated otherwise: **Argentina**, Calle 36 No 511 entre 5 y 7, T 24-2972/2549, F 24-2140; **Austria**, Calle 4 No 101, esquina 1, T 24-2852, F 24-1235; **Belgium**, Av 5 No 7408 esquina 76, T 24-2410, F 24-1318; **Brazil**, Calle 16 No 503 entre 5 y 7, T 24-2026/2141, F 24-2328; **Canada**, Calle 30 No 518, esquina 7, T 24-2516/2527, F 24-2044; **France**, Calle 14

Mojito

Every barman makes a slightly different Mojito, some are sweeter than others, but all are refreshing, tasty and light enough to be drunk at any time of day. Since the 1920s, *the* place to drink a Mojito is the *Bodeguita del Medio* in Havana, surrounded by graffiti through the ages. Imagine yourself rubbing shoulders with the likes of Ernest Hemingway, the most famous boozer of them all. To make a Mojito yourself, put half a tablespoon of sugar, the juice of half a lime and some soda water in a tall glass, stir, then add some lightly crushed mint leaves, some ice cubes, $1\frac{1}{2}$ oz light dry rum and top up with soda water. Serve with a garnish of mint leaves and a straw.

No 312 entre 3 y 5, T 24-2132/2080, F 24-1439; **Greece**, Av 5, No 7802, esquina 78, T 24-2854, F 24-1784; **Mexico**, Calle 12 No 518 entre 5 y 7, T 24-2294, F 24-2719, open 0900-1200, Monday-Friday; **Netherlands**, Calle 8 No 307 entre 3 y 5, T 24-2511/2, F 24-2059; **Peru**, Calle 36 No 109 entre 1 y 3, T 24-2477, F 24-2636; **Sweden**, Av 31A, No 1411, T 24-2563, F 24-1194; **Switzerland**, Av 5, No 2005, T 24-2611, F 24-1148; **UK**, Calle 34, No 708, T 24-1771, F 24-8104 or 24-9214 Commercial Section, open Monday-Friday 0800-1530; **Venezuela**, Calle 36A No 704 esquina 42, T 24-2662, F 24-2773. In Vedado, **Germany**, Calle B, esquina 13, T 33-2460; **Italy**, Paseo No 606 entre 25 y 27, T 33-3378, F 33-3416; **Japan**, Calle N No 62, esquina 15, T 33-3454/3508; **The US Interests Section** of the Swiss Embassy, Calzada entre L y M, T 33-3550/9. In the old city, **Denmark** and **Norway** are at the Prado No 20, Apartment 4C, T 33-8128, F 33-8127; **Spain**, Cárcel No 51 esquina Zulueta, T 33-8025-6, F 33-8006.

● **Entertainment**

Casa De La Trova: San Lázaro, entre Belascoán y Gervasio, closed for repairs 1997. There are Casas de la Trova around the country, they are houses where traditional Cuban music can be heard for free or for a minimal charge, thoroughly recommended. *Casa de la Cultura de Plaza*, Calzada y 8, Vedado, concerts and shows, different artistes, different times. For bolero admirers, try *Dos Gardenias*, with restaurant and bar, Av 7, esquina 26, Miramar, Playa, T 24-2353, open 2100-0500. UNEAC, Av 17 entre G y H, rumba Saturday and other Cuban band performances. Events listed at entrance. At the Teatro Nacional there is a piano bar upstairs where you can hear quality music, nueva trova, bolero, etc, beer US$2.50, downstairs in the theatre there are live concerts such as a Nueva Trova show for 10 pesos. You can find rumba on Wednesdays at the Teatro Mella, Línea entre A y B. Also *Palmares*, Malecón y E for rumba performances and disco dancing, 2100 until late. *Holá Ola*, Malecón, occasionally has big national groups, entry in pesos. The *Casa de la Música* in Miramar is a great place with a disco and stage in a beautiful old house, entry varies, some nights women are free and men pay US$15, inevitable soft sex trade, band comes on at 0200, so this is a real late night place. The *Hotel Nueva York*, Calle Zanja y Dragones, near the Capitolio, has a live band and singer around 2100-2330, playing in an attractive garden room attached, many plants hang down from the ceiling, nice effect. Radio Taino FM 93.3, English and Spanish language tourist station gives regular details of wide range of Cuban bands playing and venues, particularly in the programme at 1700-1900. The newspaper, *Opciones*, also has a listing of what's on.

Cinemas: best are *Yara* (opposite *Habana Libre* hotel, T 32-9430); *Payret*, Prado 503, esquina San José, T 63-3163, and *La Rampa*, Rampa esquina O, evenings only. Many others.

Jazz: *Maxim Club*, Calle 10, closed 1997 for repairs; *Coparrun*, Hotel Riviera (big names play there), jazz in the bar recommended; Friday nights at *Meliá Cohiba* from 2100; *El Zorro y el Cuevo*, 23 y O, Vedado, entry US$3, opens 2230 until 0400, gets lively around 2330; UNEAC, H y 17, Thursday nights, but check listings on gate.

Nightclubs: the *Tropicana* (closed Monday, Calle 72 No 4504, Marianao, T 33-7507, F 33-0109, 2000-0200) is a must; book with *Havanatur*, *Amistur*, Rumbos Tour, etc, US$30-55, depending on seat, drinks extra. Despite being toned down to cater for more sober post-revolutionary tastes, it is still a lively place with plenty of atmosphere, open-air (entry refunded if it rains). Drinks are expensive: a bottle of rum is US$60; payment in dollars. Bringing your own bottle seems acceptable. Foreigners may be admitted without booking if there is room. All the main hotels have their own cabarets, eg *Parisien* at Hotel Nacional, excellent long show for US$20-25, make a reservation. *Capri* is recommended, at US$15 and longer show than *Tropicana* but the drinks are expensive at US$40 for a bottle of best rum. *Aché* in the *Meliá Cohiba* and next door *Palacio de Salsa* in the *Riviera*, which is full of life and atmosphere, US$20 for a *Los Van Van* show until 0400, but if a really good band like *Médico de la Salsa* plays then entrance can be US$60, US$3 for a beer, US$5 for a cocktail. Also the *Commodore* disco (US$10), crowded, Western-style, free to Hotel Neptune guests; *Café Cantante*, Teatro Nacional, Paseo y Calle 39, Plaza de la Revolución, open nightly from 2200, 3 bands, US$10, although sometimes it is US$15, although this place is well regarded, it is popular with *jinetero/as* and lone travellers have commented on feeling uncomfortable; *La Finca* at Playas del Este. The *Cabaret Nacional*, San Rafael y Prado, is a nightclub for Cubans, you must be invited by a Cuban friend.

Music in Havana

🎵 Havana is buzzing with musical activity. Rumba, conga, son, danzón, charanga, salsa – you'll hear it all, as Cuba's greatest musicians converge on the capital. This is the place to be if you want to hear Cuba's established artists – Los Van Van, Sierra Maestra, NG La Banda, La Charanga Habanera, Isaac Delgado – a11 regularly liven up the theatres, hotels and parks. You might even get to wave a flag at Silvio, Sara or Pablito if the UJC are holding a rally in the Plaza de La Revolución. Havana offers more than star quality, however. Fancy a conga? The revived carnival parade is in February. Many of the comparsa congas parade regularly throughout the year down Paseo Martí and through Habana Vieja, and a newly established Christmas Day parade gives another chance to go wild with the farolas and tambores. A rumba? The unmissable Sábados de La Rumba are held fortnightly by the Grupo Folclórico Nacional at Calle 4 entre 5 y 7 in Vedado, you can Guaguancó with some of the best drummers and dancers in the land. You might want to practice your son – there are plenty of willing partners at the Casa 10 de Octubre (Calzada de Luyanó entre Reforma y Guasabacoa), where the septetos turn back the clock to the Havana of the 1920s. More up to date sounds can be heard at the annual Jazz Plaza festival in January, where Cuba's finest join forces with international stars for a world class event. You can peruse Cuba's musical history at the Museo Nacional de la Música (see **Other museums**). For a real history lesson, don't miss the ancient Orquesta Típica playing old Danzones with gusto in the Plaza de la Catedral. None of the band looks a day over 80.

Theatres: *Teatro Mella*, Línea entre A y B, Vedado, T 3-8696, specializes in modern dance; more traditional programmes at *Gran Teatro de la Habana* on Parque Central next to *Hotel Inglaterra*, T 613076-9, claims to be the oldest working theatre in the world, opened in 1837, wonderful baroque building which seats 2,000. The Conjunto Folklórico Nacional and Danza Contemporánea dance companies sometimes perform here, highly recommended, US$0.60. In Miramar, *Teatro Karl Marx*, Av 1 entre 8 y 10, T 300720/305521. Havana has some very lively theatre companies. *Amistur* travel agency can help with theatre and nightclub bookings.

● **Hospitals & medical services**
The *Cira García Clinic*, Calle 20 4101 esquina 41, Miramar, T 242811/14, F 241633, payment in dollars, also the place to go for emergency dental treatment, the pharmacy (T 242051) sells prescription and patent drugs and medical supplies that are often unavailable in other pharmacies, as does the *Camilo Cienfuegos Pharmacy*, L and 13, Vedado, T 333599, open daily 0800-2000. *Optica Miramar*, Calle 43 1803 entre 18 y 18A, T 242590, opthamology consultants, contact lenses, photocromic brown and grey lenses, lightweight glasses, plastic and metal frames; *Biotop*, Av 7 2603 esquina 26,

T 242377, F 242378, body and facial aesthetics, stress management, revitalizers, innovative techniques for psychological and physical evaluations, bio-feedback and alternative non-invasory techniques. *The Clínica Internacional* is at Av de las Terrazas 36, Santa María del Mar, Playas del Este, T 06872689. *Servimed* (turismo de salud) is at Calle 18 4304 entre 43 y 47, Playa, T 332658, F 332948, with information on special treatments, spas and health facilities around the country.

● **Places of worship**
Baptist church J 555, Vedado, T 322250; **Methodist** K 502, Vedado, T 320770; **Presbyterian** Salud 218, Centro Habana, T 621219; **Catholic**, Sagrado Corazón, Reina e Belascoín y Gervasio, Centro Habana, Iglesia del Carmen, Infantas e Neptuno y Concordia, Centro Habana.

● **Post & telecommunications**
Post Office: there is a post office at Oficios 102, opposite the Lonja, and postal facilities in the *Hotel Nacional*, *Hotel Plaza* (5th floor, walk through dining area and turn right on to the terrace, open 0700-1900) and in the *Hotel Habana Libre* building. Also on Calle Ejido next to central railway station and under the Gran Teatro de La Habana. For stamp collectors the

Círculo Filatélico is on Calle San José 1172 entre Infanta y Basarrata, open Wednesday, 1700-1900, Saturday 1300-1700, Sunday 0900-1200, and there is a shop on Obispo 518 with an excellent selection (Cuban stamps are very colourful and high quality). A new philatelic shop has opened in Vedado on 27 esquina L, just around the corner from the Fernando Ortíz bookshop. DHL has its central office in Miramar on Av 1 y Calle 42, T 331578, F 330999, another branch in the *Hotel Las Yagrumas*, T 650-4460, and at Calle Calzada 818 entre 2 y 4, Vedado, T 33-4351/2.

Telephones & cable offices: *Ministerio de Comunicaciones*, Av de Rancho Boyeros entre 19 de Mayo y 20 de Mayo, Plaza de la Revolución, T 810875, 820087, for national and international telegraphs (Cuban pesos). *The Empresa Telecomunicaciones de Cuba* (Etecsa) is on Av 33 1427 entre 18 y 14, Miramar, T 332476, F 332504. *Cubacel Telefonía Celular* is at Calle 28 510 entre 5 y 7, Miramar, T 332222, F 331737. The large hotels of 4 or 5 stars such as the *Habana Libre* and *Nacional* have international telephone, telex and fax facilities. At the *Hotel Plaza*, 5th floor you can send faxes, US$3 to USA, US$5.85 to UK for 1 minute, US$1 after that. Wall mounted phone takes phone cards.

● **Shopping**

Original lithographs and other works of art can be purchased or commissioned directly from the artists at the *Galería del Grabado*, at the back of the *Taller Experimental de Gráfica de la Habana*, Callejón del Chorro 62, Plaza de la Catedral (open all day, closed Sunday, T 62-0979, F 338121). You can watch the prints and engravings being made and specialist courses are available for those who want to learn the skill for themselves, for one month, US$250, or three months, US$500. The *Taller Serigrafía* is another big workshop, on Cuba 513, making screen prints; again, you can watch them being made and buy things. Reproductions of works of art are sold at *La Exposición*, San Rafael 12, Manzana de Gómez, in front of Parque Central. Handicraft and tourist souvenir markets have sprung up, especially around the Cathedral, on D and Av 1, Vedado, and on the Rampa, open Tuesday-Sunday 0900-1600; Che Guevara and religious *Santería* items lead the sales charts. The market in the Cathedral square is a platform for many talented young artists to show off their skills, you may pick up a bargain, or you may be asked to pay Miami-type prices. There is a special boutique, the *Palacio de la Artesanía*, in the Palacio Pedroso (built 1780) at Calle Cuba 64 (opposite Parque Anfiteatro) where the largest selection of Cuban handicrafts is available; the artisans have their workshops in the back of the same building (open Monday-Saturday 0900-2000) it has things not available elsewhere: jewellery, Cuban coffee, local and imported liqueurs, soft drinks, T-shirts, postcards and best retail selection of cigars (2 cigar-makers in attendance, lower prices than at factory); Visa and Mastercard accepted, passport required. *Artex* shop on Av 23 esquina L has excellent music section and tasteful T-shirts and postcards. The *Caracol* chain in tourist hotels (eg *Habana Libre*) and elsewhere, sell tourists' requisites and other luxury items such as chocolates, biscuits, wine, clothes, require payment in US$ (or credit cards: Mastercard, Visa). *La Maison* is a luxurious mansion on Calle 16, 701 esquina 7 in Miramar, with dollar shops selling cigars, alcohol, handicrafts, jewellery and perfume. There is sometimes live music in the evening in lovely open-air patio, and fashion shows displaying imported clothes sold in their own boutique, free entry. The large department stores are along Galiano (Av Italia) near San Rafael and Neptuno. Calle Monte is being redeveloped, with a variety of shops operating in dollars or Cuban pesos, starting from the Capitolio end with a food supermarket. At the other end is Cuatro Caminos market (see **Markets** below). In Miramar there is a dollar shopping complex on Av 5 y 42 and a large diplomatic store, *Diplomercado* (Av 5 esquina 24 y 26), with a bakery next door. Bread is also available at the new French bakery on Av 42 y 19 and in the Focsa shopping complex on Av 17 entre M y N. For food shopping, there is the *Focsa Supermarket*, or the *Amistad*, on San Lázaro just below Infanta. The *Isla de Cuba* supermarket on Máximo Gómez entre Factoría y Suárez has the best selection of food in Old Havana, with prices stamped on the goods to prevent overcharging. Opposite the *Plaza Hotel* is the *Peerless* and inside the small shopping centre is *El Cristal*, both of which also mark the prices on the goods. One which doesn't is *El Juvenil*, or *Los Fornos*, on Neptuno, just round the corner from the *Hotel Inglaterra*, where overcharging is common. If you eat at the restaurant here ask to see a price list as they overcharge too. Both are housed in a repainted shell of an old building. There are tourist ministores in most hotels, but they do not sell fresh food. The International Press Centre (open to the public) on La Rampa sells items like chocolate for dollars in a shop to the right of the entrance.

Markets: farmers are allowed to sell their produce (root and green vegetables, fruit, grains and meat) in free-priced city *agromercados*. You should pay for food in pesos. There are markets in Vedado at Calle 19 y B; in Nuevo Vedado, Tulipán opposite Hidalgo; in the Cerro district at the Monte and Belascoaín crossroads; and in Central Havana, the Chinese market at the junction of Zanja and Av Italia where you can eat at street food stalls (avoid Mondays, not a good day). Cadeca exchange bureaux at the first 2 listed.

Bookshops: international bookstore at end of El Prado, near Parque Fraternidad and Capitol, English, French, German books but selection poor and payment has to be in dollars. Other good bookshops near Parque Central and *La Internacional* on Calle Obispo 528 esquina Bernaza (books are very good value, also some stationery). *Librería La Bella Habana*, in the Palacio del Segundo Cabo, O'Reilly 4 y Tacón, open Monday-Saturday 1000-1800, has both Cuban and international publications. *Fernando Ortíz*, L esquina 27, quite a wide selection, mostly in Spanish and some beautiful postcards. *El Siglo de las Luces* (Neptuno), near Capitolio, good place to buy *son*, *trova* and jazz (rock) records.

Photography: films developed at *Publifoto*, Edificio Focsa, Calle M entre 17 y 19, and *Photoservice*, Calle 23 esquina P, Vedado, 0800-2200, camera repairs 0800-1700, T 33-5031 (another branch in Varadero, *Hotel Cuatro Palmas*, Av 1 entre 61 y 62, open 0900-1900. Kodak film can be bought in a number of tourist locations at reasonable prices.

● **Tour companies & travel agents**

There is a large number of state owned travel agencies, which cooperate fully with each other and have bureaux in all the major hotels (see **Information for travellers**, page 289). *Amistur*, Paseo 646, entre 19 y 17, T 33-3544/1220, F 33-3515, is more geared towards independent travellers and can book you into good hotels in all the major cities at reduced rates. They are helpful with transport and tours and can also book excursions, restaurants, theatre and nightclubs, or help you find a guide. They arrange sociocultural tours with specific interest groups if contacted in advance.

Tours can be arranged all over Cuba by bus or air, with participants picked up from any hotel in Havana at no extra charge. Examples include a tour of the city's colonial sites (US$10, 4 hours); a trip to the *Tropicana* cabaret

(US$50-60, 4 hours); Cayo Largo for the day by air with boat trip, snorkelling, optional diving, lunch (US$94, 12 hours); Guamá and the Península de Zapata with a stop en route at the *Finca Fiesta Campesina*, tour of crocodile farm, lunch (US$39, 9 hours); Viñales and Pinar del Río, visiting *mogotes*, caves and tobacco factory, lunch (US$39, 9 hours); a day on the beach at Varadero (US$27 or US$38 with lunch, 10 hours); Trinidad by air, visiting the colonial city and the Valle de los Ingenios (US$79, 12 hours); ecological tour of Las Terrazas with walking and river bathing, lunch (US$38, 10 hours).

Guides: many Cubans in Havana tout their services in their desperate quest for dollars and it can be easier to accept one of them to prevent being pestered all the time. Both male and female single travellers have recommended using a guide as long as you are careful who you choose; avoid young Cubans hanging around main tourist areas, especially if they approach you in pairs. Lots of Cubans speak English and are keen to practise it. If you feel you trust someone as a guide, make sure you state exactly what you want, eg private car, *paladar*, accommodation, and fix a price in advance to avoid shocks when it is too late. You may find, however, that the police will assume your guide is a prostitute and prohibit him or her from accompanying you into a hotel.

● **Useful addresses**

Police: T 820116. **Fire**: T 811115, 798561-69. **Asistur**: Prado 254, Old Havana, T 625519, 638284, F 338087, for medical and dental emergencies, repatriations, financial and legal problems, travel insurance claims, reservations. **Weather reports**: Observatorio Nacional, T 621051-58.

● **Transport**

The economic crisis and shortage of fuel has led to severe transport problems and public transport is only slowly recovering. Transport for tourists is organized in dollars; some of that income is being channelled into the national transport sector, now showing definite signs of improvement. The easiest way to travel out of town is to use the computer-linked tour service in most of the tourist hotels.

Local Taxis: a fleet of white 'Turistaxis' with meters has been introduced for tourists' use; payment in US$: sample fare, Ciudad Vieja to Vedado US$3.50. A cheaper way of getting around is via **Panataxi**, a company set up for the 1992 Pan American Games. Basically a call-out service, T 813311/813008/813065, Panataxis also wait just outside the Plaza de la Catedral, the *Meliá Cohiba*, on 17 entre L y M, and at the airport, or ask your hotel to call one. They are identified by their navy and yellow colour and have a new fleet of Citröen cars, so they are the most comfortable service as well as being the most reliable and still the cheapest dollar service at under US$10 from the airport to Vedado. Meters should read 2 (the standard fare) and the rate is US$0.45/km 24 hours a day. **Habanataxi** is a new call-out taxi service introduced at the end of 1997, T 419600, same basic rate of US$0.45/km within city of Havana, (US$0.34 for return service), or US$0.50/km if you take a longer trip outside the city. Licensed **Cuban peso taxis** are mostly reserved for hospital runs, funerals etc, but after completing their quotas they can now freelance. They usually have some kind of taxi sign. In the older taxis there are no meters and there is normally a fixed charge between points in or near the city. The fare should be fixed before setting out on a journey. Several private car owners operate as taxi drivers, some legitimately, others without a licence, always for dollars. Beware of private moonlighters (yellow licence plates, often identifiable by their harassment); they could charge you over the odds, generally are not paying any taxes and you have no come-back in the case of mishaps. In Habana Vieja and Vedado tricycle taxis are cheap and readily available, a pleasant way to travel. A short journey will cost US$1, or pay around US$5/hour, bargaining is acceptable.

Buses: at the end of 1997 a new service was introduced by Rumbos which covers many places of interest across Havana. For US$4/day you can get on and off a 30-seater bus along the route; buses pass every 35 minutes from 0845-2100 on the following route: Roundabout Palacio de las Convenciones (Playa), Morro-Cabaña, Calles 3 y 70, Palacio de las Bellas Artes, Acuario Nacional, Parque Central, Maqueta de la Habana, *Hotel Deauville*, *Hotel Meliá Cohiba*, *Hotel Riviera*, La Rampa, Cementerio de Colón, *Hotel Meliá Cohiba*, *Hotel Riviera*, Plaza de la Revolución, Maqueta de la Habana, *Coppelia*, Acuario Nacional, Pabellón Cuba, Calle 3 y 70, Galiano (Central Havana), Roundabout Palacio de las Convenciones, Parque Central, Museo de la Revolución, Casco Histórico, Morro-Cabaña. **Town buses** have been in crisis since 1993 but the service is now slowly recovering; buses are more frequent and therefore less crowded. There is a regular service on the *camellos*, long articulated buses on a truck bed, 20 Cuban

Castro on dying

When asked how many assassination attempts he had survived, Fidel Castro replied "If there were an Olympic event in this field, I would certainly have won the gold medal." Although in 1995 he was quoted as saying "Dying doesn't figure in my immediate plans," he later remarked in a speech in 1996 that he never expected to live to 70 but that he wanted his ideas to outlive him. "Men pass away, people stay; men pass away, ideas live on."

centavos. They cover the main suburbs, M1 to Playa, M2 to the airport, M6 to Alamar, and leave from Parque de la Fraternidad. Ask for the right queue. With all urban buses, there is a queuing ritual. Discover who is last (última) for the bus you want; when identified, ask him/her who they are behind, as people mark their places and then wander off until the bus comes. Other than the *camellos*, buses cost 40 centavos.

Bicycle hire: *Hotel Neptuno* charges US$3 for the first hour then US$1 for each subsequent hour. Also *Hotel Riviera*. Check the bicycle carefully (take your own lock, pump, even a bicycle spanner and puncture repair kit; petrol stations have often been converted into bicycle stations, providing air and tyre repairs). Cycling is a good way to see Havana, especially the suburbs; some roads in the Embassy area are closed to cyclists. The tunnel underneath the harbour mouth has a bus designed specifically to carry bicycles and their riders. Take care at night as there are few street lights and bikes are not fitted with lamps.

Car hire: Nacional Rent a Car, Av 47 4701 y 40, Reparto Kohly, Playa, T 81-0357, 20-6897, 23-7000, F 33-0742; **Havanautos**, Calle 36 505 entre 5 y 5a, Miramar, T 332369, F 331416; **Transautos**, Calle 21 entre N y O, Vedado, next to *Hotel Capri*. Hiring a car is not recommended for getting around Havana, roads are badly signed and there have been many accidents with tourists driving rental cars (see **Information for travellers**, page 302).

Airport José Martí, 18 km from Havana. A new terminal is to be built by 1998 to allow 3 million passengers a year. Turistaxi to airport, US$16-18 depending on time of day or night and destination. Panataxi are US$9-12. The Cubatur desk will book a taxi for you from the airport. The return journey in a private taxi could cost as little as US$5. The duty free shop at the airport is good value. City buses run from Terminal 4 (Air Cubana terminal) to town, ask around. To catch a bus to the airport from town, the M2 buses leave from Parque Fraternidad, but are always full, long queues, difficult with luggage.

Long distance buses Leave from the Terminal de Omnibus Interprovinciales, Av Rancho Boyeros (Independencia). See **Information for travellers** for advance booking addresses, page 304. There is also a new service, Víazul, which leaves from Av 26 entre Av Zoológico y Ulloa, Nuevo Vedado, T 811413, 811108, 815652, F 666092, with buses or minibuses usually every other day to Varadero, Trinidad, Viñales via Pinar del Río (and Varadero-Trinidad) in late 1997, with new runs to Girón (Guamá) and Santiago de Cuba expected soon.

Trains Leave from the Estación Central in Av Egido (de Bélgica), Havana, to the larger cities. The Estación Central has what is claimed to be the oldest engine in Latin America, *La Junta*, built in Baltimore in 1842. Get your tickets in advance as destinations very, the 'special' leaves every other day, with the regular on the other days, and the departure time is very approximate. Tickets easily purchased from LADIS office on the corner of Arsenal y Cienfuegos, or they have a desk in an upstairs area of the main train station (ask around and you will be led there),

pay in US$, carriage, a/c, spacious, food and drink on board. The 'special' leaves Estación Central daily at 1620, arrives Matanzas 1800, US$4, arrives Santa Clara 2033, US$10, arrives Ciego de Avila 2313, US$18, arrives Camagüey 0054, US$19.50, arrives Las Tunas 0258, US$27, arrives Holguín 0505, US$31, arrives Santiago de Cuba 0645, US$35, arrives Guantánamo 0835, US$38. The regular service prices are: Cienfuegos US$9.50, Sancti Spíritus US$13.50, Ciego de Avila US$18, Holguín US$27. A long distance bus or dollar taxi may well do the same journey in a fraction of the time, eg Havana-Pinar del Río, 2 hours or less by taxi, 7-8 hours by train. It is not unusual for the trains to break down, in fact Cubans refer to this as 'normal service'. It will be mended and carry on, but be prepared to spend a serious amount of time travelling.

Ferries There are ferries from Habana Vieja to Casablanca and Regla which depart from San Pedro opposite Calle Santa Clara. If you are facing the water, the Casablanca ferry docks on the left side of the pier and goes out in a left curve towards that headland, and the Regla ferry docks on the right side and goes out in a right curve.

Province of Havana

A SEMI-CIRCULAR province, it surrounds the city of Havana and provides lots of opportunities for excursions from the city or, if you want to do it the other way around, stay in a quiet, country or beach hotel and make your excursions into the city.

EAST OF HAVANA

The main road along the coast towards Matanzas and Varadero is called the **Vía Blanca**. There are some scenic parts, but you also drive through quite a lot of industry, such as the rum and cardboard factories at **Santa Cruz del Norte**, a thermal electricity station and many smelly oil wells. The **Hershey Railway** runs inland from the Casablanca station in eastern Havana, more or less parallel to the Vía Blanca, and is an interesting way to get to Matanzas. This electric line was built by the Hershey chocolate family in 1917 to service their sugar mill at what is now the Central Camilo Cienfuegos.

Some 60 km east of Havana is **Jibacoa** beach, which is excellent for snorkelling as the reefs are close to the beach and it is also a good area for walking.

● **Accommodation C-D** *Villa Loma de Jibacoa*, T 0692 83612, 29 rooms in stone houses with shared bathroom, TV, fridge, best for families or groups wanting to share a house; **D** *Campismo El Abra* campsite has 2-4-bed cabins

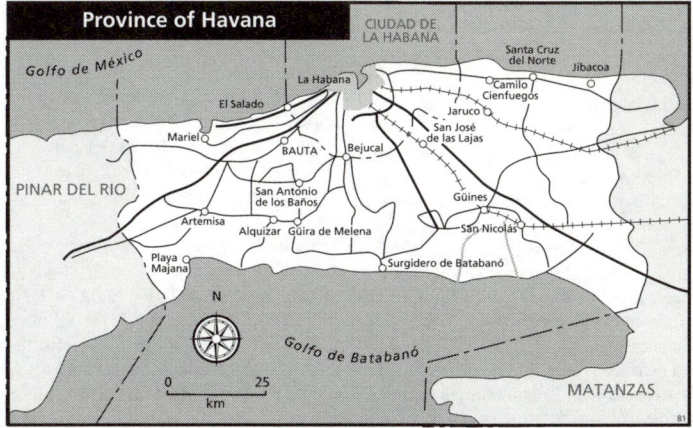

Province of Havana

Province of Havana

The Province of Havana has a northern coastline east and west of the city of Havana, the Province of Matanzas to the east, the Caribbean Sea and the Golfo de Batabanó to the south and the Province of Pinar del Río to the west. The southern coast is mostly swamp and wetlands, but access by sea to the Isla de la Juventud is from here. The province is traversed by major transport routes, both road and rail, heading out from the capital to the rest of the island, so most people are on their way to somewhere else and do not bother to stop. Much of the agriculture in the province is devoted to growing food for the city, such as cattle, pigs, fruit, vegetables and root crops, but there is also sugar cane and some tobacco. There is also a fair amount of industry, with cement works, thermal electricity plants, sugar mills and factories, alongside which you will find post-Revolutionary housing estates featuring a large amount of concrete. The capital of the province is **Bauta**, near the beginning of the Carretera Central, the old route to Pinar del Río, but it is of little interest to travellers.

Havana

Area 5,731 sq km, *Population* 680,700, *Density* 118.5 per sq km, *Urban* 78.3%

with fan, shared bathroom, organized activities including bicycles, motorbikes, volleyball, tennis, scuba diving and snorkelling, pizza house, bar, restaurant, gift shop and pool, transport to/from Havana or Varadero and booking provided by Cubamar. This resort does accept foreigners. However, there are several other places for Cubans, which do not, and which may be open only in the Cuban summer holiday season. 14 km east of *El Abra* is the Puerto Escondido marina, which has boat trips, fishing, snorkelling, scuba diving and windsurfing.

From Santa Cruz del Norte you can drive inland via the Central Camilo Cienfuegos to **Jaruco**, and 6 km to the west, the **Parque Escaleras de Jaruco**. The *escaleras*, or stairs, are geological formations in the limestone and there are caves, forests and other rock formations to see, set in some very picturesque landscape. There is a hotel in the park, but it is for Cubans only. The restaurant at the entrance is only open at weekends for lunch but there is a nice view down to the coast from the terrace.

Heading south there are towns like San José de las Lajas, **Güines** and **San Nicolás**, old towns which are now ringed

with industry and concrete housing blocks. The autopista bypasses them and travellers rarely stop there now.

THE SOUTH COAST

There is no coastal road as along the north coast, which means that although there are several nice beaches within striking distance of Havana, they are difficult to get to and beach hopping is tricky. The easiest to get to from Havana is probably **Playa Majana**, in the west of the province, access to which is off the Carretera Central, the old road to Pinar del Río. From here northwards to the **Bahía de Mariel** is the island's narrowest point. The main town on the south coast is **Batabanó**, 51 km from Havana. There has been a settlement here since the 16th century, but most travellers are only passing through on their way to **Surgidero de Batabanó** to catch the ferry or hydrofoil (*kometa*) to Isla de la Juventud. The latter is a ramshackle fishing town of wooden houses. There are several small restaurants selling fried fish, which makes a pleasant change from fried chicken, but only peso accommodation which may not accept foreigners.

WEST OF HAVANA

Heading out of the city west along the north coast on the autopista La Habana-Mariel, you come to **Playa Baracoa**, which is a nice place to come for some relaxation on the beach. 25 km west of Havana is **El Salado**, another beach with clear water, although some parts are rocky, but there is good snorkelling as a result. Taxi from Havana US$25. There is a hotel here, **B-C** *Villa El Salado*, T 805089, popular with Germans, 41 rooms in attractive setting, pool, reasonably priced restaurant, tours offered, nightclub on Saturday. Lots of watersports on offer, including rowing boat hire and scuba diving.

Don't expect a beach at **Mariel**, further west along the coast and scene of the mass exodus in 1980, known as the Mariel boatlift. This is a major industrial town, with the largest cement plant on the island, a shipyard, a thermal electricity plant and a new duty free industrial zone. If you continue along the coastal road, you enter the province of Pinar del Río on the way to Viñales.

South of the provincial capital is **San Antonio de los Baños**, a pleasant country town of some 30,000 people, set in an agricultural area where citrus and tobacco are grown. The Río Ariguanabo flows through the town, going underground by a large ceiba tree near the railway station. The town is large enough to have two museums: the **Museo del Humor**, Calle 60 y Av 45, open Tuesday-Saturday 1100-1800, Sunday 0900-1300, US$2, with an unusual collection of cartoons, drawings and other humorous items, worth visiting if you are in the area; and the **Museo Municipal**, Calle 66 entre 41 y 43, open Tuesday-Friday 1000-1800, Saturday 1300-1700, Sunday 0900-1300, with exhibitions of local historical interest. There is also an art gallery displaying the work of local artists, the **Galería Provincial Eduardo Abela** on Calle 58 3708 entre 37 y 39, closed Mondays, US$1. The reason most foreigners come here, though, is because of the hotel *Las Yagrumas*, featured in Canadian holiday brochures, which is on the banks of the river 3 km outside the town in a lovely setting. It is a low key resort of 120 rooms in a 2-storey building, the rooms overlooking the river are quieter than those looking over the pool. You can take boat trips or go fishing on the river and there is tennis, squash and an indoor games room. All-inclusive packages are available including buffet meals, tours and unlimited rum and Cuban beer.

Western Cuba

HAVANA

San Antonio de los Baños
Güira de Melena
Playa del Cajío
Cayería Las Cayamas
BAUTA
Caimito
Guanajay
Artemisa
Guanimar
Cayos los Guzmanes
Santa Fé
La Boca
Mariel
Cabañas Quiebra Hacha
El Morrillo
San Pedro
San Diego de Núñez
Bahía Honda
Luis Carrasco
Candelaria
Playa José Martí Majana
Cantón
Cayos del Hambre
Las Terrazas
Las Terrazas
San Cristóbal
Santa Cruz de los Pinos
Los Palacios
Punta Carraguao
Cayo Levisa
Pan de Guajaibón 698m
Cuevada Las Portales
Paso Real de San Diego
Cubanacán
Maspotón
Punta del Gato
Manuel Sanguily
La Palma
San Diego de los Baños
La Güira NP
Herradura
Playa Dayaniguas
Alonso de Rojas
Cayo Arenas
Cayetano
Pico Grande 521m
Viñales
Consolación del Sur
Puerta de Golpe
Playa El Guanal
Cayos de San Felipe
Cayo El Coco
Cayo Inés de Soto
Puerto Esperanza
Piloto
Las Ovas
Playa La Coloma
Cayo Real
San Lucía
Pan de Azúcar
Minas de 616m Matahambre
PINAR DEL RÍO
Llanura del Sur
Las Canas
Cayo Jutías Río del Medio
Ponó
Sumidero
San Juan y Martínez
Punta de Cartas
Bailén Cortés
Punta Tábaco
Dimas
Guane
Isabel Rubio
Las Martinas
Cabo Francés
Cayo Rapado Grande
Sierra de los Órganos NP
Mendua
Arroyo de Mantua
Sandino
Manuel Lazo
Cayo de Buenavista
La Sierra
Clavellinas
Bolívar
La Fé
Vallecito
La Bajada
Las Coloradas
María La Gorda
Cabo Francés
Golfo de México
Archipiélago de los Colorados y de Santa Isabel
Golfo de Guanahacabibes
Península de Guanahacabibes NP
Cayos de la Leña
Las Tumbas
Punta El Cajón
Cabo de San Antonio
Caleta Larga
Bahía de Corrientes
Cabo Corrientes

Sierra del Rosario
Sierra del Sur

N
50
0
km

Province of Pinar del Río

THE WEST of Cuba is blessed with an exotic landscape of limestone *mogotes*, caves and mountains, forested nature reserves and tobacco plantations. There is world class scuba diving, good beaches all round the coast and wetlands for migrant water fowl. The provincial towns and villages are quiet and agricultural, a complete contrast with Havana, from where most travellers come.

WEST FROM HAVANA

A tour to Viñales with one of the many tour companies (about US$45) is a good way of organizing a flying visit to western Cuba from Havana. You will be picked up at around 0800 from your Havana hotel, visit cigar and rum factories in Pinar del Río (you may prefer to skip these and spend an hour exploring the town), stop for a drink at *Hotel Los Jazmines* with a spectacular view of Viñales valley, lunch at Cueva del Indio (drinks and US$3 visit to a cave not included) then back to Havana, arriving at around 1800. If you want to stay more than a day, tour buses will drop you off and collect you around 1600 on the day you want to return.

A dual carriage highway has been completed almost to **Pinar del Río**, the major city west of Havana. It takes 1 hour to get to Pinar del Río on the autopista, a rather surreal experience, with modern motorway junctions but virtually no traffic using them except horse-drawn buses running to nearby villages. Some slip roads are unsurfaced, just mud and stones. Watch out for dogs sleeping peacefully in the fast lane.

Vultures can be seen circling overhead. A few kilometres from the start of the autopista, you pass a lake to the south of the road which is used for training by national canoeing and rowing teams and for international competitions. The autopista passes through flat or gently rolling countryside, with large stretches of sugar cane, tobacco fields and some rice fields, with scattered royal palms and distant views of the Cordillera de Guaniguanico, separated sharply from the southern plains by a geological fault. There are also large uncultivated areas used as rough pasture, with hump-backed zebu and other cattle, and white cattle egrets which help rid them of parasites. You can see traditional houses built of palm planks, thatched with palm leaves, and plenty of *vegas*. There are large irrigation lakes to the north of the road, but these are out of sight behind the earth dams which enclose them.

An alternative route is to leave the autopista at **Candelaria** or **Santa Cruz de los Pinos** for the Carretera Central, quite a good road which adds only 20 minutes to the journey. It passes through more

Province of Pinar del Río

The western end of the island is dominated by one of the island's three main mountain ranges, the **Cordillera de Guaniguanico**, which is divided into the **Sierra del Rosario** in the east (rising to the **Pan de Guajaibón**, at 699m its highest point) and the **Sierra de los Organos** in the west, which form a curious Chinese-looking landscape with steep-sided limestone hills and flat, fertile valleys. A fault line creates a sharp boundary between these mountains and a wide expanse of rolling farmland in the southern part of the province, centred on the pleasant but unspectacular provincial capital of Pinar del Río. This western tip of Cuba is bounded by the Gulf of Mexico to the north, the Yucatán Straits to the west, the Gulf of Batabanó to the south and the province of Havana to the east.

The province contains three major nature reserves: a 250 sq km Biosphere Reserve in the Sierra del Rosario, a 132 sq km National Monument in the Sierra de los Organos around Viñales, and a 1,175 sq km Biosphere Reserve in the Guanahacabibes peninsula at the western tip.

Pinar del Río grows about 70% of Cuba's tobacco crop and almost every agricultural area is dotted with *vegas*, curious tent-shaped windowless structures made of palm thatch which are used for drying tobacco leaves, a process which takes at least 45 days (easy to enter and take photographs). The fields are ploughed, mostly with oxen, in September and October. The crop is transplanted into the fields in November, with the leaves picked over the following months. The cigar factory in Pinar del Río has regular tours and in the harvest season it is possible to visit some villages to see an *escogida de tabaco*, where the best leaves are selected for further processing. The flat lands of San Juan y Martínez are where the very best tobacco is grown.

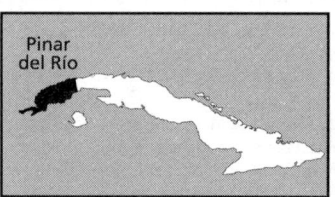

Pinar del Río

Area 10,925 sq km, *Population* 721,900, *Density* 66.1 per sq km, *Urban* 62.5%

intensively farmed countryside, with citrus and other fruit trees. Villages straggle along the road, with colonnaded single storey traditional houses and newer post-Revolution concrete block structures. There are *paladares* in some villages, including a rooftop one in Candelaria: *Fusilazo*, US$5-10, three blocks south of the Carretera Central and 500m east of the junction with the road for Soroa.

LAS TERRAZAS

On the autopista, 51 km west of Havana, the Sierra del Rosario appears on the right and a roadside billboard announces the turning to **Las Terrazas/Moka**, 4 km north of the autopista. However, after that there is little signposting through a confusing series of side roads; you will have to ask the way. There is a barrier at the entrance to the Biosphere Reserve which covers 260 sq km of the eastern Sierra del Rosario. Admission to the Reserve, US$3 (diplomats US$1, other residents US$2) unless you have a reservation at the hotel. **Las Terrazas** was built in 1971 as a forestry and soil conservation station, with nearby slopes terraced to prevent erosion. It is a pleasant settlement of white-painted houses and a long apartment block overlooking the lake of San Juan, which now houses an ecological research centre. In

Las Terrazas

Not to scale

Loma del Mulo 486m

Loma Las Peladas 380m

Buenavista

Santa Serafina

Ecological Centre

Toll

Lago de San Juan

Las Terrazas
Hotel Moka

Camping El Taburete

To Havana

Loma El Taburete 453m

La Victoria

Km 51

Toll

San Pedro

Santa Catalina

Loma del Salón 564m

Toll

Autopista Havana - Pinar del Río

Sulphur Baths

R. Bayate

To Pinar del Río

Camping La Caridad

Soroa

To Candelaria

Paths & Trails
1. Cañada del Infierno Trail
2. San Juan River Trail
3. El Taburete Path
4. Buenavista Coffee Plantation Trail
5. Las Delicias Path
6. La Serafina Path

Las Terrazas there is a *paladar* (US$7), craft workshops, a gym, a cinema and a museum which sometimes holds *canturías* or folk music sessions.

● **Accommodation** Above the village is the new 26-room **A2-A3** *Hotel Moka* run in cooperation with the Cuban Academy of Sciences as an ecotourism centre, breakfast US$5, other meals US$15, transfer from Havana US$32, a/c, satellite TV, T 085-2921/2996, 80-2694, Havana marketing office, Sr Falcón, T 33-3814/3900, F 33-5516/3814/3961. The hotel complex is beautifully designed and laid out, in Spanish colonial style with tiled roofs, staff are friendly and knowledgeable, gardens behind the hillside site have a tennis court and a pleasant swimming pool where you can bathe. Within Las Terrazas there are also *Casa del Lago*, right on the water, 2 a/c rooms, TV, bar, phone, pier; and *El Taburete Camp Site*, 54 cabañas on the hill, set in beautiful landscape near a river where you can bathe. This is an unusual opportunity to stay in a nature reserve with tropical evergreen forests, 850 plant species, 82 bird species, an endemic water lizard, the world's second smallest frog and world-class experts on tap. Even the hotel receptionist is an ecology PhD.

Hiking around Las Terrazas

The hills behind the hotel rise to the **Loma del Salón** (564m). There are several easy hiking trails: to the partly restored 19th

century **Buenavista** coffee plantation (restaurant has *pollo brujo*, US$10 for hotel guests, US$12-15 for others); 3 km along the San Juan river to the old **La Victoria** coffee plantation and sulphur springs; 4 km along **La Serafina** path to the ruins of the 19th century **Santa Serafina** coffee plantation, an excellent walk for seeing birds like the Cuban trogon, the solitaire, woodpeckers and the Cuban tody; 8 km along the Cañada del Infierno valley to the **San Pedro** and **Santa Catalina** coffee plantations. There are also more demanding whole-day hikes. The cost of a day hiking with a professional ecologist as guide is US$33-41 for one person, falling to US$14-18 with 6 people. Other activities include riding (US$6/hour), mountain bikes (US$1/hour), rowing on the lake (US$2/hour) and fishing.

SOROA

If travelling by car, you can make a detour to **Soroa** in the Sierra del Rosario, 81 km southwest of the capital, either by continuing 18 km west then southeast from Moka through the Sierra del Rosario, or directly from the autopista, driving northwest from Candelaria. It is a spa and resort in luxuriant hills. As you drive into the area from the south, a sign on the right indicates the **Mirador de Venus** and **Baños Romanos**. Past the baths is the *Bar Edén* (open till 1800), where you can park before walking up to the Mirador (25 minutes, free on foot, US$3 on a horse). From the top you get fine views of the southern plains, the forest-covered Sierra and Soroa itself. Lots of

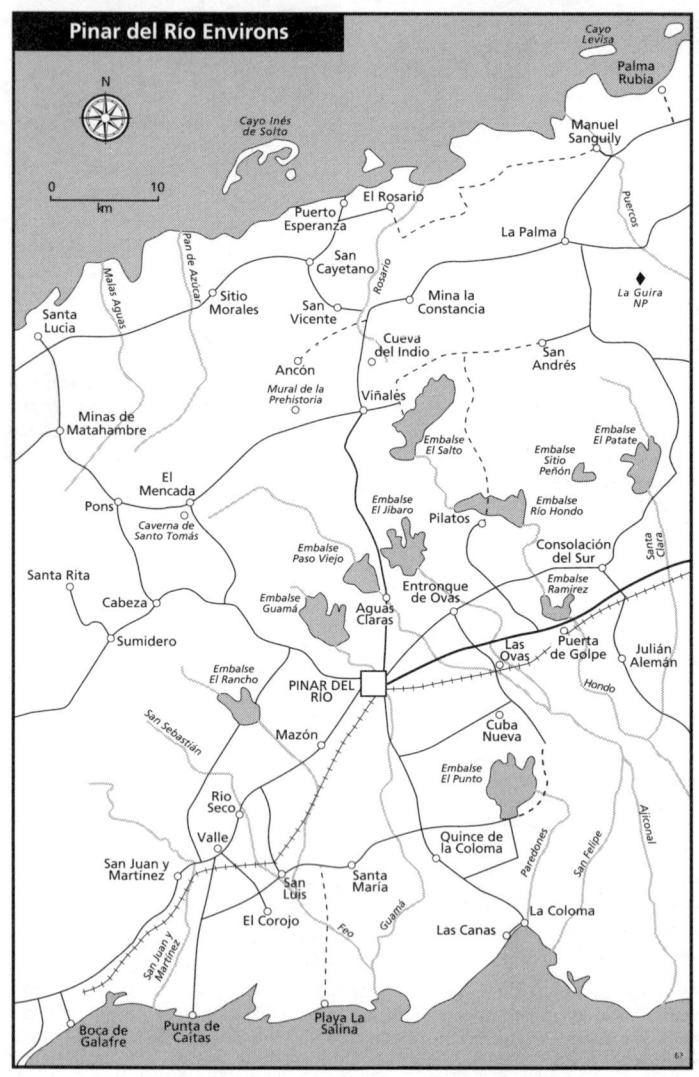

Pinar del Río Environs

N

0   10
km

Cayo Levisa
Palma Rubia
Manuel Sanguily
Cayo Inés de Solta
El Rosario
Puerto Esperanza
La Palma
Puercos
San Cayetano
Malas Aguas
Pan de Azúcar
Rosario
Santa Lucia
Sitio Morales
San Vicente
Mina la Constancia
La Guira NP
Ancón
Cueva del Indio
San Andrés
Mural de la Prehistoria
Viñales
Minas de Matahambre
Embalse El Salto
Embalse Sitio Peñón
Embalse El Patate
El Mencada
Pons
Caverna de Santo Tomás
Embalse El Jibaro
Pilatos
Embalse Río Hondo
Santa Rita
Embalse Paso Viejo
Consolación del Sur
Santa Clara
Cabeza
Embalse Guamá
Aguas Claras
Entronque de Ovas
Embalse Ramírez
Sumidero
Embalse El Rancho
Las Ovas
Puerta de Golpe
Julián Alemán
PINAR DEL RÍO
Mazón
Hondo
San Sebastián
Cuba Nueva
Río Seco
Embalse El Punto
Valle
Alcoranal
San Juan y Martínez
San Luis
Santa María
Quince de la Coloma
Paredones
San Felipe
El Corojo
Feo
Guamá
Las Canas
La Coloma
San Juan y Martínez
Boca de Galafre
Punta de Caitas
Playa La Salina

birds, butterflies, dragonflies and lizards around the path; many flowers in season.

Further north is an **Orchidarium** with over 700 species of which 250 are native to Cuba, as well as ferns and begonias (check if the orchids are in bloom before visiting, guided tours between 0830-1140, 1340-1555 daily, US$3) and the *Castillo de las Nubes* restaurant (1200-1900, entrées US$5-6). Across the road from the Orchidarium is a waterfall (250m along a paved path, entry US$2), worth a visit if you are in the area.

● **Accommodation** At the resort, **A3-B** *Horizontes Villa Soroa*, T 85-2122, 49 cabins and 10 self-catering houses, a/c, phone, radio, some have VCR and private pool, restaurant *El Centro* (quite good), lunch US$8, dinner US$10, disco, bar, Olympic-sized swimming pool, bike rental, riding nearby and handicrafts and dollar shop. Despite the gloomy cabins, it's a peaceful place. The hotel runs one day, gently paced hikes around the main sights of the area with picnic for US$10, to caves for US$12. *Pepe* at Km 5.5 north of autopista junction on the west of the main road into Soroa, is a *casa particular*. There is no officially licensed *paladar*.

SAN DIEGO DE LOS BAÑOS AND LA GÜIRA

Nearer Pinar del Río another detour north off the Carretera Central at Entronque de San Diego is to the spa of **San Diego de los Baños** and **La Güira**, also in fine scenery. In the wet season a nearby irrigation lake, the Embalse La Juventud, often floods and then this diversion becomes compulsory. San Diego de los Baños is a pretty little village, with colonnaded houses and tree lined square, right on the southern edge of the Sierra del Rosario. It has become one of the most popular health farms for its mineral waters, but not everyone who comes here is sick.

● **Accommodation** **B** *Hotel Mirador* on Calle 23 Final, T 335412, F 335410, 3-star, has a spa with warm sulphur baths, massage, swimming pool, car rental office, rooms have a/c, phone, satellite TV. *Hotel Libertad*, just west of the main square is for Cubans only. *Paladar Sorpresa* opposite *Libertad*.

A few kilometres west of San Diego an impressive neo-Gothic gateway leads to the **Parque Nacional La Güira**. Inside there are extensive neglected 19th century gardens, pools and statues, with the ruins of a Gothic mansion. There is a small bar near the entrance. Behind, the road winds up through the hills to an army recreation centre with its own swimming pool; behind this there is an enormous, cheap (US$3 main course) and rather run-down restaurant. The holiday *cabañas* further up this road are closed and the ones at the entrance are for Cubans only. The **Cueva de las Portales** just north of here was Che Guevara's HQ during the Cuban missile crisis, and there is a small exhibition of military and personal relics.

MASPOTÓN

For **Maspotón**, near **Alonso de Rojas** in the mangrove wetlands close to the south coast, leave the autopista at Los Palacios and drive south for 25 km. This is an interesting wildlife area close to the bird migration route from North to South America, but is run by Horizontes as a 134 sq km hunting resort, where migratory ducks, long-tail and white wing doves, quail, guinea fowl and pheasant can all be shot, or there is fresh water fishing. The *Club de Caza Maspotón*, Granja Arrocera La Cubana, Los Palacios, T 85-5914, has 20 a/c rooms, with restaurant, bar, shop and swimming pool, hunting equipment for rent.

PINAR DEL RIO

Phone code 82

The capital of Pinar del Río province is lively and attractive, giving a good taste of provincial Cuba. The centre consists of single-storey neoclassical houses with columns, some with other interesting architectural detail. Under the porches, there is a thriving trade in one-person businesses, from selling snacks to repairing cigarette lighters. The main tourist

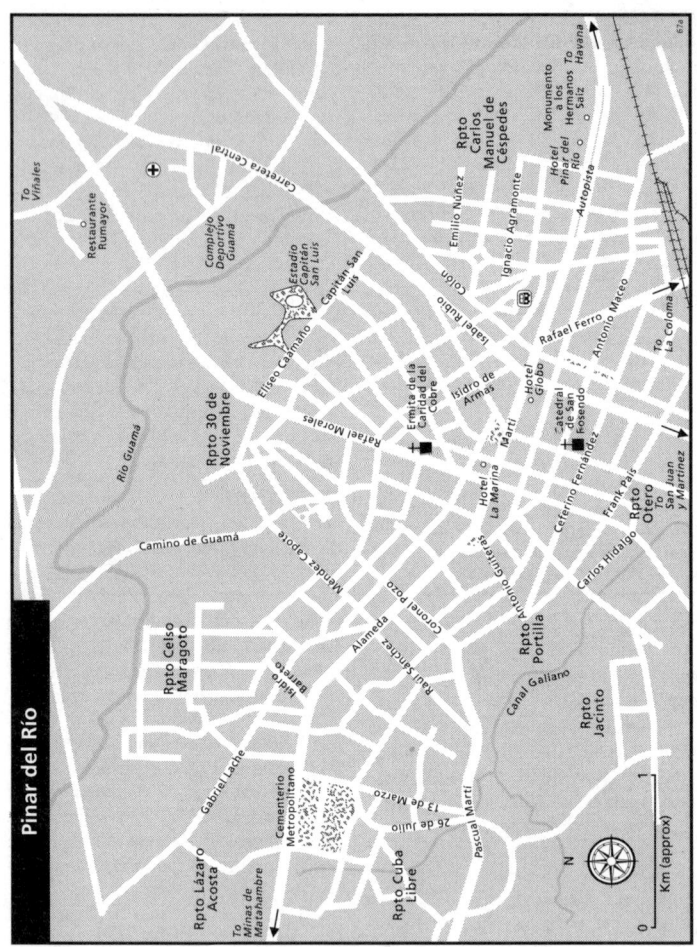

attractions are the cigar factory, which reputedly makes the best in Cuba (US$2 for a short visit, open Monday-Friday 0900-1630, Saturday 0900-1200), and the rum factory on Isabel Rubio, which makes a special rum flavoured with miniature wild guavas: *Guayabita del Pinar*, which comes either dry or sweet. This costs US$3.90 at the factory, US$5 in Havana, but only US$3 in the departure lounge at Havana airport.

Between the two is the pretty cream-coloured Cathedral of **San Rosendo**. A short walk along José Martí to the east is the **Museo de Ciencias Naturales Sandalio de Noda**, with geological and natural history, open Monday-Saturday 0800-1400. There is also a small historical museum and an art gallery.

Pinar del Río is one of several Cuban towns which have changed street names

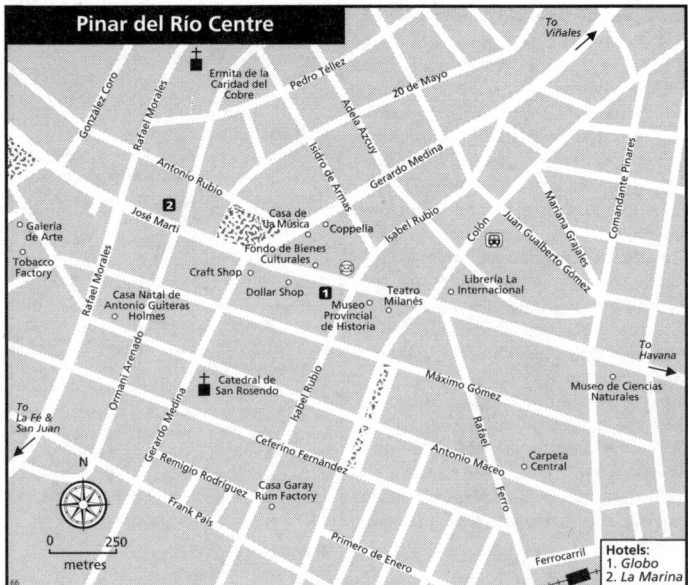

Pinar del Río Centre

To Viñales

González Coro
Rafael Morales
Ermita de la Caridad del Cobre
Pedro Téllez
20 de Mayo
Adela Azcuy
Isidro de Armas
Gerardo Medina
Antonio Rubio
José Martí
Galería de Arte
Casa de la Música
Coppelia
Isabel Rubio
Colón
Juan Gualberto Gómez
Mariana Grajales
Comandante Pinares
Tobacco Factory
Rafael Morales
Fondo de Bienes Culturales
Craft Shop
Dollar Shop
Casa Natal de Antonio Guiteras
Holmes
Ormani Arenado
Museo Provincial de Historia
Teatro Milanés
Librería La Internacional
To Havana
Catedral de San Rosendo
Gerardo Medina
Isabel Rubio
Máximo Gómez
Museo de Ciencias Naturales
To La Fé & San Juan
N
Ceferino Fernández
Remiglio Rodríguez
Frank País
Casa Garay Rum Factory
Antonio Maceo
Rafael Ferro
Carpeta Central
0 250
metres
Primero de Enero
Ferrocarril

Hotels:
1. *Globo*
2. *La Marina*

but continue to use the old ones as well as the new, official names. It can be confusing when names on the map conflict with what people really call the streets, eg Vélez Caviedes is also Ormani Arenado, while Virtudes is also Ceferino Fernández.

Excursions

The nearest beach 25 km to the south is **Las Canas**, near **La Coloma**.

The Carretera Central continues west from Pinar del Río through pleasant farming country with villages strung along the road, sugar and tobacco fields, citrus trees and pasture. There are distant views of the mountains to the north and clearly marked side roads lead south to small beaches at **Boca de Galafre** and **Bailén**. The beach chalets at *Villa Boca de Galafre* are now closed, but a little further west along the beach a new chalet complex was close to completion in 1997. The beach is sandy but holds little appeal. Several kilometres down the road to Playa Bailén and 2 km before you get to the

beach, there is a crocodile farm, where you can get uncomfortably close to the babies and can hold them. However, unless you are lucky, or come at feeding time, you are a 500m telephoto lens away from the 4-5m beasts. Entrance is US$3, photographs are US$10 and video cameras are US$50. Note that small cars are likely to get bogged down in the sandy drive of the farm. The *Villa Playa Bailén* on the beach, T 33401, is a sprawling resort stretching 2 km along the sand, with small A-frame cabins on the beach and concrete houses with self-catering facilities behind. It is very popular with Cubans in the summer months and even at other times of the year foreigners are likely to be told it is full. The beach here is sandy and deeper than at Boca de Galafre, but spoilt by the run off from the Río Cuyaguateje, which makes the water muddy and there is no reef to snorkel on.

Back on the main road, **Isabel Rubio** has a gas station with a dollar shop selling drinks, toiletries and canned foods. To the north is a waterfall, **Salto de los Portales**. Ask locally for directions. From Isabel Rubio, a very pretty way to return to Pinar del Río (about 1 hour) is through Guane, Los Portales and Sumidero. **Guane**, a large pretty village with old houses and a little baroque church, is also the railway terminus. The road runs through limestone hills, crossing the pretty **Río Cuyaguateje** several times and passing through the **Valle de San Carlos**, a spectacular narrow valley with cliffs and steep wooded hills rising on either side. Farmers grow fruit, vegetables and tobacco, with ox-drawn ploughs furrowing the bright red soil and tent-shaped drying sheds everywhere. Other roads branch off into the mountains and from Cabeza there is a road to the **Valle de Santo Tomás** (with 25 km cave system), the copper mining centre of **Minas de Matahambre** and **Cayo Jutías** on the north coast.

Local information

● **Accommodation**

Prices: **L1** over US$200; **L2** US$151-200; **L3** US$101-150; **A1** US$81-100; **A2** US$61-80; **A3** US$46-60; **B** US$31-45; **C** US$21-30; **D** US$12-20; **E** US$7-11; **F** up to US$6

As you leave the autopista on the north side of José Martí, but in walking distance of the city centre, is the **C** *Hotel Pinar del Río*, Calle Martí final, T 5070-7, excellent value, staff friendly and helpful, swimming pool, nightclub, car hire etc; **C** *Globo*, right in the centre near corner of José Martí and Isabel Rubio, beautiful tiled staircase worth a peep even if not staying.

D *Villa Internacional Aguas Claras*, T 2722, 7.5 km north on road to Viñales, 2-star, 50 a/c rooms in small chalets in beautiful landscaped garden around (unchlorinated?) pool, hot showers, restaurant has usual pork and chicken US$5 but tastier than most, beer US$0.85, excellent value, recommended; **D-E** *La Marina*, north side of José Martí close to Rafael Morales, the cheapest and really a peso hotel for Cubans.

Other hotels shown on the tourist map: *Vueltabajo*, *Lincoln* and *Italia* are currently closed. There are about 15 licensed *casas particulares* and several who are not, but you should stay clear of the latter to avoid getting yourself or Cubans into trouble. One which has been recommended is *Sr Juan Carlos Otaño*, Primero de Mayo 29, Apartment 16, also known as The Teacher, he speaks good English.

● **Places to eat**

The state-run *Rumayor*, 2 km on Viñales road, specializes in *pollo ahumado* (smoked chicken), overpriced at US$6.50, grim toilets, open 1200-2200, closed Thursday, cabaret at night, US$5, US$15 for a bottle of 5-year old Havana Club, good show. There are three *paladares*; *Nuestra Casa* on Colón 161 entre Ceferino Fernández y Vandama, pleasant, nicely decorated roof terrace, enormous meal for US$7, pork or chicken with two salads, yuca, masses of *papas fritas* and *congris*; *Don Miguel*, Ormani Arenado esquina Ceferino Fernández, good but less food for more money, overpriced mineral water; another *paladar* on José Martí opposite the Museum. The restaurant at *Hotel Pinar del Río* is more expensive at around US$12. A peso restaurant *El Bodegón* on Ormani Arenado, looks attractive but refuses to serve foreigners.

● **Entertainment**

The town is very lively on Saturday nights, and to a lesser extent on Fridays. There is live music everywhere, salsa, son, Mexican music, international stuff. The **Casa de la Música** on Gerardo Medina next to *Coppelia* has live music, but you will also find it all along José Martí, with competitions and displays. *Disco Rita*, on González Coro, is an open air venue popular with teenagers, where they play loud, US-style disco music, entry 2 pesos, the only drink on sale is neat rum at 25 pesos a bottle. The classy night life, however, is the disco in the *Hotel Pinar del Río*. There are three theatre groups, one children's and two adult's, which give occasional performances.

● **Shopping**

There is a well-stocked dollar shop on the south side of José Martí just west of Isabel Rubio. The main craft shop is on the corner of José Martí and Gerardo Medina. Photo shop on the north side of José Martí just west of Isabel Rubio, another just round the corner on Isabel Rubio just south of José Martí.

● **Transport**

Local Car hire: Havanautos and Transautos both have offices in *Hotel Pinar del Río*. Distances from Pinar del Río are 157 km to Havana, 159 km to María La Gorda, 103 km to Las Terrazas, 88 km to Soroa, 25 km to Viñales.

Road Bus: the bus station is on Colón, north of José Martí, near Gómez. Eight buses a day to Havana, first one at 0330, most of the rest early morning, last at 1400, US$7, 2 hours. May be necessary to book in advance in peak travel periods. Buses run to surrounding villages, mostly one in larly morning, one around 1800, services unreliable. **Taxi**: Long distance travel by taxi is possible but you will need very good Spanish to negotiate effectively. From Pinar del Río to Havana you might be quoted US$50, but from Havana to Pinar del Río it will be US$80. Pinar del Río to Viñales about US$20, although locals can hire a taxi for the same distance for about US$5.

Train For travel to Pinar del Río, train from Havana's Estación 19 de Noviembre/del Occidente, rather than bus, is recommended (leaves Havana 0500, book 1300 day before in peak periods, leaves Pinar del Río 1702, 8 hours, US$6); slow but comfortable, the line continues to Guane.

WEST OF PINAR DEL RIO TO PENINSULA DE GUANAHACABIBES

Follow the Carretera Central west to Isabel Rubio, after which the countryside becomes completely flat. The villages are less lively and agricultural landscapes less varied, with plantations of Caribbean Pine in some stretches. On the north side of the road 7 km west of Isabel Rubio is the turning for **Laguna Grande**, a lake where you can fish. A few miles further on at **Punta Colorada** is a small beach.

● **Accommodation** *Villa Turística Laguna Grande*, T 2430, 12 cabins with a/c, radio, TV, fridge.

The main road continues through **Sandino** and **La Fe** to **Manuel Lazo**. After this village potholes are more common and the last 15 km or so to the coast are through semi-deciduous dry coastal woodland. On reaching the coast at **La Bajada**, a very desolate little village, an immigration post will ask to see your documents.

The **Peninsula de Guanahacabibes** which forms the western tip of Cuba is a Natural Biosphere Reserve and there is a scientific station at La Bajada. The reserve covers 1,175 sq km but has not yet been developed for ecotourism. The peninsula is formed of very recent limestone, with an irregular rocky surface and patchy soil cover. There are interesting fossil coastlines, caves and blue holes; but with dense woodland on the south coast and mangrove on the north, the peninsula is uninviting for the casual hiker. However, for keen naturalists there are 12 amphibian species, 29 reptiles including iguana species, 10 mammals (including *carabalí* and *jutia conga*) and 147 bird species including 9 of the 22 which are endemic to Cuba.

To the west of La Bajada, a track for 4WD vehicles continues to **Cabo de San Antonio**, where there are a few houses and a lighthouse built in 1849 and named after the Spanish governor, Roncalli. The coastline has several pretty white sand beaches and clear waters, but is otherwise lonely and desolate.

The main road continues 12 km south to **María La Gorda**, reputedly the best diving centre in Cuba (see **Diving and marine life**, page 24). There is a small tourist development, with beach houses, **C**, a restaurant (breakfast US$5, lunch or dinner US$15, food dabolical), a bar selling sandwiches (US$2.50) and a shop with camera film and dry biscuits but not much else. A guide is available for a day's birdwatching at a nearby lake. For divers, Marsub (Calle B, esquina 15, Havana, T 33-3055, F 33-3481) organizes a package including accommodation, food, diving and transfers from Havana. The dive boat leaves 0930 and 1530 for the offshore reef (US$30 per dive, plus US$7.50 a day to rent equipment for those not on a package). There are several wrecks off the western peninsula and fresh water cave diving in the blue holes is also possible though not on offer as an organized activity. The sea is very clear, warm and calm. There is good snorkelling with small coral heads close to the white sand beach, but non-divers will find the attractions limited and would probably find a day visit to a less distant beach more satisfactory.

● **Transport** A package tour or rented car are the only practical ways to visit by land. Local buses run unreliably to María La Gorda from the equally remote villages of Las Martinas and Sandino, around 0600 and 1800. Tourists may also be able to travel on the weekly bus which takes resort staff from Pinar del Río, leaving from the Ministry of Tourism building opposite the Palacio de Justicia at 0830 on Tuesdays. For visitors arriving by yacht, María La Gorda is a port of entry. The resort can be contacted by satellite phone 00 874 683 680 510, or satellite fax 00 874 683 680 520 at US$6.50/minute. Land-based phone is 087-3121.

VINALES

Phone code 8

North of Pinar del Río, the road leads across pine-covered hills and valley for 25 km to **Viñales**, a delightful small town in a dramatic valley in the **Sierra de los Organos**. The valley has a distinctive landscape, with steep-sided limestone mountains called *mogotes* rising dramatically from fertile flat-floored valleys, where farmers cultivate the red soil for tobacco, fruits and vegetables. As in so much of rural Cuba, horses, pigs, oxen, zebu cattle and chickens are everywhere, including on the main road. An area of 132 sq km around Viñales has been declared a National Monument. Hiking in the valleys is perfectly safe, but if venturing into the mountains themselves, it would be sensible to take a local guide, at around US$5 a day.

Viñales itself is a pleasant town, with trees and wooden colonnades along the main street, red tiled roofs and a main square with a little-used cathedral and a Casa de Cultura with art gallery.

Excursions 2 km west is the **Mural de la Prehistoria**, painted by **Lovigildo González**, a disciple of the Mexican Diego Rivera, between 1959 and 1976; tourist restaurant nearby. 6 km north of Viñales is the **Cueva del Indio**, a cave which you can travel on foot or by boat (US$3 for foreigners), very beautiful. There is a restaurant nearby where tour parties are given a lunch of suckling pig (*lechón*). The

Rumbos tour includes lunch but not the cave, and not drinks taken with lunch, even water is an 'extra'. Beyond the restaurant is a little farm, well kept, with little red pigs running around, oxen and horses. Riding is US$4/hour. Rumbos also advertises day trips to a disco in the **Cueva de San Miguel**, short hiking trips to a *mogote*, visits to various caves and El Palenque de los Cimarrones, a restaurant and craft shop with a display of Cuban folklore. These are advertised as daily events, but don't rely on it.

● **Accommodation** **A3-B** *Los Jazmines* (Horizontes), Carretera de Viñales Km 25, 3 km before the town, in a superb location with travel brochure view of the valley, T 89-33404, 62 nice rooms and 16 *cabañas*, nightclub, breakfast buffet US$4 if not already included, lunch US$10, dinner US$12, unexciting restaurant, bar with snacks available, shops, (unchlorinated?) swimming pool, riding, easy transport, highly recommended; **A3-B** *Horizontes La Ermita*, Carretera de la Ermita Km 2, 3 km from town with magnificent view, T 89-3204, 62 rooms, a/c, phone, radio, shop, tennis court, wheelchair access, pool (not always usable), food not bad, breakfast included, lunch US$10, dinner US$12, recommended as beautiful, the

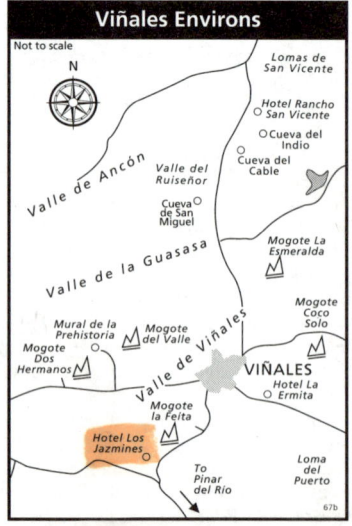

Viñales Environs

Not to scale

Lomas de San Vicente

Hotel Rancho San Vicente

Cueva del Indio

Cueva del Cable

Valle de Ancón

Valle del Ruiseñor

Cueva de San Miguel

Valle de la Guasasa

Mogote La Esmeralda

Mogote Coco Solo

Mural de la Prehistoria

Mogote del Valle

Mogote Dos Hermanos

Valle de Viñales

VIÑALES

Hotel La Ermita

Mogote la Feita

Hotel Los Jazmines

To Pinar del Río

Loma del Puerto

67b

Rocks, caves, valleys and mogotes

The rocks around Viñales are pure limestones, formed in the Jurassic period around 160 million years ago. Unlike most other rocks, limestone can be dissolved by rainwater. Rivers and streams often flow underground through extensive cave systems; most of the 10,000 recorded caves in Cuba are in the western province and one cave system in the Valle Santo Tomás consists of a total of 25 km of underground passages. Where a valley is formed in tropical limestone, often by downwards faulting of the rock, it may be filled with fertile red soil. Rotting vegetation increases the acidity of the groundwater on the valley floor. This 'aggressive' water eats into the valley sides, undercutting the rocks and producing steep cliff-like features. The valley floor is broken by isolated steep-sided hills, known to both English- and Spanish-speaking geologists by their Cuban name: *mogotes*. Other valleys (narrow gorges) are produced when the roof of a large cave collapses. Similar tropical limestone landscapes can be seen in parts of Puerto Rico and Jamaica.

Rapid drainage of rainwater into the rock produces dry growing conditions for plants. The limestone hills have a distinctive vegetation type, with palms (including the curious cork palm), deciduous trees, succulents, lianas and epiphytes. More than 20 species are endemics, found only in the Viñales area. The isolation of the *mogotes* has also produced distinctive animal species, with some types of snail found only on a single *mogote*.

farmers in the valley below are friendly and hospitable, they may invite you for a meal of their own fruit and vegetables or offer a home grown cigar; **B** *Horizontes Rancho San Vicente*, Valle de San Vicente, near Cueva del Indio, T 89-3200, 20 a/c cabañas, bar, restaurant, breakfast included, lunch US$8, dinner US$10, nightclub, shop, tourist information desk, nice pool, spa with warm sulphurous waters, mud baths with steroids, hormones, antibiotics and vitamins, other amusements on offer include physiotherapy, massage, acupuncture, digitopuncture, medical checkups. Book your hotel before you arrive as everywhere is often full. There are also several registered *casas particulares*. **Caridad Chirino**, Rafael Trejo 38, US$10, good food available.

● **Places to eat** *Paladar Restaurant*, or *Valle Bar*, T 93183, on the main street, small, friendly, recommended, *pollo frito* US$4, spaghetti US$2.50, steak, or just have a beer, US$1, and listen to the live music in the evening, can find you local accommodation with private families. Also licensed is *Casa Cocero*, which takes pesos. *Casa de Don Tomás* is the oldest house in Viñales (1879), state owned, features in Horizontes brochure.

● **Transport** Turistaxi from Havana to *Motel Los Jazmines* takes 2½ hours. Bus from Havana 0900, 3½ hours, US$8. Tour buses from Havana will drop you off if you want to stay more than a day and collect you about 1600 on the day you want to return. Truck to Pinar del Río 2 pesos.

Offshore, north of Viñales is **Cayo Levisa**, part of the **Archipiélago de los Colorados**, with a long, sandy beach and reef running parallel to the shore with good snorkelling and scuba diving (lots of fish). One small hotel, **A1** *Cayo Levisa* (Gran Caribe), 3-star, with 20 cabins, a/c, TV, restaurant, lunch US$10, dinner US$12, bar, shop, dive shop, waterskiing, windsurfing and sailing, no phone on site, in Havana T 666075 or contact Horizontes reservation centre T33-4238/4042, F 33-3161/4361. To get to Cayo Levisa go to Palma Rubia, from where it is 15 minutes by boat to the island. The Diving World dive centre has wooden boats of 10-12m for 8-14 divers. The guides and instructors are Cuban, speaking English and Spanish. There are about 15 dive sites between 15-35m deep and no more than 30 minutes away by boat.

VINALES TO HAVANA

From Viñales to Havana along the coast road takes about 4 hours by car. It is an attractive drive through sugar and tobacco plantations, pines, the mountains inland, the coast occasionally visible. All the small houses have flower gardens in front. You pass through **La Palma**, **Las Pozas** (which has a ruined church with a boring new one beside it), **Bahía Honda** and **Cabañas**; many agricultural collectives along the way. After Cabañas the road deteriorates; either rejoin the motorway back to the capital, or take the old coast road through the port of **Mariel** to enter Havana on Avenida 5.

Province of Matanzas

T HIS PROVINCE receives more visitors than any of the others because of the great attraction of the Varadero beach resort. Hotels of all sizes and to suit all budgets line the coast of this finger of land stretching out into the ocean. Many visitors never move from the beach and never find out what the rest of Cuba is like, isolated as they are within their tourist dollar enclave. The Zapata Peninsula in the south appeals to nature lovers and birdwatchers, but is more notorious for the Bay of Pigs attempted invasion, now a tourist attraction.

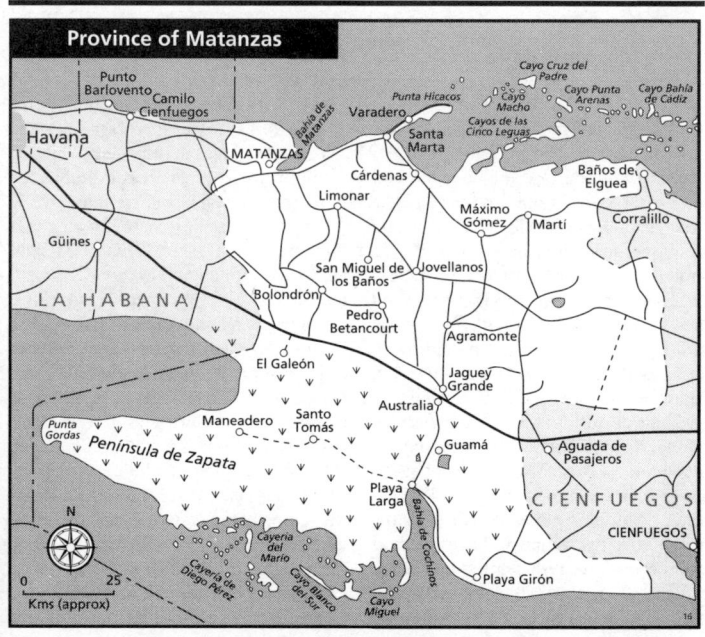

Province of Matanzas

Province of Matanzas

Matanzas province, to the east of Havana, is the second largest in the country, at 11,978 sq km. Its neighbours are La Habana to the west and Villa Clara and Cienfuegos to the east, while bounded by the Atlantic to the north and the Caribbean to the south. The province is largely flat, the highest point is the **Pan de Matanzas** at 380m. The northern coast is fringed with little coral islands covered in scrub and mangrove, many with idyllic, deserted, sandy beaches. The southern coast has one of Cuba's most notable geographic features, the **Ciénaga de Zapata**, a huge marsh covering the entire coast and the peninsula of the same name. It is a nature reserve, protecting many endemic species of flora and fauna, as well as numerous migrating birds. Despite the demands of beaches and nature tourism, Matanzas is quite an industrial province, with oil storage facilities and a supertanker base, citrus processing plants and many factories. There are 21 sugar mills in the province, but only 16 were in use for the 1997-98 grinding season. It was hoped that this would be a temporary closure to improve efficiency, with laid off workers found other jobs, rather than a western-style economic shock policy.

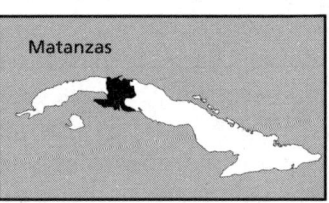

Area 11,978 sq km, *Population* 643,400, *Density* 53 per sq km, *Urban* 80.1%

MATANZAS

Population 115,000, *Phone code* 52

The old provincial town of **Matanzas** lies 104 km east of Havana along the Vía Blanca, which links the capital with Varadero beach, 34 km further east. The drive is unattractive along the coast and smelly because of the many small oil wells producing low-grade crude en route, but once you get into the hills there are good views. It is a sleepy town with old colonial buildings and a busy, ugly industrial zone. Both the rivers Yumurí and San Juan flow through the city. Walk along the riverside at dusk to watch the fishermen and take in the tranquillity and murmur of fellow observers. Most of the old buildings are between the two rivers, with another colonial district, Versalles, to the east of the Río Yumurí. This area was colonized in the 19th century by French refugees from Haiti after the revolution there. The newer district, Pueblo Nuevo,

also has many colonial houses. The industrial zone runs along the north shore of the bay, with railways running inland and around the bay to transport cargo. Matanzas has oil storage facilities, chemical and fertilizer plants, sugar, textile and paper mills and thermal power stations.

The town dates from 1693, when immigrants from the Canary Islands founded a settlement they called San Carlos y Severino de Matanzas between the rivers San Juan and Yumurí. Before that the area was known mainly for an attack in 1628 in the Bahía de Matanzas by the Dutch pirate Piet Heyn on a Spanish fleet carrying 12 million gold florins. The name Matanzas is thought to come from the mass slaughter of wild pigs to provision the fleets, but it could also refer to the killing of the Amerindians who lived here and called the bay Guanima. Around the time of the founding of the city, a fortress was built on the northern shore of the bay to keep out pirates and any

Music in Matanzas

Matanzas is a quiet town in all senses but one. If you listen carefully you can hear its unique heartbeat: one, two, one two three... With its docks and warehouses, Matanzas provided the ideal birthplace for the rumba and it is still the world capital of this exhilarating music and dance form. Families here are virtually born into the rumba: the latest incarnation of the Muñequitos de Matanzas has a young boy keeping the beat on the bamboo guagua. The Muñequitos are the acknowledged fathers and mothers of contemporary rumba, having set the standards for rumberos on their tours across the globe. Of course, the rumba Matancera bears not the slightest resemblance to its ballroom namesake. A rumba at the Casa de la Trova on Calle 85 involves intricate drumming, vocal improvisations and dancing which is by turns graceful, audacious, devotional and downright dirty. Rumba is a communal art form – the Columbia style was created by workers on the Columbia railway line; however, great names of the past are recalled in Columbias such as 'Malanga Murió'. On your way to – or staggering home from – a rumba, don't forget to stop at a bar and put a record by Matanzas' own Arsenio Rodríguez on the 1950s jukebox. Without Arsenio, there would have been no Conjunto son and thus no Latin salsa. If you've still got time, go and pay homage at the site of the dance hall where on a hot January night in 1879 Miguel Faílde created the Danzón Cubana, still the only authentic, unselfconscious marriage of orchestral sounds with African rhythms. It is now the Casa de Cultura José White, Calle 79 entre 288 y 290. Danzón is currently enjoying a revival: across Cuba, music is being reissued and orchestras are being formed. There is even a European Danzón orchestra based in Holland. The world has much to thank Matanzas for.

other invaders. The **Castillo de San Severino** is now rather dilapidated and mostly closed. The town became prosperous with the advent of sugar mills in the 1820s, followed by the railway in 1843. Most of the buildings date from this time and by the 1860s it was the second largest town in Cuba after Havana, with all the trappings of an important city such as a theatre, newspaper and library. It even became known as the 'Athens of Cuba' because of all the musicians and writers living there.

Like several Cuban towns, there are old street names and new street names, or in Matanzas' case, new street numbers. Although you will find numbers written on the streets, the locals still refer to the names. Streets running north-south in the old town have even numbers while streets running east-west have odd numbers. We have tried to list both names and numbers in our map.

Places of interest

Most visitors to Matanzas are merely passing through on their way from Havana to Varadero, but there are plenty of things to see if you are able to stop. There are several bridges in the town, but the one you are most likely to notice is the steel **Puente Calixto García**, built in 1899. By the bridge is the **Plaza de la Vigía** and the neo-classical fire station, **Parque de los Bomberos**. The **Galería de Arte Provincial** is on the plaza, open Monday 0900-1700, Tuesday-Saturday 0900-1800, US$1, and next door is **Ediciones Vigía**, where you can see books being produced. These are all handmade and in first editions of only 200 copies, so they are collectors' items, particularly if you get one signed. Also on Plaza de la Vigía is **Teatro Sauto**, a magnificent neo-classical building dating from 1862-63 and seating 775 people in three-tiered balconies for performances which have in the past included Enrico

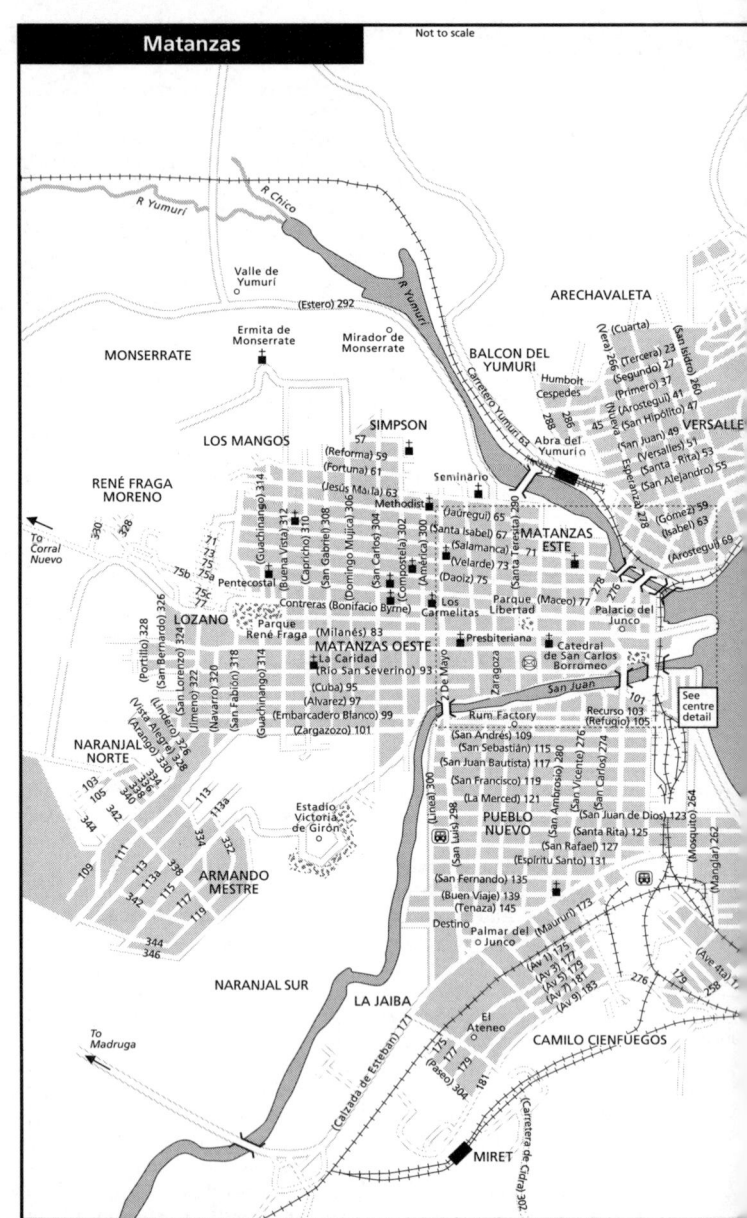

Matanzas

Not to scale

R Yumurí

R Chico

R Yumurí

Valle de Yumurí

(Estero) 292

Ermita de Monserrate

Mirador de Monserrate

MONSERRATE

ARECHAVALETA

BALCON DEL YUMURI

Carretera Yumurí 282

Humbolt Cespedes

Abra del Yumurio

45

(Cuarta)
(Tercera) 23
(Segundo) 27
(Primero) 37
(Arosteguí) 41
(San Hipólito) 47
(San Juan) 49
(Versalles) 51
(Santa Rita) 53
(San Alejandro) 55

(San Isidro) 260

VERSALLE

SIMPSON

57

(Reforma) 59

(Fortuna) 61

(Jesús María) 63

LOS MANGOS

RENÉ FRAGA MORENO

To Corral Nuevo

390
388

Seminario

Methodist

(Jáuregui) 65
(Santa Isabel) 67
(Salamanca) 71
(Velarde) 73
(Daoíz) 75

(América) 300

(Gómez) 59
(Isabel) 63

(Arosteguí) 69

MATANZAS ESTE

71

77

71
73
75
75a
75b
75c
75c
77

Pentecostal

Buena Vista 312
Caprico 310
San Gabriel 308
Domingo Mujica 306
San Carlos 304
Compostela 302

Guachinango 314

Contreras (Bonifacio Byrne)

Los Carmelitas

Parque Libertad

Palacio del Junco

LOZANO

Parque René Fraga

(Milanés) 83

MATANZAS OESTE

La Caridad

(Rio San Severino) 93

(Cuba) 95

(Alvarez) 97

(Embarcadero Blanco) 99

(Zargazozo) 101

Presbiteriana

Catedral de San Carlos Borromeo

See centre detail

101

Recurso 103

(Refugio) 105

(Portillo) 328
(San Bernardo) 326
(San Lorenzo) 324
(Jimeno) 322
(Navarro) 320
(Guachinango) 314
(Fabián) 318

(Vista Alegre) 328
(Linduro) 326
(Alvarez) 330

De Mayo

Zaragoza

San Juan

Rum Factory

(San Andrés) 109
(San Sebastián) 115
(San Juan Bautista) 117
(San Francisco) 119
(La Merced) 121

(San Antonio) 280

(San Vicente) 276

(San Carlos) 274

(Manglar) 264

NARANJAL NORTE

103
105
344
342

Estadio Victoria de Girón

109
111
113
113a
334

113
113

332

Lunai 300

PUEBLO NUEVO

(San Juan de Dios) 123
(Santa Rita) 125
(San Rafael) 127
(Espíritu Santo) 131

(San Fernando) 135
(Buen Viaje) 139
(Tenaza) 145

(Manglar) 262

ARMANDO MESTRE

113
115
119

342
344
346

To Madruga

Destino

Palmar del Junco

(Maurin) 173

El Ateneo

CAMILO CIENFUEGOS

NARANJAL SUR

LA JAIBA

(Calzada de Esteban) 171

(Paseo) 304

173

175
177
179
181

(Av 1) 175
(Av 3) 177
(Av 5) 179
(Av 7) 181
(Av 9) 183

276
179
264
258

MIRET

Carretera de Cuba 302

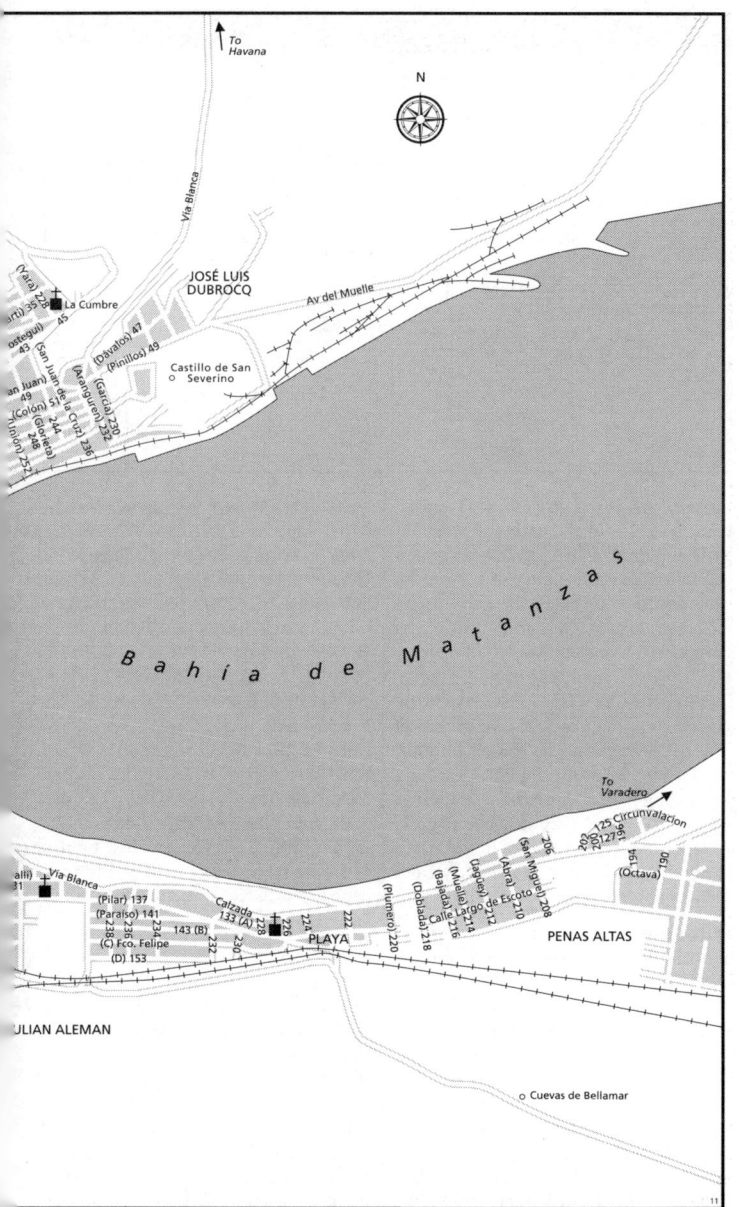

To Havana

N

Via Blanca

JOSÉ LUIS DUBROCQ

Av del Muelle

(Yara) 35
La Cumbre 45
...egui) 43
(San Juan de la Cruz) 244
(Colón) 51
(Ayuntamiento) 232
(San Juan) 49
(Dabalou) 47
(Pinillos) 49
(García) 230
(Ginoteta) 246
(Lincoln) 252

Castillo de San Severino

Bahía de Matanzas

To Varadero

Circunvalacion
125
127
200
196
202
205
194
150

(Octava)

(San Miguel) 208
(Aura) 210
Calle Largo de Escoto 210
(Muelle) 216
(Bajada) 218
Dapoley 212
(Doblada) 218
(Plumero) 220

Via Blanca
...alli)
...31

(Pilar) 137
(Paraiso) 141
(C) Fco. Felipe
(D) 153
143 (B)
234
238
236
Calzada 133 (A)
228
226
224
230
232

PLAYA

PENAS ALTAS

JULIAN ALEMAN

Cuevas de Bellamar

11

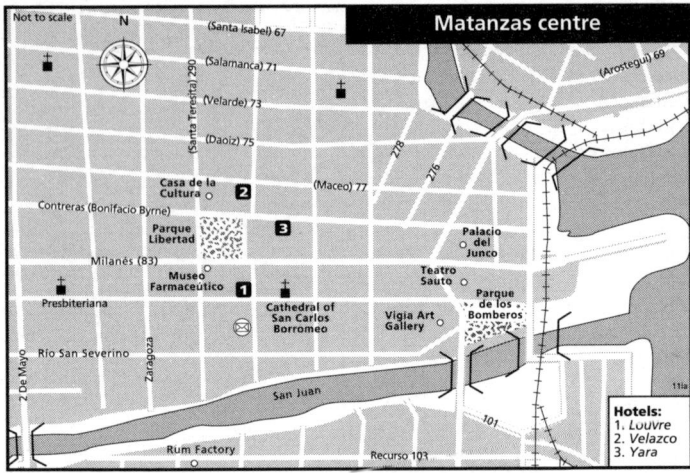

Matanzas centre

Not to scale N

(Santa Isabel) 67

(Salamanca) 71

(Velarde) 73

(Daoiz) 75

(Maceo) 77

(Arostegui) 69

Casa de la Cultura

Contreras (Bonifacio Byrne)

Parque Libertad

Milanés (83)

Museo Farmacéutico

Presbiteriana

Cathedral of San Carlos Borromeo

Palacio del Junco

Teatro Sauto

Vigía Art Gallery

Parque de los Bomberos

Río San Severino

Z De Mayo

Zaragoza

San Juan

Rum Factory

Recurso 103

Hotels:
1. Louvre
2. Velazco
3. Yara

Caruso and Anna Pavlova who toured Cuba in 1917. In the entrance there are marble statues of Greek goddesses and in the hall the muses are painted on the ceiling. Most unusually, the floor can be raised to convert the auditorium into a ballroom. The theatre was restored after the Revolution and is open to the public Tuesday-Sunday US$1. The **Palacio de Justicia** was built in 1826 and rebuilt in 1911. It is opposite the theatre and has been restored and nicely painted, serving to highlight the crumbling buildings which surround it. **Parque Libertad** is the main square, with a statue of José Martí in the middle and dominated by the former **Palacio del Gobierno**.

Museums

Visit the **Museo Farmacéutico**, Milanés 4951 entre Santa Teresa y Ayuntamiento, on the south side of Parque Libertad, T 23197, which contains the original equipment, porcelain jars, recipes and furnishings of the Botica La Francesa opened in 1882 by the Triolet family. It was a working pharmacy until 1964, when it was converted into a museum, believed to be unique in Latin America. Open Monday-Saturday 1000-1700, Sunday 0800-1200,

US$1. The **Museo Provincial**, Milanés entre Magdalena y Ayllón, T 23195, is a large museum in the former **Palacio del Junco**, built by a wealthy plantation owner and dating from 1840. The historical exhibits include an archaeological display and the development of sugar and slavery in the province. Open Monday-Saturday 1000-1700, Sunday 0800-1200, US$1. The former home of local poet, José Jacinto Milanés (1814-1863), on the street which bears his name, is now the **Archivo Histórico**. There is a statue of the poet outside the elegant **Catedral de San Carlos Borromeo**, on Milanés, first built in 1693, but rebuilt in 1878 after a fire in a neo-classical style with frescoed ceilings and walls.

Excursions

There is a wonderful view of the town and the surrounding countryside of the **Valle de Yumurí** from the ruined church of Monserrate, a good hike north up Domingo Mujica. Southeast of town are the **Cuevas de Bellamar** at Finca La Alcancía. This cave system, discovered in 1850, stretches for 3 km, with stalactites, stalagmites and underground streams. Tour parties come from Varadero so you may get herded along with a bus load, but in any case you are not allowed in unaccompanied. Open 0900-1700, entrance US$3, parking US$1, extra charges for cameras and video cameras. There are also caves at **Las Cuevas de Santa Catalina**, near Carbonera, 20 km east of Matanzas, where there are believed to be 8 km of tunnels. Amerindian paintings have been found here and the caves were used as a burial site. Another cave, **Refugio de Saturno**, is a large cave often visited by scuba divers (see **Diving and marine life**, page 28), although anyone can enjoy a swim. It is one km south of the Vía Blanca, 8 km east of the Río Canímar.

The road out to Varadero goes past the university and the Escuela Militar. 1 km past the university you come to the **Río Canímar**, which flows into the Bahía de Matanzas. Just before the bridge over the river, take the road running alongside the river towards the bay to the **Castillo del Morrillo**, built in 1720. It is now a museum (open Tuesday-Sunday 0900-1700) in memory of **Antonio Guiteras Holmes**, who was shot with the Venezuelan revolutionary, Carlos Aponte Hernández, by Batista's troops near the bridge. Bronze busts of the two men can be seen underneath a mahogany tree. Guiteras Holmes was a student leader who started a revolutionary group called Joven Cuba (Young Cuba) in 1934. He served briefly in the government which replaced Machado, but fell foul of the rising Batista. It was when he and Aponte came to Matanzas in 1935 to try and find a boat to take them into exile in Mexico that they were caught and executed. Below the bridge on the other side of the river is the *Bar Cubamar*, where you can hire rowing boats and take a trip up the river for US$2/hour. Given time and enough people, you can also organize excursions up the river with lunch and horse riding, which is a pleasant day out.

Local information
● Accommodation

Prices: L1 over US$200; **L2** US$151-200; **L3** US$101-150; **A1** US$81-100; **A2** US$61-80; **A3** US$46-60; **B** US$31-45; **C** US$21-30; **D** US$12-20; **E** US$7-11; **F** up to US$6

B-C *Hotel Canimao*, Km 4 Carretera Matanzas a Varadero, T 668021, 120 rooms on hill above Río Canímar, pool, night club, good restaurant, excursions offered on the river or to caves; another hotel outside town is **B-C** *El Valle*, T 53300/53118, 7 km northwest of Matanzas, in woodland in the Valle del Yumurí, built 1985, 42 rooms, some with shared bath, pool, bowling alley, riding, good walking. Three colonial hotels in town: **B-C** *Hotel Louvre*, 19th century building on south side of Parque Libertad, T 4074, variety of rooms and prices, opt for the a/c room with bathroom and balcony overlooking the square, beautiful mahogany furniture, rather than the small, dark, cupboard room in the bowels of the hotel; *Velazco* is on the north side of Parque Libertad, T 4443, and *Yara* is a block away on Calle 79 entre 288 y 282, T 4418, both lovely old buildings but often accept only Cubans paying in pesos with the aim of pushing foreigners out to Varadero. Private rooms are also offered but are usually expensive for what you get.

● Places to eat
Not a lot of choice here and both service and style are lacking. *Pekin*, Calle 83 entre 292 y 294, open daily 1200-1400, 1800-2100, foreigners pay in dollars; *Año 30*, Calle 272 entre 75 y 77, open Monday-Saturday 1200-1400; *Café Atenas*, Calle 83 y 272 on Plaza La Vigía, open 24 hours, pizza, spaghetti, sandwiches.

● Banks & money changers
Banco Financiero Internacional at Calle 85 y 298 for exchange facilities and cash advances on credit cards; **Banco Nacional** at Calle 83 (Milanés) y 282.

● Entertainment
The Plaza Vigía is the place to go in the evenings; locals congregate here to chat, play dominoes or draughts, or make music. The **Casa de la Trova** here, near the bridge, was where the *Muñequitas de Matanzas*, a famous rumba band, was formed. The Casa de la Cultura on Calle 79 entre 288 y 290, was formerly the Lyceum Club and is famous for being the place where the *danzón* was danced for the first time in 1879; music is performed here from time to

time. Teatro Sauto usually has live performances at the weekends.

● **Hospitals & medical services**
Facilities for foreigners are available in Varadero, but there is a pharmacy here, open 24 hours, at Calle 85 y 280.

● **Post & telecommunications**
Post Office: at Calle 85 y 290.
Telephone: office on Calle 83 y 288, open 0630-2200 every day.

● **Shopping**
Casa de Bienes Culturales La Vigía on Plaza de la Vigía, for crafts, ceramics, clothing. Librería Viet Nam on Calle 85 y 288 for books. Photo Service on Calle 288 entre 83 y 85. For food there is a vegetable market near the bridge on Calles 97 y 298, Supermercado La Reina is at Calle 85 entre 290 y 292 and bread can be bought at a snack bar on Calle 83 y 294.

● **Transport**
Bus The long distance bus station is at Calle 131 y 272, while the interprovincial terminal is at Calle 298 y 127, both in Pueblo Nuevo.

Train The journey from Havana via the Hershey Railway, the only electric train in Cuba, is memorable and scenic if you are not in a hurry (4 trains daily, 3-4 hours, from the Casablanca station, which is reached by public launch from near La Fuerza Castle). It uses a station north of the Río Yumurí in Versalles. Those who wish to make it a day trip from Havana can do so, long queues for return tickets, best to get one as soon as you arrive. There is another, newer, station south of the town at Calle 181, Miret, which receives regular and *especial* trains from Havana en route to Santiago and also has services to Sancti Spíritus, Santa Clara, Cienfuegos, Camagüey, Las Tunas, Bayamo, Manzanillo and Ciego de Avila.

VARADERO

Phone code 5

From Matanzas a good dual carriageway runs to **Varadero**, 144 km from Havana, Cuba's chief beach resort with all facilities. The toll at the entrance to the resort can be paid in pesos or foreign currency, choose your channel. Varadero is built on **Península de Hicacos**, a 20 km sandspit, the length of which run two roads lined with dozens of large hotels, some smaller ones, and many chalets and villas. Many of the villas date from before 1959. Development of the peninsula began in 1923 but the village area was not built until the 1950s. The Du Pont family bought land, sold it for profit, then bought more and built a large house, now *Las Américas* restaurant on a cliff near the new hotel of the same name, and constructed roads. Varadero is undergoing large scale development of new hotels and cabins. Joint ventures with foreign investors are being encouraged with the aim of expanding capacity to 30,000 rooms by the turn of the century.

The southern end is more downmarket, with hustlers on the beaches by day and prostitutes in the bars at night. The northern end is where the Sol Meliá and other international hotels are; you can pay to use their facilities even if you are not staying there. Check out the price of sun loungers for an indication of hotel prices, eg US$1/day at the *Internacional*, US$2/day at Sol Meliá resort. In Varadero all hotels, restaurants and excursions must be paid in US dollars. Don't bother to buy any pesos for your stay here. Book excursions at any hotel with a Tour Agency office.

Despite the building in progress it is not over-exploited and is a good place for a family beach holiday. The beaches are quite empty, if a bit exposed, and you can walk for miles along the sand, but you are totally isolated from the rest of Cuba. Beach vendors will try to sell you T-shirts, crochet work and wooden trinkets, don't buy the black coral, it is protected internationally and you may not be allowed to take it in to your country.

Places of interest

Distances are large. Avenida 1, which runs northeast-southwest the length of the spit, has a bus service; calle numbers begin with lowest numbers at the southwest end and work upwards to the northeast peninsula. Because of the relatively recent development of Varadero, there is little of historical or architectural interest, visitors spend their time on the beach, engaging in watersports or taking organized excursions, rather than sightseeing. There is a **Museo Municipal** at Calle 57 y Av de la Playa, with some Indian artefacts and paintings, open Tuesday-Saturday 0900-1800, Sunday 0900-1200, US$1. The **Centro Recreativo Josone**, Av 1 y Calle 59, is a large park with pool, bowling, other activities and a café. Towards the end of the peninsula, halfway between Marina Chapelín and Marina Gaviota, is a cave, **Cueva de Ambrosio**, where dozens of Indian drawings were discovered in 1961. Open Tuesday-Sunday 1000-1200, 1400-1600, US$2, but may be unattended unless a tour party is booked in to visit. At the far end of the peninsula the land has been designated the **Parque Natural de Varadero**. It is an area of scrub and cactus, with a lagoon where salt was once made, and several kilometres of sandy beach.

Beaches and watersports

Varadero's sandy beach stretches the length of the peninsula, broken only occasionally by rocky outcrops which can be traversed by walking through a hotel's grounds. Some parts are wider than others and as a general rule the older hotels have the best bits of beach. For instance the *Internacional*, which was the *Hilton* before the Revolution, has a large swathe of curving beach, whereas the brand new, upmarket, *Meliá Las Américas* and its sister hotels, *Meliá Varadero* and *Sol Palmeras* have a disappointingly shallow strip of sand and some rocks. However, the sand is all beautifully looked after and cleaned daily. The water is clean and nice for swimming but snorkelling is not worth the effort. For good snorkelling take one of the many boat trips out to the cays. There are three marinas: Acua, Chapelín and Gaviota, all full service with sailing tours, restaurants, fishing and diving (see **Diving and marine life**, page 23). All their services can be booked through the tour desks in hotels. Deep sea fishing costs around US$250 for

four people for half a day, but prices vary according to what exactly is on offer. The dive operators are Club Barracuda (Cubanacán), T 613481, Marina Gaviota (Gaviota Group), T 667755, and Acua Diving Club (Puertosol), T 668063. Average prices are US$35 for a single dive, US$70 for two tanks, with discounts for groups of 5,7 or 10 divers and if you have your own equipment. A 5-day ACUC certification course costs US$365. Varadero's **Dolphinarium** is at Autopista Km 12, beyond the Marina Chapelín but the one on Cayo Macho (see **Excursions** below) is a nicer location. You can indulge in almost any form of watersports, including windsurfing, parasailing, waterskiing, jet skiing and non-motorized craft such as pedalos and water bikes.

Other sports

The large hotels all offer tennis courts, some have squash courts and volleyball is played on the beach, usually organized by the hotel entertainment staff. Table tennis, billiards and other indoor games are available if the weather deteriorates or you have had enough sun. There is a **golf** course on Av Las Américas, upgraded in 1996-98 to 18 holes. The first nine holes will be opened at the beginning of 1998 with the other nine finished during the fist half of the year. The original nine holes were set out by the Du Ponts around their mansion, and the new ones extend along the Sol Meliá resorts. Bookings can be made through hotel tour desks; the golf course is owned by Rumbos in partnership with a French company.

Excursions

From Varadero it is possible to explore the interesting town of **Cárdenas** (see page 158), where the present Cuban flag was raised for the first time in 1850. The sea here is polluted with oil and the air smells of sulphur which drifts as far as Varadero if the wind is in the wrong direction when gas is released from the oil wells, often in the middle of the night. Many of the Cubans who work in the hotels live

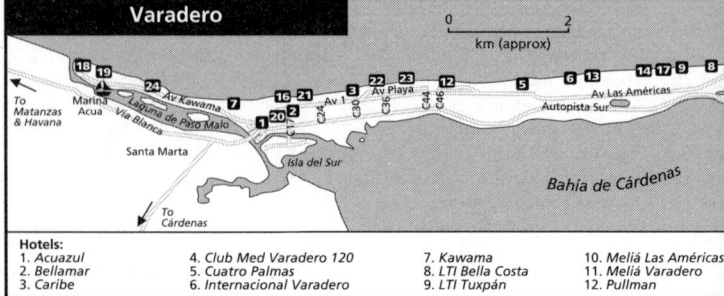

Varadero

0   2
km (approx)

Hotels:

1. *Acuazul*	4. *Club Med Varadero 120*	7. *Kawama*	10. *Meliá Las Américas*
2. *Bellamar*	5. *Cuatro Palmas*	8. *LTI Bella Costa*	11. *Meliá Varadero*
3. *Caribe*	6. *Internacional Varadero*	9. *LTI Tuxpán*	12. *Pullman*

in Cárdenas and old Canadian buses, mostly blue, go from the town all the way to the last hotel, US$1. Another excursion is to **Neptune's Cave** (thought a more appealing name than the old one, Cepero), which is south of the town of **Carboneras**, half-way between Matanzas and Varadero. It has an underground lagoon, stalagmites and stalactites, evidence of Indian occupation and was used as a clandestine hospital during the war of independence.

There are many sailing tours to the offshore cays. The *Jolly Roger* is recommended. It is not a pseudo pirate ship as in other parts of the Caribbean, but a comfortable catamaran, US$70 including lunch and open bar, good food, several stops for snorkelling or beaches. Ask for a detour to the dolphinarium on Cayo Macho if it is not already included and if your fellow passengers agree. It is isolated, apparently in the middle of nowhere, with large pens for the dolphins, US$5 for a show, US$5 to swim with them.

The cays around the Hicacos Peninsula were once the haunt of French pirates and it is supposed that the name Varadero comes from the fact that ships ran aground here, becoming *varados*. **Cayo Mono** lies five nautical miles north northeast of Punta de Morlas. During the nesting season in mid-year it becomes a seagull sanctuary for the 'Gaviota Negra' (*Anous stolidus*) and the 'Gaviota Monja' (*Sterna fuscata* and *Annaethetus*), during which time you can only pass by and

watch them through binoculars. **Cayo Piedra del Norte** is 2 miles southeast of Cayo Mono. On the cay is one of the 18 lighthouses which Marinas Puertosol intends renovating for tourism with facilities for passing yachts.

Varasub, a Japanese semi-submersible carrying 48 passengers, has 6 daily departures from the *Hotel Paradiso*, adults US$25, children US$20. Reservations can be made with Havanatur representatives or the Varasub offices: Av Playa 3606, entre 36 y 37, T 66-7279; Calle 31, entre Av 1 y Playa, T 66-7154; Av Kawama y Calle O, T 66-7165; Av de las Américas y Calle 64, T 66-7203, and others. You can also see underwater by taking a trip on the glass bottomed boat, *Nautilus*, which can take 90 passengers round the cays and operates from Marina Gaviota, US$25 including drink and hotel transfers.

For an all-round view of the peninsula, Matanzas and the Yumurí valley, you can ride in a noisy 32-seater Russian helicopter, landing in the valley for lunch, a visit to a local farm, horse riding or boating on a lake, Wednesday, Friday, Sunday, 0930-1530, US$75. Many more excursions are available from hotel tour operators, including to the Bay of Pigs, US$47, or to Trinidad, US$99 by plane.

Festival

Some years in November a festival is held in Varadero, lasting a week, which attracts some of the best artists in South America. Entrance US$2-10 per day. Carnival is

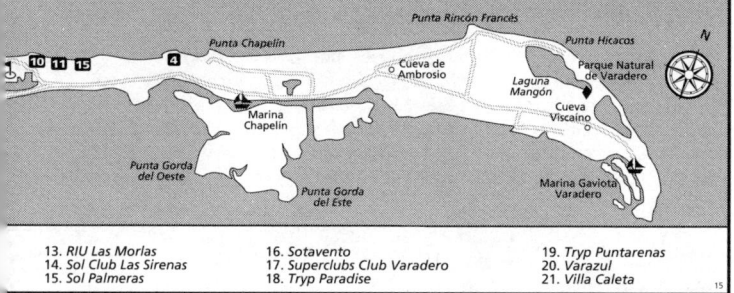

Punta Rincón Francés

Punta Chapelín · Cueva de Ambrosio · Punta Hicacos · Parque Natural de Varadero · N

Laguna Mangón · Cueva Viscaíno

Marina Chapelín

Punta Gorda del Oeste · Punta Gorda del Este · Marina Gaviota Varadero

13. RIU Las Morlas	16. Sotavento	19. Tryp Puntarenas
14. Sol Club Las Sirenas	17. Superclubs Club Varadero	20. Varazul
15. Sol Palmeras	18. Tryp Paradise	21. Villa Caleta

held in January with lots of tourist participation, encouraged by the hotel entertainment teams.

Local information

● Accommodation

(All prices high season, double. Hotels can be booked in the tourist office. Many hotels now offer all-inclusive rates, but these can be disappointing with lack of variety in food and drinks.)

> **Prices: L1** over US$200; **L2** US$151-200;
> **L3** US$101-150; **A1** US$81-100; **A2** US$61-80;
> **A3** US$46-60; **B** US$31-45; **C** US$21-30;
> **D** US$12-20; **E** US$7-11; **F** up to US$6

A Cuban-Spanish joint venture has opened three resort hotels managed by Sol/Meliá Hotels of Spain: **L1-L2** *Meliá Las Américas*, T 66-7600, F 66-7625, 5 stars, 250 rooms, suites, 125 luxury bungalows, comfortable, glitzy public areas, restaurants, breakfast recommended, nice pool but cold, good beach, golf, tennis, watersports, disco, Plaza América shopping centre alongside, new, shops still opening up; **L1-L3** *Sol Palmeras*, T 66-7013, F 66-7162, 375 rooms, 32 suites, 200 bungalows, well-landscaped, quiet, shady, attractive, cool lobby bar, 4 stars, same facilities, Chinese restaurant recommended, buffet breakfast poor; and the star-shaped **L1-L2** *Meliá Varadero*, T 66-7013, F 66-7162, 490 rooms, 5 stars, on rocky promontory, tennis, watersports, disco, nightclub, spa, sauna, jacuzzi. There is a shuttle service through the Sol/Meliá complex 0730-2300; **L3** *Cuatro Palmas Resort* (Gran Caribe), Av 1 entre 60 y 62, T 66-7640, F 66-7583, 343 a/c rooms, also in bungalows and villas hacienda style, on beach, opposite Centro Comercial Caiman in heart of hotel strip, very pleasant, pool, tennis, bicycle and moped hire, tourism bureau, Post Office, lots of services; **L3** *LTI Bella Costa*

Resort Hotel & Villas, Carretera Las Américas, T 667210/667010, F 667205, good 4-star hotel at end of one section of sandy beach with rocky ironshore, newly landscaped gardens, attractive, well run, good service, recommended, pool with swim up bar, watersports, tennis, lovely fish restaurant on small cliff overlooking sea; **L3** *LTI Tuxpán*, Carretera Las Américas, T 667560/665241, F 667561/667205, also with very good facilities; **L3-A3** *Varadero Internacional* (Gran Caribe), Av Las Américas, T 66-7038/9, F 66-7246, formerly the *Hilton*, now dated compared with Sol/Meliá resorts but has charm, 371 rooms, also new villas, Porto Carrero original painting on tiles in lobby, ghastly pink paint outside, friendly bar staff, best bit of beach on whole peninsula, nice rooms, solid wooden furniture, dodgy wiring, cheap packages available, dancing classes on beach, good value lunches, recommended cabaret.

Jamaican investors have built the 160-room, all-inclusive **Superclubs Club Varadero**, T 66-7030, F 66-7005, for singles and couples, no children under 16, a/c, phone, satellite TV, lots of activities and sports, plenty of equipment, free sunbeds for guests, 5 bars, 3 restaurants, disco, theme parties, indoor games room, gym, sauna, jacuzzis, Olympic size pool, tennis, diving and other watersports, popular, crowded even in low season. *Club Med Varadero* has also recently opened in participation with Gaviota, Autopista Sur Km 11, T 668341, F 668340, all-inclusive for ages 12 and up, 266 rooms including 18 suites, a/c, phone, TV, safety box, 3 restaurants and 3 bars, of which one is reserved for cigar smokers, lots of sports including catamarans, windsurfing, kayaks, aerobics, gymnasium, volleyball, basketball, 8 tennis courts, circus school, pool, dancing lessons, pétanque and indoor games, other things can be arranged outside the Club such as horse

Typical cocktails

🦶 Most bars have their own specialities, but there is a range which is fairly common to all. However, even the standard cocktails will taste different when made by different barmen, so don't expect a Mojito in Havana to be the same as a Mojito in Varadero. Cocktails come in all colours and flavours, short or long, and some are even striped or multicoloured. All should be presented as a work of art by the barman, who has probably spent years at his training.

A **Cubanito** is a Cuban version of a Bloody Mary, with ice, lime juice, salt, Worcestershire sauce, chilli sauce, light dry rum and tomato juice. Tomato juice is not always available everywhere.

An **Ernest Hemingway Special** is light dry rum, grapefruit juice, maraschino liqueur, lime and shaved ice, blended and served like a Daiquiri.

A **Havana Special** is pineapple juice, light dry rum, maraschino liqueur and ice, shaken and strained.

A **Mulata** is lime juice, extra aged rum, crème de cacao and shaved ice, blended and served in a champagne glass.

The old favourite, **Piña Colada**, can be found anywhere: coconut liqueur, pineapple juice, light dry rum and shaved ice, all blended and served with a straw in a glass, a pineapple or a coconut, depending on which tropical paradise you are in.
Another old recipe best served in a coconut is a **Saoco**, which is just rum, coconut milk and ice.

One to finish the day off, and maybe even yourself, is a **Zombie**, a mixture of ice, lime juice, grenadine, pineapple juice, light dry rum, old gold rum and extra aged rum, garnished with fruit.

riding, deep sea fishing and scuba diving and the usual excursions offered by all the hotel tour desks. *Brisas del Caribe* (Cubanacan) is another new and comfortable all-inclusive on Av Las Américas, T 668030, F 668005, 266 a/c rooms with satellite TV, phone, terrace or balcony and sea or garden view, 4 suites have jacuzzis, 2 restaurants, grill on the beach, 6 bars, lots of sporting facilities, pool, gym, games room, entertainment. *Sol Club Las Sirenas* is an all-inclusive in the Sol/Meliá chain, on the beach with the usual emphasis on sports and evening entertainment, restaurants specialize in Italian food, large curving pool, children welcome, very comfortable.

A1-A3 *Kawama* (Gran Caribe), Carretera de Kawama y Calle O, T 66-7155/6, F 66-7334, 202 rooms, refurbished older hotel; at the south end **A1-A3** *Paradiso*, attached to *Puntarena* (Tryp), T 66-7120, F 66-7074, with all resort facilities, 3 pools, watersports, all shared by both hotels, smart, modern, 518 rooms in total, 5 stars, good restaurants, fresh seafood,

recommended; **A2** *Acuazul*, Av 1 entre Calles 13 y 14, 156 rooms, with pool, older style, not on beach, blue and white, lots of concrete; **A2** *Villa Punta Blanca*, T 66-7090/7083, F 66-7004, 320 rooms, made up of a number of former private residences with some new complexes; **A3-C** *Villa La Herradura*, Av Playa entre 35 y 36, T 6-3703, well-equipped suites, balcony, restaurant, bar, shop, etc.

B *Villa Caribe*, Av de la Playa y Calle 30, T 66-8030, F 66-8005, 124 rooms; **B** *Los Delfines*, Av Playa y Calle 39, T 6-3630, F 66-7496; **B** *Pullman*, Av 1 entre 49 y 50, T 6-2575, F 66-7495, best value for the independent traveller, only 15 rooms, friendly, family atmosphere, very popular; **B** *Varazul*, Av 1 entre Calles 14 y 15, T 66-7132/4, F 66-7229, aparthotel, 69 rooms, quiet; **B** *Villa Sotavento*, dependency of *Acuazul*, Calle 13 between Av 1 and Av Playa, T 66-2953, 130 rooms, next to beach, clean, with bath, breakfast, US$5, buffet, very good.

In Varadero, hotels built in the 1940s and 1950s are considered 3-star and some 4-star, depending on how recently they were renovated. Rates for 3-star hotels such as *Mar del Sur*, *Club Tropical*, *Bellamar*, *Dos Mares* and *Herradura*, charge US$30-50 in high season for a double room bed and breakfast, or US$20-25 in low season. 4-star hotels like *Paradiso Puntarena*, built in the 1990s, *Punta Blanca*, refurbished, *Kawama*, refurbished, and *Varadero Internacional*, the former Hilton, can charge up to US$80-90 in high season and US$60-70 in low season, although a package deal will usually produce bargains.

● **Places to eat**
Recommended restaurants, all between US$9-15, are *Mi Casita* (book in advance), Camino del Mar entre 11 y 12, T 63787, meat and seafood, open 1800-2300; *La Cabañita* Camino del Mar esquina Calle 9, T 62215, meat and seafood, open 1900-0100; *Oshin*, Chinese, in grounds of *Sol Palmeras*, open 1200-1500, 1800-2300, good, popular, reservations essential; *Halong*, Camino del Mar esquina Calle 12, T 63787, Chinese, open 1900-2300; *El Mesón del Quijote* (Spanish) at *Villa Cuba*, Carretera Las Américas, T 63522, open 1500-2300; *Albacora*, at *Hotel Copey*, Calle C entre Av 62 y 63, T 6-3650, open 1200-1245, disappointing, all dishes except *pescado*, US$12-18, but if you want fish you may be told '*no hay*'; *Lai-Lai* bar/restaurant, Oriental, Av 1 y Calle 18, T 66-7793, 1900-0045; *Castelnuovo*, Av 1 y Calle 11, T 66-7794, 1200-2345, Italian; *Las Américas*, Av Las Américas, T 6-3856, open 1200-2215, international food, beautiful setting, food good one night, inedible the next; *El Mirador*, at *LTI Bella Costa Resort*, on cliff overlooking the sea, lovely fish restaurant, lobster US$18.50, shrimp US$14, open 1200-2300; *Bodegón Criollo*, Av Playa esquina Calle 40, T 66-7795, open 1200-0100, pleasant atmosphere, popular, music, no vegetarian food; *La Casa del Chef*, Av 1 entre 12 y 13, T 6-3606, 1200-2245, set menu US$9 including salad, black bean soup, rice, meat and chips, flan, coffee not recommended, chicken dry, fish tasteless; *La Sangría*, snack bar on sea front, Av 1 entre Calle 8 y 9, T 6-2025, open 24 hours; *Coppelia*, Av 1 entre Calle 44 y 46, T 62866, open 1000-2245, in town centre, ice cream US$0.90. It is now easier to buy food in Varadero because the new Aparthotels (*Varazul*, *La Herradura*) have a small food store.

● **Airlines**
All at the airport, Cubana T 63612-14; LTU T 61797; Martinair T 63624; Air Europa T 667317. Aerotaxi is at C 24 y Av 1, T 62929. Cubana has an office in *Iberostar Barlovento*, Calle 9 esquina 1, T 667593.

● **Entertainment**
Discos: in most large hotels. *Kastillito*, Av de la Playa y Calle 49, T 63888, open 2300-0600; *La Patana*, Canal de Kawama, T 66-7791, open 2200-0300; *La Bamba*, hottest in town at *LTI-Tuxpán*, biggest, most popular, T 667560, open 2230-0430; *Havana Club* in old *Centro Comercial Copey*, Av 2 y C 63, open 2200-0400, matinées Sunday afternoon, frequented by locals.

Nightclubs: *Cabaret Continental* at *Hotel Internacional*, US$40 with dinner, 2000, show and disco US$25 at 2200-0300, recommended by Canadians; *Cabaret Cueva del Pirata*, Autopista Sur Km 11, T 66-7751, 2100-dawn, closed Sunday.

Cinema: *Cine Varadero*, Av Playa entre C 42 y C 43.

● **Banks & money changers**
Banco Financiero Internacional, Av Playa y C 32, cash advance service with credit cards, open 0900-1900 daily.

● **Hospital & medical services**
Policlínico Internacional, Av1 y C 61, T 66-7226, 667689, 667710, international clinic, doctor on duty 24 hours, a medical consultation in your hotel will cost US$15. The clinic has an excellent international pharmacy attached, T 667226. Any diver needing treatment for the bends will be taken to the recompression chamber at the Centro Médico Sub Acuática at the *Hospital Julio M Arístegui* just outside Cárdenas.

● **Post & telecommunications**
Most hotels have post offices where you can buy stamps for use and in packets for collectors. Phone and fax services are also usually available but prices vary. The Centro Internacional de Comunicaciones is at C 64 entre Av 1 y Av 3, T 62103/62356, F 667020. For cellular phones, Cubacel is at C 25 y Av 1, Edificio La Cancha, T 667222/667198, F 667222. Etecsa is at C 18 y Av 3, T 667070, F 667050. DHL is on C 10 next to *Hotel Barlovento*, T/F 667330.

● **Shopping**
There are several art galleries and craft shops: Casa de la Artesanía, C 9 y Av Camino del Mar, T 667035; Casa de la Artesanía Latinoamericana,

Av 1 y C 64, T 667691; Casa de la Miniatura, Av Camino del Mar y C 10, T 64211; Galería de Arte y Taller de Cerámica Artística, Av 1 entre C 59 y C 60, T 63810; Galería de Arte Sol y Mar, C 34 y Av 1, T 63153; Casa de los Orishas, A 1 entre C 33 y C 34, T 63663; Arte Nuevo, Av 63 entre Av 1 y Av 2, T 61256. Photo Service has two outlets: Av Playa y C 44, open 24 hours, and Centro Comercial Copey, C 63 y Av 3, T 667753, open 0900-2100. Photo Express is at Av 1 entre C 41 y C 42, T 667015, also open 24 hours.

● **Tour companies & travel agents**
Most hotels have a tour agency on site offering local and national excursions, boat trips, etc. A recommended travel agency is *Fantástico*, Calle 24 y Playa, T 66-7061, F 66-7062, helpful multilingual guides, transfers, booking and confirmation of air tickets, air charters, car rentals, reception and representation service, linked to Cubanacan hotels.

● **Useful addresses**
Immigration and **Police**: C 39 y Av 1, T 116. Immigration is open Monday-Friday 0800-1130, 1300-1600, Saturday 0800-1130 for visa extensions.

● **Transport**
Local Car hire: Havanautos, agency in Varadero at Av 1 y C 31, T 63733, F 667029, T 63630 at airport, or through many hotels: *Hotel Siboney*, T 667094; *Hotel Internacional*, T 667038; *Hotel Kawama*, T 667139; *Hotel Cuatro Palmas*, T 667040; *Villa Tortuga*, T 667139. **Cubacar** (Cubanacan), at *Hotel Sol Palmeras*, T 667359, *Hotel LTI-Tuxpan*, T 667639, *Hotel Meliá Varadero*, T 667013 ext 8191. **Transautos**, Av 2 y C 64, T 667336, or Av 1 entre C 21 y C 22. **Nacional** (Gaviota) at C 13 entre Av 2 y Av 4, T 63706, T/F 667663. Hot tip: hire a car rather than jeep to avoid having your spare wheel stolen, insurance covers 4 wheels, not the spare (see **Information for travellers**, page 302). **Moped rental**: US$9 per hour, US$15 3 hours, extra hours US$5, a good way to see the peninsula but you will have no insurance and no helmet. **Bicycle hire**: from hotels, US$1/hour. **Horse drawn vehicles** act as taxis, usually just for a tour around town. **Taxis** (cars) charge US$0.50/km; from *Hotel Internacional* to the bank is US$3, to Plaza América US$5. The best place to hail a taxi is at any hotel as they usually wait there for fares. Cubataxi is at C 28 entre Av 1 y Av 2, T 63674; Taxi Gaviota, T 62620; Turistaxi T 63566; Taxi OK Cubanacan, T 667089.

Air The Juan Gualberto Gómez airport (VRA) had a brand new second terminal in 1997 which will increase operating efficiency and speed; the departure lounge now has a capacity for 1,500 passengers and there are state of the art methods of transferring passengers and luggage from the aircraft to the terminal. When fully operational the airport should receive international scheduled flights from Amsterdam (Martinair), Cologne/Bonn (Condor), Dusseldorf (LTU), Frankfurt (LTU and Condor), London (Cubana), Madrid (Air Europa), Montego Bay (Tropical Airlines), Montréal (Cubana), Paris (AOM French Airlines), Puerto Plata (LTU), Rome (Cubana) and Toronto (Cubana), but in the past these have been diverted to Havana. Charter flights also come to Varadero. Cubana has domestic flights from Baracoa, Cayo Coco, Havana, Holguín and Santiago. Bus from airport to the hotels US$10pp. A taxi from Varadero airport to Havana costs US$60.

Bus The interprovincial bus station is at Autopista Sur y C 36, T 63254, 62626. The *colectivos* to Matanzas outside the bus station are for Cubans only. You can, however, catch one of the blue buses to Cárdenas with the hotel staff, US$1. The easiest way to get to Havana is on a tour bus, booked through the hotel tour desk, which will pick you up at your hotel, but there is a regular bus twice a day (0805 and 1600) from Havana bus terminal to Varadero, which stops off at Varadero airport, US$8, reserve 1-2 days in advance.

Train A cheap method of getting to Varadero from Havana is to take the train to Matanzas (see above), then a taxi to Matanzas bus terminal from where you catch a bus, about 1 hour (state destination, take ticket, wait for bus and then your number to be called, and run for the bus). About 5 1/2 hours in all, if buses are running. Alternatively take the train to Cárdenas and bus from there.

CARDENAS

Population 75,000, *Phone code* 5

Cárdenas is usually visited as a day trip from Varadero and is a good way of seeing a bit of real Cuban life if you are spending an entire holiday on the peninsula. The town is 18 km southeast of Varadero on the Bahía de Cárdenas. It was founded in 1828 and is set out in very regular grid form with Calles running parallel to the sea in consecutive numbers and Avenidas crossing them. The main street is Avenida Céspedes and Avenidas are numbered from here, with those running northwest starting from Avenida 1 oeste in odd numbers, and those running southeast starting from Avenida 2 este in even numbers.

Places of interest Cárdenas was a wealthy sugar town in the 19th century which is reflected in the colonial buildings, now tatty and decrepit. Its main claim to fame is that the Cuban flag was first raised here in 1850 by the revolutionary **General Narciso López**, a Venezuelan who tried unsuccessfully to invade Cuba by landing at Cárdenas with an army of 600 men (only six of whom were Cuban) who had sailed from New Orleans. Where Av Céspedes ends at the sea, there is a monument with a huge flagpole commemorating the flag raising event on 19 May. There is also a plaque at the *Hotel Dominica*, which Narciso López occupied with his men and is now a National Monument. Unfortunately the General's attempts to free Cuba from colonial rule were unsuccessful, as he failed to get local support. One of the town's other claims to fame is that it contains the oldest statue of Christopher Columbus in the Western Hemisphere. It is in front of the cathedral in Parque Colón on Av Céspedes and was the work of a Spanish sculptor, Piquier, in 1862. Plaza Molokoff is worth a visit to see the decaying iron market building put up in the 19th century on Av 3 oeste and Calle 12. It was built in the shape of a cross and the two-storey building is surmounted by a 15m dome made in the USA.

On Calle 2 overlooking the water is the Fábrica de Ron Arrechabala, which makes both the Varadero and Bucanero label rums. The site has been a rum factory since 1878, when the Havana Club company was founded here.

Museums A local 20th century hero is remembered in his birthplace, now a museum. The **Casa Natal de José Antonio Echevarría** is on Av 4 este y Calle 12, open Tuesday-Saturday 0800-1600, Sunday 0800-1200. The house dates from 1703 but Echevarría was born here in 1932. He was a student leader killed by Batista's troops in 1957. The museum has exhibits relating to 19th century independence struggles downstairs and the 20th century Revolution upstairs. The park outside is named after Echevarría and there is a monument to him in the park. Another museum on the other side of Av 4, **Museo Oscar María de Rojas**, is notable for being one of the first museums in Cuba, dating from 1900. It is housed in the former Ayuntamiento, built in 1861, and contains a wide array of exhibits, from butterflies to Indian relics, open same hours, US$1.

● **Accommodation** C *Dominica*, Av Céspedes y Calle 9, T 521502, 25 rooms in old sugar warehouse converted to hotel in neo-classical style in 1919 and now a National Monument, basic, poor restaurant.

● **Places to eat** *Las Palmas*, Av Céspedes y Calle 16, in large, walled, colonial building with imposing dining room, worth eating here for the location if nothing else, open for food Tuesday-Sunday 1200-1400, 1800-2100, but also opens as a night club at weekends 2100-0200 with a show at 2230, US$5. *El Castillo*, Av 3 oeste y Calle 12 on Plaza Molokoff, mixed reports on this peso restaurant depending on food supply, but if it is open you should be able to get a reasonable pizza. There are a couple of *cafeterías* where you can get a sandwich and a beer, but otherwise Cárdenas is not a great culinary experience; ask around to see if any *paladares* have opened.

● **Transport** There is not much in the way of local transport; bicycles or horses are the main carriers. The bus station is on Av Céspedes y Calle 22, with services to Matanzas, Colón, Jagüey Grande, Havana and Santa Clara. To get to Varadero catch a bus from the corner of Av 13 oeste y Calle 13, they should leave every hour, but as the principal demand is from hotel workers they are more likely to run according to shifts. Cárdenas has a railway station at Av 8 este on the waterfront, but it is not on a main line. Local services run intermittently to Pedroso via Jovellanos, and Guareiras via Colón and Los Arabos.

Cuban rum

Sugar was first introduced to Cuba by Christopher Columbus, who brought sugar cane roots from the Canary Islands on his second trans-Atlantic voyage. The first rudimentary mills produced sugar cane juice but as they became more sophisticated the juice was turned into alcohol. A clear wine was made, which when distilled several times became a basic rum. In the 19th century a new manufacturing process was developed which considerably improved the quality of Cuban rum and the industry rapidly expanded with the construction of hundreds of sugar mills all over the country. The cities of Havana, Santiago de Cuba, Cienfuegos and Cárdenas all produced rum of export quality under the labels of Havana Club (founded in 1878), Bacardí, Campeón, Obispo, San Carlos, Jiquí, Matusalem, Bocoy and Albuerne.

The family firm of Bacardí was the largest in Cuba for nearly 100 years, building substantial wealth on the back of rum. After the 1959 Revolution, when the sugar industry and the distilleries were taken over by the state, the family left the island but took the Bacardí name with them. The Bacardí rum now found world wide is not distilled in Cuba. Many labels can now be found in Cuba, including the venerable Havana Club, Caribbean Club, Caney, Legendario, Matusalem, Varadero, Bucanero and Siboney.

Rums of different ages can be found. Generally the younger, light rums are used in cocktails and aged, dark rums drunk on the rocks or treated as you might a single malt whisky. Light, dry rum in Cuba is aged for 3 years, has little body and is between 40° and 60° proof. Old gold, dry rum is aged for 5 years, is amber in colour and can be drunk straight or added to cocktails for an extra kick. Extra aged rum is aged for 7 years and while occasionally added to cocktails, is usually drunk neat in a brandy glass.

South to the Bay of Pigs

24 km south of Cárdenas is **Jovellanos**, a large town with a pleasant colonial centre, Parque Central and church. It is a junction of the roads from Varadero to the Zapata peninsula and from Matanzas to Santa Clara. It is of no particular interest to travellers except that as a result of slavery and enforced migrations, the Arara people of Benin came here via Haiti and brought the sort of music with them which is normally only heard around Santiago de Cuba.

The main road from Matanzas runs east from here to **Colón**, on the main railway line from Havana. This is another 19th century town with abundant neo-classical architecture and faded grandeur. For adventurous independent travellers exploring rural Matanzas, you will be well off the tourist trail; you can stay in peso hotels here and spend pesos in restaurants and on transport.

Due south of Jovellanos you head towards the Zapata peninsula and the countryside becomes flat and uninteresting. **Jagüey Grande** is just north of the central highway from Havana to Santa Clara, and just south of it is **Central Australia**. This is primarily a sugar mill, built in 1904, but became known when Castro used it as his centre of operations to repel the Bay of Pigs invasion. The office he used is now a museum, the **Museo de la Comandancia**, open Tuesday-Sunday 0800-1700, US$1. Outside is the wreck of a plane shot down by Castro's troops.

● **Accommodation B-C** *Finca Fiesta Campesina* is a complex of 6 wooden cabins (2 quads, 4 doubles) near Central Australia, with an excellent, if somewhat pricey restaurant and food supposedly available 24 hours. An English

Cocktails first became popular after the development of ice making in the USA in 1870 and were introduced to Cuba soon afterwards. The first Cuban cocktails were the Cuba Libre and the Daiquirí, the former developed when US intervention forces brought in bottled cola drinks during the war of independence against Spain at the end of the 19th century, and the latter invented by an engineer in the Daiquirí mines in eastern Cuba. Cocktails boomed in the 1920s with an influx of bartenders and visitors from all over the world, many of whom were escaping prohibition in the USA. Many recipes were named after visiting film stars and other dignitaries and developed at *La Bodeguita del Medio* or *El Floridita*, bars still flourishing today. The Hemingway Special was created for the writer by the famous bartender, Constante, at *El Floridita*, others still found today include a Greta Garbo, Dorothy Gish and a Mary Pickford.

speaking guide is available for bird watching, diving and fishing. Book through Mario Díaz, Director, Rumbos Península de Zapata, T 0592535.

ZAPATA PENINSULA

The whole of the south coast of Matanzas province is taken up with the **Zapata Peninsula**, an area of swamps, mangroves, beaches and much bird and animal life. It is the largest ecosystem in the island and contains the **Laguna del Tesoro**, a 9.1 sq km lagoon over 10m deep. It is an important winter home for flocks of migrating birds. There are 16 species of reptiles, including crocodiles. Mammals include the jutia and the manatee, while there are over 1,000 species of invertebrate of which more than 100 are spiders. Access from Playa Larga or Guamá, inland.

There is a crocodile farm (Criadero de Cocodrilos) at the Zapata Tourist Institute in **Boca de Guamá**, open 0900-1800, where they breed the native Rhombifer (*cocodrilo*). This is all a bit touristy now and there is even a man who wrestles with the crocodiles (well, only the babies). Varadero, Havana and other hotels and tourist agencies organize day excursions including lunch, multilingual guide and a boat ride on the lagoon through the swamps to *Villa Guamá*, a replica Indian village. On one of the islets a series of life-size statues of Indians going through their daily routines has been carved by Cuban sculptor Rita Longa. If you go on your own, entrance to the crocodile farm is US$3 and the boat trip from Boca de Guamá to *Villa Guamá* is US$10(by ferry 20 minutes or speed boat 10 minutes). Tours are interesting and good value but involve a lot of travelling. Birdwatchers are advised to go there from Ancón and

Zapata Peninsula

spend a few nights, or go on a tour one day and return with the next tour the following day. You will see most at dawn before the tour buses arrive. Take insect repellent. There are supposed to be public buses from Jagüey Grande to Playa Girón, but most foreigners travel on tour buses or car. If you stay overnight you can often negotiate with a tour bus driver for a return journey to Varadero or Havana.

● **Accommodation** **B** *Horizontes Villa Guamá*, Laguna del Tesoro, T 59-2979, 59 a/c rooms in thatched cabañas on several little islands in the style of a Taino village, with bath, phone, TV, restaurant, bar, *cafetería*, nightclub, shop, tourist information desk, excursions, fishing for largemouth bass in the lake.

PLAYA LARGA

Phone code 59

The road south across the peninsula meets the coast at **Playa Larga**, at the head of the **Bahía de Cochinos**, commonly known as the **Bay of Pigs**. The US-backed invasion force landed here on 17 April 1961 but was successfully repelled. There is a small monument but most of the commemorative paraphernalia is at Playa Girón. The beach here is unexciting but the diving and snorkelling is excellent (see **Diving and marine life**, page 28) and you can walk to the reef

from the shore. East around the bay there is also a *cenote*, **Cueva de los Peces**, which is good for diving and snorkelling, and it is full of fish, as its name suggests. Playa Larga is also a good place to come to explore the nature reserves of the Zapata Peninsula. It is difficult to travel by car, but well worth while, as you will see large numbers of birds including numerous flamingoes, ospreys and other water birds. The **Laguna de las Salinas**, 25 km southwest, is the temporary home of huge numbers of migratory birds in November-May. At the end of the road at La Salina you can get a boat to one of the out-lying islands, **Cayo Blanco del Sur**, to see the dense, strange vegetation and, if you are lucky, some of the elusive animals. West of Playa Larga, a track leads to **Santo Tomás** where, in addition to waterfowl, you can see the Zapata wren, the Zapata rail and the Zapata sparrow. However, you can not explore alone, and no one is allowed into the reserves without a guide. Park headquarters are near the *Hotel Playa Larga*, here you can get permission to enter and pay the admission fee of US$10 per person as well as find a guide. Just as important, don't go anywhere without your insect repellent. The Park also runs a number of rare bird (Cuban parrots and Cuban parakeets), turtle and fish breeding programmes which are housed in various sites not far from the Park's headquarters between Playa Larga and Palpite. Not far from the *Hotel Playa Larga* there is a good site for watching birds such as hummingbirds and the Cuban trogon.

● **Accommodation** C *Villa Horizontes Playa Larga*, at Playa Larga, T 59-7219, sometimes fully booked with tour groups, 59 a/c spacious rooms in fairly basic one- or two-bedroomed bungalows with bath, Russian fridges and a/c, some of which work, radio, TV, water goes off at night, restaurant, bar, nightclub, shop, birdwatching and watersports. Most people prefer to travel on to stay at Playa Girón.

PLAYA GIRON

Phone code 59

Playa Girón and the **Bay of Pigs** can also be reached by taxi from Cienfuegos(1½ hours). If you do not want to stay overnight, ask the driver to wait while you visit the beach and tourist complex, and the site of national pilgrimage where, in 1961, the disastrous US-backed invasion of Cuba was attempted. There is an instructive museum full of details of how the invasion was repelled within 72 hours, with 200 CIA-trained Cuban exiles killed, 1,197 captured and 11 planes shot down. Monuments to those who died defending Castro's Cuba are scattered along the coast. Outside the museum is a British Sea Fury fighter aircraft used by Castro's air force against the invaders. The museum is open daily 0900-1700, US$2, additional US$1 to see a 15-minute film and US$1 to take photos.

The resort at Playa Girón is isolated and small with little entertainment or nightlife. It is named after a 17th century French pirate, Gilbert Girón, who frequented the area and presumably also appreciated its isolation. A stay of a few nights would be plenty to explore the area and take advantage of the scuba diving and snorkelling. The beach is walled in and therefore protected, but the sea is rocky. Further along the shore, however, there is another long sandy beach, and 8 km southeast is Caleta Buena, a pretty cove with lots of coral and fish, making it great for snorkelling and diving. There are also caves in the area for divers to explore. The dive operation at the resort offers courses and packages of dives which can be tied in with accommodation.

● **Accommodation** C *Villa Horizontes Playa Girón*, T 59-4118, 292 rooms in bungalows or blocks of rooms, a/c with bath, buffet meals, bar, pool, disco, tourist information desk, shop, car rental (make sure they give you a full tank of fuel as there is no gas station nearby).

Province of Cienfuegos

THE PROVINCE of Cienfuegos is small, with only a southern coast, but the city of Cienfuegos is well worth a visit. Despite being surrounded by industry, the old centre retains its charm and has some fascinating architectural gems. Outside the city the botanical gardens should not be missed, and for those who aim to scuba Cuba, the diving is good around the coast.

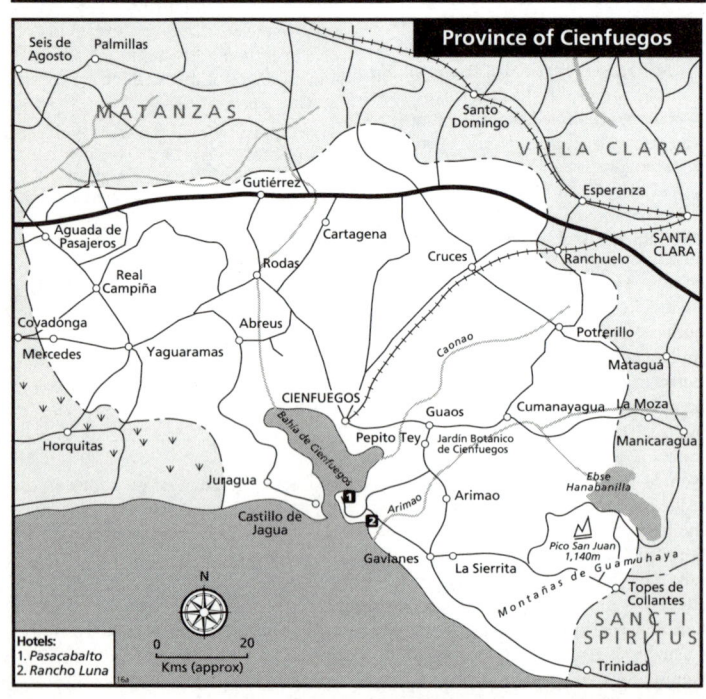

Province of Cienfuegos

Seis de Agosto
Palmillas
MATANZAS
Santo Domingo
VILLA CLARA
Gutiérrez
Esperanza
Aguada de Pasajeros
Cartagena
Cruces
Ranchuelo
SANTA CLARA
Real Campiña
Rodas
Covadónga
Abreus
Potrerillo
Mercedes
Yaguaramas
Caonao
Matagua
CIENFUEGOS
Guaos
Cumanayagua
La Moza
Horquitas
Pepito Tey
Jardín Botánico de Cienfuegos
Manicaragua
Juragua
Embse Hanabanilla
Castillo de Jagua
Arimao
Arimao
Pico San Juan 1,140m
Gavianes
La Sierrita
Montañas de Guamuhaya
Topes de Collantes
N
SANCTI SPIRITUS
Trinidad

Hotels:
1. *Pasacabalto*
2. *Rancho Luna*

0   20
Kms (approx)

Province of Cienfuegos

Small, and with only a short coastline on the Caribbean, Cienfuegos is bounded by Matanzas to the west, Villa Clara to the north and east, and Sancti Spíritus to the southeast. Cienfuegos is largely low lying, devoted to growing sugar cane with lots of sugar mills dotted around. In the east of the province, however, the **Montañas de Guamuhaya** rise to their highest point at Pico San Juan (1,140m) before spreading into the neighbouring provinces.

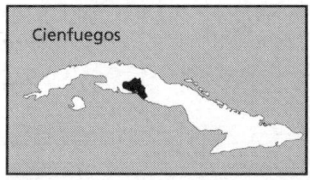

Cienfuegos

Area 4,178 sq km, *Population* 386,100, *Density* 92.4 per sq km, *Urban* 80.5%

CIENFUEGOS

Phone code 432

Cienfuegos, on the south coast, is an attractive seaport and industrial city 80 km from Trinidad and 70 km from Santa Clara. The main street, running north-south, is Calle 37, called the Prado and similar to the Prado in Havana, with a central promenade down the middle of the road where people stroll or sit. The Prado is the principal street in the city centre, but further south, between Avenida 40 and Avenida 22 where it runs beside the water, it is called the Malecón. The palm trees and the view across the Bahía de Cienfuegos make this a lovely walk. The bay can be seen from quite a few places in the centre of the city but there is no beach and the land by the water is usually unattractive and dirty. Part of Avenida 54 from Calle 31 to the Prado is closed to traffic. Known as the Boulevard, it has small trees, cafés and restaurants as well as many shops. The central square is the **Parque José Martí**, which is a pleasant plaza with benches, a rotunda bandstand and a statue of the ever-present José Martí. The arch on the west side of the square symbolizes the entrance to the city and is supposed to be similar to the Arc de Triomphe in Paris, having been built by the French founders of Cienfuegos.

Places of interest

There are interesting colonial buildings around the Parque José Martí. On the east side on Calle 29 is **La Catedral Purísima Concepción**, built in 1868, which has a somewhat neo-gothic interior with silvered columns. Mass is at 0730 and the church is open until 1200. On the north side on Avenida 56 is the majestic building of the old **Colegio San Lorenzo**, not open to the public but a site of former resistance. Next door is Cienfuegos' gem, the **Teatro Tomás Terry**, built in 1889 after the death of the Venezuelan Tomás Terry, with the proceeds of a donation by his family. It was inaugurated in 1890 with an audience of 1,200. The lobby has a statue of Terry and is decorated with fine paintings and ornate gold work. The interior is largely original with wooden seats. Note the ceiling with exquisite paintings of muses and two portraits of Cuban writers. Over the stage is a large grinning mask representing comedy. The two sets of boxes nearest the stage were traditionally used by mourners who were not supposed to be at the theatre but did not wish to miss the performance. They had a separate door so that they could enter and leave the theatre and watch the performance unseen by the rest of the audience. The theatre is open daily 0900-1800, guided tour available, free but tip expected, push open the gate across the entrance and wait for a guide. The most notable building on the west side is the **Palacio de Ferrer**, now the **Casa de Cultura Benjamín Duarte**. It is a beautiful building dating from 1894 with

a magnificent tower on the corner designed to keep an eye on the port and shipping (great views, US$1 to climb the tower). The opera singer, Caruso, stayed at the Palacio de Ferrer when he came to Cienfuegos to sing at the theatre in 1920. It is a little neglected now, but worth seeing for the marble floor, staircases and walls carved in Italy and assembled at the palace. Also note the Italian ceramic wall tiles in gold, white and blue which change colour in the sunlight, and the plasterwork on the walls and ceiling. Open Monday-Saturday 0800-1800, US$1, guided tours in Spanish. Several rooms are used for music, dance, theatre and art, especially for children. The grand grey and white building on the south side of the square is the **Antiguo Ayuntamiento**, the old town hall where Fidel Castro spoke to the people on 6 January 1959 after the revolution. About 3 km east of the centre is the **Cementerio Tomás Acea**, noted for its grand replica of the Parthenon at the entrance.

Museums

On the south side of the Parque Martí, on Avenida 54, the **Museo Provincial** (formerly the casino) is open 0800-1630 daily, US$0.50, but it suffered hurricane damage in 1996 and upstairs is closed. There is one room open of period furniture and two more of contemporary art. There are two other museums: the **Histórico Naval Nacional** (Naval Museum) at Cayo Loco was closed in 1997 because of hurricane damage, but was expected to reopen; the **Museo Hermanas Giralt (de la Clandestinidad)** on Avenida 42 entre Prado y Calle 39 has exhibits about the revolution. The **Galería de Arte de Cienfuegos** on Boulevard (Avenida 54) entre Calle 33 y 35, has a small selection of art. The **Galería de Arte Universal** is on the north side of the Parque José Martí, Avenida 56 entre Calle 25 y 27.

Excursions

15 km east of Cienfuegos on the road to Trinidad between the villages of San Antón and Guaos is the **Jardín Botánico de Cienfuegos**, a national monument founded in

1901 by Edwin F Atkins, the owner of a sugar plantation called Soledad, nowadays Pepito Tey. Atkins turned over 4.5 hectares of his sugar estates to study sugar cane, later including other trees and shrubs which could be used as raw materials for industry. In 1919 Harvard University became involved in the studies and it became known as the Harvard Botanical Station for Tropical Research and Sugar Cane Investigation. After the Revolution the State took charge of the gardens in 1961, renaming them and employing scientific personnel to preserve and develop the many tropical species now found there. Different sections of the gardens are devoted to areas such as medicinal plants, orchids, fruit trees, bamboos and one of the world's most complete collection of palm trees. It is a fine garden and a nice place to wander around, but it received a lot of damage from Hurricane Lili in 1996. See if you can get a guide as it will be much more interesting. Open 0800-1600 every day, US$2.50. The entrance is not well signed, look out for two rows of palm trees leading to the garden from the entrance at the road.

If you are in need of some sea and sand, the **Playa Rancho Luna** is about 18 km from Cienfuegos, near the *Hotel Rancho Luna*. The beach is quite nice but nothing special and there is a run down restaurant. If you continue along the road past the beach you get to the *Hotel Pasacaballos*. There is a jetty here and another further along a rough track to the left, from where you can get a little ferry (US$1) which constantly plies across the mouth of the Bahía de Cienfuegos to the village on the western side, site of the **Castillo de Jagua**. The castle was built at the entrance to the bay in 1733-1745 by Joseph Tantete, of France. There is only one entrance via a still-working drawbridge across a dry moat. Walk up the spiral staircase in the tower to a terrace which gives a view of the narrow entrance to the bay and the Escambray mountains beyond. You can also see the *Hotel Pasacaballos* and a housing project for the nuclear power station still under construction nearby. The courtyard of the castle has a prison, a chapel (the frescoes of which are being restored) and a rain water cistern. There

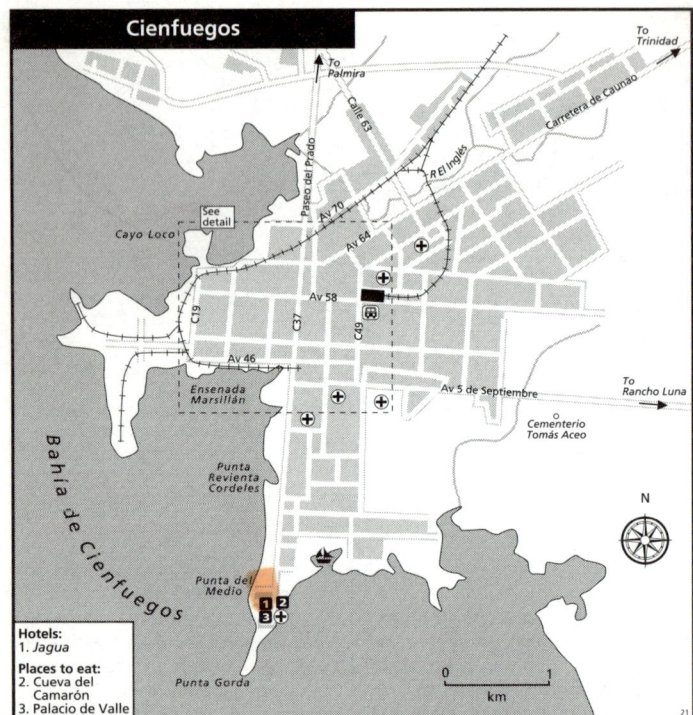

Cienfuegos

To Palmira

To Trinidad

Carretera de Caunao

Calle 63

Paseo del Prado

R El Inglés

Av 70

Av 64

See detail

Cayo Loco

Av 58

C19

C37

C49

Av 46

Ensenada Marsillán

Av 5 de Septiembre

To Rancho Luna

Cementerio Tomás Aceo

Bahía de Cienfuegos

Punta Revienta Cordeles

Punta del Medio

Hotels:
1. *Jagua*

Places to eat:
2. Cueva del Camarón
3. Palacio de Valle

Punta Gorda

0   1
km

N

is a restaurant but service is slow and food not very good. The castle is open 0800-1700 every day, entrance US$1 includes a tour. If you take a taxi or private car to the ferry ask the driver to wait for an hour while you tour the castle and walk around the village.

Festivals

Christmas is celebrated with a huge street party; rum is drunk from all manner of containers and there is dancing to a band on the *Hotel Jagua* promenade.

Local information
● **Accommodation**

Prices: L1 over US$200; **L2** US$151-200; **L3** US$101-150; **A1** US$81-100; **A2** US$61-80; **A3** US$46-60; **B** US$31-45; **C** US$21-30; **D** US$12-20; **E** US$7-11; **F** up to US$6

A1-B *Jagua* (Gran Caribe), Punta Gorda, Calle 37 No 1, T 3021-4, F 66-7454, 145 a/c rooms with view over bay, comfortable, *Palacio de Valle* restaurant next door, gorgeous decor, live piano music, simple but good food in snack bar, DHL office in hotel. Many of the hotels are out of town or booked solid by Cubans.

B *Hotel Pasacaballo*, Carretera a Rancho Luna, Km 22, T 9-6280/90, and **B** *Rancho Luna*, Km 16, T 4-8120/3, F 33-5057, 225 rooms with balcony, poor service, salt water pool, scuba diving, are seaside complexes with cafeteria etc.

People offering private accommodation meet buses and trains but charge you for gasoline to their houses. **D** Dr R Figueroa, Calle 35 4210, entre 42 y 44, T 9108, price negotiable; also his brother, Dr A Figueroa, Av 56 3927, entre 39 y 41, T 6107, hot shower, nice family, excursions offered, will take you anywhere as long as you pay for the gasoline.

● Places to eat

The place to go for its style, if not for the food, is *Palacio de Valle*, by *Hotel Jagua*, a building dating from 1894 in a mixture of architectural styles but with Arab influences predominating, incredibly ornate ceilings and other decorations, the building was bought by Alejandro Suero Balbín and given to his daughter as a wedding present upon her marriage to Sr Valle, open 1145-2300 for food, from 1000 for drinks, meals US$10-22, speciality seafood, upstairs on the roof is a bar with good views and another restaurant in the garden; in the same area on Calle 37 adjacent to the hotel is *Los Laureles* where meals are cheaper; also on Calle 37 opposite the hotel is *Cueva del Camarón*, nice place to eat, clean, open 1200-2300, meals around US$10-25; *37 y 42*, Calle 37 4204 entre 42 y 44, T 6027, open 1100-0100 or 0200, meals around US$6-10; *El Criollito*, Calle 33 5603 entre 56 y 58, T 5540, open 24 hours, meals US$7-8 include salad, chips, rice and coffee, tasty fish, live music; *La Verja*, Boulevard (Av 54) entre 33 y 35, open 1200-1800 daily, quite a nice setting but food unappetizing, no fish or chicken, meals around US$6; *El Cochinto*, Prado y Calle 4 near *Hotel Jagua*, not a great choice but you pay in pesos, open 1900-2100; *1819*, Av Prado, limited choice, menu in dollars or pesos; plenty of *paladares* on the Prado; *Coppelia* ice cream, on Prado entre Av 52 y 56, open Tuesday-Sunday 1100-2300. Some restaurants in Cienfuegos will serve only Cubans.

● Bars

El Palatino is on the south side of Parque José Martí entre Calle 25 y 27. *El Polinesio*, on the east side of Parque José Martí on Calle 29 entre Av 56 y 54, open 1000-1600, 1830-2200 every day except Monday, bit of a dark dive. The restaurant of the same name next door is also dark, open 1830-2300.

● Entertainment

Music: the Casa de la UNEAC is like a Casa de la Trova, with live local music on the west side of Parque José Martí, Calle 25, open Sunday 1000-1300, 1500-2300, and sometimes other days too.

Cinema: *Cine Prado*, is on Prado entre Av 54 y 56; *Cine Luisa* is on Prado entre Av 50 y 52.

● Banks & money changers

The **Banco Financiero Internacional** is on Av 54 esquina 29, T/F 33-5603, open 0800-1500 Monday-Friday, 3% commission on travellers' cheques. Cash advances on credit cards.

● Hospitals & medical services

The *International Clinic* is at Punta Gorda on Calle 37 202, opposite the *Hotel Jagua*, T/F 8959, offering 24-hour emergency care, consultations, laboratory services, X-rays, pharmacy and other services. There is usually someone who speaks a language other than Spanish. If the front door is shut, knock. Visa and Mastercard accepted. There is a pharmacy on Prado esquina Av 60, open 24 hours every day.

Castillo de Jagua

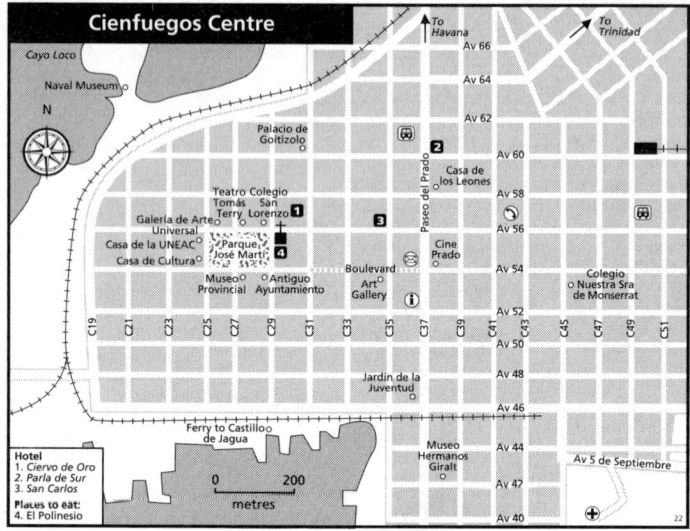

Cienfuegos Centre

To Havana
To Trinidad

Av 66
Av 64
Av 62
Av 60
Av 58
Av 56
Av 54
Av 52
Av 50
Av 48
Av 46
Av 44
Av 47
Av 40

Cayo Loco
Naval Museum
N
Palacio de Goitizolo
Casa de los Leones
Paseo del Prado
Teatro Colegio Tomás San Terry Lorenzo
Galería de Arte Universal
Casa de la UNEAC
Casa de Cultura
Parque José Martí
Museo Provincial
Antiguo Ayuntamiento
Cine Prado
Boulevard Art Gallery
Colegio Nuestra Sra de Monserrat

C19 C21 C23 C25 C27 C29 C31 C33 C35 C37 C39 C41 C43 C45 C47 C49 C51

Jardín de la Juventud

Ferry to Castillo de Jagua

Hotel
1. Ciervo de Oro
2. Perla de Sur
3. San Carlos
Places to eat:
4. El Polinesio

Museo Hermanos Giralt

Av 5 de Septiembre

0   200
metres

22

● Shopping

For souvenirs there is a small shop next to Teatro Terry which sells T shirts, books, maps, CDs, cassettes etc, open Monday-Saturday 0900-1800, Sunday 0900-1200. The dollar store *Glamour* (Tienda Panamericana) on Calle 35 entre Av 56 y 54, sells some food and clothes.

Photography: *Photo Service* on Boulevard (Av 54) entre Calle 31 y 33, and a larger branch at Punta Gorda on Calle 37 opposite the *Hotel Jagua*, open 0800-2200.

● Tour companies & travel agents

Rumbos Cuba office is on the west side of Parque José Martí, Calle 25 entre Av 56 y 54, open 0800-2000 every day. They offer local and extended tours: day trip to Playa Sirena on Cayo Largo, US$64 including flight, lunch; US$27 day trip to El Nicho near Lago Hanabanilla where there is a nice waterfall; US$17 day trip to Trinidad; US$17 to Hacienda La Vega, a farm trip.

● Transport

Local Coches: horse-drawn carriages operate in Cienfuegos. **Car hire**: Transautos is in *Hotel Jagua*. The Bahía filling station is on Prado esquina Av 40.

Bus Terminal at Calle 49 esquina Av 56. Tickets may be purchased 1 hour or so in advance from the small office with a brown door next to the Salón Reservaciones. To Havana, daily, 0600, 1000, 1230, 1500, 2350, 5 hours, US$14. From Havana, 0630, 1220, 1630, 1945, 2130. To Santiago de Cuba, every other day, 1700, US$31. To Camagüey, every other day, 0800, 1400. To Trinidad, 0630, arrive 1200, US$3. To Santa Clara, 0500, 0910, 1550, 1½-2 hours, US$2.50.

Train Terminal at Calle 49 esquina Av 58. To Havana, direct or via Santa Clara, on alternating days, 1030, 9 hours, US$9.50, or 1430, arrive Santa Clara 1700, Havana 2300, US$12.10, all services generally slow and uncomfortable.

Province of Villa Clara

O NE OF the central provinces of Cuba, with sandy beaches
on the coral cays along its northern shore and attractive
reservoirs where you can fish or hike, its capital, Santa
Clara, is best known for being the site of the last and definitive
battle of the Revolution, when Che Guevara and his men captured
an armoured troop train and subsequently the city.

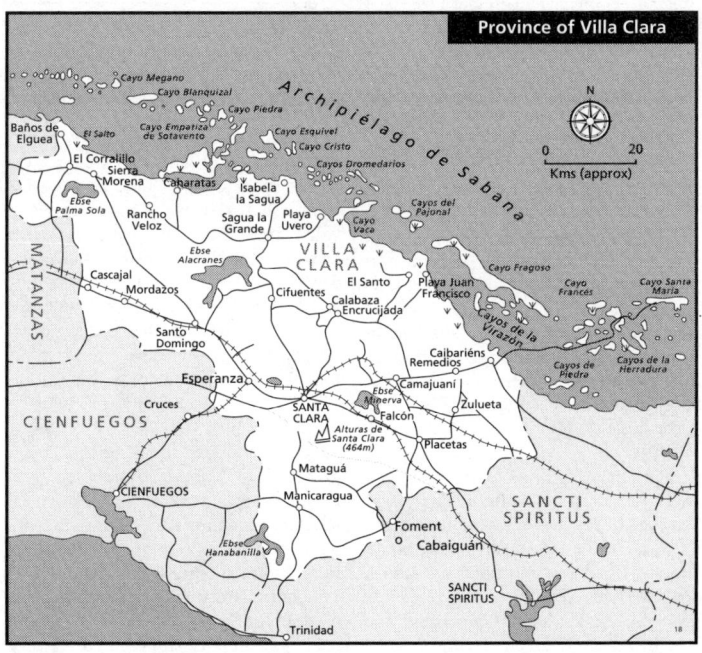

Province of Villa Clara

The northern coast of Villa Clara is fringed with numerous cays in the Archipiélago de Sabana. These coral islands have many sandy beaches and beautifully clear water, but tourism is still in its infancy. The land is low lying and there are mangroves and swamps along much of the coast. Further inland, towards the capital, Santa Clara, the land rises gently to the Alturas de Santa Clara, a range of hills reaching 464m at its highest point. The southernmost point of the province is in the Montañas de Guamuhaya, around Embalse Hanabanilla. Villa Clara has no outlet to the Caribbean Sea, being bounded to the south and east by Sancti Spíritus, to the south and west by Cienfuegos and to the northwest by Matanzas. Its port on the north coast is Caibarién, but much of its trade is also done through Cienfuegos. Sugar cane is grown on the northern plains and there are several mills providing employment.

Cattle are more common in the southern hills. There are several lakes and dams in the province. Embalse Alacranes is the second largest reservoir in the country, while Embalse Hanabanilla, the third largest, is very attractive and used for recreational purposes as well as water supply, with hunting and fishing both popular. The province boasts the largest river to drain into the Atlantic, Río Sagua la Grande, at 144 km long.

Villa Clara

Area 8,662 sq km, *Population* 825,800, *Density* 95.3 per sq km, *Urban* 74.1%

SANTA CLARA

Population 200,000; *Altitude* 112m; *Phone code* 422

300 km from Havana and 196 km from Varadero, **Santa Clara** is a pleasant university city in the centre of the island. Its main industry is a large factory making electrical domestic goods. There are not as many colonial buildings as in cities such as Camagüey or Santiago de Cuba, but there is lots of activity, mainly because of the large student population, and it is worth spending some time here.

The village of Santa Clara was founded on 15 July 1689, after the population of San Juan de los Remedios migrated from the coast to the interior to escape pirate attacks. Land was parcelled out and a powerful landholding oligarchy was formed. The settlement grew and the economy prospered on the fortunes of stockbreeding, crops and the exploitation

of the Malezas copper mines, while taking advantage of its favourable location on the main trading route through the island. In 1827 when the island was divided into three departments, Santa Clara was one of the sections of the central department. In 1867 the town became a city and in 1873 the railroad arrived, linking it with Havana. In 1895 when the island was further divided, this time into six provinces, Santa Clara became the capital of Las Villas, which included within its boundaries what is now Villa Clara, Cienfuegos, Sancti Spíritus and the Península de Zapata. The 1975 administrative reorganization sharply reduced the provincial territory, renaming it as Villa Clara, with Santa Clara as its capital and dividing it into 13 municipalities.

Santa Clara was the site of the last battle of the Cuban revolution in December 1958 before Castro entered Havana. Batista was on the point of sending an

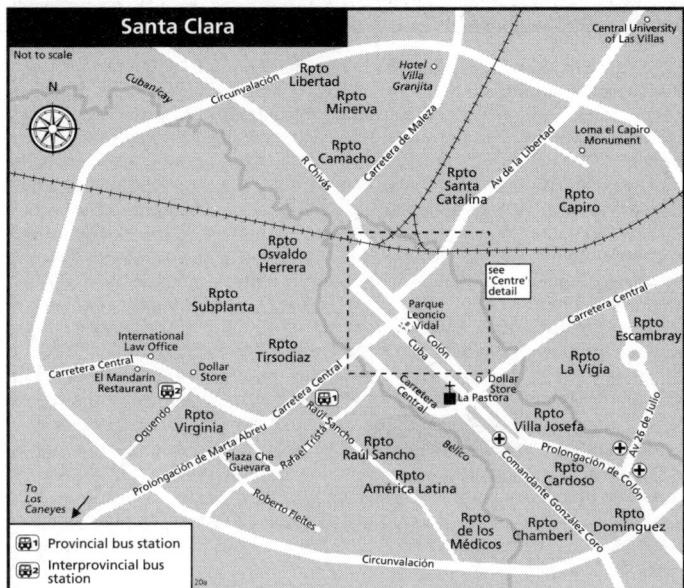

Santa Clara

Not to scale

N

Cubanicay
Circunvalación
R. Chivas
Carretera de Maleza
Carretera Central
Av de la Libertad
Central University of Las Villas
Loma el Capiro Monument

Rpto Libertad
Rpto Minerva
Hotel Villa Granjita
Rpto Camacho
Rpto Santa Catalina
Rpto Capiro

Rpto Osvaldo Herrera
Rpto Subplanta
International Law Office
Carretera Central
El Mandarin Restaurant
Dollar Store
Rpto Tirsodiaz
Rpto Virginia
Oquendo
Prolongación de Marta Abreu
Plaza Che Guevara
Rafael Tristá
Raúl Sancho
Roberto Fleites

Parque Leoncio Vidal
Cuba
Colón
see 'Centre' detail
Carretera Central
Dollar Store
La Pastora
Bélico
Carretera Central
Rpto Escambray
Rpto La Vigía
Rpto Villa Josefa
Prolongación de Colón
Comandante González Coro
Av 26 de Julio
Rpto Cardoso
Rpto Domínguez

Rpto Raúl Sancho
Rpto América Latina
Rpto de los Médicos
Rpto Chamberi

To Los Caneyes

Circunvalación

20a

🚌1 Provincial bus station
🚌2 Interprovincial bus station

---

armoured train with military supplies including guns, ammunition and soldiers to Santiago de Cuba to counter attack the revolutionaries. However, **Che Guevara** and his troops were hiding in the outskirts of Santa Clara (on the Loma de Capiro and in the university) waiting for the train. On 28 December 1958 it was ambushed in the afternoon. The soldiers on the train surrendered quickly and the fighting for the train was soon over, but the battle for the city lasted nearly four days until 1 January 1959 when news spread that Batista had fled the country. It is said that the capture of the train was the decisive factor in the triumph of the revolution and it is now a major tourist attraction (see below, **Places of interest**).

Places of interest

Parque Leoncio Vidal is the central plaza of the city, a pleasant park with trees and a central bandstand. The roads around the edge are for pedestrians only and until 1894 there was racial segregation with a fence dividing the inner and outer footpaths: white people walked in the centre of the park while blacks were only allowed around the edge. In 1996 the plaza was declared part of the National Heritage. There is a bronze statue of **Marta Abreu de Estévez**, one of the benefactors of Santa Clara. On the north side of the park on the corner of Calle Máximo Gómez is **Teatro La Caridad**, built in 1884-85 with money raised by Marta Abreu de Estévez containing frescoes by Camilo Zalaya. In its heyday it attracted artistes such as Enrico Caruso who sang there. It has been restored several times and is a National Monument. Every year a winter jazz festival is held which attracts many international jazz musicians. Also on the park is the **Biblioteca Provincial José Martí** housed in the neoclassical **Palacio Provincial** built at the beginning of the 20th century and one-time headquarters of Batista's po-

Ernesto 'Che' Guevara: Rise and Fall of the New Man

Beginning with the triumph of the Revolution on 1 January 1959, Cubans rallied to Guevara, the ascetic outsider with a dramatic appearance and an unfamiliar accent. Nicknamed 'Che' after an Argentine figure of speech, Guevara routinely spoke at Castro's side and was seen as the Revolution's second leader. His position was won through public support; a charismatic orator, Guevara appealed to the idealism of the young, calling for the birth of a 'New Man', or a revolutionary society based on moral, rather than material incentives. His eloquence on behalf of the poor and dispossessed made him a global spokesman for the Third World, but it proved easier to be against what Che was against than for what he was for. Once in power, Guevara endorsed show trials and summary executions of opponents and later, as head of the Central Bank and the Ministry of Industry, his Socialist economic reforms produced chaos even by his own account. Frustrated by Fidel Castro's increasing reliance on the Soviet Union, Guevara quit Cuba in 1965, first to join a doomed rebellion in the Congo, then, in late 1966, to launch his own guerrilla column in Bolivia. On 8 October 1967, in an operation coordinated by the CIA, Guevara was captured and executed by Bolivian troops. His remains were repatriated to Cuba 30 years later, to be interred in a bronze mausoleum at the site of his great victory in Santa Clara. Guevara remains an enigmatic figure, seen as both an inspiring idealist and an inflexible ideologue. Despite his position as the Revolution's greatest hero, 'El Che' has also become a symbol of dissent for those Cubans who recall his energy and optimism at a time when the Cuban Revolution seems to lack both.

Mausoleum of Che Guevara

lice force. Its stock of books is limited and poor but the architecture rewards a visit.

Heading east on Calle Independencia towards Camajuaní between Río Cubanicay and the railway line is the **Monumento a la Toma del Tren Blindado** where four of the carriages of Batista's troop train are preserved. The train, carrying 408 heavily armed troops and weapons, was attacked and taken on 28 December 1958 by 18 guerrillas under the command of Che Guevara in a heroic battle lasting only 1 hour. The carriages are arranged in a small park amongst clusters of angular pillars and an inscription on an obelisk describes the event. There is a museum inside the wagons showing weapons and other things carried on the train. Open Tuesday-Saturday 0900-1200, 1500-1900, Sunday 0900-1200. There is also a monument on top of **El Capiro**, the hill where Che and his troops waited to attack the train. You can get an excellent view of the city from here, just as Che did in 1958.

A monument to Che has been built in the **Plaza de la Revolución Ernesto Guevara**, with a huge bronze statue of Che on top of a large concrete plinth, a bas relief scene depicting Che in battle and an inscription of a letter from Che to Fidel. It is on Prolongación Marta Abreu after the Carretera Central forks to the north, look out for La Victoria service station, entrance on Calle Rafael Tristá, which runs parallel. The monument complex, inaugurated on 28 December 1988, was designed by **José Delarra**, who went on to construct 14 further sculptures symbolizing the feats of the guerrilla and his invading forces in Villa Clara province. The remains of Che and his comrades who fell in Bolivia have been interred at this site, with environmental work designed to be in keeping with the harsh surroundings in which they fought. Under the monument is a museum, the **Museo Histórico de la Revolución**, with good displays in Spanish about Che's life and role in the revolution, with many

photos, uniforms and personal effects, as well as displays of the battle in Santa Clara, recommended, open Tuesday-Sunday 0900-1200, 1400-1700, US$2. The Plaza de la Revolución has enough spotlights to light a football stadium, major speeches and commemorative events take place here and on 28 December there is an annual concert with Cuban and Latin American singers.

Museums

The **Museo de Artes Decorativas** is on the same side of the park as the theatre between Calle Lorda and Luis Estévez. Furniture, paintings, porcelain and glassware are exhibited in rooms around a central courtyard, each furnished in the style of the 18th, 19th, or 20th centuries. The museum is open Monday 1300-1800, Wednesday and Thursday 0900-1200, 1300-1800, Friday and Saturday 1300-1800, 1900-2200, but check the times as they can vary, entrance US$2.

Churches

The 20th century **Cathedral, Iglesia Parroquial Mayor de las Santas Hermanas de Santa Clara de Asís** is on Calle Marta Abreu, entre Alemán y Fabián, open daily 0900-1200. It is not especially interesting but there is a story to the 3m-high white marble statue of the Virgin Mary, officially known as La Inmaculada Concepción, but also called La Virgen de la Charca (Virgin of the pond). The statue was commissioned by a local association of Catholic women and blessed on Mother's Day, 12 May 1957. It stood originally at the entrance to the city but in the 1960s it was discarded in a ditch where it sank in the mud. It remained there until 1986 when it was disturbed by road building machinery and attracted huge interest with hundreds of people trying to help to clean up the Virgin. However, it was removed again and it was not until 1995, when a new Diocese of Santa Clara was created, that the rather damaged and soiled Virgin was put at the entrance to the Cathedral.

Other churches are scattered around the city. **Nuestra Señora del Carmen** is north of Parque Vidal, built in 1748 with a tower added in 1846, it has a beautiful altar. In the square outside there is a monument to the 13 families who founded the city. **Nuestra Señora del Buen Viaje**, east of the Parque on Pedro Estévez with Pardo, is a mixture of styles. Another Catholic church to the south of the Parque is **la Santísima Madre del Buen Pastor**.

Excursions

The colonial town of **San Juan de Remedios** is only 43 km east, beyond Camajuaní; there are organized tours with Rumbos, or you can hire a car or taxi driver. It is usually done as a day trip because there is no accommodation. Remedios was the eighth *villa* founded by the Spaniards, around 1513-15 by Vasco Porcallo de Figueroa and for 160 years it was the main settlement in the area. It was never given the status of one of the original *villas* because Porcallo de Figueroa refused to allow the construction of a city hall. Its location was changed a couple of times, however, in 1544 and 1578, and when pirate attacks and other commercial incentives encouraged some of the inhabitants to move inland to Santa Clara, it began to decline. Not long after the founding of Santa Clara, a fire in Remedios in 1692 hastened this trend. The present town was built following the fire and there are many beautiful colonial buildings, particularly around the **Plaza Martí**, which has a fine collection of royal palms and a gazebo in the centre. The **Iglesia San Juan Bautista de Remedios** was built in 1692 on the remains of a 1570 church, making it one of the oldest churches in Cuba. Note the carved ceiling which was once hidden by plaster but now restored. Also on the square is the **Museo de Música Alejandro García Caturla**; García Caturla was a musician who was murdered in 1940, aged 34, for upsetting the local social order by working with the poor and marrying a black woman. Apart from its colonial architecture, Remedios' other claim to fame is its carnivals, called *parrandas*. Two sections of the town compete against each other in games and festivities, with the winning district being the one to make most noise. Since the Revolution this carnival has been held on 24 July or the last Saturday in July and celebrations go on all night and into the dawn.

Local festivals

On 12 August there is a festival held at the corner of Parque Vidal. It is very popular as many Cubans are on holiday and make the most of the traditional local food, music and dancing, but hotel reservations should be no problem.

Local information
● **Accommodation**

Prices:
L1 over US$200; **L2** US$151-200; **L3** US$101-150; **A1** US$81-100; **A2** US$61-80; **A3** US$46-60; **B** US$31-45; **C** US$21-30; **D** US$12-20; **E** US$7-11; **F** up to US$6

A3 *Villa Granjita*, outside town at Km 5 on the Maleza road, T 26051/2, 40 rooms in thatched cabañas among fruit trees, cable TV, a/c, phone, pool, bar, shop, night time entertainment around the pool.

B *Los Caneyes* (Horizontes), Av de los Eucaliptos y Circunvalación, T 4512/5, F 33-5009 (outside the city), thatched public areas with 91 cabins, a/c, hot showers, TV, facilities for the disabled, pool, disco, evening entertainment by the pool, good buffet, supper US$12, breakfast US$4, excellent value, car rental, medical services, shop, tourism bureau, hairdresser, game shooting and fishing can be arranged, popular hotel for tour parties and hunters.

C *Santa Clara Libre*, central, 1956 concrete building on Parque Vidal with bullet holes on the façade preserved from the December 1958 battle when some of the police were using the building to defend the city from the revolutionaries, T 27548/27550, a/c and fans, phones, some rooms have TV, clean, water shortages, reasonable lunch, disco, car rental, observation deck with bar on top of the building, from where you get a great view of the city, cinema on ground floor.

There are several peso hotels in the centre: *Modelo*, *América* and *Central*, where power

Footprint Handbooks

...step inside
a world other travel
guides miss

Win a 7 night Cuban Highlights Tour
for two courtesy of Hayes and Jarvis

We want to hear your ideas for further
improvements as well as a few details about
yourself so that we can better serve your needs
as a traveller.

Well established as one of the UK's leading
long haul tour operators Hayes and Jarvis
prides itself on providing good quality, reliable
arrangements at sensible prices for the discerning
traveller. Every reader who sends in the completed
questionnaire will be entered in the Footprint
Prize Draw.

Mr ☐ Mrs ☐ Miss ☐ Ms ☐   Age............

First name ....

Surname..

Permanent Address..

....

....

Postcode/Zip...

Country...

Email...

Occupation..

Title of Handbook..

Which two destinations would you most
like to visit in the next two years?

....

....

How did you hear about us?
    Recommended ☐   Bookshop   ☐
    Used before   ☐   Media/press article ☐
    Library   ☐   Internet   ☐

There is a complete list of Footprint
Handbooks at the back of this book.
Which other countries would you like
to see us cover?

....

Offer ends 31 May 1999. Prize winners will be
notified by 30 June 1999 and holidays are subject
to availability. Hayes and Jarvis may offer an
alternative tour if the prize is no longer featured
at time of travel.

If you do not wish to receive information from
other reputable businesses, please tick box ☐

Footprint Handbooks

6 Riverside Court
Lower Bristol Road
Bath BA2 3DZ
T 01225 469141
F 01225 469461
handbooks@footprint.cix.co.uk
www.footprint-handbooks.co.uk

Win a 7 night Cuban Highlights Tour for two courtesy of Hayes and Jarvis

HAYES and JARVIS
HOLIDAYS WORLDWIDE

Footprint Handbooks
6 Riverside Court
Lower Bristol Road
Bath
BA2 3DZ
England

Affix
Stamp
Here

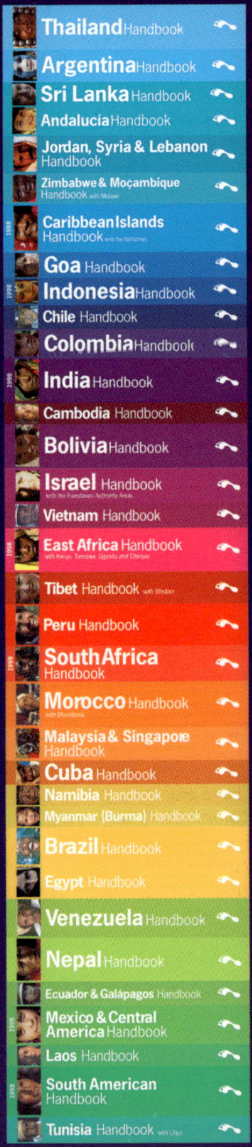

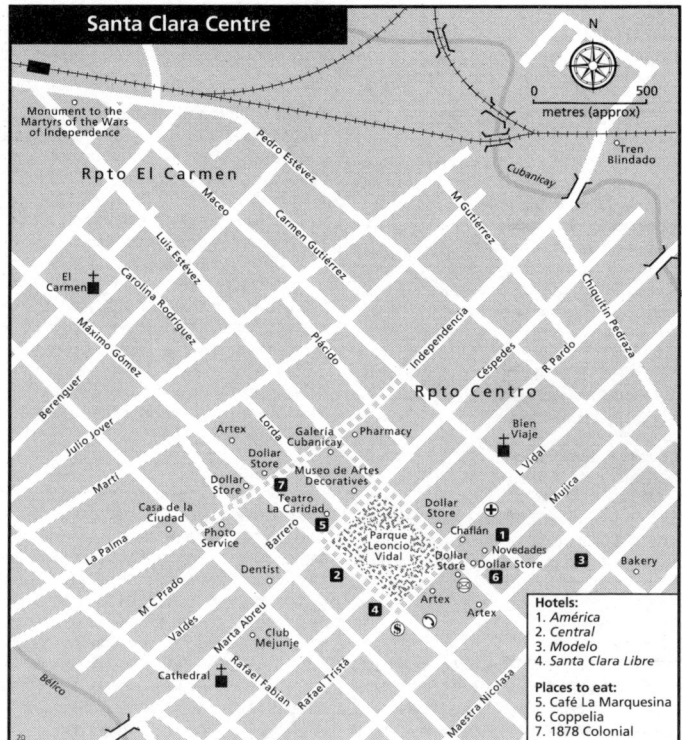

Santa Clara Centre

N

0   500
metres (approx)

Monument to the
Martyrs of the Wars
of Independence

Pedro Estévez

Tren
Blindado

Cubanicay

Rpto El Carmen

Maceo

Carmen Gutiérrez

M. Gutiérrez

Luis Estévez

Chiquín Pedraza

El
Carmen

Carolina Rodríguez

Plácido

Máximo Gómez

Independencia

Céspedes

R. Pardo

Berenguer

Rpto Centro

Julio Jover

Lorda

Artex   Galería   Pharmacy
            Cubanicay

Bien
Viaje

L. Vidal

Marti

Dollar
Store

Dollar
Store

Museo de Artes
Decoratives

Músca

Casa de la
Ciudad

Teatro
La Caridad

Dollar
Store

La Palma

Photo
Service

Barrero

Parque
Leoncio
Vidal

Chaflán   1

Novedades

3   Bakery

Dentist   2

Dollar
Store   Dollar Store

6

M C Prado

Artex

Valdés

Marta Abreu

4

Artex

Bélico

Club
Mejunje

Rafael Fabián

Rafael Trista

Maestra Nicolasa

Cathedral

Hotels:
1. *América*
2. *Central*
3. *Modelo*
4. *Santa Clara Libre*

Places to eat:
5. Café La Marquesina
6. Coppelia
7. 1878 Colonial

cuts and water shortages are common, but foreigners are not encouraged to stay there and you may be refused a room. Lodging can be found in private homes for around US$15.

● **Places to eat**

1878 Colonial, Calle Máximo 8, near the Boulevard, T 22428, offers a variety of creole dishes, mainly pork in different styles, bar in the patio; *El Marino*, Paseo de la Paz y Carretera Central, T 5594, seafood, *paellas* a speciality; *La Carreta*, Carretera Central, creole food in cosy environment; *Mandarín*, Chinese, Carretera Central beyond bus stations, reservations needed with Islazul on Calle Lorda, or T 91010, open 1830-2230; other state-owned restaurants are *Cubanicay* on the top floor of a 12-storey building in Reparto El Sandino, T 27888, and *El Nuevo Artesano* on the Parque Central, all of which are only average, better

food is served at *paladares*, which offer a wider variety of dishes and taxi service. *Sol de Cuba* on Machado (Candelaria) entre Alemán y Carretera Central, up spiral staircase, limited menu, US$6-8 for main dish, make sure rice and salad are included, not charged extra, slightly overpriced; *Rincón Criollo*, Cuba 410, entre Serafín Sánchez y Estrada Palma, T 7-1309, chicken and pork dishes US$2-3, others can be ordered, lunch 1200-1500 by reservation, dinner 1800-2400, food OK, nice surroundings, clean; *La Casona*, Carretera Central 6 entre Padre Chao y Marta Abreu, just by Río Bélico, T 5027, meals US$1-2 for main dish, side dishes US$0.25, very tasty, nice old house with beautiful tiled floor with a rose design, friendly hosts, open 1200-2400, very clean, proprietor Orlando Molina is a manager at the nearby *Los Caneyes* hotel restaurant; *La Terraza*, Serafín Sánchez 5 entre Cuba y Colón, T 73117, open 1200-2400, tables on upper storey terrace, main dishes US$2-3 including rice and salad; *El Rápido* café, on Calle Lorda near Plaza, hot dogs, pizzas, sandwiches, beer, billiards table, only US dollars, also on Calle Marta Abreu, opposite interprovincial bus station, if you have a wait; dollar shop next door sells food and bread as well as clothes, shoes, etc; *Coppelia* ice cream, Calle Colón just off Parque Vidal, corner of Calle Mujica, 1000-2330; *La Marquesina*, 24-hour café next to theatre, pleasant place for a drink or snacks, music, used to be part of the theatre but now belongs to Rumbos SA, popular with young people at night, only US dollars; another dollar cafeteria is *Europa* on the corner of Boulevard and Luis Estevez; *El Recres* is a tiny bar on the park, next to the hamburger bar. On Calle Maceo and Nazareno there is a bakery and cafeteria with good quality bread, cakes and pastries, priced in dollars.

● **Banks & money changers**

The Cadeca office for changing currency and traveller's cheques (4% commission) is at Parque Vidal on the corner of Calle Rafael Tristá and Cuba, T 5690. However there is nowhere in town where you can get dollars with a credit card or traveller's cheques, you have to go to Cienfuegos.

● **Entertainment**

Club Mejunje (mishmash), 2½ blocks west from Parque Vidal, Calle Marta Abréu 107 entre Fabián y Juan Bruno Zayas, cultural centre and **Casa de la Trova** in a backyard full of artefacts and graffiti-covered walls, opens 1700, Wednesday-Sunday, free, pay for rum in pesos, composers, singers, musicians and friends sing, play and drink together, friendly, welcoming, enjoyable. Larger events are staged in the courtyard, wide variety ranging from concerts to theatre, from shows for kids to shows for gays, 5 pesos for Cubans, US$1 for foreigners. Comedians, rock bands and other entertainers can be seen at Parque del Humor, Chaflán, off Parque Vidal, open Tuesday-Sunday at 1500 and 2000, and on Sunday also at 0900. There is a cinema on the ground floor of the *Hotel Santa Clara Libre* on Parque Vidal and the best local disco is in the basement, *Disco Basement* opens Tuesday-Sunday 2230-0400, US$5 per person.

● **Hospitals & medical services**

The best hospital for foreigners is the *Arnaldo Milián Castro Hospital*, at Circunvalación and Av Escambray in the Residencial Escambray area to the south of the town, T 72016/71234. If you need a taxi to take you there, T 26956. Ambulance T 22259/23965. There is a 24-hour pharmacy at Luis Estévez 8 on the corner with Boulevard.

● **Post & telecommunications**

Post Office: Calle Colón just off Parque Vidal, opposite *Coppelia* ice cream parlour, open 0800-1800 Monday-Saturday.

Telephones: the phone code for Santa Clara is 422, but for other towns in the province it is 42. The office for international phone and fax is on Calle Cuba 7 entre Parque Vidal y Machado, open Monday-Saturday 0700-2200, Sunday 0700-1200, calls to the USA US$3/minute, minimum 4 minutes, to the UK US$5.85/minute but no minimum time. Send and receive faxes, F 735009. Postcards and stamps also sold. International phone calls can be made from *Hotel Santa Clara Libre*, US$3/minute to the USA, US$6 to the UK.

● **Shopping**

The road behind the theatre which runs between Calles Maceo and Juan Bruno Zayas is known locally as Boulevard. It is pedestrianized and locals shop here for clothes and other items, there are some cafés, dollar stores, a cinema and a store with some handicrafts. Next to the theatre on the corner of Parque Vidal and Lorda is a small shop selling T shirts, books about Che, cassettes and CDs, nicknacks and maps. On the south side of Parque Vidal, a dollar store, *Artex*, sells a few handicrafts, cassettes, CDs, toiletries, drinks, a few books in English principally on Fidel and Che, T shirts and nicknacks. *Novedades* is a dollar store selling some food and drink and clothes on Calle Colón, just off Parque Vidal, next to *Coppelia* ice cream parlour. *Galería Cubanicay* on Calle Luis Estévez 9 has various handicrafts and art. *Photo Service* at Boulevard 57 develops and sells film, eg Kodachrome Elite US$9.55, Agfa black and white US$4.65, open 0800-2200. There is a small daily agromercado selling some fruit and vegetables on Calle Sandino near the Estadio Sandino baseball stadium. Another, *Agromercado La Toronja*, is on Calle Cuba entre Síndico y Gral Roloff (also known as Caridad)

● **Sports**

You can swim at the *Hotel Los Caneyes* for US$2.50, which entitles you to US$2 worth of drinks at the bar. Bring your own towel. Fishing and duck shooting expeditions are organized to Embalse Alacranes and Embalse Hanabanilla, enquire at *Hotel Los Caneyes*.

● **Tour companies & travel agents**

Islazul is at Calle Lorda 6 entre Parque Vidal y Boulevard, just off Parque Vidal by the theatre, but may be moving, open Monday-Friday 0800-1130, 1300-1545, mostly hotel and restaurant reservations. *Rumbos Cuba* desk in *La Marquesina* café, tours arranged, French and English spoken. Their main office is in *Hotel Los Caneyes*. A morning tour of the city costs US$10; 2-hour cigar factory US$9; trip to Remedios and lunch US$21; to Lago Hanabanilla with boat trip and lunch US$32; a fishing trip on the lake US$48, and others.

● **Useful addresses**

Immigration: there is an immigration office for visa extensions on Sexta 9, entre Carretera Central y Av Sandino, English spoken, T 212523. **Police**: the Police Station is on Calle Colón entre Serafín García (Nazareno) y Morales(Síndico), near Parque Vidal, T 116. **Services**: there is a public toilet at the corner of Calle Luis Estévez y Boulevard, small charge.

● **Transport**

Local Horse-drawn *coches*, or taxi-buses go all over town and down Calle Marta Abreu to the bus stations, 1 peso. There are also some buses, 40 centavos. Taxi service T 26856/26956, or pick up a private car. **Car hire** can be arranged at the hotels.

Air There is no airport and no airline offices in Santa Clara.

Bus From Havana, US$16, 4 hours. The provincial bus station for destinations within Villa Clara, is on Calle Marta Abreu, T 26284, 1 km from centre, on corner with Calle Pichardo, white building. The interprovincial bus station for long distances is on the same road with Oquendo, T 92114, 1 km further out, in blue building.

Train The railway station, T 22895, is north of Parque Vidal on Estévez and is much more central than either of the bus stations. There are daily trains to Havana and Santiago; the *especial* stops here heading east at 2048 and west at 0253. There is a train to Bayamo/Manzanillo at 0418, which on the return journey to Havana leaves Santa Clara at 0843. Similarly a train to Camagüey leaves at 2327, returning to Havana and passing through Santa Clara at 2338; to Sancti Spíritus at 1319, returning to Havana at 0025. Two daily trains run Cienfuegos-Sancti Spíritus, passing through Santa Clara around 0700-0730 and 1730. None of these times is reliable and the train may not even appear at any time.

LAKE HANABANILLA

30 km south of Santa Clara the road to Trinidad passes through **Manicaragua**, a large town of some 80,000 inhabitants set in rolling hills covered with tobacco fields, and then rises into the Escambray mountains. The man-made reservoir, **Hanabanilla**, is the third largest in the country and has the largest hydroelectricity station, but looks natural. It is in very attractive landscape with lovely views. It has been a resort area for a long time because of its popularity with the shooting/fishing fraternity. The lake is stocked with largemouth bass and other fish and there are plenty of wild duck, quail, pheasants and other game birds. This does, of course, also make it interesting for twitchers. You can take a boat trip on the lake (boat rentals US$20/hour) to the *Restaurante Río Negro* (7 km from the hotel and accessible only by boat) and the Trucha Falls, and go hiking or horse riding in the mountains. The resort area can get crowded with Cubans at the weekends, but you don't need to walk far to get peace and quiet. Lake Hanabanilla can be visited as a day trip from Santa Clara, Cienfuegos, Trinidad or Sancti Spíritus, but an overnight stay would be more rewarding and it is a convenient place to stay between the towns. There is almost no public transport to the lake despite assurances of the occasional bus from Manicaragua, so car hire or private transport is essential.

● **Accommodation**   **B-C** *Hanabanilla*, T 86392, on the northwest edge of the lake, rates vary with the season, 127 rooms, a/c, phone, radio, pool, bar and grill, restaurant with Cuban and international food, *Mirador Bar* on the top floor has excellent view, disco, tours offered, fishing tackle available.

THE COAST

In the extreme west of the province, 136 km from Santa Clara, is **Elguea**, a health resort with sulphur springs which are used to treat arthritis, rheumatism and skin diseases. Thermal waters come in different temperatures and there are medicinal muds for a variety of complaints. Quali-fied medical assistance is available, along with masseurs. There are beaches at **El Salto** and **Ganuza**, nearby, where there are no hotels but you can find accommodation at local resorts, *campismo*. The nearest ho-tel is outside **Coralillo**, **D-E** *Hotel Elguea*, Circuito Norte, T 668020/686290, 139 rooms with TV, fridge, pool, tennis, gym, fishing.

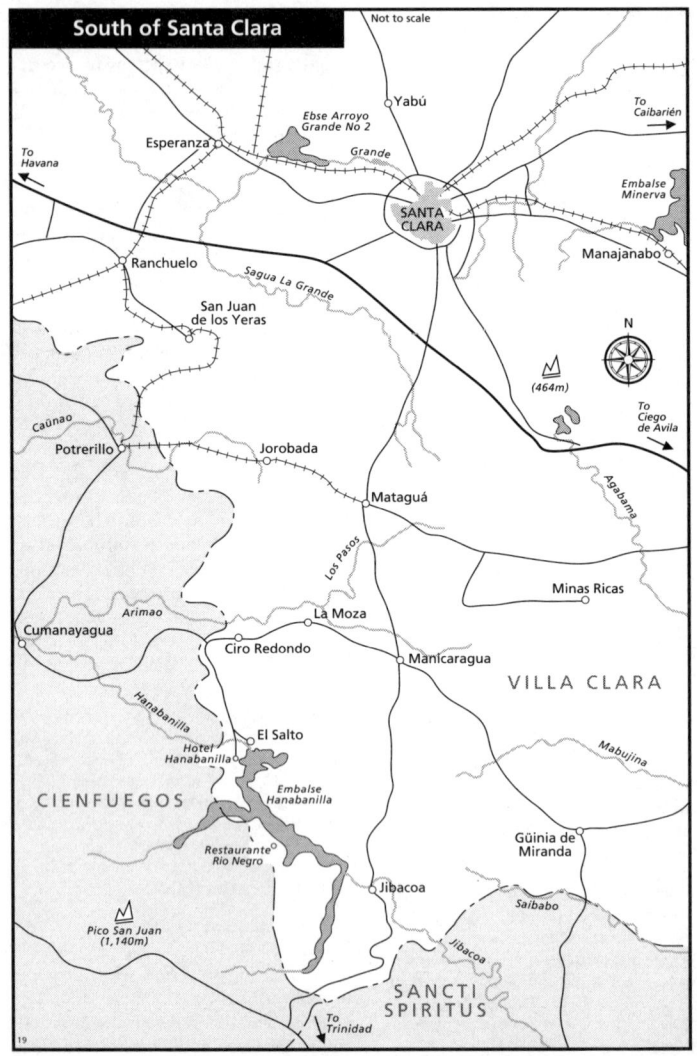

In the extreme east of the province, 8 km beyond Remedios and 51 km from Santa Clara, is the main port of **Caibarién**. There is a beach here but this is surpassed by the newly-accessible cays which are still virgin territory. In 1996 a stone causeway was completed which now links the port with **Cayo Santa María** and others in between. Hotels are planned in the near future once foreign investment is secured, possibly in 1998.

Calalú

Calalú is an Afro-Caribbean soup, which varies from island to island according to the available ingredients. Its basis is the green leaves of the *malanga*, or dasheen plant, which has a tuber resembling a sweet potato, but any green leaves can be substituted, such as spinach, leaf beet, chard or Chinese leaves. Any edible green leaves will do, even the young leaves of yams, yucca or squashes.

90 gm bacon or ham
250 gm fresh white fish, crab, shrimp or lobster
1 kg *malanga* leaves, washed
$\frac{3}{4}$ litre chicken stock
1 onion, chopped
3 cloves of garlic, chopped
3 cloves
3-5 spring onions, chopped
2-3 sprigs of thyme
2-3 sprigs of parsley, chopped
1 hot chilli, chopped
8 tablespoons of coconut milk
250 gm *quimbombó* (okra)
salt, pepper and hot sauce to taste

Lightly fry the bacon or ham cut into little pieces and reserve any fat which is left; if there is less than 4-5 tablespoonfuls make up to that amount with oil and fry in it the fish or seafood cut into small pieces. Put the bacon, *malanga* leaves, onion, garlic, cloves, spring onions, thyme, parsley, and chilli into the stock and boil until the bacon is soft. Add the fish or seafood, the coconut milk and the *quimbombó*, sliced or whole. When the *quimbombó* is cooked season with salt, pepper and hot sauce. Serve with rice or bananas and hot sauce for those who like extra. Some people beat the soup to make it thick and add little pieces of crispy bacon or pork crackling.

Province of Sancti Spíritus

E
AST OF Villa Clara, the next province is Sancti Spíritus, known for the splendour of the colonial city of Trinidad rather than the provincial capital, although the city of Sancti Spíritus was one of the earliest towns founded in the 16th century and should not be missed. Architecturally, Trinidad is perhaps the most important town in Cuba, its colonial gems suspended in a time warp and protected by its status as a UNESCO World Heritage Site.

Province of Sancti Spíritus

The province of Sancti Spíritus has a short Atlantic coastline which includes the Cayos de Piedra and a beach at La Victoria, but its Caribbean coastline is much longer, making it a triangular province. It is bordered by Villa Clara to the west, Cienfuegos to the southwest and Ciego de Avila to the east. The flatlands of the northern coast rise to the Sierra de Meneses, and the flatlands of the southern coast rise in the west to the Montañas de Guamuhaya. Much of the southeast of the province is flat, with mangroves and wetlands along the coast, and this area contains the largest man made reservoir in the country, Embalse Zaza, through which flows the second longest river in the country, the Río Zaza, 144.7 km long. Most tourism is concentrated on Trinidad, but the lake is popular for fishing and duck shooting. Much of the province's economy depends on sugar cane and cattle, but there is also some tobacco grown on the hills and rice paddies in the low lying south.

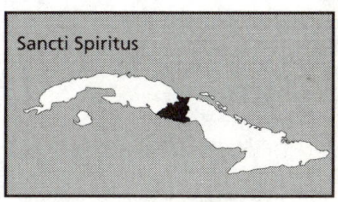

Area 6,744 sq km, *Population* 453,300, *Density* 67 per sq km, *Urban* 69.1%

TRINIDAD

Population 60,000, *Phone code* 419

Trinidad, 133 km south of Santa Clara is a perfect relic of the early days of the Spanish colony: beautifully preserved streets and buildings with hardly a trace of the 20th century anywhere. It was founded in 1514 by Diego Velázquez as a base for expeditions into the 'New World'; Cortés set out from here for Mexico in 1518. The five main squares and four churches date from the 18th and 19th centuries; the whole city, with its fine palaces, cobbled streets and tiled roofs, is a national monument and since 1988 a UNESCO World Heritage Site.

A thriving economy soon grew up around the settlement, originally based on livestock, with the export of leather, meat and horses. This prize inevitably attracted the attention of adventurers and there was a particularly severe period of attacks between 1660-1688. Mansfield from Port Royal in Jamaica and Legrand from Tortuga looted and set fire to the town, destroying the original archives of the church and the city hall. Unlike other populations who moved inland to escape pirate attacks, the inhabitants of Trinidad decided to stay and defend their wealth with their own fleet, inflicting several defeats on British and Dutch corsairs in the 17th and 18th centuries. After the British took Havana in 1797 they tried and failed to invade Trinidad and Sancti Spíritus, an event which is portrayed in the coats of arms of both cities. After a time sugar was introduced, most successfully, and by 1797 there were 56 sugar mills and 11,697 slaves, imported to work in the sugar cane fields. Trade, the arts and sciences all expanded on the back of the sugar prosperity. Alejandro de Humboldt visited and studied the fauna and flora around Trinidad. The first printing press was opened and the first newspaper began to circulate. Schools of languages, music and dance were opened and a wide variety of artisans set up businesses, including gold and silversmiths. In 1827 the Teatro Cándamo opened its doors. The well off patricians built huge mansions for themselves (now museums) and sent their children to European universities. However, the Industrial Revolution and the increase in sugar beet grown in Europe sounded the death knoll for an economy based on slave labour and in the second half of the 19th century Trinidad went into decline. Construction ceased and the city remained frozen in time with its cobbled streets and red tiled roofs.

Plazas and churches

The **Plaza Mayor** is the centre of the town, elegantly adorned with glazed earthenware urns. Around the plaza are the Museo Romántico and the Museo Arqueología as well as the cathedral, **Iglesia Parroquial de la Santísima Trinidad**, built between 1817 and 1892 and consecrated in the latter year. The altars are made of precious woods, such as cedar, acacia, caoba and grenadine and were built in 1912-1922 by a French priest, Amadeo Frieory, a Swiss Brother Lucas and two Cuban carpenters. It is the largest church in Cuba and is renowned for its acoustics. On the left at the front of the church is a crucifix of the brown-skinned Christ of Veracruz, who is

the patron of Trinidad. The church is open 1130-1300, 1930-2000, mass daily at 2000-2100 when tourists are excluded. **Parque Céspedes** has shaded archways of vines and trailing plants. To the west is the fine building of the local government, Poder Popular Municipal, and to the south is the **Iglesia de San Francisco de Paula**. The **Plaza Santa Ana**, now officially known as the **Parque Isidoro Armenteros**, is a little to the northeast of the centre. On the north side is the ruined church, the **Ermita de Santa Ana** and on the east is a yellow colonial building housing the *Restaurante Santa Ana*.

Museums

The **Museo Romántico**, Calle Hernández 52, next to the church of Santísima Trinidad on the main square, is excellent. It has a collection of romantic-style porcelain, glass, paintings and ornate furniture which belonged to the Conde de Brunet family, dating from 1830-1860 displayed in a colonial mansion, with beautiful views from the upper floor balconies. No cameras allowed, open Tuesday, Thursday

Plaza Mayor dominated by the Iglesia de la Santísima Trinidad

0800-2200, Saturday-Monday, Wednesday, Friday 0800-1800, US$2, T 4363. Locals come here for their wedding photos. **Museo Municipal de Historia** is on Calle Simón Bolívar 423, an attractive building but rather dull displays in 8 rooms of scientific, historical and cultural displays, walk up the tower for a good view of Trinidad, open Sunday, Monday, Tuesday, Thursday 0900-1800, Wednesday, Friday 0900-2200, US$1.50, T 4460. These two museums are very popular with tour parties and can get very crowded, particularly on Wednesdays. It then becomes very difficult to get up the narrow staircase to the tower and roof view. Other museums worth visiting include the **Museo de Arqueología Guamuhaya**, Simón Bolívar 457, esquina Villena, Plaza Mayor, with a general view of developments from pre-Columbian to post-conquest times, T 3420, open Monday, Wednesday 0900-2200, Sunday, Tuesday, Thursday, Friday 0900-1700, US$1; **Museo de Arquitectura Colonial**, Desengaño 83, T 3208, exhibits specifically on the architecture of Trinidad, particularly aspects of the 18th and 19th centuries, open Monday, Thursday

---

Trinidad street names, old and new

Maps of Trinidad can be unbelievably difficult to follow because of the use of old and new street names. Locals of course switch from one to the other, but to the average traveller the possession of a map with completely different street names to those written on the walls can be frustrating. Here is a list of some of the changes:

New name	Old name
Vicente Suyama	Encarnación
Isidoro Armenteros	San Antonio
Juan M Márquez	Amargura
Ciro Redondo	San José
Fernando Hernández	Cristo
Piro Guinart	Boca
Ruben Martínez Villena	Real del Jigüe
Simón Bolívar	Desengaño
Francisco Javier	Rosario
Antonio Maceo	Gutiérrez
José Martí	Jesús María
Gustavo Izquierdo	Gloria
Patricio Lumumba	Cañada
Almirante Colón	Colón
Jesús Menéndez	Alameda
Ernesto Valdes Muñoz	Media Luna
Rita M Montelier	La Rosa
José Mendoza	Santa Ana
Julio A Mella	Guásima
Lino Pérez	San Procopio
Camilo Cienfuegos	Santo Domingo
Miguel Calzada	Borrel
Francisco Cadahia	Gracia
Schmidt	Smith
Agustín Bernaz	Paz
Abel Santa María	Lirio
Independencia	Nueva
Peterssen	Del Coco

0900-2200, Saturday, Sunday, Tuesday, Wednesday 0900-1700, US$1; **Museo Nacional de Lucha Contra Bandidos**, Calle Hernández esquina Piro Guinart, housed in the old San Francisco convent, exhibits about the campaign in the Escambray mountains, open Tuesday, Friday 0900-2200, Wednesday, Thursday, Saturday, Sunday, 0900-1700, US$1, T 4121.

Places of interest

The **Casa de la Cultura** is on Calle Zerquera 406 entre Muñoz y Lumumba, open 0700-2300 every day. A small gallery has art for sale, there is a small shop and a Sala de Teatro y Danza open for special events.

The **Casa de la Música** has two entrances. There is a **Casa de la Trova** (see **Entertainment**, page 192) for music in an

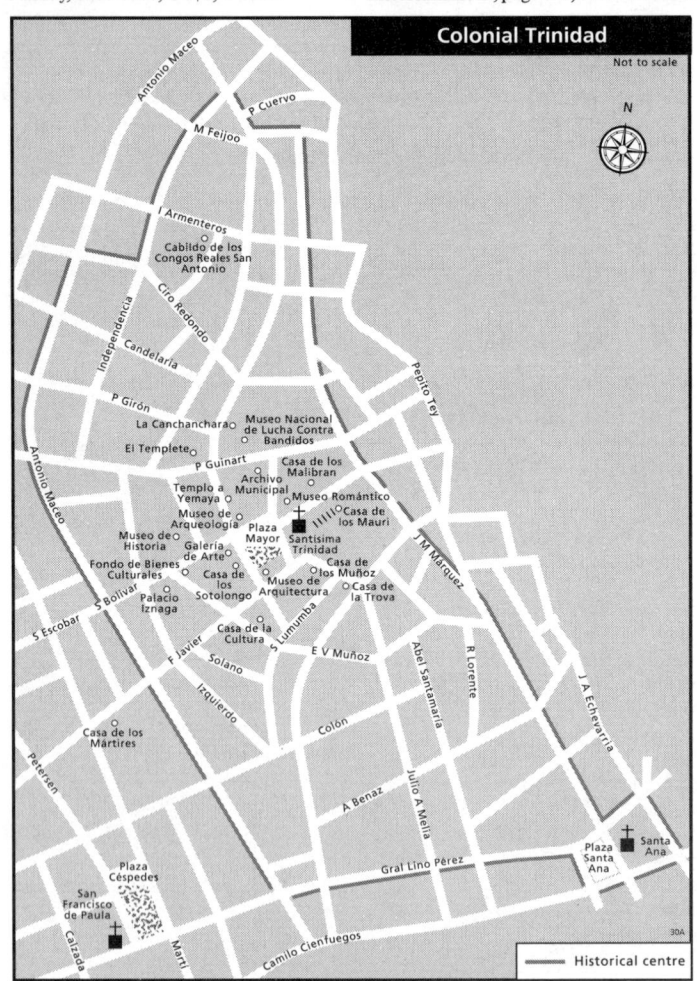

Colonial Trinidad

Not to scale

N

Cabildo de los Congos Reales San Antonio

Museo Nacional de Lucha Contra Bandidos

La Canchanchara

El Templete

Casa de los Malibran

Archivo Municipal

Templo a Yemaya

Museo Romántico

Museo de Arqueología

Casa de los Mauri

Museo de Historia

Plaza Mayor

Santísima Trinidad

Galería de Arte

Fondo de Bienes Culturales

Casa de los Sotolongo

Casa de los Muñoz

Palacio Iznaga

Museo de Arquitectura

Casa de la Trova

Casa de la Cultura

Casa de los Mártires

Plaza Céspedes

San Francisco de Paula

Plaza Santa Ana

Santa Ana

30A

Historical centre

The old San Francisco Convent, now the Museo Nacional da Lucha Contra Bandidos

open air shell of a house, entrance on Calle Márquez, open Monday-Saturday from 2200 until late for music performed by live bands and on Sunday from 1400 for singing groups, going on until late with *música mecánica*. The other part of the casa, a green house, has an entrance at the top of the steps leading from Hernández just east of Santísima Trinidad (nice, small, open air bar on the right half way up the steps), open 0800-0200. There is a music shop selling CDs, cassettes and also instruments, with a small display of the history of music in Trinidad. These two places join back to back.

The **Piro Guinart Cigar Factory** is on Maceo esquina Colón, opposite the *Restaurante Colonial*. It is not very big and the tour is free but tips are gratefully received; it is all right to take photos. Open Monday-Saturday 0700-1200, 1300-1600, but only a few people work on Saturdays.

El Alfarero ceramics factory making earthenware pots on Calle Andrés Berro can be visited. There is no organized tour but it is open for you to wander around, watch the pots being thrown and glazed and buy anything if you want. Open Monday-Saturday 0730-1200, 1300-1600, go east on Maceo until you get to a school,

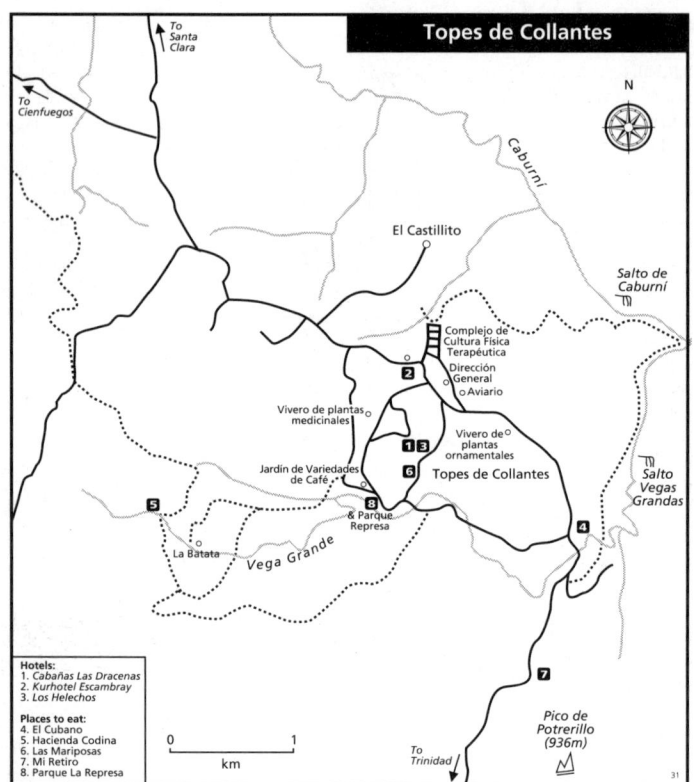

Topes de Collantes

To Santa Clara

To Cienfuegos

Caburní

El Castillito

Salto de Caburní

Complejo de Cultura Física Terapéutica

2

Dirección General

Aviario

Vivero de plantas medicinales

Vivero de plantas ornamentales

1 **3**

Jardín de Variedades de Café

6   Topes de Collantes

5

8

Parque Represa

Salto Vegas Grandas

4

La Batata

Vega Grande

Hotels:
1. Cabañas Las Dracenas
2. Kurhotel Escambray
3. Los Helechos

Places to eat:
4. El Cubano
5. Hacienda Codina
6. Las Mariposas
7. Mi Retiro
8. Parque La Represa

0   1
km

To Trinidad

7

Pico de Potrerillo (936m)

where you turn left. El Alfarero is the low yellow building two blocks on the right hand side.

Excursions

Parque Natural Topes de Collantes

Inland from Trinidad are the beautiful, wooded Escambray mountains, whose highest point is Pico San Juan, also known as La Cuca, at 1,140m. Rivers have cut deep valleys, some of which, such as the Caburní and the Guanayara, have attractive waterfalls and pools where you can swim. 110 sq km of the mountains have been classified as the **Parque Natural Topes de Collantes** which contains many endemic species of fauna and flora. There

is no public transport but day trips are organized to Topes de Collantes by Rumbos. A Jeep Safari for 6 hours costs US$25, minimum 3 passengers, lunch not included. A Truck Safari, minimum 10 passengers, including lunch, costs US$37, both take in swimming in a waterfall. You can see hummingbirds and the tocororo, the national bird of Cuba. A great day out. Hiring a private car with driver to Topes de Collantes and the **Salto de Caburní** will cost you about US$15-20. Private tours do not go to the same places as jeep tours, whatever anybody tells you. There is also a huge hospital in the mountains, *Kurhotel Escambray*, which offers special therapeutic treatments for patients from all over the world, and a hotel **C** *Los Helechos*, T 40117, F 40288, 38 rooms, restaurant, bar, cafeteria, thermal pool, gym, massage, sauna, steam baths, bowling alley, shop, tourism bureau, car hire.

There are several paths in the area and walking is very rewarding with lovely views and lush forest, although Hurricane Lili passed through here in 1996 and took many trees with her. Take the road which forks right (north) at the *Kurhotel Escambray* for the Caburní falls, park at the house at the end of the road if you have a car, and from there it is a 2 km walk to the waterfall through the forest with good views. A guide at the house will take you for US$1, but it isn't really necessary. You can swim in the cold pools at the bottom of the 62m falls or take a path to the right a few hundred metres before the falls for swimming in the river below. Another 2 km walk leads west from the hotels to **La Batata**, a cave with an underground river making pools in which you can swim. The temperature of the water never exceeds 20C. Just northwest of here, but best reached on another path, is the restaurant at *Hacienda Codina*, often combined with a trip to the Cueva del Altar, the orchid gardens and a *mirador*/lookout.

12 km north of Topes near Guanayara, there is another waterfall, the **Salto El Rocío**, with swimming in the Poza del Venado by the Río Caballero. There is a restaurant nearby, the *Casa de la Gallega*, where you can have a chicken lunch Galician style.

Alberto Delgado monument

About 4 km from Trinidad on the Cienfuegos road on the way to the turning for the Topes de Collantes national park, there is a small monument to **Alberto Delgado**. Turn south on the road by the stone wall with his name on it and there is a small monument and cave by the Río Guaurabo. Alberto Delgado was a revolutionary who infiltrated the group of US backed counter revolutionaries known as G2, working

from the Escambray mountains. As a result of his activities a group of 90 counter revolutionaries was caught. However, intelligence sources in Cuba and Miami identified him as a spy and a message to that effect was sent from Radio Swan (on Swan Island near Miami) to G2 in the mountains. Delgado was captured and executed by the counter revolutionaries by being hung from a tree in the vicinity of the monument. On the other side of the river from the monument is the house of the Finca Maisinicú, where Alberto Delgado lived.

Torre de Manaca Iznaga and Valle de los Ingenios

Rumbos will also take you to the **Torre de Manaca Iznaga** in the village of the same name about 15 km from Trinidad on the road to Sancti Spíritus, or you can hire a private car to take you for about US$10. The legend goes that there were two rival brothers, one wanted to build a tower and the other wanted to dig a hole as deep as

---

The little blue train to Manaca Iznaga

A fun way to see the Valley of the Sugar Mills and visit the tower is to take a tiny passenger train (really a bus on train wheels) which will take you past small villages, sugar mills and cane fields. The trains are spartan and often crowded. The little blue train leaves Trinidad daily at 1000 and 1740 and takes about 30 minutes to get to Manaca Iznaga, allowing you about an hour there before you catch the return train. A little brown train with two or three coaches leaves Trinidad daily at 0900, 1300 and 1700 and takes 40 minutes to get to Manaca Iznaga, fare 50 centavos. If you have already seen the tower, or just like train journeys, you can do a return trip on the blue train to Meyer, 2 hours, 80 centavos, or on the brown train to Condado, 2 hours 10 minutes, 60 centavos.

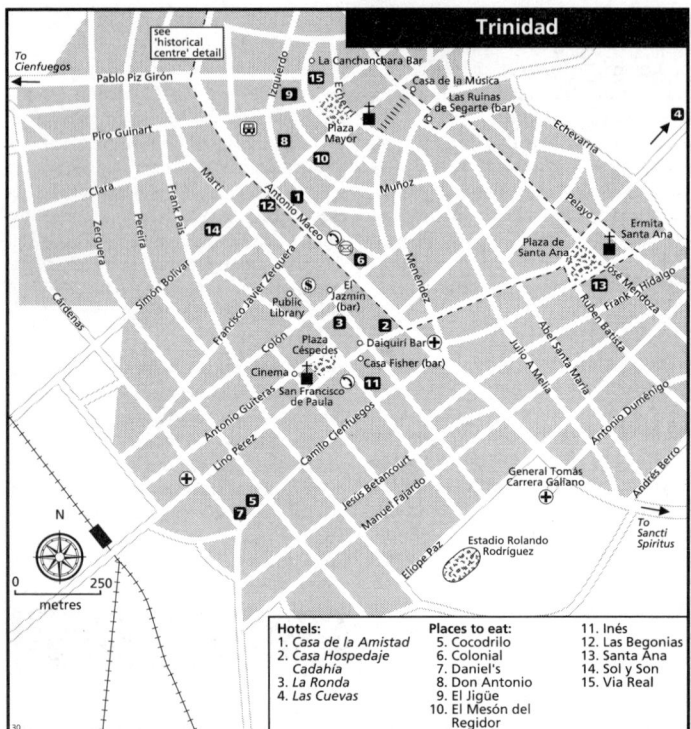

Trinidad

Hotels:
1. *Casa de la Amistad*
2. *Casa Hospedaje Cadahía*
3. *La Ronda*
4. *Las Cuevas*

Places to eat:
5. Cocodrilo
6. Colonial
7. Daniel's
8. Don Antonio
9. El Jigüe
10. El Mesón del Regidor

11. Inés
12. Las Begonias
13. Santa Ana
14. Sol y Son
15. Via Real

the tower was high. In fact there is only a tower, built between 1835-1845. It is 43.5m high, has seven floors and 136 steps to the top. It was built as a lookout to watch the slaves working in the valley at the sugar mills. There were two bells in the tower, one was rung when it was time for the slaves to stop work and take a meal in a communal eating house, the other was rung if an escape was discovered, alerting the slave catchers, or *rancheros*. One of the bells, dating from 1846, can be seen on the path leading to the tower. It has now been given UNESCO World Heritage status alongside Trinidad city, because of its historical importance. There is a great view of the surrounding countryside including the **Valle de los Ingenios** (Valley of the Sugar Mills) and the Escambray Moun-

tains as well as the roof tops of the village below. Open 0900-1600 or 1700, entrance US$1. The *Manaca Iznaga* restaurant is in the old plantation house, a yellow colonial building, open 0900-1700 daily, meals US$7-8, and there is a small shop. Look out for the large sugar cauldrons lying around the village.

On the same road, 5 km from Trinidad is a *mirador*, or look out point, from where you get a fine view of the Valley of Sugar Mills and the Escambray mountains, with the sea on the opposite side. There is a nice bar at the *mirador*, and if a tour group turns up there is often a demonstration of a sugar press.

Excursions are offered by Rumbos, eg US$12 for a city tour including the Valley of the Sugar Mills *mirador*, the tobacco and ceramics factories, museums and *La Canchanchara*; US$50 for a trip to the Zapata peninsula, minimum 12 people; US$99 to Cayo Largo; US$43 to Río Negro in the Escambray mountains to Lago Hanabanilla; US$26 for a sea safari to Cayo Blanco with snorkelling and other trips to Havana or Cienfuegos with flights over Trinidad.

Local information
● Accommodation

Prices: **L1** over US$200; **L2** US$151-200; **L3** US$101-150; **A1** US$81-100; **A2** US$61-80; **A3** US$46-60; **B** US$31-45; **C** US$21-30; **D** US$12-20; **E** US$7-11; **F** up to US$6

A3-B *Motel Las Cuevas* (Horizontes), Finca Santa Ana, T 419-4013/9, on a hill 10 minutes' walk from town (good road), nice view of the sea, 114 very comfortable rooms in 60 chalets and apartments with a/c, phone, radio, hot water, and very clean, 2 swimming pools, bar, beer US$1.50, discotheque from 2200 in cave below reception, entrance US$2(most rooms are far enough away not to be disturbed by noise), dollar shop, Post office, exchange facilities, car and motorbike rental, tour agencies (Cubatur and Rumbos), restaurant with buffet meals, breakfast US$4, evening meal US$12, not bad.

C-D *La Ronda*, Calle José Martí 238 entre Colón y Lino Pérez, T 2248, TV, clean, restaurant and bar.

D *Bárbara Vásquez* hostal, Simón Bolívar 312 entre José Martí y Maceo, T 4107, clean room, fan, hot water, not far from historic centre; **D** *Casa de Huésped Mercedes Albalat Milord*, José Martí 330 entre Rosario y Desengaño, T 3350, large house full of antiques, quiet, good food on request, lobster recommended, will guide if you want; **D** *Casa Hospedaje Lic Balbina Cadahía Benavente*, Calle Maceo 355 entre Lino Pérez y Colón, CP 62600, T 2585, breakfast US$2, meals US$6, extremely nice family, old colonial house, hot water shower, will arrange trips, highly recommended; **D** *Casa de la Amistad*, Izquierdo 69 entre Bolívar y Zerrano, T 3824, 2280, run by the Instituto Cubano de Amistad con los Pueblos (ICAP), 2 rooms each with 2 beds, a/c, clean, meals available; **D** *Finca María Dolores*, Carretera Circuito Sur, T 3581, also called *Casa de Campesino*, 3 km from Trinidad on the road to

Cienfuegos, in a nice setting of grass and shrubs near Río Guaurabo, 20 brick cabañas, 2 single beds, a/c, shower, clean, restaurant, shop, bar, quiet spot but sometimes noisy in the evening as it is an all-dancing, all-singing tour group destination, horse riding, cock fighting, milk the cows; **D-E** *Hospedaje Yolanda*, Piro Guinart 227 entre Izquierdo y Maceo, opposite the bus station, rooms vary, hot water shower, a/c.

E *Maritza Hernández*, Francisco Cadahía 223 entre Colón y Lino Pérez, T 3160, warmly recommended, she speaks only Spanish (her son speaks some) but is fluent in sign language, 2-3 rooms, family atmosphere, pleasant courtyard, sitting room, wonderful rocking chairs, excellent meals, US$7 for dinner, king prawns, huge whole fish, etc, with lots of rice, beans, salad, more than you can eat, generous breakfast US$2.50; **E** *Aleida Calzada*, Juan Manuel Márquez 20 entre José Mendoza y Jesús Menéndez.

Camping: campsites at Ancón beach (see page 193) and La Boca (5-bed apartments). Camping at Base Manacal in the mountains: tent or small hut for US$5 per day.

● Places to eat

El Jigüe, Calle Real 69 esquina Guinart, T 4316, open 1100-1700 only unless a group comes in and then they open at night, live music, good food and atmosphere, most dishes US$7-8, chicken special US$12, lower prices for groups of over 10 people, recommended. A Rumbos restaurant is *El Mesón del Regidor*, Simón Bolívar 424, opposite Calle Toro, T 3756, open 0900-1800 daily, US$7-8; *Vía Real*, Villena 74, open 0900-1700, US$6-7 for a meal, quite good; *Las Begonias*, Calle Maceo esquina Simón Bolívar, open 1000-2200, dishes around US$5-8; *Santa Ana*, on Plaza Santa Ana, is open 0900-2200 every day, house special pork US$12, other dishes US$5-8; *Café Jazmín*, Colón y Maceo, more of a bar than a restaurant, open 0900-2200 every day, tables in the courtyard, interesting old fashioned pharmacy, Laboratorio Verde, nearby at Colón 47. The price of beer in some restaurants drops from US$2 to US$0.60 after 1700 when the tourist tours leave but all the state-run places shut then too. Family-run restaurants, *paladares*, have opened. Some which have been recommended include *Paladar Inés*, José Martí 160, entre Lino Pérez y Camilo Cienfuegos, T 3241, open 1200-2300, US$5-7 including rice, salad, etc, nice place; *Daniel's*, Camilo Cienfuegos 20, T 4395, open 1100 until everyone leaves, some courtyard tables, US$5-6 including side dishes, also rooms

US$15, a/c, but may be noisy from restaurant music downstairs; *Cocodrilo*, next door at Camilo Cienfuegos 28, entre Cárdenas y Zerquera, T 2108, open 0900-2400, nice old house, meals US$8, house pork special called Cocodrilaso US$7, also rooms for US$10; *Colonial*, Maceo 402, esquina Colón, open daily 0900-2200, US$5-6, nice place, locally popular; *Sol y Son*, Simón Bolívar 283, entre Frank País y José Martí, run by English-speaking ex-architect Lázaro, open 1200-2400, in 19th century house, nice décor, courtyard, vegetarian special US$4.50, tasty stuffed fish US$7, all meals cost US$3 extra if you go with a guide, highly recommended; *Restaurante Don Antonio*, Calle Izquierdo entre Frank País y Simón Bolívar, open 0800-late, in nice old colonial house with ornate columns and tiled floor, meals around US$6-8. On the road to Cienfuegos, *Finca María Dolores*, see above, under **Accommodation**, serving creole food, 0900-1600, has a collection of tropical birds, cockfighting, spit-roast pig and a fiesta on Thursday, 1800-2300.

● **Bars**
Casa Fisher, Calle Lino Pérez entre Cadahía y José Martí, in a nice old colonial house built in 1870, open 0900-0100; *Bar Daiquirí*, Lino Pérez entre Cadahía y José Martí, open 24 hours, also gallery of local art, seems pretty dead between 1700-0100, but kicks into life around 0200 when the *Las Cuevas* nightclub closes, unaccompanied Cuban women are not generally admitted, though this does not stop a large number of them hanging around outside, beer US$1, mojito US$2, zombie US$4; *Bar Las Ruinas de Segarta*, Calle Alameda entre Márquez y Galdós, in nice ruined courtyard, open 24 hours, also does fried chicken for US$1.50.

● **Banks & money changers**
Banco Nacional is on José Martí 264 entre Zerquera y Colón, open Monday-Friday 0800-1300, will change traveller's cheques for dollars. You can not get cash on a credit card, Cienfuegos is the nearest place for that. There are *cambios* in *Hotel Las Cuevas*, *Hotel Ancón* and *Hotel Costa Sur*, where you can change traveller's cheques for dollars.

● **Entertainment**
One block from the church is the **Casa de la Trova**, open weekend lunchtimes and evenings, entry free. Excellent live Cuban music with a warm, lively atmosphere. There are mostly Cubans here, of all age groups, and it's a great place to watch, and join in with, the locals

having a good time. All drinks paid for in dollars. Another venue for live music is *La Canchanchara*, Calle Villena 70, T 4345. Open 0900-1900, cocktails, no food, serves a drink of the same name in small earthenware pots created out of rum, sugar, honey and lime. More touristy than **Casa de La Trova** (cigar and souvenir shop), but good traditional music at lunchtimes.

Cinema: *Cine Romello Cornello*, is on Parque Céspedes and has a show at 2000, 40 centavos. For up to date times and programme see the billboards just inside the doors. Some English films are shown.

● **Hospitals & medical services**
The *Clínica Internacional* run by Servimed is on Calle Lino Pérez 103 esquina Anastasio Cárdenas, T 3391, modern, with out-patient consultations, laboratory tests, X-rays, pharmacy, dentistry and 24-hour emergency care. It is better to come here rather than to the general hospital as they have more medical supplies. A consultation fee is US$25, a call out fee US$40.

● **Library**
The **Public Library** is on Calle José Martí 265 entre Zerquera y Colón, open Monday-Friday 0800-2200, Saturday 0800-1700. The literary archives of Trinidad are in the **Archivo Histórico Municipal de Trinidad** on Calle Piro Guinart entre Hernández y Villena, open Monday-Friday 0800-1700.

● **Places of worship**
Templo a Yemaya, Calle Villena 59 entre Piro Guinart y Simón Bolívar, a place of *santería* worship which anyone can visit, open 24 hours, where you will see dolls on the altars and Afrocuban symbols on the walls.

● **Post & telecommunications**
Post Office: Calle Antonio Maceo 418 entre Zerquera y Colón, also for international **telephones** and fax, US$12 to the USA for the first 4 minutes, all other countries US$6/minute, open Monday-Saturday 0800-1800.

● **Shopping**
Caracol on Calle Maceo esquina Zerquera for souvenirs, T shirts, postcards etc. *Bazar Trinidad* on Calle Maceo 451, esquina Zerquera, on the opposite corner from *Caracol*, for postcards, curios, pictures, T shirts, typical Cuban handicrafts. *Tienda de Arte Amelia Pelaez*, Calle Simón Bolívar esquina Calle Valdés Muñoz. At Calle Toro a whole street is devoted to handicraft stalls, especially crochet and needle work, with

some books and stamps and sometimes a band playing, it is called **Candonga**, or Mercado Popular de Artesanía. *Galería de Arte Universal*, Villena 43 opposite the Plaza Mahor, has contemporary Cuban art for sale, open 0800-1700 most days but until 2200 on Tuesdays and Thursdays. *Tienda Panamericana* is a dollar store on Calle Lino Pérez entre Cadahía y José Martí, selling some food, clothes and toiletries. *Tienda La Cochera* is another dollar store with a small selection of souvenirs, drinks, postcards, toiletries, T shirts, on Simón Bolívar, round the corner from the Museo Romántico. For food and drink, *El Partón*, on Calle Hernández next to the Museo Romántico sells ice cream, drinks and beer, but there is nowhere to sit. There is a store on Calle Zerquera esquina Calle Izquierdo, open 0930-2330, which sells some food and drink with a good selection, and another on Calle Maceo esquina Calle Lino Pérez which sells food, clothes and toiletries.

Photography: *Photoservice* is on Calle José Martí entre Colón y Lino Pérez, open 0800-2000, film about US$5-7 per roll, also sometimes has bread.

● **Sports**
Hotel Las Cuevas allows tourists who are not their guests to use their **swimming** pool free of charge, showers available.

● **Useful addresses**
Immigration: Rumbos Cuba on Calle Maceo esquina Zerquera can renew visas and tourist cards within a day or less, open every day 0800-2000. **Police**: the main police station is 1 km from the centre of town on Calle 1 in Reparto Armando Mestre. There is a sub-station at the corner of Colón and José Martí. For any problem T 2168.

● **Tour companies & travel agents**
Rumbos Cuba office is on Maceo esquina Zerquera, open daily 0800-2000, can arrange tours and excursions and find out any information for travellers, will renew tourist cards, book flights from Trinidad and deal with Cubana enquiries. Staff speak French, English, German and Italian.

● **Transport**
Local Car hire: Nacional Rent A Car is on José Martí 164 entre Cienfuegos y Lino Pérez, T 4101, open 0800-2200 every day, but if all the cars are hired out then it closes, there is only a tiny sign on the door, it is next to *Paladar Inés*. There is also car hire at *Hotel Las Cuevas* and *Hotel Ancón*. Cupet station on Calle Frank País esquina Zerquera. **Taxi**: Cienfuegos-Trinidad

US$75; tour US$30 pp including lunch. A taxi *particular* from Sancti Spíritus costs US$12, 1 hour, 70 km.

Air The airport was being expanded in 1997 and at the time of writing there were no flights to Trinidad, although there was a bus transfer link from Cienfuegos airport. Once the work is completed there will be regular flights with fares of about US$40 one way, US$80 return from Havana.

Bus Terminal on Piro Guinart entre Izquierdo y Maceo. Bus for Havana leaves 1330 every other day, arrives 1930, US$21 a/c, US$17 without a/c; also every other day Víazul a/c minibuses carrying 8 foreigners at 1500, US$25, comfortable, buy tickets in advance if possible. To Sancti Spíritus, daily, 0400, 0700, 0930, 1200, 1500, 2000, all take 2 hours except 0400, 1200, which take 2 hours 40 minutes, 2.10 pesos. To Cienfuegos, daily, 0900, 1415, US$3. *Camión* (truck) leaves every other day, 0700, 1300, 2 hours, 2.30 pesos. To Santa Clara, daily, 1715, arrive 2030, US$6. Ticket office open daily, 0800-1130, 1330-1700. Transport to the east of Cuba is difficult from Trinidad as it is not on the Carretera Central. Best to go to Sancti Spíritus through beautiful hilly scenery (see below) and bus from there. As elsewhere, severe shortages and huge queues, trucks and tractors with trailers may be laid on as a back-up.

Train The station is south of the town, walk south straight down Lino Pérez until you get to the railway line, turn left and you will see a shelter and an old building beyond which is the 'office'. Get a numbered ticket at the office and get on the train in numbered order (its a stampede nonetheless). Go early for a low number for a window seat (fight your way to the front). Pay the fare (exact change only) on board to the conductor. Trains are liable to delays and cancellations so it is best to call ahead and check times etc, T 3348. See **Excursions** above for destinations.

PLAYA ANCON

Nearby are the excellent beaches of **La Boca** (8 km), a small fishing village, restaurant on beach, some buses or taxi, or rent a bicycle from local people for about US$1. Private accommodation with Iliana Serrano, Villa La Piedra, Calle Real 47. You can hire a private car for about US$10 to take you from Trinidad to La Boca then on to Playa Ancón where you can be

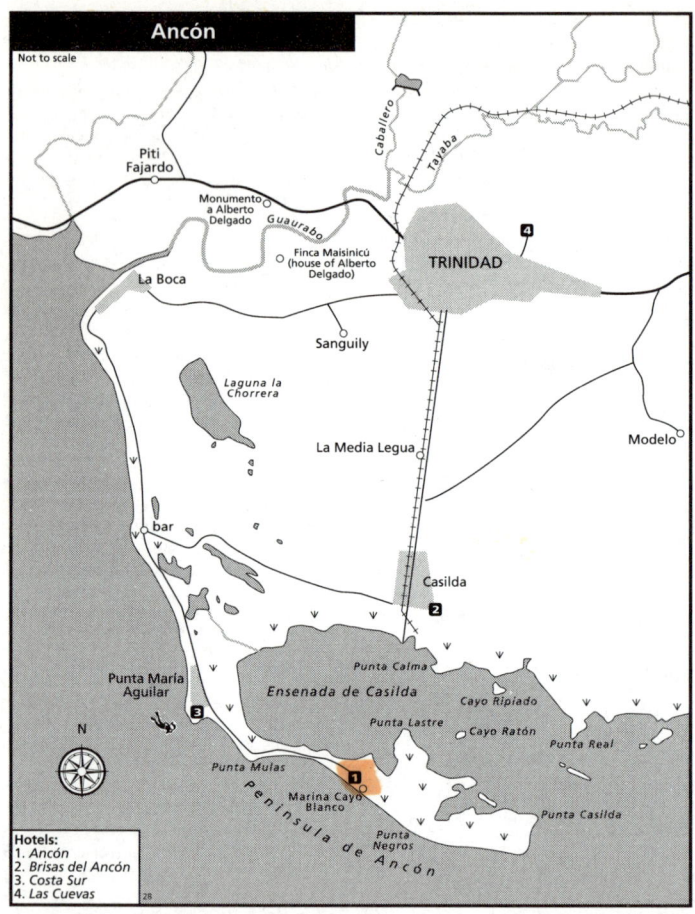

Ancón

Not to scale

Piti
Fajardo

Monumento
a Alberto
Delgado

Guaurabo

Finca Maisinicú
(house of Alberto
Delgado)

La Boca

Caballero

Tayaba

TRINIDAD 4

Sanguily

Laguna la
Chorrera

La Media Legua

Modelo

bar

Casilda 2

Punta Calma

Punta María
Aguilar

Ensenada de Casilda

Cayo Ripiado

3

Punta Lastre

Cayo Ratón

Punta Real

N

Punta Mulas

Marina Cayo
Blanco

1

Punta
Negros

Punta Casilda

Peninsula de Ancón

Hotels:
1. Ancón
2. Brisas del Ancón
3. Costa Sur
4. Las Cuevas

28

dropped off and collected at an appointed time. The return journey will be via a different route through **Casilda**, a rather scruffy fishing village 6 km south of Trinidad across a tidal flat where there are lots of birds. Casilda is a run down port used mainly for exporting sugar, where you can see the ruined Catholic church, **Ermita de Santa Elena**. There is a basic peso hotel but it is not particularly recommended despite the price as it is still about 11 km to the beach. If you are cycling this route

you may be pleased to know that there is a breezy bar at the point where the road La Boca-Ancón meets the road Casilda-Ancón, where you can get a coke for US$1.

The best beach resort near Trinidad is **Playa Ancón** not a town as such, just two resort hotels. The beach is lovely, pure white sand and clean turquoise water, highly recommended. There is good diving less than 300m offshore, near the *Hotel Costa Sur* (see **Diving and marine life**, page 28). A metered taxi from Trinidad costs

US$5.20 to *Hotel Costa Sur* via La Boca, which is 16 km. Some people hire bicycles in Trinidad to do a circular day trip.

Southeast of Playa Ancón is **Cayo Blanco de Casilda** where there is a beautiful beach with lovely white sand, 2 hours by boat. A small cay to the east is excellent for watching sea birds and pelicans, while to the west of Cayo Blanco there is some lovely coral 18-40m deep where you can find a wide variety of fish, turtles, lobster and crab. A day trip with snorkelling is organized by both hotels for US$25-35 (children half price), minimum 20 passengers, and diving can be done through the Marina Cayo Blanco (Puertosol), just east of *Hotel Ancón*. The Marina also lays on fishing trips to several locations; a boat for a party of four to go deep sea fishing all day costs around US$250, while fishing from a launch is US$50/day.

● **Accommodation** A2 *Ancón* (Gran Caribe), F 66-7424, price room only though they encourage you to go all-inclusive, including three meals, drinks and such extras as snorkels, bicycles and horse riding, 279 rooms, hexagonal pool, good restaurant, snack bar by the pool does filling pizzas US$3-4, hot dogs US$2.50, disco and many facilities, including scuba diving and watersports, best beach here, popular with families; **A2-A3** *Costa Sur* (Horizontes), T 6100/2524, 131 rooms and chalets, new block best, occasional hot water, a/c, bath, phone, balconies with mostly broken chairs, restaurant, good value breakfast buffet for US$3.50, dinner buffet US$10, not bad, bar, beer US$2, mojito US$2, nightclub, pool, shop, car rental and taxis, lovely beach if a bit narrow. The rainforest tour to Topes de Collantes offered by both hotels for US$30 pp is superb (minimum 3 people, but can negotiate higher price for 2), knowledgeable and adaptable guides, good hiking, swimming through a river inside a cave coming out behind a waterfall, through which you have to dive (see Trinidad **Excursions**, page 188).

● **Places to eat** Apart from the hotels above, there is the *Grill del Caribe* along the beach northwest of the *Hotel Ancón*, which makes a change from hotel food but is poor value, a salad (plate of tomatoes) is US$1.

SANCTI SPIRITUS

Population 80,000; *phone code* 41

Sancti Spíritus, the provincial capital, about 80 km northeast of Trinidad and 90 km southeast of Santa Clara, can be reached by road from Cienfuegos, Santa Clara or Trinidad. In the San Luis valley, or Valle de los Ingenios (Valley of the Sugar Mills), between Trinidad and Sancti Spíritus are many ruined sugar mills, plantation houses and slave quarters, including Manaca Iznaga (see page 189). It is one of Cuba's seven original Spanish towns and has a wealth of buildings from the colonial period. Much of its history is linked with that of Trinidad, both towns were founded by Diego Velázquez, both grew on the back of sugar and slavery, both fought off pirate attacks. Sancti Spíritus was founded in 1514 on the Río Tuinicú, moved to its present location on the Río Yayabo in 1522 and sacked by pirates in 1665. The town grew as sugar became important and its geographical position made it an excellent agricultural market town. There are many sites commemorating those who fought in the 19th century wars of independence, the local hero being Major General Serafín Sánchez Valdivia. At the end of the Revolution in 1958, rebel forces were led into the city under the command of Armando Acosta Cordero and Sancti Spíritus was liberated on 23 December. Fidel Castro arrived on 6 January 1959. With the administrative changes in 1975, Sancti Spíritus became the capital of the new province of Sancti Spíritus.

Places of interest

The **Iglesia Parroquial Mayor del Espíritu Santo** on Plaza Honorato dates from 1522 when it was a wooden construction. The present building, of stone, replaced the earlier one in 1680, but it is acknowledged as the oldest church in Cuba because it still stands on its original foundations. The church has been declared a National Monument but it is not

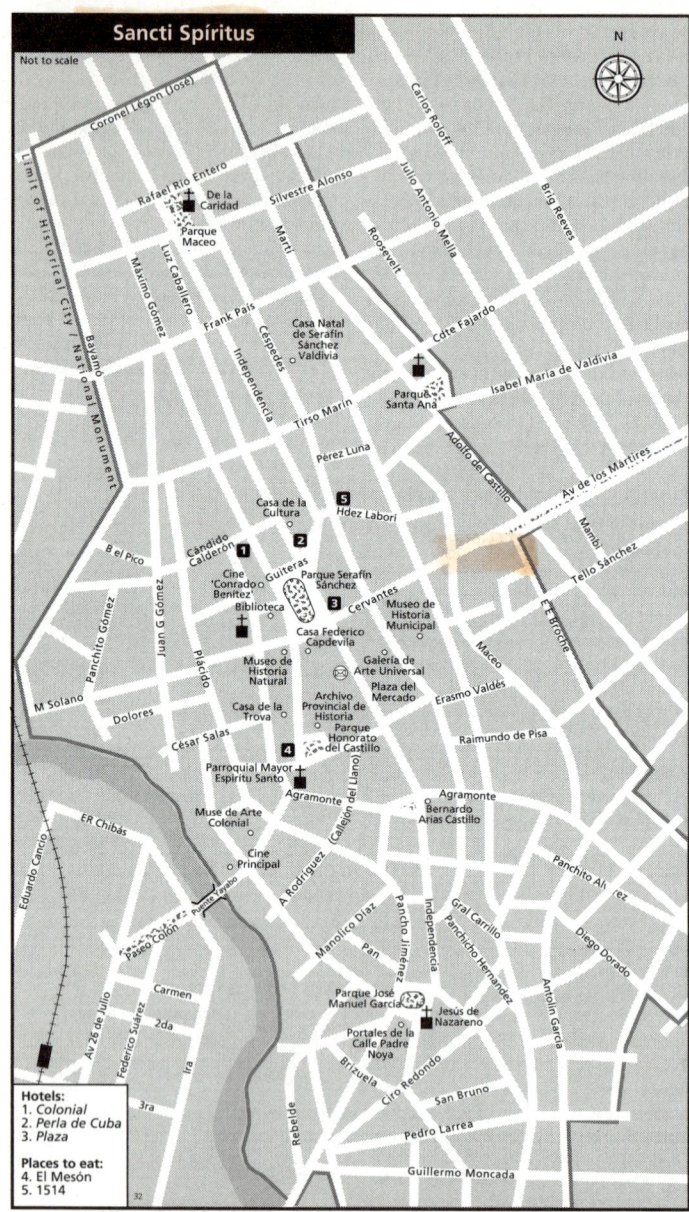

Sancti Spíritus

N

Not to scale

Hotels:
1. *Colonial*
2. *Perla de Cuba*
3. *Plaza*

Places to eat:
4. El Mesón
5. 1514

always open so you may not be able to look inside. The **Puente Yayabo** is considered a particular feature of Sancti Spíritus and is the only one of its type left on the island. The bridge was built in 1815 with five arches made of lime, sand and bricks. It is now also a National Monument. The river itself has given its name to the *guayaba*, or guava, which grows along its banks, and also to the *guayabera*, a loose man's shirt without a tail worn outside the trousers and without a tie. The former **Teatro Principal** next to the bridge was built in 1839 and was the scene of all the major cultural, social and political events of the city. **Calle Llano** is a twisty street, with cobblestones right to the edge of the Yayabo river. **Parque Serafín Sánchez** is the centre of activity in the city where all major roads converge. **Parque Antonio Maceo**, on which stands the **Iglesia de la Caridad**, was the place where the Communist Party of Sancti Spíritus was founded on 7 December 1930. The **Real Cárcel** (Royal Prison) has been preserved as a site of historical interest. It was built in the mid-19th century and used initially to incarcerate runaway slaves and then to imprison hundreds of Cubans who fought for independence.

Museums

The **Museo de Arte Colonial**, Calle Plácido Sur 74, is housed in the former palace of the Iznaga family, who made their fortune out of sugar and were hugely influential with links to the military and bureaucracy of the province. The museum has a collection of 18th and 19th century furniture. Open Tuesday-Saturday 0830-1700, Sunday 0800-1200, US$1. The **Galería de Arte Universal** is in the house of the local artist Oscar Fernández Morera on Céspedes Sur, whose works are on permanent display, originals as well as reproductions. The **Museo Provincial de Sancti Spíritus** on Céspedes Sur 11 gives a general historical perspective of the region, from pre-Columbian times to the present day. There are several houses where famous *independentistas* (people who fought for independence) were born or lived: **Casa Natal de Serafín Sánchez Valdivia**, who fought in three wars in the 19th century, collaborated with José Martí and reached the rank of Major General before being killed in battle in 1896, is at Céspedes Norte 112; **Casa Natal de Honorato del Castillo** who started the war in Sancti Spíritus in 1868 and was a part of the Constituent Assembly of Guáimaro; **Casa Natal de Manuel Mendigutía** the secretary to Carlos Manuel de Céspedes, the first president of the Republic in Arms. There is also the **Museo de Historia Natural** on the southwest corner of Parque Serafín Sánchez which has a planetarium.

Excursions

Many of the excursions included in the Trinidad section can also be done from here, particularly the Valley of the Sugar Mills which lies between the two towns. **Embalse Zaza** is a popular excursion for hiking, birdwatching, shooting and fishing, or just to go to the hotel (see below) and laze around the pool. The hotel can get busy at weekends. In September there is an annual international fishing tournament here. For those with their own transport (or hired private car), you can tour the north coast, where there is a beach at La Victoria, a spa at San José del Lago and a cave system at Cueva Grande de Judas. Mayajigua is the main town in this area, founded in 1820, and reasonable for a break in the driving.

Local information
● Accommodation

Prices: **L1** over US$200; **L2** US$151-200; **L3** US$101-150; **A1** US$81-100; **A2** US$61-80; **A3** US$46-60; **B** US$31-45; **C** US$21-30; **D** US$12-20; **E** US$7-11; **F** up to US$6

A2-A3 *Rancho Hatuey*, T 26015, modern hotel on hill 4 km north of town just off Carretera Central, 38 overpriced rooms in main building or in cabaña, pool, restaurant, bar, quiet.

B-C *Zaza* (Horizontes), T 26012/25334, 10 km outside the town on the Zaza artificial lake, at Finca San José, 128 a/c rooms with bath, phone, restaurant, bar, nightclub, pool, games room, shop, car rental, medical services, tourism bureau, rather run down but pleasant and good value, shooting and fishing can be arranged.

C *Los Laureles*, T 23913, 5 km north of town, 50 rooms, pool, nightclub, used by Cubans, pleasant.

There are three peso hotels in town around Parque Serafín Sánchez which may accept foreign guests if you ask: **C** *Plaza*, 27 rooms; **E** *Colonial*, Máximo Gómez Norte 23, T 25123, 20 rooms; *Perla de Cuba*, on the north side of the Parque, under renovation. For private accommodation, **E** *Sergio Orihuela Ruíz*, room in apartment, Agramonte 61, Apto 5 Altos entre Jesús Menéndez y Llano, CP 60 100, T 23828, 5 minutes' walk from station, opposite Iglesia Parroquial Mayor del Espíritu Santo, English spoken, meets most trains. Ask around in the Parque or in restaurants for other accommodation, mostly **D-E**.

● **Places to eat**
El Mesón, on Plaza Honorato del Castillo, in a building which was the first Post Office, closed Monday; *Restaurante 1514*, Céspedes Norte 52, open 1200-1400, 1830-2030, closed Thursday. These two are state-owned but there are more *paladares* opening, ask around. Street stalls also sell snacks including pizza, which are good value.

● **Entertainment**
The **Casa de la Trova** is at Máximo Gómez Sur 26, for music. There is a cinema on Parque Serafín Sánchez and also in what was once the Teatro Principal. There is a Rumbos Bar on Independencia Norte 32.

● **Hospitals & medical services**
Pharmacy at Independencia Sur 15 opposite the Post Office.

● **Post & telecommunications**
Post Office: is at Independencia Sur 8, south of Parque Serafín Sánchez.

● **Shopping**
There is a large dollar store on Independencia Sur on the corner of Parque Serafín Sánchez. Librería Julio Antonio Mella, Independencia Sur 29, is a reasonable bookshop; there is a second hand bookshop nearby at Independencia Sur 25.

● **Transport**
Local Taxi: you can negotiate a private taxi (*particular*) to take you to Trinidad for about US$25 or less, depending on the quality of your Spanish.

Bus The bus station is 2 km east of town on the Carretera Central. Buses to Trinidad several daily, 70 km, 2 hours; Ciego de Avila several daily, 75 km, 2 hours; Santa Clara several daily, 86 km, 2 hours; also long distance buses to Havana, Holguín, Santiago daily.

Train Station at end of Av Jesús Menéndez and more convenient for the town centre than the bus station. Daily trains to Santa Clara (2 hours), Cienfuegos (5 hours) at 0430 and 1410, and Havana (9 hours), this one is supposed to leave Sancti Spíritus at 2145. Sancti Spíritus can also be reached by getting the 'special' from Havana to Santiago and changing at Guayos, 15 km north. All times very approximate and length of journey can be double.

Province of Ciego de Avila

O FF THE northern coast are Cayo Coco and Cayo Guillermo, beach resorts with excellent deep sea fishing, diving and snorkelling. Scuba divers also rate highly the cays off the southern coast which make up the western half of the Jardines de la Reina archipelago. Game shooting is organized and freshwater fishing must be about the best on the island. However lovers of colonial architecture may be disappointed as there is little of historical interest.

Province of Ciego de Avila

Ciego de Avila is sandwiched between the provinces of Sancti Spíritus and Camagüey and before the administrative reorganization of 1975 was actually part of the latter. It is the flattest province, with no part rising above 50m. Its northern coastline is low lying and swampy with mangroves. The **Laguna de la Leche**, Cuba's largest natural lake at 68.2 sq km, is called the 'Milk Lake' because of its cloudy white appearance, caused by lime deposits under the water, and its salinity makes it very popular with several thousand flamingoes. Offshore, but connected to the mainland by a long causeway, is Cayo Coco and other smaller cays where tourism is being developed and several large hotels have been built. The central part of the province is used for cattle ranching. Sugar is grown widely and there are citrus and pineapple plantations. To the south there are more mangroves along the coast and more cays with a wealth of marine life (see **Diving and marine life**, page 26). The two main cities of Ciego de Avila and Morón lie in the centre of the province. In the late 19th century the Spanish built a road, sentry towers and other fortifications north-south from Morón to Júcaro via Ciego de Avila to try and contain independence fighters. The ruins of some of these fortifications can still be seen in places. They were unsuccessful in keeping out the rebels; in 1876 General Manuel Suárez took Morón, in 1895 General Antonio Maceo crossed the line north of Ciego de Avila, as did Camilo Cienfuegos in 1958.

Ciego de Avila

Area 6,910 sq km, *Population* 396,600, *Density* 57.4 per sq km, *Urban* 74.4%

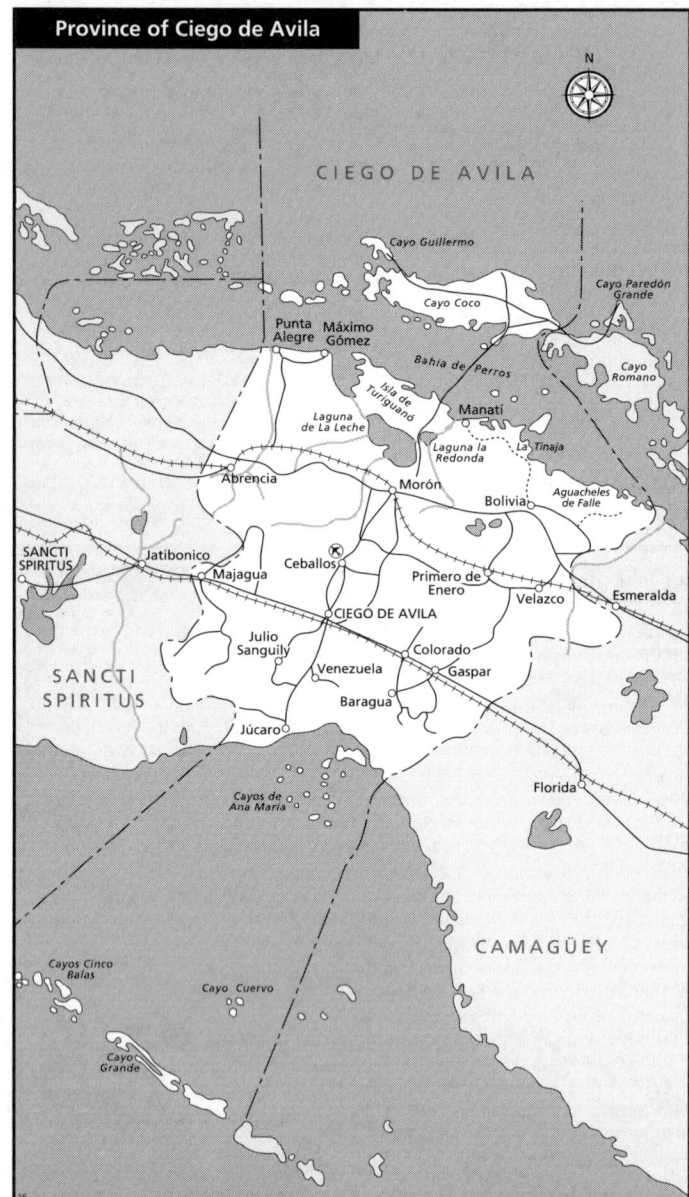

Province of Ciego de Avila

CIEGO DE AVILA

Population 85,000; *Phone code* 33

Ciego de Avila was founded in 1849 on the site of an hacienda granted to Alonso de Avila, one of Velázquez' commanders, and consequently is short of fine historical buildings and monuments. It is an agricultural market town with a large thermal electricity plant. The main road from Havana to Camagüey passes straight through the middle of town and most people just keep going.

Places of interest

The main square is the **Parque Martí**, with a statue of José Martí dating from 1925 in the centre. On the south side of the Parque are the church and the former town hall, **Ayuntamiento**, built in 1911, which is now the provincial government's headquarters. The **Teatro Principal**, built in 1927 is on Joaquín Agüero y Honorato del Castillo, and the **Galería de Arte Provincial** is on Calle Independencia entre Honorato del Castillo y Maceo. The **Museo Provincial** is in an old school building the other side of the railway on José Antonio Echevarría 25, with exhibitions of local history including the region's part in the Revolution, open Tuesday-Saturday 0800-1200, 1300-1700, Sunday 0800-1200, entrance US$1.

Excursions

South of Ciego de Avila there are mangrove and lagoons where bird watchers and hunters will find migrant waterfowl, snipe, doves, quail and guinea fowl. It is 25 km to **Júcaro** on the coast, from where the dive boats leave to go out to the Jardines de la Reina archipelago. Puertosol runs the marina here, which has moorings for 6 boats, catering and VHF/HF communications systems. Bonefishing is available all year round. Fantástico Tours organizes coach tours of the area, to Morón (see below), jeep tours to villages, horseriding, boat trips, fishing and tours of the northern cays.

Local information
● Accommodation

Prices: **L1** over US$200; **L2** US$151-200; **L3** US$101-150; **A1** US$81-100; **A2** US$61-80; **A3** US$46-60; **B** US$31-45; **C** US$21-30; **D** US$12-20; **E** US$7-11; **F** up to US$6

2 km outside town is **B** *Hotel Ciego de Avila*, Carretera de Ceballos, T 28013, with 144 rooms in a modern, 5-storey block, pool, taxis, Havanautos car hire, good food.

C *Santiago-Habana*, Chicho Valdés y Honorato del Castillo, T 25703, 76 overpriced rooms on the main road through town, run down but convenient if you need to be central.

● Places to eat

There is the usual crop of low quality state run restaurants, including *Mesón El Fuerte*, Av Las Palmas on Plaza Camilo Cienfuegos; *Moscú*, Chicho Valdés 78, closed Wednesday; *Solaris*, on west side of Parque Martí, top floor of 12-storey building; *El Colonial*, Independencia 110, nice courtyard; *La Romagnola*, Chicho Valdés y Marcial Gómez, Italian; *Rumbos 12*, Parque Martí, same building as *Solaris*, 24-hour bar where you can get fried chicken and cold beer. *Paladares* are springing up and it would be best to investigate some of these, ask around.

● Airlines

Cubana office at Chicho Valdés 83 entre Maceo y Honorato del Castillo, T 25316.

● Entertainment

Casa de la Trova at Libertad 130 y Simón Reyes.

● Post & telecommunications

Post Office: at the corner of Chicho Valdés y Marcial Gómez. Salón de Llamadas Nacionales e Internacionales on Parque Martí in the 12-storey building.

● Transport

Local Car hire: Havanautos is at *Hotel Ciego de Avila*.

Air There is an airport at **Ceballos**, 24 km north of Ciego de Avila, Aeropuerto Máximo Gómez (AVI), which receives weekly scheduled flights from Cologne/Bonn and from Frankfurt with Condor, from Dusseldorf with LTU, and from Buenos Aires and Paris with Cubana, as well as twice weekly flights from Havana with Cubana. Charter flights also use this airport from time to time to get holiday makers out to the resort hotels on Cayo Coco.

Bus The bus station is on the Carretera Central just east of the zoo. There are buses to all the

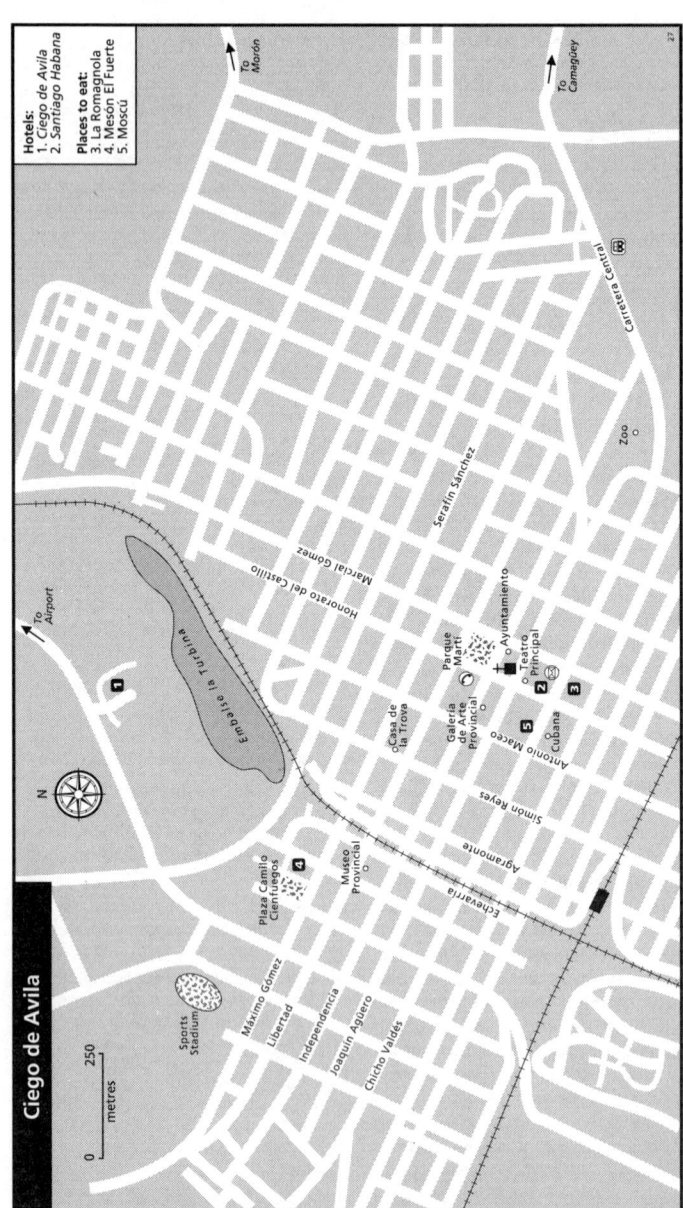

Ciego de Avila

0 250 metres

N

Hotels:
1. Ciego de Avila
2. Santiago Habana

Places to eat:
3. La Romagnola
4. Mesón El Fuerte
5. Moscú

To Morón

To Camagüey

Carretera Central

Zoo

Serafín Sánchez

Marcial Gómez

Honorato del Castillo

To Airport

Embalse la Turbina

Ayuntamiento

Parque Martí

Teatro Principal

Casa de la Trova

Galería de Arte Provincial

Cubana

Antonio Maceo

Simón Reyes

Agramonte

Plaza Camilo Cienfuegos

Museo Provincial

Echeverría

Máximo Gómez

Libertad

Independencia

Joaquín Agüero

Chicho Valdés

Sports Stadium

places on the main road from Havana to Santiago and a lot of others besides, such as Manzanillo, Holguín and Niquero. However, by the time the long distance buses get here they are nearly always full.

Train Three trains daily to Havana. Most trains go through at night to Holguín, Matanzas and Santiago.

MORON

Population 45,000; *Phone code* 335

Morón was founded in 1750 and is about 40 km northeast of Ciego de Avila. It is promoted as the Ciudad del Gallo, Cockerel City, and there is even a monument to the bird which tourists are taken to see. A **Museo Municipal** is at Calle Castillo 164 and there is a **Casa de la Trova** on Calle Libertad entre Martí y Narciso López.

Apart from tourists passing through here on their way to Cayo Coco, the main visitors to this area are here for the shooting and fishing. Northeast of Morón, Horizontes organizes shooting for game birds and waterfowl at **Aguachales de Falla** and other lakes close by. The hunting season runs from 15 November to 15 March and a licence costs US$25. On top of that you pay for hire of a 12-bore shotgun, about US$8/day, ammunition US$12 and transport rental US$0.80/km.

11 km from Morón, beside the road and before the Isla de Turiguanó, is **Lago La Redonda**. It covers an area of 26 sq km, with four main canals and a channel network, with an average depth of 1m. Red mangroves grow in abundance and you may see the *tocororo*, the national bird. The lake is full of fish, principally the largemouth bass. A record was set in the 1980s when a group of Americans caught 5,078 fish in five days. There is a Puertosol marina at the lake, where you can arrange fishing trips and hire rods, boats and guides, and a restaurant/bar where non-fishing visitors can sit and watch the water. Fishing is available all year, there is no closed season.

About 40 km west of Morón, where the land becomes more hilly and picturesque, is **Florencia**. This is a place where organized excursion parties come from the cays to sample Cuban country life. Horseriding is available in the hills, you can swim in the mineral waters of a river pool, have a lunch of suckling pig on the banks of the river and watch a rodeo. Independent travellers may not get the rodeo, but if a visit is timed not to coincide with a tour party, they could benefit from all the other activities in peaceful surroundings.

● **Accommodation B** *La Casona de Morón* (Horizontes), Cristóbal de Colón 41, T 33-4563, F 33-5301, also known as the *Club de Caza y Pesca*, 7 a/c rooms, colonial building, TV, minibar, restaurant, grill, bar, night club, pool, cambio, used by hunters. On the south side of town, on Av Tarafa, is **B** *Morón*, T 33-3076/3901, F 33-3076, 3-star, smart, renovated 1994, 144 rooms with balcony, 8 suites, 3 restaurants, 2 coffee shops, bars, pool, games room, good a/c and food, tourism bureau, medical services, car hire, currency exchange, shop, shooting arranged with guide and dog. There is also a cheap, peso hotel, *Perla del Norte*, on Av de Tarafa, 54 rooms, but you probably won't get in. Private rooms may be offered.

● **Transport Train** Morón is on the railway line from Santa Clara to Nuevitas. Most tourists move around on tour buses, but if you have a car, there is a gas station near the *Hotel Morón*.

CAYO COCO

Cayo Coco has become a focal point in the Government's 'ecotourism' interests, although the hotels are large, luxury resorts with foreign investment. It is a large island of mostly mangrove and bush which shelter many migratory birds as well as permanent residents. The island is connected to the mainland just north of Morón by a 27 km causeway across the Bahía de Perros. There is an airstrip for an air taxi service, with day trips and 2-night packages from Havana, but international flights and other large aircraft come in to the airport north of Ciego de Avila. The Atlantic side of the island has excellent beaches, particularly **Playa Los**

Flamencos (15 minutes' drive from hotels), with some 5 km of white sand and shallow, crystalline water. At certain times of the year you will see flamingos, after whom the beach is named. Beach bar and horses for hire. Anyone looking for solitude can explore **Playa Prohibida**, appropriately named as the Government has banned construction here in the interests of ecology. Cayo Coco is very isolated and

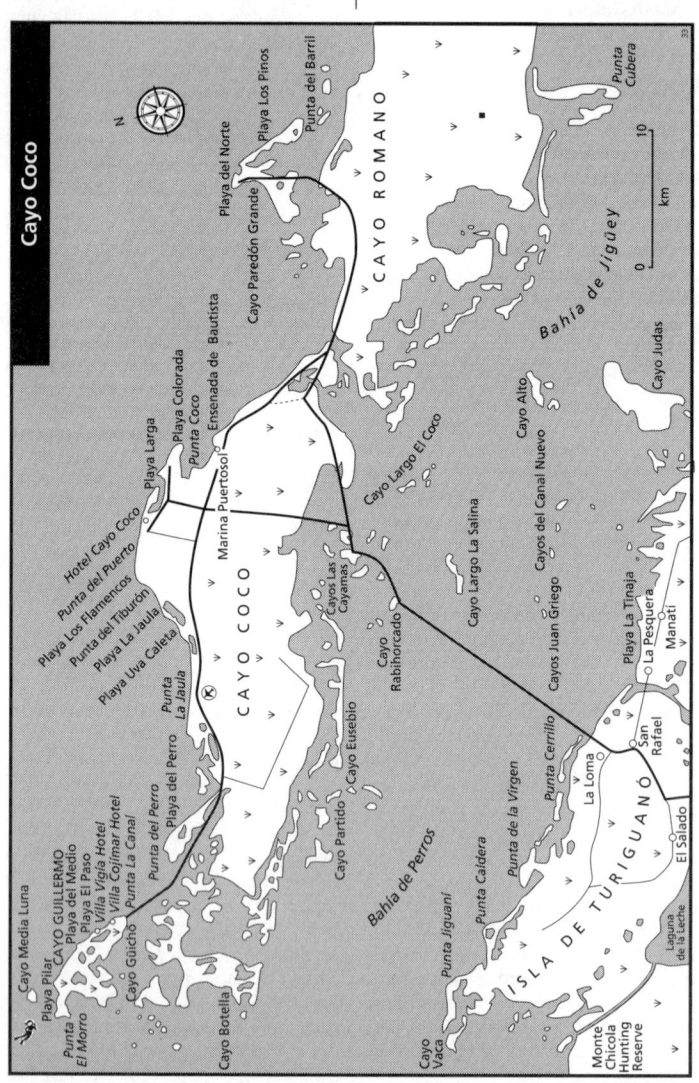

Cayo Coco

nearly all foreigners are here on a package of a week or so and do not go far. Marina Puertosol offers deep sea fishing and there is good diving (see **Diving and marine life**, page 28).

Cayo Guillermo, a 13 sq km cay with 5 km of beach, is protected by a long coral reef which is good for diving with plentiful fish and crustaceans, while on land there are lots of birds. The author Ernest Hemingway came here to fish, which is why there are references to him in the names of hotels. Fishing is still superb around here and if tired of deep sea fishing you can make an excursion to one of the freshwater lakes mentioned above. Marina Puertosol is based at *Hotel Villa Cojímar* for fishing, snorkelling and diving.

● **Accommodation On Cayo Coco**: *Tryp Cayo Coco*, Spanish and Cuban, all-inclusive, 458 rooms in bungalows in replica of old colonial village, 5 restaurants, 2 bars, piano bar, 2 snack bars, 2 pools, shops, disco, watersports (extra charge for motorized watersports), volleyball, floodlit tennis, badminton, beach a bit disappointing but facilities well planned; second hotel alongside under construction 1996. A joint French-Cuban venture is to construct 1,300 rooms on the cay by 2001. **On Cayo Guillermo**: *Villa Cojímar* (Gran Caribe), T 301725/26, F 301727, 218 rooms, phone, TV, minibar, fridge, a/c, kitchenette, restaurant, snack bar, buffet, bar, Cuban and international cuisine, credit cards accepted, tennis, water sports, pool, disco, medical services, shops, foreign exchange, Post Office, fax service, tourist bureau, car rental, all-inclusive luxury resort. *Villa Vigía* (Gran Caribe), T 301760, F 301748, 264 rooms in cabins with red tiled roofs, all the same facilities and all-inclusive luxury.

● **Transport** Only tour buses go to Cayo Coco, there are no public buses and a checkpoint at the beginning of the causeway effectively prevents Cubans without permission from visiting the cay.

Province of Camagüey

CAMAGÜEY is the largest of Cuba's 14 provinces. The countryside is flat and fertile, with cattle roaming the grasslands dotted with royal palms. Camagüey city is a colonial gem and should not be missed, although most tourists head instead for the Santa Lucía beach resort for sun, sea and sand.

Province of Camagüey

Situated in the central part of the island between the provinces of Ciego de Avila to the west and Las Tunas to the east, Camagüey is mostly low lying. Its highest point, at 330m, is in the Sierra de Cubitas to the north of Camagüey city. The Atlantic north coast is broken by a series of large coral cays which make up the Archipiélago de Camagüey. There is great potential for tourism here, with long sandy beaches, crystal clear water and fantastic diving on the reef, but so far there has been little development except at Playa Santa Lucía in the east. Behind the protective cays, the land is marshy, until it rises gently to the Sierra de Cubitas where there are caves and rocky spurs. Nuevitas is the main port on the north coast and there is considerable heavy industry in the area. The southern, Caribbean coast of the province is mostly swampy. There is a fishing port at Santa Cruz del Sur, but otherwise little habitation in the wetlands. Offshore the sea is dotted with tiny uninhabited cays which are part of the Archipiélago Jardines de la Reina. Previously one of Fidel Castro's favourite fishing spots, the cays are now visited mostly by scuba divers on liveaboard boats.

Beef and dairy farming occupies much of the land and many of the province's traditions revolve around cowboys and their activities, such as rodeos. There are also many poultry farms in the central part around Camagüey and Minas. Sugar cane is grown in the north and south of the province, with sugar mills near Florida, Carlos Manuel de Céspedes, Brasil, Senado, Vertientes, Batalla de las Guásimas, Cándido González, Haití and Hatuey. There are also rice fields in the west around El Trece and El Alazán. Some citrus is grown and processed in the north near Solas.

Camagüey

Area 15,990 sq km, *Population* 774,100, *Density* 48.4 per sq km, *Urban* 75%

Province of Camagüey

CAMAGÜEY

Population 350,000, *Phone code* 322

Camagüey is the largest province in the country with more than 14,000 sq km. The city of the same name which is the capital of the province was originally called Puerto Príncipe until 9 June 1903. The village of Santa María de Puerto del Príncipe was first founded in 1515 at Punta del Guincho in the Bahía de Nuevitas but the site was unsatisfactory because of lack of water and poor soil fertility. In 1516 the first settlers moved to Caonao (an Indian word for gold or place where gold can be found), an aborigine chiefdom near the Río Caonao. However, in 1527 the enslaved Indians rose up against the Spanish colonizers and burned down the town. The settlers then moved again, further inland, between the Río Tínima and the Río Hatibonico, where the village was finally established.

Moving inland was no protection against pirate attacks. During the 17th century as the settlement became prosperous on the back of raising livestock and later sugar, it was the target of the Englishman Henry Morgan in 1668 and of French pirates led by François Granmont in 1679. However, despite the looting the town continued to grow throughout the 18th century, although its architects took the precaution of designing the layout to foil pirate attacks. No two streets run parallel, to create a maze effect, which is most unlike other colonial towns built on the grid system. On 12 November 1817, Fernando VII, the king of Spain, declared Puerto Príncipe a city with a coat of arms.

Several revolutionary events of the 19th century are remembered in Camagüey. In 1812 eight black slaves fighting for independence under the command of

José Antonio Aponte, were executed. In 1826, Aguero Velazco was hanged in what is now Parque Agramonte. Joaquín de Aguero y Aguero and his followers took arms against the colonial power in 1851, but their movement failed and they were executed by firing squad. In 1868, when Carlos Manuel de Céspedes initiated the struggle for independence, many Camagueyans supported him, including Ignacio Agramonte, Salvador Cisneros Betancourt, Maximiliano Ramos, Javier de la Vega and others who are remembered in street names, monuments and museums.

Churches

Nuestra Señora de la Merced, a National Monument on Av Agramonte on the edge of the Plaza de los Trabajadores, was built in 1747 as a church and convent at what was then the edge of town but is now in the centre. Over the years it has been transformed into a baroque church and a diocesan house with lodging for specific activities held by the church. In 1906 a fire burned the altar, which was reconstructed in Spain in a neo-gothic style. As the city

expanded the cemetery had to be closed, but the catacomb can still be seen. The ceiling of the church shows early 20th century paintings, although it badly needs restoring. On the walls are four 17th century and eight 18th century paintings, but the most important treasure in the church is the Santo Sepulcro constructed in 1762 with the donation of 23,000 silver coins. Before the Revolution, it was taken in procession along the streets of Camagüey; now it is done inside the church. The church has been under restoration for many years and is still not completed. It has an external clock, which was the first public clock in Camagüey, and a library. There is always someone around to show visitors the church and provide information.

Nuestra Señora de la Soledad is on República at the corner of Ignacio Agramonte. It is one of the oldest churches in town. In 1697 the Presbyterian Velasco started the construction of a hermitage which was concluded in 1701 and transformed into a parish by the bishop Diego Evelino de Compostela. In 1733

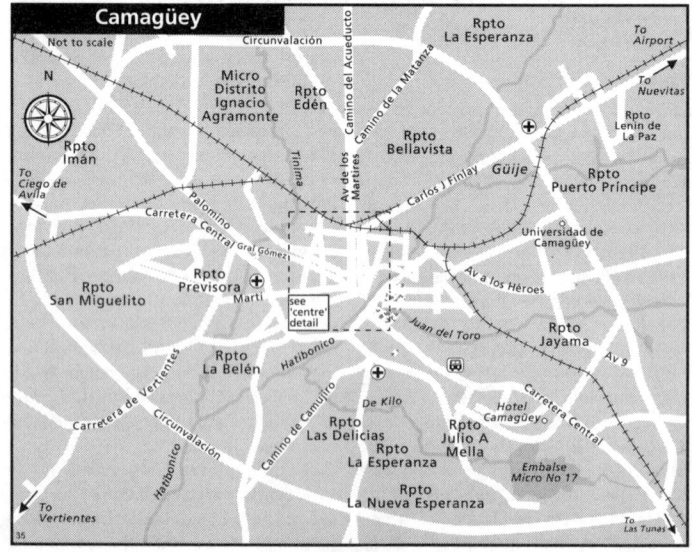

Camagüey

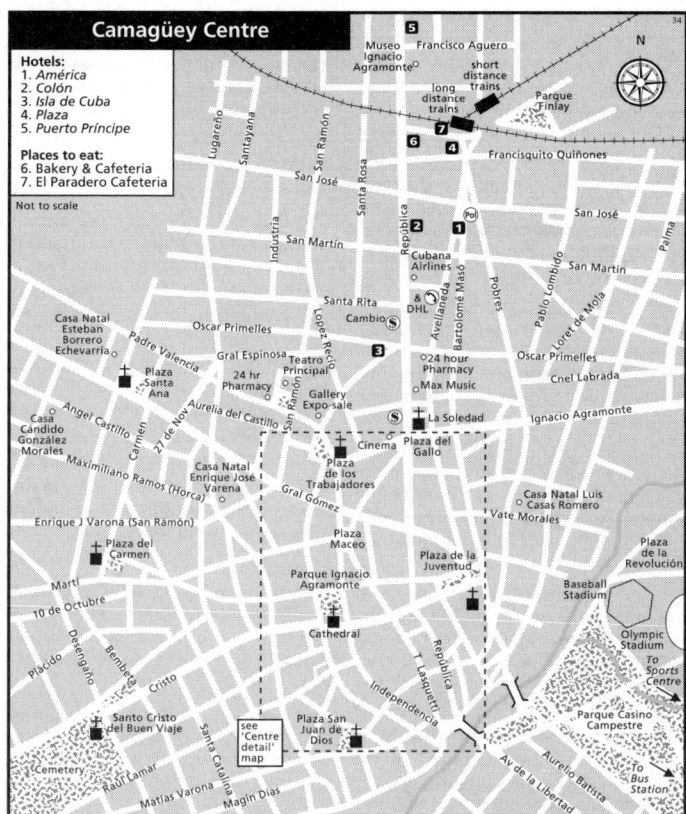

Camagüey Centre

34

N

Museo Ignacio Agramonte
Francisco Aguero
short distance trains
long distance trains
Parque Finlay

5

7
6
4

Hotels:
1. *América*
2. *Colón*
3. *Isla de Cuba*
4. *Plaza*
5. *Puerto Príncipe*

Places to eat:
6. Bakery & Cafeteria
7. El Paradero Cafeteria

Not to scale

Francisquito Quiñones

Lugareño
Santayana
San Ramón
Santa Rosa
San José

Industria

San Martín

San José
Palma

República
Pobres
Bartolomé Masó
Avellaneda

(Pol)
1

Cubana Airlines
2
San Martín
Pablo Lombido
Lore de Mola

Santa Rita
& DHL
Cambio (S)

Casa Natal Esteban Borrero Echevarría

Oscar Primelles
Padre Valencia
Gral Espinosa
Teatro Principal
3
24 hr Pharmacy
López Recio
San Ramón

Oscar Primelles
Cnel Labrada

24 hour Pharmacy
Max Music
Gallery Expo-sale
(S)
La Soledad
Ignacio Agramonte

Plaza Santa Ana
Angel Castillo
Carmen
27 de Nov
Aurelia del Castillo

Casa Cándido González Morales

Maximiliano Ramos (Horca)

Casa Natal Enrique José Varena
Gral Gómez
Plaza de los Trabajadores
Cinema
Plaza del Gallo

Casa Natal Luis Casas Romero
Vate Morales

Enrique J Varona (San Ramón)

Plaza del Carmen

Martí

Plaza Maceo

Parque Ignacio Agramonte

Plaza de la Juventud

Plaza de la Revolución

Baseball Stadium

Olympic Stadium
To Sports Centre

10 de Octubre

Bembeta
Cristo
Desengaño

Cathedral

República
T Lasqueti

Independencia

Plácido

Santo Cristo del Buen Viaje
see 'Centre detail' map
Plaza San Juan de Dios
Parque Casino Campestre

Raúl Lamar
Cemetery

Matías Varona
Magín Dias

Santa Catalina
Aurelio Batista
Av de la Libertad
To Bus Station

---

the current church was started, although construction was not finished until 1776. **San Juan de Dios**, another National Monument, was built in 1728 as a church with a hospital attached, the first hospital in the village for men which also contained a home for the aged. Apparently this is the only church in Latin America which has the Holy Trinity as its central image. The **Plaza San Juan de Dios** was created at the beginning of the 19th century when two houses were bought to make the plaza. At around this time the church's tower was moved to the front. On 12 May 1813 the body of Ignacio Agramonte was deposited in the hospital for identification before being take to the cemetery. In 1902 the hospital was closed and later converted to a military infirmary. It was used to house the homeless after the hurricane in 1932 and was inaugurated as a modern hospital in 1952. Cobblestones were laid in the plaza in 1956. After changing hands several times, the hospital building is now occupied by the Centro de Provincial de Patrimonio and there are plans to turn it into a luxury hotel.

Santa Iglesia Catedral is on the south side of Parque Ignacio Agramonte. Construction was started after the town fire of 1616 with the intention of it being the largest parish church in Puerto Príncipe, with two chapels and a cemetery. In the 19th century the chapels were demolished and a different shape was given to it in 1875. In 1937 the sculptor Juan Albaijez carved a statue of Christ which was placed inside the church. It is currently closed for renovations, having nearly fallen to pieces. **Nuestra Señora de Santa Ana**, along General Gómez, was started in 1697 with a single nave. Over the years it was gradually enlarged with a tower added in the middle of the 19th century. **Nuestra Señora del Carmen**, on the west side of Plaza Carmen, was started in 1732 by Eusebia de Varona y de la Torre, who wanted to build a three-nave temple for the Jesuits. However, they did not like its location, which at that time was on the outskirts of the town, and they demolished it. 100 years later, her heirs with the help of Padre Valencia, built the women's hospital of Nuestra Señora del Carmen, which was finished in 1825. A church was built alongside the hospital, originally with only one tower, but a second was added in 1846, making it the only two-towered church in Camagüey. The **Sagrado Corazón de Jesús**, on Luaces, overlooking the Plaza de la Juventud, is a beautiful neogothic church built in 1920. It used to have wonderful stained glass windows depicting scenes from the gospel, but most were destroyed by stone throwing after the Revolution. At the west end of Calle Cristo is **Santo Cristo del Buen Viaje**, built as a small hermitage in 1794 by Emeterio de Arrieta with one nave. In the 19th century two naves and a tower were constructed.

Places of interest

The **Parque Casino Campestre** on the eastern side of the Río Hatibonico, was the first place in Cuba to have cattle shows. In the 19th century it was used for fairs, dances and other social activities but in the 20th century its purpose and structure has been changed. Trees have been planted and there are monuments to Salvador Cisneros Betancourt, to the Unknown Soldier, and to teachers. Next to the park there is a monument erected in 1941 to Barberán and Collar, the first pilots to cross the Atlantic at its widest point, in a flight from Sevilla. It took them 39 hours and 55 minutes.

Museums

Museo Provincial Ignacio Agramonte, Av de los Mártires 2 esquina Ignacio Sánchez, first built as a cavalry barracks in 1848, it was converted to the *Hotel Camagüey* from 1905-43. After considerable restoration the museum was inaugurated on 23 December 1955 (the anniversary of Agramonte's birth). There are exhibitions of history, natural history, paintings and furniture of the 17th and 18th centuries.

Padre Valencia and the white vulture

Camagüey's lepers were first housed in a timber and thatched shelter, but in 1815-19 Padre Valencia raised money locally to build a new hospital for leprosy sufferers, with a chapel, hermitage and cemetery, known as San Lázaro. Padre Valencia continued to raise money and look after the sick until his death, whereupon the whole enterprise fell apart, no one took care of the inmates and they began to starve. The story goes that they were sitting on the patio one day, watching the circling vultures waiting for them to die, while remembering the good old days when they had plenty to eat and shared their leftovers with the birds. Suddenly a white vulture landed on the patio, which they managed to catch. They exhibited this rarity to earn money for their keep, believing it to be the soul of Padre Valencia come down from heaven to help them. You can see the white vulture on display in Matanzas' museum of natural history. Today the site of San Lázaro is the School of Arts 'José White'.

Tinajón - vessel of love and bondage

🐾 The logo of Camagüey is the *tinajón* and the city is known as the city of the *tinajones*. The story goes back to the time when the first settlers had serious problems with water, which was in short supply. However, it rained a lot in the region and the Spanish potters found a solution by storing water in pots similar to those brought from Spain containing wine and oil. From that time on the *tinajón* became a feature of every Camagueyan house or patio. Legend has it that if a girl offers a visitor water from a *tinajón*, he should not refuse it, but before accepting it he should know that if he drinks he will fall in love with the girl and never leave the city.

Open Tuesday-Saturday 0900-1700, Sunday 0800-1200, US$1. The **Museo Casa Natal Ignacio Agramonte** is one of the most impressive museums in the country (Av Ignacio Agramonte 59, T 9-7116, open Tuesday-Saturday 1000-1800, US$1). Ignacio Agramonte y Loynaz, one of the national heroes of the struggle against the Spanish, was born here on 23 December 1841. Agramonte, a cattle rancher, led the rebellion in this area and in July 1869 forces under his command bombarded Camagüey. However, he was killed in action in 1873. When he took up arms against the colonial power in 1868 all his goods were confiscated by the state. The ground floor of the house was turned into a market while the second storey was occupied by the Spanish council. Later the ground floor became a bar and a post office. In the second half of the 20th century the house was restored and turned into a museum exhibiting objects relating to the life of this revolutionary. **Casa Jesús Suárez Gayol** was the home of one of the Cuban guerrillas who lost his life in Bolivia in 1967 alongside Che Guevara. The museum has exhibits about Camagüeyans, particularly students, who were active revolutionaries in the struggle for independence.

Local information
● **Accommodation**

> **Prices: L1** over US$200; **L2** US$151-200; **L3** US$101-150; **A1** US$81-100; **A2** US$61-80; **A3** US$46-60; **B** US$31-45; **C** US$21-30; **D** US$12-20; **E** US$7-11; **F** up to US$6

A3 *Villa Maraguán* (Cubanacán), Circunvalación Este, on outskirts, T 7-2017, 7-2170, 32 rooms and 2 suites with terrace, 3 bars, restaurant, cafetería, car rental, pool, open air night time entertainment when tour parties are staying, video and games room, squash, billiards, table tennis, volleyball, children's playground, horseriding, medical services.

B *Hotel Camagüey* (Horizontes), Av Ignacio Agramonte, T 72015/82490, good condition, modern, Soviet influenced architecture, pool, disco show, bar in the lobby and on second floor, cafetería, buffet restaurant US$10, car hire; **B** *Puerto Príncipe*, Av de los Mártires 60 y Andrés Sánchez, La Vigía (in town), T 82469/82403, near museum and railway station, 77 rooms, a/c, bar, very slow restaurant, choose a room away from the nightclub on roof open until 0130 every night; **B** *Gran Hotel*, Maceo 67, T 92093/4, colonial style, under renovation 1997, central, swimming pool being added, restaurant on top floor, good view, also cafetería and snack bar; **B-D** *Colón*, Calle República 472 entre San José y San Martín, T 83346, 83368, old style built in 1920s, central, poor restaurant, snack bar better, two grades of rooms, the better ones have a/c, ice box, TV.

C-D *Plaza* (Islazul), Calle Van Horne 1, entre República y Avellaneda, T 8-2413, 8-2457, 67 rooms with TV, fridge, colonial building right by railway station, ask for room at the back away from traffic noise, mediocre restaurant, bar, Altamira travel agency on the ground floor next to the shop.

D *Isla de Cuba*, República y San Estéban, T 91515, in the heart of the city, 43 rooms, two grades.
América is a peso hotel on Avellaneda at the intersection with San Martín, T 82135, small, cosy hotel with a/c, nice variety of dishes in the restaurant, bar, you will probably be told the hotel is full.

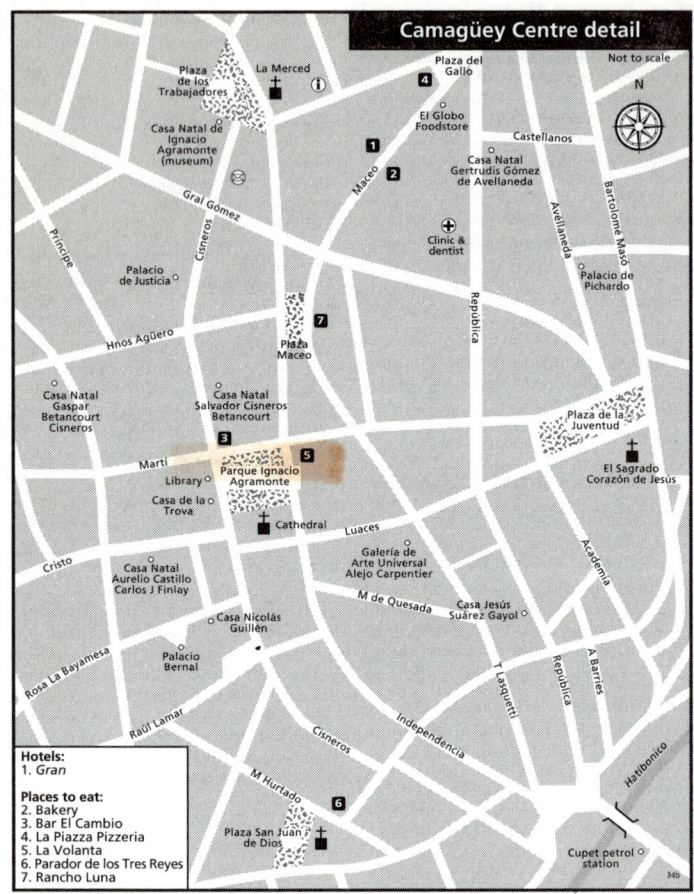

Camagüey Centre detail

Not to scale

Plaza de los Trabajadores

La Merced

Plaza del Gallo

4

El Globo Foodstore

Castellanos

Casa Natal de Ignacio Agramonte (museum)

Casa Natal Gertrudis Gómez de Avellaneda

1

Maceo

2

Gral Gómez

Cisneros

Avellaneda

Bartolomé Masó

Príncipe

Clinic & dentist

Palacio de Justicia

República

Palacio de Pichardo

Palacio de Justicia

Hnos Agüero

7

Plaza Maceo

Casa Natal Gaspar Betancourt Cisneros

Casa Natal Salvador Cisneros Betancourt

Plaza de la Juventud

Martí

3

Parque Ignacio Agramonte

5

El Sagrado Corazón de Jesús

Library

Casa de la Trova

Cathedral

Luaces

Galería de Arte Universal Alejo Carpentier

Academia

Cristo

Casa Natal Aurelio Castillo Carlos J Finlay

M de Quesada

Casa Jesús Suárez Gayol

República

A Barries

Casa Nicolás Guillén

Palacio Bernal

Rosa La Bayamesa

Raúl Lamar

Cisneros

Independencia

T Lasguetti

Hatibonico

M Hurtado

6

Plaza San Juan de Dios

Cupet petrol station

Hotels:
1. *Gran*

Places to eat:
2. Bakery
3. Bar El Cambio
4. La Piazza Pizzeria
5. La Volanta
6. Parador de los Tres Reyes
7. Rancho Luna

Private rooms can be found around the city, you will be approached on the street.

● **Places to eat**

State-run restaurants, apart from those in hotels, include *Rancho Luna*, on Plaza Maceo, open 1200-1400, 1800-2200, and *La Volanta*, on Parque Agramonte, open 1200-2300, both of which offer Cuban food and you will be asked to pay in dollars. You can pay in pesos at *Pizzería La Piazza* on Agramonte on the corner with Maceo, but there may be a queue. On the Plaza de San Juan there are the *Parador de los Tres Reyes* and

the *Campana de Toledo*, two small colonial-style restaurants serving Spanish food, pleasant, live music, meals from US$8. Near the railway station there is *El Paradero* cafetería and bar open 24 hours and a bakery and cafetería also open 24 hours. *Bar El Cambio* on Parque Agramonte is good. There are several shops where you can buy food, but to find out how the locals cope, go to the Agromercado near the river. As well as fruit and vegetables there is a small place where you can order cooked food and lots of people will try to sell you snacks.

● **Airlines**
Cubana is at República 400 esquina Correa, open Monday-Friday 0700-1500, Saturday 0700-1100, T 92156/91338.

● **Banks & money changers**
The **Banco Financiero Internacional** is on Plaza Maceo for all financial and exchange services including cash advances on credit cards. There is a *cadeca* for currency exchange on República entre Primelles y Santa Rita. The **Banco de la República** is on República opposite Iglesia La Soledad.

● **Entertainment**
Every Saturday night a *Noche Camagueya* is held along Calle República, when the street is closed to traffic and there is music everywhere and traditional food. The Ballet de Camagüey, ranked second in the country after Havana's ballet company, often performs at the Teatro Principal, on Padre Valencia 64, T 93048. There are three cinemas: Casablanca, T 92244; Guerrero, T 92874 and Encanto, T 95511. Folk music is played at the **Casa de la Trova**, on the west side of Parque Agramontes between Martí and Cristo, closed Mondays.

● **Hospitals & medical services**
24-hour pharmacy on the corner of Avellaneda y Primelles. There is a children's hospital on the east side of the river in the block formed by Dolores Betancourt, Domingo Puente, Palmira and Javier de la Vega, T 97538. The Policlínico Finlay is on Av Carlos J Finlay heading towards the airport. Policlínica Pirra is squeezed between the railway station and the Agramonte museum. The *Provincial Hospital* is west of the centre, T 91902/82012/83213. Amalia Simoni Clinic is out on the road to Nuevitas, just past the junction with Circunvalación, T 61011/61234.

● **Post & telecommunications**
The central **Post Office** is just off the Plaza de los Trabajadores on Cisneros. The DHL headquarters and international phone service is on Avellaneda entre Correa y San Esteban.

● **Shopping**
For handicrafts try the Gallery Expo-sale on the north side of the Plaza de los Trabajadores. The Galería de Arte Universal Alejo Carpentier is at Luaces 153 with San Pablo. Photo service is on Agramonte with Lope Recio. Artex dollar shops almost opposite Photo service on Agramonte and also on República opposite Cubana and on Cisneros, just north of Parque Agramonte. Max

Music sells CDs, cassettes etc, on República two blocks north of Iglesia La Soledad.

● **Transport**
Local Car hire: Havanautos is at *Hotel Camagüey*. There are Servi Cupet gas stations by the river on Carretera Central with Av de la Libertad, and a couple of blocks further south on the other side of the Carretera Central. **Taxi**: service T 81247/98721. For a tourist taxi T 72428.

Air There is supposed to be a bus from Parque Finlay by the railway station out to the Ignacio Agramonte International Airport (CMW). The airport is 9 km from the centre on the road to Nuevitas, T 61010. Cubana flies daily from Havana and once a week from London Gatwick. There are also charter flights from Toronto and Europe depending on the season.

Bus Ticket agency T 71602. The Interprovincial bus station is southwest of the centre along the Carretera Central. Three buses a day to Havana, daily to Holguín, Manzanillo, Santiago de Cuba, Cienfuegos, Guantánamo, Matanzas, Sancti Spíritus, Las Tunas, Bayamo, Ciego de Avila and Baracoa. A truck to Las Tunas is 5 pesos. If you go to the *terminal amarillo* on the edge of town you can pick up cheap transport as it becomes available, eg a shared *taxi particular* to Ciego de Avila is US$3.

Train Railway station T 92633/81525. Train ticket agency T 83214, foreigners pay in dollars at Ladis office upstairs above the main ticket office opposite *Hotel Plaza*. The station is divided into long distance, south of the railway by *Hotel Plaza*, and short distances within the province, north of the railway between Joaquín de Aguero and Manuel Benavides. The 'special' from Havana gets in to Camagüey at 0054 on its way to Santiago and Guantánamo. Another train leaves Havana at 1835, arriving Camagüey 0455, returning from Camagüey at 1825, arriving Havana 0435.

NORTHEAST TO THE COAST

The road and railway head northeast out of Camagüey past the brewery and the airport through pastures and chicken farms to the coast. The first town of any size is **Minas**, 60 km away, with a population of about 20,000. There is no reason to stop here except to see the place where they make violins and other musical instruments. The Fábrica de Instrumentos Musicales is on Calle Camilo Cienfuegos

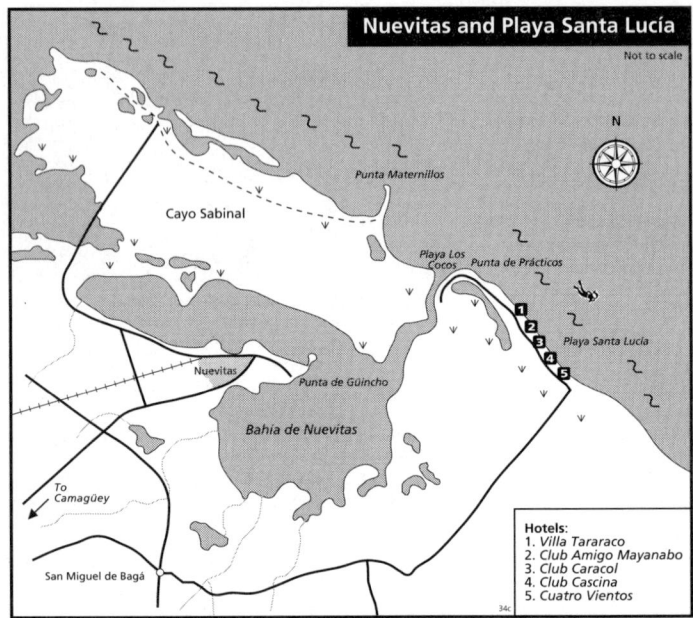

Nuevitas and Playa Santa Lucía

Not to scale

N

Punta Maternillos

Cayo Sabinal

Playa Los Cocos

Punta de Prácticos

1
2
3   Playa Santa Lucía
4
5

Nuevitas

Punta de Güincho

Bahía de Nuevitas

To Camagüey

San Miguel de Bagá

Hotels:
1. *Villa Tararaco*
2. *Club Amigo Mayanabo*
3. *Club Caracol*
4. *Club Cascina*
5. *Cuatro Vientos*

on the east of town, open Monday-Saturday, US$2. There is a peso hotel by the railway tracks. After Minas, road and railway diverge, passing through cattle country before joining again and terminating together at the port of **Nuevitas** 87 km from Camagüey. Nuevitas has always been a busy port, primarily for the export of sugar and with a thriving fishing industry, but the outskirts are now dominated by heavy industry including a large cement works and fertilizer plant fuelled by a huge thermoelectric power station. It is not a tourist town although there are pretty parts, such as the plaza with its huge tree and old church, and the wooden houses on the two main streets. On no account swim in the bay because of pollution. Nuevitas is not much of a place to stay, but there is a hotel, the **D** *Caonaba*, T 44265, on the road to Camagüey, 48 rooms, simple, depends on its Cuban clientele but will give you a room if there is one.

PLAYA SANTA LUCIA

Santa Lucía is a beach resort 112 km northeast, or two hours by bus, from Camagüey, where the sand stretches some 20 km along the northern coast near the **Bahía de Nuevitas**. This is a beautiful beach, protected by an offshore reef which contains over 50 species of coral and is much sought after by divers (see **Diving and marine life**, page 28). The water is clear and warm, with an average temperature of 24°C. You can sometimes see dolphins near the shore and there are flamingoes in the salt flats inshore. It is a lovely place to come and relax but be aware that it is remote, there is no real town as such, and excursions inland can therefore be time consuming and expensive. Most people who stay here are on package tours for a week or so and see little of Cuba. However, hotel tour desks can offer you an excursion to Camagüey city, Trinidad or Santiago overnight, air taxi to Cayo Kawama, to

Havana by plane, several helicopter trips, a boat ride in Bahía de Nuevitas, hunting, fishing and diving etc. 8 km from Santa Lucía there is **Playa Los Cocos**, which is even better than Santa Lucía. The sand here is very white and the water crystal clear. There are some bars and the *Lazo Lobster House*.

● **Accommodation A1-A3** *Cuatro Vientos* (Cubanacán), the newest on the beach, 4-star, full board or room only, 196 rooms and suites, a/c, TV, all facilities, disco show, pool with children's area, 2 restaurants, snack bar, aqua bar, shops, beauty salon, diving and aerobics lessons, tennis, volleyball, horseriding, watersports; *Villa Tararaco*, (Cubanacán) T 36222/36310, 30 rooms and 1 suite with terrace, TV, restaurant, bar, live music, car and bicycle hire, billiards, child care, diving and watersports, under restoration in 1997; **A2** *Club Amigo Mayanabo* (Cubanacán), T 36184-5, on the beach, 3-star, simple but good value as price is all-inclusive, 201 double rooms, 12 triples, 12 suites, a/c, pool, daily organized activities, night club on the jetty, restaurant, bars, cafeteria, shops, post office, car hire, table tennis, pool table, beach volleyball, watersports include windsurfing, catamarans and snorkelling, fishing or horse riding can be arranged; **A3** *Club Caracol*(Golden Tulip), T 30402-3, 36429, F 7335043, 4-star, sea front in large gardens, 150 2-storey cabañas with sea view, a/c, TV, ice box, phone, free form pool with children's area, jacuzzi, disco, buffet restaurant, snack bar, barbecue and beach grill, aqua bar, shops, beauty parlour, tennis, volleyball, aerobics, bicycles, table games, watersports include windsurfing, pedal boats, kayaks, snorkelling, entertainment includes Cuban dance lessons, price quoted is room only but most guests are all-inclusive; **A2** *Club Cascina Santa Lucía*, next to the *Caracol*, you get to the beach through its grounds, 3-star, usually all-inclusive, 246 simple rooms, 40 suites or 12 bungalows, a/c, TV, buffet restaurant, grill, snack bar, disco, pool with children's area and swim-up bar, games room, gym, aerobics, massage, lots of activities and trying to cater for all ages.

● **Places to eat** State-run restaurants include *La Brisas*, creole; *Bonzai*, Chinese; and *La Casa del Pescador*, for seafood. There are also *paladares* where you can eat for a more reasonable price.

FLORIDA

46 km northwest of Camagüey on the road and railway to Ciego de Avila, is **Florida**, a town of some 40,000 inhabitants, with hospitals and clinics, museum, art gallery, Casa de Cultura, cinema, hotel and restaurants. There are a couple of sugar mills and factories making construction materials, textiles and a brewery. Tour buses pass through here, but few foreigners stop long. However, there are a number of lagoons in the area and Florida is used as a base for shooting and fishing expeditions. The reservoirs Porvenir and Muñoz nearby and Mañana de Santa Ana, southeast of Camagüey, are used for organized 6-hour trout fishing sessions. The area is also popular for shooting duck, quail, doves and guinea fowl, amongst other game birds, so if you stay at the local hotel you may find your fellow guests are hunters.

● **Accommodation C** *Horizontes La Casona de Florida*, Carretera Central Km 2, T 53011, 74 rooms with bath and TV, pool.

GUAIMARO

Heading southeast by road towards Las Tunas, you can stop in **Guáimaro**, just before the provincial border. It is a small town about 80 km from Camagüey, with a population of about 20,000 and an agricultural fair every October. However it is notable for its historical connections: Carlos Manuel de Céspedes was elected first president of the Republic here by the constituent assembly of 1869, whose other task was to draw up the first Cuban constitution. Seventy years later the town got round to commemorating the event with a monument in Parque Constitución dedicated to the men who fought for Cuban independence including Céspedes and José Martí.

● **Accommodation D** *Guáimaro*, T 82102, 40 rooms on the east side of town on the Carretera Central.

Province of Las Tunas

AN AGRICULTURAL province, travellers could be forgiven for not noticing Las Tunas on their way from Camagüey to Holguín or Bayamo, as only about 65 km of the road actually passes through the province. On the other hand, the provincial capital would make a convenient break in the journey, or you could get well off the beaten track by visiting the beaches of the northern coast.

Province of Las Tunas

Las Tunas borders Camagüey to the west and Holguín and Granma to the east. It is only 6,589 sq km of mostly low lying farming land, although the central part of the province around the city is part of the Holguín ridge and more hilly. There are three large bays on the northern coast: Bahía de Manatí, Bahía de Malagueta and Bahía de Puerto Padre de Chapata, which offer safe harbour and fishing ports. The southern coast opens on to the Golfo de Guacanayabo, and is marshy with mangroves. Beef cattle and sugar cane are the main agricultural activities. The capital, **Victoria de las Tunas**, also known as **Las Tunas**, or even just **Tuna**, is located in the centre of the province, which was formerly part of Oriente.

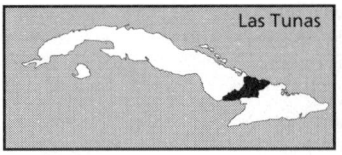

Las Tunas

Area 15,990 sq km, *Population* 774,100, *Density* 48.4 per sq km, *Urban* 75%

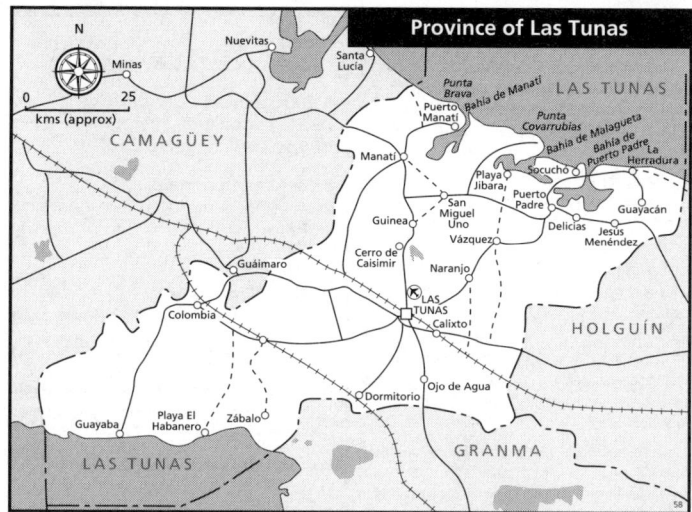

Province of Las Tunas

LAS TUNAS

Population 120,000; *Phone code* 31

Victoria de las Tunas was founded in the 1750s but was never more than a market town until Las Tunas became a province in its own right in 1975 and needed a capital city. The Carretera Central linking Havana with the east of the country runs through the middle of the town, although there is now a Circunvalación running round the south so that you can avoid the centre all together if you want to. The town centre is effectively the junction of three roads, the tree-lined Vicente García (the Carretera Central), Angel Guardia and Francisco Varona, at the Parque Vicente García, where there is a small church. There is a memorial to General Vicente García just off the Parque and his name crops up frequently in the town, having led the struggle for independence in the area in 1868 and having captured the town in 1876.

Places of interest

In 1976 a Cubana plane en route from Caracas to Havana was blown up just after takeoff from a stop in Barbados by a bomber who left a device under his seat when he disembarked in Barbados. 73 people, including the Cuban fencing team, were killed. The **Memorial a los Mártires de Barbados**, in the park along Vicente García by the river, contains photos of all the victims around the walls. Entrance US$1. Local history is displayed in the **Museo Provincial General Vicente García**, on Vicente García opposite the Parque. The birthplace of a local 19th century poet has been made into a museum, the **Casa Natal Juan Cristóbal Nápoles y Fajardo**, on Lucas Ortíz.

Excursions

Close to Las Tunas you can get out to the *Motel El Cornito*, see below, where you can relax, walk or fish in the river and reservoir. Further afield you can drive to the north coast to the beaches on Punta Covarrubias or Playa La Herradura. There is no tourist development along this stretch of coast and you are likely to have the place to yourself.

Festivals

There is a Fiesta Cucalambé at the *Motel El Cornito* in June or July for folk music and an agricultural fair in La Tunas in December.

Local information

● Accommodation

C *Las Tunas*, Av 2 de Diciembre y Carlos J Finlay, T 45014/45169, on a hill on the road out to the hospital, southeast of the town, 142 rooms in modern 4-storey block, restaurant, cafeteria, pool (not always filled), car rental.

There are peso hotels, which might be worth trying if you want to stay in the centre of town: *Santiago*, Angel Guardia 112, T 43396, 32 rooms, just off Parque Vicente García; *Ferroviario*, opposite the railway station, T 42601, 20 rooms in old hotel.

D *Motel El Cornito*, 7 km west of town, off Carretera Central, T 45015, 129 rooms in blocks or bungalows, basic and uncomfortable but attractive setting in park with bamboo groves and reservoir, fishing in the Río Hormiguero, restaurant, evening entertainment, amusement park next door.

There is an office of Campismo Popular on Angel Guardia near the *Hotel Santiago*, which has information on rustic lodging and campsites in remote places.

● Places to eat

The food is not bad at the *Majibacoa* in the *Hotel Las Tunas*. The only other state restaurant is the *Restaurante 1876*, Vicente García, near the park by the river, open 1200-2300, specializes in pork. *Paladares* are a better bet, but these change frequently.

● Airlines

Cubana office on Lucas Ortíz y 24 de Febrero, T 42702, or at the airport T 43266.

● Entertainment

Casa de la Cultura, Vicente García 8 entre Francisco Vega y Francisco Varona.

● Post & telecommunications

Telephone office on Angel Guardia, just east of the Parque.

● Transport

Local Most local transport is by horse and cart or other non-motorized transport such as *bici-taxis*. **Car hire**: there is a **Havanautos** desk in the *Hotel Las Tunas*.

Air There is an airport (VTU) 11 km from Las Tunas which receives Cubana flights 4 times a week from Havana.

Bus The bus station is just south of the main Parque on Francisco Varona, T 43801. Long distance buses are already full when they pass through Las Tunas and you just have to hope that someone is getting off here. Local buses use the terminal near the railway station. A truck to Camagüey is 5 pesos.

Train The railway station is northeast of the centre, with daily trains to Holguín, Santiago, Matanzas and Havana.

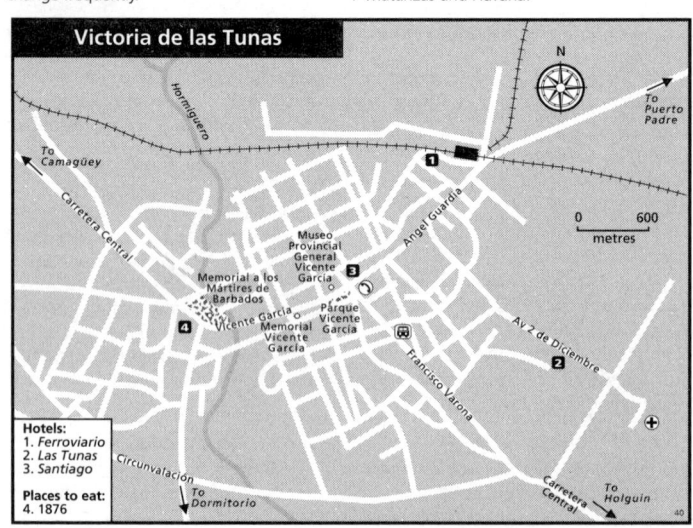

Province of Holguín

THE COUNTRYSIDE of Holguín is attractive, hilly and covered with luxuriant vegetation. There are picture book views of hillsides dotted with royal palms, towering over thatched cottages, called *bohíos*, while the flatter land is green with swathes of sugar cane. Tourism has been developed along the coast, which is indented with horseshoe shaped bays and sandy beaches, protected by a coral reef, but the resorts are low-key and pleasant.

Holguín, the city of parks, was founded in 1545. There are many statues and monuments to national heroes, several of which are around the Plaza de la Revolución on the edge of the city, the location of the City Hall and the Provincial Communist Party building. Several attractive excursions can be made from the city.

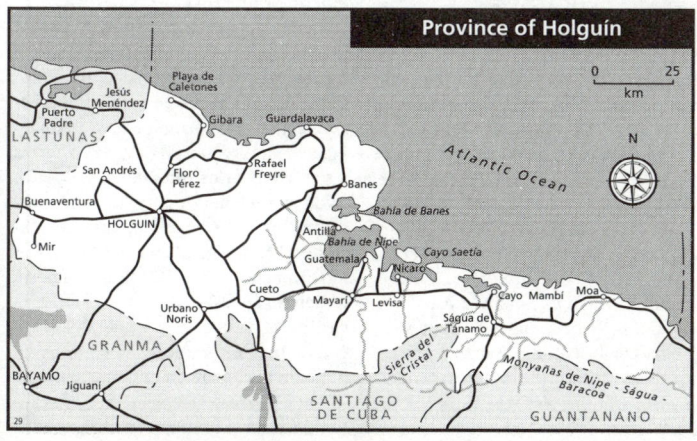

Province of Holguín

Holguín lies in the east of the country, stretching along the north coast and indented by many bays. Its neighbours are Las Tunas to the west, Bayamo to the southwest, Santiago de Cuba to the south and Guántanamo to the southeast. The capital, Holguín, lies in a range of hills which stretch from Las Tunas to the coast at Punta de Mulas, while the eastern part of the province takes in the foothills of the Sierra del Cristal and the Montañas de Nipe-Sagua-Baracoa. The local economy is traditionally based on sugar and there is a sugar mill at Rafael Freyre, but cattle, corn, coffee and beans are also grown. Further to the east of the province is the hugely important nickel and cobalt plant with shipping facilities at Moa, which is receiving large amounts of foreign investment, particularly from Canada. Other mining and industrial plants include chrome processing in Mayarí, and nickel, iron and steel at Nícaro. Tourism is now a major employer and brings foreign exchange to the local people. The area around Guardalavaca has a collection of hotels catering for most budgets with a sprinkling of all-inclusives, but there is not the tourist infrastructure you find in Varadero. This buoyant economy supports a growing population which has made the province the second after Havana City to exceed 1 million inhabitants.

Columbus is believed to arrived at the Bahía de Bariay in 1492, where he landed on 28 October and claimed that it was the most beautiful country he had ever seen. The indigenous people probably thought so too, since archaeological explorations have shown that there were primitive cultures here some 6,000 years ago. Seboruco man is thought to have been the first inhabitant of what is now the province of Holguín.

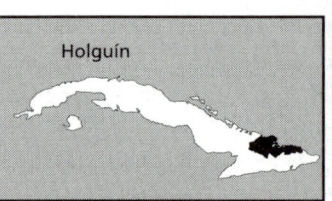

Area 9,300 sq km; Population 1,013,600, Density 109 per sq km, Urban 58.3%

HOLGUIN

Population 250,000, Phone code 24

Holguín is the provincial capital, with easy access to some of the best beaches in the country. The town was founded in 1545 and named after García Holguín, a captain in the Spanish colonization force. It officially received the title of Ciudad de San Isidro de Holguín on 18 January 1752, when the population numbered 1,426.

The city has a university, a paediatric hospital, coffee roasting plant, brewery and baseball stadium and is busy, although all traffic moves at the pace of the thousands of bicycles which throng the streets.

Places of interest

Holguín is known as the 'city of the parks', four of which, **Parque Infantil**, **Parque Carlos Manuel de Céspedes**, the **Plaza Central** and **Parque José Martí**, lie between the two main streets: Antonio Maceo and Libertad (Manduley). There is a statue of **Carlos Manuel de Céspedes** in the parque named after him, he is remembered for having freed his slaves on 10 October 1868 and starting the war of independence. The 1820 church, **Iglesia de San José** is also in the square. The Plaza Central is named after **General Calixto García Iñiguez** (statue in the centre), who was born in Holguín in 1837 and took part in both wars of independence. He captured the town from the Spanish in 1872

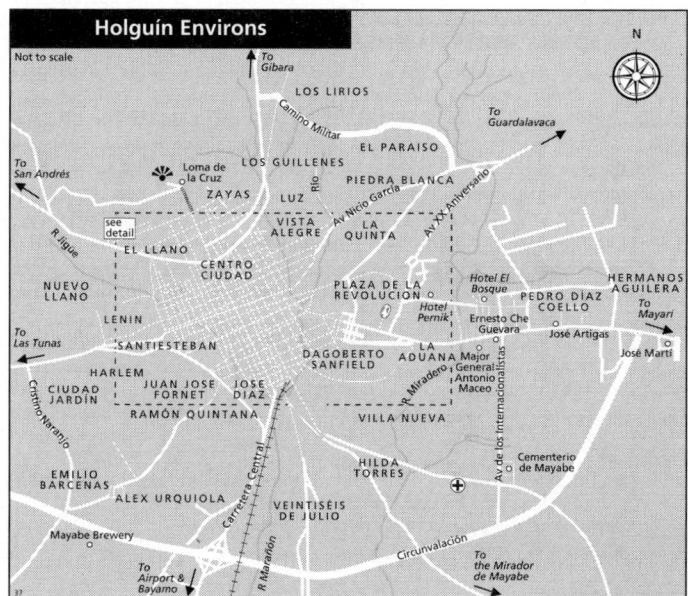

Holguín Environs

Not to scale

N

To Gibara

LOS LIRIOS

Camino Militar

To San Andrés

LOS GUILLENES

EL PARAISO

Loma de la Cruz

ZAYAS

LUZ

PIEDRA BLANCA

Av Nicio García

To Guardalavaca

see detail

EL LLANO

VISTA ALEGRE

LA QUINTA

Av XX Aniversario

CENTRO CIUDAD

NUEVO LLANO

PLAZA DE LA REVOLUCION

Hotel El Bosque

PEDRO DIAZ COELLO

HERMANOS AGUILERA

LENIN

Hotel Pernik

Ernesto Che Guevara

To Mayarí

To Las Tunas

SANTIESTEBAN

DAGOBERTO SANFIELD

ADUANA

José Artigas

José Martí

HARLEM

JUAN JOSE FORNET

JOSE DIAZ

R Mirador

Major General Antonio Maceo

RAMÓN QUINTANA

VILLA NUEVA

Av de los Internacionalistas

CIUDAD JARDIN

Cristino Naranjo

EMILIO BARCENAS

HILDA TORRES

Cementerio de Mayabe

ALEX URQUIOLA

VEINTISEIS DE JULIO

Carretera Central

Av de Mayabe

Mayabe Brewery

Circunvalación

To the Mirador de Mayabe

To Airport & Bayamo

R Marañón

and again occupied it in 1898 after helping the US forces defeat the colonial power in Santiago de Cuba. His statue is in the centre and his birthplace on Calle Miró 147, one block from the plaza, is now a museum, **Casa Natal de Calixto García**, open Monday-Friday 0800-1700, Saturday 0800-1300, US$1. Around the plaza are the **Commander Eddy Suñol Theatre** (he fought against Batista), the Library, **Galería Bayado** (ceramics, carvings, furniture, all for sale, courtyard at back with small bar, singing, music at night), **Casa de Cultura** (handicrafts, dancing), cafetería and both peso and dollar stores. On the north side of the square is the **Museo Provincial**, known as *La Periquera*, parrot cage, because of the brightly coloured soldiers known as *periquitos*, parakeets, who used to stand guard outside when the building was used as an army barracks in the 19th century. It was built between 1860-1868 and is now a National Monument. On 30 October 1868, 500 armed *independistas* attacked the building shouting ¡Viva Cuba! but failed to take it because of its strategic defences. The most important item on display here is the Hacha de Holguín, a precolumbian axe head carved with the head of a man, measuring 350mm in length and 76mm at its widest point. It was found in 1860 on one of the hills around the city and is believed to be about 500 years old. It has become the symbol of Holguín. The museum is open Monday-Friday 0900-1700, Saturday 0900-1300, US$1, US$3 with camera). Off the square on Maceo 129, the **Museo de Ciencias Naturales** is full of stuffed animals, but is popular, open Sunday-Thursday 0900-1700, Saturday 1300-1700, US$1. **Parque Peralta** is another square between Maceo and Manduley, named after Julio Grave de Peralta, who led the Holguín independence struggle against Spain in 1868. The **Cathedral** is on this square, built in 1720 but frequently altered or improved.

Above the city is **La Loma de la Cruz**, a strategic hill with a cross on top. On 3 May 1790, a Franciscan priest, Antonio de Alegría, came with a group of religious people and put up the cross, 275m above sea level, 127m above the town. All the streets of the town were laid out from that strategic point, which has a look out tower, built by the Spanish during the 10 Years War. In 1929 stone steps were begun up the hill, which were finished 3 May 1950. Every 3 May locals celebrate the Romerías de la Cruz de Mayo. There is a road round the side of the hill, but if you wish to walk up straight up the 458 steps, there are lots of benches for resting on. The way is lit up at night with street lights. Candles are lit and offerings of coins are made at the cross, but you are more likely to meet gangs of boys waiting

Ajiaco (Gran sopa de Cuba)

There are many different recipes for *ajiaco*, which is found in most Latin American countries. In Cuba, each city seems to have its own variations on this hearty soup which originates partly in Spain, but also has ingredients from Africa and from the Amerindians who gave the world ají, or chilli pepper. This recipe comes from Trinidad and Cienfuegos and has more meat than some other, peasant variations.

125 gm salt or dried beef
¼ chicken, cut into 2-3 pieces
250 gm fresh beef, suitable for soup
250 gm pork, cut into 2-3 pieces
250 gm pork ribs
3½ litres water
4 tablespoons lard
1 onion, peeled and chopped
3 cloves of garlic, peeled and crushed
1 green pepper (not hot), finely chopped
8 small ripe tomatoes (or purée), seeds removed, finely chopped
1 cob of yellow sweet corn, sliced into rounds
1 large green banana, peeled and chopped
1 kg mixed squash, sweet potato, yucca, dasheen, yams or other starchy vegetables
1 large lime
250 gm ground or grated yellow maize
1 tablespoon milk
salt

Cut the salt beef into 3-4 pieces and soak overnight. Next morning discard the water and put the meat and the chicken in a very large pot with the water. Bring to the boil and simmer for about 1 hr. Add the pork and the ribs. Cook for another hour skimming off any scum or excess fat. In 2 spoonfuls of lard, fry the onion, 2 cloves of garlic, green pepper and tomatoes until soft. Add to the meat and then add the sweet corn, banana and mixed vegetables. Always toss the banana in lime juice before adding to food to stop it discolouring. While the soup continues to cook, make some corn dumplings. Mix the ground maize with I teaspoonful of salt, 1 clove of garlic, milk and the rest of the lard. Carefully put spoonfuls of this mixture on top of the soup. Cover and leave to simmer very gently, so that the dumplings don't break up, for about another hour. If at the end you want a thicker soup, mash some of the root vegetables with a little of the stock and return it to the soup. Season to taste. Serve hot with bread. Serves 6.

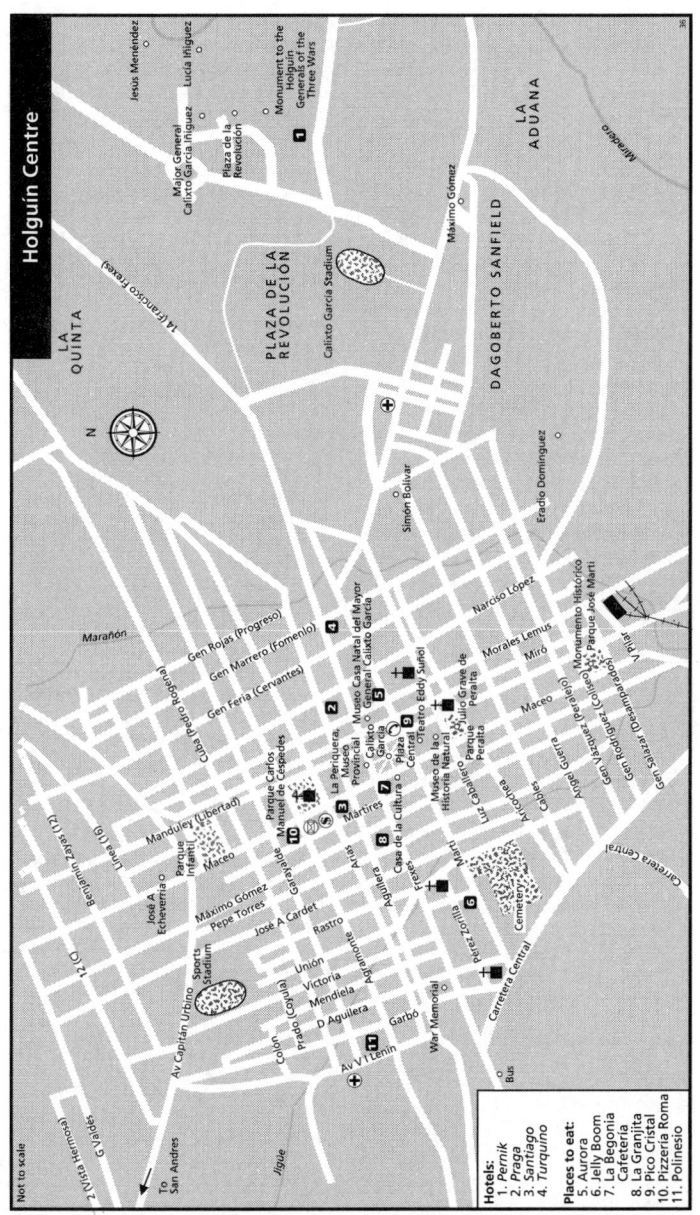

Holguín Centre

Not to scale

N

LA QUINTA

La (Francisco Fexeu)

PLAZA DE LA REVOLUCIÓN

Calixto García Stadium

Jesús Menéndez

Lucía Iñiguez

Major General Calixto García Iñiguez

Plaza de la Revolución

Monument to the Holguín Generals of the Three Wars ❶

LA ADUANA

Máximo Gómez

Mirador

DAGOBERTO SANFIELD

Simón Bolívar

Marañón

Gen Rojas (Progreso)

Gen Marrero (Fomento)

Gen Feria (Cervantes)

Cuba (Pedro Rogena)

Parque Carlos Manuel de Céspedes

La Periquera, Museo Provincial

Museo Casa Natal del Mayor General Calixto García

Calixto García ❺

Parque Central

Museo de la Historia Natural

Teatro Eddy Suñol

Julio Grave de Peralta

Parque Peralta

Narciso López

Morales Lemus

Miró

Maceo

Eradio Domínguez

❹

❷

❸

Parque Infantil

Manduley (Libertad)

Maceo

Garayalde

Mártires

Arias

Aguilera

Casa de la Cultura

Luz Caballero

Aricochea

Cables

Angel Guerra

Gen Vázquez (Coliseo)

Gen Rodríguez (Desampazados)

Monumento Histórico

Parque José Martí

Gen Salazar (Venegas)

V Pita

Carretera Central

José A Echeverría

Máximo Gómez

Pepe Torres

José A Cardet

Rastro

Frexes

Martí

Pérez Zorrilla

Cemetery

Av Capitán Ubino

Benjamín Zayas (12)

Línea (16)

Colón (Coyula)

Prado (Coyula)

Unión

Victoria

Mendiela

D Aguilera

Garbó

Av V I Lenin

War Memorial

Sports Stadium

To San Andrés

2 (Vista Hermosa)

G Valdés

Jigüe

Bus

Carretera Central

Hotels:
1. Pernik
2. Praga
3. Santiago
4. Turquino

Places to eat:
5. Aurora
6. Jelly Boom
7. La Begonia Cafetería
8. La Granjita
9. Pico Cristal
10. Pizzería Roma
11. Polinesio

❿ 🔟 ❻ ❽ ❼ ❾

for tourists than religious devotees. A policeman is usually on patrol in the morning.

Excursions

The **Mirador de Mayabe** is a popular excursion for Cubans and tour parties. A restaurant and hotel have been built on a hillside a few km out of town with a splendid view over the valley and the whole city. Water towers stand out like mushrooms in the distance. The restaurant has good Cuban food, open air but under cover and the usual strolling musicians. There is a swimming pool perched on the edge of the hill and beside it a bar, where Pancho, the beer-drinking donkey entertains guests. Actually he is confined in a very small pen beside the bar and it is unlikely that the quantity of beer does him any good, but apart from an air of boredom he seems quite healthy and happy. *La Finca Mayabe* has a second restaurant, normally open only for tour parties, with a *bohío*, and a collection of chickens, turkeys, ducks etc which you might find around a typical farmer's house.

About 27 km north of Holguín on the coast is the pretty little town of **Gibara** (*Population* 16,000). It is believed that Columbus first landed near here at Cayo Bariay on 27 October 1492. The hill nearby, the Silla de Gibara, he referred to as shaped like a saddle and it became a landmark and navigation reference point. The town was not founded until 1827, but it became an important port for the area and there is still a thriving fishing industry, specializing in lobsters. The main square has a fine row of big African oak trees around it and there are many large and pleasant old houses dating from the 19th century in the town. On Independencia there are two museums, the **Museo Municipal** and the **Museo de Historia Natural**, which have exhibitions about the area. There is a small peso hotel but foreigners usually come on day trips from Guardalavaca or Holguín.

Local information
● **Accommodation**

Prices: L1 over US$200; L2 US$151-200; L3 US$101-150; A1 US$81-100; A2 US$61-80; A3 US$46-60; B US$31-45; C US$21-30; D US$12-20; E US$7-11; F up to US$6

B *Pernik*, T 48-1011/1140, near Plaza de la Revolución on Av Jorge Dimitrov y Av XX Aniversario, 202 rooms, mostly overnighters passing through, shops, bar, restaurant, empty swimming pool, TV, a/c, nice view from top floor rooms, blue furniture, small bathrooms, adequate.

C *Villa El Bosque*, T 48-1012, just off Av Jorge Dimitrov, 69 rooms in spread out villas, patio garden, fridge, basic shower room, TV, a/c, also 2 suites, **A3**, good security, car rental, large pool, *El Pétalo* disco, popular. **C** *El Mirador de Mayabe* (Islazul), T 422160, T/F 425347, outside the town, see **Excursions** above, has 24 rooms in cabins under the trees, tiled floors, a/c, TV, wooden furniture, fridge, hot water, adequate bathroom, quiet, also a suite and **A3** 4 rooms in a house at the top of the hill with a fantastic view.

In the centre are **D** *Turquino*, T 46-2124 on Martí, 40 rooms with bath, TV, basic; and 3 peso hotels, *Santiago*, *Praga* and *Majestic*, which only occasionally take foreigners and have little to recommend them. Famous guests at the *Majestic* in the 1950s included Fidel Castro in room 13 and the Mexican singer Jorge Negrete, but now it is more of a short-stay hotel, painted red.

For a *casa particular*, **D**, Eddy G Osorio, Calle Frexes 166 entre Morales Lemus y Narciso López, with bath, very good breakfast for US$1.50.

● **Places to eat**
There are several *paladares*. *Aurora*, on Martí, has a good reputation and is popular; *Jelly Boom*, also on Martí, near the cemetery, is supposed to be the best in town; ask around for others as they change quickly; *Pizzería Roma* on Maceo with Agramonte at the corner of Parque Céspedes, is state-run; *La Begonia*, is a *cafetería* on the Plaza Central, outdoors under a flowering creeper, very pretty, good for a Mayabe beer, meeting place for *jineteras*. For ice cream, *Coppelia* is on Parque Peralta. The two main hotels are farther far away from the restaurants and their own food is not recommended; *Taberna Pancho* is in the area, though, on Av Jorge Dimitrov, round the corner from the *Pernik* and serves beer and a reasonable burger.

● **Airlines**
Cubana is in Edificio Pico de Cristal, Calle Libertad esquina Martí, 2do Piso Policentro, T 425707, F 468111.

● **Entertainment**
Teatro Comandante Eddy Suñol on Parque Calixto García, has performances of local and touring groups. During the day videos are shown on three TVs sitting on the stage, while backstage workers carry on behind them getting ready for the evening performance. **Casa de la Trova** on Plaza Calixto García near *La Begonia*, open daily except Monday, good music and dance. *Cabaret El Nocturno*, on road to Las Tunas, show with different Latin American music followed by salsa and dance music disco.

● **Hospitals & medical services**
The main hospital is west of the town centre on Av V I Lenin. A new hospital is being built, but only very slowly because of the shortage of raw materials. East of the centre there is a paediatric hospital, by the coffee roasting plant and just before you get to the Calixto García sports stadium. There are medical services at the hotels *Pernik* and *El Bosque*.

● **Post & telecommunications**
The **Post Office** is on Maceo, opposite Parque Céspedes. DHL is on Libertad, opposite the Plaza Central, open Monday-Friday 1000-1200, 1300-1600, alternate Saturdays 0800-1500. Telecorreos on the Plaza Central charges US$5.85/minute to Europe, US$3/minute to North America, minimum 4 minutes, for phone calls. For a fax you have to go to *Hotel Pernik*, where they charge a commission of US$1.

● **Shopping**
There is a bookshop on the east side of the Plaza Central by the telephone office, which has a reasonable selection of books and maps and a very helpful guard who knows what they have in stock. There is a dollar shop on the corner of the square but it is not of great interest to foreigners. A peso store on the square is almost empty and only has things no one wants to buy.

● **Transport**
Local There is very little motorized public transport. The city is choked with *bicitaxis*, bicycles with an extra wheel and seat on the side, or cart behind, or horse drawn buses and taxis, charging 50-80 centavos. Out of town people wait at junctions for the *Amarillos* (traffic wardens dressed in yellow) to stop any truck or large vehicle and bundle on as many passengers as possible.

Bus The interurban bus terminal, notable for the number of horses, rather than vehicles, is on Av de los Libertadores after the coffee roasting plant and opposite the turning to Estadio Calixto García. The interprovincial bus terminal is west of the centre on the Carretera Central. A *colectivo* to Las Tunas costs 20 pesos.

Air Frank País international airport (HOG), 8 km from the centre, receives direct scheduled flights from Amsterdam (Martinair), Dusseldorf (LTU), Paris, Buenos Aires and Bogotá (Cubana), while others connect through Havana. There are also charter flights from other cities which vary according to the season. There are domestic flights from Havana and Varadero.

Train Holguín is on the Havana-Santiago line (see Havana, **Transport**, page 126).

The road from Holguín past Rafael Freyre to the beach resort of Guardalavaca is broad with a good surface, lined with trees and empty of traffic. There is a cart track on either side for oxen and horses, so even these will not slow you up. The Amarillos are out in force at every junction, organizing lifts on trucks, while other people improvise, getting the whole family on a bicycle or a motorbike.

GUARDALAVACA

Guardalavaca has been developed as a tourist resort along a beautiful stretch of coastline, indented with horseshoe bays and sandy beaches. The resort is in two sections: the older part is rather like a village, apartments for workers are here and there are a few shops, discos, bank, restaurant and bus stop, while two newer hotels further west on the beach Estero Ciego (also referred to as Playa Esmeralda), are very isolated and there is nothing to do outside the hotels. Nevertheless, Estero Ciego beach is idyllic, a very pretty horseshoe shape with a river coming down to the sea in the middle and rocks at either end providing good snorkelling opportunities. There is a reef offshore for diving, which is very unspoilt and has a lot to offer. The hills surrounding the beach are green and wooded, helping to make the two Sol hotels here unobtrusive.

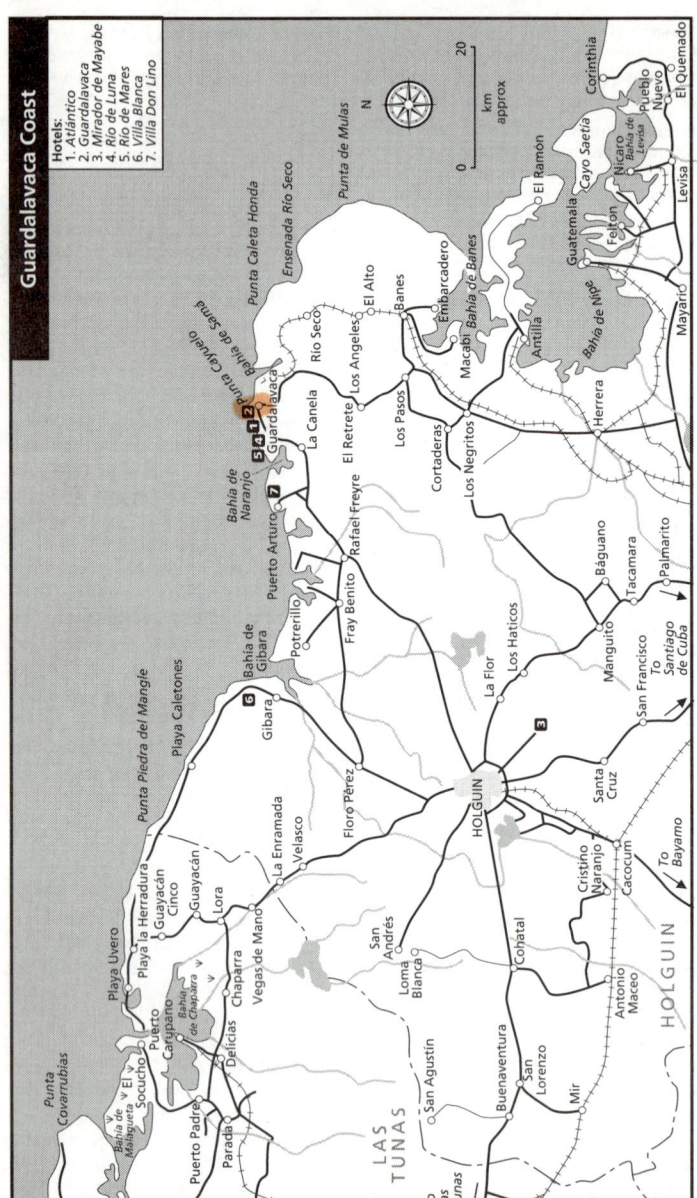

Guardalavaca Coast

Hotels:
1. Atlántico
2. Guardalavaca
3. Mirador de Mayabe
4. Rio de Luna
5. Rio de Mares
6. Villa Blanca
7. Villa Don Lino

N

0   km   20
         approx

Excursions

The lagoon in the **Bahía de Naranjo** is being developed as a small marina, where sailing trips and fishing expeditions can be arranged. Near the mouth of the lagoon is an aquarium, 10 minutes by boat from the dock, with dolphins and a sea lion, and a restaurant. A visit here is often included in tours of the area with a show. An evening excursion costs US$45, including dolphin show, extra US$8 to swim with the dolphins, lobster supper and an Afro-Cuban show.

West along the coast, **Playa Pesquero** is visited by tour parties on a boat excursion and is mostly empty, although it fills up with Cubans on holiday in July/August. It is a lovely sandy beach, the east end is better for children as there are strong currents and deceptive sand bars to the west. There is a lifeguard on duty even out of season. There are plans to build a hotel here with Italian investment.

The tour desks in the hotels have lots of excursions on offer along the coast and inland, even to Santiago de Cuba. Alternatively you can hire a car, scooter or bike, or contract a local private driver to take you wherever you want, eg to Gibara for US$25 return with the option of having a meal with a Cuban family. Private operators can not pick you up from your hotel, so you have to meet in the Centro Comercial or on the main road.

A few km from Guardalavaca on a hill with a wonderful view, is the **Museo Aborigen Chorro de Maita**, a small but well-presented museum displaying a collection of 56 skeletons dating from 1490-1540, exactly as they were found. One is of a young Spaniard of about 22 years of age with his arms crossed for a Christian burial, but the rest are Amerindians, buried in the Central American style, lying flat with their arms folded across their stomachs. Excavations took place in 1986 and a total of 108 skeletons were found (including the Spaniard), but they are not all displayed here. The aborigines had malformed their skulls from birth, which can be seen clearly. The tallest was 1m 75cm, although the average was 1m 56cm. Open Tuesday-Saturday 0900-1700, Sunday 0900-1300, US$1 per photo, plus US$5 per film, small shop with souvenirs.

If you are on an organized tour you may be taken to see the little village primary school just down the hill and you will pass the rural clinic where the doctor lives and works, looking after his allotted 120 families. A farmer at the bottom of the hill is pleased to see visitors and show them around his land, where he grows enough food for his extended family. According to Cuban rules he is allowed to keep everything he grows on his 7 hectares, but if he wants more land he has to give a proportion to the state. It is interesting to see how he grows his fruit and vegetables, with herbs dotted around, and he is likely to take his machete to bits of his produce for you to taste. The livestock are kept close to the house and fed coconuts. Ask to see his 1948 Plymouth car, which is a treasure.

It is a pleasant drive about 30 km to **Banes** over the hills through rolling fields of sugar interspersed with royal palms. This town is not usually on the itineraries of tour parties even though its church, **Iglesia de Nuestra Señora de la Caridad** was the site of the marriage of Fidel Castro to Birta Díaz Balart on 12 October 1948. Having visited the Museo Aborigen Chorro de Maita, however, you may be interested to see the **Museo Indocubano Bani**, Gen Marrero 305 y Av José Martí, which has a good collection of pre-columbian artifacts, probably the best in Cuba, open Tuesday-Saturday 0900-1700, Sunday 0800-1200, US$1. The town of Banes was originally the site of the Bani chieftancy and the museum contains treasures discovered by the many archaeological digs in the area. The **D** *Motel Oasis* is just west of the town, T 3447, with 28 rooms, restaurant and bar, used mostly by Cubans.

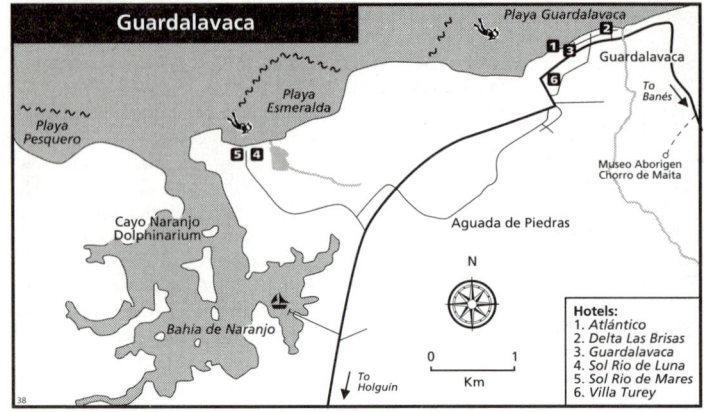

Hotels:
1. Atlántico
2. Delta Las Brisas
3. Guardalavaca
4. Sol Río de Luna
5. Sol Río de Mares
6. Villa Turey

Local information
● Accommodation

> Prices: **L1** over US$200; **L2** US$151-200; **L3** US$101-150; **A1** US$81-100; **A2** US$61-80; **A3** US$46-60; **B** US$31-45; **C** US$21-30; **D** US$12-20; **E** US$7-11; **F** up to US$6

Delta Las Brisas opened 1994 and became all-inclusive 1996, 230 good sized sea view or inland rooms all same price, a/c, satellite TV, phone, balcony, 3 restaurants, 3 bars, non-motorized watersports included, small man-made beach, nice pool, organized entertainment, family rooms with garden, kids kamp, tour desk, car rental; **A1-A2** *Atlántico*, T 30180/30280, F 30200, on beach, 233 rather small rooms with shower, adequate but nothing special for the price, parts under renovation 1997, shops, pool, tennis, long dark corridors; **A1** *Villa Turey*, opposite bus station, not on beach, spread out villas and apartments around pool, 136 rooms, 3 suites (with 2 bedrooms, 2 bathrooms upstairs, sitting room, kitchenette and toilet downstairs), large rooms, cupboards, TV, safe box, balconies, 2 restaurants, shop, short walk to beach through other hotels; **A2-A3** *Guardalavaca*, T 30121, F 24-30145 (in Holguín), 234 smallish rooms, TV, basic bathroom, shower, outside a/c, restoration 1996/97.

Along the coast at Estero Ciego are the best hotels in the area, *Sol Río de Luna* (all-inclusive), T 2430102, F 335571, and sister hotel next door, **L3-A3** *Sol Río de Mares*, T 337013,

F 337162, upmarket, half board only, most people on discounted packages, comfortable, open, well-designed for ventilation, not so good when it rains, pool, restaurants, bars, organized entertainment, some of it excruciatingly embarrassing, lovely beach, diving and other watersports, shade, sunbeds US$2. The older, rustic *Don Lino* hotel further west along the coast was closed in 1997.

● Places to eat
El Cayuelo, short walk along coast from *Las Brisas*, good for lobster. Most hotel restaurants in the hotels offer buffet meals which get very dull after a few days. There are restaurants in the Centro Comercial but no *paladares* in the area.

● Watersports
There are dive shops on the beach near the *Atlántico* and the *Sol Río de Mares*, offering courses and fun dives. The **Sea Lovers Diving Centre** at the latter hotel has dives at 0900 and 1400 (US$30, US$140/5 dives, equipment US$10 or US$35/5 dives), and snorkelling trips at 1100 (US$8, plus US$5 for equipment), several good dive sites on the reef offshore, can be rough at certain times of the year, no jetty so you have to swim and carry tank and gear out to boat. Good, well-maintained equipment and safety record. Safety not so good with other watersports, where life-jackets are not always offered or worn. The lifeguard on duty is not always in his chair. Hobie cats US$10/hour, windsurfers and kayaks US$5/hour, pedalo bikes US$2/hour.

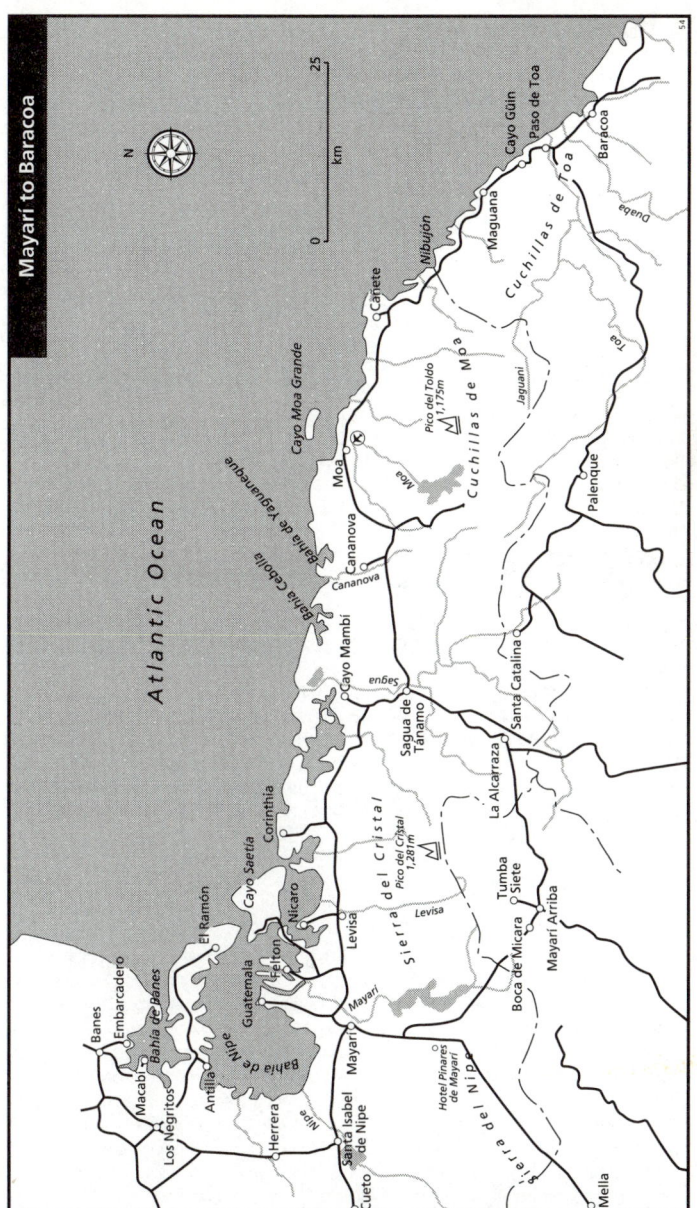

HOLGUIN TO BARACOA

On the road from Holguín to Baracoa is the small town of **Mayarí** (*Population* 23,000) founded in 1814 on the river of the same name. It is the sort of place people pass through on their way round the coast to Moa or inland and up into the mountains to Santiago de Cuba, but hardly anyone bothers to stop. The setting is very pretty, with the Sierra del Cristal as a backdrop. 6 km from Mayarí is a large cave, **Farallones de Seboruco**, where in 1945 an archaeological exploration revealed evidence that it had been used by people living there 5,000 years ago. Inland and up in the hills the soil turns to a deep red; known as *mocarrero*, it is 85% iron. Visit the scientific station at the **Jardín de Pinare National Park**. There are trails in the park through 12 different eco-systems. The **Salto de Guayabo** is 85m high, one of the highest waterfalls in Cuba, and there is a tremendous view across the fall, down the valley to the Bahía de Nipe. In February 1997 a forest fire destroyed more than 100 hectares of pine forest in the Mayarí Arriba area. Seek local information on where to walk.

● **Accommodation** There is a peso hotel in town, but if you need a stop in the area you would do better to drive another 30 km south and up into the hills to **A3** *Pinares de Mayarí*, T 53157, mountain lodge style, rustic timber and stone, isolated, pool, nature trails, pine trees, lake, restaurant, bar, billiards, horse riding, mostly used by eco-tour groups, check before arriving that they are open as they sometimes close if no party is expected. Alternatively, if you prefer the beach, go northeast to **Cayo Saetía**, where there is a small resort hotel, **A2** *Villa Cayo Saetía*, T 25350, on the island in the Bahía de Nipe. There are some lovely beaches here and it is popular with day-trippers from the Guardalavaca hotels who come by noisy Russian

Nickel

🐾 Cuba is currently the sixth largest producer of refined nickel in the world, but has more than a third of the world's known reserves. Output of nickel and cobalt fell from a peak of 46,600 tonnes in 1989 to 26,772 tonnes in 1994, but a rehabilitation of the Moa plant raised production to 43,900 tonnes in 1995 and 56,000 tonnes in 1996. Potential output is theoretically 100,000 tonnes a year for over 200 years. The Moa Bay plant is jointly owned by Sherritt international and the Cuban government and it produced 27,000 tonnes in 1996, up from 20,000 in 1995. The Pedro Alba mine was built in 1944 by the Americans and the Moa Bay nickel plant was opened in 1959, but after the Revolution it was nationalized in 1960 and since then it has been operated by Cubaniquel. Sherritt now produces an intermediate product in Cuba: nickel and cobalt contained in sulphide, which is then shipped to Canada and ends up as part of its Canadian refined output. Cubaniquel has two refineries producing nickel oxide: Nicaro, which has a capacity of 23,000 tonnes a year, and Punta Gorda, with 30,000 tonnes a year. A US$145 million investment programme is upgrading all three and building a new facility at Las Camariocas, 10km from Punta Gorda, with a capacity of 30,000 tonnes a year, which was 75% complete in 1997.

Sherritt is not the only foreign company to be interested in Cuban mining. Gencor (South Africa) is looking at San Felipe, another eastern deposit with a 30-year mine life, and completion of the Las Camariocas smelter, abandoned in the early 1990s after the collapse of the Soviet bloc. Western Mining (WIMS of Australia) is interested in a greenfield site at Pinares de Mayarí, where there is a substantial laterite deposit. Reserves at the site are estimated at 200 million tonnes of ore containing 1% nickel and 0.1% cobalt. They could start producing in 2000 and because it is a new project it would not fall foul of the US Helms Burton legislation which has so plagued Sherritt International.

helicopter. It is also promoted as a place to shoot wild fowl and hunt introduced animals such as zebra and antelope.

The coastal road continues east to **Moa** (*Population* 30,000), an industrial complex of little interest to the average traveller, but a major attraction for Canadian employees of Sherritt (see box, page 230). There is a hotel here, **C** *Miraflores*, T 66103, west of the town on a hill, a modern block close to the smelter workers' apartment buildings. There is also the Orestes Acosta Airport (MOA), 3 km from town, which receives two scheduled Cubana services a week from Havana. The Cubana office is at Av del Puerto, Rolo Monterrey, T 024-67916. The journey from Moa to Baracoa is 74 km and takes about 2 hours, depending on whether you are in a truck or car. It is a spectacular ride along the coast with the mountains of the **Cuchillas de Moa** and the **Cuchillas de Toa** coming down to the sea, indented by many rivers and bays. The highest peak is the **Pico del Toldo**, at 1,175m.

Maize

Europeans first discovered maize, the basic cereal of the Amerindians, in the far eastern region of Cuba, at Punta de Maisí, which was the name of the local cacique. The indigenous people practised a primitive cultivation and used maize in a variety of ways in their cooking, many of which are in use today. Variously called majisi, maisi or mais, the Spanish later changed the 's' to a 'z' and it became maíz, or maize in English. Other cereals were later imported to feed the African slaves and their masters, such as rice and wheat. Potatoes, which originated in South America, were introduced to Spain before making their way back across the Atlantic to Cuba. Maize is often considered a poor man's food, partly because during the depression of the 1930s it was the staple diet and consumed every day. Traditional recipes use maize with crab, or in sweets, puddings and fritters. Tamales, maize parcels stuffed with pork, turkey or chicken, are eaten on festive occasions.

Maize fritters
$1/2$ litre young corn off the cob, grated or ground
2 beaten eggs
$1/2$ cup (4 oz) sugar
1 teaspoon salt
1 teaspoon ground aniseed (optional)

Mix all the ingredients together and deep fry in spoonfuls.

Cosubé
$1 1/2$ cups cornflour
1 cup castor sugar
1 teaspoon salt
$1/2$ teaspoon ground aniseed or zest of lime or orange to flavour
2 tablespoons melted margarine or oil
2 tablespoons dry white wine
1 beaten egg

Mix together the first four ingredients, then add the fat, mixed with the wine and egg. Mix well. Roll out until about 1 cm thick, and cut into shapes. Place the shapes on a greased baking sheet, dust them lightly with sugar and bake in a moderate oven (350F, 150C, gas mark 4) for 10 minutes, or until they start to turn golden. Remove from the baking tray and leave to cool on a rack. Can be stored in a tin.

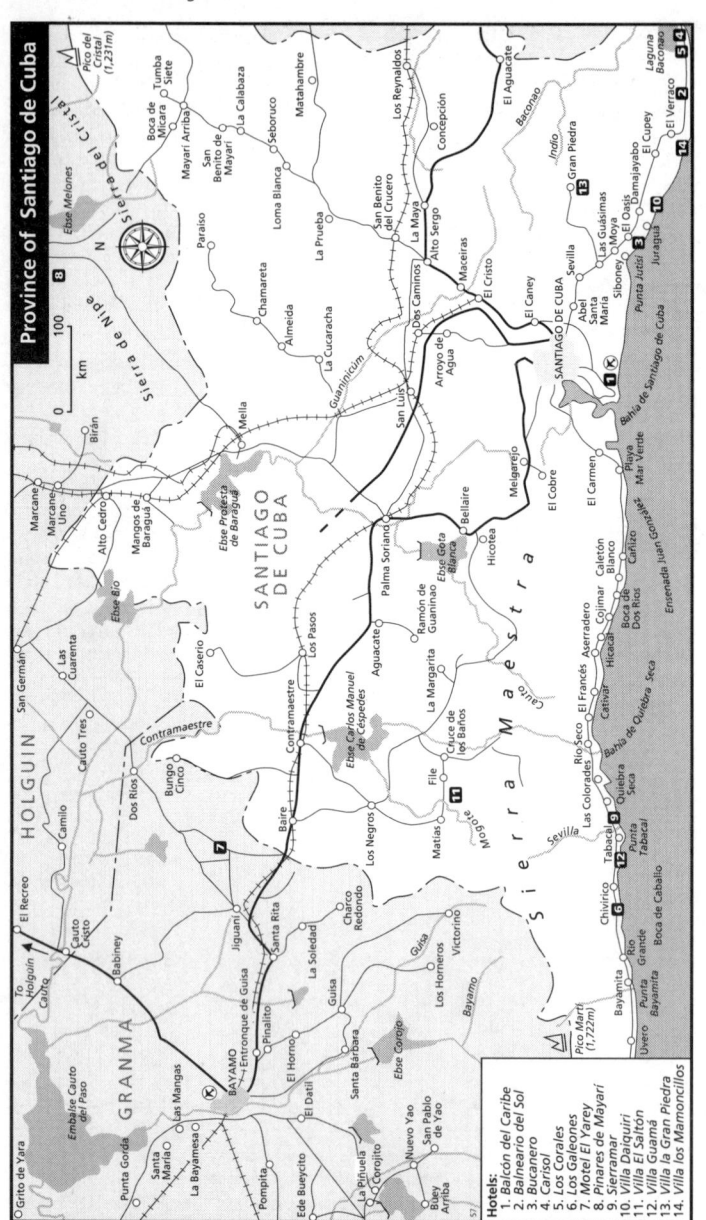

Province of Santiago de Cuba

Pico del Cristal (1,231m)

Sierra del Cristal

Sierra de Nipe

HOLGUIN

GRANMA

SANTIAGO DE CUBA

Sierra Maestra

SANTIAGO DE CUBA

Bahía de Santiago de Cuba

Pico Martí (1,722m)

Laguna Baconao

Hotels:
1. Balcón del Caribe
2. Balneario del Sol
3. Bucanero
4. Carisol
5. Los Corales
6. Los Galeones
7. Motel El Yarey
8. Pinares de Mayarí
9. Sierramar
10. Villa Daiquirí
11. Villa El Saltón
12. Villa Guamá
13. Villa la Gran Piedra
14. Villa los Mamoncillos

Province of Santiago de Cuba

THE SIERRA MAESTRA dominates this, the most mountainous province in the country. Its capital, Santiago de Cuba is one of the oldest towns on the island, protected from the sea in an attractive bay surrounded by mountains. All along the coast there are beaches and tourist attractions, while inland there is good hiking.

Province of Santiago de Cuba

The Province of Santiago de Cuba is bordered by Holguín to the north, Guantánamo to the east, the Caribbean Sea to the south and Granma to the west. Almost the whole of the province is mountainous and clad in the pine forests of the Sierra Maestra. Its highest point is Pico Turquino, 1,974m and the highest mountain in Cuba. The main agricultural activities are sugar, citrus, banana, cocoa and coffee, there is also some copper mining, a good deal of heavy industry around the capital and a growing tourist industry. The province has been the site of many battles during the wars of independence and the Revolution, which are remembered in numerous monuments. These, and the natural beauty of the landscape are attracting greater numbers of visitors.

Santiago de Cuba

Area 6,170 sq km, *Population* 1,016,600, *Density* 164.8 per sq km, *Urban* 69.7%

SANTIAGO DE CUBA

Phone code 226

Santiago de Cuba, near the east end of the island, 970 km from Havana, is Cuba's second city. It is not a colonial gem along the lines of Havana or Trinidad, but it does have an eclectic range of architectural styles from colonial to art deco. The city centre is cluttered, with the feel of an overgrown country village, featuring many beautiful pastel coloured buildings in much better condition than many of those in the capital. The Vista Alegre barrio is an outstanding example of a leafy Cuban suburb, with grand art nouveau buildings, an early 20th century contrast to the Mudejar style of the city centre.

History

Santiago de Cuba was one of the seven towns (*villas*) founded by Diego Velázquez. It was first built in 1515 on the mouth of the Río Paradas but moved in 1516 to its present location in a horseshoe valley surrounded by mountains. It was Cuba's capital city until replaced by Havana in 1553 and capital of Oriente province until 1976. During the 17th century Santiago was besieged by pirates from France and England, leading to the construction of the Castillo del Morro, still intact and now housing the piracy museum. Because of its location, Santiago has been the scene

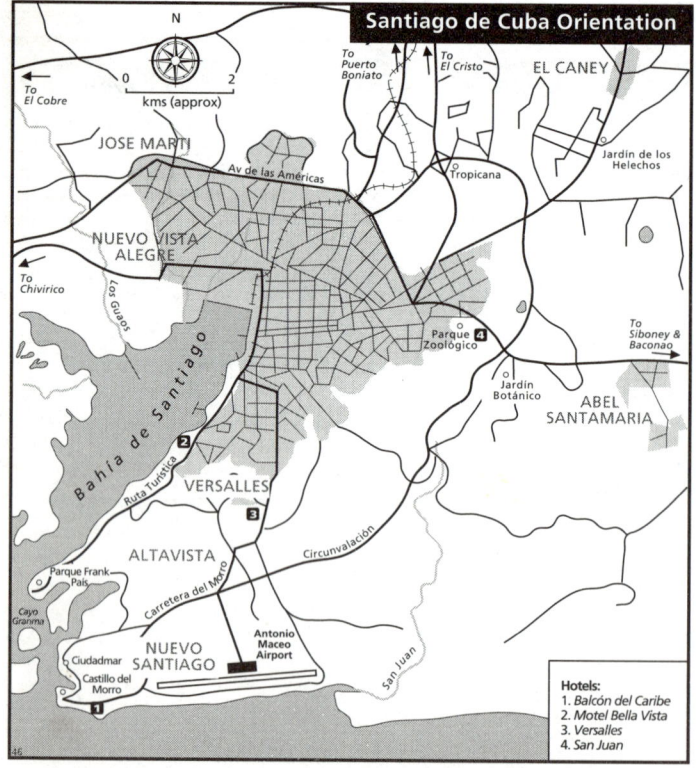

Santiago de Cuba Orientation

Hotels:
1. *Balcón del Caribe*
2. *Motel Bella Vista*
3. *Versalles*
4. *San Juan*

of many migratory exchanges with other countries; it was the first city in Cuba to receive African slaves, many French fled here from the slaves' insurrection in Haiti in the 18th century and Jamaicans have also migrated here from the neighbouring island. Santiago is more of a truly ethnic blend than many other towns in Cuba.

It is known as the 'heroic city' (*Ciudad Héroe*) or '*capital moral de la Revolución Cubana*'. One of Cuba's foremost revolutionaries of the 19th century, General Antonio Maceo, is honoured in the **Plaza de la Revolución**, to the northeast of the centre, with a dramatic monument to the revolution made of galvanized steel in searing, solid Soviet style, and a gargantuan bronze statue of the general on horseback surrounded by huge iron machetes rising from the ground at different angles. Fidel has made many stirring speeches from the platform and you can picture the plaza filled to capacity to hear him. The national hero, José Martí, is buried in Santa Ifigenia cemetery, just west of the city. The city played a major role in the early days of the Revolution in the 1950s and boasts two major landmarks of the clandestine struggle: the Moncada Garrison, now a school and museum, scene of Fidel Castro's first attack on the Batista regime in 1953, and *La Granjita Siboney*, the farmhouse where 100 revolutionaries gathered the night before the attack on the Garrison, which is also now a museum.

The Padre Pico steps in Santiago

The revolution in Haiti at the end of the 18th century brought a large influx of French immigrants to Cuba, many of whom settled in the south west of Santiago de Cuba in an area known as Loma Hueca. They built a theatre there called El Tivoli, the name by which the neighbourhood came to be identified. The hill leading up to the Tivoli area was so steep that it had to be paved in staggered form, and these steps were named Loma de Corbacho, after the grocery store on one of the corners.

Decades later, in the Republic's first year, Emilio Bacardí, in his function as mayor, had the steps renovated. Locals wanted them to be named in his honour, but he proposed the name 'Padre Pico', in memory of Bernardo del Pico, a priest who had helped the poor in Santiago.

The Padre Pico steps gained further historical status when Castro chose their strategic location to fire the opening shots in his first offensive against Batista in 1956. The steps give commanding views of the bay and the mountains around Santiago, and now form an essential part of any walking tour of the city.

Places of interest

Parque Céspedes is in the centre of town and everything revolves around it. Most of the main museums are within easy walking distance. The *Hotel Casa Granda* flanks the entire east side of the small park. The **Cathedral**, Santa Iglesia Basílica Metropolitana, is on the south side, entrance on Félix Peña. The first building on the site was completed in 1524, but four subsequent disasters, including earthquakes and pirate attacks meant that the cathedral was rebuilt four times. The building now standing was restored in 1818, with more new decoration added in the early 20th century. It is open 0800-1200 daily, services Monday, Wednesday 1830, Saturday 1700, Sunday 0900, 1830. The west side of the park is occupied by a rather ugly bank, next to the beautiful 16th century **Casa de Diego Velázquez**. On the north side the **Casa del Gobierno** features a strong Moorish influence, particularly in the patio. This building is not open to the public, but is used for government functions. Parque Céspedes is now very heavily policed because of hustlers and has changed so much that if you

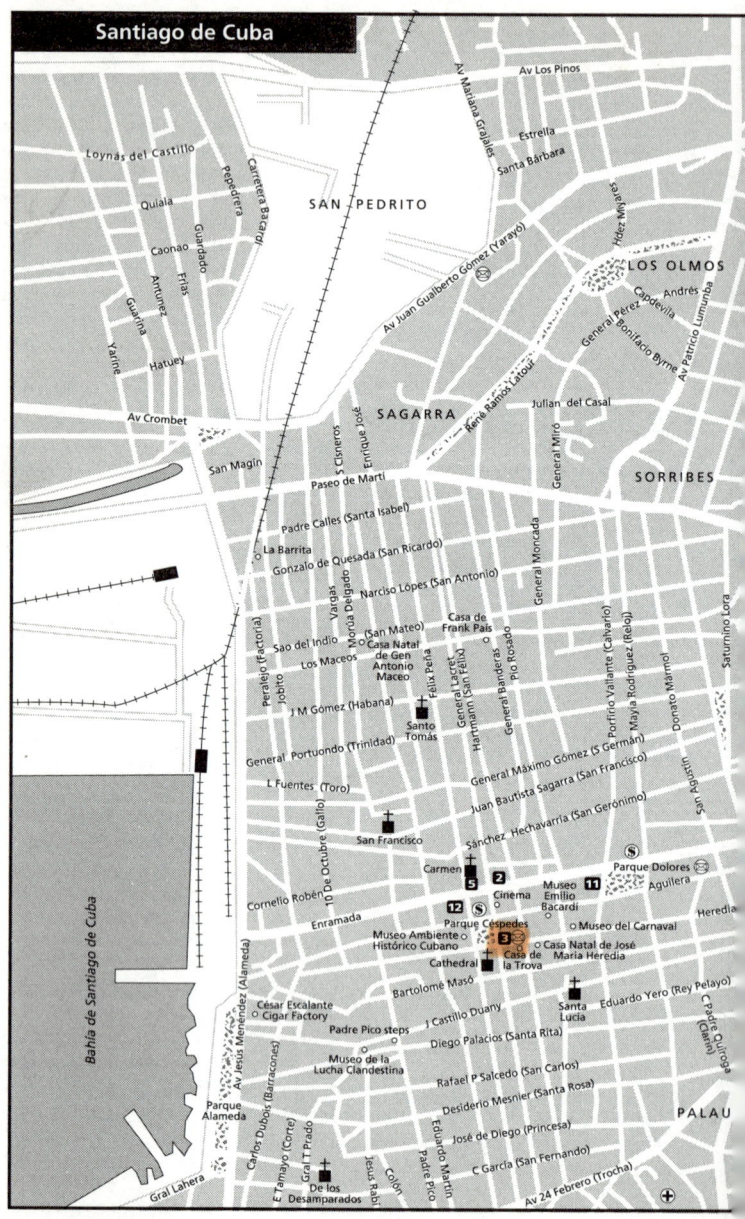

Santiago de Cuba

Av Los Pinos

Loynas del Castillo

Estrella

Santa Bárbara

Quiala

SAN PEDRITO

Caonao

Frías

Arnunez

Guarina

Yarine

Hatuey

Av Juan Gualberto Gómez (Yarayo)

Andrés

Candevila

LOS OLMOS

General Pérez

Bonifacio Byrne

Av Patricio Lumumba

Av Crombet

Julian del Casal

SAGARRA

René Ramos Latour

General Miró

SORRIBES

San Magín

Paseo de Martí

Padre Calles (Santa Isabel)

La Barrita

Gonzalo de Quesada (San Ricardo)

General Mordaca

Narciso López (San Antonio)

Casa de
Frank País

Sao del Indio

(San Mateo)
Casa Natal
de Gen
Antonio
Maceo

Porfirio Valiente (Calvario)

Mayía Rodríguez (Reloj)

Donato Mármol

Saturnino Lora

Peralejo (Factoría)

Jobito

Vargas

Morua Delgado

Los Maceos

J M Gómez (Habana)

Felix Peña

General Lacret

Hartmann (San Félix)

General Banderas

Pío Rosado

Santo
Tomás

General Máximo Gómez (S Germán)

L Fuentes (Toro)

General Portuondo (Trinidad)

Juan Bautista Sagarra (San Francisco)

San Agustín

10 De Octubre (Gallo)

Sánchez Hechavarría (San Gerónimo)

San Francisco

Carmen **5** **2**

Cinema

Museo
Emilio
Bacardi

11

Parque Dolores

Aguilera

Cornelio Robén

12

Parque Céspedes

Museo del Carnaval

Enramada

Museo Ambiente
Histórico Cubano

3

Heredia

Cathedral

Casa de
la Trova

Casa Natal de José
María Heredia

Bartolomé Masó

Santa
Lucía

Eduardo Yero (Rey Pelayo)

César Escalante
Cigar Factory

J Castillo Duany

Padre Pico steps

Diego Palacios (Santa Rita)

Museo de la
Lucha Clandestina

Rafael P Salcedo (San Carlos)

Desiderio Mesnier (Santa Rosa)

José de Diego (Princesa)

PALAU

Parque
Alameda

Carlos Dubois (Barracones)

Av Jesús Menéndez (Alameda)

Gral T Prado

Eduardo Martín

Padre Pico

Colón

Jesús Rabí

C García (San Fernando)

Bahía de Santiago de Cuba

Gral Lahera

E Tamayo (Corte)

De los
Desamparados

Av 24 Febrero (Trocha)

P Padre Quiroga (Gallo)

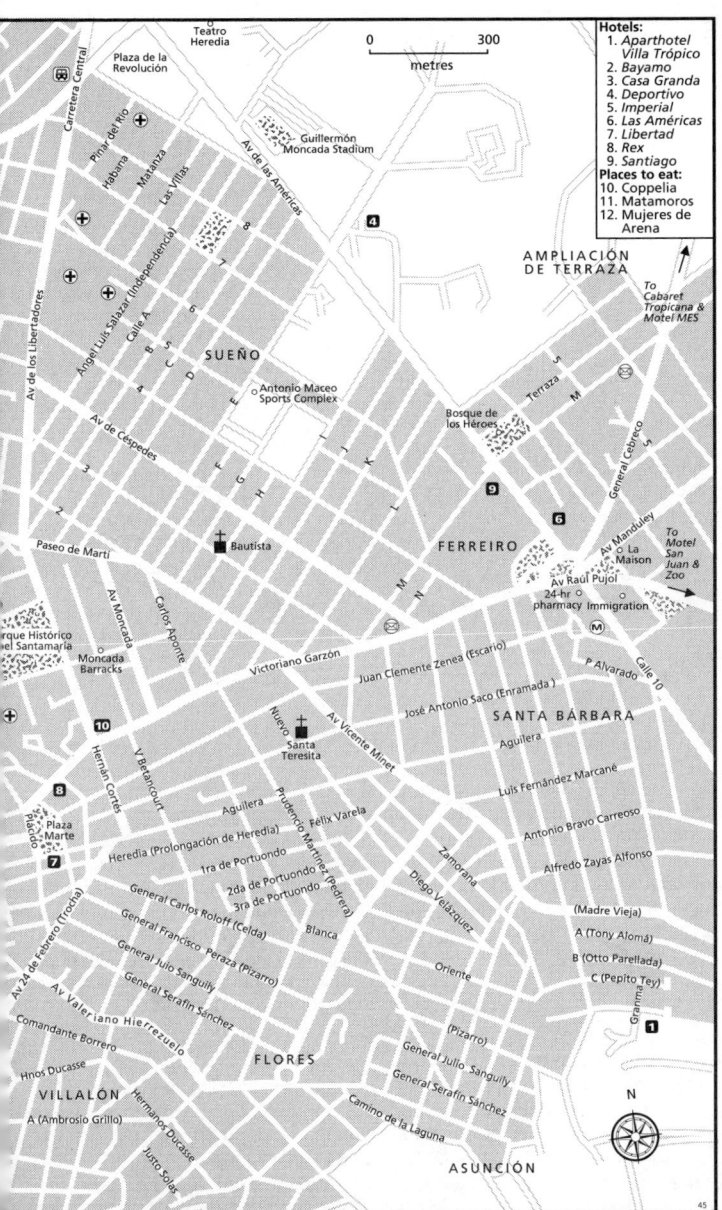

Teatro Heredia

Plaza de la Revolución

0   300
metres

Hotels:
1. *Aparthotel Villa Trópico*
2. *Bayamo*
3. *Casa Granda*
4. *Deportivo*
5. *Imperial*
6. *Las Américas*
7. *Libertad*
8. *Rex*
9. *Santiago*
Places to eat:
10. Coppelia
11. Matamoros
12. Mujeres de Arena

Carretera Central

Pina del Río
Habana
Matanza
Las Villas
Ángel Luis Sabaza (Independencia)
Calle A
B
C
D
E
F
G
H
I
J
K
L
M
N

Av de las Américas

Guillermón Moncada Stadium

AMPLIACIÓN DE TERRAZA

To Cabaret Tropicana & Motel MES

SUEÑO

Antonio Maceo Sports Complex

Av de los Libertadores

Av de Céspedes

Bosque de los Héroes

Terraza

General Cebreco

Paseo de Martí

Bautista

FERREIRO

Av Manduley

La Maison

To Motel San Juan & Zoo

Av Raúl Pujol

24-hr pharmacy   Immigration

Av de Moncada

Carlos Aponte

rque Histórico el Santamaría

Moncada Barracks

Victoriano Garzón

Juan Clemente Zenea (Escario)

P. Alvarado

Calle 10

Hernán Cortés

V. Betancourt

Nuevo

Santa Teresita

José Antonio Saco (Enramada)

SANTA BÁRBARA

Aguilera

Av Vicente Minet

Luis Fernández Marcané

Plaza Marte

Aguilera

Prudencio Martínez (Pedral)

Félix Varela

Antonio Bravo Carreoso

Heredia (Prolongación de Heredia)

1ra de Portuondo

Zamorana

Alfredo Zayas Alfonso

General Carlos Roloff (Celda)

2da de Portuondo
3ra de Portuondo

Diego Velázquez

(Madre Vieja)

General Francisco Peraza (Pizarro)

Blanca

A (Tony Alomá)

Av 24 de Febrero (Trocha)

General Julio Sanguily

B (Otto Parellada)

General Serafín Sánchez

Oriente

C (Pepito Tey)

Av Valeriano Hierrezuelo

Comandante Borrero

(Pizarro)

Granma

Hnos Ducasse

FLORES

General Julio Sanguily

VILLALÓN

Hermanos Ducasse

General Serafín Sánchez

A (Ambrosio Grillo)

Justo Solas

Camino de la Laguna

ASUNCIÓN

N

45

The Cathedral

want a peaceful hour of sitting alone and watching the world go by, this is the place to do it, for you will be entirely left alone.

The **Cementerio Santa Ifigenia**, northwest of the city, is on Av Crombel, Reparto Juan G Gómez, entrance US$1, extra US$1 to take pictures, guided tour in Spanish and English. The cemetery features José Martí's mausoleum, a huge structure with a statue of Martí inside, designed to receive a shaft of sunlight all morning. Martí is surrounded by six statues of women, representing the six Cuban provinces of the 19th century. Along the path leading up to the mausoleum are signposts commemorating successful independence battles, each decorated with a quote by Martí. Also in the cemetery is the grave of Frank País, a prime mover in the revolutionary struggle.

Another historical site, southeast of the centre, is the huge ceiba tree in the grounds of the *Motel San Juan* (formerly *Leningrado* hotel), beneath which Spain and the USA signed the surrender of Santiago on 16 July 1898; at the Loma de San Juan nearby are more monuments of the Hispano-Cuban-American war (only worth visiting if staying at the *San Juan*, or going to the zoo and amusement park behind the hotel). The **zoo** is on Av Raúl Pujol, esquina Padre de las Casas, open Tuesday-Sunday 0900-1700, US$1, to see all the usual animals.

10 minutes from the centre of Santiago there is the Bacardí rum factory, or La

Daiquirí

The recipe for the Daiquirí cocktail was first created by an engineer in the Daiquirí mines near Santiago de Cuba. Known as a Daiquirí Natural (1898), it includes the juice of half a lime, ½ tablespoon sugar, 1½ oz light dry rum and some pieces of ice, which you put in a shaker, shake and serve strained in a cocktail glass, with more ice if you want. The idea of using shaved ice came later, added by Constante, the bartender at *El Floridito* in the 1920s. It was a favourite of Ernest Hemingway; he described it in his book, *Islands in the Stream*, and drank it in the company of Jean-Paul Sartre, Gary Cooper, Ava Gardner, Marlene Dietrich, Tennessee Williams and others. The recipe for this Daiquirí includes 1½ tablespoons of sugar, the juice of half a lime, some drops of maraschino liqueur, 1½ oz light dry rum and a lot of shaved ice. Put it all in a blender and serve in a champagne glass. Other refinements are the strawberry Daiquirí, the banana, peach or pineapple Daiquirí or even the orange Daiquirí, made with the addition of fruit or fruit liqueur. The resulting mound of flavoured, alcoholic, crushed ice should be piled high in a wide, chilled champagne glass and served with a straw -.aaah!

Barrita, but you can only go in the museum and bar, the factory is closed to visitors since tourists 'stole' the technology by taking too many photos.

Churches

There are several interesting churches in Santiago: **Iglesia de la Santísima Trinidad**, Félix Peña y San Jerónimo, built late 18th century with some neoclassical features; two blocks west is **Iglesia San Franciso**, on Calle San Francisco, also 18th century; **Iglesia de Santa Lucía**, Santa Lucía esquina Pío Rosado, a small church worth visiting for the architecture in the surrounding streets; three blocks south of the Museo de la Lucha Clandestina is **Iglesia de los Desamparados**, on General T Padro; **Iglesia Santo Tomás** is an 18th century church on Habana y Félix Peña.

Plazas

Plaza Marte, a short walk up Aguilera from Parque Céspedes, is a pick-up and drop-off point for most urban transport. Go there if you want to get a taxi/moped late at night. The bus stop for other *repartos* including Vista Alegre is on the corner of Aguilera and Plaza Marte. **Plaza Dolores** is worth noting as a point of reference if walking between Plaza Marte and Parque Céspedes. It is known as 'Bulevar', though

it is really just a widening of Aguilera. It has a coffee house, *La Isabelica* on the corner and a chain of Rumbos-run restaurants for wealthy tourists. The junction of Victoriano Garzón and Avenida Las Américas, where the hotels *Santiago* and *Las Américas* are situated, is known locally as 'Ferreiro', and is where you can catch a bus to any part of town and get a taxi, official or otherwise. Take care at night, as the three small squares at this junction are not lit. **Parque Histórico Abel Santamaría** is a small square commemorating one of Fidel's comrades who was captured by Batista's troops and had his eyes gouged out. The park is on the site of the hospital he was occupying at the time of his capture, and since then all eye hospitals in Cuba have been named after him.

Museums

Of the several museums, the best is the **Museo de Ambiente Histórico Cubano** located in Diego Velázquez' house (the oldest in Cuba, started in 1516, completed 1530), at the northwest corner of Parque Céspedes, Félix Peña 612. Velázquez lived on the top floor, while the ground floor was used as a contracting house and a smelter for gold. It has been restored after its use as offices after the Revolution and is in two parts, one 16th century, one 18th century.

Each room shows a particular period, demonstrating the development of Cuban material culture, featuring furniture, china, porcelain, crystal; there is also a 19th-century extension. Visitors are permitted to wander in and out of the rooms freely, there are no ropes barring entry into any areas, you could even sit on the chairs. Open Monday-Saturday 0900-1700, Sunday 0900-1300, US$1, with guided tour in English or German, camera fee US$1.

Two blocks east of the Parque, opposite the Palacio Provincial is the **Museo Emilio Bacardí**, named after industrialist Emilio Bacardí Moreau, the main benefactor and collector of much of the museum's contents. This was the second museum founded in Cuba and has exhibits from prehistory to the Revolution downstairs, one of the most important collections of Cuban colonial paintings upstairs, while outside on one side there is a reconstruction of a typical colonial street front and a nice courtyard. The archaeology hall has mummies from Egypt and South America, including a Peruvian specimen over 1,000 years old. The Egyptian mummy dates back to the 18th dynasty, 2,000 years ago, and was personally acquired by Emilio Bacardí and brought back to Cuba. There are also exhibits of ancient art, ethnology, documents of the history of Santiago and a hand-made torpedo used by the rebels during the first war of independence. Entrance on Pío Rosado esquina Aguilera, open Tuesday-Saturday 0900-1800, Sunday 0900-1300, US$2, T 28402.

Visit the **Museo Histórico 26 de Julio**, Av Moncada esquina General Portuondo, open Monday-Saturday 0800-1800, Sunday 0800-1200, US$1. Formerly the Moncada Garrison, it was attacked (unsuccessfully) by Castro and his revolutionaries on 26 July 1953. When the revolution triumphed in 1959, the building was turned into a school. To mark the 10th anniversary of

La Casa Natal de José María Heredia

José Martí said of Heredia: "The first poet in America is Heredia. Only he has captured in his poetry the sublimity, fire and ostentation of its nature. He is as volcanic as its entrails and as calm as its mountain peaks." In his short but eventful life Heredia created a poetic canon which transformed the form and content of Latin American poetry.

Jose María de Heredia y Heredia was born on 31 December 1803 in Santiago de Cuba, the city his parents had fled to from Santo Domingo in 1801 from the invading Haitian troops. He had an itinerant childhood, the family being constantly uprooted by his father's work; they left their first house in Santiago de Cuba when Heredia was only 3 years old. He then spent time in the USA and Santo Domingo, as well as Havana and Matanzas. At the age of 20 he was exiled to the USA for his involvement in an independence conspiracy. There he wrote his ode 'Niagra', establishing him as a world-class poet. His death in Mexico aged 36 cut short a tragic life in exile for a man devoted to his country.

The house where Heredia was born still stands, at Heredia y San Félix, in spite of efforts by the colonial rulers of the 19th century to have it demolished. An association made up of influential people like Emilio Bacardí succeeded in buying the house, agreeing to hand over its restoration to the municipal government in 1902. Today it has regained its original prestige as a national monument, and is the most important of the numerous other cultural sites on Calle Heredia, the street formerly called Calle Catedral. The house is a now museum dedicated to the poet's life, as well as a cultural centre and meeting point for current local poets.

the attack, one of the buildings was converted to a museum, featuring photos, plans and drawings of the battle. All commentaries are in Spanish. Bullet holes, filled in by Batista, have been reconstructed on the outer walls. The **Museo Casa Natal de Frank País** (General Banderas 226 y Los Maceos, T 52710), is in the birthplace of the leader of the armed uprising in Santiago on 30 November 1956, who was shot in July 1957. His tomb is in Santa Ifigenia cemetery and features in a guided tour. The **Museo de la Lucha Clandestina** was founded to mark the 20th anniversary of the armed uprising in Santiago, Central Ermita and other parts of Oriente on 30 November 1956. The purpose of the museum is to highlight the support given by the local urban population during the battle in the Sierra Maestra and has an exhibition of the citizens' underground struggle against the dictatorship. Housed on two floors, exhibits revolve around Frank País, from his early moves to foment a revolutionary consciousness to his integration into the Movimiento 26 de Julio under Fidel Castro. The building was originally the residence of the Intendente, then was a police HQ, a key target of the 26 July revolutionary movement, now completely restored after having been stormed and gutted during the revolution. It is a beautiful yellow building with a nice courtyard at the top of picturesque Calle Padre Pico (steps), corner of Santa Rita and Jesús Rabí, and affords good views of the city (T 24689). Open 0900-1700 Tuesday-Sunday, US$1, a guide speaking 'Spanlish' will take you round if you can't read Spanish. The **Casa Natal de Antonio Maceo** was the birthplace, on 14 June 1845, of Antonio Maceo y Grajales, one of the greatest military commanders of the 1868 and 1895 wars of independence. The museum houses his biography and details of his 32 years' devotion to the struggle for independence. The house,

built between 1800-1830, is on Los Maceo 207 entre Corona y Rastro, open Monday-Saturday 0800-1830. The **Museo de Holografía** is housed below the monument in the Plaza de la Revolución, and features holograms mostly of things associated with the revolution, like guns. Open Tuesday-Saturday, 1000-1700, Sunday 1300-1700, US$1.

The **Museo del Carnaval** exhibits a collection of instruments, drums and costumes from Santiago's famous July carnival. If you are not going to be there in July, this is the best way to get a flavour of the celebrations. On Calle Heredia esquina Pío Rosado, open Tuesday-Saturday 0900-1800, Sunday 0900-1200, US$1. The **Centro Cultural Africano Fernando Ortíz** on Av Manduley 106 displays items of African culture, open 0900-1700. The **Casa del Caribe**, off Av Manduley on Calle 13 esquina Calle 8 is a world renowned cultural centre. If you are interested in *Santería*, there is a musical and religious ceremony at 0930 on Wednesdays. The **Museo de la Religión** displays religious items particularly concerning *Santería*, but there are no written explanations of the exhibits, not even in Spanish, so it is best to ask for a guide. The museum is on Calle 13 206, esquina Calle 10, open Monday-Saturday 0830-1700, free. The **Museo de la Imagen**, on Calle 8 106, Reparto Vista Alegre, T 42234, displays cameras, photographs, cine (film) and television, open Monday-Saturday 0900-1700, US$1. On Heredia near the Casa de la Trova is the **Casa Natal de José María Heredia**, the birthplace of Santiago's most famous poet. It is now a cultural centre and there is a poetry workshop here on Fridays from 1700. Two contemporary art galleries are **Galería Oriente**, underneath the *Hotel Casa Granda* on Parque Céspedes, and **Galería de Confronta**, on Calle Heredia. The **Museo de Música** is above the Casa de la Trova (see **Entertainment**, page 250).

Gun emplacements at Castillo del Morro

Excursions
South of Santiago

The Ruta Turística runs along the shore of the Bahía de Santiago to the **Castillo del Morro**, a clifftop fort with the **Museo de la Piratería**, a museum of the sea, piracy and local history, charting the pirate attacks made on Santiago during the 16th century. Pirates included the Frenchman Jacques de Sores and the Englishman Henry Morgan, and you can see many of the weapons used in both attack and defence of the city (closed for renovations in 1997 but usually open Tuesday-Sunday 0900-1800, T 9-1569). You can wander around the fort even if the museum is still closed. It has many levels and fascinating rooms whose purpose can be easily guessed, such as the prison cells, the chapel and the cannon-loading bay. From the roof you can admire the thrilling views over the Bay of Santiago and Cayo Granma and you can follow some 16th century steps almost down to the waterline. There is a narrow, grass-covered passage which eventually leads down to a small beach, which you can also get to by road. There is a good restaurant on a terrace with a great view, main dish US$6. Turistaxi to El Morro, US$10 round trip with wait. Transport along the road passes the ferry at Ciudadmar to the resorts of **Cayo Granma** and La Socapa in the estuary (hourly, 5 cents each way). Cayo Granma was originally Cayo Smith, named after its wealthy owner; it became a resort for the rich. Now most of its 600 inhabitants travel to Santiago to work. There are no vehicles; there are three *paladares* serving seafood in an idyllic setting looking across the bay towards Santiago, the most recommended is *El Marlen*.

East of Santiago

Excellent excursions can be made to the **Gran Piedra** (26 km east) a viewpoint from which it is said you can see Haiti and Jamaica on a clear day, more likely their lights on a clear night. It is a giant rock weighing 75,000 tonnes, 1,234m high, reached by climbing 454 steps from the road ('only for the fit'). Hand carved wooden curios are sold by artisans on the steps. Along the road to Gran Piedra look out for small monuments to fallen heroes of the Revolution. They are in groups of three and their names and occupations are carved on boulders or sculptures. There are no buses but a private car will charge you about US$15 there and back (the tour desk in any hotel will arrange a tour, good value). **A3-B** *Motel Gran Piedra,* T 5913/51098, 2-star, accepts Visa, bungalows with a bedroom, kitchen, sitting

Road Rage in Cuba

The lack of traffic congestion in Cuba is one of the positive benefits of the US blockade, along with the absence of McDonalds, Burger King, and walking teenage adverts for Nike and Reebok. The few car-owners are either employed by the state to ferry tourists around in their battered but beautiful Chevies and Cadillacs, or they hawk their services illegally in public squares near hotels. Their constant pestering can get on your nerves, but if the idea of being sealed in an air-conditioned mini-bus with 15 other tourists doesn't appeal to you, it is a good way to explore the more remote attractions on the island. You can hire a private car plus driver for about $50 a day and he will take you virtually anywhere. It was during one such journey that I experienced the Cuban version of road rage. I was travelling from Santiago de Cuba, the island's second largest city, to a beach resort about 50 km away. On a deserted coastal road, we suddenly found ourselves sandwiched between the only other two vehicles in sight: a truck full of farm produce in front, and a black '50s Buick behind. This car made several clumsy attempts to overtake us, before swerving out alongside us on a curve, almost forcing us to plunge into the ditch at the edge of the road. Then it screeched around the truck and disappeared into the horizon.

The truck later turned off. As we gathered speed we caught up with the Buick. An empty beer can was tossed out of the driver's window in response to our presence, and there seemed to be arms waving out of all the windows. We still had about 25km to go before we reached our destination, but the driver turned off the main road when we reached a small town. The Buick had also turned off, and I realized with horror that we were following it. I tried to get an explanation from the driver and my guide, but in the heat of the moment they had reverted to obscure Cuban slang, which my rudimentary Castillian was unable to penetrate. I tried bluntly asking whether I'd be expected to join in the imminent confrontation, but my questions were dismissed with non-committal shrugs.

Both cars slowed to a halt in a deserted gravel patch outside the town. By then I was cowering behind the back seat, hoping that my $50 payment would exclude me from whatever was going to happen. The occupants of the Buick alighted: five burly Cuban youths; baseball caps the wrong way round, mirrored shades, muscles – in a word, they looked hard. Cans of beer were tossed to the ground as they paced the gravel. My driver and the guide got out of the car, slamming the doors behind them. I took this to signify that I had been granted some kind of amnesty from the proceedings.

What followed took the drama into the realms of the absurd. The two drivers marched up to each other and shook hands. I watched the potential scene of ugly violence transform into something resembling a summit meeting. Everyone shook hands, the pecking order tacitly established; after the drivers, the guide shook hands first with the Buick driver, then with all the passengers, who went on to shake hands with our driver. A few words of apology and acknowledgement were muttered. The fact that the Buick driver had been in the wrong was the undisputed and unspoken basis of the meeting. I watched from the car, moved by the spectacle, almost tempted to get out and shake hands with everyone too, but I knew I had no part in this ritual.

I thought of the nasty scene which could have been taking place in front of my eyes, had I been in Britain. But this is Cuba, where an old-fashioned form of politeness and social ritual dominates every situation, from the vagaries of courtship and marriage, right down to the way you conduct yourself on the road.

Gavin Clark

room, bathroom and balcony. 2 km before La Gran Piedra are the **Jardines de la Siberia**, on the site of a former coffee plantation, an extensive botanical garden; turn right and follow the track for about 1 km to reach the gardens. The **Museo La Isabelica** is at Carretera de la Gran Piedra Km 14, a ruined coffee plantation once owned by French emigrés from Haiti, the buildings of which are now turned into a museum (open Tuesday-Saturday 0900-1700, Sunday 0900-1300, US$1) housing the former kitchen and other facilities on the ground floor with farming tools and archaeological finds. Upstairs is the owners' house in authentic 19th-century style. On view in the ground floor are instruments of slave torture. After the slave revolt in Haiti, large numbers of former slave owners were encouraged to settle in the Sierra de la Gran Piedra. This influx led to the impact of Haitian/French culture on Santiago, especially in music. Here they built 51 *cafetales*, using slave labour. During the Ten Years War (1868-78) the revolutionaries called for the destruction of all the *cafetales*. The owner, Victor Constantin Cuzeau, named the plantation after his lover and house slave, but when Céspedes freed the slaves he fled and Isabelica was thrown by the former slaves into a burning oven.

On the Carretera Siboney at Km 13½ is **La Granjita Siboney**, the farmhouse used as the headquarters for the revolutionaries' attack on the Moncada barracks on 26 July 1953. It now has a museum of uniforms, weapons and artefacts used by the 100 men who gathered here the night before, as well as extensive newspaper accounts of the attack (open Tuesday-Sunday 0900-1700, T 9836, entry US$1). The road is lined with stone tributes commemorating the spots were revolutionaries were killed. **Siboney**, 16 km east of the city is the nearest beach to Santiago. Right on the beach are pleasant and unpretentious **D** cabins with two bedrooms, the office is at the entrance to the village. You will be approached with

offers of private rooms to rent and there are numerous street food stalls and *paladares*, mostly frequented by Cubans although you will be charged in dollars. Take bus 214 from near bus terminal. Very crowded at weekends. Further east along the coast is the 200-room **A3** *Club Amigo Bucanero*, 3-star, Carretera Baconao Km 4, Arroyo La Costa, T 7293/7216, car hire, accepts credit cards. About 20 km from Santiago, or half way between Siboney and Juraguá, look for a sign on the left to *Finca Del Porvenir*. This turning leads to a nice freshwater swimming pool with a bar and restaurant. The pool looks a bit green at first, but is actually clean and a wonderful place to stop off and cool down after sweating along the dusty highway. Entrance US$1. **Juraguá** is an even nicer beach than Siboney; it is a bit run down and not really geared towards tourism but further development is projected in this area. There is a bar if you are desperately thirsty. You can scuba dive.

At Km 24 is the **Valle de la Prehistoria**, a huge park filled with life-size carved stone dinosaurs and stone age men. Great for the kids but due to the total absence of shade it is like walking around a desert. Take huge supplies of water and try to go early or late. Entrance US$1, extra US$1 to take photos. Nearby is **Mundo de Fantasía**, a small amusement park also good for kids. Admission appears to be free, ask the stone clown at the entrance. Also in the area is an old car and trailer museum, **Museo de Transporte**, turn left at the junction for Daiquirí. The old classic American cars are well kept, though some of them are now being brought out to be used as taxis in Santiago to entertain the tourists (admission free, recommended).

Daiquirí beach (turn right at Km 25) is beautiful and quiet and the resort there was due to re-open Summer 1997, entrance US$2 if not staying the night. Facilities for tourism are good, with scuba diving and a disco. **A3** *Daiquirí* (Cubanacán), T 24849/ 24724, 150 rooms, 3-star, takes Visa; also **C** cabins, bookable

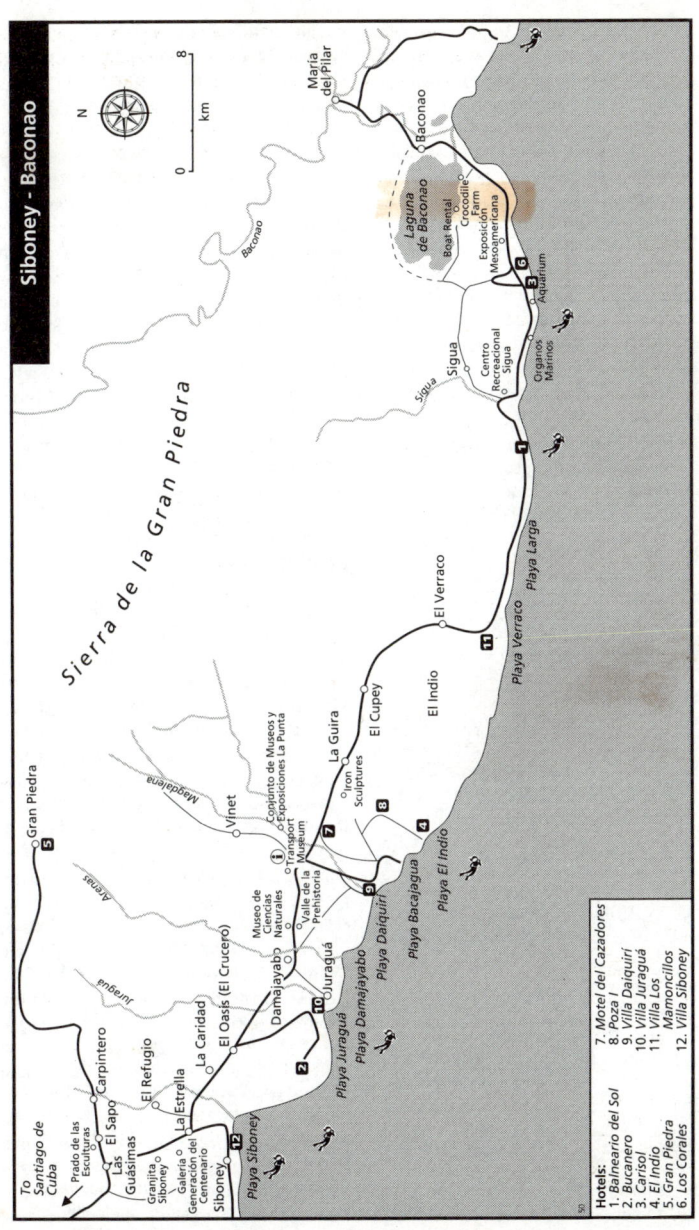

Siboney - Baconao

Sierra de la Gran Piedra

Hotels:
1. Balneario del Sol
2. Bucanero
3. Carisol
4. El Indio
5. Gran Piedra
6. Los Corales
7. Motel del Cazadores
8. Poza I
9. Villa Daiquiri
10. Villa Juraguá
11. Villa Los Mamoncillos
12. Villa Siboney

in any hotel or agency in Santiago. The road starts to get really bad after Daiquirí and is full of holes all the way to Laguna Baconao. If you are using a private car, make sure the driver knows about this, or he will not be happy when he feels his suspension cracking underneath him. There are no buses to **Parque Bacanao**, a sprawling chain of tourist attractions in buildings mostly in need of repair; a private car hired for a whole day will cost about US$50. The next beach, 1 km after Daiquirí, is **Culebrín**, featuring a seawater swimming pool and a few tourist facilities like cabins. Continuing east at Km 35 is **Comunidad Artística Verraco**, a small artists' community, where you can buy original artwork.

● **Accommodation** On the coast near here is **A3** *Balneario del Sol*, Carretera Baconao Km 39, T 6005, a 3-star resort with 123 rooms, car hire, Visa accepted. On the way to Laguna Baconao are two more resort hotels, **L3** *Carisol*, T 28519, 3-star, and **A3** *Los Corales*, T 27191, both of which are near **Playa Cazonal**, which is a very high quality beach for this area.

An Aquarium and Dolphinarium (entrance US$3) on this stretch of the coast has three sea-lion and dolphin shows daily, however small the audience. The show is of a high standard and visitors are invited to dive in and play with the dolphins for an extra US$5, highly recommended. The aquarium has many species of fish as well as turtle and sharks (feeding time is spectacular). There is a basic refreshment bar where you can get a sandwich for US$1 and a beach with trees for shade but no facilities, if you want a quick dip while waiting for the next dolphin show. **Laguna Baconao** is a large murky lake, which is used to breed the dolphins for the nearby dolphinarium. Flanking the lake is a crocodile sanctuary, but this is not for animal lovers. Just for fun, a man jumps in with the crocodiles and taunts them with a stick. They are kept in small enclosures with barely enough water to drink.

West of Santiago

10 km west of Santiago is **El Sanctuario**

de Nuestra Señora de la Caridad del Cobre ('El Cobre') where the shrine of Cuba's patron saint, the Virgen de la Caridad del Cobre, is built over a working copper mine. The story goes that in the 17th century, three fishermen were about to capsize in Nipe Bay, when they found a wooden statue of the Virgin Mary floating in the sea. Their lives were saved and they brought the statue to its current resting place above the altar. Downstairs there are many tokens of gratitude left by Cubans who have been helped by the Virgin in some way, eg for their son to escape to Miami on a raft, in some medical problem or in some sporting event. It is quite common to see nuns dragging the infirm from a minivan into the church. The interesting collection of personal offerings at foot of the statue includes a gold model of Fidel Castro. There is a pilgrimage here on 12 September, when the accommodation will be fully booked. There is a hostal behind the church, where foreigners can stay if there is room; everybody pays the nominal fee of 10 pesos and the setting is idyllic, surrounded by the lush vegetation of the Sierra Maestra. Watch out for the touts swarming around you when you get out of the car; they will try to sell you souvenirs and pieces of copper. It is probably best to take a bit of copper and offer 50 cents or some pesos, otherwise they will be waiting for you when you leave the church. Fortunately they are not allowed inside. There is no bus, so either hire a car and driver, about US$10, or get on a truck at the bus station for a few pesos.

There is a small, busy beach about 10 km west of Santiago called **Mar Verde**; then **Huencabón**, nothing special, then **Caletón Blanco**, 30 km west of Santiago, a nice beach, mostly frequented by Cubans. Like all the beaches in this area it is quite narrow, with white sand, but no facilities. A seawater swimming pool next to the sea has the remains of a diving board. Hold your breath as youths throw themselves 2m or so into the air above the pool, getting the distance they need over

El Cobre

the water to avoid being smashed on the pool's edge. When they are not doing that, the pool is a pleasant place to take a dip if you want the Caribbean without the waves. About 25 km inland from there you will find **B** *El Saltón*, T 61175, a mini-resort advertised as 'stress relief', where there is a waterfall and several natural pools to bathe in. Further along is **El Francés**, said to be the best beach in the west.

Festivals

The **Festival del Caribe** begins in the first week in July with theatre, dancing and conferences, and continues later in July to coincide with the Moncada celebrations on 26 July. The **Carnival**, already in full swing by then (as it was in 1953, the date carefully chosen to catch Batista's militia drunk and off-guard and use the noise of the carnival to drown the sound of gun-fire), traditionally stops for a day of more serious celebration, then continues on 27 July. Carnival is 18-29 July, taking in Santiago's patron saint's day, 25 July. This carnival is regaining its former glory and is well worth seeing. Visit the **Museo del Carnaval** on Calle Heredia 301 esquina Pío Rosado, to get the feel of it. Photos, costumes and musical instruments depict the history of the carnival and the cultures which influenced it. At the end is a fun painted collage of places in Santiago. Open Tuesday-Sunday 0900-1700, entrance US$1, cameras US$1, a guided tour is available, music is performed on Sunday at 1100 and Wednesday at 1500.

Other events include the **Festival de Baile**, which takes place in the streets 15-19 May; **Expocaribe**, based in Teatro Heredia, an annual festival celebrating Caribbean culture in the last week in May; **Festival del Pregón**, also known as Fruta del Carey, a festival of song in September when people dress up in traditional costumes and sell fruit in the street while singing; **Festival de la Trova**, a festival of folk music is held in September or October, the exact date depends on funding; **Festival Internacional del Coro** is a new festival held in December every five years, with one due at the end of 1997.

Local information
● Accommodation

> **Prices: L1** over US$200; **L2** US$151-200; **L3** US$101-150; **A1** US$81-100; **A2** US$61-80; **A3** US$46-60; **B** US$31-45; **C** US$21-30; **D** US$12-20; **E** US$7-11; **F** up to US$6

L2-A2 *Casa Granda* (Gran Caribe) Heredia 201 entre San Pedro y San Félix, near Parque Céspedes, T 86600, F 86035, elegant building opened in 1914 and patronized by many famous movie stars and singers as well as sports champions Joe Louis the boxer and Babe Ruth the baseball player, 4-star, 58 renovated rooms and suites, a/c, fax service, laundry, car hire, satellite TV, nanny service, post office, disabled access and one room for handicapped people, Havanatur and Asistur offices, excellent central location with terrace bar overlooking park, fifth floor bar with even better views over city, restaurant, snack bar, café, open 2000-0300, good.

L3 *Hotel Santiago* (Cubanacan), Av Las Américas entre 4 y M, T 42612/42680, F 41756, 5-star, 302 rooms, clean, good service, excellent breakfast buffet US$7, good *La Cubana* restaurant, highly recommended, open 1200-2100, swimming pool, tennis, sauna, discotheque, car hire, has post office and will change almost any currency into dollars.

A2 *Versalles* (Cubanacan), Carretera del Morro Km 1, T 91014/91016/91504, 3-star, 61 rooms, takes Visa, very near airport.

B *Balcón del Caribe* (Islazul), next to Castillo del Morro, T 9-1011, 3-star, 72 rooms overlooking the sea, quiet, pool, tourist office, simple Cuban food, cold water in bungalows, pleasant but inconvenient for the town; **B** *Las Américas* (Horizontes), T 4-2011, F 86075, Av de las Américas esquina General Cebreco, easy bus/truck access to centre, private cars around bus stop in plaza opposite hotel, 3-star, 68 rooms, recommended, lively, restaurant not recommended except for breakfast, hustlers on terrace café, discotheque noisy but rooms mostly quiet, fills up with *jineteras*, non-residents may use swimming pool, helpful Rumbos

agent, nice reception staff, safety deposit, Havanautos in front of hotel, bicycle hire; **B** *Motel San Juan* (Horizontes), Km 1 Carretera a Siboney, T 42478/42490, F 86137, out of town but nice location, turistaxi US$3.95, private car US$2, a complex with cabins, 112 very nice rooms, large and clean, intermittent hot water, pool, bar and several restaurants, good breakfast, high quality by Cuban standards, accepts pesos, queues at weekends and during festivals, car hire, private car into town US$2; **B** *Villa* (Gaviota), Av Manduley 502, entre 19 y 21, Reparto Vista Alegre, T 41368/41346, 3-star, car hire, tourist office, nearby pool for guests, quiet, no credit cards.

C *Rancho Club Motel* (Islazul), Carretera Central Km 4.5, Altos de Quintero, T 33202/33280, 29 rooms; **C-D** *MES* (Horizontes), Calle L esquina 7, Reparto Terrazas (about 5 blocks north of *Las Américas*), T 4-2398, 2-star, 16 rooms, clean, TV and fan, 2 rooms share bath and fridge, food OK; **C-D** *Libertad* on Plaza Marte, T 23080, good central location, good value if slightly downmarket, very noisy fans, there is an annex, *Rex* nearby on Av Garzón 10, T 26314, where the rooms are better, clean, with soap, toilet paper and towels, but the a/c is still noisy and the water is not always on, you have to register at the *Libertad* first.

E *Imperial*, Saco 251, T 28917, basic, central, peso hotel.

Private accommodation available for about US$10-15; touts around Parque Céspedes, also near all hotels. A recommended family is **D** Hermes Domínguez and Dalgis López Sablón, Féliz Peña 455 (altos), CP 90100, T 20060, some rooms a/c, breakfast US$3, dinner US$5, large portions, good. Due to open in February 1998, Grethel Suárez Sánchez, Alfredo Zayas 513 entre 13 y Anacaona, Santa Bárbara, CP 90300, T 43177, room with double bed and private bathroom, expected to be worth recommending.

● Places to eat

The hotels have restaurants and mostly serve buffet meals. Three restaurants run by Rumbos (*Combinado* is the collective name) on Plaza Dolores (known as Búlevar locally), Italian, Chinese and creole food, quite expensive and low on local atmosphere; opposite them on Búlevar is *Matamoros*, which is better although prices are quite high with a system of US$1=1 peso; also *Las Enramadas*, Búlevar, good atmosphere, cheap, basic food, nice setting. *Las Acacias* in *Hotel Villa*, Av Manduley 502, T 41368, open 1900-2300, Creole Cuban food;

Santiago 1900, Bartolomé Maso y Hartmann, T 23507, open 1900-2400, average prices, good food; *La Taberna de Dolores*, Aguilera esquina Reloj, T 23913, Spanish food, open 1900-2400, prices in pesos but tourists pay 1:1 in dollars. The *Terrace Coffee Bar* at the *Casa Granda* is open 24 hours and is a nice place for a drink, look out for Tony, the deaf-mute magician who is there in the evening, the *Roof Garden* at the top of the same hotel is open 2000-0300. *Coppelia* ice cream on Félix Peña under the cathedral, open Monday-Friday 1000-2100, Saturday-Sunday 1100-2200, no queuing if you have dollars. *Isabelica*, Aguilera esquina Plaza Dolores, open 24 hours, serves only coffee, US$0.85, cigars rolled, bohemian hangout, watch out for hustlers; *Casa del Té*, Aguilera esquina Lacret, grow their own herbs, cheap herbal tea available.

Lots of good *paladares* (official ones have a sign outside) around Calles Heredia and Aguilera, and in Reparto Vista Alegre, near the hotels *Santiago*, *Las Américas* and *San Juan*. *Mujeres de Arena*, Félix Peña 554 entre Aguilera y Enramada, main dish US$3-7, side dishes extra, simple décor but food delicious and nicely presented, open all the time; *Paladar Mireya*, Padre Pico 368-A, Frente a la Escalinata, US$5-6 including rice and salad, open 1200-2400, in smokey back room; *Doña Cristina*, Padre Pico, recommended; *La Palmita*, Calle 3 610, entre K y L, Reparto Sueño, Creole food, recommended; *El Balcón*, Independencia 253, Reparto Sueño, T 2-7407, good food, US$3, open 24 hours, popular with locals; *Terrazas*, Calle 5 50 entre M y Terraza, Ampliación de Terraza, T 4-1491, *paladar* on the upper floor open daily 1000-2400, tasty food, nicely presented, chicken US$6, pork US$5, recommended, if the gate is locked, whistle; *Casa Pita*, Calle 8 208 entre Calles 7 y 9, Vista Alegre, is open 1200-1500, 1900-2300, maximum US$10, good food. Street stalls sell snacks in pesos, usually only open until early evening, some only at lunchtime. Most things cost 1 peso. Avoid *fritos*, they are just fried lumps of dough; most reliable thing is cheese, pork or egg sandwich; pizza is usually dry bit of dough with a few gratings of cheese. Lots of stalls along 'Ferreiro' or Av Victoriano Garzón, these are open later than others, especially up near *Hotel Las Américas*. Also lots around bus station on Libertadores and few along the bottom part of Aguilera, between Parque Céspedes and Plaza Dolores.

● **Bars**
Kontiki, Enramada esquina San Pedro; terrace bar in *Hotel Casa Granda* (see above), overlooking Parque Céspedes; new bar (unnamed as we went to press) for tourists on corner of Parque Céspedes y Aguilera.

● **Airlines**
Cubana office on Félix Peña 673 entre Heredia y San Basilio, near the cathedral, open Monday-Friday 0900-1700, Saturday 0900-1400, T 24156/51579/22290. Aerocaribbean office under *Hotel Casa Granda*. Local and inter-Caribbean (some destinations) flights can also be booked in the Rumbos office on Heredia esquina Parque Céspedes and at the Havanatur office under the *Casa Granda*.

● **Banks & money changers**
Possible to get US dollar cash advance on Visa at **Banco Financiero Internacional**, corner of Parque Céspedes at Santo Tomás y Aguilera, T 22101, open Monday-Friday 0800-1600, they also change foreign currency and travellers' cheques. BICSA, is on Enramada opposite Plaza Dolores, for changing foreign currency and travellers' cheques. Travellers' cheques can be changed in any hotel except those in the Islazul chain; commission is usually 2-3%. *Hotel Santiago* will change virtually any cash currency into dollars. Travellers' cheques can be changed in the Havanatur office in *Casa Granda*. In the Asistur office under *Casa Granda* you can get cash advance on all major credit cards including American Express and Diners Club; they will also change American Express travellers' cheques, the only place who will do so in all Cuba. Dollars can be changed into pesos in the street, usually near a bank, but for the sake of security only change small amounts, US$5-10. There is no commission but you will usually get about 10% less than the official rate anyway.

● **Cultural centres**
Casa de Africa, Av Manduley, includes craftwork shop and has Afro-Cuban music in the evenings. **La Conga de los Hoyos**, Moncada y Av José Martí, specializes in conga music, promotes festival 24 June with conga drummers in the streets. **El Tívoli**, Santa Rosa y Jesús Rabi, promotes influence of French culture, named after neighbourhood where French settled in 18th century, fleeing from slave uprising in Haiti. **La Tumba Francesa**, Reloj y Habana, like its counterpart in Guantánamo, it celebrates Haitian influence on Cuban culture, with traditional costumes, music, dancing and handicrafts. **UNEAC** national art and literature centre on Bartolomé Maso y Pío Rosado. **Casa del Caribe**,

Calle 13 154 esquina Calle 8, Vista Alegre, T 42285, extensive library of Caribbean subjects, publishes magazine called *Caribe*, Afro-Cuban music and dance Saturday nights. **Centro de Estudios Africanos Fernando Ortiz**, Av Manduley y Calle 5, Vista Alegre, US$1 entrance, artefacts and research centre. **Hermanos Saiz** on Heredia, cultural centre which promotes poetry.

● **Entertainment**

Club Tropicana Santiago, local version of Havana show, on Autopista Nacional Km 1.5, T 43036/43610, open 2000-0300, book direct or through a travel agent in any hotel, eg Rumbos US$50 including transport. **Casa de la Trova**, Calle Heredia 206 around the corner from *Casa Granda*, 2 daily shows of music, morning and evening, traditional, acoustic Son music, open until 2400, US$1, nice venue in beautiful building with patio where the bands play at night, also bar. *Grupo Folklórico del Oriente*, Calle San Francisco y San Félix, folk groups play daytime till lunchtime, then again in the evening. *Sala de Dolores* on Plaza Dolores has classical and choral concerts. Lively nightly disco in *Santiago* and *Las Américas* hotels, to which Cubans are welcome, American disco music, hardly any salsa, *jinetera* pick-up places. Two discos on Heredia, one of them opposite the **Casa de la Trova**, mostly for the under-20s. *Buró de Información Cultural* on Plaza Marte has live music in its patio bar every night. *Casa del Caribe* (see above, **Cultural centres**, page 249) on Calle 13 154 esquina Calle 8, T 42285, live Afro-Cuban music and dance at weekends.

● **Hospitals & medical services**

Clínica Internacional, Calle 13 y 14, Reparto Vista Alegre, T 42589, along Av Raúl Pujol away from the city, opposite *Motel San Juan*, especially for tourists, has a dentist as well, everything payable in dollars, the best clinic to visit to be sure of immediate treatment. There is a **pharmacy** next door to the **Casa de la Trova** on Heredia and another, open 24 hours, on Victoriano Garzón y Calle 10.

Music in Santiago de Cuba

Santiago is overflowing with musical talent. Even the cockerels crow in time to the son. Santiago is son's spiritual home. At the Casa de la Trova on Calle Heredia images of old soneros look down on the musicians, as elegant Santiaguerans lose themselves in the dance and the rum flows free. Although Cuba's most famous groups rarely venture out to Santiago (the impressive Heredia theatre has a reputation for turning on the sound half way through the night), the city has enough supreme musicians of its own. The ancient and ironically named Estudiantina Invasora, the young Grupo Turquino and the multi-talented Sonora La Calle are all worth catching. Rumba in Santiago has its place in the carnival parade. While the band takes a rest, the Columbia Santiaguera strikes up for the dancers. There is also a regular rumba on Sunday mornings at the Museo del Carnaval on Heredia (almost opposite the Trova). For a calmer session you can enjoy choral, orchestral and chamber music at the Sala Dolores (on Plaza Dolores). There is an annual Festival Internacional del Coro in December. You can experience Santiago's African roots at the occasionally wonderful peñas at the Casa del Caribe on Calle B or the Casa de Africa on the evocatively named Avenida Manduley, both in Vista Alegre. Stunning shows by Cutumba, Cocoyé, and Guillermón Moncada celebrate all of Oriente's music and dance traditions. Other groups such as the Cabildo Isuama and the Tumba Francesa keep alive the memories of Africa. July in Santiago is super-hot, and so is the music. In early July, the Festival del Caribe brings groups from all over the Caribbean for street shows, theatre events and a big parade. Carnival follows almost immediately, when the comparsas and paseos parade their congas around the streets in spectacular style, past stages set up for live bands and kiosks selling beer and *frituras*. To conga properly you'll need your wooden sandals (chancletas), curlers, shorts and a boob tube (bajo y chupa, literally 'down and suck'). To join the musicians you need the brake drum off a 1953 Chevy. Maybe it's better simply to *arrollar y gozar*.

● **Language schools**
The only place to learn Spanish is the Universidad de Oriente, on the outskirts of town, but it is not well-organized.

● **Laundry**
Abatur, Av de Céspedes, near *Hotel Santiago*.

● **Post & telecommunications**
Post Office: main Post Office is on Aguilera y Clarín, near Plaza Marte. There is another one at Aguilera 310 and one on the corner of Heredia with San Félix, open 0700-2000, where you can make phone calls within Cuba. The *Casa Granda* has its own post office, as does *Hotel Santiago*.

Telephones: Etecsa is on Aguilera, just before Plaza Dolores, open 24 hours. For calls outside Santiago, Centro de Comunicaciones Nacional e Internacional, Heredia y Félix Peña, by the cathedral. You can not make collect calls from hotels, only from private houses.

● **Shopping**
Casa de la Artesanía, under the cathedral in Parque Céspedes, T 23924, open 0800-1730, also on Lacret 724 entre San Basilio y Heredia, T 24027; *Cubartesana* on Félix Peña esquina Masó under the cathedral; *Salón Artexanda* on Heredia 304 entre Pío Rosado y Calvario. Handicrafts are sold on the street on Heredia entre Hartmann and Pío Rosado.

Bookshops: *Librería Internacional* on Heredia under the cathedral has a selection of paperbacks in English and postcards, open 0800-2000. There is also a bookshop on Av Victoriano Garzón near Plaza Marte (pesos) and *Ho Chi Minh* at the top of Enramada, also pesos.

Photography: *Photoservice* has two shops near Parque Céspedes, one on General Lacret under the Cathedral, and one on Félix Peña entre Aguilera y Enramada; there is another on Victoriano Garzón entre Calle 6 y 7, Reparto Santa Bárbara, across the road from *Hotel Las Américas*. There are also other photo shops on Enramada (Saco).

Music: *Casa de la Trova* sells CDs and tapes; *Artex* on Aguilera sells CDs, tapes and videos for dollars; *Enramadas* and *Siglo XX*, both on Enramada, are large stores with stalls inside selling records, books, clothes, jewellery, ornaments etc in pesos. On Enramada there is a second hand record shop.

La Maison on Av Manduley has expensive European clothes for dollars; there is a *Benet-*

ton under the Cathedral. Several dollar stores can be found in the Parque Céspedes area, ask for 'shopping', especially on Calle Saco. There is a good bread shop (dollars) called *Doña Neli* on Aguilera at Plaza Marte, just down from *Hotel Libertad*. *Panadería El Sol* is on Plaza Marte entre Saco y Aguilera. *Casa de Miel*, General Lacret, sells honey. *La Bombonera* is a dollar store selling food very near Parque Céspedes on Aguilera entre General Lacret y Hartmann, open Monday-Saturday 0900-1800, Sunday 0900-1200. Food market on Ferreiro opposite *Hotel Las Américas*.

● **Sport**
Baseball: is played from January onwards at the Estadio Guillermo Moncada on Av Las Américas, T 41090/41078.

Hunting: can be done around Parque Baconao, contact Coto El Indio, T 43445.

● **Tour companies & travel agents**
Rumbos Cuba is on Heredia opposite *Casa Granda* hotel, open 0800-1700 for tours and later for car hire. Organized city tours with guide, also day trips to all destinations around Santiago. Prices vary according to season and number of people, tour to Gran Piedra US$35 for one person, US$25 for 2 people, US$20 for three, then progressively lower to ten people when it stays the same however many there are. There is a day trip to Pico Turquino/Sierra Maestra/Comandancia de la Plata, all the revolutionary spots, costing US$120 for one, US$60 for two, US$40 for three and so on; to Baracoa US$60 for 8 hours minimum 4 people including breakfast and lunch or 2-3 day trips; also flights and trips to Jamaica and Santo Domingo. Havanatur main office is near La Maison on Av Manduley, T 43603, with another office under the *Hotel Casa Granda*, offering the same as Rumbos but slightly more expensive. They have very good guides who are fluent in most European languages. All the main hotels have tour agencies, usually outlets of Rumbos or Havanatur, and you can save time by using them rather than going to the main office. Islazul only deals with tourism for Cubans.

● **Useful addresses**
Immigration: Inmigración y Extranjería on Av Raúl Pujol y Calle 1, Reparto Santa Bárbara.
Police: T 116. The central police station is Unidad 2, Calle Corona y San Gerónimo. Near to the hotels *Santiago* and *Las Américas* is Unidad 4, on Aguilera near the hospital and the market.

Fire: Calle Martí 517, T 23242. **Asistur**: *Hotel Casa Granda*, Calle Heredia esquina San Pedro, T 86600, for all health, financial, legal and insurance problems for foreign tourists.

● **Transport**

Local Bus: regular bus service between Plaza Ferreiro (top of Av Victoriano Garzón) and Plaza Marte/Parque Céspedes. Buses run until about 0100 and the fare is always 20 centavos. If there is no sign of a bus, catch a truck, ask driver the destination, pay flat rate 1 peso. Horse drawn coches are also 1 peso. Bus number 214 goes to Playa Siboney; 207 to Juraguá; no bus at present to Parque Baconao; no bus to El Cobre, but many trucks go there from the main bus terminal. **Car hire**: Transautos are based in the hotels *Casa Granda*, *Motel San Juan* and *Libertad*, and also have an office at the airport. Havanautos are based in the Cupet Cimex (gas station), T 42806/43111, and have a desk in the Rumbos offices on Heredia opposite *Casa Granda*, also in hotels *Las Américas* and *Casa Granda*. Cubacar has an office in the *Hotel Santiago* and at *Los Corrales* in Parque Baconao. **Taxis**: there are three types: *Turistaxi* are the most expensive, eg US$8 from airport to town centre; *Taxis OK*

owned by Cubanacan are also expensive; *Cubataxi*, T 51038/9, are the cheapest (name on windscreen), eg airport to town US$5. The taxi fare from the bus station to Plaza Marte is US$1, to Parque Céspedes US$1-2. You can also get a private taxi, lots of them hanging around Parque Céspedes and Plaza Marte, but they will charge about the same as a Cubataxi. The difference is if you want to do a longer journey, you can negotiate a price, eg Castillo del Morro, US$10, Parque Baconao US$50. You will be continually offered private taxis every time you go out, but if you are extremely unlucky and 'there's never one when you need one', go to one of the three little plazas in front of *Hotel Las Américas* and you'll find one. Motorbike transport can be arranged at Plaza Marte for about US$1. Bici-taxis cost US$0.50.

Air Airport Antonio Maceo (SCU), 8 km from town, T 91014, 91830, F 86184. Daily flight to/from Havana, Baracoa Sunday, Varadero Monday and Friday. Cubana also has international flights to Santiago from Frankfurt, Lisbon, Paris, Rome, Santo Domingo and Vitoria (Spain), while Tropical Airlines flies from Kingston, Jamaica. There are connecting flights from Mexico via Havana. On arrival you are greeted by several

Our Man in Havana

🐾 Graham Greene's first visit to Cuba was in 1957 to research *'Our Man in Havana'*. He was originally going to set it in Lisbon, but decided on a more exotic location; he planned to sell the film rights to the novel before it was even written. He immediately took a liking to the unlimited decadence Havana had to offer, and spent much of his time at the Shanghai theatre, a club which featured live sex shows. Greene's former connections with the British SIS (Secret Intelligence Service) gave him access to political society. He based some of the characters in *'Our Man'* on Batista's soldiers: Captain Segura, with his cigarette case made of human skin, was based on the real-life Capitán Ventura. The plot of the novel involves a vacuum cleaner salesman being mistaken for a secret agent, who for fear of being discovered as a fraud, tries to carry out the orders given to him by providing diagrams of vacuum cleaner parts, pretending they are in fact the plans for an arsenal of nuclear weapons.

Greene's training as a secret agent allowed him to infiltrate all levels of political life: he made contact with Castro's rebel forces in the Sierra, offering them any help they needed. He was asked to smuggle a suitcase of warm clothes, to help them survive the freezing night time temperatures of the Sierra Maestra, through customs on a Havana-Santiago flight.

In 1959, when Greene arrived for the second time in Havana to assist director Carol Reed in the filming of his novel, the Revolution had already triumphed. Greene's small act of support in 1957 had not been forgotten, and Castro gave his personal seal of approval to the film, although he felt it didn't capture the full extent of Batista's evil.

taxi drivers, some of whom even manage to get right into the arrivals building; these are unofficial taxis but reasonably priced and safe, they should charge no more than US$5 to anywhere in town.

Long distance bus Terminal near Plaza de la Revolución at the top of Av de los Libertadores/Carretera Central. Jump queue paying in dollars, but if the bus is full you will not get a seat with any currency, so it is best to get there either the day before or at least a couple of hours in advance. Buy ticket in office on Calle Yarayo (the first street on the left going north from the terminal) before boarding, open daily 0600-1400. To **Havana** daily at 1600; **Moa**, 0700, US$9; **Manzanillo**, 0720, US$9; **Niquero/Bayamo**, 0720, US$7.50; **Baracoa**, 0640, US$9; **Guantánamo** (Baracoa bus), US$3. If you pay in pesos it is 5 pesos to Guantánamo, 9 pesos to Baracoa and 15 pesos in a *colectivo* to Guantánamo. Also trucks available at terminal to most destinations, drivers shout destination prior to departure, pay in pesos. For a long journey avoid trucks without any kind of cover, or you will burn.

Train Book tickets in advance in LADIS office on Aguilera near Plaza Marte. Terminal at north end of Malecón (Av Jesús Menéndez), new terminal being built further north, stalled for some time but supposed to be finished by end-1997. Train travel is not as reliable or comfortable as bus travel. Take sweater for Havana journey, freezing a/c. Daily to Manzanillo 0545, US$8; Camagüey 0855, US$13; Santa Clara and Havana 1635, arriving Santa Clara 0238 US$24, Havana 0700 US$35.

WEST FROM SANTIAGO

West from Santiago runs a wonderful coastal road along the **Sierra Maestra** with beautiful bays and beaches, completely deserted, some with black sand. It is only possible to visit by car. Many of the villages have connections with historical revolutionary events.

● **Accommodation** There are two all-inclusive SuperClubs hotels in the **Chivirico** area (formerly Delta properties): **L3** *Sierra Mar*, on Playa Sevilla, Carretera de Chivirico Km 62, T22-26337, 194 rooms and 6 suites, modern resort in terraced style, a/c, satellite TV, small beach, watersports, freeform pool on terrace with bar and good sea view, 2 restaurants, 3 bars, shop, free bikes, many activities such as horse rental, helicopter ride into the mountains, sports, gymnasium, kids' club, the only Super-Clubs resort in Cuba where children are welcome, tours and car hire, weddings arranged free of charge including cake, champagne, marriage certificate and public notary; further west past Chivirico is the smaller *Los Galeones*, Carretera Chivirico, for singles and couples over 16 only, marketed to honeymooners, weddings arranged free of charge, 32 rooms including 1 suite on a cliff overlooking the Caribbean, a/c and fan, satellite TV, 300 winding steps lead down to the sea, restaurant, bar, special scuba training pool, bowling, volleyball, car rental, courtesy bus to *Sierra Mar*.

El Uvero, about 60 km from Santiago, has a monument marking the attack by Castro and his men on the Batista troop HQ on 28 May 1957. The building which was attacked is now a small museum. About 20 km further west is a turning for **Pico Turquino** (1,974m), just before the village of Ocujal. You can drive a short distance and park and walk. This is the highest peak in the Sierra Maestra. At **La Plata**, about 150 km from Santiago in the mountains, is a little museum about the Cuban guerrillas' first successful battle. There is no curator so ask the local people to open it.

Province of Granma

CONTINUING west, you enter the province of **Granma**, created out of the former Oriente province in 1975 and named after the boat which brought Castro and his comrades to Cuba to start the Revolution. The area is studded with memories of the guerrilla struggle and the hills are full of evocative plaques commemorating the events immediately after their landing.

Province of Granma

Granma occupies the western end of the Sierra Maestra and the flatlands and swamps to the north of the mountains. Many of the country's major rivers drain into the Golfo de Guacanayabo, the longest being the Río Cauto. The capital of the province is **Bayamo**, which has good transport links, while **Manzanillo** is its main port. The southern coast has the best beaches and several resort hotels are clustered around **Marea del Portillo**.

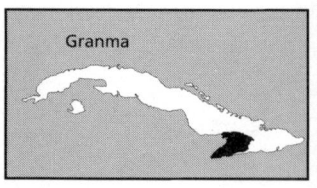

Granma

Area 8,372 sq km, *Population* 819,500, *Density* 97.9 per sq km, *Urban* 57.3%

The road from Santiago continues along the coast to **Pilón** (*Population* 12,000), a small town with a harbour, from where the road turns inland towards the Golfo de Guacanayabo.

● **Accommodation** At Marea del Portillo before you get to Pilón, there are two more resort hotels popular with Canadian package tours: **A3-B** *Marea del Portillo*, T 23-594001/2, hot water, phone, TV to rent US$3/day, shop; **A2-B** *Farallón del Caribe*, T 23-594081-7, F 597080, a/c, TV, hot water, phone for international calls, nice position. Watersports, scuba diving, snorkelling and sailing can be arranged at both resorts.

From Pilón you can take a road inland across the peninsula past **Ojo de Agua**. Just after the village there are three separate signs and plaques marking the spots where three groups of men who disembarked from *Granma* crossed the road in underground water conduits, before heading into the Sierra Maestra. The signs have the emblems of five palms in a heart, because the men arranged to reassemble at a place called **Cinco Palmas**. The spot near Ojo de Agua has the actual conduit through

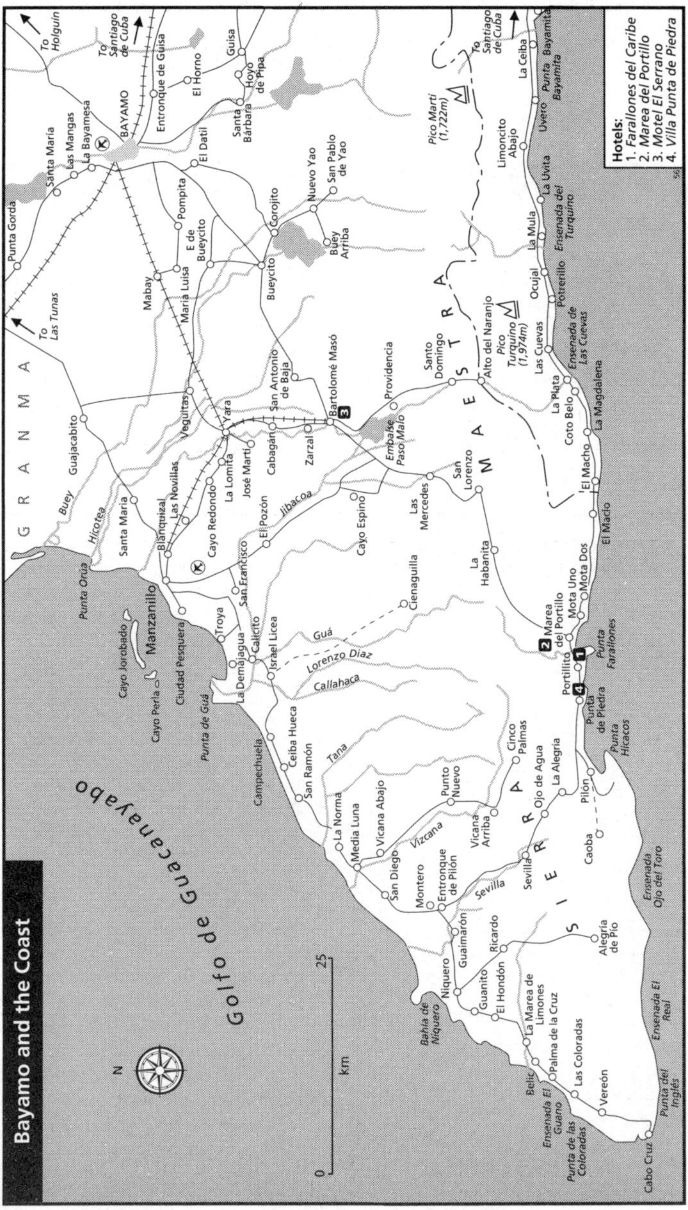
Bayamo and the Coast
N
0
25
km
Golfo de Guacanayabo
G R A N M A
S I E R R A M A E S T R A
To Las Tunas
To Holguín
To Santiago de Cuba
To Santiago de Cuba
BAYAMO
Manzanillo
Punta Gorda
Santa María
Las Mangas
La Bayamesa
El Datil
Entronque de Guisa
El Horno
Guisa
Hoyo de Pipa
Santa Bárbara
San Pablo de Yao
Nuevo Yao
Corojito
Buey Arriba
Bueycito
E de Bueycito
Pompita
Mabay
María Luisa
Veguitas
Yara
Guajacabito
Santa María
Blanquizal
Las Novillas
Cayo Redondo
La Lomita
José Martí
Cabagán
San Antonio de Baja
Zarzal
Bartolomé Masó
Providencia
Embalse Paso Malo
Santo Domingo
Alto del Naranjo
Pico Turquino (1,974m)
Pico Martí (1,722m)
San Lorenzo
Las Mercedes
Cayo Espino
El Pozón
Jibacoa
San Francisco
Buey
Hicotea
Punta Orúa
Cayo Jorobado
Cayo Perla
Ciudad Pesquera
Punta de Guá
Troya
La Demajagua
Calicito
Israel Licea
Cienaguilla
Guá
Lorenzo Díaz
Callahaca
La Habanita
Marea del Portillo
Mota Uno
Mota Dos
El Macío
El Macho
Coto Belo
La Magdalena
La Plata
Las Cuevas
Ensenada de Las Cuevas
Ocujal
Potrerillo
La Mula
Ensenada del Turquino
La Uvita
Limoncito Abajo
Uvero
Punta Bayamita
La Ceiba
Bayamita
Portillito
Punta Farallones
Punta de Piedra
Punta Hicacos
Cinco Palmas
La Alegría
Ojo de Agua
Pilón
Caoba
Campechuela
Ceiba Hueca
San Ramón
Tana
La Norma
Media Luna
Vicana Abajo
Punto Nuevo
Vicana Arriba
Vizcana
San Diego
Montero
Entronque de Pilón
Sevilla
Ensenada Ojo del Toro
Guaimarón
Ricardo
Alegría de Pío
Niquero
Guanito
El Hondón
Bahía de Niquero
La Marea de Limones
Palma de la Cruz
Las Coloradas
Belic
Vereón
Ensenada El Real
Ensenada El Guano
Punta de las Coloradas
Cabo Cruz
Punta del Inglés
Hotels:
1. Farallones del Caribe
2. Marea del Portillo
3. Motel El Serrano
4. Villa Punta de Piedra

which Fidel and his group went, sitting at the side of the road. The road follows the Río Sevilla to join up with the Manzanillo-Niquero road running down the other side of the peninsula to **Cabo Cruz** at the tip.

Turn left to **Niquero** from where a dirt road leads to the spot where Castro's 82 revolutionaries disembarked from the yacht, *Granma*, on 2 December 1956 in a mangrove swamp just southwest of **Playa Las Coloradas**. By the road is a small

Santiago de Cuba to Manzanillo by bus

The buses vary in quality. Some are air conditioned, but even the others have a window by every seat, so breezes pass through the bus. There is enough space under the seat for a holdall or small suitcase, but other luggage goes in the hold. Security did not seem to be a problem; on the advice of a Cuban on the bus I left my bag under the seat while we went for lunch. The Cubans travel with so little cash that to run off at some deserted pit stop with a tourist's bag did not seem like a very attractive idea. All the Cuban travellers are going from one specific place to another, and they seemed to be much more simple folk than the hustlers you encounter in the heart of the city. You do not get hassled on the buses like in the city. People chat to you or attach themselves to you, for little else than to relieve the boredom of a 5-hour journey. I bought lunch for the woman and her daughter who'd been chatting to me and giving me oranges for the first 2 hours of the trip. Lunch came to about 6 pesos a head.

The first part of the journey is through flat land, past the messy outskirts of the city. The hills in the distance are the beginning of the Sierra Maestra. The road is good, giving a smooth ride. On both sides farmland stretches into the hills, mostly with sugarcane. After one hour and 25km, you arrive at San Luis, a nondescript village where vendors sell you snacks through the window (load up on breakfast in San Luis if you missed it in Santiago). Next stop, 45km from San Luis, is Contramaestre, bigger than San Luis and more colonial and rustic. There isn't time to get off the bus, but fruit is sold through the windows. You can get *refrescos* to drink, but these are made with tap water, so avoid if you haven't had your hepatitis jab. Next stop was a roadside café for lunch. We stopped here for about half an hour, and there were toilets. On the menu was one choice: chicken and yams, at only 6 pesos. Make sure you have at least 30 pesos for this bus journey, though if you only have dollars the private vendors will gladly accept them, but you'll get pesos in the change. I found it easier to forget about dollars outside the tourist centres; it also helps send beggars scurrying away, when they ask for a dollar, and you whip out your grubby wad of peso bills and tell them it's all you have.

After a few more small stops, the bus reaches Bayamo, a largish town 4 hours and approximately 125km from Santiago. You can get off the bus for about 15 minutes and get a bite to eat or a drink from a private vendor in the terminal (terminals have no official facilities except toilets). The police got on the bus while we waited at Bayamo and did a quick search. When they asked who I was, half the passengers leapt to my defence, assuring them that I was only a tourist. One Cuban was taken away for having a few kilos of coffee over the limit. An hour and a half later (56km) we arrived in Manzanillo, at the tiny bus terminal 2km from the city centre. Huge murals of Che and Camilo Cienfuegos greet you outside the terminal. Lots of classic US automobiles are waiting to take you anywhere in town or the *Hotel Guacanayabo* for about 10-20 pesos.

Gavin Clark

park where a replica of *Granma* can be seen and a 2 km concrete path through the swamp takes you to a rather ugly concrete jetty and a plaque marking the occasion. Every year on 2 December, hundreds of youths re-enact the whole journey from Mexico, disembarking here and heading off into the Sierra Maestra, worth visiting at that time. The dirt road ends at Cabo Cruz at the tip of the peninsula.

MANZANILLO

Phone code 23, *Population* 100,000

You can make a circular route back to Santiago via **Manzanillo**, a small seaside town and principal port of Granma province with not much to offer to the foreign tourist. It is rather lacking in character and atmosphere, but its one advantage is that due to lack of tourism, visitors will not be subject to the constant attention and hassle common in tourist destinations; the people of Manzanillo seem completely uninterested in the activities of foreigners in their midst and you can stroll about the town at your leisure virtually ignored. Another advantage of the absence of tourism is that there are few dollar facilities; you can pay for nearly everything in pesos, so for the budget

traveller who wants to hang on to dollars for later, Manzanillo is a good stop-off point.

The **Malecón** is disappointing, being a grey stretch of stony beach lined with the odd concrete shell housing a cheap peso restaurant where you may be the only customers for lunch. The Malecón leads to the centre of the village, around the **Parque Céspedes**. Here is the *glorieta* (gazebo), maintained in pristine condition and considered a symbol of the city. The square is surrounded by restaurants and snack bars, all of whom charge in pesos. On José Martí there are cheap stalls selling essential commodities for Cubans, also the usual mini-*paladares*. The **Casa de la Trova** is the centre of nightlife on Saturdays, and you can mingle with Cubans in a natural environment, without feeling segregated in a tourist-only exclusion zone, as in the big cities.

Places of interest

A small, colonial church, the **Iglesia de la Purísima Concepción**, is on Maceo, overlooking Parque Céspedes. The **Museo Histórico Municipal** is on José Martí 226, with artefacts of the *conquistadores* in one section and relics of the clandestine struggle in the other.

Manzanillo

Not to scale

Golfo de Guacanayabo

To Bayamo

Barrio de Oro

Rpto Caymari

Nuevo Manzanillo

Rpto Pérez

Valerino

Ciudad Pesquera

Rpto Vázquez

Estadio Wilfredo Pagés

Rpto Horacio Rodríguez

Cemetery

Av de Céspedes

Av Camilo Cienfuegos

To Niquero

To Airport

Hotels:
1. Guacanayabo

Places to eat:
2. Balcón del Guacanayabo

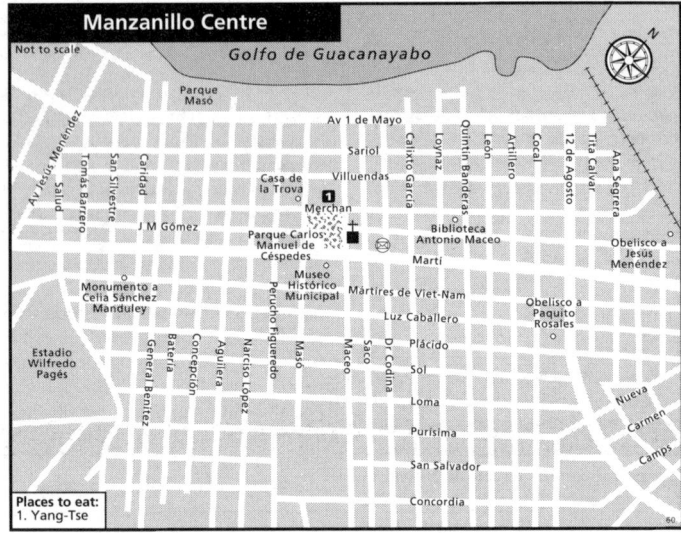

Manzanillo Centre

Not to scale

Golfo de Guacanayabo

N

Parque Masó

Av 1 de Mayo

Av Jesús Menéndez
Tomás Barrero
Salud
San Silvestre
Caridad

Sariol
Villuendas
Casa de la Trova

J M Gómez

Merchan

Parque Carlos Manuel de Céspedes

Calixto García
Loynaz
Quintín Banderas
León
Artillero
Cocal
12 de Agosto
Tita Calvar
Ana Segrera

Biblioteca Antonio Maceo

Martí

Obelisco a Jesús Menéndez

Museo Histórico Municipal

Monumento a Celia Sánchez Manduley

Perucho Figueredo

Mártires de Viet-Nam

Luz Caballero

Obelisco a Paquito Rosales

Estadio Wilfredo Pagés

General Benítez
Batería
Concepción
Aguilera
Narciso López
Maso
Maceo
Saco
Dr Codina

Plácido

Sol

Loma

Purísima

San Salvador

Concordia

Nueva
Carmen
Camps

Places to eat:
1. Yang-Tse

Excursions

The ruins of the Demajagua sugar mill are in the hills outside Manzanillo. This is the place where, in 1868, Carlos Manuel de Céspedes cast the first stone in the First War of Independence by liberating his slaves. The **Parque Nacional de Demajagua** is 10 km south of Manzanillo. The mill was named after the bell formerly used to call the slaves to work, which then became the symbol of the call to revolution when he freed his slaves and set off to rebel against Spanish colonial rule. **Playa de los Coloradas** (see page 256) is only 80 km from Manzanillo and a reasonable excursion. The *Hotel Guacanayabo* will organize a bus trip there in high season, but only with a minimum of 30 people. They also run day trips to **Cayo Perla** for US$15 per person, or less for a large group, including food. There is a nice beach, but nothing else.

Local information
● **Accommodation**

Prices: **L1** over US$200; **L2** US$151-200;
L3 US$101-150; **A1** US$81-100; **A2** US$61-80;
A3 US$46-60; **B** US$31-45; **C** US$21-30;
D US$12-20; **E** US$7-11; **F** up to US$6

C *Guacanayabo* (Islazul), Av Camilo Cienfuegos, T 54012/5, 53590, F 4139, Visa/Mastercard, car hire, post office, 24-hour doctor, very helpful, change travellers' cheques, views of swimming pool from most rooms, full of noisy children during their holidays, very loud disco music all day and evening, staff unaccustomed to foreign tourists, hotel caters mostly for Cubans, to get to town centre, walk down steps to the right of the entrance, down the street with blocks of apartments to seafront and catch a horse and cart. The tourist bureau in the hotel has some day trips but if you go out of season they probably won't be running.

Private accommodation can easily be arranged in the town centre, just hang around Parque Céspedes until you are approached.

● **Places to eat**

All the restaurants charge in pesos; most of them are in and around Parque Céspedes, but avoid the cheaper establishments (the ones with just a concrete bar and plastic plates) as you run the risk of a stomach infection. The best restaurant is housed in a former Chinese place called *Yang Tse* on Parque Céspedes. Other restaurants have very basic menus, usually consisting of two or three dishes. To escape the heat, there is a nice coffee bar on the corner of Maceo and Merchan; to enjoy the heat, there is a snack bar with large terrace opposite the coffee bar. There are mini-*paladares* all along José Martí, selection not as good as in Santiago, but ice creams (1 peso) are nice.

● **Airlines**
Cubana is on Maceo 70 entre Merchan y Villuendas, T 2800.

● **Entertainment**
Casa de la Trova on the corner of Masó y Merchan. There is a folklore music show at the art gallery building on the south corner of Parque Céspedes on Thursdays at 2030.

● **Hospitals & medical services**
The *Hospital Celia Sánchez Manduley* is on Av Camilo Cienfuegos, 10 minutes' walk from the *Hotel Guacanayabo* (turn left outside the main entrance). Medical services for foreigners are free and you will be seen quickly, but take an interpreter if you don't have good Spanish. Prescriptions can be taken to the pharmacy in the hospital, where you pay in pesos (antibiotics and drops for an ear infection cost only 5 pesos). Doctor on call 24 hours at *Hotel Guacanayabo*, can treat minor ailments.

● **Shopping**
Two souvenir shops on Parque Céspedes, one of them has Che Guevara T-shirts for US$4, compared with US$15 in the hotel, also a small but interesting selection of books, mostly revolutionary history.

Manzanillo to Bayamo by train

First of all the price: it was almost embarrassing to hand over 1.25 pesos for a 2 hour journey, but there was no separate ticket office for tourists. You bought your tickets from a man slouched against the wall outside the station. It would be wise to buy them about an hour in advance in a small place like Manzanillo, to avoid the crowds rushing for tickets. Perhaps even more forward planning would be necessary further down the line (Manzanillo is the end of the line), although the train gradually filled up so that a third of passengers were standing. I took this to mean that there was no particular limit in numbers. You're supposed to sit in your numbered seat but nobody does. I was whisked off by the couple I'd been chatting to in the station, to take our seats together in an empty carriage. The views as the train leaves Manzanillo are of farms, which get larger and larger as you travel into the countryside, after which you only see well-cultivated farmland on a bigger scale, including banana, sugar cane and tobacco fields. My fellow passengers were eager to tell me about every farm, horse or cow that we passed on the way out of Manzanillo; I found everyone extremely friendly, and devoid of any phoney kind of '*amistad*' with tourists before stinging them for drinks, food etc. There was nothing to eat or drink (nor a toilet) on the train, but vendors sold things through the windows at most stations. Advisable to take a bottle of water for a longer journey, and be prepared for the train to stop in the middle of nowhere for no apparent reason.

Although my destination was the nearby Bayamo, my fellow passengers were headed all the way to Santiago on this train. However, when we reached Bayamo, an announcement said the train was broken, and the journey would be terminated there. My friends seemed to accept this without complaint, saying it happened all the time. They didn't even seem to be headed to the station to get a refund or anything. They were very proud people, preferring to bundle me onto a horse and cart to take me to my hotel than for me to see them organize their journey among the chaos. I gathered they were to get a bus or a truck, whatever was available, for the rest of their journey. According to them, and in my experience too, buses were more reliable for longer journeys, at least in Oriente.

Gavin Clark

● **Transport**
Local Plenty of 1950s American cars at the bus station, 10 pesos to the hotel. Horses and carts from the hotel to the centre, 1 peso.

Bus The bus station is at Km 2 on the Bayamo road. To Bayamo at 0600, 1500, US$2,50; also daily buses to Havana and Santiago de Cuba.

Train Station is 10 blocks east of Parque Céspedes on José Martí. To Bayamo 0900, 1345, 1700, 2 hours, 1.35 pesos (tourists do not have to pay in dollars); to Havana at 2100, Santiago 1410, Guantánamo 0505, Jiguaní 0905, 1735.

BAYAMO

Phone code 23

Bayamo is the capital of the province of Granma. It was the second town founded by Diego Velázquez in November 1513 and has been declared a *Ciudad Monumento Nacional*. However, it was burned to the ground by its own population in 1869 as an act of rebellion against the colonial Spanish; consequently the town has little to offer in the way of colonial architecture and is really rather uninteresting. Bayamo has a shabby, lacklustre atmosphere compared with other small towns in the Oriente. Hurried rebuilding after the big fire led to a hotchpotch of architectural styles, the centre having many low, box-like buildings reminiscent of provincial suburbs in Spain.

The people are sometimes indifferent to tourists; there are a few hustlers, but a complete lack of dollar facilities in the town centre. Every Saturday there is a *Noche Cubana*, when the whole of General García fills with stalls, ad hoc bars, pigs on spits, and the restaurants all put tables on the road. Everything is sold in pesos, even in the established bars along this street. If you need to stop over in Bayamo en route to the Sierra Maestra, you can at least drink as many daiquirís as you want at about 5 pesos each (US$0.25).

Places of interest
The **Iglesia de Santísimo Salvador** in the Plaza del Himno Nacional is a 16th century church which was badly damaged by

the 1869 fire, but is currently under restoration, open Tuesday-Friday 1500-1700. The local museum is the **Museo Provincial** on Maceo 58, T 4125, open Tuesday-Saturday 0800-1400, Sunday 0900-1300. Next door is the **Casa Natal de Carlos Manuel de Céspedes**, open Tuesday-Saturday 0900-1700, Sunday 0900-1200, a museum dedicated to the life of the main campaigner of the 1868 independence movement, who was born here.

Excursions
Carmen Prieto and Gladys Avalle, Public Relations Officers at the *Hotel Sierra Maestra*, are very helpful with information on all tours in this area, whether you take one of their organized ones or not. There is an organized trip (which you can equally well do on your own) to the **Parque Nacional Sierra Maestra**, taking you by truck to **Alto de Naranjo**, 20 km south of Bartolomé Masó, then a 3 km walk to the **Comandancia de la Plata**, Castro's mountain base prior to the revolution. The trip can be done in one day, or with an overnight stay in cabins with the usual tourist facilities. **Pico Turquino** (see page 253) can also be visited on this route. Other excursions include a morning's visit to the national monument **Dos Ríos** to the northeast of Bayamo, where José Martí was killed on 19 May 1895, a tour of a farming cooperative or a day trip to the **Botanical Gardens**.

Local information
● **Accommodation**
A3 *Sierra Maestra* (Islazul), Carretera Central via Santiago de Cuba, T 481013, 2 km from city centre, 204 rooms, delightful post-revolution 1960s building, thoroughly kitsch interior, avoid rooms overlooking noisy pool, plenty of nightlife, 3 bars, disco, mostly Cubans, helpful staff, car hire, credit cards accepted. Cheaper is *Villa Bayamo* (2-star) on the Carretera Manzanillo Km 5.5, T 423102/423124, 34 rooms, 1 km from city centre. Under construction in 1997 was the *Royalton* (Islazul), due to open by the end of the year, on Maceo y Joaquín Palma, very central location. *Hotel Central*, Av General García, is a basic, peso hotel, very central, next to *Restaurante 1513*.

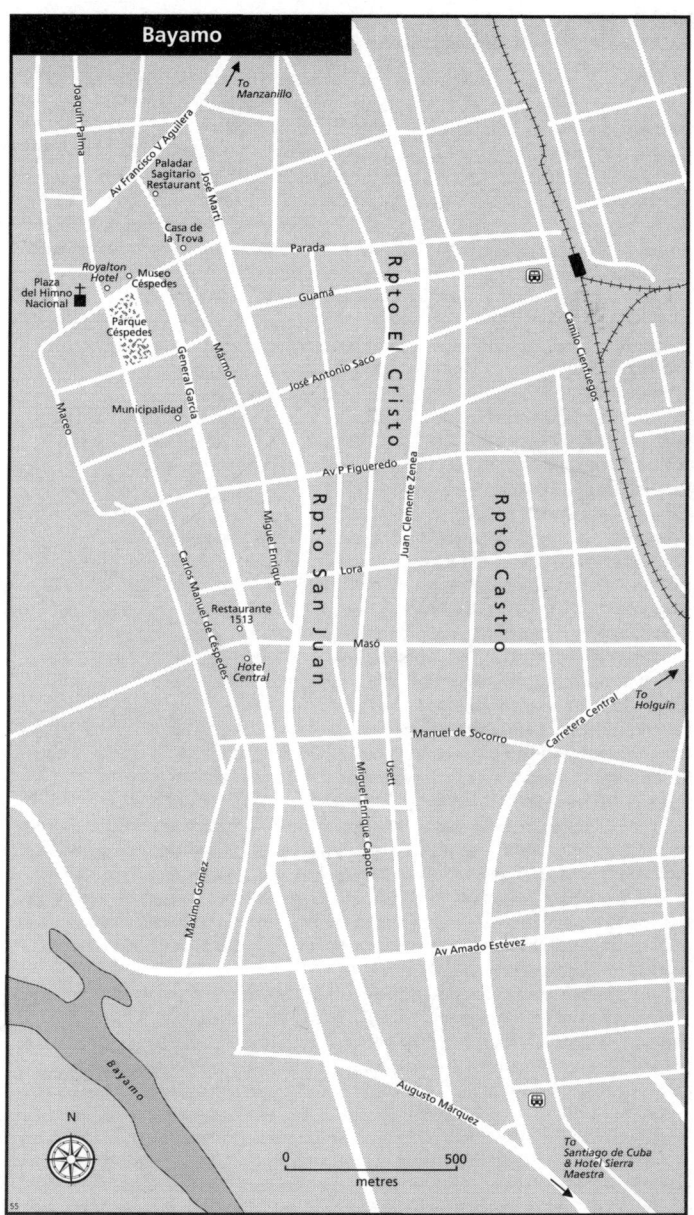

Bayamo

To Manzanillo

Joaquín Palma

Av Francisco V Aguilera

José Martí

Paladar Sagitario Restaurant

Casa de la Trova

Parada

Royalton Hotel

Museo Céspedes

Plaza del Himno Nacional

Parque Céspedes

Guamá

Rpto El Cristo

Camilo Cienfuegos

Maceo

General García

Mármol

Municipalidad

José Antonio Saco

Av P Figueredo

Juan Clemente Zenea

Rpto Castro

Carlos Manuel de Céspedes

Miguel Enrique

Rpto San Juan

Lora

Restaurante 1513

Masó

Hotel Central

Manuel de Socorro

Carretera Central

To Holguín

Máximo Gómez

Miguel Enrique Capote

Usett

Av Amado Estévez

Bayamo

Augusto Márquez

To Santiago de Cuba & Hotel Sierra Maestra

N

0   500
metres

Bayamo to Guantanamo by bus

🐾 My first and only grievance was that there was no transport immediately available from the *Hotel Sierra Maestra* to the bus station. When I saw the poorly-staffed reception, with a huge crowd of complaining guests around it, I knew I'd never get them to call me a taxi in time to catch my 0900 bus. I walked in the end, finding no form of transport on the way, the kilometre to the bus terminal. Bayamo has quite a busy terminal, and like anywhere else in Cuba, if you get there late and all the seats have been sold, they're hardly going to chuck some Cuban off the bus just because a dollar-wielding tourist wants to get on. So I'd recommend buying tickets for this journey (Bayamo-Guantánamo or Santiago) well in advance. I was fortunate enough to be offered assistance by a guy in the terminal in finding a truck going to Guantánamo (or to Santiago, where I could easily have got another one to Guantánamo). When eventually I was told by the ticket vendor that another bus to Guantánamo had appeared, not on the timetable at all, I had to go and find the helpful guy with the trucks to hand him a dollar: he hadn't expected it, his search for a truck had been a purely friendly gesture.

I was charged $12 for the journey to Guantánamo. The bus left at 1000. The first part of the view is of lots of tiny little nondescript towns (because of the basic concrete architecture, I got the impression that building work on these places was done mostly after the Revolution). The roads leaving Granma province are good, the journey smooth; as long as you sit right by an open window it shouldn't get too hot. The passengers on this bus were not as friendly as others I'd encountered. There was a bunch of rowdy guys who kept breaking into song in an aggressive way, they might have been Haitian or Dominican, their Spanish had a foreign lilt to it. One of them found an excuse to fiddle around with something under my seat from behind; luckily I'd placed my bag so there was no entry to it from that side. I kept the straps tied around my ankles for the rest of the journey.

From Jiguaní, about 25km from Bayamo, you begin to see the Sierra Maestra mountains in the distance, which last, with varying proximity, all the way to the outskirts of Santiago. The rest is of course well-tilled farmland, where during the afternoon, the sweating backs of farm labourers (you never see them lounging around on tea-breaks) made the heat inside the bus seem like nothing. Once the sun ceases to be directly above the bus, and starts to come into the windows, the journey gets increasingly uncomfortable; for this reason it is best to get your journeys started as early as possible.

The bus pulled in at Santiago to the exalted cries of people who had apparently been expecting it for some time, probably having missed another bus. These cries soon turned to groans when they were told they couldn't get straight on the bus, but had to go and queue up for tickets in the office. One guy simply couldn't stand it, and tried to fight his way past the resistant driver on to the bus. He was restrained, and the driver made an impassioned speech to the waiting hordes, who thanks to his skill as an orator, shuffled off obediently to the ticket office.

The road to Guantánamo was a bit more hilly than the one going west of Santiago, the scenery more rugged and picturesque. There were hardly any stops for food in this direction. There was something of the frontier or port town about Guantánamo: first of all the taxi driver refused to take a black guy on crutches as well as me, even though I said he should; he then picked up a friend of his to give him a free lift, while I paid a dollar. They were both cagey and suspicious at first, especially when I questioned the price, and it took an exaggerated display of smiling camaraderie to get them on my side. The driver claimed that the black guy he'd refused to take was a dodgy character who'd run off without paying him some other time.

Gavin Clark

● **Places to eat**
Restaurante 1513, General García esquina General Lora, T 425921, open 1200-2200, small but recommended by many Bayameros; *Bayamo*, in *Villa Bayamo* (see above), open 1900-2215, also *Bar Terraza*; *XXX Aniversario*, Carretera Central via Manzanillo, T 43182, open 1200-2100. Lots of *paladares* and bars along General García, all charge in pesos, best every Saturday night during *Noche Cubana*, some only open on Saturday; *Sagitario*, Marmol 107, across the street is *Bartería*, on Av Francisco V Aguilera, both recommended by locals.

● **Airlines**
Cubana at José Martí 58 entre Parada y Rojas, T 423916.

● **Banks & money changers**
Banco Nacional de Cuba, Saco y General García.

● **Cultural centres**
Casa de la Cultura José Fornaris, General García 15, T 422209; Casa de la Cultura Josué País, Heredia 204 entre San Félix y San Pedro, T 7804; Casa de la Cultura Miguel Matamoros, Lacret 653, T 5710. Galería Provincial, General García 174 esquina Luz Vázquez, T 423109; Galería de Arte, José Martí 224.

● **Entertainment**
Casa de la Trova on the corner of Maspote and José Martí has shows during the afternoon and every night, quite touristy in high season. **Cabaret Bayamo** opposite *Hotel Sierra Maestra*, on Carretera Central, T 421698, open 2100-0200.

● **Hospitals & medical services**
24-hour chemist at General García 53.

● **Post & telecommunications**
The **Post Office** is on Parque de la Revolución.

● **Shopping**
Cheap peso nick nacks in a few shops along General García.

● **Tour companies & travel agents**
Islazul office on General García 207, open 0830-1700, also tourist information in *Hotel Sierra Maestra* and occasionally maps, but it is difficult to get information about day trips as they do not cater for many foreign visitors.

● **Transport**
Local Horse and cart, 7 pesos from bus station to *Hotel Sierra Maestra*. **Car hire**: the **Havanautos** office is in Cupet Cimex gas station next to the bus station, T 423223.

Air Carlos Manuel de Céspedes airport is 4 km out of town; flight to Havana 3 times a week.

Bus The terminal is on the corner of Carretera Central and Jesús Rabi, T 424036. Bus to Santiago 0900, US$10; to Guantánamo US$12, sometimes there is a direct bus, otherwise change at Santiago or get a truck from there. If you miss a bus or it is full, another may turn up unannounced, or ask around the terminal for a shared truck or car to Santiago, lots of them going.

Train Station is at Saco y Línea. Daily trains to Santiago and Havana; four daily to Manzanillo.

Province of Guantánamo

G UANTANAMO is the most easterly and most mountainous province on the island. The range of the Montañas de Nipe-Sagua-Baracoa runs through the province, ending in the Atlantic Ocean on the northern coast and the Caribbean Sea to the south. The area is notable for its fauna and flora, with many endemic species, and also for the US naval base housing the rare species of US 'imperialists' in Cuba. Guantánamo, the provincial capital has one major difference from other Cuban colonial towns. The large influx of Haitian, French and Jamaican immigrants in the 19th century means that the architecture has much less of a Spanish colonial feel; the narrow, brightly coloured buildings with thin wooden balconies and wrought ironwork are more reminiscent of New Orleans than Madrid.

Province of Guantánamo

Guantánamo province is bounded by Holguín and the Atlantic Ocean to the north, the Caribbean Sea to the south and Santiago de Cuba to the west. The most eastern point of Cuba, Punta de Maisí, is only 80 km from Haiti across the Windward Passage, and on a clear night you can see the lights of the neighbouring island from the lighthouse here. The Nipe-Sagua-Baracoa mountains rise from both coastlines but divide the province in its climate and landscape. The northern coast, around Baracoa, faces the prevailing winds and is the wettest region in the country, while the southern coast, around Guantánamo, is sheltered, dry and the hottest part of the country. The north is green, lush and tropical, while the south is arid and cacti happily grow here.

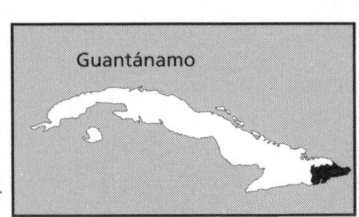

Guantánamo

Area 6,178 sq km, *Population* 507,300, *Density* 82 per sq km, *Urban* 59.4%

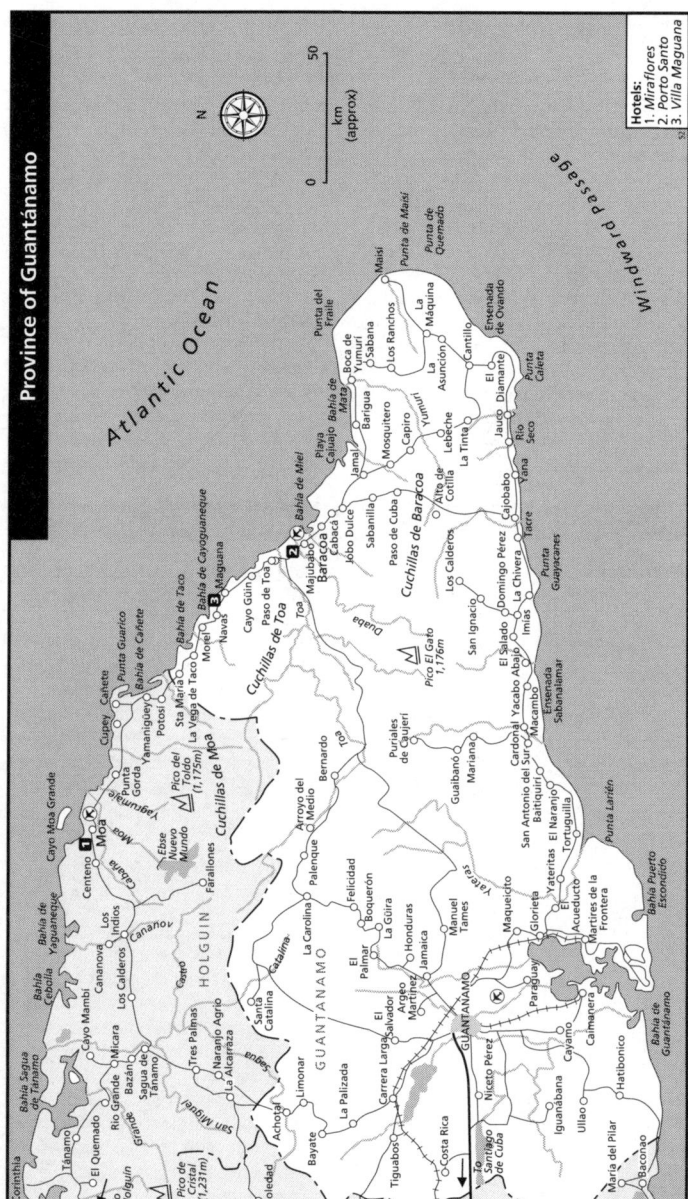

Province of Guantánamo

Hotels:
1. *Miraflores*
2. *Porto Santo*
3. *Villa Maguana*

N

0   50

km
(approx)

Atlantic Ocean

Windward passage

GUANTANAMO

Population 205,000; *phone code* 21

80 km from Santiago on the Baracoa road, Guantánamo is the capital of the province of the same name. It is close to the US naval base of Guantánamo (which cannot be easily visited from Cuba), which was established at the beginning of the 20th century in the area known as Caimanera. The base is so little a part of the town that you will not, except in conversation, come across it unless you make a specific trip to Mirador de Malones to view it through binoculars.

The town of Guantánamo was founded in 1819 and was called Santa Catalina del Saltadero del Guaso until 1843. It lies north of the Bahía de Guantánamo, between the Jaibo, Bano and Guaso rivers which flow into the bay. Guantánamo is a pleasant, fairly well-restored colonial town. It has its own *Tumba Francesa*, a colourful folk dance tradition originating in Haiti, based in the centre of the town.

A number of streets have had their names changed, but locals often do not even know the official title. Avenida de los Estudiantes is known as Paseo, while Bartolomé Masó is known as Carretera.

Places of interest

The central square is the **Plaza Martí**, with a church in the centre. The Post Office and the **Casa de la Cultura** are on the west side and the *Tumba Francesa* on the east. 2 km north, the **Plaza de la Revolución** has a modernist carved stone monument to the

Music in Guantánamo

The name of Guantánamo is known the world over, thanks to the son 'Guajira Guantanamera' which is the climax of the show for all but the most principled groups. (the way to look cool and Cuban is to cry "AE SALA", after the first 'Guantanamera' and "SONGOLOQUESONGO" after the second). The words to the verses are noble and mournful, based as they are on the poetry of José Martí. 'Guajira' is a rural style of son and is similar to the simple, improvising 'Nengón' which developed in the mountains surrounding Guantánamo. The Valera Miranda family, still living in the hills, have kept this style alive. In Guantánamo itself, Nengón became the 'Son Changüí' which, with its African thumb bass (Marímbula) and old style bongos has stayed true to the roots of the original son. Changüí is tremendously complex, with backbeats, cross rhythms and constant bongo improvisation but for many it is the most beautiful form of son. Catch it at the Casa de la Trova. Local grandad made good Elio Revé Matos (1930-1997), created a new changüí which brought him national fame (and a contract with Peter Gabriel) during the 1970s and 1980s. His background, like many Guantanamerans, is in the coffee plantations established in the Sierra by French landowners following the Haitian revolution in 1791. The Tumba Francesa de Santa Catalina was created during the 1890s by newly freed blacks in order to preserve the rich cultural heritage that had been developed on the plantations. One of only three such organizations still surviving (the other two being in Santiago and Sagua de Tánamo), the Tumba Francesa in Guantánamo still fulfils its original purpose. To the urgent rhythms of the great *Premier* drums and the wooden *Catá* (both of which have their origins in the Dahomeyan region of Africa), the elderly patrons recreate the dances of their great-great-grandparents. The singer (or *Composé*) organizes the dance, calling the musicians to order and setting in train the ancient movements of the *Mason, Yuba* or *Frente*. Queen of Composé was Tecla Benet Danger, the only woman Catá player in Cuba who died recently, having sung and played until the age of 91.

Guantánamo

To Autopista Nacional

3 **2**

Plaza de la Revolución

Space Capsule Museum

Bano

N

To Baracoa

2 de Octubre

Ahogados

José Martí

General Pedro A Pérez

Narciso López

Paseo (Av de los Estudiantes)

Cinema

Prado

Museo Municipal

Cubana

Aguilera

Los Maceos

Flor Crombet

Casa de Cultura

Plaza Martí

Tumba Francesa

1

Carretera (Bartolomé Masó)

Calixto García

Camilo Cienfuegos

Guaso

To bus station

Jaibo

To Caimanera

0		800

metres

Hotels:
1. *Brasil*
2. *Guantánamo*

Places to eat:
3. *Caribe*

heroes of all the wars of independence. The **Museo Municipal**, housing artefacts from the history of Guantánamo is in a former prison on José Martí, open Tuesday-Saturday 0800-1800, Sunday 0800-1200. There is also a small museum near the Plaza de la Revolución which contains the space capsule in which the first Cuban went into space.

Excursions

There is a day tour of Guantánamo city, *La Tumba Francesa*, Zoológico de Piedra and Changüí (a traditional form of music played on a farm a short distance from the city while visitors have a good lunch, join in the dance and meet the musicians). The **Zoológico de Piedra** is an outdoor museum of carved stone animals, set in a

Guantánamo to Baracoa by tour bus

First we were taken to the Zoológico de Piedra, then for lunch at the Finca Changüí (see **Excursions**, page 267); after that the real journey to Baracoa began, with no more signs of civilization except for the US naval base, quite far below the road (you need an organized tour with good binoculars to see anything of interest). The road winds through the mountains, with many minor holes, causing the driver to dodge around them sometimes. Arid but plentiful vegetation lines the road, the sea is visible for the early stages of the journey, with splendid views of the glimmering Caribbean Sea on the right. The bus stopped at a low altitude for everyone to stretch their legs. Only a hundred yards below the road was a beach which, with a bit of a scrabble down the hill, could be reached for a last dip in the sea before it became the Atlantic. The road rose more steeply after that, snaking its way through more lush, but not yet tropical, mountain greenery. We stopped once more at a point from where both the Caribbean and the Atlantic could be viewed.

We turned off at Cajobabo for the inland road to Baracoa. Winding through the mountains, the scenery getting greener and more jungly, the last 25km or so is a stretch of road known as 'La Farola'; here all conversation in the bus stops and everyone just gawps out of the window, at this wet, lush, bright green mini-Amazon jungle. The bends and swoops in the road make it even more spectacular, as you get to see it from various different angles.

If you are staying at the *Hotel Castillo*, or even if you aren't, the best place for a first view of the town of Baracoa is from the entrance, perched on top of a cliff right in the town, from where you can see across the rooftops into the bay, as well as the tropical scenery in the mountains behind the town.

Gavin Clark

beautiful hillside location with tropical vegetation. Many are bizarre, from tiny stone lizards to huge bison. All are carved directly from the rocks in their natural setting and you can buy miniature replicas from the sculptor on the way out. The tour is organized by Havanatur, US$22, with an excellent guide in an a/c minibus, daily during high season, Tuesday and Saturday in low season, 0900 outside *Hotel Guantánamo*. There is also a trip with the same sights going on to Baracoa on the same day, US$40.

Local information
● **Accommodation**
C *Guantánamo* (Islazul), Ahogados, esquina 13 Norte, Plaza Mariana Grajales, Reparto Caribe, T 381015, F 382406, 15 minutes' walk from the centre, 3-star, 112 rooms, 12 cabins, pool, 2 bars, food average, clean, a/c, 2 bars and busy restaurant, food average, disco, mostly Cuban clientèle, telephone service to Havana

and beyond; C *La Lupe* (Islazul), Carretera del Salvador Km 2, T 326168/326180, 2-star but much nicer than *Guantánamo*, a bit far out of town, nice pool, peaceful atmosphere, 50 rooms, mostly cabins, sports area, a/c, restaurant, bar; C *Casa de Los Ensueños*, Ahogados esquina 15 Norte, Reparto Caribe, T 326304, 3 rooms, a/c, TV, bar, 24-hour room service. G *Brasil*, Calixto García, in town centre, the only peso hotel which accepts foreigners.

● **Places to eat**
Restaurante Caribe, on top of a tower block near *Hotel Guantánamo*, local food, pay in pesos. Plenty of *paladares*, most of whom charge in pesos although they will, of course, accept dollars. Price should be about 45 pesos per person, but some raise it for tourists. Two *paladares* on Av de los Estudiantes (Paseo) and a number of street stalls selling pork sandwiches for 5 pesos, some are there every day, all of them at weekends. Other *paladares* off Plaza Martí in the centre.

● **Airlines**
Cubana is at Calixto García 817 entre Prado y Aguilera, T 34533.

● **Banks & money changers**
Banco de Crédito at Calixto García esquina Carretera, changes travellers' cheques into dollars.

● **Cultural centres**
Casa de la Cultura on General Pérez, southwest corner of Plaza Martí, exhibitions of photography and painting, usually organized by UNEAC, whose office is on José Martí near Plaza Martí.

● **Entertainment**
Cinema: on Av de los Estudiantes, on the corner of the road to *Hotel Guantánamo*.

● **Post & telecommunications**
The **Post Office** is on Plaza Martí.

● **Shopping**
A couple of good peso bookshops, one just off Plaza Martí on Calixto García, much better stocked than those in Havana or Santiago. The demand is not so high here for literature, so several classics have been sitting on the shelves for years. *Tumba Francesa* (see **Excursions**, page 267) sells good quality Haitian-style handicrafts and souvenirs; the shop is right on Plaza Martí, opposite the church.

● **Tour companies & travel agents**
Peter Hope, Public Relations Officer at the *Hotel Guantánamo*, is the fount of all tourist information in the area and runs all the guided tours for foreigners. He works for Islazul but represents Havanatur as well. He can arrange tours to Mt Malones, where you can view the US base through Soviet binoculars, US$6. He speaks English, German and French and is based in room 117, *Hotel Guantánamo*, Monday-Saturday. Islazul office is on Los Maceos entre Narciso López y Paseo.

● **Transport**
Local Car hire: Havanautos office is at Cupet Cimex gas station at the beginning of the Baracoa road.

Air Aeropuerto Mariana Grajales (GAO) is 16 km from Guantánamo, off the Baracoa road. Daily (except Saturday) scheduled flight at 0600 from Havana, returning 0915, plus a Saturday flight at 1635.

Bus The bus terminal, T 326016, is 5 km from the centre. Private cars and taxis run from the train and bus station to *Hotel Guantánamo*/town centre, US$1. Daily bus to Havana, 4 buses to Santiago, 1 bus to Baracoa.

Train The station is in the centre on Calixto García. Daily trains to Santiago, Havana and Holguín.

BARACOA

150 km east of Santiago, close to the most easterly point of the island, Baracoa is an attractive place surrounded by rich, tropical vegetation and the perfect place to come and spend a few relaxing days on the beach. It was the first town founded in 1512 by Diego Velázquez, with the name Nuestra Señora de la Asunción de Baracoa, and for three years it was the capital of Cuba. Up until the 1960s it was really only accessible by sea until the viaduct, **La Farola** was built. This is one of the most spectacular roads, 30 km long, joined to the mountain on one side and supported by columns on the other. It is well worth the trip from Santiago (4 hours' drive) for the scenery of this section of road, which winds through lush tropical mountains and then descends steeply to the coast. Look out for people selling *Cucurucho*, a delicious mixture of coconut, fruit and sugar served in a cone of palm leaves and costing about 3 pesos.

Baracoa is a charming town, noted for its friendly inhabitants. The name Baracoa is an Indian word meaning 'existence of the sea'. It is a UNESCO biosphere, with more than ten rivers, including the **Río Toa**, 120 km long and the widest river in Cuba. Another river, the **Río de Miel**, carries the legend that if you swim in it you will come back to Baracoa one day. There are many beautiful waterfalls, 120 different types of tree and lots of coconuts. 80% of Cuba's coconut production comes from here. It is the wettest region in Cuba with annual rainfall of 2m in the coastal zone to 3.6m in the middle and upper Toa Valley. White water rafting is possible down the Río Toa, with different levels of difficulty.

Christopher Columbus arrived in Baracoa on 27 November 1492. He planted a cross, now housed in the church, and described a mountain in the

Baracoa

Atlantic Ocean

Malecón

Máximo Gómez

10 de Octubre

Flor Crombet

Paladar La Colonial

Frank País

Cira Frías

Casa de la Trova

Félix Ruenes

Cubana Airlines

Céspedes

Coroneles Galana

José Martí

Rodney Coutin

Reyes

To Museo

To Bus terminal & La Punta

Mariqui

José Martí

Plaza Independencia

Antonio Maceo

Antonio Maceo

Fondo de Bienes Culturales

Paladar El Moro

Rupert López

Calixto García

Robert

L Sánchez

Abel Díaz

Moncada

7 de Abril

Paraíso

N

To Airport, Moa & Hotel Porto Santo

Pier

0   200
metres

Hotels:
1. *El Castillo*
2. *La Rusa*
3. *Plaza*

shape of an anvil (*yunque*) which was thereafter used as a point of reference for sailors. The first maps of Cuba drawn by an Englishman showed the **Yunque de Baracoa** mountain, copies of which can be seen in the museum. Baracoa is full of references to Columbus' stay here. *Porto Santo* marks the place where he was married in 1511, the same year that the capital of Cuba was moved from Baracoa to Santiago de Cuba by Diego Velázquez. Between 1639 and 1742, Baracoa's three forts were built. The oldest, **El Castillo**, also known as Seboruco of Sanguily, now the *Hotel Castillo*, was destroyed in 1652 by the French. The others were **Fuerte de la Punta**, now restaurant *La Punta*, and **Fuerte Matachín**, now the municipal museum. Baracoa became a refuge for French exiles after the revolution in Haiti, and they brought with them coffee and cacao farming techniques as well as their own style of architecture, which contributed greatly to the buildings we can see now; like Guantánamo,

they have much less of a Spanish colonial style than other towns in Cuba. The French also created the first drinking water plant. In 1856, Céspedes spent five months in isolation in Baracoa as a punishment. The war of independence of 1895 saw many revolutionaries disembarking at Baracoa.

Baracoa has 56 archaeological sites, with many traces of the three Indian groups who lived there: the Siboney, the Taino and the Guanturabey. There is one surviving community of 300 Indians, called the **Yateras**, dating back to the Spaniards' arrival. They are integrated with the rest of society but only marry among themselves and maintain their traditions. They live in an isolated region along the shores of the Río Toa, but a visit can be organized through Alejandro Hartmann in the Museo Municipal, minimum six people.

Places of interest

The **Iglesia de la Asunción** was built in 1512, burnt down by the French in 1652 and rebuilt in 1805. The church contains the cross, known as the **Cruz de la Parra**, said to have been planted there by Columbus. Catholics and restorers have carved off slices over the years, with the result that the cross has diminished to almost half its former size. Belgian historians confirmed in 1989 that the cross did indeed date from Columbus' time. The best time to be sure of finding the church open is during Mass on Sunday. **Museo Municipal**, in the Matachín fort at the end of the Malecón to the east of the town (turn right as you come in from La Farola), is a small museum with interesting but rather antiquated displays on the history of the town from prehistoric times to memorabilia of La Rusa (see box, page 272) who died in 1978. There is a large cauldron for making sugar and the only armaments magazine of its type in Cuba dating from 1739. In 1838 the Queen of Spain presented Baracoa with its own coat of arms, now on display in the museum. The English-speaking conservation officer, Daniel Salomon Paján, is happy to give further information on local history and legends. Open daily 0800-1800, US$1.

The **Parque Central**, or **Parque Independencia**, is halfway down Antonio Maceo. It has many peso stalls selling good snacks and sandwiches at lunchtime and evening; there is also a Rumbos dollar drinks kiosk. All the young people hang out here every night, it is great for people watching but you will get pestered a lot by harmless hustlers with rooms to rent, pesos to exchange etc, unless you are with Cubans, in which case you'll be left alone. It is the hub of activity every Saturday, when Antonio Maceo fills up with stalls selling food and drink and the whole town comes out to dance to street musicians and have a party, or *noche Cubana*.

Excursions

All organized excursions are best arranged through Wilder Laffita, a very efficient Public Relations Officer at the *Hotel Porto Santo*, T 43590, who works for Gaviota and is also the guide for all local ecotourism walks. A city tour, minimum 6 people, will cost US$8 per person. A day trip with lunch to **Playa Maguana**, a beautiful white sand beach 22 km from Baracoa is US$28. Alternatively hire a private car for about US$10, 1 hour on an unpaved road. There are many families living near the beach who will cook lunch for you; the best is Ramona, but ask around. There is also bungalow accommodation, **C** *Villa Maguana*, with only four double rooms and a restaurant, run by Islazul.

The **Río Yumurí** (US$28 with lunch) is 30 km east of Baracoa. This is the most spectacular of Baracoa's rivers, running through two deep canyons. The organized trip includes a visit to a farm where they cultivate cacao. Fishing trips can also be arranged in the village of Yumurí. If you don't want to take the tour, rent a private car (US$10) or take a *colectivo* taxi or truck to the Río Yumurí where the road ends. A canoe will ferry you across or you can hire one to take you upriver for US$1. You can continue walking upriver and swim, very quiet and peaceful. You can take a trip to the top of **El Yunque**, 575m above sea level, to view the breathtaking scenery and panorama of banana and coconut palms, or take a long walk up the **Río Toa** through the UNESCO biosphere forest, followed by a 45-minute return boat journey along Cuba's widest river. **Terrazas de Yara** are caves featuring ancient cave drawings, which you can visit only on an organized tour. **Playa Duaba** is a point 6 km from Baracoa where the river meets the sea; you can swim in both and eat at *Finca Duaba*, where the food is good but the service not fantastic. You can hire horses here. Historically, Duaba is notable for being the place where General Antonio Maceo landed on 1 April 1895 to start the second War of Independence.

Local information
● Accommodation

Prices: **L1** over US$200; **L2** US$151-200;
L3 US$101-150; **A1** US$81-100; **A2** US$61-80;
A3 US$46-60; **B** US$31-45; **C** US$21-30;
D US$12-20; **E** US$7-11; **F** up to US$6

B *El Castillo*, Calixto García, Loma del Paraíso, T 214-2103/2115, 35 a/c rooms with bath, phone, TV in lobby lounge, recommended, friendly staff, food OK, excellent views, very good breakfast; **A1-B** *Porto Santo*, T 214-3578/3590, 36 rooms, 24 *cabañas* or suites, a/c, bath, restaurant, bar, shop, beautiful swimming pool, car hire, next to airport, beach, peaceful atmosphere, friendly, highly recommended, speak to Wilder Laffita, Public Relations Officer, to organize excursions (see above); **C-D** *La Rusa* (Islazul), a bright yellow building on the Malecón, Máximo Gómez 13, T 4-3011/4-3570, e-mail islazul@gtmo.cu, named after the Russian lady, Magdalena Menasse (see box below), who used to run the hotel and whose photos adorn the walls, famous guests have included Fidel Castro, accommodation now basic, food average, nice location, good *paladar* opposite.

Private accommodation easily arranged, ask in Parque Central in front of church or contact **Rafael**, at Félix Ruenes 29, T 43441; *Ranchos*, on Mariana Grajales, T 43361, a *paladar* with 2 rooms to let, soon they'll be letting the whole house; **Ikira Mahíquez Machado**, Maceo 168-A entre Céspedes y Ciro Frías, T 42466, 2 rooms, also a separate part of the house with kitchen and garage, nice building, recommended.

● Places to eat
The isolation of Baracoa has led to an individual local cuisine, mostly featuring coconut milk and fish. Don't miss the *cucurucho*, see above. Lots of *paladares*, many of which are well-established, most offer pork, chicken, fish, turtle, some offer lobster, all of a high standard. One of the best is *Walter's*, on Rubén López 47, T 4-3380, US$5-7 for a good dinner; *La Colonial*, José Martí 123, T 43161, excellent subdued candlelit atmosphere, extensive menu, highly recommended; *Ranchos*,

Myths and legends of Baracoa

Economic growth picked up in Baracoa at the beginning of the 20th century with bananas. A railway was built to transport them and trade in bananas was established with the USA. However, two diseases endemic to bananas wiped out the industry in 1945. Superstitious blame was placed on a mysterious man called 'El Pelú', who had arrived in Baracoa in 1897. Children had laughed at his strange appearance and, offended, he had placed a curse on the village. No one took any notice of it until the banana crisis of 1945. Even today, people still refer to the 'curse of El Pelú', and in Baracoa El Pelú is generally held to bring bad luck.

In the 1930s 'La Rusa' arrived in Baracoa. Magdalena Rovieskuya was the daughter of a general in the Russian aristocracy, who had left Russia in 1917 to travel the world. She came to Baracoa, built a hotel (still called *La Rusa*) on the Malecón and became very popular with the local people, who affectionately called her 'Mimá'. In the 1950s she was on the point of leaving but decided to stay and give her full support to the Revolution. She helped the Red Cross and supplied funds for the rebels to buy arms. Fidel and Che stayed in her hotel during the clandestine struggle. She died in 1978, on her deathbed donating a diamond bracelet to the Festival Mundial de Los Estudiantes.

There are many species of flora and fauna endemic to the Baracoa area and it is famous for its multicoloured snails, called *polimitas*. Legend has it that they came to Baracoa to find peace and took their bright colours from the sun, earth, sea and sky. They are sometimes sold around Boca de Yumurí, but they are now rather rare.

A local story explains the origin and size of the Río Toa, the widest river in Cuba. It is believed that there was an Indian tradition to banish naughty children to the mountains to learn good behaviour. Once there, the grief-stricken children cried so much that their torrent of tears formed a river.

Mariana Grajales 30, T 43361, nice patio, also rooms to rent, see above; *El Moro*, Antonio Maceo 110, open very late, good atmosphere, sometimes live music. The fort at La Punta, which juts out into the bay west of the town, has been converted to a pleasant, breezy, open air restaurant, *La Guama*, although everyone refers to it as La Punta, nice setting, creole food, recommended, main courses (described on the menu as 'mean' plates) US$3-5.50.

● **Bars**
El Patio, in the Fondo de Bienes Culturales (see below), snack bar run by Rumbos open all day until 2300, also beer; Rumbos also has a 24-hour kiosk in the Parque Central; *La Punta* has a 24-hour bar; the bar in *Hotel El Castillo* is open until 0100; you can get a beer in *Paladar El Moro* until about 0200.

● **Airlines**
Cubana is on José Martí 181, T 42171.

● **Banks & money changers**
Banco Nacional de Cuba is on Maceo but will change only travellers' cheques, you can not get cash advance on credit cards. *Porto Santo* and *El Castillo* hotels both change travellers' cheques.

● **Cultural centres**
Fondo de Bienes Culturales on Maceo 120, T 43627. As well as a tasteful souvenir shop full of local artists' work, wooden carvings, paintings etc, information about local artists. Baracoa has its own school of *artesanía*, where artists train in traditional methods using wood and coconut shell, producing the work on sale in the shop. The very friendly and helpful English-speaking Alberto Matos Llime is worth talking to if you have any questions about local history and culture.

● **Entertainment**
Casa de la Trova, José Martí 149, traditional music, Tuesday-Sunday from 2100, US$1, good son and friendly atmosphere. **Casa de la Cultura**, Maceo 122, has live music in its patio. There is a nightly show of Afro-Cuban music by Yambú Akalé at *Restaurante La Punta*, which is highly recommended, US$4, very interesting to

see all the costumes and instruments. **Dancing Light** on Maceo just before Parque Central, disco for young Cubans although tourists will not feel out of place, drinks in dollars for tourists, quite a small place but lively, check out break-dancing show nightly by local youths. There is also nightly dancing and live music at *Porto Santo* and *El Castillo*, the former is livelier. **Cineteatro El Encanto**, Maceo, next to Parque Central, for movies and cultural events.

● **Hospitals & medical services**
Hospital Octavio de la Concepción y de la Pedraja, on Carretera Guantánamo. Policlínica in the small barrio next to *Hotel Porto Santo*, where you pay in pesos, there is also a dentist here. Clínica Dental in Barrio de la Punta, near the fort. 24-hour pharmacy on Maceo 132.

● **Post & telecommunications**
Post Office: on Maceo 136, open 0800-2000. Phone boxes next to it.

● **Shopping**
Bookshop on José Martí 195. Handicrafts at Fondo de Bienes Culturales (see above).

● **Transport**
Local The best way to get around Baracoa is by *bicitaxi*; most of them wait on Maceo outside the Fondo de Bienes Culturales, they charge 1 peso to go anywhere in town and US$1 from the centre to *Hotel Porto Santo*/airport. Getting from *Porto Santo* into town is difficult as there are no *bicitaxis* or taxis outside the hotel, unless you get reception to call you a cab; walk down to the barrio at the bottom of the hill and wait around on the bridge for a *bicitaxi*. **Car hire**: at the Servi Cupet station, Guantánamo road Km 4.

Air Airport 100m from *Hotel Porto Santo*. Cubana flight to Havana Tuesday, Friday 1045, to Santiago Sunday, 1200, US$18. All times subject to frequent change.

Bus Main bus terminal at the end of Martí near Av de los Mártires, T 4-2239, 4-3670, for buses to Havana, Santiago (1350, 6 hours, US$9, get there an hour in advance, the day before in busy periods), Camagüey, Guantánamo. Trucks to Guantánamo, Moa and other destinations from 2nd bus terminal on Coroneles Galana.

The Islands
Isla de la Juventud

THERE ARE three good reasons for visiting the Isla de la Juventud: diving, birdwatching and checking out Cuban provincial life away from tourist resorts. With its history as a prison island, there has been very little development, and what there is has been concentrated around Nueva Gerona and the port area. The Isla is a good place to go for a weekend out of Havana, although if you plan to see the whole island you will need more than one weekend.

The Isla was always an enclave, whether populated by pirates post-Columbus, or by US businessmen and communities of Japanese farmers in the first quarter of the 20th century. In recent decades its population has been swelled by tens of thousands of Cuban and Third World students, giving rise to the modern name of **Isle of Youth**. Early aboriginal inhabitants called it **Camaraco**, **Ahao** or **Siguanea**. The abundant pine and later casuarina (Australian pine) trees gave

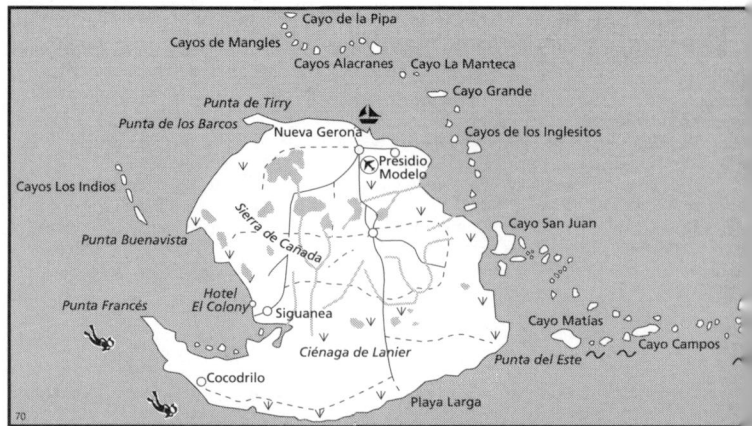

Isla de la Juventud and Archipiélago de los Canarreos

In the Gulf of Batabanó is the **Isla de la Juventud** (Isle of Youth), 97 km from the main island, It is the second largest island in the Cuban archipelago, measuring 54 km from north to south and 58 km from east to west. Its 2,205 sq km area makes it bigger than countries like Grenada, Dominica, Guadeloupe, St Lucia or Martinique, though its population is much smaller. The Isla is the centre of administration for the 2,398 sq km 'Special Municipality', which includes Cayo Largo and the other islets of the **Archipiélago de los Canarreos**. Much of the island is flat, with a large area taken up with swamp in the Ciénaga de Lanier in the southern half of the island. The northern half is more hospitable and here there are marble hills near the capital, **Nueva Gerona**, and the slate hills of Sierra del Cañada in the west. The area around the Presidio is particularly beautiful, with its low green hills and citrus plantations. Mangroves line much of the coast, a haven for wildlife and migrating birds. After the Revolution youth brigades were mobilized to plant citrus, and now the major economic activities are citrus cultivation and processing (in conjunction with Chilean capital), marble quarrying (mainly for tourism and export), fishing and tourism. A Canadian/Cuban joint venture plans a 1998 start-up at the Delita mine which has estimated deposits of 1.75 million ounces of gold and close to 14 million ounces of silver.

The south coast's white sand beaches are currently inaccessible but are zoned for tourism development in partnership with a Canadian company, though not in the short term. There is so far no infrastructure and the area can be visited only with official permission, but roads are virtually non-existent. West coast beaches have black sand.

Isla de la Juventad

Area 2,398 sq km, *Population* 77,300, *Density* 33.2 per sq km, *Urban* 87.2%

Isla de la Juventud and Archipiélago de Los Canarreos

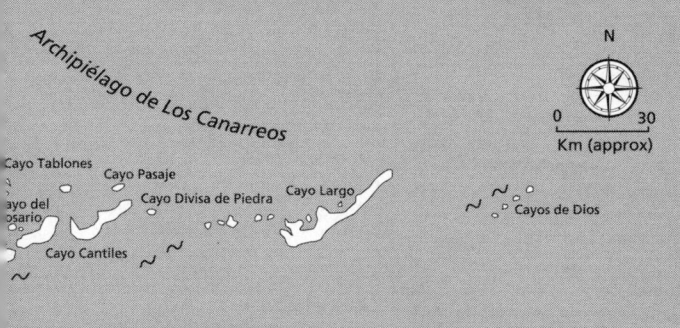

Isla de la Juventud's wild and marine life

Fauna and flora

There are many endemic birds on the Isla de la Juventud and also many migrating water fowl, particularly in the Ciénaga de Lanier, the second largest swamp in the Cuban archipelago, where you can also find crocodiles. There are few facilities for birdwatchers and roads are very poor in the south, but on the other hand keen twitchers and birds alike find it remarkably unspoilt.

Diving and marine life

Underwater there are even more attractions, with some of the best scuba diving in the whole country (see **Diving and marine life**, page 24). **The Centro Internacional de Buceo (International Scuba Diving Centre) El Colony** has excellent facilities and there is a recompression chamber. Courses are offered, but they are only valid in Cuba. For US$56 you get a bus to the marina, dive at 0930, lunch at the restaurant, do a second dive and then back to the hotel at 1630. Equipment costs extra.

The area around Punta Francés in the west is probably the best, with caves, tunnels and all manner of sea creatures including turtles, which are protected. There are over 40 different corals and innumerable fish. The area is a marine reserve and you may only dive with an official operator, not on your own. You may not fish around here, but the marina can arrange for a fishing trip round to the south of the island if you wish.

The Marina El Colony has mooring for 15 boats, a liveaboard with a capacity for 8 divers and other facilities. Accommodation on dry land is at the *Hotel El Colony*. Other watersports are also available at the *Hotel El Colony*, such as catamarans, US$10/hour, a 2-person kayak, US$6/hour and a single kayak, US$4/hour.

rise to the name **Isla de Pinos** (Isle of Pines) by which it was known officially before the revolutionary authorities re-named it, and local inhabitants (and their baseball team) are still called *pineros* by other Cubans. It earned its place in world literature as the supposed model for Robert Louis Stevenson's *Treasure Island*. Yet another, unofficial, name, **La Isla de las Cotorras** (Island of the Parrots) is a reminder of just one of the feathered species which inhabit the island's pinewoods, though the Ciénaga de Lanier marshland extending east-west across the island is the chief magnet for ornithologists. Columbus named the island **San Juan Evangelista** (St John the Evangelist) when he arrived in June 1494. In the 16th and 17th centuries its use as a base by French and British pirates (including Welshman Henry Morgan who later gained respectability as governor of Jamaica) earned it another name, the **Isla de Piratas** (Isle of Pirates). Place names like Estero de los Corsarios date from that era, as does Punta Francés, the lair of the French pirate Leclerc. Francis Drake also fought the Spaniards in the surrounding seas, and wrecked galleons from this era add interest to modern-day diving. The biggest draw, however, is the superb coral reef, acclaimed by Jacques Cousteau and others. Spain colonised the island in the 19th century, naming it **Colonia Reina Amalia**, but from the 19th century until the Revolution its main function was as a prison and both José Martí and Fidel Castro served time there.

Isla de la Juventud

Cayo de la Pipa
Cayos de Mangles
Cayos Alacranes
Cayo La Manteca
Cayo Grande

N

0   30
Km (approx)

Punta de Tirry
Punta de los Barcos
NUEVO GERONA
Playa Bibijagua
Cayos de los Inglesitos

Cayos Los Indios
La Demajagua
El Abra
Presidio Modelo

Mina de Oro
La Fé
Cayo San Juan

Punta Buenavista
La Victoria
Julio Antonio Mella
La Reforma

Sierra de Cañada

Punta Francés
Hotel El Colony
Argelia Libre
Siguánea

Cayo Piedra
Cayo Matías

Ciénaga de Lanier
Punta del Este
Cayo Campos

Cocodrilo

Playa Larga

70a

NUEVA GERONA

Phone code 61

The capital, **Nueva Gerona**, dates from the 19th century and remains the only substantial settlement. Surrounded by small rounded hills, it is a pleasantly laid-back country town with a slow pace and shoe shiners. There has recently been a proliferation of private tourist-related businesses, but apart from at the ferry terminal, you will not be harassed. As most development has taken place post-1959 (the island's entire population was just 10,000 in 1959), there are few historically interesting buildings. The town centre is set out on the grid system where each block is about 100m, with even numbered calles running east-west and odd numbered calles north-south. The Río Las Casas runs through the town heading northwards out to sea, and this has traditionally been the main route to the Cuban mainland. The boat which served as a ferry from the 1920s until 1974, *El Pinero*, has been preserved by the river at the end of Calle 28. The Parque Central is two blocks west of the river, between calles 28 and 30, and 37 and 39. The Parque attracts 'retired' men during the day and comes alive at night; it is also a good place to enquire about cars and guides. Ask anyone, as everyone has a contact. The church of **Nuestra Señora de los Dolores** is on the north side of the square. A church was first built on this site in 1853, but was blown away by a hurricane in 1926. The present one, in colonial style, was built in 1929. Padre Guillermo Sardiñas, parish priest here in the 1950s, was the only priest to join Fidel Castro on his revolutionary campaign in the Sierra Maestra, leaving the Isla in 1957 to take up arms. To make the most of a day in town, you could ask the local ICAP office to arrange visits to places of social interest, where the rarity of visitors ensures a genuine welcome. A visit to the pottery, **Fábrica de Cerámica**, on Calles 37 y 30, near *Coppelia*, whose design department seems to be stuck in a time-warp, should be considered a last resort.

Museums

The **Museo Municipal** is in the building which was once the Casa de Gobierno, built in 1853, one of the oldest on the island. It is on the south side of the Parque Central, on Calle 30, and has a small historical collection of items of local interest. Open Tuesday-Saturday 0800-1700, Sunday 0900-1300. The **Museo de la Lucha Clandestina**, on Calle 37 y 30, near *Coppelia*, has a collection of photos and other material relating to the Revolution and the uprising against the dictator, Batista. Open Tuesday-Saturday, 0900-1700, Sunday 0800-1200. The **Planetario y Museo de Historia Natural**, Calle 41 y 52, has exhibits relating to the natural history, geology and archaeology of the island, with a replica of the cave painting. Open Tuesday-Thursday 0800-1900, Friday 1400-2200, Saturday 1300-1700, Sunday 0900-1300, US$1. Outside the town, 3 km

west just off the road to La Demajagua, is **Museo Finca El Abra**. This is where José Martí came on 17 October 1870, to spend 9 weeks of exile and hard labour quarrying marble in the Sierra de las Casas before being deported to Spain. The farmhouse belonged to a friend of his family and is in a lovely setting with a backdrop of hills, approached along an avenue of oak trees. It is a pleasant walk from town. You can see the contents of the house and kitchen and some of Martí's belongings. Open Tuesday-Sunday 0900-1700.

Excursions

It is worthwhile renting a car and driver/guide simply for the drive as there are some particularly beautiful areas with green rolling hills and citrus plantations. A good day's sightseeing will take in the Model Prison, the crocodile farm and the *Hotel El Colony*, where you can hire a kayak for an hour. If you hope to see the whole island, plan to spend more than a weekend, particularly if you want to see all the caves. Roads are generally in good condition.

4 km east of Nueva Gerona in Reparto Chacón, is the **Presidio Modelo** (the Model Prison), built 1926-32 by the dictator Machado to a high-security 'panopticon' design first developed by Jeremy Bentham in 1791 to give total surveillance and control of the inmates. It is a sinister and impressive sight of huge circular buildings, very atmospheric, especially towards dusk and although the building is now decaying, you can still imagine the horrors of incarceration here. The iron work has been removed for other uses, but everything else remains. You can wander around the guard towers and circular cell blocks, and see the numbered, tiered cells. Offer the guide a tip to let you see the interior. The museum is open Monday-Saturday 0800-1700, Sunday 0800-1300, US$2, cameras US$1. Pictures, beds and belongings have been carefully preserved. Inmates have included many fighters in the independence struggle, Japanese Cuban internees in the Second World War, and Fidel Castro and fellow Moncada rebels imprisoned 1953-1955. Fidel and the other Moncada prisoners were held for 19 months in the medical wing, which is now the museum. Castro returned in 1959 to propose the development projects which were to transform it into the Isle of Youth. He closed the prison in 1967. The route to El Presidio is lined with boards bearing internationalist political messages and striking designs. The schools for international students, mostly from Africa (Mozambique, Angola, South Africa, Ethiopia) and Vietnam are also located along the highway. Students here start their studies at secondary level and return to their countries at technical or postgraduate level. Their education is free. Students are taught on the basis of work and study and contribute to citrus cultivation.

The **Cueva del Punta del Este** contains paintings attributed to the original Siboney inhabitants. There are actually 7 caves 59 km southeast of Nueva Gerona and the only way to get there is by hotel rental car or hotel bus, ie an organized excursion, US$92 flat rate divided between however many passengers there are. They were discovered in 1910 by a shipwrecked French sailor and contain 235 pictures on the walls and ceilings, painted long before the arrival of the Spanish. They are considered the most important pictographs in the Caribbean and have been declared a national monument. It is believed that they might represent a solar calendar.

The **Cocodrilo** crocodile farm is a one-hour drive (any car) south and west from Nueva Gerona, including several kilometres of dirt road. Entry US$3, well worth it. You have a guided tour by the knowledgeable caretakers (in Spanish) of the hatchery and the breeding pens where the crocodiles stay for 4-5 years until they are released.

Festival

Nueva Gerona has a grapefruit festival in February/March.

Local information
● **Accommodation**

> Prices: **L1** over US$200; **L2** US$151-200; **L3** US$101-150; **A1** US$81-100; **A2** US$61-80; **A3** US$46-60; **B** US$31-45; **C** US$21-30; **D** US$12-20; **E** US$7-11; **F** up to US$6

Hotels can be booked through Amistur. Main tourist hotel is **C** *El Colony* (3-star), T 98181/2, 98240, F 335212, 77 a/c rooms in main block and cabañas, single and triple available, discounts for stays of over a week, TV, 40 minutes by road from Nueva Gerona's small airport, once part of the Hilton chain, established as a diving hotel before Cuba reappeared on the world tourist map, diving centre with access to 56 buoyed diving locations, swimming and snorkelling not great because of shallow water and sea urchins, but beach is white sand, lovely setting, and there is a pool, 3 restaurants, snack bar, store, basket ball, volleyball, tennis and squash courts, horse riding, disco Saturdays

2100-0600, car rental, excursions, busy with package tourists, so accommodation could be hard to find. **C** *Villa Gaviota* (3-star) on the outskirts of Nueva Gerona on the road to La Fe beside the river, T 23290, has 20 rooms, single and triple available, extra cots for children, a/c, fridge, TV, phone, pool where national swimming team trains, good service at poolside bar, restaurants, squash court and gymnasium, disco Thursday-Sunday 2130-0400, techno music, young crowd, dance and werobics classes advertised, the nicest dollar place to stay if you are not diving or on a package, Havanautos for car and motorcycle rental. 1 km south of *Gaviota* is **D** *Rancho del Tesoro*, T 24069, in woods close to the Río Las Casas, 60 rooms in blocks. In Nueva Gerona, **D** *La Cubana*, Calle 39 y 16 above Cubana, 17 rooms with bath, but basic, formerly for Cubans only . Other peso places to stay include **D** *Los Codornices*, T 24981, on the way to the airport, 40 rooms in a block or in cabañas, pool, own transport needed. *Campismo Arenas Negras*, T 25266, is east of Nueva Gerona at Playa Bibijagua, a black sand beach, 59 very basic peso cabañas. Also *Campismo* at Calle José Martí 1423, prices vary, reservations at Oficina de Campismo, Calle 37 y 22, T 25266. The best option price-wise is to stay in private homes at US$10-15 per room. People will approach you at the ferry dock. Don't be hustled off immediately, but don't be too suspicious either. One recommended contact is **Roberto Figuerero Rodríguez**, Calle 35 1809, entre 18 y 20, Apto 1, T 4892, friendly and above board, will also help with cars and drivers and information in general.

● **Places to eat**
If you are on a package you will probably take all your meals in hotels. Private restaurants are few and aimed mainly at locals. The best bet is to eat in people's homes, where you can get an excellent meal for US$5-6, with lobster, rice, beans, fried plantain etc, drinks extra. *El Tocororo*, opposite the park on Calles 39 y 16, Cuban dishes, pay in pesos, breakfast 0700-0900, lunch 1200-1400, dinner 1800-2000, but times seem flexible; *El Cochinito*, Calle 39 y 24, state run, open 1400-2200, specializes in pork; *Cabaret El Dragón*, Calle 39 y 26, also state run but Chinese and Cuban food, restaurant and bar, open 1600-2200, Monday-Thursday, 1600-0030 Friday-Sunday, cabaret at weekends, deluxe atmosphere, upscale crowd; there is a Mercado Agropecuario at Calle 41 y 40, where you can get fresh fruit and vegetables and there are a few basic places to eat in this area where you can pay in pesos. For ice cream, *Coppelia* is at Calle 37 y 32.

● **Bars**
Casa de los Vinos, Calle 20 y 41, open Monday-Wednesday 1400-2200, Friday-Sunday 1400-2400, popular peso drinking spot with grapefruit, melon, tomato and grape wines, drink orders finish at 2300, so order early, wine served in earthenware jugs, advisable to take glasses, avoid the snacks; *Taberna Gerona*, Calle 39 y 22, open daily 1100-2100, Cuban food and pub atmosphere, very friendly, strictly pesos.

● **Entertainment**
El Patio, Calle 24 entre 37 y 39, open 2100-0300, cabaret, 2 shows nightly at weekends, at 2200 and 0100, entry US$3, lots of Cubans and popular; *La Movida* disco, Calle 34 entre 18 y 20, outdoors, US$3, Cubans pay in pesos, young student crowd, starts at 2200; *Villa Gaviota* disco, Thursday-Sunday, 2130-0400, entry US$1, cave-like atmosphere, picks up after midnight, young crowd, techno music; *Casa de la Cultura*, Calle 37 y 24, check the schedule posted outside for dance events; beside the Servi Cupet petrol station on Calle 39 y 30, no sign outside, café where you can dance, open 24 hours, total mix of music, comfortable and friendly, best place in Nueva Gerona.

● **Airlines**
Cubana at Calle 39 1415 entre 16 y 18, Nueva Gerona, T 061 22531/24259.

● **Banks & money exchange**
Banco Nacional, Calle 39 y 18, open Monday-Friday 0800-1400, Saturday 1300-1500; Caja Popular de Ahorro, Calle 39 y 26, open Monday-Friday 0800-1700. Best to bring enough cash from the mainland.

● **Hospitals & medical services**
Pharmacy at Calle 39 y 24, open Monday-Friday 0800-2200, Saturday 0800-1600. Take plenty of insect repellent, particularly if you are heading for the Ciénaga or out to the *Hotel Colony*.

● **Shopping**
There is a bookshop, *Librería Frank País*, Calle 22 y 39, mostly Spanish books. Photoservice is on Calle 39 y 20. Handicrafts in the Mercado Artesanal at Calle 24 y 35. For local artwork there is the Centro de Desarrollo de las Artes Visuales, Calle 39 y 26. Food can be bought in the market (see above) or at the Cubalse Supermarket, Calle 35 entre 30 y 32, open Monday-Saturday 1000-1800.

● **Sport**

You can go paragliding with the *Club Parapente*, run by instructor, Reynaldo Prendes, who lives at Calle 16 4304 entre 43 y 45, no club house yet. Prices unknown, but very friendly people, who are more than willing to take foreigners for a glide on their double paragliders.

● **Transport**

Local Travel to anywhere on the island can be difficult although nearly every car will turn into a taxi on request. Fares within Nueva Gerona and to main hotels about US$2. Local transport is often by horse and cart, recommended for short distances, the drivers are willing to show you the sights and give you an impromptu history lesson. Buses run to La Fe, the *Hotel Colony*, Playa Bibijagua, and there is a bus marked 'Servicio Aereo', which runs between the airport and the cinema in Nueva Gerona, but don't rely on any of these to run on a regular basis. **Car hire:** Havanautos has an office in Nueva Gerona at Calle 32 y 39, T 24432, but the dollar hotels also have car hire desks. The best way to see the island is to hire a private car with a driver/guide, which costs about US$40-60 a day. Motorbike hire from the hotels is US$7/hour.

Air The Rafael Cabrera airport (GER) is nearly 5 km from town and there are three scheduled 40-minute flights a day from Havana in Cubana Antonov AN-24 aircraft, one at 0715, one at 2000 and one at either 0930 or 1730 depending on the day of the week. They return at 0815, 1045 or 1830, and 2100, so you could do a day trip if you wanted. Fare US$20 one way, book in advance.

Sea An interesting way of getting to the Isla is by the 106-passenger *kometa*, (a vintage Soviet hydrofoil) from Surgidero de Batabanó on the mainland south coast. There is a morning crossing and an evening crossing, which take 2 hours, US$11. Connecting bus from Havana, 1 hour, from bus terminal on Boyeros at 0700 and 1300. Book a couple of days in advance at the terminal at the far end of the Boyeros entry, between 0600-1200, 2 pesos, at the office in the terminal. Snacks available at the terminal. On the *kometa* try for Salón A, the only one with a view. Those paying in dollars are usually directed to Salón C, with freezing air conditioning. Snacks available in pesos and beer at US$1. Customs entry both ways, remember 20-kilo weight limit. Alternatively a ferry crosses on the same route Wednesday, Friday and Sunday at 1930 from Havana train station and takes 6 hours, US$8.

In Havana tickets are sold at the station office. In Nueva Gerona the terminal is on the Río Las Casas at the end of Calle 22 and the ticket office is open daily 0600-1300. Fares in dollars, you must take your passport.

CAYO LARGO

Cayo Largo, east of Isla de la Juventud, is a westernized, all-inclusive island resort reached by air. There are few Cubans on the island and it is not recommended for independent travellers wanting to see Cuba. On the other hand, if you want a few days on the beach with nothing but water-sports to entertain you, then you should enjoy the resort.

The land

(*Area* 38 sq km) Cayo Largo is at the eastern end of the Archipiélago de los Canarreos, 114 km east of Isla de la Juventud and 80 km south of the Península de Zapata. It is a long, thin, coral island, 26 km long and no more than 2 km wide. There are beautiful white sandy beaches protected by a reef, all along the southern coast which, together with the cristal clear, warm waters of the Caribbean, make it ideal for tourism. A string of hotels lines the southern tip of the island and these are practically the only employers on the island so that its economy depends entirely on tourism. The northern coast is mostly mangrove and swamp, housing hungry mosquitoes as well as numerous birds (pelicans being the most visible) and iguanas. Turtles lay their eggs at Playa Tortuga in the northeast, and there is a turtle farm at Combinado northwest of the airstrip.

Beaches and watersports

The best beach on the island is **Playa Sirena**, which faces west and is spared any wind or currents which sometimes affect the southern beaches. It is also spared any hotels along its 2 km of white sand and so everyone comes on a day trip for around US$25. Snorkelling and scuba diving can be done at Playa Sirena, 10 minutes' boat ride from the hotels,

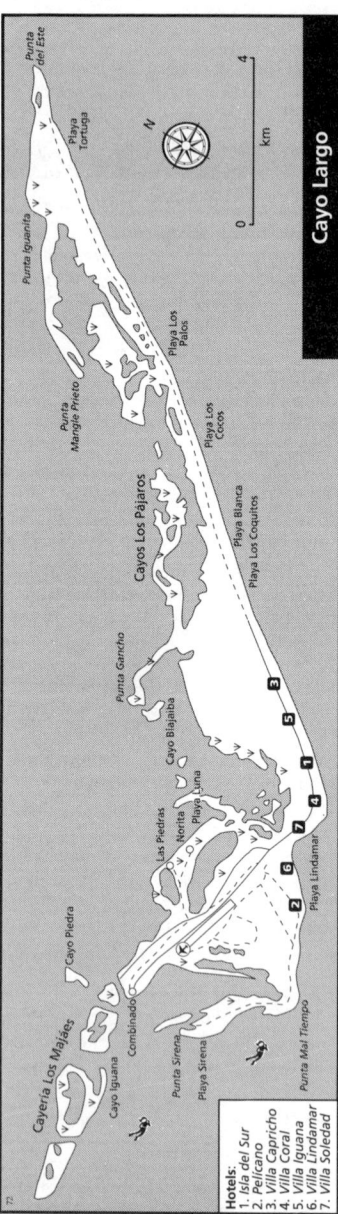

Cayo Largo

Hotels:
1. Isla del Sur
2. Pelícano
3. Villa Capricho
4. Villa Coral
5. Villa Iguana
6. Villa Lindamar
7. Villa Soledad

and there is a restaurant for lunch. Snorkelling is also good further east at **Playa Los Cocos**, which you can reach by bicycle. If there is a problem with the weather and the currents become dangerous, red flags will be flown to forbid swimming.

Scuba diving is good around the island, although perhaps not as spectacular as in some other areas of Cuba (see **Diving and marine life**, page 24). There is an extensive reef with gorgonians, sponges and lots of fish, while north of the island you will find large pelagics. We have received complaints about the scuba diving operation, which was reported to be lax about service, safety and checking divers' qualifications, but we understand that management changed in 1997, so it may have improved. The Marina Puertosol has a liveaboard dive boat with space for 14 divers.

Sailing is popular and there is a bareboat yacht charter fleet run by Cubanaútica (T 48220, F 48221 in Havana). The Marina Cayo Largo del Sur at Combinado has 50 moorings for visiting yachts, who don't have to buy a tourist card to come here if they are not going on to anywhere else in Cuba, because the island is a free port. To clear customs, call the marina on VHF 6, or maritime security (*seguridad marítima*) on VHF 16. There are also 8 a/c rooms with private bath at the *Villa Internacional* with restaurant if you want to stay on dry land.

There is deep sea fishing for marlin and other big fish, with international fishing tournaments held here. Other watersports include windsurfing, kayaking, jet skis, catamarans, banana rides, glass bottomed boats and snorkelling, organized by the Puertosol marina at its three nautical bases.

Very tame iguanas can be spotted at another nearby cay, **Cayo Rico** (day-trips available for US$37 from Cayo Largo) and also on the appropriately named **Cayo Iguana**. Hotel expansion is planned to cater for watersport tourism. **Cayos Rosario** and **Avalos**, between Juventud and Largo, have not yet been developed.

Island information
● Accommodation

There are several hotels here at present, all in the Gran Caribe chain and grouped together under the name of the *Isla del Sur Hotel Resort*, T 535 48111/48150, F 535 48201, with all facilities shared and included in the package cost, which can be as low as US$400 per person for 4 nights, including air and ground transport from Havana, breakfast and dinner buffet. You may have to wear a coloured plastic bracelet to indicate which package you are on. Prices include 3 meals and free use of all water sports and other activities such as tennis, horse riding and volleyball. Always check what is included in your package. Medical facilities, laundry, Post Office and fax services are all available.

Villa Capricho, 75 rooms in thatched A-frame *cabañas*; *Hotel Isla del Sur*, 57 rooms; *Villa Coral*, 60 bungalows; *Villa Iguana*, 52 bungalows; *Villa Lindamar*, 63 cabañas; *Villa Soledad*, 43 bungalows; *Hotel Pelícano*, T 535 48333-6, F 535 48166, 230 rooms including 12 suites, set apart from the others and more isolated. The hotels and the thatched *cabañas* are low-lying and pleasantly spread out in gardens by the beach, all rooms are a/c, with private bath, telephone and satellite TV. There is no private accommodation on the island and you will not need any pesos.

● Places to eat

There are several buffet restaurants and thatched snack bars (*ranchones*) attached to the hotels, as well as a seafood restaurant at the *Pelicano* which has to be booked, a highly recommended Italian place at the *Villas* and a good pizzería. Food is reported to be plentiful and fresh. You will not find any *paladares* here but there is lots of lobster.

● Entertainment

There is usually evening entertainment in the hotels and a disco, *El Marinero* at the *Hotel Pelícano*, but better is the *Discoteca Blue Lake* at the airport, to which there is a minibus shuttle service from the hotels after 2300.

● Transport

Local Car hire: hardly worth it for such a small island, but should you want it there are Havanautos and Transautos at the *Hotel Pelícano*. Motorcycles, bicycles, and jeeps are also available.

Air The only scheduled international flight to Cayo Largo del Sur airport (CYO) is from Toronto on Saturdays, with Cubana. Aerogaviota flies from Aeropuerto Playa Baracoa, Havana, a former military air base. A day trip from Havana is US$94 including transfers and lunch but you have to pay extra for watersports and boat trips; there are also flights from Varadero, or by light plane or boat from Isla de la Juventud, or by charter plane from Grand Cayman.

Information for travellers

BEFORE TRAVELLING

ENTRY REQUIREMENTS

● **Visas**

Visitors from the majority of countries need only a 30-day **tourist card** to enter Cuba, as long as they are going solely for tourist purposes and are staying in an hotel. A tourist card may be obtained from Cuban embassies, consulates, airlines, or approved travel agents (price in the UK £15 from the consulate, or from travel agents, some other countries US$15). From some countries (eg Canada) tourist cards are handed out by the tour operator or on the plane and checked by visa control at the airport; the first one is free but replacements cost US$10. To get a tourist card at a Consulate you have to fill in an application form, photocopy the main pages of your passport (valid for more than 6 months after departure from Cuba), submit confirmation of booking your accommodation and your return or onward flight ticket. Immigration in Havana airport give you only 30 days on your tourist card. You can get it extended a further 30 days at Immigration in Miramar (see below) or some other towns.

Travellers who will be staying with friends or in any type of private accommodation are not normally granted a tourist card unless they have a pre-booked hotel voucher for part of their stay. If you have not obtained one in advance you will be asked to pay for a minimum of 3 nights in a hotel upon arrival in Cuba before being admitted to the country. Officially you have to request authorization from the Immigration Office if you want to stay outside hotels, but no one ever does as far as we know.

Nationals of countries without visa-free agreement with Cuba, journalists, students and those visiting on other business must check what visa requirements pertain and, if relevant, apply for an **official/business visa**. For this you must submit two application forms, two passport photos, your passport (tell them whether you want the visa in your passport or on a separate piece of paper), and a letter from the Cuban organization or company which has invited you. In the UK a business visa costs £32, plus £13 for the fax that has to be sent to Cuba in connection with the application. A journalist from Trinidad and Tobago paid US$50 for a visa plus an additional US$60 for a press card in Havana. A business visa is issued for one entry into Cuba and can take at least 10 days to process.

There is also a **family visa**, for those who are visiting relatives, valid for one entry into Cuba. You have to fill in an application form naming the relative who has invited you (in duplicate), submit your passport (valid for 6 months after your departure from Cuba) and pay a fee of £45.

The US government does not normally permit its citizens to visit Cuba. US citizens should have a US licence to engage in any transactions related to travel to Cuba, but tourist or business travel are not licensable, even through a third country such as Mexico or Canada. For further information on Cuban entry and customs requirements, US travellers should contact the Cuban Interests Section, an office of the Cuban government at 2630 16th Street NW, Washington DC 20009, T 202 797-8518. They could also contact *Marazul Tours*, 250 West 57th St, Suite 1311, New York City, 10107 New York, T 212-582 9570, or Miami T 305-232 8157 (information also from *Havanatur*, Calle 2 No 17 Miramar, Havana, T 33-2121/2318).

The Cuban Interests Section in Washington DC will process applications for visas. Visas can take several weeks to be granted, and are apparently difficult to obtain for US citizens other than businessmen, guests of the Cuban Government or Embassy officials. However, a British citizen was able to obtain a Tourist Card there in half an hour (US$26, photographs essential). When the applicant is too far from a Cuban consulate to be able to apply conveniently for a visa, he may apply direct to the Cuban Foreign Ministry for a visa waiver. US citizens on business with Cuba should contact Foreign Assets Control, Federal Reserve Bank of New York, 33 Liberty Street, NY 10045.

Many travellers conceal their tracks by going via Mexico, the Bahamas, or Canada, when only the tourist card is stamped, not the passport. The Cuban Consulate in Mexico City refuses to issue visas unless you have pre-arranged accommodation and book through a travel agent; even then, only tourist visas are available, US$20. In Mérida, a travel agent will arrange your documents so you do not need to go to a Consulate for a visa.

Visitors travelling on a visa must go in person to the Immigration Office for registration the day after arrival. The office is on the corner of Calle 22 and Av 3, Miramar. When you register you will be given an exit permit.

Travellers coming from or going through infected areas must have certificates of vaccination against cholera and yellow fever.

The Cuban authorities do not insist on stamping your passport in and out but they often do so. They will stamp your tourist card instead if you ask.

TOURIST INFORMATION
● Local tourist office
The Government has a decentralized system for receptive tourism and there is a large number of state-owned travel agencies/tour companies, which cooperate fully with each other and with the tourism bureaux in the major hotels. Their main function is to sell excursions and package tours. Individual tourism is relatively new but growing, with agencies like *Amistur*, overseas agent Cubanacán.

● Tourist offices overseas
The Cuba Tourist Office also has offices in: **Canada**, 440 Blvd René Levesque, Suite 1402, Montréal, Quebec H2Z 1V7, T (514) 875-8004/5, F 875-8006; 55 Queen Street E, Suite 705, Toronto, M5C 1R5, T (416) 362-0700/2, F 362-6799.

Belgium, Robert Jones Straat 77, Brussels 18, T 02-343-0022; **France**, 280 Bd Raspail, 75014 Paris, T 14-538-90-10, F 14-538-99-30; **Italy**, Via General Fara 30, Terzo Plano, 20124 Milan, T 66981463, F 6690042; **Spain**, Paseo de la Habana No 28 iro derecha, 28036 Madrid, T 411-3097, F 564-5804; **Switzerland**, Gesellschaststrasse 8, 3012 Berne, Case Postale 52725, T/F 31 3022111; **UK**, 167 High Holborn, London WC1V 6PA, T 01891-880-820, 0171-240-6655, F 0171-379-5455.

Russia, Room 627, Hotel Belgrado, Kutuzovskii 14KB7, Moscow, T 2-48-2454/3262, F 2-43-1125.

Argentina, Paraguay 631, 2° piso A, Buenos Aires, F 311-4198, T 311-5820; **Mexico**, Insurgentes Sur 421 y Aguascalientes, Complejo Aristos, Edificio B, Local 310, México DF 06100, T 574-9651, F 574-9454.

● **Travel agents abroad**

In the **UK**, there are some 32 agents who sell holidays in Cuba including: *Regent Holidays*, 15 John Street, Bristol BS1 2HR, T (0117) 9211711, F (0117) 9254866, ABTA and AITO members, holding ATOL and IATA Licences; *Trips Worldwide*, 9 Byron Place, Clifton, Bristol BS8 1JT, T (0117) 9872626, F (0117) 9872627, Email: enquires@trips.demon.co.uk, ATOL, member of LATA, specialists in holidays to help you get off the beaten track; *South American Experience Ltd*, 47 Causton Street, Pimlico,

London SW1P 4AT, T 0171-976 5511, F 0171-976 6908, IATA, ATOL; *Progressive Tours*, 12 Porchester Place, Marble Arch, London W2 2BS, T 0171-262 1676, F 0171-724 6941, ABTA, ATOL, IATA; *Aquatours*, T 0181 255 8050, F 0181 255 8052; *Interchange*, Interchange House, 27 Stafford Road, Croydon, Surrey CR0 4NG, T 0181 681 3612, F 0181 760 0031; *Journey Latin America*, 14-16 Devonshire Road, Chiswick, London W4 2HD, T 0181 747 8315, F 0181 742 1312; *Regal Diving*, T 01353 778 096, F 01353 777 897; *Steamond-Latin American Travel*, T 0171 730 8646, F 0171 730 3024; *Travelcoast*, T 0181 891 2222, F 0181 892 9588; *Cubanacan UK Ltd*, Skylines, Unit 49, Limeharbour Docklands, London E14 9TS, T 0171-537-7909, F 0171-537-7747. Check with these agents for special deals combined

UK experts to cuba since 1975

Accommodation throughout the Island.

Flexible arrangements.

All holidays covered by our

ABTA and CAA bonds.

Regent Holidays UK Ltd.

15 John Street, Bristol BS1 2HR

Tel (0117) 9211711 Fax: (0117) 9254866

Email: regent@regent-holiday.co.uk

TRIPS
Worldwide

*A wonderful way to
plan your travel in...*

CUBA

We organise fly-drive, tailor made,
scuba diving and ecological
tours of Cuba

**COSTA RICA,
CUBA, DOMINICA,
GUATEMALA, GUYANA,
HONDURAS, MEXICO,
SURINAME, TRINIDAD &
TOBAGO.**

PHONE: 0117 987 2626
FAX: 0117 987 2627

with jazz or film festivals. *Cubanacan SA*, Calle 148/11 y 13, Playa, Aptdo Postal 16046, Zona 16, Havana, T 7-219-457/200-569/336-006, operates all diving packages, as well as Veracuba excursions by bus or fly/drive packages; Club Amigo all-inclusives; Servimed health organization for special treatments; Cubacar car hire; Tropicana Club; ExpoCuba at Havana International Conference Centre.

A recommended agent in **Eire** for assistance with Aeroflot flights is *Concorde Travel*, T Dublin 763232; Cubatur agent is *Cubatravel*, T Dublin 713385. See page 286 under **Documents** for *Marazul Tours* in the USA.

If travelling from **Mexico**, many agencies in the Yucatán peninsula offer packages, very good value and popular with travellers wanting to avoid Mexico City. From Cancún Cubana flights cost US$225 return, although you can get special deals for US$170; Aerocaribe charges US$286. Flights are heavily booked. A recommended agency is *Viñales Tours*, in Mexico City at Oaxaca 80, Col Roma, T 208 9900, F 208 3704, http://www.spin.com.mx/vinales, e-mail jmcelis@spin.com.mx; in Guadalajara at Av Adolfo López Mateos Norte 1038-9, T 817 2069, F 3-817 2983, e-mail vinales@infosel.net.mx; and in Havana at Av 3 B No 9207 entre 92 y 94, Miramar, T 241051/3, F 241054, e-mail vintours@ceniai.inf.cu.

From **Canada**, *Air Canada Vacations* has year-round packages or air tickets only to Varadero, from economy to first class hotels; *Canadian Holidays* (division of Canadian Airlines) to Varadero and other destinations including ecological tour of Sierra Maestra, direct flights to Varadero from Vancouver, Edmonton, Calgary, Winnipeg, in high season, also from Halifax to Havana, Varadero and Santiago in February-May; *Alba Tours*, year-round packages up to 4 weeks to all parts of the island, or flights only; *Magna Holidays* books individual travel and custom tours out of Toronto including health tourism,

bird watching, bass fishing and duck shooting; *Sunquest Vacations* offers 3-5 star hotels in Varadero and Havana with direct flights from Vancouver/Edmonton/Calgary to Varadero in high season, connecting flights through Toronto/Montréal at other times, http://www.sunquest.ca; *Air Transaat Holidays* has direct flights from Vancouver and Calgary to Varadero in high season and hotels from all-inclusive to optional meal plans in Varadero, Holguín (Guardalavaca), Manzanillo and Santiago, family plans in Varadero; *Signature Vacations* has a range of 3-5 star hotels and direct flights from Ottawa in high season; *Hola Sun* has year round packages with basic to 5 star hotels, coach tours, car rental, insurance, to Havana, Ciego de Avila, Camagüey, Santiago, Cienfuegos, Holguín and Varadero. The **Canadian-Cuban Friendship Association**, Box 57063-2458 E Hastings Street, Vancouver, BC, V5K 5G6, coordinates specialist group tours, eg medical, children's study, cycling tours, also lots of information on who is doing what in Canadian-Cuban aid and cultural exchange, membership Can$10/year, newsletter.

From **Venezuela**, *Ideal Tours*, Centro Capriles, Plaza Venezuela, T (010 582) 793-0037/1822, have 4-day or 8-day package tours depending on the season, flight only available. From **Jamaica**, *UTAS Tours* offer weekends in Cuba for US$199 including flight, hotel etc, PO Box 429, Montego Bay, T (809) 979-0684, F 979-3465.

In the **Bahamas**, *Havanatur* in Nassau, T 242 394-7195, F 242 394-5196 (ask for Joba), sells package tours to Cuba and has charter flights to Havana or Holguín (see **Getting there** page 292). Havanatur's Havana based reps for the Nassau-Havana route are efficient and helpful, Iris and Laura speak excellent English, Calle 2 17 entre 1 y 3, Miramar, T 247413. A package includes the tourist card, hotel, breakfast, transfer to and from Havana hotel and city tour of Havana, prices start at US$239 for return flight plus 2 nights at *Hotel Inglaterra*, double occupancy, US$269 single occupancy. You can use these 2 nights at the beginning and end of your visit, and travel on your own in between. Less efficient is the Nassau agency, **Majestic**, T 242 322-2606, F 242 326-1995, whose staff are on commission and don't cooperate with each other. Phone first on voice line to get a name, then ensure that all subsequent dealings are with the same person, otherwise multiple bookings/cancellations may result. Payment will have to be in cash or by credit card in Nassau; by bankers draft sent in advance by courier; or by telegraphic transfer. It is preferable if possible to deal with Havanatur direct in Nassau. There are weekly charter flights from **Martinique** via **Guadeloupe** which can be booked through *Laroc Voyages SA*, Zijambette, BP 292-97286 Lamentin, Cedex 02, Martinique, T 603701, F 603898. From **Haiti**, the travel agency *La Citadelle*, Place du Marron Inconnu in Port-au-Prince, T 23-5900, has flights if you book 2 weeks in advance for US$300 return to Havana or US$190 return to Santiago.

● **Local travel agents**

Several state-owned tour companies offer day trips or excursion packages including accommodation to many parts of the island as well as tours of colonial and modern Havana. Examples (1 day, except where indicated): Viñales, including tobacco and rum factories, US$39; Guamá, US$39; Cayo Coco (by air), US$89; Soroa, US$29; Varadero, US$27; Cayo Largo (by air), US$94; Trinidad (by air), daytrip US$79 or US$139 including overnight stay; Santiago de Cuba (by air) and Baracoa, US$159 including 1 night's accommodation, recommended, you see a lot and cover a lot of ground in 2 days. Tours can also be taken from any beach resort. Guides speak Spanish, English, French, Italian or German; the tours are generally recommended as well-organized and good value. A common complaint from

individual tourists is that, when they sign up for day trips and other excursions (eg Cayo Largo), they are not told that actual departure depends on a minimum number of passengers (usually 6). The situation is made worse by the fact that most tourists are on pre-arranged package tours. They are often subject to long waits on buses and at points of departure and are not informed of delays in departure times. Always ask the organizers when they will know if the trip is on or what the real departure time will be.

● **Travel assistance**

Asistur, Paseo del Prado 254, entre Animas y Trocadero, Habana Vieja, for 24-hour service T 33-8527, 62-5519, F 33-8088, cellular Asis 2747, linked to overseas insurance companies, can help with emergency hospital treatment, robbery, direct transfer of funds to Cuba, etc. Also office in *Hotel Casa Granda*, Santiago.

● **Working in Cuba**

Those interested in joining International Work Brigades should contact Cuba Solidarity Campaign, c/o The Red Rose, 129 Seven Sisters Road, London N7 7QG, or 119 Burton Road, London SW9 6TG.

WHEN TO GO

Northeast trade winds temper the heat. Average summer shade temperatures rise to 33°C (91.4°F) in Havana, and higher elsewhere. In winter, day temperatures drop to 20°C (68°F). Average rainfall is from 860 mm in Oriente to 1,730 mm in Havana; it falls mostly in the summer and autumn, but there can be torrential rains at any time. Hurricanes come in August-November. The best time for a visit is during the cooler dry season (November to April). In Havana, there are a few cold days, 8°-10°C (45°-50°F), with a north wind. Walking is uncomfortable in summer but most offices, hotels, leading restaurants and cinemas are air-conditioned. Humidity varies between 75% and 95%.

HEALTH

Sanitary reforms have transformed Cuba into a healthy country, and tap water is generally safe to drink (check if renting privately), although bottled and mineral water are recommended. Doctors abroad will advise you to get Hepatitis A and typhoid inoculations.

Medical service is no longer free for foreign visitors in Havana, Santiago de Cuba, and Varadero, where there are international clinics that charge in dollars (credit cards accepted). Visitors requiring medical attention will be sent to them. Emergencies will be handled on an ad hoc basis. Check with your national health service or health insurance on coverage in Cuba and take a copy of your insurance policy with you. Remember you can not dial any toll-free numbers abroad so make sure you have a contact number. Charges are generally lower than those charged in Western countries. According to latest reports, visitors are still treated free of charge in other parts of the country, with the exception of tourist enclaves with on-site medical services.

Bring all medicines you might need as they can be difficult to find. You might not be offered even a painkiller if you have an accident, as they are in very short supply.

Between May and October, the risk of sunburn is high, sun blocks are recommended when walking around the city as well as on the beach. In the cooler months, limit beach sessions to 2 hours.

Always carry toilet paper with you, it is not available in public toilets and even some hotels do not have it.

MONEY

● Currency

The monetary unit is the peso Cubano. The official exchange rate is US$1=1 peso. Watch out for pre-1962 peso notes, no longer valid. There are notes for 3, 5, 10, and 20 pesos, and coins for 5, 20, and 40 centavos and 1 peso. You must have a supply of 5 centavo coins if you want to use the local town buses (20 or 40 centavos) or pay phones (very few work). The 20 centavo coin is called a *peseta*. In 1995 the Government introduced a new freely 'convertible peso' on a par with the US dollar with a new set of notes and coins. It is fully exchangeable with authorized hard currencies circulating in the economy.

● Exchange

As a result of currency reforms the black/street exchange rate fell from 130 pesos Cubanos = US$1 in May 1994 to 20 pesos = US$1 in May 1997, depreciating to 23 pesos = US$1 on 14 November 1997. Official Casas de Cambio (CADECA) rates fluctuate between 19-24 pesos to the dollar and there is now virtually no black market. The 'peso convertible' is equal to the dollar and can be used freely in the country. Cubans are allowed to hold US$ and to have a bank account. There is very little opportunity for foreigners to spend pesos Cubanos unless you are self-catering or travelling off the beaten track and you are advised to change only the absolute minimum, if at all. Food in the markets (*agromercados*), at street stalls, on trains, postcards, stamps and books, popular cigarettes, but not in every shop, can be bought in pesos. You will need pesos for the toilet, rural trains, trucks, food at roadside cafeterias during a journey and drinks and snacks for a bus or train journey. Away from tourist hotels, in smaller towns such as Manzanillo or Bayamo, there are very few dollar facilities and you will need pesos for everything. Visitors on pre-paid package tours are best advised not to acquire any pesos at all. Bring US$ in small denominations for spending money, dollars are now universally preferred. You will only be able to change a US$50 or US$100 note in one of the large hotels or on production of a passport (if change is available). The hotel cambios sometimes make an irritating US$0.50 charge for

Insurance tips

Insurance companies have tightened up considerably over recent years and it is now almost impossible to claim successfully if you have not followed procedures closely. The problem is that these often involve dealing with the country's red tape which can lead to some inconvenience at best and to some quite long delays at worst. There is no substitute for suitable precautions against petty crime.

The level of insurance that you carry is often dictated by the sums of medical insurance which you carry. It is inevitably the highest if you go through the USA. Also don't forget to obtain sports extensions if you are going to go diving, rafting, climbing etc. Most policies do not cover very high levels of baggage/cash. Don't forget to check whether you can claim on your household insurance. They often have worldwide all risks extensions. Most policies exclude manual work whilst away although working in bars or restaurants is usually alright.

Here are our tips: they apply to most types of policies but always check the details of your own policy before you leave.

1.   Take the policy with you (a photocopy will do but make sure it is a complete one).

2.   Do not travel against medical advice. It will invalidate the medical insurance part of the cover.

3.   There is a 24 hour medical emergency service helpline associated with your insurance. You need to contact them if you require in-patient hospital treatment or you need to return home early. The telephone number is printed on the policy. Make sure you note the time of the call, the person you were talking to and get a reference number. Even better get a receipt from the telephone company showing the number you called. Should you need to be airlifted home, this is always arranged through the insurance company's representative and the hospital authorities. Ironically this can lead to quite intense discussions which you will not be aware of: the local hospital is often quite keen to keep you!

4.   If you have to cancel your trip for whatever reason, contact your travel agent, tour operator or airline without delay.

5.   If your property is damaged by an airline, report it immediately and always within 3 days and get a "property irregularity report" from them.

6.   Claims for baggage left unattended are very rarely settled unless they were left in a securely locked hotel room, apartment etc; locked in the boot of a car and there is evidence of a forced entry; cash is carried on your person or is in a locked safe or security box.

7.   All loss must be reported to the police and/or hotel authorities within 24 hours of discovery and a written report obtained.

8.   If medical attention is received for injury or sickness, a medical certificate showing its nature must be obtained, although some companies waive this if only out-patient treatment is required. Keep all receipts in a safe place as they will be needed to substantiate the claim.

9.   Check your policy carefully to see if there is a date before which claims must be submitted. This is often within 30 days of returning home. It is now usual for companies to want your policy document, proof that you actually travelled (airline ticket or travel agent's confirmation of booking), receipts and written reports (in the event of loss). **NB** photocopies are not accepted.

splitting a US$100 bill. US dollars are the only currency accepted in all tourist establishments.

Travellers' cheques expressed in US or Canadian dollars or sterling are valid in Cuba. TCs issued on US bank paper are not accepted so it is best to take Thomas Cook or Visa. Amex TCs are accepted if issued in Europe. Commission ranges from 2-4%. Don't enter the place or date when signing cheques, or they may be refused.

There are branches of the **Banco Financiero Internacional** and CADECAS (exchange houses) for changing money legally. Non-dollar currencies can be changed into dollars. The BFI charges a 3% commission to change travellers' cheques into dollars cash, but not to change sterling, whereas the cambio in the *Hotel Nacional* charges 3% commission to change any currency. Visitors have difficulties using torn or tatty US dollar notes.

● **Credit cards**

Credit cards acceptable in most places are Visa, MasterCard, Access, Diners, Banamex (Mexican) and Carnet. No US credit cards accepted so a Visa card issued in the USA will not be accepted. American Express, no matter where issued, is unacceptable. Many restaurants which claim to accept credit cards make such a performance that it is not worthwhile. A master list of stolen and rogue cards is kept at the *Habana Libre* and any transaction over US$50 must be checked there; this can take up to 3 hours. You can obtain cash advances with a credit card at 63 locations in Havana, Pinar del Río, Playas del Este, Matanzas, Varadero, Cayo Largo, Cienfuegos, Sancti Spíritus, Ciego de Avila, Camagüey, Holguín, Bayamo and Santiago de Cuba, including branches of the Banco Financiero Internacional, but best to bring plenty of cash as there will often be no other way of paying for what you need. For Visa or MasterCard problems go to Av 23 entre L y M, Vedado, or phone the credit card centre on T 34-4444, F 33-4001. If you get really stuck and need money sent urgently to Cuba, you can get money transferred from any major commercial bank abroad direct to Asistur (see below, **Travel Assistance** page289) immediately for a 10% commission.

GETTING THERE

AIR

The frequency of these **scheduled** flights depends on the season, with twice weekly flights in the winter being reduced to once a week in the summer. Some of the longer haul flights, such as to Buenos Aires, are cut from once every 2 weeks in winter to once a month in summer. There are **charters** from Vancouver with Air Transat, from Cancún, Mexico, and between Santiago de Cuba and Montego Bay, Jamaica. Regular charters between Cayo Largo and Grand Cayman. Occasional charters between Providenciales, Turks and Caicos Islands and Santiago de Cuba. The Cuban air charter line AeroCaribbean has an arrangement with Bahamasair for a (nearly) daily service Miami-Nassau-Havana, changing planes in Nassau; the Cuban tourist agency *Amistur* organizes the service. This route is probably the cheapest and quickest from the USA, flight one way US$140, round trip US$180 (see **Travel agents abroad** page 287). Havanatur has 8 weekly charter flights, 5 to Cancún and 3 to Nassau, in 1997 it inaugurated a flight between Holguín and Nassau. At certain times of year there are special offers available from Europe; enquire at specialist agents. There are also many combinations of flights involving Cuba and Mexico, Venezuela, Colombia and the Dominican Republic; again ask a specialist agent.

Mexicana de Aviación organizes package tours. Several Canadian tour operators have departures from Toronto and Montréal and run package tours to Cuba for all nationalities. Package tours also available from Venezuela, the Bahamas and Jamaica (see **Travel agencies** page 287).

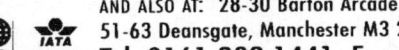

Getting there by air						
	Havana	**Varadero**	**Holguín**	**Santiago**	**Ciego de Avila**	**Cayo Largo**
From Europe						
Amsterdam		Martinair	Martinair			
Barcelona	Cubana / Iberia					
Berlin	Cubana					
Brussels	Cubana					
Cologne/Bonn		Condor			Cubana	
Copenhagen	Cubana					
Dusseldorf		LTU	LTU		LTC	
Frankfurt	Cubana	Condor / LTU			Condor	
Las Palmas	Cubana					
Lisbon	Cubana			Cubana		
London Gatwick	Cubana	Cubana				
Madrid	Cubana / Iberia / Spanair / Air Europa	Air Europa				
Manchester	Cubana					
Moscow	Cubana / Aeroflot					
Munich			Condor			
Paris	Cubana / AOM	AOM	Cubana	Cubana	Cubana	
Rome	Cubana	Cubana		Cubana		
Santiago de Compostela	Cubana					
Shannon	Aeroflot					
Vitoria	Cubana			Cubana		
From North America						
Cancún	Aerocaribe / Cubana / Aviateca / Mexicana					
Mérida	Aerocaribe					
Mexico City	Cubana / Mexicana de Aviación					Cubana
Monterrey	Aerocaribe					
Montréal	Cubana	Cubana				

Getting there by air						
	Havana	**Varadero**	**Holguín**	**Santiago**	**Ciego de Avila**	**Cayo Largo**
Oaxaca	Aerocaribe					
Toronto	Cubana / Lacsa	Cubana				
Tuxtla Gutiérrez	Aerocaribe					
Veracruz	Aerocaribe					
Villahermosa	Aerocaribe					
From Central & South America						
Bogotá	Cubana / Avianca					
Buenos Aires	Cubana		Cubana		Cubana	
Caracas	Cubana					
Cayenne	Air France					
Guatemala City	Aviateca					
Guayaquil	Cubana / Tame					
Managua	Aviateca					
Mendoza	Cubana					
Montevideo	Cubana					
Panama City	Cubana / Copa					
Quito	Cubana / Tame					
Rio de Janeiro	Cubana					
San José	Cubana / Lacsa					
San Salvador	Aviateca					
Santiago de Chile	Cubana					
São Paulo	Cubana					
From the Caribbean						
Curaçao	Cubana					
Fort-de-France	Cubana / Air France					
Kingston	Cubana			Tropical		
Montego Bay	Cubana / Air Jamaica	Tropical				
Nassau	Aero Caribbean		Aero Caribbean			
Pointe-à-Pitre	Cubana / Air France					
Puerto Plata		LTU				
Santo Domingo	Cubana / Lacsa			Cubana		

SEA
● Ports of entry
Havana, Cienfuegos and Santiago receive tourist cruise vessels. There are several marinas, including the Hemingway, Tarará and Veneciana (in Havana), Acua, Chapelín, Gaviota (in Varadero), and Cayo Largo. Arriving by yacht, announce your arrival on VHF channel 16, 72 or 55B.

CUSTOMS
Personal baggage and articles for personal use are allowed in free of duty; so are 200 cigarettes, or 50 cigars, or 250 grams of tobacco, and 2 bottles of alcoholic drinks. Visitors importing new goods worth between US$100 and US$1,000 will be charged 100% duty, subject to a limit of 2 items a year. No duty is payable on goods valued at under US$100. You may take in up to 10 kg of medicine. It is prohibited to bring in fresh fruit and vegetables, which will be confiscated if found. Many things are scarce or unobtainable in Cuba: take in everything you are likely to need other than food (say razor blades, medicines and pills, heavy duty insect repellent, strong sun protection and after-sun preparations, toilet paper, tampons, reading and writing materials, photographic supplies, torch and batteries).

ON ARRIVAL
● Airport
On arrival immigration can be painfully slow if you come off a busy Iberia DC10 flight but speedy off smaller Cubana aircraft. At Havana airport there are taxi dispatchers who can get you in a taxi or minibus for US$12, cheaper than Turistaxi which charges US$15 to the centre on a meter.

● Clothing
Generally informal. Summer calls for the very lightest clothing. Sunglasses, sun factor and some kind of head cover recommended for those with fair complexions. A jersey and light raincoat or umbrella are needed in the cooler months; a jersey is also needed if you plan to travel on air conditioned internal flights or trains, which are very cold.

● Gifts
If you are planning to stay with Cubans, whether with friends or in private rented accommodation, there are some items in short supply in Cuba which they may appreciate: T-shirts (preferably with something written on them), household medicines such as Paracetamol, cosmetics, cotton wool, washing up or kitchen cloths, neutral shoe polish , refillable cigarette lighters, and for children, pens and pencils. The list of items in short supply changes according to whether foreign exchange is available to pay for imports.

● Hours of business
Government offices: 0830-1230 and 1330-1730 Monday to Friday. Some offices open on Saturday morning. Banks: 0830-1200, 1330-1500 Monday to Friday. Shops: 0830-1800 Monday to Saturday, 0900-1400 Sunday. Hotel tourist (hard currency) shops generally open 1000-1800 or 1900.

● Official time
Eastern Standard Time, 5 hours behind GMT; Daylight Saving Time, 4 hours behind GMT. However, Cuba does not always change its clocks the same day as the USA or the Bahamas. On Sunday, 5 October 1997, Cuba moved its clocks back 1 hour, which appeared to take everybody by surprise in the travel industry, including Cubans, and all flight times for the following week were changed on minimal notice. Best to check in the spring and autumn so that you are not caught out with missed flights and buses etc.

● Photography
It is forbidden to photograph military or police installations or personnel, port, rail or airport facilities. A fee is charged for photographs in some museums and national monuments.

● **Public Holidays**

Liberation Day (1 January), Victory of Armed Forces (2 January), Labour Day (1 May), Revolution Day (26 July and the day either side), Beginning of War of Independence (10 October).

● **Security**

In general the Cuban people are very hospitable. The island is generally safer than many of its Caribbean and Latin neighbours, but certain precautions should be taken. Visitors should never lose sight of their luggage or leave valuables in hotel rooms (most hotels have safes). Do not leave your things on the beach when going swimming. Guard your camera closely. Pickpocketing and purse-snatching on buses is quite common in Havana (especially the old city) and Santiago. Also beware of bagsnatching by passing cyclists. Walking in Havana involves a constant escort of small children, or even teenagers, asking for chewing gum and small change. This is an issue of social concern because of what it could lead to as much as because of the general harassment. You need to be equipped with pockets full of little gifts or a very hard heart. In the capital, street lighting is poor so care is needed when walking or cycling the city at night. Some people recommend walking in the middle of the street. The police are very helpful and thorough when investigating theft, ask for a stamped statement for insurance purposes. In the event of a crime, make a note of where it happened. Visitors should remember that the government permitting Cubans to hold dollars legally has not altered the fact that some of the local population will often do anything to get hard currency, from simply asking for money or dollar-bought goods, to mugging. Latest reports suggest that foreigners will be offered almost anything on the street 'from cigars to cocaine to chicas'. Buying cigars on the street is not recommended, they are often not genuine and may be confiscated at customs if you cannot produce an official receipt of purchase.

Prostitution is common, beware of sexually transmitted diseases. If you are a man out alone at night you will find the market very active and you will be tugged at frequently, mostly by females, but around *Coppelia* the prostitutes are mostly males. Cubans who offer their services (whether sexual or otherwise) in return for dollars are known as *jineteros*, or *jineteras* ('jockeys' because they 'ride on the back' of the tourists). Hotels and restaurants often prevent *jineteras* and other Cuban companions from entering their premises, in an attempt to isolate dollar-paying foreigners from locals. If you or your travelling companion is dark-skinned you may suffer from this policy. Dave Winter (Editor, *Pakistan Handbook*) writes "When in India, most Indians thought that my dark-skinned French girl-friend was Indian. In Pakistan they assumed that she was Pakistani. While researching the *Israel Handbook*, it was always assumed that she was Israeli (or Arab, when in the Palestinian areas). On this holiday to Cuba, not only was it assumed by most people that we encountered that she was Cuban, but also that she was a 'companion' that I had 'rented' for a couple of weeks. This became a real pain in the arse every time we went into our hotel, or a bar or restaurant."

Take extra passport photos and keep them separate from your passport. If you have to get more photos there is a place in Havana next to the International Press Centre at Calle 213 esquina O which does them for US$4, with a wait of about an hour.

● **Shopping**

Essentials, rent and most food, are fairly cheap; non-essentials are very expensive. Everything is very scarce, although imported toiletries and camera film (Kodak print and Elite slide film, from Mexico), are reasonably priced. A sandwich in a restaurant or bar costs about US$4, a coffee costs US$1. The street price of a bottle of rum ranges from US$2-4 for poor quality to US$4-8 for a 5-year-old rum, beware of some diabolical doctoring processes. A beer costs US$0.75-1.50 in both restaurants and shops. Compared with much of Latin America, Cuba is expensive for the tourist, but compared with many Caribbean islands it is not dear. If you are buying souvenirs to take home, remember to keep the official receipt in case you have to show it at customs on departure.

● Tipping

Tipping customs have changed after a period when visitors were not allowed to tip in hotels and restaurants. It is now definitely recommended. Tip a small amount (not a percentage) in the same currency as you pay for the bill (typically US$1-2 on a US$25 meal). At times taxi drivers will expect (or demand) a tip. Turistaxis are not tipped, but the drivers still appreciate a tip. Musicians in bars and restaurants depend on your tips, give generously, they are worth it. If you want to express gratitude, offer a packet of American cigarettes. Leaving basic items in your room, like toothpaste, deodorant, paper, pens, is recommended. Tourism workers regularly donate tips to the national health service, for the purchase of equipment for cancer treatment in children etc. However, any evidence of malpractice should be reported to the management.

● Voltage

110-230 Volts. 3 phase 60 cycles, AC. Plugs are usually of the American type, an adaptor for European appliances can be bought at the Intur shop at the *Habana Libre*. In some new tourist hotel developments, however, European plugs are used, with 220 volts, although they often provide adaptors, check in advance if it is important to you.

● Weights and measures

The metric system is compulsory, but exists side by side with American and old Spanish systems.

ON DEPARTURE

It is advisable to book your flight out of Cuba before actually going there as arranging it there can be time-consuming. Furthermore, it is essential to reconfirm onward flights as soon as you arrive in Cuba and certainly 48 hours prior to departure, otherwise you will lose your reservation. Independent travellers should have tickets stamped in person, not by an agent and, for Mexico, should make sure they have a Mexican tourist card and that Cuban departure tax is collected. The airport departure tax is US$15. The international terminal is Terminal 1. On departure, check in, pay tax at separate booth, go upstairs for immigration control and X-ray. Seating in the departure lounge is uncomfortable. Restaurant OK for sandwiches or full meals, welcome during 3-hour check-in. Last chance to hear live Cuban band while eating. Limited shops, lots of rum, coffee, a few books and magazines. Poor selection of cigars and overpriced, eg US$113 for 25 Montecristo No 3, as against US$89 at the Partagas factory in Havana. The Cubita coffee on the other hand was marginally cheaper than in the dollar shops in town, at US$5.60 for a 440g pack, and the *Guayabita del Pinar* flavoured rum costs US$3.90 at the factory, US$5 in Havana, but only US$3 in the departure lounge at Havana airport.

WHERE TO STAY

● Hotels

Accommodation for your first day should be booked in advance of travelling. You have to fill in an address on your tourist card and if you leave it blank you will be directed to the reservations desk at the airport, which is time consuming. A voucher from your travel agent to confirm arrangements is usual and the hotels expect it as confirmation of your reservation. This can be done abroad through travel agencies, accredited government agencies, or through Turismo Buró desks in main hotels. It's a good idea to book hotel rooms generally before noon. In the peak season, December to February, it is essential to book in advance. At other times it is possible to book at hotel reception. Prices given in the text are high season (15 December-15 March); low season prices are about 20% lower. Shop around for prices, eg one reader was quoted US$48 in the *Hotel Presidente* by Cubatur, US$42 when contacting the hotel direct, and US$28 through the agency Mexihabana, who have an office in the hotel. After 31 August many hotels go into hibernation and offer limited facilities, eg no restaurant, no swimming pool.

All hotels are owned by the government, solely or in joint ventures with foreign partners. All Cubanacán hotels are 4-5 star and were finished after 1991, they are the most expensive and are usually joint ventures. Gaviota hotels date from after 1990 and some of them are joint ventures, eg *Gaviota Club Med* and *Sol Club Sirenas*, both all-inclusives in Varadero. Gran Caribe also has 4-5 star hotels while Horizontes hotels are 3-star and Islazul has the cheaper end of the market, mostly for national tourism but foreigners are welcome. A 3-star hotel in Varadero costs US$30-50d bed and breakfast in high season, US$20-25 in low season, while a 4-star hotel will charge US$ 80-90 and US$60-70 respectively. Most 3-star hotels were built in the 1940s and 1950s and are showing their age, but some have been refurbished and are now considered 4-star.

● **Camping**
Official campsites are opening up all over the island; they are usually in nice surroundings and are good value. One such is El Abra International Campsite halfway between Havana and Varadero, which has extensive facilities (car hire, bicycles, mopeds, horses, watersports, tennis etc) and organizes excursions. Camping out on the beach or in a field is forbidden. Cubamar, Calle 15 No 752 esquina Paseo,

Vedado, T 30-5536/9, F 33-3111, will arrange bookings and transport to villa or cabin-style accommodation in most provinces, open Monday-Friday 0830-1700, Saturday-Sunday 0830-1200.

● **Private accommodation**
Cuba is geared more to package tourism than to independent visitors but self-employment is opening up opportunities which can prove rewarding for the visitor. Lodging with a family is possible (at US$10-25 per day) following new legislation in 1997 introducing taxation on a practice which had been going on for some time. Cubans are now allowed to rent out their houses, apartments or rooms, subject to health and hygiene regulations and incorporation into the tax system. Hustlers on the street will offer accommodation, but it is safer to arrange rooms through contacts if you can. A guide or hustler taking you to a private home will expect US$5 commission, which goes on your room rate. *Paladares*, private restaurants, can be a good source of information on places to stay; if they are not renting rooms themselves, they are bound to know someone who is. You should consider the location of private houses as local transport is usually difficult (is there a phone to call for a taxi?), check whether there is regular water, enquire about availability of food and if you have 24-hour access (eg a key). Remember that Cubans can buy peso food with ration coupons only. This food is not enough to feed a visitor and any extra food has to be bought in dollars, so either bring your own supply or pay tourist prices. Security is not a major issue in Cuba but you should always be careful with your belongings. **Note** It is best to check that the *casa particular* you stay in is legally registered and pays taxes. If you stay at an illegal residence and it is discovered, the Cuban family will be in big trouble. If you are asked, and don't want to be an informer, try forgetting all your Spanish. Be prepared for long waits for everything: buses,

cinemas, restaurants, shops etc. Service has improved somewhat in Havana tourist facilities with foreign investment and the passage of new legislation allowing employees to be sacked if they are not up to the job. Officials in the tourist industry, tour guides, agencies and hotel staff are generally efficient and helpful 'beyond the call of duty'. Take care with unofficial guides or 'friends' you make; if they take you to a bar or nightclub or restaurant you will be expected to pay for them and pay in dollars.

FOOD AND DRINK

FOOD

Visitors should remember that eating is often a problem and plan ahead. If you are going to a concert or the theatre (performances start at 2030 or 2100 in Havana). You will only be able to get a meal beforehand if you go to a *paladar*.

Breakfast can be particularly slow although this is overcome in the larger hotels which generally have buffets (breakfast US$3, lunch and dinner US$10-20). If not eating at a buffet, service, no matter what standard of restaurant or hotel, can be very slow (even if you are the only customers). Look out for the *oferta especial* in small hotels which gives guests a 25% discount on buffet meals in larger hotels. Also, the 'all-you-can-eat' vouchers for buffets in tourist hotels do not have to be used in the hotel where bought. Breakfast and one other meal may be sufficient if you fill in with street or 'dollar shop' snacks. All towns and cities have peso street stalls for sandwiches and snacks; change about US$10 for a 2-week stay if planning to avoid restaurants.

In Havana the peso food situation is improving. The Ministry of Agriculture has set up many *organopónicos* in the city to provide the capital with fresh vegetables grown under organic conditions and avoid transport costs. Outside Havana, including Havana province, shortages are not so bad. Self-catering has become easier with the farmers' markets and the new fish shops. The dollar shops sell mostly imported supplies. Tourists do not have access to local stores, or *bodegas*, as these are based on the national ration card system. Cubans are rationed to one small round bread a day and local products such as rice, beans, sugar and coffee, although available to dollar holders are severely rationed to Cuban families. Milk is allowed only for children up to the age of 7; chicken and beef are rare.

For vegetarians the choice is very limited, normally only cheese, sandwiches, spaghetti, pizzas, salads and omelettes. Even beans are usually cooked with meat or in meat fat. Generally, although restaurants have improved in the last few years,

Green banana soup

2 green bananas (plátanos)
1 large lime
1½ litres of stock (beef or chicken)
salt to taste

Peel and roughly chop the bananas and mix with half the lime juice. Put the banana in the stock, bring it to the boil and simmer, covered, until the banana is soft. Mash the banana with a little of the stock (or put it in the blender to make a purée) and return to the rest of the stock. Add the rest of the lime juice, season and simmer for 20 minutes. Serves 6.

An alternative method of making green banana soup is to slice a green banana thinly, fry the slices in oil and then crush them, using this to thicken a hot stock. Add some lime juice before serving.

Hatuey – freedom fighter and beer brand name

The first Cuban resistance fighter we know of was an Indian chief called Hatuey, who has now become a symbol of rebellion. He lived at the time of the Spanish invasion and when he discovered what the Spanish really wanted from his island he tried to mobilize his people. However, he was no match for the better-armed Spaniards, who chased him into the mountains, captured him and burnt him alive. The story goes that when approached by a priest and asked whether he would like to make a last request, confess and make his peace with God, he asked whether there would be Spanish people in heaven. When told that there would, he declined the offer saying he certainly didn't want to go there.

It took nearly four centuries before Cuban freedom fighters expelled the Spanish and gained their independence, limited though it was, and 1998 sees the centenary of that event. Cuba's former ally, the USA, will be noticeably absent from the celebrations, but Spanish investors and tourists have returned in great numbers and will no doubt join in the fiestas. Many thousands of other foreigners will also participate, now that Cuba is firmly established on the package holiday circuit with tourist facilities of international quality. Demand for beer to quench their thirst will no doubt be strong. A Hatuey *Cerveza* will do the trick.

the food in Cuba is not very exciting or enjoyable. There is little variety in the menu and menu items are frequently unavailable. Always check restaurant prices in advance and then your bill. Private restaurants are better; these *paladares* are now licensed, subjected to health inspections and regulations, and taxed, which may limit their scope in the short term.

The national dish is *congris* (rice mixed with black beans), roast pork and yuca (cassava) or fried plantain. Pork is traditionally eaten for the New Year's celebrations, so before then all the pigs which have been fattened on people's balconies or smallholdings are on the move (in various forms) in the backs of trucks, cars and bicycles to be sold privately or at the markets. Salads in restaurants are mixed vegetables which are slightly pickled and not to everyone's taste.

DRINK

Hatuey was the best of Cuba's many beers, named after an Indian chief ruling when the Spanish arrived, but in late 1997 it was unavailable because of a patent battle. Cristal is now probably the best, made by Cervecería Mayabe, in Holguín, which also makes Mayabe. Lagarto has also been recommended. The alcohol content of beers varies, eg a can of Hatuey contains 5.4% alcohol/volume, while a bottle of the same beer is only 4.8%; a bottle of Mayabe beer is 3.5% and a can of Cerveza Cristal is 4.9%.

GETTING AROUND

AIR TRANSPORT

Cubana de Aviación services between most of the main towns. From Havana (January 1998 prices) to Camagüey (US$60 one way), Holguín (US$74), Baracoa (US$80), Guantánamo (US$80), Manzanillo (US$66), Moa (US$80), Nueva Gerona/Isla de Juventud (US$22), Bayamo (US$66), Ciego de Avila (US$50), Las Tunas (US$66), Santiago (US$80), Cayo Largo and Cayo Coco (US$50), Varadero (US$24), all have airports. Return fare is twice the single fare. Tourists must pay airfares in US$; it is advisable to prebook flights at home as demand is very heavy, although you can get interprovincial flights from hotel tour desks if you are on a package. It is difficult to book flights from one city to another when you are not at the point of departure, except from Havana, the computer is not able to cope. Airports are usually a long way from the towns, so extra transport costs will be necessary. Delays are common. Cubana flights are very cold, take warm clothes and possibly some food for a long flight.

Although theoretically possible to get a scheduled flight as listed above, it is often only possible for tourists to travel on excursions: day trips or packages with flights, accommodation, meals and sightseeing.

Aerogaviota is a charter airline with national and international flights to Central America and the Caribbean, using 20-seater YAK-40 planes and 8-seater MI-8 helicopters.

LAND TRANSPORT

● Motoring

Petrol for foreigners is available in Cupet stations, costs US$0.75 per litre and must be paid for in US$. If possible, get the rental company to fill the car with fuel, otherwise your first day will be spent looking for petrol. One reader had to wait some hours near Playa Larga for the local fuel 'delivery vehicle', a horse and cart with two petrol drums, to arrive, and on another occasion when they stopped on the *autopista*, the driver had to siphon out petrol from another driver's tank while trying to avoid the watchful gaze of a policeman who was sitting nearby. Needless to say, the siphoned fuel cost a hugely inflated price. Hiring a car is recommended, in view of difficulties of getting seats on buses and trains and you can save a considerable amount of time but it is the most expensive form of travel. Breakdowns are not unknown, in which case you may be stuck with your rented car many kilometres from the nearest place that will accept dollars to help you. Be careful about picking up hitchhikers, although it can be an interesting and pleasant way of meeting Cubans as well as being a useful talking road map.

Autopistas are incredibly empty of traffic. As a result, Cubans have been using the hard surface for other purposes, such as drying rice on the roadside. A military band was seen practising as though the soldiers were on a parade ground. The dogs on the side of the road are often not dead, just asleep. On the other hand, the autopistas are good places to shop for fresh fruit and vegetables, vendors stand by the roadside or sell from broken down trucks. Most ordinary roads are in reasonable condition with hardly any potholes, but minor roads can be very badly maintained and signposting is uniformly atrocious.

● Car hire

Through state rental companies at the International Airport and most large hotels. Nacional Rent A Car is at Av 47, 4701 y 40, Rpto Kohly, Playa, Havana, T 81-0357, 23-7000, 20-6897, F 33-0742; in Matanzas (Varadero), T 056-2968/2620; Sancti Spíritus (Trinidad), T 042-40117/40330; Holguín, T 024-30102/30115; Santiago de Cuba, T 0226-41368; Isla de la Juventud, T 2-3290, 24486. Minimum US$40 a day (or US$50 for a/c) with limited mileage of 100 km a day, and US$8-20 a

	Bayamo	Camagüey	Cienfuegos	Guantánamo	Havana	Holguín	Matanzas	Pinar del Río	Santa Clara	Santiago de Cuba
Baracoa	313	524	853	116	1051	348	989	1192	793	193
Bayamo		211	540	197	738	71	676	879	480	120
Camagüey	211		329	408	527	208	465	668	269	331
Cárdenas	628	417	171	825	146	625	56	287	148	748
Ciego de Avila	321	110	219	518	397	318	335	538	139	441
Cienfuegos	540	329		737	246	537	199	387	61	660
Guantánamo	197	408	737		935	232	873	1076	677	77
Havana	738	527	246	935		735	90	141	258	858
Holguín	71	208	537	232	735		673	876	477	155
La Fé	989	778	497	1186	251	986	341	110	509	1109
Las Tunas	82	129	458	279	656	79	594	7979	398	202
Manzanillo	60	271	600	257	798	131	736	39	540	180
Matanzas	676	465	199	873	90	673		231	196	796
Nuevitas	286	75	404	483	602	283	540	743	344	406
Palma Soriano	73	284	613	124	811	108	749	952	553	47
Pinar del Río	879	668	387	1076	141	876	231		399	999
Sancti Spíritus	395	184	145	592	343	3924	281	484	85	515
Santa Clara	480	269	61	677	258	77	196	399		600
Santiago de Cuba	120	331	660	77	858	155	796	999	600	
Trinidad	468	257	72	665	318	465	271	459	122	588

Approximate distances in kilometres

day optional insurance, or US$50-88/day unlimited mileage; cheaper rates over 7 days. Visa, Mastercard, Eurocard, Banamex, JCB and Carnet accepted for the rental, or cash or traveller's cheques paid in advance, guarantee of US$200-250 required; you must also present your passport and home driving licence. In practice, you may find car hire rates prohibitively expensive when small cars are 'unavailable' and a 4-door sedan at US$93, unlimited kilometres, insurance included, is your only option. Staff have been reported as 'unhelpful' in finding what you want.

However, it pays to shop around, even between offices of the same company: the US$93 quoted for a 4-door sedan by Transautos next to the *Hotel Capri*, was US$10 less at Transautos at the *Hotel Nacional*, while the Transautos office at the *Hotel Plaza* did have a small car (really small) for US$60/day with no a/c, uncomfortable but economical in fuel consumption. Cubans are not allowed to hire cars, so even if you have organized a local driver you will have to show a foreign driving licence. Fly and drive packages can be booked from abroad through Cubacar, part of the Grupo Cubanacán, who have a wide range of jeeps and cars all over the country and can even arrange a driver at US$70 for 8 hours, or US$90 for 12 hours (e-mail pmando@cubacar.cha.cyt.cu). Or you can do it through a travel agency, eg in the UK, Journey Latin America, T 0181-747-8315, who can organize rentals of Suzuki Samurai jeeps (or equivalent). Most vehicles are Japanese makes, Suzuki jeeps can be hired for 6-12 hours in beach areas, US$11-22, plus US$8 insurance, extra hours US$5. Watch out for theft of radio and spare tyre; you will have to pay about US$350 if stolen unless you take out the costly extra insurance. Moped rental at resorts is around US$5-9/hour, cheaper for longer, US$25-30/day, US$80/week.

● **Bicycles**

For people who really want to explore the country in depth and independently, cycling around is excellent, although you are advised to bring your own bike and all spare parts. Iberia and Cubana airlines both accept bicycles as normal luggage as long as you do not take more than 20kg, but some charters, such as Marti-nair, charge extra. It is best to pack your bicycle in cardboard, with the front wheel turned 90°, the tyres half flat and the saddle off. A good quality bicycle is essential if you are going to spend many hours in the saddle, although that does not mean it has to be very sophisticated. We have heard from cyclists who have toured Cuba without gears, although they did have plenty of muscle.

Most of Cuba is flat, the road network is good and there is little traffic. In towns traffic tends to move at the speed of the hoards of bicycles imported by the government when the fuel shortage started to bite. In cities there are *parqueos bicicletas* where you can store your bike while walking around. If you need a lift, through the mountains, or across monotonous sugar cane fields, long distance trucks often take passengers with

bikes, ask the *Amarillos* who organize informal transport at road junctions outside towns. Cycling can get very hot, so you are advised to do long distances early in the morning between 0600-1000. Take plenty of food and water with you as supplies along the way can not be guaranteed. Carry a refillable bottle, preferably in a 'cool bag', take energy food, a bicycle repair kit, good tyres and spare tyres, so that you can change the tyres on the road and repair them in the evening, a spare brake cable, a hat and sun protection, and light clothing, it is too hot for cycling shorts.

For organized cycling tours of Cuba contact Bike Tours, in the UK, T 01225 480 130, F 01225 480 132; Fietsvakantiewinkel, Spoorlaan 19, 3445 AE Woerden, Holland, T 31-3480-21844, F 31-3480-23839. You may also be able to join a group of Cuban students (mostly English speaking) through the Club Ciclocaribe Olímpico, Comité Olímpico Cubano, Calle 13 esquina C 601, Vedado, Zona Postal 4, CH, Cuba, CP 10400.

● **Bus**

The local word for bus is *guagua*. In Havana there are huge double jointed buses pulled by a truck, called *camellos* (camels) because of their shape, also irreverently known as 'Saturday night at the cinema' because they are full of 'sex, crime and alcohol'. The urban bus fare throughout Cuba is 20 centavos for *camellos* and 40 centavos for all others, and it helps to have the exact fare. In the rush hours they are filled to more than capacity, making it hard to get off if you have managed to get on. Buses are running but fuel shortages limit services. Urban tickets can only be bought in pesos Cubanos.

For bus transport to other provinces from Havana there is a dollar ticket office in the Terminal de Omnibus Nacional, Boyeros y 19 de Mayo (3rd left via 19 de Mayo entrance), T 70-3397, open daily 0700-2100, very helpful staff. You don't have to book in advance but it might be wiser to do so. There may be cancellations. Another service is Víazul (Viaje Azul), at Av 26 entre Av Zoológico y Ulloa, Nuevo Vedado, T 811413/811108/815652, F 666092, open 0900-2300, with long distance buses and minibuses every other day to Varadero US$8, Cienfuegos US$20, Trinidad US$25, Santiago de Cuba US$51, fares one way. There is a weight limit for luggage of 20 kilos on all long distance bus journeys and the bus-hoverfoil to Isla de la Juventud.

It is theoretically possible to pay for tickets in pesos but, apart from all the complications of doing so, you will be depriving a Cuban of a seat. If you want the hassle, tickets between towns must be purchased in advance from: Oficina Reservaciones Pasajes, Calle 21, esquina 4, Vedado (main booking office for buses and trains from Havana to anywhere in the country, one-way only, open Monday to Friday 1200-1745, organized chaos); Plazoleta de la Virgen del Camino, San Miguel del Padrón; Calzada 10 de Octubre y Carmen, Centro; Terminal de Omnibus Nacional, Boyeros y 19 de Mayo (all in Havana). Look for notices in the window for latest availabilities, find out who is last in the queues (separate queues for buses and trains, sometimes waiting numbers issued), and ask around for what is the best bet. Maximum 3 tickets sold per person. Seat reservations are only possible on a few long distance routes (eg Havana-Trinidad Express) but you still need pesos Cubanos, or a Cuban entrepreneur to obtain one. Cubans queue professionally and make a profit out of selling places near the top of the queue. You may end up paying the same as if you'd gone to the dollar ticket office. Away from the capital and off the beaten tourist track, it is not so controversial to pay in pesos, in fact in many cases you will have no other option.

● **Hitchhiking**

With the shortage of fuel and decline in public transport since 1991, Cubans have taken to organized hitchhiking to get about. At every major junction outside towns throughout Cuba you will find the *Amarillos*, traffic wardens dressed in yellow, who organize a queue, stop traffic to find out where the trucks or vans are going, and load them with passengers. You pay a nominal amount in pesos, eg 6 pesos for a 4-hour ride Cienfuegos-Havana in an open truck.

● **Taxis**

There are three types of taxis: tourist taxis, Cuban taxis and private taxis (*particulares*). The best you can do is avoid the most expensive tourist taxis, which accept only dollars, have a meter and are costly. See **Transport** under Havana (page 126). **Dollar tourist taxis** can be hired for driving around; you pay for the distance, not for waiting time. On short routes, fares start at US$1. Airport to Havana (depending on destination), US$9-12 with Panataxi, to Playas del Este US$25, to Varadero US$71; Havana to Varadero US$65; Varadero airport to Varadero hotels US$13; Santiago de Cuba airport to *Hotel Las Américas* US$8, to *Balcón del Caribe* US$5. Cuban taxis, or *colectivos* also operate on fixed routes and pick you up only if you know where to stand for certain destinations. Travelling on them is an adventure and a complicated cultural experience. If you are lucky enough to get into a *colectivo*, sit at the back. The person in front pays the metered price starting from the time it is switched on. Anybody joining along the way pays a flat rate of 1 peso. If somebody charters the taxi first and sits at the back, the person joining later and sitting in front will have to pay the meter if the first customer in the back gets out first. Otherwise, if the first customer in is also the last out, he/she pays the full metered price independent of where he/she sat. Got that? Cubans are not allowed to carry foreigners in their vehicles, but they do; private taxis, *particulares*, are considerably cheaper than other taxis, eg airport to Havana centre

US$8-12, from Havana to Santa María del Mar beach US$8-10, from Santiago to the airport US$5. A *particular* who pays his tax will usually display a 'taxi' sign, which can be a hand-written piece of board, but have a private registration plate. Some have meters, in others you have to negotiate a price in either pesos or dollars, although as a foreigner you will be urged to pay in dollars. If not metered, 10 km should cost around US$5. For long distances you can negotiate with official taxis as well as *particulares*, and the price should be around US$10/hour. Taxis can work out cheaper than going on organized tours, if you are prepared to bargain. As a general rule, the cost will depend on the quality of your Spanish and how well you know the area. We have received reports of a Dutch family paying US$80 to travel from Havana to Viñales by taxi, although someone else was quoted US$50 to travel back to Havana by taxi.

● **Train**
Recommended whenever possible, although delays and breakdowns must be expected. Be at station at least 30 minutes before scheduled departure time. Fares are reasonable but have to be paid for in dollars, which will usually entitle you to a waiting area, seat reservation and being allowed to board before the big rush starts. There is a dollar ticket office in every station. Alternatively, the Tourist Desks in some of the larger hotels sell train tickets to foreigners, in dollars. Long distance trains allow only seated passengers, are spacious and comfortable, but extremely cold unless the air conditioning is broken, so take warm clothes. All carriages are smokers. Bicycles can be carried as an express item only. There is no food service except on the *especial*, when a trolley passes through once with sandwiches and juice, followed later by coffee (pay in pesos). Sometimes there are additional sandwiches and drinks for sale at a bar (dollars only), but it is advisable to take food with you.

NB Travel between provinces is usually booked solid several days or weeks in advance. If you are on a short trip you may do better to go on a package tour with excursions.

COMMUNICATIONS

● **Language**
Spanish, with local variants in pronunciation and vocabulary. English is becoming more commonly used; it is a university entrance requirement and encouraged by the influx of Canadian tourists. German, Italian and French are now spoken by people working in the tourist industry and tour guides are usually multilingual.

● **Language study**
Any Cuban embassy will give details, or, in Santiago, contact Cecilia Suárez, c/o Departamento de Idiomas, Universidad de Oriente, Av Patricio Lumumba, Código Postal 90500, Santiago de Cuba. Spanish courses at the University of Havana cost US$300-350 depending on the level and begin the first Monday of every month. For language combined with social study, contact Projecto Cultural ELI, PO Box 12227, 6000 Luzern 12, Switzerland, T/F 4141 360 8764, e-mail proyectocultural@compuserve.com, www.idiomas.ch/cuba.htm, 2-week courses all year.

● **Postal services**
When possible correspondence to Cuba should be addressed to post office boxes (Apartados), where delivery is more certain. Stamps can only be bought at Post Offices, or at certain hotels. Hotels will charge you in dollars, making the stamps very expensive, but you pay in pesos at the Post Offices. All postal services, national and international, have been described as appalling. Letters to Europe, for instance, take at least 4-5 weeks, up to 3 months. Cubans will stop you in the street and ask you to bring letters out of Cuba for them. Telegraphic services are adequate. You can send telegrams from all post offices in Havana.

Telegrams to Britain cost 49 centavos a word. The night letter rate is 3.85 pesos for 22 words.

● **Telecommunications**
Local telephone calls can be made from public telephones for 5 centavos. To phone abroad on a phone with international dialling facility, dial 119 followed by the country and regional codes and number. A telephone call to Europe costs US$6/minute. The cost of phoning the USA is US$4.50/minute from Havana, US$3 from Varadero and Guardalavaca hotels. Many hard currency hotels and airports (including Havana departure lounge and Santiago) have telephone offices where international calls can be made at high prices. No 'collect' calls allowed and only cash accepted. Collect calls to some places, including London, are possible from private Cuban telephones. At least one Havana hotel, the *Nacional*, can arrange for you to direct dial foreign countries from your room. Phonecards are in use at Etecsa call boxes, in different denominations from US$10-50, much cheaper for phoning abroad, eg US$10 for a 4-minute call to France. Telephone sockets (for computer users) are standard US type. The cost of these calls is high, connections are hard to make and you will be cut off frequently. In 1994 the US Federal Communications Commission approved applications from 5 US companies to provide direct telephone services to Cuba and for AT&T to expand its existing service. Mobile phones are commonly used in Cuba.

The international phone code for Cuba is 53. Codes for major towns are: Havana 7; Pinar del Río 82; Viñales 8; Nueva Gerona 61; Cárdenas and Varadero 5; Girón and Playa Larga 59; Matanzas 52; Cienfuegos 432; Rancho Luna 43; Santa Clara 422; rest of Villa Clara province 42; Arroyo Blanco 418; Jatibonico 41; Sancti Spíritus 41; Topes de Collante 42; Trinidad 419; Ciego de Avila, Cayo Coco and most of the province 33 except Morón 335; Camagüey 322; rest of Camagüey province 32; Las Tunas and most of the province 31; Bayamo, Manzanillo and all of Granma province 23; Holguín, Guardalavaca and all the province 24; Santiago de Cuba 226; Palma Soriano 225; El Cobre 22; Baracoa and Guantánamo 21; Isla de la Juventud 61.

MEDIA

● **Newspapers**
Granma, mornings except Sunday and Monday; *Trabajadores*, Trade Union weekly; *Tribuna* and *Juventud Rebelde*, also only weekly. *Opciones* is a weekly national and international trade paper. *Granma* has a weekly edition, *Granma International*, published in Spanish, English, French and Portuguese, and a monthly selected German edition, all have versions on the Internet, Website: http://www.granma.cu; main offices: Avenida General Suárez y Territorial, Plaza de la Revolución, La Habana 6, T 81-6265, F 33-5176, Telex: 0511 355; in UK 928 Bourges Boulevard, Peterborough PE1 2AN. *El País* is the Mexican edition of the Spanish newspaper, available daily, 2 days late. Foreign (not US) newspapers are sometimes on sale at the telex centre in *Habana Libre* and in the *Riviera* (also telex centre, open 0800-2000). The previous day's paper is available during the week. Weekend editions on sale Tuesday.

● **Television**
There are two national channels: Cubavisión and Tele Rebelde, which broadcast around 5-6 hours a day beginning at 1800. The Sun Channel can be seen at hotels and broadcasts a special programme for tourists 24 hours a day. Some of the upmarket hotels also have satellite TV.

Rounding up

ACKNOWLEDGEMENTS

For their help in the research and preparation of this Handbook I should like to thank the following: Angie Todd, our resident correspondent in Havana, who despite the difficulties in communications, managed to keep me informed and updated right up to the deadline; Gavin Clark, whose enthusiasm for travel and all things Cuban has enlivened much of the text; Mark Wilson, geology correspondent for the *Caribbean Islands Handbook*, who overcame numerous obstacles to get to Cuba; Hilary Emberton, who researched many colonial cities; Rigoberto Herrera Romero, who has answered questions and helped with Varadero; Orestes Cordovi Quintana with Holguín; and Arnaldo Iglesias who provided much information on Camagüey, Playa Santa Lucía and Santa Clara.

Angie Todd had help with fact finding from Frank Sánchez and Brian López, to whom she is most grateful, and would like to give a special mention to Arelys Jañez, guide at the Maqueta de la Habana, for a fascinating account of the development of Havana. We are also grateful to Ellen Rosenzweig for letting us use her e-mail and Angie's friends who we woke up in the night to receive faxes.

Gavin Clark would like to thank Grethel Suárez Sánchez, a continual source of help and information in Santiago de Cuba, Peter Hope for help with transport and research in Guantánamo and Baracoa, Wilder Laffite Lanañino, Public Relations Officer at *Hotel Porto Santo*, who was extremely helpful on Baracoa, Daniel Salomon Paján, conservation officer at the Museo de Baracoa, for useful historical information, Alberto Matos Llime, promoter at Galería Yara, for more information on Baracoa, and Yenima Soto, Press Officer, plus all the staff at Casa de las Américas, Havana, for information on Cuban art.

Hilary Emberton would like to thank Marjorie Zimmerman, Panfilo Barbón and Yvonne Pedraza (general Cuba) as well as Francisco López Cala and Enrique Pérez Pozo of Rumbos, Santa Clara, José Ramírez Pupo in Santiago, Balbina Cadahía Benavente, Richardo Valladares Sabín and Armando Valladares Cadahía in Trinidad.

310

Arnaldo Iglesias would like to thank Gustavo Sed, Altamira Travel Agency, Andrea, Camilita, Karen and Dianelis.

Not forgetting Rhoda Williams, for secretarial help and for being a great travelling companion who helped me sample all those rum cocktails in half the time it would have taken me on my own, but with twice the pleasure.

Thanks are also due to all the travellers and correspondents who contributed to the 1998 edition of the *Caribbean Islands Handbook*.

Finally, special thanks to Ben Box, editor of the *South American Handbook*, and our daughters, Katie and Jenny, for their tolerance, encouragement and complete conviction that Mummy's book is by far the best on Cuba.

FURTHER READING

The Penguin History of Latin America, by Edwin Williamson (1992), is an excellent general history of Cuba's colonial past and independence and revolutionary struggles, set in the context of what else was happening in the Spanish empire and independent Latin American republics. *The Cambridge Encyclopaedia of Latin America and the Caribbean*, edited by Simon Collier, Thomas E Skidmore and Harold Blakemore (2nd edition 1992) is also useful and includes much cultural, geographical and economic information on Cuba in the Latin American context. For an introduction to Cuban literature and writings on Cuba, *The Traveller's Literary Companion, The Caribbean*, by James Ferguson with chapters on Cuba and Puerto Rico by Jason Wilson (1997), is very good and includes a good reading list.

The best history specifically on Cuba is *Cuba, or the Pursuit of Freedom*, by Hugh Thomas (1971). Other books which can be recommended include: *Guía de Arquitectura La Habana Colonial*, La Habana, Sevilla 1995, useful guide book to Old Havana, with maps, ground plans and photos; *Rumba, Dance and Social Change in Comtemporary Cuba*, Yvonne Daniel, Indiana University Press, 1995, in the series: Blacks in the Diaspora (ISBN 0-253-31605-7, paperback ISBN 0-253-20948-X), good general book on Cuba as well as on music, portrait of life on the streets, the author is a professional dancer who completed her research in 1991; *Machos, Maricones and Gays, Cuba and Homosexuality*, Ian Lumsden, Temple University Press, Philadelphia, 1996, also in the UK by Latin American Bureau (ISBN 1-56639-371-X), very readable account of the attitudes of Cubans towards gays since the days of slavery, with related treatment of blacks and women; *Afro-Cuba, an Anthology of Cuban Writing on Race, Politics and Culture*, edited by Pedro Pérez Sarduy and Jean Stubbs, published by Ocean Press, Melbourne, Australia, 1993, and Latin American Bureau (ISBN 0-906156-75-0), a collection of fiction, theatre, poetry, historical and political commentary, a bit of everything dealing with the relationship between Africa and Cuba; *Cuba, the Test of Time*, Jean Stubbs, published by Latin American Bureau, London, 1989 (ISBN 0-906156-42-4), short analysis of the first 30 years of the Revolution from the historical and economic viewpoint, still useful even without the upheaval of the 1990s; *In Focus: Cuba, A Guide to the People, Politics and Culture* by Simon Calder and Emily Hatchwell, published by Latin American Bureau (ISBN 0 906156 95 5), one of an excellent series of books on Latin American and Caribbean countries, with descriptions of history, economic, politics and culture.

See the **Literature** section (page 69) for noteworthy Cuban novelists and poets, the **Music** section (page 74) for a bibliography on Cuban music and the section on **Religion** (page 59) for writing on *santería* and AfroCuban religion.

MAPS

Get your maps in Cuba if you can wait, they are generally more reliable and up to date than any of the foreign maps we have seen, although even then not perfect, although it depends on what you are looking for and how much detail you want. Mapa Geográfico is one of the best maps, with a large map of Cuba, accompanied by several smaller maps of towns, regions and routes. It is one of the more accurate and up to date. For individual states and areas there are very good provincial maps going under the name of Mapa Turístico, usually including the provincial capital and sometimes other places of interest, but you will probably only find them in the relevant province. One shop to try for maps of all kinds including nautical maps is *El Navegante*, Mercaderes entre Obispo y Obrapía in Old Havana.

Words and phrases

NO AMOUNT of dictionaries, phrase books or word lists will provide the same enjoyment as being able to communicate directly with the people of the country you are visiting. Learning Spanish is a useful part of the preparation for a trip to Cuba and you are encouraged to make an effort to grasp the basics before you go. As you travel you will pick up more of the language and the more you know, the more you will benefit from your stay. The following section is designed to be a simple point of departure.

General pronunciation

The stress in a Spanish word conforms to one of three rules: 1) if the word ends in a vowel, or in **n** or **s**, the accent falls on the penultimate syllable (*ventana, ventanas*); 2) if the word ends in a consonant other than **n** or **s**, the accent falls on the last syllable (*hablar*); 3) if the word is to be stressed on a syllable contrary to either of the above rules, the acute accent on the relevant vowel indicates where the stress is to be placed (*pantalón, metáfora*). Note that adverbs such as *cuando*, 'when', take an accent when used interrogatively: *¿cuándo?*, 'when?'

Vowels

a   not quite as short as in English 'cat'
e   as in English 'pay', but shorter in a syllable ending in a consonant
i   as in English 'seek'
o   as in English 'shop', but more like 'pope' when the vowel ends a syllable
u   as in English 'food'; after 'q' and in 'gue', 'gui', **u** is unpronounced; in 'güe' and 'güi' it is pronounced
y   when a vowel, pronounced like 'i'; when a semiconsonant or consonant, it is pronounced like English 'yes'
ai, ay   as in English 'ride'
ei, ey   as in English 'they'
oi, oy   as in English 'toy'

Unless listed below **consonants** can be pronounced in Spanish as they are in English.

b, v   their sound is interchangeable and is a cross between the English 'b' and 'v', except at the beginning of a word or after 'm' or 'n' when it is like English 'b'
c   like English 'k', except before 'e' or 'i' when it is as the 's' in English 'sip'
g   before 'e' and 'i' it is the same as **j**
h   when on its own, never pronounced
j   as the 'ch' in the Scottish 'loch'
ll   as the 'g' in English 'beige'; sometimes as the 'lli' in 'million'
ñ   as the 'ni' in English 'onion'

rr trilled much more strongly than in English

x depending on its location, pronounced as in English 'fox', or 'sip', or like 'gs'

z as the 's' in English 'sip'

GREETINGS, COURTESIES

excuse me/I beg your pardon *permiso*
Go away! *¡Váyase!*
good afternoon/evening/night *buenas tardes/noches*
good morning *buenos días*
goodbye *adiós/chao*
hello *hola*
how are you? *¿cómo está?/¿cómo estás?*
I do not understand *no entiendo*
no *no*
please speak slowly
  hable despacio por favor
please *por favor*
pleased to meet you *mucho gusto/ encantado/encantada*
see you later *hasta luego*
thank you (very much) *(muchas) gracias*
what is your name *¿cómo se llama?*
yes *sí*

BASIC QUESTIONS

how do I get to_? *¿cómo llegar a_?*
how much does it cost? *¿cuánto cuesta?*
how much is it? *¿cuánto es?*
is this the way to the church?
  ¿la iglesia está por aquí?
what for? *¿para qué?*
what time is it? *¿qué hora es?*
when does the train leave? *¿a qué hora sale el tren?*
  - arrive? *- llega -*
when? *¿cuándo?*
where is_? *¿dónde está_?*
why? *¿por qué?*

BASICS

bank *el banco*
bathroom/toilet *el baño*
cash *el efectivo*
exchange house *la casa de cambio*
exchange rate *la tasa de cambio*
notes/coins *los billetes/las monedas*
police (policeman) *la policía (el policía)*

post office *el correo*
supermarket *el supermercado*
telephone office *el centro de llamadas*
travellers' cheques *los travelers/los cheques de viajero*

GETTING AROUND

aeroplane/airplane *el avión*
airport *el aeropuerto*
bus station *la terminal (terrestre)*
bus stop *la parada*
bus *el bus/el autobus/la guagua etc*
first/second class *primera/segunda clase*
on the left/right *a la izquierda/derecha*
second street on the left *la segunda calle a la izquierda*
straight on *derecho*
ticket office *la taquilla*
ticket *el boleto*
to walk *caminar*
train station *la estación (de tren/ferrocarril)*
train *el tren*

ACCOMMODATION

aspirin *la aspirina*
blankets *las mantas*
blood *la sangre*
Chemist *farmacia*
clean/dirty towels *toallas limpias/sucias*
condoms *los preservativos*
contact lenses *las lentes de contacto*
contraceptive (pill) *anticonceptivo (la píldora anticonceptiva)*
diarrhoea *la diarrea*
doctor *el médico*
fever/sweat *la fiebre/el sudor*
(for) pain *(para) dolor*
head *la cabeza*
hot/cold water *agua caliente/fría*
noisy *ruidoso*
period/towels *la regla/las toallas*
pillows *las almohadas*
room *el cuarto/la habitación*
sheets *las sábanas*
single/double *sencillo/doble*
stomach *el estómago*
to make up/clean *limpiar*
toilet paper *el papel higiénico*
with private bathroom *con baño*
with two beds *con dos camas*

TIME

at one o'clock *a la una*
at half past two/ two thirty *a las dos y media*
at a quarter to three *a cuarto para las tres or a las tres menos quince*
it's one o'clock *es la una*
it's seven o'clock *son las siete*
it's twenty past six/six twenty *son las seis y veinte*
it's five to nine *son cinco para las nueve/ son las nueve menos cinco*
in ten minutes *en diez minutos*
five hours *cinco horas*
does it take long? *¿tarda mucho?*

Monday *lunes*
Tuesday *martes*
Wednesday *miércoles*
Thursday *jueves*
Friday *viernes*
Saturday *sábado*
Sunday *domingo*

January *enero*
February *febrero*
March *marzo*
April *abril*
May *mayo*
June *junio*
July *julio*
August *agosto*
September *septiembre*
October *octubre*
November *noviembre*
December *diciembre*

NUMBERS

one *uno/una*
two *dos*
three *tres*
four *cuatro*
five *cinco*
six *seis*
seven *siete*
eight *ocho*
nine *nueve*
ten *diez*
eleven *once*
twelve *doce*
thirteen *trece*
fourteen *catorce*

fifteen *quince*
sixteen *dieciseis*
seventeen *diecisiete*
eighteen *dieciocho*
nineteen *diecinueve*
twenty *veinte*
twenty one, two *veintiuno, veintidos etc*
thirty *treinta*
forty *cuarenta*
fifty *cincuenta*
sixty *sesenta*
seventy *setenta*
eighty *ochenta*
ninety *noventa*
hundred *cien or ciento*
thousand *mil*

KEY VERBS

To Go
ir
I go voy; you go (familiar singular) vas; he, she, it goes, you (unfamiliar singular) go va; we go vamos; they, you (plural) go van.

To Have (possess)
tener
tengo; tienes; tiene; tenemos; tienen (also used as To Be, as in 'I am hungry' tengo hambre)
(**NB** haber also means to have, but is used with other verbs, as in 'he has gone' ha ido.)
he; has; ha; hemos; han.
Hay means 'there is'; perhaps more common is No hay meaning 'there isn't any')

To Be (in a permanent state)
ser
soy (profesor - I am a teacher); eres; es; somos; son

To Be (positional or temporary state)
estar
estoy (en Londres - I am in London); estás; está (contenta - she is happy); estamos; están.

This section has been compiled on the basis of glossaries compiled by André de Mendonça and David Gilmour of South American Experience, London, and the Latin American Travel Advisor, No 9, March 1996.

CUBA FOOD VOCABULARY

avocado *aguacate*
bakery *panadería*
banana chips *mariquitas*
beans *frijoles*
beef *carne de res*
beef steak or pork fillet *bistec*
boiled rice *arroz blanco*
bread *pan*
breakfast *desayuno*
butter *mantequilla*
cassava, yucca *yuca*
cheese *queso*
chewing gum *chicle*
chicken *pollo*
chilli pepper or green pepper *ají*
clear soup, stock *caldo*
cod, salt cod *bacalao*
cooked *cocido*
dining room *comedor*
egg *huevo*
family restaurant *paladar*
fish *pescado*
fork *tenedor*
fried *frito*
garlic *ajo*
grapefruit *toronja*
grill *parrilla*
guava *guayaba*
ham *jamón*
hamburger *hamburguesa*
hot, spicy *picante*
ice cream *helado*
jam *mermelada*
knife *cuchillo*
lime *limón*
lobster *langosta*
lunch *almuerzo*
margarine, fat *manteca*

meal, supper, dinner *comida*
meat *carne*
minced meat *picadillo*
mixed salad *ensalada mixta*
okra *quimbombó*
omelette *revoltillo*
onion *cebolla*
orange *naranja*
pepper *pimiento*
plantain, green banana *plátano*
pork *cerdo*
potato *papa*
prawns *camarones*
raw *crudo*
restaurant *el restaurante*
rice and black beans *moros y cristianos*
rice and kidney beans *congri*
roast *asado*
root or starchy vegetables *viandas*
salad *ensalada*
salt *sal*
sandwich *bocadillo*
sauce *salsa*
scrambled eggs *huevos revueltos*
seafood *mariscos*
small sandwich, filled roll *bocadito*
soup *sopa*
spoon *cuchara*
squash *calabaza*
squid *calamares*
supper *cena*
sweet *dulce*
sweet potato *boniato*
to eat *comer*
toasted *tostado*
turkey *pavo*
turtle *tortuga*
vegetables *legumbres/vegetales*
without meat *sin carne*
yam *ñame*

CUBA DRINK VOCABULARY

aged rum *ron añejo*
beer *cerveza*
boiled *hervido*
bottled *en botella*
camomile tea *manzanilla*
canned *en lata*
carbonated water *agua mineral con gas*
cocktail *coctel*
coconut milk *leche de coco*
coffee *café*
cold *frío*
condensed milk *leche condensada*
cup *taza*
drink *bebida*
drunk *borracho*
fruit milk shake *batido*
glass *vaso*
glass of liqueur *copa de licor*

hot *caliente*
ice *hielo*
juice *jugo*
milk *leche*
mint *menta*
red wine *vino tinto*
rough rum, firewater *aguardiente*
rum *ron*
small, strong coffee *cafecito*
soft drink *refresco*
soft fizzy drink *la gaseosa/cola*
still mineral water *agua mineral natural (sin gas)*
sugar *azúcar*
sugar cane juice *guarapa*
tea *té*
to drink *beber/tomar*
water *agua*
white coffee *café con leche*
white wine *vino blanco*

Useful Cuban words and phrases

Pronunciation
Cubans, like many other Latin Americans, often drop the letter S in the middle or end of the word, replacing it with a slight aspiration, eg *dos* becomes *do'h*, and *espera* becomes *e'hpera*.

'jockey', escort *jinetero/a*
1 peso convertible note *chavito*
bus *guagua*
buzz off, go away *lárgate*
camel, long bus pulled by a truck engine *camello*
car, vehicle *carro*
dollar (slang) *fula, fao*
dollar store, shop *tienda*
foreigner (slang) *yuma*
freelancer, entrepreneur *cuentapropista*
horse drawn vehicle *coche, carretón*
private home (room rental) *casa particular*
private restaurant *paladar*
queue, line *cola, fila*
state exchange bureau *Cadeca*
train/bus station *terminal de trenes/bus*
what's up? *¿qué bolá?*
you're welcome *por nada*

CDR
Comités de Defensa de la Revolución (a mass organization with a representative office in every block to keep an eye on everybody)

UJC
Unión de Jóvenes Comunistas (young Communists league)

Health in the Caribbean

S TAYING healthy in the Caribbean is straightforward. With the following advice and precautions you should keep as healthy as you do at home and most travellers experience no problems at all beyond an upset stomach. Obviously this in part depends on how you are travelling: the beach tourist who stays in good hotels is much less at risk than the backpacker who slings his hammock in the back of beyond. Most of the islands have a tropical climate but this does not mean that tropical diseases as such are a great problem or even the main problem for visitors. Should you fall ill, remember that throughout the islands there are well qualified doctors who speak good English (or French or Spanish). Medical practices may vary from those you are used to but there is likely to be better experience in dealing with locally occurring diseases. Most of the better hotels have a doctor on standby so do not be afraid to ask at reception. If you do fall ill in Cuba and you are not at a hotel, go to the local hospital or International Clinic. See Health page 17.

BEFORE TRAVELLING

Take out medical insurance. Make sure it covers all eventualities especially evacuation to your home country by a medically equipped plane, if necessary. You should have a dental check up, obtain a spare glasses prescription, a spare oral contraceptive prescription (or enough pills to last) and, if you suffer from a chronic illness (such as diabetes, high blood pressure, ear or sinus troubles, cardiopulmonary disease or a nervous disorder) arrange for a check-up with your doctor, who can at the same time provide you with a letter explaining the details of your disability in English or, if necessary, French or Spanish. Check the current practice in countries you are visiting for malaria prophylaxis (prevention) if you are going to the Guianas, Dominican Republic or Haiti.

CHILDREN

More preparation is probably necessary for babies and children than for an adult and perhaps a little more care should be taken when travelling to remote areas where health services are primitive. This is because children can become more rapidly ill than adults (on the other hand they often recover more quickly). Diarrhoea and vomiting are the most common problems, so take the usual precautions, but more intensively. Breastfeeding is best and most convenient for babies, but powdered milk is generally available and so are baby foods. Papaya, bananas and avocados are all nutritious and can be cleanly prepared. The treatment of diarrhoea is the same as for adults, except that it should start earlier and be continued with more persistence. Children get dehydrated very quickly in hot countries and can become drowsy and unco-operative unless cajoled to drink water or juice plus salts. Upper respiratory infections, such as colds, catarrh and middle ear infections are also common and if your child suffers from these normally take some antibiotics against the possibility. Outer ear infections after swimming are also common and antibiotic eardrops will help. 'Wet wipes' are always useful and sometimes difficult to find in the Caribbean, as in some places such as Cuba, are disposable nappies.

MEDICINES AND WHAT TO TAKE WITH YOU

There is little control on the sale of drugs and medicines in some of the Caribbean. You may be able to buy any and every drug in pharmacies without a prescription. Be wary of this because pharmacists can be poorly trained and might sell you drugs that are unsuitable, dangerous or old. Many drugs and medicines are manufactured under licence from American or European companies, so the trade names may be familiar to you. This means you do not have to carry a whole chest of medicines with you (except in Cuba, where there are shortages, see Health page 17) but remember that the shelf life of some items, especially vaccines and antibiotics, is markedly reduced in hot conditions. Buy your supplies at the better outlets where there are refrigerators, even though more expensive and check the expiry date of all preparations you buy. Immigration officials occasionally confiscate scheduled drugs (Lomotil is an example) if they are not accompanied by a doctor's prescription.

Self-medication may be forced on you by circumstances so the following text does include the names of drugs and medicines which you may find useful in an emergency or in out-of-the-way places and you may like to take some of the following items with you from home:

Sunglasses – ones designed for intense sunlight
Earplugs – for sleeping on aeroplanes and in noisy hotels
Suntan cream – high protection factor
Insect repellent – containing DET for preference

Mosquito net – lightweight permethrin-impregnated for choice

Tablets – for travel sickness

Tampons – can be expensive in some countries

Condoms

Contraceptives

Water sterilizing tablets

Antimalarials

Anti-infective cream eg Cetrimide

Dusting powder for feet etc – containing fungicide

Antacid tablets – for indigestion

Sachets of rehydration salts plus anti-diarrhoea preparations

Painkillers such as Paracetamol or Aspirin

Antibiotics – for diarrhoea etc

A simple first aid kit

Small pack containing a few sterile syringes and needles and disposable gloves – the risk of catching hepatitis etc from a dirty needle used for injection is now negligible in the Caribbean but some may be reassured by carrying their own supplies – available from camping shops and often at airports.

VACCINATION AND IMMUNIZATION

Smallpox vaccination is no longer required anywhere in the world. Neither is yellow fever vaccination unless you are going to or are coming from South America. The cholera epidemic in South and Central America has not spread to any of the Caribbean islands but they are all on the alert for the possibility. Although cholera vaccination is largely ineffective, immigration officers may ask for proof of such vaccination if coming from a country where the epidemic has occurred.

Typhoid A disease spread by the insanitary preparation of food. A number of new vaccines against this condition are now available; the older T AB and monovalent typhoid vaccines are being phased out. The newer, eg Typhim Vi, cause fewer side effects, but are more expensive. For those who do not like injections, there are now oral vaccines.

Poliomyelitis Despite its decline in the world this remains a serious disease if caught and is easy to protect against. There are live oral vaccines and in some countries injected vaccines. Whichever one you choose it is a good idea to have a booster every 3-5 years if visiting developing countries regularly.

Tetanus One dose should be given with a booster at 6 weeks and another at 6 months and 10 yearly boosters thereafter are recommended.

Children should already be properly protected against diphtheria, poliomyelitis and pertussis (whooping cough), measles and HIB, all of which can be more serious infections in the Caribbean than at home. Measles, mumps and rubella vaccine is also given to children throughout the world, but those teenage girls who have not had rubella (German measles) should be tested and vaccinated. Hepatitis B vaccination for babies is now routine in some countries. Consult your doctor for advice on tuberculosis innoculation: the disease is still present on some of the Islands – BVI, Grenada, Guadeloupe, Haiti and Martinique.

Infectious Hepatitis is less of a problem for travellers than it used to be because of the development of two extremely effective vaccines against the A and B form of the disease. It remains common, however, in some of the islands. A combined hepatitis A and B vaccine is now licensed and has been available since 1997 – one jab covers both diseases.

Other Vaccinations Might be considered in the case of epidemics, eg meningitis. There is an effective vaccination against rabies which should be considered by all travellers, especially those going through remote areas or if there is a particular occupational risk, eg for zoologists or veterinarians.

FURTHER INFORMATION

Further information on health risks abroad, vaccinations etc, may be available from a local travel clinic. If you wish to take specific drugs with you such as antibiotics these are best prescribed by your own doctor. Beware, however, that not all doctors can be experts on the health problems of remote countries. More detailed or more up-to-date information than local doctors can provide are available from various sources. In the UK there are hospital departments specializing in tropical diseases in London, Liverpool, Birmingham and Glasgow and the Malaria Reference Laboratory at the London School of Hygiene and Tropical Medicine provides free advice about malaria, T 0891 600350. In the USA the local Public Health Services can give such information and information is available centrally from the Centres for Disease Control (CDC) in Atlanta, T (404) 3324559.

There are in addition computerized databases which can be accessed for destination – specific up-to-the-minute information. In the UK there is MAST A (Medical Advisory Service to Travellers Abroad) T 0171 631 4408, Tx 8953473, F 0171 436 5389 and Travax (Glasgow, telephone 0141 946 7120 extension 247). Other information on medical problems overseas can be obtained from the book by Richard Dawood (Editor) – Travellers' Health, How to Stay Healthy Abroad, Oxford University Press 1992 £7.99 (new edition imminent). We strongly recommend this revised and updated edition, especially to the intrepid traveller heading for the more out of the way places. General advice is also available in the UK in 'Health Information for Overseas Travel' published by the Department of Health and available from HMSO and 'International Travel and Health' published by WHO Handbooks on First Aid are produced by the British & American Red Cross and by St John's Ambulance (UK).

ON THE WAY

For most travellers a trip to the Caribbean means a long air flight. If this crosses time zones then jetlag can be a problem where your body's biological clock gets out of synchrony with the real time at your destination. The main symptoms are tiredness and sleepiness at inconvenient times and, conversely, a tendency to wake up in the middle of the night feeling like you want your breakfast. Most find that the problem is worse when flying in an easterly direction. The best way to get over jetlag is probably to try to force yourself into the new time zone as strictly as possible which may involve, on a westward flight, trying to stay awake until your normal bedtime and on an eastward flight forgetting that you have lost some sleep on the way out and going to bed relatively early but near your normal time the evening after you arrive. The symptoms of jetlag may be helped by keeping up your fluid intake on the journey, but not with alcohol. The hormone melatonin seems to reduce the symptoms of jetlag but is not presently licensed in most of Europe although can be obtained from health food stores in the USA.

On long-haul flights it is also important to stretch your legs at least every hour to prevent slowing of the circulation and the possible development of blood clots. Drinking plenty of non-alcoholic fluids will also help.

If travelling by boat then sea sickness can be a problem – dealt with in the usual way by taking anti-motion sickness pills.

STAYING HEALTHY

INTESTINAL UPSETS

The thought of catching a stomach bug worries visitors to the Caribbean but there have been great improvements in food hygiene and most such infections are preventable. Travellers' diarrhoea and vomiting is due, most of the time, to food poisoning, usually passed on by the insanitary habits of food handlers. As a general rule the cleaner your surroundings and the smarter the restaurant, the less likely you are to suffer.

Water purification

There are a number of ways of purifying water in order to make it safe to drink. Dirty water should first be strained through a filter bag (camping shops) and then boiled or treated. Bringing water to a rolling boil at sea level is sufficient to make the water safe for drinking, but at higher altitudes you have to boil the water for longer to ensure that all the microbes are killed.

There are sterilizing methods that can be used and there are proprietary preparations containing chlorine (eg Puritabs) or Iodine (eg Pota Aqua) compounds. Chlorine compounds generally do not kill protozoa (eg giardia).

There are a number of water filters now on the market available both in personal and expedition size. They work either on mechanical or chemical principles, or may do both. Make sure you take the spare parts or spare chemicals with you and do not believe everything the manufacturers say.

Foods to avoid Uncooked, undercooked, partially cooked or reheated meat, fish, eggs. Raw vegetables and salads, especially when they have been left out and exposed to flies. Stick to fresh food that has been cooked from raw just before eating and make sure you peel fruit yourself. Wash and dry your hands before eating – disposable wet-wipe tissues are useful for this.

Shellfish eaten raw are risky and at certain times of the year some fish and shellfish concentrate toxins from their environment and cause various kinds of food poisoning. The local authorities notify the public not to eat these foods. Do not ignore the warning. Heat treated milk (UHT) pasteurized or sterilized is becoming more available in the Caribbean as is pasteurized cheese. On the whole matured or processed cheeses are safer than the fresh varieties. Fresh unpasteurized milk from whatever animal can be a source of food poisoning germs, tuberculosis and brucellosis. This applies equally to ice cream, yoghurt and cheese made from unpasteurized milk, so avoid these homemade products – the factory made ones are probably safer.

Tap water is rarely safe outside the major cities, especially in the rainy season and stream water, if you are in the countryside, is often contaminated by communities living surprisingly high in the mountains. Filtered or bottled water is usually available and safe, although you must make sure that somebody is not filling such bottles from the tap and hammering on a new crown cap. If your hotel has a central hot water supply this water is safe to drink after cooling. Ice for drinks should be made from boiled water, but rarely is so stand your glass on the ice cubes, rather than putting them in the drink. The better hotels have water purifying systems.

TRAVELLERS' DIARRHOEA

This is usually caused by eating food which has been contaminated by food poisoning germs. Drinking water is rarely the culprit. Sea water or river water is more likely to be contaminated by sewage and so swimming in such dilute effluent can also be a cause.

Infection with various organisms can give rise to travellers' diarrhoea. They may be viruses, bacteria, eg Escherichia coli (probably the most common cause worldwide), protozoal (such as amoebas and giardia) salmonella and cholera. The diarrhoea may come on suddenly or rather slowly. It may or may not be accompanied by vomiting or by severe abdominal pain and the passage of blood or mucus when it is called dysentery. How do you know which type you have caught and how to treat it?

If you can time the onset of the diarrhoea to the minute ('acute') then it is probably due to a virus or a bacterium and/or the onset of dysentery. The treatment in addition to rehydration is Ciprofloxacin 500 mg every 12 hrs; the drug is now widely available and there are many similar ones.

If the diarrhoea comes on slowly or intermittently ('sub-acute') then it is more likely to be protozoal, ie caused by an amoeba or giardia. Antibiotics such as Ciprofloxacin will have little effect. These cases are best treated by a doctor as is any outbreak of diarrhoea continuing for more than 3 days. Sometimes blood is passed in amoebic dysentery and for this you should certainly seek medical help. If this is not available then the best treatment is probably Tinidazole (Fasigyn) 1 tablet four times a day for 3 days. If there are severe stomach cramps, the following drugs may help but are not very useful in the management of acute diarrhoea: Loperamide (Imodium) and Diphenoxylate with Atropine (Lomotil). They should not be given to children.

Any kind of diarrhoea, whether or not accompanied by vomiting, responds well to the replacement of water and salts, taken as frequent small sips, of some kind of rehydration solution. There are proprietary preparations consisting of sachets of powder which you dissolve in boiled water or you can make your own by adding half a teaspoonful of salt (3.5 grammes) and 4 tablespoonsful of sugar (40 grammes) to a litre of boiled water.

Thus the lynch pins of treatment for diarrhoea are rest, fluid and salt replacement, antibiotics such as Ciprofloxacin for the bacterial types and special diagnostic tests and medical treatment for the amoeba and giardia infections. Salmonella infections and cholera, although rare, can be devastating diseases and it would be wise to get to a hospital as soon as possible if these were suspected.

Fasting, peculiar diets and the consumption of large quantities of yoghurt have not been found useful in calming travellers' diarrhoea or in rehabilitating inflamed bowels. Oral rehydration has on the other hand, especially in children, been a life saving technique and should always be practised, whatever other treatment you use. As there is some evidence that alcohol and milk might prolong diarrhoea they should be avoided during and immediately after an attack.

Diarrhoea occurring day after day for long periods of time (chronic diarrhoea) is notoriously resistent to amateur attempts at treatment and again warrants proper diagnostic tests (most towns with reasonable sized hospitals have laboratories for stool samples).

There are ways of preventing travellers' diarrhoea for short periods of time by taking antibiotics, but this is not a foolproof technique and should not be used other than in exceptional circumstances. Doxycycline is possibly the best drug. Some preventatives such as Enterovioform can have serious side effects if taken for long periods.

Paradoxically constipation is also common, probably induced by dietary change, inadequate fluid intake in hot places and long bus journeys. Simple laxatives are useful in the short-term and bulky foods such as maize, beans and plenty of fruit are also useful.

HEAT AND COLD

Full acclimatization to high temperatures takes about 2 weeks. During this period it is normal to feel a bit apathetic, especially if the relative humidity is high. Drink plenty of water (up to 15 litres a day are required when working physically hard in the tropics) use salt on your food and avoid extreme exertion. Tepid showers are more cooling than hot or cold ones. Large hats do not cool you down, but do prevent sunburn. Remember that, especially in the highlands, there can be a large and sudden drop in temperature between sun and shade and between night and day, so dress accordingly. Warm

Accidents will happen

It was 1996, and Eileen, a retired travel agent from Canada, was enjoying a bit of R&R with friends in one of her favourite countries: Cuba. It was all going well; they had stayed a few days in Guardalavaca and had arranged a tour to Guantánamo to see the US Naval Base, via Sherritt's nickel plant at Moa, ending up in Santiago overnight. So far so good. Then Eileen slipped on the steps at her hotel, broke her thigh and began some first hand research into the Cuban health service.

"The first thing I advise: medical insurance, and take a copy of your policy with you. Read it carefully before you leave home, know what it covers, and most important, the phone number to call. In the case of Cuba, I called the medical insurance head office, and asked which telephone number to call (the toll free numbers do not work from there and Cuba does not accept collect calls). They advised me to use a telephone number in Brighton, England! It was put through the hotel operator and I paid US$90, but this can be put on a credit card, at least from the hotel.

As for the International Clinic charges in Santiago, the bill was US$192 (which can be put on a credit card), which included: the ambulance from the hotel to the clinic and back and later to the airport; X-rays (which I took home with me to Canada); a small cast to immobilize my leg (which the doctors, drivers, cleaning lady, bus driver, desk clerk and many others, signed) and the constant attention of at least two doctors in my hotel room at any given time. After the initial phone call, Medex took over, called the doctor and talked to him in Spanish, then someone else called me and told me that they were sending an air ambulance from Canada to pick me up. Later that evening I was taken by ambulance with the help of my good doctor Carlos, to the airport, where the sky ambulance was waiting. They put me on board, had IVs and goodness knows what else going in minutes, and off we went (my sister included) by Lear Jet to Toronto. My break was pinned there. A week later I was taken again by air to Vancouver and by ambulance to my home town, where I spent a further week in hospital, all on the insurance.

Cuba is very progressive in medicine and medical care is free for their citizens, but they lack many ingredients to make pharmaceuticals. I did not even have a pain killer offered to me. Fortunately my resourceful friend had some with her. It is best to bring prescription drugs, aspirins, anti-histamines, insect repellent, band-aids, sunscreen etc with you as these things are not readily available in Cuba, even in some tourist shops."

Author's note: Eileen is now back on her feet and looking at travel brochures.

jackets or woollens are essential after dark at high altitude. Loose cotton is still the best material when the weather is hot.

INSECTS

These are mostly more of a nuisance than a serious hazard and if you try, you can prevent yourself entirely from being bitten. Some, such as mosquitoes are, of course, carriers of potentially serious diseases, so it is sensible to avoid being bitten as much as possible. Sleep off the ground and use a mosquito net or some kind of insecticide. Preparations containing pyrethrum or synthetic pyrethroids are safe. They are available as aerosols or pumps and the best way to use these is to spray the room thoroughly in all areas (follow the instructions rather than the insects) and then shut the door for a while, re-entering when the smell has dispersed. Mosquito coils release insecticide as they burn slowly. They are widely available and useful out of doors. Tablets of insecticide which are placed on a heated mat, and plugged into a wall socket are probably the most effective. They fill the room with insecticidal fumes in the same way as aerosols or coils.

You can also use insect repellents, most of which are effective against a wide range of pests. The most common and effective is diethyl metatoluamide (DET). DET liquid is best for arms and face (care around eyes and with spectacles – DET dissolves plastic). Aerosol spray is good for clothes and ankles and liquid DET can be dissolved in water and used to impregnate cotton clothes and mosquito nets. Some repellants now contain DET and permethrin insecticide. Impregnated wrist and ankle bands can also be useful.

If you are bitten or stung, itching may be relieved by cool baths, antihistamine tablets (care with alcohol or driving) or mild corticosteroid creams, eg hydrocortisone (great care, never use if any hint of infection). Careful scratching of all your bites once a day can be surprisingly effective. Calamine lotion and cream have limited effectiveness and antihistamine creams are not recommended – they can cause allergies themselves.

Bites which become infected should be treated with a local antiseptic or antibiotic cream, such as Cetrimide as should any infected sores or scratches.

When living rough, skin infestations with body lice (crabs) and scabies are easy to pick up. Use whatever local commercial preparation is recommended for lice and scabies. Crotamiton cream (Eurax) alleviates itching and also kills a number of skin parasites. Malathion lotion 5% (Prioderm) kills lice effectively, but avoid the use of the toxic agricultural preparation of Malathion, more often used to commit suicide.

TICKS

Usually attach themselves to the lower parts of the body, often after walking in areas where cattle have grazed. They take a while to attach themselves strongly, but swell up as they start to suck blood. The important thing is to remove them gently, so that they do not leave their head parts in your skin because this can cause a nasty allergic reaction some days later. Do not use petrol, vaseline, lighted cigarettes etc. to remove the tick, but, with a pair of tweezers remove the beast gently by gripping it at the attached (head) end and rock it out in very much the same way that a tooth is extracted. Certain tropical flies which lay their eggs under the skin of sheep and cattle also occasionally do the same thing to humans with the unpleasant result that a maggot grows under the skin and pops up as a boil or pimple. The best way to remove these is to cover the boil with oil, vaseline or nail varnish so as to stop the maggot breathing, then to squeeze it out gently the next day.

SUNBURN

The burning power of the tropical sun, especially at altitude, is phenomenal. Always wear a wide brimmed hat and use some form of suncream lotion on untanned skin. Normal temperate zone suntan lotions (protection factor up to 7) are not much good; you need to use the types designed specifically for the tropics or for mountaineers or skiers with protection factors up to 15 or above. These may be available in all the islands. Glare from the sun can cause conjunctivitis, so wear sunglasses, especially on tropical beaches, where high protection factor sunscreen should also be used.

AIDS

In the Caribbean AIDS is increasing but is not wholly confined to the well known high risk sections of the population, ie homosexual men, intravenous drug abusers and children of infected mothers. Heterosexual transmission is now the dominant mode and so the main risk to travellers is from casual sex. The same precautions should be taken as with any sexually transmitted disease. The AIDS virus (HIV) can be passed by unsterilized needles which have been previously used to inject an HIV positive patient, but the risk of this is negligible. It would, however, be sensible to check that needles have been properly sterilized or disposable needles have been used. If you wish to take your own disposable needles be prepared to explain what they are for. The risk of receiving a blood transfusion with blood infected with the HIV virus is greater than from dirty needles because of the amount of fluid exchanged. Supplies of blood for transfusion should now be screened for HIV in all reputable hospitals, so again the risk is very small indeed. Catching the AIDS virus does not always produce an illness in itself (although it may do). The only way to be sure if you feel you have been put at risk is to have a blood test for HIV antibodies on your return to a place where there are reliable laboratory facilities. The test does not become positive for some weeks.

MALARIA

In the West Indies, malaria is confined to the island of Hispaniola, being more prevalent in Haiti than the Dominican Republic. It also exists in parts of the Guianas (seek up-to-date advice on the type in the location to be visited). It remains a serious disease and you are advised to protect yourself against mosquito bites as above, and to take prophylactic (preventive) drugs. Start taking the tablets a few days before exposure and continue to take 6 weeks after leaving the malaria zone. Remember to give drugs to babies and children also. The subject of malaria prevention is becoming more complex as the malaria parasite becomes immune to some of the older drugs. However, at the present time Chloroquine should give sufficient protection. You can catch malaria even when taking these drugs, though it

is unlikely. If you do develop symptoms (high fever, shivering, headaches), seek medical advice immediately. If this is not possible and the likelihood of malaria is high the treatment is Chloroquine, a single dose of 4 tablets (600 mgs) followed by 2 tablets (300 mgs) in 6 hours and 300 mgs each day following. Pregnant women are particularly prone to malaria and should stick to Proguanil for prophylaxis. The risk of malaria is obviously greater the further you move from cities and into rural areas with primitive facilities and standing water.

INFECTIOUS HEPATITIS (JAUNDICE)

The main symptoms are pains in the stomach, lack of appetite, lassitude and yellowness of the eyes and skin. Medically speaking there are two main types. The less serious, but more common is hepatitis A for which the best protection is the careful preparation of food, the avoidance of contaminated drinking water and scrupulous attention to toilet hygiene. The other, more serious, version is hepatitis B which is acquired usually as a sexually transmitted disease or by blood transfusion. It can less commonly be transmitted by injections with unclean needles and possibly by insect bites. The symptoms are the same as for hepatitis A. The incubation period is much longer (up to 6 months compared with 6 weeks) and there are more likely to be complications.

Hepatitis A can be protected against with gamma globulin. It should be obtained from a reputable source and is certainly useful for travellers who intend to live rough. You should have a shot before leaving and have it repeated every 6 months. The dose of gamma globulin depends on the concentration of the particular preparation used, so the manufacturers advice should be taken. The injection should be given as close as possible to your departure and as the dose depends on the likely time you are to spend in potentially affected areas. Again follow the manufacturer's instructions. Gamma globulin has really been superseded now by a proper vaccination against hepatitis A (Havrix), which gives immunity lasting up to 10 years. After that boosters are required. Havrix monodose is now widely available as is junior Havrix. The vaccination has negligible side effects and is extremely effective. Gamma globulin injection can be a bit painful, but it is cheaper than Havrix and may be more available in some places.

Hepatitis B can be effectively prevented by a specific vaccine (Engerix) – 3 shots over 6 months before travelling. If you have had jaundice in the past it would be worthwhile having a blood test to see if you are immune to either of these two types, because this might obviate the necessity and cost of vaccination or gamma globulin. There are other kinds of viral hepatitis (C, E, etc) which are very similar to A and B, but vaccines are not available as yet.

SNAKE BITE

This is a very rare event indeed for travellers. If you are unlucky (or careless) enough to be bitten by a venomous snake, spider, scorpion or sea creature, try to identify the creature, but do not put yourself in further danger. Snake bites in particular are very frightening, but in fact rarely poisonous – even venomous snakes bite without injecting venom. What you might expect if bitten are: fright, swelling, pain and bruising around the bite and soreness of the regional lymph glands, perhaps nausea, vomiting and a fever. Signs of serious poisoning would be the following symptoms: numbness and tingling of the face, muscular spasms, convulsions, shortness of breath and bleeding. Victims should be got to a hospital or a doctor without delay. Commercial snake bite and scorpion kits are available, but usually only useful for the specific type of snake or scorpion for which they are designed. Most serum has to be given intravenously so it is not much

good equipping yourself with it unless you are used to making injections into veins. It is best to rely on local practice in these cases, because the particular creatures will be known about locally and appropriate treatment can be given.

Treatment of Snake Bite Reassure and comfort the victim frequently. Immobilize the limb by a bandage or a splint or by getting the person to lay still. Do not slash the bite area and try to suck out the poison because this sort of heroism does more harm than good. If you know how to use a tourniquet in these circumstances, you will not need this advice. If you are not experienced, do not apply a tourniquet.

Precautions Avoid walking in snake territory in bare feet or sandals – wear proper shoes or boots. If you encounter a snake stay put until it slithers away, and do not investigate a wounded snake. Spiders and scorpions may be found in the more basic hotels. If stung, rest and take plenty of fluids and call a doctor. The best precaution is to keep beds away from the walls and look inside your shoes and under the toilet seat every morning.

Certain tropical sea fish when trodden upon inject venom into bathers' feet. This can be exceptionally painful. Wear plastic shoes when you go bathing if such creatures are reported. The pain can be relieved by immersing the foot in extremely hot water for as long as the pain persists.

OTHER AFFLICTIONS

PRICKLY HEAT

A very common intensely itchy rash is avoided by frequent washing and by wearing loose clothing. Cured by allowing skin to dry off through use of powder and spending two nights in an air-conditioned hotel!

ATHLETES FOOT

This and other fungal skin infections are best treated with Tolnaftate or Clotrimazole.

DENGUE FEVER

This is increasing worldwide including in South and Central American countries and the Caribbean. It can be completely prevented by avoiding mosquito bites in the same way as malaria. No vaccine is available. Dengue is an unpleasant and painful disease, presenting with a high temperature and body pains, but at least visitors are spared the more serious forms (haemorrhagic types) which are more of a problem for local people who have been exposed to the disease more than once. There is no specific treatment for dengue – just pain killers and rest.

TYPHUS

Can still occur carried by ticks but is exceptionally rare in the Caribbean. There is usually a reaction at the site of the bite and a fever. Seek medical advice.

INTESTINAL WORMS

These are common and the more serious ones such as hookworm can be contracted from walking barefoot on infested earth or beaches. Some cause an itchy rash on the feet 'cutaneous larva migrans'.

LEPTOSPIROSIS

Various forms of leptospirosis occur throughout the Caribbean, transmitted by a bacterium which is excreted in rodent urine. Fresh water and moist soil harbour the organisms which enter the body through cuts and scratches. If you suffer from any form of prolonged fever consult a doctor.

WHEN YOU RETURN HOME

Remember to take your antimalarial tablets for 6 weeks after leaving the malarial area. If you have had attacks of diarrhoea it is worth having a stool specimen tested in case you have picked up amoebas. If you have been living rough, blood tests may be worthwhile to detect worms and other parasites. If you have been exposed to bilharzia (schistosomiasis) by swimming in lakes etc check by means of a blood test when you get home, but leave it for 6 weeks because the test is slow to become positive. Report any untoward symptoms to your doctor and tell the doctor exactly where you have been and, if you know, what the likelihood of disease is to which you were exposed.

The above information has been compiled for us by Dr David Snashall who is presently Senior Lecturer in Occupational Health at the United Medical Schools of Guy's & St Thomas' Hospitals in London and Chief Medical Advisor of the British Foreign and Commonwealth Office. He has travelled extensively in Central and South America and the Caribbean, worked in Peru and in East Africa and keeps in close touch with developments in preventative and tropical medicine.

Travelling with children

Cubans love children and the experience of travelling with children in Cuba can be rewarding for both parents and offspring. Children are good conversation starters and will help you to break the ice (if there is any) and bring you into closer contact with Cuban families. The children will love the beaches and the sea of course, but inland there are lots of opportunities for entertaining them, with trips to amusement parks, caves, rivers, farms and animals everywhere. Travelling with children generally presents no special problems – in fact the path is often smoother for family groups. Officials tend to be more amenable where children are concerned and they are pleased if your child knows a little Spanish. Moreover, even thieves and pickpockets seem to have some of the traditional respect for families, and may leave you alone because of it!

TRAVEL

People contemplating overland travel in Cuba should remember that a lot of time can be spent waiting for buses and trains. On bus journeys, if the children are good at amusing themselves, or can readily sleep while travelling, the problems can be considerably lessened. If your child is of an early reading age, take reading material with you as it is impossible to find locally. A bag of say, 30 pieces of Duplo or Lego can keep young children occupied for hours. Travel on trains, while not as fast or at times as comfortable as buses, allows more scope for moving about, but you have to remember that the length of a train journey can be double what is scheduled because of frequent breakdowns.

FOOD

Food can be a problem if the children are not adaptable. It is easier to take biscuits, drinks, bread etc with you on longer trips than to rely on meal stops where the food might not be to taste. Bananas are safe, easy to eat and nutritious; they can be fed to babies as young as 6 months and most older children like them. Similarly avocados, if they are in season and available. Buy what you can when you see it, particularly at roadside stops where farmers sell their own produce. Remember that there are no fast food chains in Cuba but roadside stalls in towns sell slabs of pizza, which can fill a nagging hole and satisfy a child. In restaurants, you can ask for children's portions or divide one full-size helping between two children. It is advisable to take all your own baby food and nappies/diapers if travelling with babies, as you can not rely on them being available.

HOTELS

In hotels try to negotiate family rates. If charges are per person, always insist that two children (if small enough) will occupy one bed only, therefore counting as one tariff. If rates are per bed, the same applies. In either case you can almost always get a reduced rate at cheaper hotels. In the resort hotels there is a standard reduction for children or they go free if sharing a room with two adults. Several hotels are now offering kids clubs which amuse the children all day and allow adults to go off and do their own thing. Babysitting services are usually available too.

TOILETS

Hotels will always have toilets somewhere near the reception area; state run restaurants will also have toilets for customers' use but not all private restaurants have them; public toilets can be found in the centre of most towns, but you can not rely on it. There are unlikely to be any facilities for changing babies' nappies/diapers and remember to take a good supply of toilet paper as it is not usually supplied.

TEMPERATURE CONVERSION TABLE

°C	°F	°C	°F
1	34	26	79
2	36	27	81
3	38	28	82
4	39	29	84
5	41	30	86
6	43	31	88
7	45	32	90
8	46	33	92
9	48	34	93
10	50	35	95
11	52	36	97
12	54	37	99
13	56	38	100
14	57	39	102
15	59	40	104
16	61	41	106
17	63	42	108
18	64	43	109
19	66	44	111
20	68	45	113
21	70	46	115
22	72	47	117
23	74	48	118
24	75	49	120
25	77	50	122

The formula for converting °C to °F is:
$$°C \times 9 \div 5 + 32 = °F$$

WEIGHTS AND MEASURES

Metric

Weight
1 Kilogram (Kg) = 2.205 pounds
1 metric ton = 1.102 short tons

Length
1 millimetre (mm)= 0.03937 inch
1 metre = 3.281 feet
1 kilometre (km) = 0.621 mile

Area
1 heactare = 2.471 acres
1 square km = 0.386 sq mile

Capacity
1 litre = 0.220 imperial gallon
$\qquad$ = 0.264 US gallon

Volume
1 cubic metre (m³) = 35.31 cubic feet
$\qquad$ = 1.31 cubic yards

British and US

Weight
1 pound (lb) = 454 grams
1 short ton (2,000lbs) = 0.907 m ton
1 long ton (2,240lbs) = 1.016 m tons

Length
1 inch = 25.417 millimetres
1 foot (ft) = 0.305 metre
1 mile = 1.609 kilometres

Area
1 acre = 0.405 hectare
1 sq mile = 2.590 sq kilometre

Capacity
1 imperial gallon = 4.546 litres
1 US gallon = 3.785 litres

Volume
1 cubic foot (cu ft) = 0.028 m³
1 cubic yard (cu yd) = 0.765 m³

NB 5 imperial gallons are approximately equal to 6 US gallons

Schedule of events in Cuba

MUSIC AND DANCE

Theme	Date	Location
Huella de España Festival	15-22 April 1998	Havana
Days of the Dance	25 April- 7 May 1998	Havana
Dance Fiesta	26 April- 1 May 1998	Villa Clara
International Guitar Festival and Contest	7-17 May 1998	Havana
Overseas Chinese Festival	2-7 June 1998	Havana
XI EL SINOR Festival	16-28 June 1998	Havana
XII Boleros de Oro Festival dedicated to Mexico	18-28 June 1998	Havana
XVIII Caribbean Culture Festival	3-9 July 1998	Santiago de Cuba
FOLKCUBA	6-18 July 1998	Havana
CUBALLET	4-31 August 1998	Havana
CUBADANZA	5-16 August 1998	Havana
VIII Theatre Festival of Camagüey	25 September- 4 October 1998	Camagüey
Havana Festival of Contemporary Music	1-9 October 1998	Havana
V International Festival IMAGO	20-23 October 1998	Havana
Iberian-American Culture Fiesta (Andalusia and Chile)	24-30 October 1998	Holguín
XVI International Ballet Festival	28 October- 7 November 1998	Havana
International Festival of University Theatre	16-18 November 1998	Matanzas
II National Festival of Esperanto Culture	20-22 November 1998	Santiago de Cuba
XX Festival of the New Latin America Cinema	1-15 December 1998	Havana
International Jazz Festival "JAZZ PLAZA"	December 1998/1999	Havana
CUBALLET	January 1999/2000	Havana
FOLKCUBA	January 1999/2000	
International Contest of Dance	April 1999/2000	

Bienal de La Habana	May 1999	Havana
Theme	**Date**	**Location**
Caribbean Cultural Festival FIESTA DEL FUEGO	July 1999/2000	Santiago de Cuba
International Festival of Music Benny Moré	August 1999	
Festival IMAGO	October 1999	Havana
International Festival of the New Latin America Cinema	December 1999/2000	Havana
Guitar Festival and Contest	May 2000	Havana

SPORT			
Theme	**Name**	**Date**	**Location**
Sport	World Cup "José Ramon Fonst"	February 1999/2000	
Archery	Norceca Dianas Doradas	25 April-3 May 1998	Ciego de Avila
	Pan-American Games (Americas Cup)	19-28 June 1998	Havana
Athletics	Memorial Barrientos	March 1999/2000	
Badminton	Central American and Caribbean Championship	23 August-1 September 1998	Havana
Bowling	Isla Tournament	13-19 April 1998	Havana
	Bolihabana Tournament	6-12 July 1998	Havana
	Isla Melia-Cohiba Tournament	24-30 August 1998	Havana
Cycling	Intercontinental Track Cup	7-13 April 1998	Havana
Fencing	Ramón Fonts World Cup	10-17 June 1998	Havana
GRD	Interclub Cup	1-8 August 1998	Havana
Handball	Cuba Cup	9-16 November 1998	Pinar del Río
Hockey	Pan American Tournament World Cup	October 2000	
Judo	José Ramón Rodríguez	14-22 June 1998	Camagüey
	Japanese Immigration Anniversary	16-20 June 1998	Las Tunas
Pelota	Capitán San Luis Cup	8-19 June 1998	Havana

Skating	Latin American Race Championship	15-19 July 1998	Havana
Theme	**Name**	**Date**	**Location**
Table tennis	Latin American Championship	11-20 April 1998	Havana
	The 32 Latin American Best Tournament	25-30 November 1998	Havana
Taekwondo	Cuba Cup	13-18 May 1998	Matanzas
Tennis	Davis Cup	27 March-5 April 1998	Matanzas
	Challenger Tournament	9-19 April 1998	Havana
	Davis Cup	3-13 July 1998	Matanzas
Weight lifting	Iberoamerican Championship	May 2001	

WATER SPORTS			
Theme	**Name**	**Date**	**Location**
Aquabike	Open of the Americas Aquabike International	24-26 April 1998	Havana
Diving	Cuba and Canamex Cup	19-24 May 1998	Havana
Fishing	I International Fly Fishing Tournament	April 1998	Cayo Largo del Sur
	48th Ernest Hemingway International Marlin Fishing Tournament	May 1998	Havana
	IV Gregorio Fuente Betancourt Tournament (Marlin)	June 1998	Varadero
	V The Old Man and the Sea International Marlin Fishing Tournament	18-22 July 1998	Havana
	17th International Blue Marlin Fishing Tournament	September 1998	Havana
	VI La Hispanidad International Fishing Tournament (Marlin)	8-12 October 1998	Havana
	6th International Marlin Fishing Tournament	October 1998	Santiago de Cuba
Hobbie cat	Regatta Copa del Caribe	27 October-2 November 1998	Matanzas
Kayak	Descent of the Sagua River	31 March-6 April 1998	Villa Clara
	Cup of the Americas	December 1998	Havana

Theme	Name	Date	Location
Rowing	Regatta Copa BOHEMIA of Rowing	8-22 July 1998	Havana and Cienfuegos
	26th of July Cuba Rowing Cup Regatta	24-27 July 1998	Varadero
	World Master Championship	July 2001	
Sailboat-cruiser	III Havana Cup Regatta	22-29 May 1998	Havana
	IV Morro Castle Regatta	26-27 May 1998	Havana
	Havana Merry Christmas Regatta	22-27 December 1998	Havana
Sailing	World Championship Table M-F	March 2001	
Ski	Caribbean Open Water Ski	19-21 June 1998	Varadero
Swimming	Marathon/25m Tournament	10-15 April 1998	Matanzas
	Caribbean Championship	July 2000	

Source: Buró de Comvenciones, Edificio Focsa, Calle M e/ 17 y 19, Vedado, La Habana, T 31-3600, F 33-4261, e-mail: buroconv@buroconv.mit.cma.net

Year planner

1998

J	F	M	A	M	J	J	A	S	O	N	D
					1						
					2			1			1
			1		3	1		2			2
1			2		4	2		3	1		3
2			3	1	5	3		4	2		4
3			4	2	6	4	1	5	3		5
4	1	1	5	3	7	5	2	6	4	1	6
5	2	2	6	4	8	6	3	7	5	2	7
6	3	3	7	5	9	7	4	8	6	3	8
7	4	4	8	6	10	8	5	9	7	4	9
8	5	5	9	7	11	9	6	10	8	5	10
9	6	6	10	8	12	10	7	11	9	6	11
10	7	7	11	9	13	11	8	12	10	7	12
11	8	8	12	10	14	12	9	13	11	8	13
12	9	9	13	11	15	13	10	14	12	9	14
13	10	10	14	12	16	14	11	15	13	10	15
14	11	11	15	13	17	15	12	16	14	11	16
15	12	12	16	14	18	16	13	17	15	12	17
16	13	13	17	15	19	17	14	18	16	13	18
17	14	14	18	16	20	18	15	19	17	14	19
18	15	15	19	17	21	19	16	20	18	15	20
19	16	16	20	18	22	20	17	21	19	16	21
20	17	17	21	19	23	21	18	22	20	17	22
21	18	18	22	20	24	22	19	23	21	18	23
22	19	19	23	21	25	23	20	24	22	19	24
23	20	20	24	22	26	24	21	25	23	20	25
24	21	21	25	23	27	25	22	26	24	21	26
25	22	22	26	24	28	26	23	27	25	22	27
26	23	23	27	25	29	27	24	28	26	23	28
27	24	24	28	26	30	28	25	29	27	24	29
28	25	25	29	27		29	26	30	28	25	30
29	26	26	30	28		30	27		29	26	31
30	27	27		29		31	28		30	27	
31	28	28		30			29		31	28	
		29		31			30			29	
		30					31			30	
		31									

Year planner

1999

J	F	M	A	M	J	J	A	S	O	N	D
					1						
					2			1			1
			1		3	1		2			2
1			2		4	2		3	1		3
2			3	1	5	3		4	2		4
3			4	2	6	4	1	5	3		5
4	1	1	5	3	7	5	2	6	4	1	6
5	2	2	6	4	8	6	3	7	5	2	7
6	3	3	7	5	9	7	4	8	6	3	8
7	4	4	8	6	10	8	5	9	7	4	9
8	5	5	9	7	11	9	6	10	8	5	10
9	6	6	10	8	12	10	7	11	9	6	11
10	7	7	11	9	13	11	8	12	10	7	12
11	8	8	12	10	14	12	9	13	11	8	13
12	9	9	13	11	15	13	10	14	12	9	14
13	10	10	14	12	16	14	11	15	13	10	15
14	11	11	15	13	17	15	12	16	14	11	16
15	12	12	16	14	18	16	13	17	15	12	17
16	13	13	17	15	19	17	14	18	16	13	18
17	14	14	18	16	20	18	15	19	17	14	19
18	15	15	19	17	21	19	16	20	18	15	20
19	16	16	20	18	22	20	17	21	19	16	21
20	17	17	21	19	23	21	18	22	20	17	22
21	18	18	22	20	24	22	19	23	21	18	23
22	19	19	23	21	25	23	20	24	22	19	24
23	20	20	24	22	26	24	21	25	23	20	25
24	21	21	25	23	27	25	22	26	24	21	26
25	22	22	26	24	28	26	23	27	25	22	27
26	23	23	27	25	29	27	24	28	26	23	28
27	24	24	28	26	30	28	25	29	27	24	29
28	25	25	29	27		29	26	30	28	25	30
29	26	26	30	28		30	27		29	26	31
30	27	27		29		31	28		30	27	
31	28	28		30			29		31	28	
		29		31			30			29	
		30					31			30	
		31									

Writing to us

Many people write to us - with corrections, new information, or simply comments. If you want to let us know something, we would be delighted to hear from you. Please give us as precise information as possible, quoting the edition and page number of the Handbook you are using and send as early in the year as you can. Your help will be greatly appreciated, especially by other travellers. In return we will send you details about our special guidebook offer.

For hotels and restaurants, please let us know:

- each establishment's name, address, phone and fax number
- number of rooms, whether a/c or air-cooled, attached (clean?) bathroom
- location - how far from the station or bus stand, or distance (walking time) from a prominent landmark
- if it's not already on one of our maps, can you place it?
- your comments - either good or bad - as to why it is distinctive
- tariff cards
- local transport used

For places of interest:

- location
- entry, camera charge
- access - by whatever means of transport is most approriate, eg time of main buses or trains to and from the site, journey time, fare
- facilities - nearby drinks stalls, restaurants, for the disabled
- any problems, eg steep climb, wildlife, unofficial guides
- opening hours
- site guides

Tinted boxes

Illustrations

Index

344

346

Notes

Maps

Map Symbols

Administration

International Border
State / Province Border
Cease Fire Line

Neighbouring country
Neighbouring state

State Capitals
Other Towns

Roads and travel

Main Roads
(National Highways)
Other Roads
Jeepable Roads, Tracks
Railways with station

Water features

River — *Paradise River*
Lakes, Reservoirs, Tanks
Seasonal Marshlands
Sand Banks, Beaches
Ocean
Waterfall
Ferry
Reefs
Dive sites
Boat anchorage
Windsurfing

Topographical features

Contours (approx),
Rock Outcrops
Mountains
Mountain Pass
Gorge
Escarpment
Palm trees
Deciduous/fir trees

Cities and towns

Built Up Areas

Main through routes
Main streets
Minor Streets
Pedestrianized Streets
One Way Street
National Parks, Gardens, Stadiums

Fortified Walls
Airport
Banks
Bus Stations (named in key)
Hospitals
Market
Police station
Post Office
Telegraphic Office
Tourist Office

Key Numbers

Bridges
Stupa
Mosque
Cathedral, church
Guided routes

National parks, trekking areas

National Parks and
Bird Sanctuaries
Hide
Camp site
Refuge
Motorable track
Walking track

Other symbols

Archaeological Sites
Places of Interest
Viewing point
Golf course
Volcano